W9-CLG-142

Books on intellectual development usually cover one of two separate developmental periods: the formation of intelligence and basic cognitive skills that occurs until adolescence, and the maintenance, decline, or improvement of these intellectual skills across the adult life-span. Robert Sternberg and Cynthia Berg have integrated research on those two periods, in a comprehensive introduction to the major approaches to intellectual development. The six approaches covered are from the psychometric, Piagetian, neo-Piagetian, information-processing, learning, and contextual perspectives. Two chapters are devoted to each perspective, one on childhood and one on adulthood, and the authors have drawn connections between the two periods so that their accounts are tied together across the life-span.

Robert J. Sternberg is IBM Professor of Psychology and Education at Yale University and an author of many books, including *Metaphors of Mind*, *The Psychologist's Companion*, and *Beyond IQ: A Triarchic Theory of Human Intelligence*. Cynthia A. Berg is Assistant Professor in the Department of Psychology at the University of Utah.

Intellectual development

Intellectual development

Edited by

ROBERT J. STERNBERG

Yale University

CYNTHIA A. BERG

University of Utah

CAMBRIDGE
UNIVERSITY PRESS

Published by the Press Syndicate of the University of Cambridge
The Pitt Building, Trumpington Street, Cambridge CB2 1RP
40 West 20th Street, New York, NY 10011-4211, USA
10 Stamford Road, Oakleigh, Melbourne 3166, Australia

© Cambridge University Press 1992

First published 1982
Reprinted 1993, 1994

Printed in the United States of America

Library of Congress Cataloging-in-Publication Data is available.

A catalogue record for this book is available from the British Library.

ISBN 0-521-39456-2 hardback
ISBN 0-521-39769-0 paperback

To our children: *Sara and Seth Sternberg*
Erik Berg

Contents

Contributors

Cynthia A. Berg
Department of Psychology
University of Utah
Salt Lake City, UT 84112

Thomas R. Bidell
Department of Human
    Development and Psychology
Larsen Hall
Appian Way
Harvard University
Cambridge, MA 02138

Sherrie Bieman-Copland
Psychology Department
University of Waterloo
Waterloo, Ontario
Canada N2L 3G1

Jeffrey Bisanz
Department of Psychology
University of Alberta
Edmonton, Alberta
Canada T6G 2E9

James A. Blackburn
School of Social Welfare
University of Wisconsin
Milwaukee, WI 53201

Richard L. Canfield
Human Development and Family
    Studies
Cornell University
Ithaca, NY 14853

Robbie Case
School of Education
Stanford University
Stanford, CA 94305

Stephen J. Ceci
Human Development and Family
    Studies
Cornell University
Ithaca, NY 14853

Neil Charness
Psychology Department
University of Waterloo
Waterloo, Ontario
Canada N2L 3G1

Elaine Clark
Dept. of Educational Psychology
University of Utah
327 Milton Bennion Hall
Salt Lake City, UT 84112

Roger A. Dixon
Department of Psychology
University of Victoria
Victoria, BC
Canada V8W 2Y2

Kurt W. Fischer
Department of Human
    Development and Psychology
Larsen Hall   Appian Way
Harvard University
Cambridge, MA 02138

Michael K. Gardner
Department of Educational
  Psychology
University of Utah
327 Milton Bennion Hall
Salt Lake City, UT 84112

Scott M. Hofer
Department of Psychology
University of Southern California
Los Angeles, CA 90089-1061

John L. Horn
Department of Psychology
University of Southern California
Los Angeles, CA 90089-1061

Robert Kail
Department of Psychological
  Sciences
Purdue University
West Lafayette, IN 47907

Bonnie G. Kanner
Department of Psychology
Clark University
Worcester, MA 01610-1477

Gisela Labouvie-Vief
Department of Psychology
Wayne State University
Detroit, MI 48202

Diane E. Papalia
Psychiatry Department
Memorial Sloan-Kettering Cancer
  Center
New York, NY 10021

Timothy A. Salthouse
School of Psychology
Georgia Institute of Technology
Atlanta, GA 30332

Robert J. Sternberg
Department of Psychology
Yale University
Box 11A Yale Station
New Haven, CT 06520-7447

James V. Wertsch
Department of Psychology
Clark University
Worcester, MA 01610-1477

Preface

The goal of *Intellectual Development* is to provide in one volume a comprehensive yet readable introduction to the major approaches to the study of intellectual development during childhood and adulthood. Our text is unique in its crisscrossing of two major periods of development with six major approaches to development, yielding 2 × 6, or 12, chapters plus introductory and concluding chapters (for a total of 14). The two major periods of development, of course, are childhood and adulthood. The six major approaches are the psychometric, Piagetian, neo-Piagetian, information-processing, learning, and contextual. Thus, each of the main chapters deals with an approach to intellectual development, as realized through theory and research on either childhood or adulthood. Authors have drawn connections between the two periods, so that their accounts are tied together across the life-span.

Our book is intended as an advanced undergraduate or introductory graduate text – main or supplementary – but can be read as an introduction to the study of intellectual development by anyone interested in the field. By inviting authors who adhere to different approaches, we have been able to achieve a balance that would be difficult in a single-authored work, and we have also been able to give the flavor of each approach. Because the approaches are diverse, we have written introductory and concluding chapters that help tie the strands together.

We are grateful to our current editor, Julia Hough, for her support of the project, as well as to Susan Milmoe, the editor who originally contracted the project, and to Helen Wheeler, the editor who saw the project through most of its intermediate stages.

1 Perspectives for viewing intellectual development throughout the life course

Cynthia A. Berg

What has one voice and is four-footed, two-footed, and three-footed? The task of characterizing intellectual development throughout the life course can be likened to the situation that faced the Thebans as they tried to solve this riddle of the Sphinx. Oedipus gave the correct answer to this riddle: man, as man is four-footed as a baby, crawling on all limbs, is two-footed during the vast majority of the life-span, and in old age occasionally uses a cane as a third foot. Theorists and researchers of intellectual development, however, have largely addressed the riddle of intellectual development by segregating the life-span into two major periods, those of child development and adult development. This book brings together theorists who focus on these different portions of the life-span in an attempt to illustrate how work on intellectual development can benefit from issues and problems that arise from an examination of how intelligence is formed, is maintained, declines, and improves throughout the course of life. The hope is that by the viewing of intellectual development as occurring in the same organism through time, a deeper look at the consistencies and inconsistencies in the descriptions and explanations of intellectual development will be possible.

In addition to presenting a picture of intellectual development throughout the life-span, the book offers a fairly diverse representation of intellectual development from a variety of different perspectives. Perhaps now more than at any other time in the history of work on intellectual development, great diversity exists in the types of theoretical perspectives that guide research, with no one perspective dominating the field. Six different theoretical perspectives on intellectual development are offered: psychometric, Piagetian, neo-Piagetian, information-processing, learning, and contextual. Although these encompass a fairly broad view of the major theoretical perspectives guiding the field of intellectual development, clearly some perspectives are missing (e.g., comparative, biological, artificial intelligence). The six perspectives presented here are included because of their pre-

Preparation of this chapter was made possible, in part, by grant HD 25728 from the National Institute of Child and Human Development and the National Institute of Aging. I thank Katerina Calderone, Barbara Ross, and Robert Sternberg for their helpful comments on an earlier draft of this essay.

1

dominance in guiding current research on the developing human's intelligence. In this introduction, I aim (1) to survey what is meant by intellectual development as seen from each of these perspectives, providing some historical background on the perspectives, and (2) to examine what we learn by considering intellectual development across childhood and adulthood.

Perspectives on the nature of intellectual development

To some individuals the word "intelligence" may be synonymous with intelligence testing and how well one scores on an intelligence test. The intelligence testing movement, however, and the psychometric perspective associated with it, is only one perspective of many employed in examining intellectual development. Although there is great diversity currently in the perspectives used to approach intellectual development, diverse views have existed since the early 1900s, when the field of intelligence testing first began. For instance, in 1921 the editors of the *Journal of Educational Psychology* (Intelligence and its measurement, 1921) solicited definitions of intelligence from several experts within the psychometric and "classical learning perspective" on intelligence. Their views included elementary cognitive processes (e.g., sensation, perception, attention), higher-order cognitive processes (e.g., abstract reasoning, problem solving, decision making), knowledge, speed of mental processing, the ability to adapt to one's environment, biological and physiological prewirings, and emotional and motivational components, among others. Sternberg and Detterman (1986) replicated this study with experts in 1986, finding at least as much diversity among views of intelligence as was found in 1921, if not more.

Divergence in views of intellectual development is not restricted to experts, as revealed by investigations of the beliefs children and adults of various ages hold about intelligence. Yussen and Kane (1981) found that young children believe intelligence consists of physical characteristics as well as the way in which individuals manage specific tasks. Sternberg, Conway, Ketron, and Bernstein (1981) found that lay adults see intelligence as a large constellation of behaviors reflecting practical problem solving, verbal ability, and social competence. Berg and Sternberg (in press) found that adults across the life-span view intelligence as consisting of dimensions such as interest in, and ability to deal with, novelty, verbal competence, and everyday competence, among other factors. The diversity present in laypersons' views of intelligence matches, if not exceeds, the diversity present in experts' views of intelligence.

The six perspectives on intellectual development offered in this volume entail differing views on how intelligence is formed, maintained, declines, and improves across the life-span. Even within a particular perspective, often a slightly different focus is adopted by those who use the perspective to study intellectual development during childhood from that adopted by those who use it to study development during adulthood. The differences in views of intelligence result, at least in part, from the perspectives' being at different points in development, with some in their relative infancy and some in advanced old age. That is, some perspectives have existed since the inception of formal psychological work on intelligence, whereas others are quite new in their formulation and empirical instantiations. These perspectives are also intertwined in that many of them developed in direct response to perceived inadequacies in other perspectives.

The advantages of viewing intellectual development from these six different perspectives are numerous. The primary advantage is that the picture constructed of what changes with age is much more complete when viewed from varying perspectives rather than from only one perspective. Each perspective affords a deeper look at a particular facet of intelligence. The psychometric perspective focuses on the intellectual products that characterize intelligence at different points during development (e.g., optimal performance on a particular measure of intelligent functioning). Other perspectives, such as the information-processing and neo-Piagetian, are more interested in the processes (e.g., mental processes, representations, and strategies) by which intellectual products are constructed. The Piagetian perspective focuses on the universal features of intellectual development characterizing most children or adults at a particular developmental period, whereas other perspectives focus on the differences among individuals. By examining all of these perspectives on intellectual development in one place, we may begin to understand a larger piece of the puzzle of intellectual development. In addition, such an integration of different perspectives on child and adult intellectual development may be a beginning step toward initiating theories of intellectual development that take into account multiple facets of intelligence across the full life course.

These six perspectives on intellectual development have been guided by different questions and issues. The following sections offer central questions guiding each perspective, as well as brief descriptions of the answers provided. In addition, a very brief historical view of the perspectives will be given in order to facilitate an understanding of the relation among the perspectives. Understanding the different questions directing each perspective, and the historical context of such questions, helps explain the variability in the methods and paradigms used in the following chapters to describe intellectual changes with age.

The psychometric perspective

The psychometric perspective has had the longest tradition in the field of intellectual development, with Sir Francis Galton's work on intelligence tests in the 1880s generally regarded as the first on formal mental tests (Gardner & Clark, this volume; Kail & Pellegrino, 1985; Sternberg & Powell, 1983). Galton undertook his work in order to understand the implications of Darwin's theory of evolution for the study of intellectual development. Whereas Galton's mental tests consisted of basic physical–sensory abilities, Binet and others devised tests of intelligence that involved higher-order intellectual abilities such as attention, verbal comprehension, and reasoning. Binet is often recognized as the creator of the first intelligence test, when he was commissioned to identify children who would be unable to profit from public school instruction.

The question guiding the psychometric perspective to intellectual development has been that of how to characterize intellectual differences between individuals at various developmental periods. The view of intelligence coming from the psychometric perspective depends heavily on the tests used to measure intelligence. The psychometric perspective begins its investigation into the nature of intelligence by measuring the performance of individuals on specific intelligence tests. Statistical procedures such as factor analysis then summarize such individual difference data and illuminate the structure underlying the organization of individuals' performance on such intelligence tests.

As Gardner and Clark describe, the types of intellectual abilities found to characterize differences between individuals during infancy are perceptual–motor and sensory in nature (e.g., watching a ball swing from a string, grasping blocks and placing them in the correct cubicles). During later childhood a variety of different intellectual abilities distinguish individuals, such as verbal and mathematical skills, abstract and visual reasoning, and components of memory. Many of the intellectual abilities found to distinguish between individuals during childhood continue to distinguish between individuals during adulthood. As reviewed by Horn and Hofer, two broad constellations of abilities have been found to be useful during adulthood in characterizing differences between individuals: (1) crystallized intelligence, abilities that are influenced by acculturation and formal schooling (e.g., measures of vocabulary and world knowledge), and (2) fluid intelligence, abilities that require adaptation to new situations and that depend more on biological and physiological influences than on formal schooling (e.g., measures of abstract reasoning).

The Piagetian perspective

Piaget's perspective on intellectual development was formed during his early psychological studies in Binet's psychometric laboratory in 1919. Piaget's dissatisfaction with Binet and Simon's psychometric tasks, and the scoring of such tasks on a pass–fail system, led to the development of Piaget's "clinical method," in which the reasoning behind a child's answer was examined extensively. These investigations led Piaget to conclude that children's reasoning at different ages represented qualitatively different ways of thinking.

A central question guiding the Piagetian perspective on intellectual development has been that of how to characterize the universal changes in mental functioning that take place from infancy to adolescence. Piaget (1952) characterized intellectual development as a process of constructing knowledge from our interactions with the environment, a process resulting in cognitive structures that were representative of a particular developmental period, or stage. Piaget viewed intelligence as the instrument that enables people to achieve an equilibrium between their cognitive structures and their environment: Intelligence "is the form of equilibrium towards which the successive adaptations and exchanges between the organism and his environment are directed" (1950, p. 6). Piaget identified four broad stages of intellectual development, which differed in the types of cognitive structures (described in terms of their logical properties) used to interact with the environment: (1) sensorimotor stage, (2) preoperational stage, (3) concrete operational stage, and (4) formal operational stage. Piagetian theorizing and research have focused on the similarities in cognitive structures among individuals at a given developmental period or stage. As Bidell and Fischer so eloquently discuss, the Piagetian focus on similarities between individuals of a given age has drawn attention away from the extensive literature illustrating variability in cognitive development.

Because Piaget posited that people achieve a final state of equilibrium between their cognitive structures and environment during the formal operational stage, occurring typically during adolescence, theorizing and research on intellectual development during adulthood were not given priority. But researchers who examine adult development and aging have investigated adults' performance on many of the tasks designed to tap the last two stages in Piaget's model – concrete operations and formal operations – in order to understand how Piaget's theory applies to adult development. Blackburn and Papalia point out that the Piagetian perspective was found to need revision in order to address issues of concern during adult intellectual development (see also Labouvie-Vief).

The neo-Piagetian perspective

As both Case and Labouvie-Vief detail, the neo-Piagetian perspective evolved sometime during the 1970s as an increasing number of concerns and criticisms were raised about Piaget's theory. Such concerns centered around the logical nature of the cognitive structures posited to underlie intellectual development and the viability of Piaget's universal theory of intellectual development for all children and for individuals past adolescence. The question directing theorizing and research in this area has been that of how best to revise and extend Piaget's perspective in order to address criticisms of Piaget's theory. Although the neo-Piagetian perspective preserves general Piagetian ideas of intellectual development (e.g., the essential concept of cognitive structures), several underlying postulates have been modified, with specific neo-Piagetian theorists extending Piaget's theory in different directions. (See Case for an extensive discussion of similarities and differences between neo-Piagetian and Piagetian perspectives.) In general, however, neo-Piagetian theorists can be characterized as being particularly interested in (1) understanding how cognitive structures are applied more locally within a domain and not universally across domains, (2) understanding individual differences in cognitive structures or their application, and (3) characterizing the integration of cognitive and emotional or affective structures.

Within child development, much of the neo-Piagetian research has involved a more fine-grained analysis of several Piagetian tasks, which were designed to illuminate cognitive structures representative of a particular stage. As Case's chapter illustrates, the detail of such an analysis is aimed at revealing the activation, integration, and consolidation of substructures operating for a given individual on a particular task. Such refined analyses elucidate processes of intellectual development not only between stages, but also within stages.

In the adult development literature, neo-Piagetian research and theorizing describes cognitive developments that occur beyond the last stage in Piaget's model (i.e., formal operations). Cognitive development during adulthood involves dialectical forms of thought, which are characterized by contradiction and change rather than by thinking that attempts to resolve contradictions, as in Piaget's equilibrium model. Labouvie-Vief reviews neo-Piagetian theories and research that illustrate how logical reasoning is integrated with affective and emotional ways of understanding.

The information-processing perspective

Although roots of the information-processing perspective can be traced back to nearly the late 1800s (see Lachman, Lachman, & Butterfield, 1980; Sternberg & Powell, 1983), most pinpoint its revival and current conception to two works published in the 1960s (Miller, Galanter, & Pribram, 1960; Newell, Shaw, & Simon, 1960), with much of the developmental work occurring in the 1970s and 1980s. This approach grew, in part, out of dissatisfaction with the classical learning perspective's emphasis on intellectual behaviors, to the exclusion of the mental processes by which such behaviors are produced.

A central question for the information-processing perspective is that of how to characterize the processes by which an individual produces intellectual performance. More specifically, the focus is on what occurs between the input of information and the output of specific intellectual responses and how this changes across development. The information-processing perspective characterizes the process between input and output in terms of mental processes, representations, accessing knowledge, strategies, executive processes that monitor the system, and the availability of resources needed for this process. The information-processing perspective characterizes human thought as akin to the way in which computers access and process information.

As reviewed by Kail and Bisanz, during child development increases in performance on a variety of intellectual tasks are explained by changes in the strategies children use to approach tasks and by increases in mental effort that can be apportioned to tasks. Salthouse reviews how during adult development the concern is to describe the impairment in processing information with advancing age in terms of the use of ineffective strategies, deficits in processes that allow for retrieving information, and the amount of processing resources available for any given task.

The learning perspective

The traditional, or "classical," learning perspective on intellectual development had its roots in the work of Thorndike and others in the early 1900s, with many of the learning theories of intellectual development published in the 1960s and 1970s by Bijou & Baer (1965), Gagne (1965), the Kendlers (Kendler & Kendler, 1975), and White (1965). (See Sternberg & Powell, 1983 for a review.) The learning perspective presented by Canfield and Ceci and by Charness and Bieman-Copland retains some of the concepts of the traditional learning perspective while adopting many of the cognitive constructs of the information-processing perspective, and it can best be viewed as a hybrid learning model. This hybrid learning model was addressed to weaknesses in the information-processing perspective, which had under-emphasized the content of knowledge as a locus of developmental changes.

A guiding question for the new learning perspective on intellectual development is, How does the amount and organization of knowledge affect intellectual development? Learning is depicted as the accumulation of information that is fine-tuned to be at the appropriate level of generality and specificity, and that can be restructured when new organizations of knowledge are needed. Development is likened to a process of becoming more expert with regard to one's knowledge base, although experience will not always guarantee optimal performance on a particular task.

During child development, the interest is in how children accumulate knowledge and how content knowledge is restructured and fine-tuned into mature organizations of knowledge. In general, young children can be thought of as relative novices, whereas older children and adults can be considered relative experts in terms of their knowledge base (although Canfield and Ceci point out exceptions to this general rule). The message from the learning perspective is that differences in intellectual performance between young and older children are due, in part, to differences in the amounts and kinds of knowledge children possess about a host of concepts, knowledge that affects the efficiency of cognitive processes.

During adult development and aging, the main concern is with how to reconcile research that demonstrates decrements with adult age on a variety of intellectual tasks with the view that older adults should possess a richer and more extensive knowledge base due to their lifelong experience. Charness and Bieman-Copland note that there are disadvantages as well as advantages to having a larger knowledge base. Relevant to the advantages of learning, older adults' expertise in specific domains of knowledge (e.g., bridge, typing) often compensates for declining performance in lower-level cognitive processes. Related to the disadvantages of learning, Charness and Bieman-Copland discuss research that illustrates how a large and well-organized knowledge base may have negative consequences for the speed of using the knowledge base and for its proper activation.

The contextual perspective

The contextual perspective is perhaps the newest one on intellectual development in the field. Although the particular contextual perspective advanced by Wertsch and Kanner, the Vygotskian perspective, dates back to the late 1920s and early 1930s, its introduction to child development in the United States began in the 1970s and 1980s. The incorporation of contextual themes and research in adult intellectual development is also rather recent, as Dixon notes. The contextual perspective grew out of a concern that previous theories of intellectual and cognitive development were overly normative, in characterizing only universal aspects of intellectual development.

A guiding question for the contextual perspective has been, How does intellectual development reflect the specific contexts – sociocultural, biological, historical – in which intelligence is displayed? A distinctive component of this perspective is that intellectual development is posited to be disparate across groups of individuals who are situated in different contexts: Intellectual development might evince varying trajectories in different contexts, certain contexts may require the development of specific dimensions of intelligence, and different historical periods may have consequences for the form of intellectual development.

Wertsch and Kanner focus on a specific contextual perspective, the Vygotskian approach, which has greatly influenced the thinking of several contemporary contextual theorists and researchers in child development. The Vygotskian perspective emphasizes that individual intellectual functioning has its origins in intellectual interactions with other people. Individuals in a given culture provide guidance as to the efficient and appropriate means for solving intellectual problems, guidance that becomes internalized with development.

Dixon examines a variety of different contextual approaches to the study of intellectual development during adulthood. These contextual approaches share the notion that the intellectual performance of adults must be understood in the context of the relationship between changing (and perhaps declining) intellectual abilities and the changing contextual demands present in adults' environments (e.g., retirement, loss of spouse, declining health). Dixon reviews research that illustrates how older adults compensate for declining memory by using external aids (e.g., writing down information to be remembered) and by interacting with other people.

These six perspectives on intellectual development across the life course, when taken together, paint a complex, rich, and detailed view of the changes that occur across development in intelligence. Each perspective adds an important, if not essential, dimension of intelligent functioning. The psychometric perspective begins by surveying the landscape of intelligence with a focus on intellectual products and the organization of such products throughout the life course. Several perspectives, then, further examine the intellectual products, identified by the psychometric perspective, in an effort to understand the processes and structures that produce intellectual products at different ages. The Piagetian perspective posits that broad universal logical cognitive structures contribute to intellectual products across development, structures that change with development. The neo-Piagetian perspective also emphasizes that intellectual products arise from cognitive structures. However, such structures are not exclusively logical in nature nor are they universally applied across tasks or across persons. The information-processing perspective takes a more microanalytic approach at understanding how intellectual products are formed, examining the processes, representations, and strategies individuals use on specific intellectual tasks. The learning perspective adds an important component to the information-processing perspective in that the actual content of knowledge is extensively examined and the consequences of knowledge for the efficient use of processes, representations, and strategies. Finally, the contextual perspective takes the intellectual products and processes investigated by the other perspectives and reminds us that these take place in a larger sociocultural context. This larger context has enormous consequences for the form and content, as well as the quality of the intellectual products and processes.

Taken collectively, the six perspectives are in many ways complementary and advance a more complete picture of intellectual development than is possible within any one particular perspective. Work on intellectual development is also greatly enriched when understood in the context of a single organism developing intelligence across the life-span.

What do we learn by examining intellectual development across the life course?

The field of intellectual development is largely segregated into theorists and researchers who examine intellectual development during childhood and those who examine intellectual development during adulthood. This isolation is exemplified by two different handbooks that deal with issues in child development (*Handbook of Child Psychology*) and adult development and aging (*Handbook of the Psychology of Aging*) and two different societies and journals for researchers in child development (Society for Research in Child Development publishing *Child Development*) and adult development (Gerontological Society publishing *Journal of Gerontology*). Traditionally, the issues in child intellectual development were slightly different from those in adult intellectual development. That is, researchers examining intelligence during childhood described and explained the growth of intellectual functions, whereas researchers examining intelligence during adulthood described and explained the decline of intellectual functions. Aspects of growth, decline, and maintenance of intellectual functioning, however, can now be found in both the child and adult development literatures (see Baltes, 1987), as discussed in the chapters that follow.

Although, as yet, very few theories of intellectual development explicitly deal with intellectual development across child and adult development (see, e.g., Pascual-Leone, 1983, 1984), many theories of intellectual development now are beginning to address issues at both ends of the life-span. These theories include the neo-Piagetian theories of Case (1985) and Labouvie-Vief (1982), the triarchic theory of Sternberg (Berg & Sternberg, 1985; Sternberg, 1985), and the contextual theory of Baltes and his colleagues (Baltes, 1987; Baltes, Dittmann-Kohli, & Dixon, 1984). Viewing intellectual development as a process that needs to be described and explained across the life course reveals many lessons from which researchers in both child development and adult development can benefit. (See also Sternberg, 1988.) Three such lessons are explored in the next section: (1) that the development of intelligence does not stop in adolescence, (2) that there is great variability in the course of intellectual development, and (3) that similarities in performance between young children and older adults may not be due to similar mechanisms.

The development of intelligence does not stop in adolescence

If the present book included only chapters dealing with intellectual development during childhood, one would get the impression that intellectual development ends sometime during adolescence. This impression would be most prominent when examining intellectual development through particular perspectives but probably would be drawn within any one perspective. Although some perspectives are quite explicit that intellectual development is complete during adolescence, others make this assumption somewhat implicitly, as theorizing and research have ended with adolescence.

The Piagetian perspective is perhaps the most explicit in positing that intellectual development is complete with the development of the formal operational structures, which occurs sometime during adolescence. Neo-Piagetians, drawing from the Piagetian perspective, typically choose to characterize intellectual development only until around the age of 20. However, they are less likely to state explicitly that intellectual development ends where their theory leaves off. Within the psychometric perspective (see Gardner & Clark), many of the intelligence tests (e.g., Stanford-Binet, Differential Ability Scales, Kaufman Assessment Battery) discontinue gathering norming data sometime around adolescence (ages 12–18).

The information-processing, learning, and contextual perspectives are much more ambiguous as to when intellectual development is complete. Information-processing research certainly demonstrates that older children (often even in early adolescence) use similar processes, strategies, and representations with the same speed and efficiency as young adults. Research within the learning perspective also shows that adolescents are similar to young adults in the content and organization of their knowledge base. In the contextual perspective, adolescent children have acquired many of the tools and means for solving intellectual problems from their more knowledgeable elders.

It is important to note that much of the work in child development uses young adults (often college students) as the comparison group, implying that young adulthood or late adolescence is the pinnacle of intellectual development. Work in adult intellectual development also most frequently uses young adults as the comparison group. Much of the empirical work described in the following chapters questions whether young adulthood should be considered to be the apex of intelligence, particularly work within the neo-Piagetian perspective. A lifelong perspective on intellectual development reorients work in adolescence from a time of finishing touches to a time of increased growth and specialization. In addition, such a lifelong perspective implies a deeper look at the intellectual developments of young and middle-aged adulthood, as well as those occurring during late adulthood.

Great variability in the course of intellectual development

A theme that runs throughout this volume is the enormous variability in the course of intellectual development. That is, individuals differ in the trajectory of intellectual development across the life course, and at any developmental point individuals can differ in their level and form of intelligence. The six perspectives have varied in their resistance to incorporating such variability into their theories. Biddell and Fischer note how this message of variability is somewhat of a revelation to those adopting a Piagetian perspective to intellectual development. The Piagetian perspective often regarded variability within stages or across stages as error. Addressing this error as a phenomenon in need of explanation itself was one contribution of the neo-Piagetian perspective, although neo-Piagetians still focus mainly on the structural similarities across children and adults at a particular stage.

Although the psychometric perspective is based on the notion that individuals differ in their intelligence, the organization of abilities and the trajectory of intellectual development (e.g., decline in fluid intelligence, maintenance of crystallized intelligence during adulthood) is posited to be quite similar across children and adults. Recent work by Horn (this volume) and Schaie and Willis (1986) begins, however, to investigate individual differences in the longitudinal trajectories of individual intellectual development, identifying those whose intelligence remains stable, declines, or increases during adulthood.

The information-processing perspective on intellectual development also has typically focused on changes in the average performance of children and adults in components of memory and processing. The field of information processing, however, is well suited to the study of individual differences (Hertzog, 1985; Hunt, Frost, & Lunneborg, 1973; Sternberg, 1980).

The learning and contextual perspectives have perhaps more directly dealt with individual variability at any given developmental level and variability in the course of intellectual development, than the other perspectives. Dixon notes that one of the basic tenets in the contextual perspective is that individual variability in the expression and trajectory of intelligence is to be expected, as individuals are dealing with different environmental demands. Canfield and Ceci and Charness and Bieman-Copland, from the learning perspective, also point to such variability, as individuals differ in their relative position on the novice-to-expert continuum on any particular task.

Similarities in performance between young children and older adults may not be due to similar mechanisms

Throughout the chapters, the reader will be struck again and again with the apparent similarities in performance between young children and older adults, similarities that arise within a variety of different perspectives. Blackburn and Papalia review research indicating that older adults solve many of the Piagetian tasks at a level similar to that of preoperational children (approximately 7 years of age and occasionally younger). The neo-Piagetian perspective also alludes to similarities between older adults and young children in attentional capacity or working memory. Research using the information-processing perspective also points to several similarities between older adults and young children: Both (1) do not use efficient strategies for remembering new information, (2) are slow in processing information, and (3) display relatively unsophisticated regulation of their cognitive processes.

Such similarities in the intellectual performance of young children and older adults might lead one to conclude that such similarities arise from comparable sorts of mechanisms. However, by taking a life-course view of intellectual development, such a conclusion would be, at least in part, erroneous. Within the Piagetian perspective, the poorer performance of preoperational children on concrete operational tasks is explained as occurring because preoperational children have not yet acquired the cognitive structures required to reason correctly about such tasks. Such an explanation seems unlikely when applied to the poor performance of older adults. Although some have argued that older adults may lose the relevant cognitive structures appropriate for the tasks, most explanations for older adults' poorer performance center on the lack of educational or occupational demands that require them to reason in a formal logical fashion.

From the information-processing perspective, young children's use of inefficient or more primitive strategies is often described as due to the child's relatively undeveloped knowledge base regarding numbers, words, and objects. The learning perspective, however, asserts that older adults are more familiar or expert with items such as numbers and words, from their lifelong experience. Thus, to utilize the same explanation for children's and older adults' use of ineffective strategies does not seem plausible.

In some instances, similarities in performance between young children and older adults are explained via the same mechanism. For instance, information-processing models of both child and adult intellectual development use the notion of a reduction in the availability of processing resources as the locus for the slower speed of mental processes in both young children and older adults.

A lifelong perspective allows us to compare the mechanisms used to account for growth in intellectual development during childhood and growth, maintenance, and decline in intellectual development during adulthood. In-depth examination and comparison of such mechanisms afford greater precision as to the conditions under which such mechanisms will operate similarly on intellectual performance. Such an examination may lead to proposals of single mechanisms that could account for the total of intellectual development across the life course (see the concept of M-space in Pascual-Leone's theory; Pascual-Leone, 1984).

In conclusion, the chapters in this book argue convincingly for two sorts of rapprochement: (1) that among researchers and theorists who adopt different perspectives on intellectual development and (2) that among researchers and theorists examining intelligence during childhood and adulthood. Each rapprochement highlights the fact that different perspectives on intellectual development need not be at odds, but that each perspective may add to the puzzle of intellectual development, helping us construct a more nearly complete picture. In addition, viewing intellectual development as it occurs in the same organism over the course of life may allow us to crack the riddle of intellectual development.

References

Baltes, P. B. (1987). Theoretical propositions of life-span developmental psychology: On the dynamics between growth and decline. *Developmental Psychology*, *23*, 611–626.

Baltes, P. B., Dittmann-Kohli, F., & Dixon, R. A. (1984). New perspectives on the development of intelligence in adulthood: Toward a dual-process conception and a model of selective optimization with compensation. In P. B. Baltes & O. G. Brim (Eds.), *Life-span development and behavior* (Vol. 6, pp. 33–76). New York: Academic Press.

Berg, C. A., & Sternberg, R. J. (1985). A triarchic theory of intellectual development during adulthood. *Developmental Review*, *5*, 334–370.

Berg, C. A., & Sternberg, R. J. (in press). Adults' conceptions of intelligence across the adult life span. *Psychology and Aging*.

Bijou, S. W., & Baer, D. M. (1965). *Child development* (Vol. 1). New York: Appleton-Century-Crofts.

Case, R. (1985). *Intellectual development: Birth to adulthood*. Orlando, FL: Academic Press.

Gagne, R. M. (1965). *The conditions of learning*. New York: Holt, Rinehart, & Winston.

Hertzog, C. (1985). An individual differences perspective: Implications for cognitive research in gerontology. *Research on Aging*, *7*, 7–45.

Hunt, E. J., Frost, N., & Lunneborg, C. (1973). Individual differences in cognition: A new approach to intelligence. In C. Bower (Ed.), *Advances in learning and motivation* (Vol. 7). New York: Academic Press.

Intelligence and its measurement: A symposium (1921). *Journal of Educational Psychology*, *12*, 123–147, 195–216, 271–275.

Kail, R., & Pellegrino, J. W. (1985). *Human intelligence: Perspectives and prospects*. New York: Freeman.

Kendler, H. H., & Kendler, T. S. (1975). From discrimination learning to cognitive development. In W. K. Estes (Ed.), *Handbook of learning and cognitive processes* (Vol. 1). Hillsdale, NJ: Erlbaum.

Labouvie-Vief, G. (1982). Growth and aging in life span perspective. *Human Development*, *25*, 65–88.

Lachman, R., Lachman, J. L., & Butterfield, E. C. (1980). *Cognitive psychology and information processing*. Hillsdale, NJ: Erlbaum.

Miller, G. A., Galanter, E., & Pribram, K. H. (1960). *Plans and the structure of behavior*. New York: Holt, Rinehart & Winston.

Newell, A., Shaw, J., & Simon, H. A. (1960). Report on a general problem-solving program.

In *Proceedings of the International Conference on Information Processing.* Paris: UNESCO.

Pascual-Leone, J. (1983). Growing into human maturity: Toward a metasubjective theory of adulthood stages. In P. B. Baltes & O. G. Brim (Eds.), *Life-span development and behavior* (Vol. 5, pp. 118–156). New York: Academic Press.

Pascual-Leone, J. (1984). Attentional, dialectic, and mental effort: Towards an organismic theory of life stages. In M. L. Commons, F. A. Richards, & C. Armon (Eds.), *Beyond formal operations* (pp. 182–215). New York: Praeger.

Piaget, J. (1950). *The psychology of intelligence.* London: Routledge & Kegan Paul.

Piaget, J. (1952). *The origins of intelligence in children.* New York: International Universities Press.

Schaie, K. W., & Willis, S. (1986). Can decline in adult intellectual functioning be reversed? *Developmental Psychology, 22,* 223–232.

Sternberg, R. J. (1980). Sketch of a componential subtheory of intelligence. *Behavioral and Brain Sciences, 3,* 573–584.

Sternberg, R. J. (1985). *Beyond IQ: A triarchic theory of human intelligence.* Cambridge: Cambridge University Press.

Sternberg, R. J. (1988). What theorists of intellectual development among children can learn from their counterparts studying adults. In E. M. Hetherington, R. Lerner, & M. Perlmutter (Eds.), *Child development in life-span perspective* (pp. 259–275). Hillsdale, NJ: Erlbaum.

Sternberg, R. J., Conway, B. E., Ketron, J. L., & Bernstein, M. (1981). People's conceptions of intelligence. *Journal of Personality and Social Psychology, 41,* 37–55.

Sternberg, R. J., & Detterman, D. K. (1986). *What is intelligence?* Norwood, NJ: Ablex.

Sternberg, R. J., & Powell, J. S. (1983). The development of intelligence. In P. H. Mussen (Series Ed.), with J. Flavell & E. M. Markman (Vol. Eds.), *Handbook of child psychology* (Vol. 3, pp. 341–419). New York: Wiley.

White, S. H. (1965). Evidence for a hierarchical arrangement of learning processes. In L. P. Lipsitt & C. C Spiker (Eds.), *Advances in child development and behavior* (Vol. 2). New York: Academic Press.

Yussen, S. R., & Kane, P. (1981). Children's concept of intelligence. In S. R. Yussen (Ed.), *The growth of reflection in children.* New York: Academic Press.

2 The psychometric perspective on intellectual development in childhood and adolescence

Michael K. Gardner and Elaine Clark

Introduction and definition of the psychometric approach

The psychometric approach to intellectual development seeks to define and quantify dimensions of intelligence, primarily through the collection of individual differences data and through the construction of reliable and valid measurement scales (i.e., mental tests). Although this definition is accurate, it may be more meaningful to consider the types of questions the psychometric approach attempts to answer. Siegler and Richards (1982) list the following: "How can intellectual development be quantified? How can such quantifications be used to predict later intellectual achievements? How can the intelligence of individual children be meaningfully compared? What factors make up intelligence, and do the factors change with age?" (p. 900). What is clear from these questions is that psychometric approaches to intelligence have had two major thrusts (Kail & Pellegrino, 1985). The first has been educationally oriented and pragmatic. How can we measure intelligence and sort individuals accordingly? The second has been research-oriented and theoretical. What are the relevant dimensions of intellectual variability within the human mind? Different scholars have made contributions to these two separate areas, and the relative lack of overlap has left the field more disjointed than is desirable. Nonetheless, psychometrics has had a major impact on psychology, and beyond. In discussing the development of the first IQ test, Jenkins and Paterson (1961, p. 81) stated, "Probably no psychological innovation has had more impact on the societies of the Western world."

In this chapter we begin by discussing some of the assumptions underlying the psychometric approach to intellectual development. We then discuss theoretical conceptions of intelligence that have grown out of the psychometric perspective. Next we present a review of some of the more popular current intellectual assessment instruments derived through psychometrics. After that review we address a number of psychometric issues that pertain to development in particular. Finally, we briefly discuss future directions and give our conclusions concerning the psychometric perspective.

16

Assumptions underlying the psychometric approach

Three basic assumptions underlie the psychometric approach. Although some (e.g., Sternberg, 1977) have doubted the appropriateness of this approach for the task of delineating the nature of intelligence, we present the assumptions here to illustrate the character of the psychometric perspective.

1. *The nature of intelligence and intellectual development can be fruitfully studied by examining individual differences in performance on tasks.* Whereas experimental psychologists perform *true experiments* (Campbell & Stanley, 1963) psychometric researchers rely on correlational data. Their interest lies in determining the rank ordering of individuals, and the stability of that rank ordering from one task to the next. If several tasks display the same rank ordering of individuals, they may indicate a single underlying ability. For example, if the same people score high on tests of solving analogies, vocabulary, sentence completion, and completing figural matrices, it is reasonable to infer that these people possess more of something (intelligence) that contributes to performance in numerous cognitive areas than do others who score low on the same tests.

It is important to realize that the study of individual differences is only one part of the overall picture of the development of intellectual ability. It is logically independent of the growth of the average level of intellectual functioning (McCall, 1981). Ignoring the difference between these two types of information can lead to absurd conclusions. For example, Bloom (1964) claimed that 50% of an individual's adult intelligence is developed by the age of 4. The basis of his claim was the fact that IQ at 4 years and at 17 years were correlated approximately 0.71; that is, they share 50% variance. But as McCall (1981) noted, the claim is based solely on the stability of individual differences and not on the level of intellectual functioning. Indeed, the 4-year-old's mean performance level is far less than 50% of the 17-year-old's.

2. *Mathematical techniques, such as factor analysis, can inform us about the structure of mental abilities.* We stated that psychometrics is based on correlational data. Psychometricians have developed sophisticated statistical techniques known as *factor analysis* to reduce large tables of correlations to some smaller number of underlying dimensions of variability known as *factors.* These techniques were originally developed to help discover the structure of mental abilities. Although factor analysis is a general data analytic approach that can be applied to any correlation matrix, it is still used in the abilities area to develop and improve tests and to support or refute theories of mental structure.

Although psychometricians have found factor analysis a useful tool, it can be abused (Guilford, 1952; McNemar, 1951). Results from factor analysis are strongly dependent on decisions made by the researcher while conducting the analysis. Should factors (abilities) be uncorrelated (orthogonal factors) or should they be allowed to correlate (oblique factors)? How many factors should be extracted? What method of extraction should be used? Should the extracted factors be rotated, and if so, to what criteria should they be rotated? Differences in the answers to these questions can lead to different factorial structures given the same set of original data. Finally, a well-known adage among factor analysts is that you only get out of a factor analysis what you put in. This means that the selection of tests to be factor-analyzed and the population of subjects to whom the tests are administered will play a crucial role in the outcome of a factor analysis. The point we wish to make is that blind reliance on factor analysis to determine the structure of human abilities is a mistake. The technique must be used appropriately, and its results should be confirmed by other converging operations (Garner, Hake, & Eriksen, 1956).

3. *The development of assessment instruments for measuring intellectual performance is as important a goal as building theories of intelligence.* Because psychometrics always had a pragmatic side, developing assessment instruments has been on an equal footing with theory building. A major goal of the psychometric approach is to order individuals according to their various abilities. These data can then be used to solve practical problems such as selecting personnel or determining eligibility for special services.

Such real-world applications have forced to the forefront issues of test reliability and validity. Reliable tests are consistent measures, yielding the same information over different testing occasions (test–retest reliability), different sets of items (alternate forms reliability), and different items within the same test (internal consistency reliability) (Anastasi, 1988). Valid tests measure what they intend to measure (Anastasi, 1988), and they usually predict valued outcomes (predictive validity). Reliability is a precondition for validity. Good tests have high degrees of both reliability and validity.

Psychometrics' emphasis on the pragmatic has been a benefit. When theoretical notions of intelligence have become bogged down, psychometricians still have been able to make progress on the development of reliable and valid (in the predictive sense) tests of intellectual ability. Those practical achievements have then served as an impetus for theoreticians to explain the empirical relations found. In short, pragmatics and theoretical knowledge, while sometimes growing up apart, have challenged each other and spurred the search for an all-encompassing theory of human ability and its development.

Theoretical conceptions of intelligence within the psychometric approach

Theoretical conceptions of intelligence within the psychometric approach are best understood by following the history of their development, which is

Reliable = yields same info over diff occasions

traced in this section. Theories have differed considerably in the number of mental abilities posited, as well as their organization. In particular, there has been a tension between theories that have proposed a single over-arching general intelligence, and those that have proposed multiple abilities to the exclusion of general intelligence. Some theorists have resolved the conflict by proposing a hierarchical ordering of abilities, including both general and specific abilities.

1) test-retest
2) alt forms
3) int consist.

A second conflict regards the nature of tests that best measure intelligence. Some psychologists believed that the best way to understand the mind was to analyze it into simpler components. They were of the opinion that intelligence could best be measured by tests of physical abilities and the ability to make simple sensory discriminations. The hope was that these more "atomistic" measurements could be combined to yield an index of the complex concept of intelligence. Other psychologists believed a more direct approach was appropriate. To measure a complex mental characteristic such as intelligence, one should measure complex mental operations such as judgment and reasoning. We now turn to this dilemma over the content of measures of intelligence.

Valid = measure what it intends to measure & is predictive

Physical–sensory testing

The story begins in Britain in the 1880s. Sir Francis Galton, cousin of biologist Charles Darwin, initiated interest in the study of individual differences. He believed that mental ability was inherited, just as physical characteristics were (Sternberg & Powell, 1983). He also believed that brighter and duller individuals could be distinguished by two characteristics (Galton, 1883): (1) overall energy level (brighter individuals had more energy); and (2) sensitivity to stimuli (brighter individuals had greater sensitivity to small differences between stimuli). Following up on these beliefs, Galton collected measures from 9,337 individuals at the South Kensington Museum in London (Brody & Brody, 1976). The measures were primarily tests of strength and sensory acuity. Unfortunately, Galton never conducted a validity test of his data; that is, he never looked to see if his physical measures were related to ratings of mental acumen. Such tasks fell to those he had influenced.

One of those influenced by Galton was James McKeen Cattell (Brody & Brody, 1976). Cattell, who coined the term *mental test* (Cattell, 1890), was intrigued by individual differences (Kail & Pellegrino, 1985) and encouraged his students to study the correlates of mental ability within the physical–sensory testing tradition. One student, Clark L. Wissler, conducted a validity study that stilled interest in the approach almost entirely. Wissler (1901) investigated the relationship between students' grades at Columbia and 21 simple measures such as strength of hand, visual acuity, cancellation of "A's," and reaction time. His results were quite disappointing. Although the grades correlated among themselves at a fairly substantial level, the correlations between the various physical–sensory tests and grades were quite low. Wissler acknowledged that "if we accept the conclusions of this research as final, an individual must be regarded as the algebraic sum of a vast array of small abilities of almost equal probability, the resulting combination conforming to the laws of chance" (Wissler, 1901, p. 42).

Complex mental testing

Not all psychologists interested in individual differences agreed with Galton and Cattell about the importance of physical–sensory testing. Among them was Alfred Binet, who coauthored a paper (Binet & Henri, 1895) criticizing the physical–sensory approach even before Wissler's results had appeared. Binet felt an adequate test of mental ability should be concerned with the higher mental processes, and should sample a large number of these processes. He and Henri described their conception of a better intelligence test. It included measures of 10 different faculties, with an emphasis on processes such as imagination, attention, and comprehension.

Stella Sharp, a student of Edward Titchener's at Cornell, set about testing the usefulness of the Binet-type measures (Sharp, 1899). Sharp's tests were heavily weighted toward memory (Sternberg & Powell, 1983), which was not in accord with Binet and Henri's (1895) proposals. Also, Sharp's subject population (seven Cornell graduate students) had an extremely restricted intellectual range. Not surprisingly, her results were only marginally more encouraging than Wissler's. In her balanced presentation of the results, however, she concluded that complex mental tests held more hope for measuring intellectual ability than simple sensory or physical tests did.

Sharp's findings might have had a similar chilling effect on the complex mental testing movement, but a practical problem arose that increased interest in mental testing. In 1904 a commission was set up by the French minister of public instruction in Paris to develop tests that would identify children who were retarded and who could not, therefore, benefit from regular public school instruction. These children would then be placed in a special class more suited to their needs. Binet and Simon (1905) developed a set of 30 different tests arranged in ascending order of difficulty, and weighted heavily toward the higher mental functions such as judgment, comprehension, and reasoning (Anastasi, 1988). The difficulty level of items was determined empirically on a standardization sample of 50 normal children, aged 3 to 13 years, and some retarded children and adults. This test has become known as the 1905 Binet scales.

The test was revised in 1908, and again in 1911. In the 1908 revision the concept of mental age became explicit (Anastasi, 1988). Also, provisions were made to distinguish among the abilities of normal children, as well as to distinguish the mentally defective from the normal. The scales became very popular and were introduced in the United States by Goddard (1908, 1910). These initial American versions of the Binet scales were very similar to their French counterparts, and were used primarily to evaluate the mentally retarded (Sattler, 1988). Goddard also altered Binet's conception of intelligence in presenting the Binet scales to an American audience. Whereas Binet had conceptualized intelligence as a constellation of interrelated mental faculties (primarily higher faculties) that were open to environmental modification, Goddard presented intelligence as a single, underlying mental capability that was primarily determined by heredity (Tuddenham, 1962).

The Binet scales began their rapid rise to prominence in the United States when Lewis Terman (1916) modified earlier versions by adding tests, extending the age range (now 3 through 18 years), and standardizing the test on an American sample (Sattler, 1988). Terman also added a new concept to mental testing with the advent of the 1916 Stanford-Binet: the intelligence quotient (IQ). IQ was obtained by dividing the child's mental age, which was determined by how many items he or she passed on the test, by the child's chronological age (Bayley, 1970). Determining IQ in this way (the ratio method) is problematic, as we point out in a later section. However, the ratio IQ remained in use until the 1960 revision of the Stanford-Binet (Terman & Merrill, 1960). The Stanford-Binet recently underwent a fourth revision (Thorndike, Hagen, & Sattler, 1986a, 1986b) and is still a popular individual test of intelligence.

Factor-analytic theories

At about the same time Cattell and Binet were conducting their research on intelligence, Charles Spearman (1904a, 1904b) began investigating mental ability in England. Spearman advocated a correlational approach, and criticized previous research for its lack of methodological rigor. One issue he raised was the problem of unreliability of measures. Because unreliability lowers correlations between measures, he proposed correcting obtained correlations for attenuation due to unreliability.

Spearman conducted a study he hoped would be a methodologically sound investigation of intelligence and that had the characteristics of those conducted by Galton and Cattell. From a student population, Spearman collected three measures of relative sensory discrimination (discrimination of pitches, shades of gray, and weights) and four measures of intelligence (school achievement, school achievement corrected for age, teachers' impressions of students, and "common sense" as evaluated by an interview). He then calculated the correlations among the measures and their probable errors. His results were as follows: Measures of intelligence were intercorrelated 0.55 on average; sensory measures were intercorrelated 0.25 on average; and measures of intelligence were correlated with sensory measures 0.38 on average. Spearman then corrected the correlation between measures of intelligence and sensory measures for unreliability of the measures. In applying his correction formula, however, he assumed that departures from unity of the intercorrelations among the sensory measures, and among the intelligence measures, were solely due to unreliability in the measures. This is certainly not the case. Application of his correction formula led to the astounding conclusion that the correlation between the sensory measures and the intelligence measures was 1.00 – a finding that led Spearman to postulate the *Universal Unity of the Intellective Functions.* Essentially this stated that all intellectual functions are based on a common ability. Although this ability contributes on all tasks, some skill at each task is also due to a specific ability relating only to that particular task.

Spearman's findings proved to be the beginning of his (1927) two-factor theory of intelligence. He claimed that all intellectual tasks were governed by two factors: a general factor, *g*, that contributed to all tasks, and a specific factor, *s*, that contributed only to a specific task. There were as many *s* factors as there were tasks, but there was only a single *g* factor, and it accounted for the positive intercorrelations among intellectual tests. Spearman also developed the basics of the mathematical model, factor analysis, that allowed one to calculate *g*. His *g* was essentially the first unrotated principal factor in the data set.

Spearman was never very clear on exactly what *g* was. At one level, he claimed that *g* was nothing more than that which was common to all tests of intellectual ability. Although certainly correct, this operational definition is not very enlightening. At a slightly deeper level, Spearman claimed *g* was the eduction of relations and correlates. These were two of three basic principles he had earlier proposed as part of a theory of cognition (Spearman, 1923). The eduction of a relation is knowing how two things are related – for instance, that black and white are opposites. The eduction of a correlate is knowing what thing satisfies a particular relation to a given object or word – for example, that *animal* is the superset of mammal. Spearman felt analogies were particularly good measures of *g* because they tapped the eduction of relations and correlates.

At a metaphorical level, Spearman equated *g* with mental energy. In this sense *g* referred to some sort of potentiality that individuals possessed in differing degrees. Spearman believed that the output of this energy was a constant, and that new activities would begin when others ceased to keep the output level the same. Although the mental energy metaphor is probably not correct, the notion of native potential that it engendered was quite close to what many members of the general public believed.

1940

bond theory

A slightly different conception of *g* came from a group of psychologists known as "bond theorists" (Brown & Thomson, 1940; Thomson, 1951; Thorndike, 1925). These psychologists did not differ with Spearman's idea of general intelligence, but offered a different explanation of how it arises. They claimed that the mind was composed of a large number of mental bonds. Each task called upon a different subset of these bonds for its solution. Tasks were correlated to the extent that they shared bonds. General intelligence was an indicator of the total number of bonds an individual possessed.

American psychometrician L. L. Thurstone (1931, 1938, 1947) disagreed with Spearman concerning a single, general intelligence. Instead, Thurstone supposed that performance was governed by some small number of "group factors" – factors that played a role in some, but not all, of the tests in a battery. Spearman's theory, by contrast, did not admit the existence of any group factors (although by the time of his death Spearman had been forced to admit that this was a mistake [Sternberg & Powell, 1983]). This difference in theoretical positions was due to differences in the way each theorist performed his factor analysis. Because the mechanics of factor analysis are often difficult to disentangle from the theoretical positions being espoused, such disputes can arise. Usually it is later shown that such disputes are not substantive in nature; rather, they are due to differences in emphasis or differences in decisions made during data analysis.

Thurstone 1938

Thurstone (1938) applied his new techniques in a study that involved 56 tests taken by 218 college students. He identified a total of nine factors, two of which seemed less well defined than the other seven. These seven factors became known as the primary mental abilities, and they consisted of Number, Memory, Perceptual Speed, Space, Verbal Fluency, Verbal Comprehension, and Inductive Reasoning. Thurstone (Thurstone & Thurstone, 1941) developed a set of tests, the *Primary Mental Abilities Tests*, for assessing these abilities in high school and college age individuals. Recently, Schaie (1985) revised the test to assess older adult subjects. A version of the test is available for young children as well.

7 factors

Although it seemed that Thurstone had proved Spearman's general intelligence incorrect, a methodological problem forced Thurstone and Spearman to acknowledge a common ground. Thurstone discovered that in practice he could achieve simple structure only by allowing his primary mental abilities to correlate with one another. But factors that correlate can be factor-analyzed, just as tests that correlate can be factor-analyzed. When this is done, a general factor appears at a higher level. Thus, just as Spearman was forced to accept the existence of group factors, Thurstone was forced to accept the existence of general intelligence as a higher order factor (Sternberg & Powell, 1983).

Cyril Burt (1940, 1949) and Philip E. Vernon (1950, 1965) have proposed hierarchical models of intelligence based on factor analysis that offer a rapprochement between Spearman's general intelligence model and Thurstone's primary mental abilities approach. Because Vernon's is the more widely discussed, we present it here. Vernon's model begins in a top-down approach by extracting a general factor (Kail & Pellegrino, 1985). The residual correlations are then factor-analyzed and two major group factors are extracted: a Verbal–Educational factor and a Spatial–Practical–Mechanical factor. These group factors can be further analyzed, yielding minor group factors at the third level. Beneath these factors, at the fourth level, are factors specific to individual tests.

John Horn and Raymond B. Cattell (1966; Cattell, 1963, 1971) have proposed a different multilevel theory of intellectual ability focusing on the distinction between *fluid intelligence* and *crystallized intelligence*. Horn and Cattell's analysis begins similarly to Thurstone's. They take a large battery of ability tests and perform a factor analysis allowing correlated factors, then rotate to a simple structure criterion. This produces a set of primary abilities, which are somewhat more numerous than Thurstone's. These primary abilities are then factor-analyzed in a second-order factor analysis. From this analysis Horn and Cattell extract a number of factors, but the two most robust are labeled g_f, Fluid Intelligence, and g_c, Crystallized Intelligence.

Horn and Cattell interpret fluid intelligence as the basic biological capacity of an individual, whereas crystallized intelligence represents the products of acculturation, or acquired knowledge. A similar distinction was made by Hebb (1939, 1942). Hebb defined intelligence A, which represents potential, and intelligence B, which represents realized intelligence (Brody & Brody, 1976). Horn and Cattell (1966) have reported different developmental courses for fluid and crystallized intelligence. Fluid intelligence peaks somewhere during the twenties, and declines thereafter, while crystallized intelligence remains constant or increases throughout the life-span (Sternberg & Powell, 1983). For a more complete description of Horn's position on intellectual development during adulthood, see Chapter 3 of this volume.

Perhaps the factor analyst whose theory has been most at odds with the mainstream of psychometric theorizing on mental abilities is J. P. Guilford. Guilford's structure of intellect theory, as originally proposed (Guilford, 1967; Guilford & Hoepfner, 1971), differed from previous theories in three major ways. First, it was a hypothetical model that Guilford tried to verify using factor analysis. Previous theorists had relied on factor analysis to discover the structure that a model should take, rather than to test a proposed model. Second, it proposed an extremely large number of factors: 120 in all. These resulted from the crossing of five types of mental operations (cognition, memory, divergent production, convergent production, and evaluation) with four types of stimulus content (figural, symbolic, semantic, and behavioral) and six types of performance products (units, classes, relations, systems, transformations, and implications). Later (Guilford, 1977) the number of factors was increased to 150 when the figural stimulus content was replaced by auditory and visual stimulus contents. Third, Guilford had required all these first-order factors to be independent of each other (i.e., uncorrelated).

Several problems have plagued Guilford's theory. First, tests associated with each of Guilford's factors have been so specific that they lack predictive validity (Brody & Brody, 1976; Caldwell, Schrader, Michael, & Meyers, 1970; Holly & Michael, 1972). Second, the replicability of Guilford's factor structures has been challenged (Horn & Knapp, 1973). Guilford has used Procrustean rotation (rotation to maximize fit to a predetermined set of factor loadings) in his analyses. As Horn and Knapp (1973) demonstrated, Guilford's data fit randomly generated theories as well as they fit the structure of intellect model. Finally, Guilford's original position that all his factors were orthogonal seems at odds with the overwhelming majority of data on human abilities (Brody & Brody, 1976). The finding of positive correlations among (appropriately scored) tests of intellectual ability has been so noticeable it even has a name: the positive manifold.

Eventually Guilford (1982) modified his theory to admit the existence of higher-order factors. First-order factors still correspond to the 150 separate structure of intellect abilities. Second-order factors now correspond to collapsing two of the three structure of intellect dimensions over a third. This can be accomplished by collapsing over any of the three dimensions (operations, contents, or products), and yields a total of 85 second-order factors (Kail & Pellegrino, 1985). Third-order factors correspond to collapsing over two of the three dimensions. There are 16 of these, and they correspond to the list of the 5 operations, 5 contents, and 6 products. Despite these changes in Guilford's theory, the structure of intellect model seems to be farthest from the consensus of factor-analytic theorists. Probably Vernon's hierarchical model is closest to that consensus.

To summarize, work on psychometric theories of intelligence began from two very different perspectives. One was dominated by the belief that intelligence could be linked to simpler physical and sensory attributes. This approach died out, although new versions of it have been resurrected in the information-processing arena (e.g., Jensen, 1987). The other perspective held that intelligence could best be studied by focusing on higher mental processes such as reasoning and judgment. This approach met with some early disappointments, but the pragmatic success of the Binet scales in the educational field helped revive it. It eventually became the primary psychometric approach to studying intelligence.

The development of factor analysis provided a means of generating, and occasionally testing, theories of mental ability. Over time, these theories have become both more sophisticated and more diverse. Few theorists now doubt the existence of a general intelligence or a set of interrelated group factors, but theorists do differ on which level of analysis is the more important. Finally, it should be remembered that it is difficult to disentangle the portions of a factor-analytic theory that are dictated by the data from the mathematics of factor analysis (with its inherent limitations). This means that only some portions of a factor-analytic theory are psychological in nature; other portions are an artifact of the data analytic technique employed (Sternberg, 1977). These problems have been reduced in recent years by the development of new psychometric techniques such as confirmatory factor analysis and structural equation modeling (Joreskog & Sorbom, 1989).

Measurement instruments derived from the psychometric approach

This section reviews some of the more widely used intelligence tests derived from the psychometric approach. The tests developed for child, adolescent, and adult populations have been, for the most part, loosely based on theories of intelligence. All have the ability to derive a single number summarizing performance, and therefore they implicitly affirm general intelligence. Most developers of these tests, however, have also claimed that intelligence is more than can be captured in a single score. Unfortunately, these authors rarely specify just what this "more" consists of.

Infant tests, however, have been developed with theories of cognitive development in mind, rather than theories of intelligence. They tend to include very different items at different ages, and are better as a measure of current cognitive functioning than as a predictor of later intellectual performance. All of the tests (infant and noninfant) have reasonably strong psychometric properties, although in some cases the norms are not current. It is important to be acquainted with these tests, because they often serve as the data on which new psychometric theories are built.

Stanford-Binet Intelligence Scale, Fourth Edition (SB4)   1986

The *Stanford-Binet Intelligence Scale: Fourth Edition* was published in 1986 (Thorndike, Hagen, & Sattler, 1986a, 1986b). The SB4 represents the most extensive, and perhaps the most important, revision of the Binet (Anastasi, 1989). It "concentrates on quantifying the attribute that a century of psychometrics has proved central to educational and vocational success" (Cronbach, 1989, p. 775). The SB4 was restandardized on a nationally representative sample of more than 5,000 individuals between the ages of 2 and 23. The test authors sought to maintain continuity with previous editions by retaining certain item types, and like its predecessors, the test is heavily weighted toward verbal items. The content, however, has been

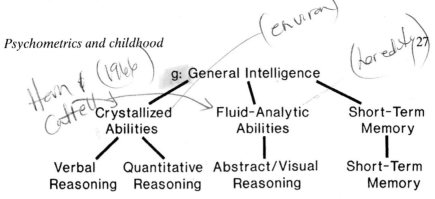

Figure 2.1. Theoretical model of intelligence for the Stanford-Binet, Fourth Edition. (Adapted with permission of The Riverside Publishing Company from *Stanford-Binet Intelligence Scale Guide for Administering and Scoring the Fourth Edition* by R. L. Thorndike, E. P. Hagen, and J. M. Sattler. The Riverside Publishing Company, 8420 W. Bryn Mawr Avenue, Chicago, IL 60631. Copyright 1986.)

expanded to include tests of quantitative skill, spatial reasoning, and short-term memory. Items were selected on the basis of a hierarchical model of intelligence consisting of three separate levels, with the first level representing *g*, and the second and third representing group factors. (See Figure 2.1.) There are three factors in level 2: Crystallized Abilities, Fluid-Analytic Abilities, and Short-Term Memory; and four more specific factors in level 3: Verbal Reasoning, Quantitative Reasoning, Abstract/Visual Reasoning, and Short-Term Memory. Level 3 factors are measured by 15 individual subtests: vocabulary, comprehension, absurdities, verbal relations, quantitative, number series, equation building, pattern analysis, copying, matrices, paper folding and cutting, bead memory, and memory for sentences, digits, and objects.

Whereas previous Binet items were grouped by age, in the SB4 items are categorized according to content areas (subtests). Because not all items are suitable for all ages, no one person is administered all 15 subtests. An adaptive format based on chronological age and vocabulary subtest performance is used to help ensure that only items appropriate for an individual's developmental level are administered. Unfortunately, this means that there is no comparable battery of subtests given for the various ages, thus limiting both inter- and intra-individual comparisons across the broad age range that the SB4 covers. Nonetheless, the SB4 compares favorably with other commonly used intelligence scales for both normal and exceptional populations, and represents significant advances in the methodology of test construction.

Wechsler intelligence scales

The first of the Wechsler scales, the *Wechsler-Bellevue Intelligence Scale*, was published in 1939 (Wechsler, 1939) and later revised in 1955 and 1981.

The most current version is the 1981 scale, the *Wechsler Adult Intelligence Scale–Revised* (WAIS-R; Wechsler, 1981). The Wechsler scales were initially intended to assess the intellectual skills of older adolescents and adults. However, there have been two downward extensions of the original scale, the *Wechsler Intelligence Scale for Children* (WISC), first published in 1949 and revised as the WISC-R in 1974 (Wechsler, 1974), and the *Wechsler Preschool and Primary Scale* (WPPSI), published first in 1967 and revised in 1989 as the WPPSI-R (Wechsler, 1989). The revisions of the scales have represented significant improvements in the technical quality of test construction; however, they have done little to advance theoretical conceptions of intelligence. An overriding theme has been Wechsler's view of intelligence as a "global capacity" that consists of a number of interrelated functions. The scales have, therefore, historically consisted of a number of verbal and performance subtests that yield verbal, performance, and full scale deviation IQ scores. Factor-analytic studies have generally supported a two-factor structure for the scales (Verbal Comprehension and Perceptual Organization), although in the case of the WISC-R (Kaufman, 1975) and WAIS-R (Waller & Waldman, 1990) a third factor has been identified (Freedom from Distractibility). Although Wechsler believed that patterns of subtest performance would be diagnostically useful (e.g., diagnosing learning disabilities), the lack of empirical support for this (Matarazzo, 1972) and the lack of uniformity across the various subtests (i.e., the highest scale score possible differs for different subtests) makes such a practice questionable. Nonetheless, the Wechsler scales are often the tests of choice for children and adults with learning problems. This is in part due to the test's admirable technical qualities.

The WAIS-R, the scale used for individuals 16 through 74, was restandardized on approximately 1,800 individuals. The test comprises six verbal subtests (information, digit span, vocabulary, arithmetic, comprehension, and similarities) and five performance subtests (picture completion, picture arrangement, block design, object assembly, and digit symbol). The WISC-R, designed for children 6 years to 17 years, has a very similar structure to the WAIS-R. The WISC-R was restandardized on approximately 2,000 school-age children, but unfortunately the norms are dated (a new version, the WISC-III, is expected soon). The test consists of six verbal subtests (information, similarities, arithmetic, vocabulary, comprehension, and digit span) and six performance subtests (picture completion, picture arrangement, block design, object assembly, coding, and mazes). The WPPSI-R, a scale designed to test abilities of children between the ages of 3 years and $7\frac{1}{4}$ years was restandardized on 1,700 children. The WPPSI-R consists of six performance subtests (object assembly, geometric design, block design, mazes, picture completion, and animal pegs) and six verbal subtests (information, comprehension, arithmetic, vocabulary, similarities, and sentences). Though similar in structure and content to its predecessor, the WPPSI, the test has undergone a number of changes, including the addition of new items and the removal of obsolete items, the addition of a subtest (object assembly), and an extension in the age range (formerly the test began at 4 years).

Differential Ability Scales (DAS)

The DAS (Elliott, 1990) was developed from the British Ability Scales (Elliott, Murray, & Pearson, 1979) and standardized on more than 3,400 U.S. children. The test, consisting of both a cognitive and an achievement battery, is suitable for children $2\frac{1}{2}$ years to 18 years. The two batteries of tests were co-normed for the purpose of analyzing ability–achievement discrepancies used in diagnosing learning disabilities. The achievement battery consists of three brief, but reliable, tests: Basic Number Skill, Spelling, and Word Reading (the use of this battery is restricted to children 5 years and older). The cognitive battery includes 17 subtests that are divided into two age levels, preschool ($2\frac{1}{2}$ to 6 years) and school age (6 to 18 years). The core cognitive subtests include block building, verbal comprehension, picture similarities, naming vocabulary, early number concepts, copying, pattern construction, recall of designs, word definitions, matrices, similarities, and sequential and quantitative reasoning. Other diagnostic subtests include matching letterlike forms, recall of digits, recall of objects, recognitive of pictures, and speed of information processing.

The actual number of subtests administered depends on the child's age, as well as the reason for testing. Although the majority of children are administered the core–diagnostic subtests recommended for their age, additional subtests outside their age level can be administered. This "out-of-level" testing was designed to ensure that the brighter, younger child as well as the less capable, older child would be administered appropriate subtests. The scores on the subtests can be combined to yield an index of general cognitive ability, as well as three cluster scores (verbal ability, nonverbal reasoning ability, and spatial ability). Innovative procedures (e.g., tailored test administration) and improvements in test construction methodology (e.g., more relevant assumptions in calculating internal consistency reliability) make the DAS an attractive candidate for assessing mental functioning.

Kaufman Assessment Battery for Children (K-ABC)

The K-ABC was published in 1983 (Kaufman & Kaufman, 1983) as a measure of intelligence for children $2\frac{1}{2}$ years to $12\frac{1}{2}$ years. The K-ABC, which was standardized on 2,000 children, was developed on the basis of a model of simultaneous and sequential processing of information, and consists of two sections, one measuring mental processing and the other measuring achievement. Sequential processing, the ability to solve problems in a serial order, is measured by three subtests (hand movements, number recall, and word order), and simultaneous processing, or the ability to solve a problem by integrating information simultaneously, is measured by seven subtests (magic window, face recognition, Gestalt closure, triangles, matrix analogies, spatial memory, and photo series).

The K-ABC has commendable psychometric properties. Unfortunately, what is meant by simultaneous and sequential processing remains unclear. In fact, the distinction between the mental-processing and achievement sections is vague (i.e., mental processing is required to perform well on the achievement subtests). Another problem concerns the K-ABC's use with minority populations. Although the K-ABC is composed of mostly non-verbal items intended to reduce the impact of cultural biases, the normative data underrepresent Hispanics and low-income blacks. Sattler (1988) goes so far as to recommend that the K-ABC not be used as a primary instrument to assess intelligence in most cases.

McCarthy Scales of Children's Ability (MSCA)

The MSCA is a test for children $2\frac{1}{2}$ years to $8\frac{1}{2}$ years of age. Though dated (McCarthy, 1972), it is considered by some to be the test of choice for preschool testing (Cronbach, 1989). The MSCA is a well-standardized instrument based on approximately 1,000 children. The scale, which consists of 18 subtests, yields a general cognitive index and five factor scores: verbal, quantitative, perceptual-performance, memory, and motor. Because the five scales are not factorially independent, they do not represent distinct abilities. This makes the MSCA a better measure of general ability than specific ability.

Group tests of intelligence

Group tests of intelligence are often used as an initial screening device to determine those who may need further individual evaluation. Some of the most commonly used group tests are the *Multidimensional Aptitude Battery* (Jackson, 1984), *Cognitive Abilities Tests* (Thorndike & Hagen, 1986), *Otis-Lennon School Ability Test* (Otis & Lennon, 1989), *Henmon-Nelson Tests of Mental Ability* (Lamke, Nelson, & French, 1973), and *Kuhlmann-Anderson Measure of Academic Potential* (Kuhlmann & Anderson, 1982). It is beyond the scope of this chapter to review these tests in detail, but reviews may be found in various editions of Buros's *Mental Measurements Yearbook* (e.g.,

Conoley & Kramer, 1989) and *Test Critiques* (e.g., Keyser & Sweetland, 1988).

Infant scales

Although the tests just reviewed are widely used, they are generally inappropriate with very young children. The following scales, however, were developed with the capacities of the infant and the young child in mind.

Bayley Scales of Infant Development. The Bayley Scales of Infant Development (Bayley, 1969) were based on the results of the Berkeley Growth Study (Honzik, MacFarlane, & Allen, 1948), and standardized on more than 1,200 infants and children. The test, suitable for children 2 months to 30 months old, yields indices of mental development and psychomotor development. There is also an infant behavior–rating scale to record systematically observations of a child's behavior. The test correlates moderately with other scales (e.g., Stanford-Binet) on a concurrent basis. The norms are dated, but the test provides valuable information about early cognitive development and is considered by some to be the best measure of infant development (Sattler, 1988).

Denver Developmental Screening Test–Revised (DDST-R). The DDST-R was published in 1975 by Frankenburg, Dodds, Fandal, Kazuk, and Cohrs (1975). This screening test was originally designed to assess developmental delays in infants and children between birth to 6 years of age. The revised test is essentially the same. It assesses four behavioral domains – language, fine motor, gross motor, and personal–social behavior – and, like its predecessor, bases the scores on direct observation. Further, the revised version has retained the norms from the 1967 standardization on about 1,000 children. The only significant change is the interpretation of test scores. Basically, a child's performance on the DDST-R is less likely to result in an abnormal classification (e.g., DDST scores interpreted as deviant would be interpreted as questionable on the DDST-R). Concurrent correlations with other intelligence tests have generally been high.

Gesell Developmental Schedule. The Gesell schedule was first published in 1940 and, according to Anastasi (1988), represented a pioneering attempt at systematically and empirically evaluating early child development. The schedule was developed based on data collected during a longitudinal study on "normal" early childhood development. As with the original schedule, the latest revision by Ilg and Ames (1965) covers five areas: adaptive, fine motor, gross motor, language, and personal–social. Data are gathered from direct observation, and they have been shown to be particularly useful in identifying neurologically based cognitive deficits in children 4 weeks to 5 years old (Knobloch & Pasamanick, 1974).

Issues of childhood and adolescent development within the psychometric approach

Up to this point our discussion of the psychometric perspective has been rather general and has not explicitly raised the role of development in psychometric conceptions of intelligence. This section reviews a number of issues that relate specifically to development.

Is intellectual development linear?

As discussed earlier, the Stanford-Binet used a ratio method of calculating IQ until its third revision in 1960 (Bayley, 1970). The ratio method assumes that mental age grows linearly throughout childhood and adolescence. Without this assumption, IQs of children with different chronological ages could not be compared. This assumption may be true during some portions of childhood, but it clearly does not hold up during adolescence and infancy. Tests such as the Stanford-Binet are not used with infants, so they pose no problem; but during adolescence, the rate of growth of mental age begins to slow (Bayley, 1970). Because chronological age continues to grow linearly, a simple ratio IQ begins to lose its meaning.

This problem can be overcome by adjusting ratio IQs as a function of the chronological age of the child, but the simpler solution is to use a deviation IQ, in which a child is compared to other children of the same age in the norming sample. Thus, IQ represents relative position in a normal distribution with a given mean (usually 100) and a given standard deviation (usually 15 or 16). In this sense, a deviation IQ is not a "quotient" at all.

Today the deviation method is used almost exclusively. It circumvents the invalid assumption that intellectual skills grow linearly. The ratio IQ is known mostly because of its historical role.

Why don't infant tests of intelligence predict later intelligence levels very well?

McCall, Hogarty, and Hurlburt (1972) compiled data from previous studies by Anderson (1939), Bayley (1949), Cavanaugh, Cohen, Dunphy, Ringwell, and Goldberg (1957), Escalona and Moriarty (1961), Honzik (1938), Moore (1967), Nelson and Richards (1938, 1939), and Werner, Honzik, and Smith (1968) in an effort to determine how well childhood IQ could be predicted

Table 2.1. *Median correlations between infant tests and childhood IQ for normal children*

	Age in infancy (months)			
Childhood age (years)	1–6	7–12	13–18	19–30
8–18	.01	.20	.21	.49
5–7	.01	.06	.30	.41
3–4	.23	.33	.47	.54

Source: Adapted by permission from McCall, Hogarty, and Hurlburt, 1972, p. 729; copyright 1972 by the American Psychological Association.

from infant IQ scores. These results are displayed in Table 2.1. The table shows that the relationship between infant IQ and childhood IQ is quite small, especially when the infant test was given early in infancy. Why aren't the correlations higher?

McCall et al. (1972) point out that the lack of correlation is not due to reliability problems with the infant tests. They suggest that the notion of a developmentally constant g is in error. Instead, there are differing competences at different periods of infancy. Some of these competences serve as the developmental base for succeeding ones and thus are correlated with them. However, these early competences are not correlated with distal behaviors, such as those represented on later childhood IQ tests, until relatively late in infancy. McCall et al. present a longitudinal set of factor analyses (for 6, 12, 18, and 24 months) for items from the Gesell, with extracted components correlated across ages (with the analyses separated by gender). The results supported the notion of a core of perceptual–motor behaviors in early infancy that gradually transformed into a core of verbal behaviors in later infancy. The authors noted that these trends meshed nicely with Piaget's theory of development during the sensorimotor period.

Although we agree with McCall et al. (1972) that the nature of what we call intelligence changes with age during the first few years of life (e.g., Siegler & Richards, 1980), we disagree with them that their results shed much light on the nature of this intelligence. It must be remembered that you can only get out of a factor analysis what you put into it. Because the Gesell items on which infants are rated change as a function of age, it would be impossible to find the same competences at each age. The competences found are a reflection of the Gesell item pool. It may or may not be the case that the Gesell accurately depicts all important changes in infant competences during the first two years of life.

Despite our criticisms of their study, McCall et al. (1972) correctly point out that infants have a set of developmental competences that evolve over the early years into more adultlike skills. As soon as the content of IQ test items stabilizes (around 3 to 4 years), and the tests assess adultlike skills, moderate correlations with later IQ are found. Thus, the lack of correlation appears to be due to the qualitatively different competences of infants and children, whatever the exact nature of these competences may be.

What are the contributions to intelligence of heredity and environment, and how do they change with age?

The debate over the relative contributions of heredity and environment to intelligence still rages. McCall (1981) has proposed a model of how the influence of heredity and environment change with age. He borrows two terms, *creod* and *canalization*, from Waddington (1957) and Scarr-Salapatek (1976). *Creod* refers to a species-typical path along which nearly all members of the species tend to develop. *Canalization* refers to the degree of deviation from that species-typical path. If development is highly canalized, there is little deviation from the path, even under quite extreme environmental and genetic circumstances. If development is poorly canalized, changes in environment and genetic make up can result in significant individual differences. McCall's proposition is that mental development is highly canalized until 18 to 24 months of age. During this early period, only the most severe of environmental and genetic circumstances can cause the infant to develop abnormally (e.g., not develop language). After this period, mental development becomes progressively decanalized, with both environment and genetics leading to stable individual differences. This tendency toward differentiation is counteracted, to some degree, by the cumulative effects of past experience. There is a developmental inertia that tends to keep individuals developing along the same paths. As age increases, this inertia also increases. The result is that as age increases, greater environmental or genetic influences are necessary to change the ongoing course of development. McCall points out that his model nicely accounts for the uniformity of development during the first 18 months of life, and for the fact that measures of infant intelligence fail to correlate well with later measures of individual differences in mental functioning.

We presented McCall's (1981) canalization model because it specifically addresses the roles of heredity and environment and how those roles change over time. We also wish to point out that his model is a rather general one, and that it has not been tested in a rigorous way. We believe the current facts warrant only the following statement: Heredity, environment, and their interaction all play some role in mental development (Sternberg &

Powell, 1983). Beyond that, the issue is unclear, and remains likely to be so for some time to come.

Interest in this question often derives from an interest in the social policy implications of the heritability of intelligence. The two issues, however, are relatively independent. If IQ were 80% inherited, one could equally well conclude that (1) no money should be spent on the least able because they are least likely to benefit from it, or (2) most of our money should be spent on the least able because they are in greatest need of whatever environmental changes can be brought about. Although the relative contributions to intelligence of heredity and environment may be a scientific question, social policy is a value question and must eventually be dealt with on those grounds.

How can factor analytic theories of intelligence account for developmental changes?

Most factor analytic theories of intelligence were developed with adolescents and adults in mind. How can such theories cope with the developmental changes that take place during infancy and childhood? Sternberg and Powell (1983) list four ways these theories can accommodate developmental change.

Changes in the number of factors with age. The most popular proposal of this kind is the differentiation hypothesis: The number of factors increases with advancing age through childhood. Garrett (1946) has been a proponent of this view and has suggested it might offer a synthesis of Spearman's and Thurstone's positions. In early childhood g would be predominant, but by later childhood g would become differentiated into the primary mental abilities.

Other researchers (e.g., Balinsky, 1941) have suggested a dedifferentiation of factors during adulthood and old age. These researchers suggest either that the number of factors becomes smaller with increasing age or that the degree of correlation among correlated factors increases. Reinert (1970), in a review of studies addressing both variants of the differentiation hypothesis, reports that the empirical evidence is mixed and no clear-cut conclusion can be reached.

Changes in the relevance or weights of factors with age. In this case the total number of factors may not change with age, but their relative importance in explaining individual differences data may. Thus, what makes one individual more intelligent than another can be different at different ages. Theories of this type (e.g., Hofstaetter, 1954) generally posit Perceptual–Motor factors (during infancy) giving way to Verbal–Symbol Manipulation factors (during childhood). In Hofstaetter's (1954) analysis of Bayley's (1933, 1943, 1949, 1951) Berkeley Growth Study, the most important factor up to 20 months of age was Sensorimotor Alertness. Between 20 and 40 months, this factor was eclipsed by a Persistence factor. From 48 months onward the most important factor was the Manipulation of Symbols, or Abstract Behavior. The other factors (i.e., Sensorimotor Alertness and Persistence) that had been important previously waned in significance.

Changes in the content (names) of factors within a given factor structure. This type of developmental accommodation presumes a stable factor structure over time, with the content or names of those factors changing at different developmental periods. Often these theories are interested in a single predominant factor (à la Spearman's g). An example is the study by McCall et al. (1972) already cited. Their primary concern was the changing nature of the first principal component extracted from the Gesell. At 6 months this component was associated with the manipulative exploration of objects that produce perceptual contingencies. At 12 months it was associated with the imitation of simple fine motor and elementary verbal behavior. By 18 months this component was related to verbal labeling and comprehension, and by 24 months it was related to verbal fluency and grammatical maturity. Thus, although the nature of the first principal component changed throughout infancy, the focus of the research was on this first principal component.

Changes in factor scores of fixed factors with age. These theories do not postulate qualitatively different factor models at different developmental periods. Instead, they assume that the amount (but not the importance or weights) of each factor changes over time. An example might be the fluid and crystallized intelligence model of Horn and Cattell (1966; Cattell, 1963, 1971) discussed earlier. Fluid intelligence (for a given individual) is assumed to increase in amount until the twenties and to decrease thereafter. Crystallized intelligence, however, is assumed to increase or remain constant throughout the life-span.

These four types of change can be mapped onto existing psychometric theories to help the theories account for developmental changes in intelligence. Given that the psychometric theories were developed independently of findings in developmental psychology, changes such as those proposed by Sternberg and Powell (1983) are almost certainly necessary if psychometric theories of intelligence are to be considered complete descriptions of intellectual development.

Are the same tests of intelligence appropriate across the life-span?   𝑁𝑜

To some extent, this question was addressed earlier in the section on tests of intelligence. At that point we noted that infant tests of intelligence are very different in their content from tests aimed at older children and adults. But what if we consider only children from age 4 through adulthood? Can very similar tests be used across this vast age range? Structurally similar tests of intelligence would be applicable if the structure of intelligence remains stable across the age range. As we have already pointed out, many theorists disagree with this proposition, positing either differentiation of abilities with age from childhood through adolescence (e.g., Burt, 1954; Garrett, 1946) or differentiation in early adulthood and dedifferentiation in later adults (e.g., Balinsky, 1941).

Cunningham (1981; Cunningham & Birren, 1980) has investigated the possibility of changes in the structure of abilities with increasing age. Consistent with the review of the data pertaining to the differentiation hypothesis by Reinert (1970), the results were mixed. Cunningham and Birren (1980), using a LISREL (linear structural relations) data analytic approach, found evidence that the factor structure changes with age, but is stable under variations of cohort and time. A longitudinal study of Army Alpha data showed that the age-related changes occurred only in their oldest subjects: 60-year-olds. When these same subjects were tested as college freshmen and 50-year-olds, no differences were found. Furthermore, the factor structure of these subjects as college freshmen did not differ from that of college freshmen during the 1970s.

The difference found in Cunningham and Birren's (1980) oldest group was not a difference in the number of factors (as a dedifferentiation hypothesis might suggest) but, rather, a stronger relationship between verbal comprehension and a speed-related factor. Thus, as people grow older, speed of response becomes more intimately associated with mental ability. Cunningham's (1981) later work confirmed these basic finding: the number of factors remain stable with age, the interrelation among factors increases, particularly with regard to the influence of speed.

With regard to intelligence tests, there is considerable evidence that the constructs represented by the basic factors of ability do not change with age. However, tests with a strong speed component (and virtually all intelligence tests include such a component) may show different relationships to other tests across the life-span. Thus, speeded tests of intelligence must be interpreted carefully when comparing individuals of different ages.

Future directions and conclusions

As is evident from the structure of this chapter, most empirical measures of intellectual development have developed apart from theoretical conceptions of intelligence, particularly factor analytic theories. In addition, most factor-analytic theories were developed with older adolescents and adults in mind;

current tests are not based on theory

issues of development were, at best, an afterthought. How can psychometric theories be more closely linked to assessment instruments?

First, the psychometric theories can be modified, along the lines presented by Sternberg and Powell (1983), to recognize explicitly issues of development. Second, the development of intelligence and ability tests can be both theory- and data-driven, rather than purely data-driven (i.e., selecting items almost exclusively on the basis of their ability to discriminate individuals). To the extent that our theorizing about intelligence has improved since the time of Binet and Wechsler, this should lead to better tests. A number of recent theories of intelligence (e.g., Sternberg's [1985] triarchic theory of intelligence, and Gardner's [1983] theory of multiple intelligences) have increased optimism that theory can indeed be linked to testing.

Another issue that has concerned educators is how tests can be linked to instructional interventions. Current assessment instruments can fathom the depth of intellectual ability, but provide few clues as to how to improve intellectual functioning. Previous efforts to bridge the gap between assessment and instruction have been largely unsuccessful. Most studies have failed to demonstrate that children and adolescents who have specific cognitive abilities learn best under a specific instructional strategy, and that those who have different skills benefit from a different strategy (Cronbach & Snow, 1977; Ysseldyke & Marston, 1990). This has led to interest in curriculum-based assessment (see Shapiro & Derr, 1990, for review). In this approach, students are tested on material presented in the curriculum, rather than on general knowledge and abilities. Although curriculum-based tests are not intended to replace norm-referenced intelligence measures, they provide useful information for student placement decisions and instructional planning.

The future, we believe, will see greater linkages: linkages among theory, assessment, and instruction. Theory will begin to inform assessment (i.e., tests will have greater construct validity). Assessment techniques, which have already acknowledged developmental differences among infants, children, and adolescents, will begin to be reflected in theories of intellect. Finally, assessment techniques will begin to address the instructional needs of educators. The psychometric perspective will be stronger once these linkages have been fully formed.

References

Anastasi, A. (1988). *Psychological testing* (6th Ed.). New York: Macmillan.
Anastasi, A. (1989). Review of the Stanford-Binet Intelligence Scale, Fourth Edition. In J. C. Conoley & J. J. Kramer (Eds.), *The tenth mental measurements yearbook*. Lincoln: University of Nebraska Press.

Anderson, L. D. (1939). The predictive efficiency of infancy tests in relation to intelligence at five years. *Child Development, 10*, 203–212.

Balinsky, B. (1941). An analysis of the mental factors of various age groups from nine to sixty. *Genetic Psychology Monographs, 23*, 191–234.

Bayley, N. (1933). Mental growth during the first three years: A developmental study of 61 children by repeated tests. *Genetic Psychology Monographs, 14*, 1–92.

Bayley, N. (1943). Mental growth during the first three years. In R. G. Barker, J. S. Kounin, & H. F. Wright (Eds.), *Child behaviour and development*. New York: McGraw-Hill.

Bayley, N. (1949). Consistency and variability in the growth of intelligence from birth to eighteen years. *Journal of Genetic Psychology, 75*, 165–196.

Bayley, N. (1951). Development and maturation. In H. Helson (Ed.), *Theoretical foundations of psychology*. New York: Van Nostrand.

Bayley, N. (1969). *Bayley Scales of Infant Development: Birth to two years*. San Antonio, TX: Psychological Corporation.

Bayley, N. (1970). Development of mental abilities. In P. H. Mussen (Ed.), *Carmichael's manual of child psychology, Vol. 1* (3rd ed., pp. 1163–1209). New York: Wiley.

Binet, A., & Henri, V. (1895). La psychologie individuelle. *Année Psychologique, 2*, 411–465.

Binet, A., & Simon, T. (1905). Methods nouvelles pour le diagnostic du niveau intellectuel des anormaux. *Année Psychologique, 11*, 191–244.

Bloom, B. S. (1964). *Stability and change in human characteristics*. New York: Wiley.

Brody, E. B., & Brody, N. (1976). *Intelligence: Nature, determinants, and consequences*. New York: Academic Press.

Brown, W., & Thomson, G. H. (1940). *The essentials of mental measurement* (4th ed.). Cambridge: Cambridge University Press.

Burt, C. (1940). *The factors of the mind*. London: University of London Press.

Burt, C. (1949). Alternative methods of factor analysis and their relations to Pearson's method of "principal axes." *British Journal of Psychology, Statistical Section, 2*, 98–121.

Burt, C. (1954). The differentiation of intellectual abilities. *British Journal of Psychology, 24*, 76–90.

Caldwell, J., Schrader, D. R., Michael, W. B., & Meyers, C. E. (1970). Structure-of-intellect measures and other tests as predictors of success in tenth-grade modern geometry. *Educational and Psychological Measurement, 30*, 437–441.

Campbell, D. T., & Stanley, J. C. (1963). *Experimental and quasi-experimental designs for research*. Chicago: Rand McNally.

Cattell, J. M. (1890). Mental tests and measurements. *Mind, 15*, 373–380.

Cattell, R. B. (1963). Theory of fluid and crystallized intelligence: An initial experiment. *Journal of Educational Psychology, 54*, 105–111.

Cattell, R. B. (1971). *Abilities: Their structure, growth, and action*. Boston: Houghton Mifflin.

Cavanaugh, M. C., Cohen, I., Dunphy, D., Ringwell, E. A., & Goldberg, I. D. (1957). Prediction from the Cattell Infant Intelligence Scale. *Journal of Consulting Psychology, 21*, 33–37.

Conoley, J. C., & Kramer, J. J. (1989). *The tenth mental measurement yearbook*. Lincoln: University of Nebraska Press.

Cronbach, L. J. (1989). Review of the Stanford-Binet Intelligence Scale, Fourth Edition. In J. C. Conoley & J. J. Kramer (Eds.), *The tenth mental measurement yearbook*. Lincoln: University of Nebraska Press.

Cronbach, L. J., & Snow, R. E. (1977). *Aptitudes and instructional methods*. New York: Irvington.

Cunningham, W. R. (1981). Ability factor structure differences in adulthood and old age. *Multivariate Behavioral Research, 16*, 3–22.

Cunningham, W. R., & Birren, J. E. (1980). Age changes in the factor structure of intellectual abilities in adulthood and old age. *Educational and Psychological Measurement, 40*, 271–290.

Elliott, C. D. (1990). *Differential Abilities Scale: Introductory and technical handbook.* San Antonio, TX: Psychological Corporation.

Elliott, C. D., Murray, D. J., & Pearson, L. S. (1979). *British Ability Scales.* Windsor, U.K.: National Foundation for Educational Research.

Escalona, S. K., & Moriarty, A. (1961). Prediction of school-age intelligence from infant tests. *Child Development, 32*, 597–605.

Frankenburg, W. K., Dodds, J. B., Fandal, A. W., Kazuk, E., & Cohrs, M. (1975). *Denver Developmental Screening Test–Revised.* Denver: Denver Developmental Materials.

Galton, F. (1883). *Inquiries into human faculty.* London: Macmillan.

Gardner, H. (1983). *Frames of mind: The theory of multiple intelligences.* New York: Basic Books.

Garner, W. R., Hake, H. W., & Eriksen, C. W. (1956). Operationism and the concept of perception. *Psychological Review, 63*, 149–159.

Garrett, H. E. (1946). A developmental theory of intelligence. *American Psychologist, 1*, 372–378.

Goddard, H. H. (1908). The Binet and Simon tests of intellectual capacity. *Training School, 5*, 3–9.

Goddard, H. H. (1910). A measuring scale of intelligence. *Training School, 6*, 146–155.

Guilford, J. P. (1952). When not to factor analyze. *Psychological Bulletin, 49*, 26–37.

Guilford, J. P. (1967). *The nature of human intelligence.* New York: McGraw-Hill.

Guilford, J. P. (1977). *Way beyond the IQ: Guide to improving intelligence and creativity.* Buffalo: Creative Education Foundation.

Guilford, J. P. (1982). Cognitive psychology's ambiguities: Some suggested remedies. *Psychological Review, 89*, 48–59.

Guilford, J. P., & Hoepfner, R. (1971). *The analysis of intelligence.* New York: McGraw-Hill.

Hebb, D. O. (1939). Intelligence in man after large removals of cerebral tissue: Report of four left frontal lobe cases. *Journal of General Psychology, 21*, 73–87.

Hebb, D. O. (1942). The effect of early and late brain injury upon test scores, and the nature of normal adult intelligence. *Proceedings of the American Philosophical Society, 85*, 275–292.

Hofstaetter, P. R. (1954). The changing composition of intelligence: A study of the *t*-technique. *Journal of Genetic Psychology, 85*, 159–164.

Holly, K. A., & Michael, W. B. (1972). The relationship of structure-of-intellect factor abilities to performance in high school modern algebra. *Educational and Psychological Measurement, 32*, 447–450.

Honzik, M. P. (1938). The constancy of mental test performance during the preschool period. *Journal of Genetic Psychology, 52*, 285–302.

Honzik, M. P., MacFarlane, J. W., & Allen, L. (1948). The stability of mental test performance between two and eighteen years. *Journal of Experimental Education, 17*, 309–324.

Horn, J. L., & Cattell, R. B. (1966). Refinement and test of the theory of fluid and crystallized general intelligences. *Journal of Educational Psychology, 51*, 253–270.

Horn, J. L., & Knapp, J. R. (1973). On the subjective character of the empirical base of Guilford's structure of intellect model. *Psychological Bulletin, 80*, 33–43.

Ilg, F. L. & Ames, L. B. (1965). *School readiness: Behavior tests used at the Gesell Institute.* New York: Harper & Row.

Jackson, D. N. (1984). *Multidimensional Aptitude Battery (MAB): Manual.* Port Huron, MI: Research Psychologists Press.

Jenkins, J. J., & Paterson, D. G. (Eds.). (1961). *Studies in individual differences.* New York: Appleton-Century-Crofts.

Jensen, A. R. (1987). Individual differences in the Hick paradigm. In P. A. Vernon (Ed.),

Speed of information-processing and intelligence (pp. 101–175). Norwood, NJ: Ablex.
Joreskog, K. G. & Sorbom, D. (1989). *LISREL 7 users reference guide*. Mooresville, IN: Scientific Software.
Kail, R., & Pellegrino, J. W. (1985). *Human intelligence: Perspectives and prospects*. New York: Freeman.
Kaufman, A. S. (1975). Factor analysis of the WISC-R at 11 age levels between $6\frac{1}{2}$ and $16\frac{1}{2}$ years. *Journal of Consulting and Clinical Psychology, 43*, 135–147.
Kaufman, A. S., & Kaufman, N. L. (1983). *K-ABC: Kaufman Assessment Battery for Children*. Circle Pines, MN: American Guidance Service.
Keyser, D. J., & Sweetland, R. C. (1988). *Test critiques, Vol. VII*. Kansas City, MO: Test Corporation of America.
Knobloch, H., & Pasamanick, B. (1974). *Gesell and Amatruda's developmental diagnosis* (3rd ed.). New York: Harper & Row.
Kuhlmann, F., & Anderson, R. G. (1982). *Kuhlmann-Anderson Measure of Academic Potential* (8th ed.). Bensenville, IL: Scholastic Testing Service.
Lamke, T. A., Nelson, M. J., & French, J. L. (1973). *The Henmon-Nelson Tests of Mental Ability, 1973 Revision*. Boston: Houghton Mifflin.
Matarazzo, J. D. (1972). *Wechsler's measurement and appraisal of adult intelligence*. Baltimore: Williams & Wilkins.
McCall, R. B. (1981). Nature-nurture and the two realms of development: A proposed integration with respect to mental development. *Child Development, 52*, 1–12.
McCall, R. B., Hogarty, P. S., & Hurlburt, N. (1972). Transitions in infant sensorimotor development and the prediction of childhood IQ. *American Psychologist, 27*, 728–748.
McCarthy, D. A. (1972). *Manual for the McCarthy Scales of Children's Abilities*. San Antonio, TX: Psychological Corporation.
McNemar, Q. (1951). The factors in factoring behavior. *Psychometrika, 16*, 353–359.
Moore, T. (1967). Language and intelligence: A longitudinal study of the first eight years. Part I. Patterns of development in boys and girls. *Human Development, 10*, 88–106.
Nelson, V. L., & Richards, T. W. (1938). Studies in mental development: I. Performance on Gesell items at six months and its predictive value for performance on mental tests at two and three years. *Journal of Genetic Psychology, 52*, 303–325.
Nelson, V. L., & Richards, T. W. (1939). Studies in mental development: III. Performance of twelve-month-old children on the Gesell schedule and its predictive value for mental status at two and three years. *Journal of Genetic Psychology, 54*, 181–191.
Otis, A. S., & Lennon, R. T. (1989). *Otis-Lennon School Ability Test* (6th ed.). San Antonio, TX: Psychological Corporation.
Reinert, G. (1970). Comparative factor analytic studies of intelligence throughout the human life-span. In L. R. Goulet & P. B. Baltes (Eds.), *Life-span developmental psychology: Research and theory* (pp. 467–484). New York: Academic Press.
Sattler, J. M. (1988). *Assessment of children* (3rd ed.). San Diego: Author.
Scarr-Salapatek, S. (1976). An evolutionary perspective on infant intelligence: Species patterns and individual variations. In M. Lewis (Ed.), *Origins of intelligence*. New York: Plenum.
Schaie, K. W. (1985). *Schaie-Thurstone Adult Mental Abilities Test: Manual*. Palo Alto, CA: Consulting Psychologists Press.
Shapiro, E. S., & Derr, T. F. (1990). Curriculum-based assessment. In T. B. Gutkin & C. R. Reynolds (Eds.), *The handbook of school psychology* (2nd ed.). New York: Wiley.
Sharp, S. E. (1899). Individual psychology: A study in psychological method. *American Journal of Psychology, 10*, 329–391.
Siegler, R. S., & Richards, D. D. (1980). College students' prototypes of children's intelligence. In *Proceedings of the 85th Conference of the American Psychological Association*, New York.

Siegler, R. S., & Richards, D. D. (1982). The development of intelligence. In R. J. Sternberg (Ed.), *Handbook of human intelligence* (pp. 897–971). Cambridge: Cambridge University Press.

Spearman, C. (1904a). The proof and measurement of association between two things. *American Journal of Psychology, 15,* 72–101.

Spearman, C. (1904b). General intelligence, objectively determined and measured. *American Journal of Psychology, 15,* 201–293.

Spearman, C. (1923). *The nature of "intelligence" and the principles of cognition.* London: Macmillan.

Spearman, C. (1927). *The abilities of man.* New York: Macmillan.

Sternberg, R. J. (1977). *Intelligence, information processing, and analogical reasoning: The componential analysis of human abilities.* Hillsdale, NJ: Erlbaum.

Sternberg, R. J. (1985). *Beyond IQ: The triarchic theory of human intelligence.* Cambridge: Cambridge University Press.

Sternberg, R. J., & Powell, J. S. (1983). The development of intelligence. In J. H. Flavell & E. M. Markman (Vol. Eds.), *Handbook of child psychology: Vol. III. Cognitive development* (4th ed., pp. 341–419). New York: Wiley.

Terman, L. M. (1916). *The measurement of intelligence.* Boston: Houghton Mifflin.

Terman, L. M., & Merrill, M. (1960). *Stanford-Binet Intelligence Scale. Manual for the third revision: Form L-M.* Boston: Houghton Mifflin.

Thomson, G. H. (1951). *The factorial analysis of human ability* (5th ed.). London: University of London Press.

Thorndike, E. L. (1925). *The measurement of intelligence.* New York: Teachers College, Columbia University.

Thorndike, R. L., & Hagen, E. P. (1986). *Cognitive Abilities Test.* Chicago: Riverside Publishing.

Thorndike, R. L., Hagen, E. P., & Sattler, J. M. (1986a). *The Stanford-Binet Intelligence Scale: Fourth Edition. Guide for administering and scoring.* Chicago: Riverside.

Thorndike, R. L., Hagen, E. P., & Sattler, J. M. (1986b). *The Stanford-Binet Intelligence Scale: Fourth Edition. Technical manual.* Chicago: Riverside.

Thurstone, L. L. (1931). Multiple factor analysis. *Psychological Review, 38,* 406–427.

Thurstone, L. L. (1938). *Primary mental abilities.* Chicago: University of Chicago Press.

Thurstone, L. L. (1947). *Multiple factor analysis.* Chicago: University of Chicago Press.

Thurstone, L. L., & Thurstone, T. G. (1941). Factorial studies of intelligence. *Psychological Monographs,* No. 2.

Tuddenham, R. D. (1962). The nature and measurement of intelligence. In L. J. Postman (Ed.), *Psychology in the making* (pp. 469–525). New York: Knopf.

Vernon, P. E. (1950). *The structure of human abilities.* New York: Wiley.

Vernon, P. E. (1965). Ability factors and environmental influences. *American Psychologist, 20,* 723–733.

Waddington, C. H. (1957). *The strategy of the genes.* London: Allen & Son.

Waller, N. G., & Waldman, I. D. (1990). A reexamination of the WAIS-R factor structure. *Psychological Assessment, 2,* 139–144.

Wechsler, D. (1939). *The measurement of adult intelligence.* Baltimore: Williams & Wilkins.

Wechsler, D. (1974). *Wechsler Intelligence Scale for Children–Revised.* New York: Psychological Corporation.

Wechsler, D. (1981). *Wechsler Adult Intelligence Scale–Revised.* New York: Psychological Corporation.

Wechsler, D. (1989). *Wechsler Preschool and Primary Scale of Intelligence–Revised.* San Antonio, TX: Psychological Corporation.

Werner, E. E., Honzik, M. P., & Smith, R. S. (1968). Prediction of intelligence and achievement at 10 years from 20 months pediatric and psychologic examinations. *Child Development, 39,* 1063–1075.

Wissler, C. L. (1901). The correlation of mental and physical tests. *Psychological Review Monograph Supplement, 3*(6).

Ysseldyke, J. E., & Marston, D. (1990). The use of assessment information to plan instructional interventions: A review of the research. In T. B. Gutkin & C. R. Reynolds (Eds.), *The handbook of school psychology* (2nd ed.). New York: Wiley.

3   Major abilities and development in the adult period

John L. Horn and Scott M. Hofer

Objectives and orientation of the chapter

The focus of this chapter is on intellectual development in what we refer to as the "vital period of life," which extends from (approximately) 20 to 80 years of age. It is "vital" because adults of this period have the primary responsibility for maintaining and enhancing the culture. Indeed, their job is to make sure someone is around to have a culture. We deal primarily with broad capabilities rather than elementary capacities. The view will be from the bird's eye looking down on the forest of human cognitive capabilities.

Mostly, we describe "normal aging," but we confess to a belief that no one is quite normal and that underlying the average and typical are many of the same influences that produce the "abnormal." Much of the discussion is aimed at understanding what have been regarded as "normal" aging declines in major intellectual capabilities of reasoning and memory. A purpose of the chapter is to provide a sound basis for designing better research on the relations between controllable factors of living and the declines and enhancements in cognitive capabilities.

We focus on theory, but theory that is based on evidence derived from tests of refutable hypotheses and research in which the results could have been different from what they were found to be. We focus on a particular form of theory, namely, multivariate theory derived from the study of individual differences. Consider next the general features of this form of theory.

Theory for the organization of this chapter

Often multivariate individual differences theory is referred to as "psychometric theory" and is said to represent the "psychometric approach" (e.g., Gleitman, 1986). This is not a good way to characterize the theory. Let us look at why this is true.

The term *metric* in *psychometric* refers to measurement and the term *psycho* refers to *psychological*, so the term *psychometric theory* means theory based on measurement of psychological phenomena. Multivariate individual differences theory is psychometric in this sense. But every other scientific theory of cognitive processes is also psychometric, since measurement is an essential basis for any scientific theory. (The simplest form of measurement is classification.) All theories of cognition thus are, if they are scientific, "psychometric theories." The term *psychometric theory* does not distinguish multivariate individual differences theory from other cognitive theories.

The individual differences paradigm. What is usually meant when one refers to psychometric theory and the psychometric approach is an individual differences (ID) paradigm for studying human capabilities. This approach – this research design – differs in important ways from other approaches. Thus, although *psychometric theory* is a misnomer for distinguishing this chapter from others, an important distinction is adumbrated by the term.

The ID approach is different from the approach most often used to study cognitive processes, namely, the comparison-of-averages (CA) approach. The CA approach can be illustrated with research on short-term memory scanning done by S. Sternberg (1966, 1975). He demonstrated that as the length of lists of stimuli to which a person is exposed increases, the reaction time (RT) to identify subsequently an element of such a list also increases. It takes longer, cognitively, to process a long list than a short one – in identifying a particular element. To demonstrate this Sternberg effect with a CA design, one might show a group of, say, 20 people a list of, say, three letters, show another group of 20 people a list of four letters, show subjects in a third group a list of five letters, and after each presentation of a list require subjects to respond as quickly as possible to indicate if a letter flashed on a screen was a member of the list to which they had just been exposed. In such a study the group average RT for those exposed to five-letter lists is found to be longer than the group average RT for those exposed to four-letter lists, which in turn is longer than the group average RT for those exposed to three-letter lists. In obtaining the average RT within groups in such a CA study, and testing to show that the group averages are different, one implicitly assumes that differences between individuals (i.e., the IDs) are error.

What the CA approach treats as error the ID approach treats as the phenomenon of interest. To demonstrate the Sternberg effect with an ID design one would, under standardized conditions, show each of many individuals a number of the same lists (e.g., of three, four, and five items long), require these individuals to respond as quickly as they could to indicate whether or not a letter had been a member of the previously presented list, and obtain the sum (or average) RT over all presentations for each individual. When all subjects respond to all items the sum RT and the average RT, for a subject, are equivalent. If the Sternberg effect is an effect that shows up in differences between individuals, the sum RT score is an estimate of the effect in an individual. To test the hypothesis that the effect does, indeed, distinguish individuals, the individual sum RT scores are tested to establish that the between-sum differences are significant. (The within-subject variability, over different items, is regarded as error in this test.) This test is usually done by calculating the intercorrelations among different indicators of the effect (the different RTs for different letters) and further calculating the internal consistency reliability of the indicators. If the correlations are positive, indicating that individual differences are consistent (across different presentations of lists with varying lengths), then the internal consistency reliability will be large for the sum RT scores. A finding that the internal consistency reliability is large (significant) is mathematically equivalent to a finding that the between-individual means are significantly different. This evidence thus demonstrates that the Sternberg effect distinguishes individual differences.

The ID and CA approaches are thus complementary. The CA approach is aimed at demonstrating an effect for people in general, regardless of individual differences, whereas the ID approach is aimed at demonstrating that an effect reliably characterizes differences between people.

Usually an effect indicated by the ID approach can be indicated also by the CA approach, and vice versa. The Sternberg effect, for example, is indicated by both approaches (e.g., Horn & Donaldson, 1980). Similarly, as problems of various kinds are made more difficult, people on the average take longer to solve them and make more errors – effects shown by the CA approach – and for many kinds of such cognitive tasks individual differences in solution time and in number of errors made are reliable – the effects are shown by the ID approach.

Factor analysis extension of the paradigm. Thus, cognitive processes indicated by the ID approach can, in principle, be indicated by the CA approach, and vice versa. But the two approaches can, and in available studies commonly do, reveal different information. This is true because the basic design of each approach is elaborated, and the elaborations are based on different assumptions and permit different kinds of relationships to be identified.

Theory is always (in any science) dependent on the methods used to study phenomena (Kuhn, 1970). But the phenomena are the same regardless of the methods used for study. The same processes underlie behavior whether we study them with the CA approach or the ID approach. In principle, what is revealed by one approach should be revealed also, although in a different way, by application of the other approach. But psychology is a young science. We are still largely in the infancy of verifying that the findings seen in ID study are also seen in CA studies, and vice versa (Horn, Donaldson

& Engstrom, 1981; Hunt, 1978, 1980; Hunt, Frost & Lunneborg, 1973; Pellegrino & Glaser, 1979; R. Sternberg, 1979; R. Sternberg & Detterman, 1979).

An important elaboration of the ID approach is factor analysis. The serious student of human thinking must understand factor analysis – the assumptions and logic (not necessarily the details of calculation) – because a very large part of contemporary scientific theory about human intelligence and cognitive processing is based on models of this method. There is no comparable elaboration of the CA approach. Applications of factor analysis thus lead to results not found with the CA approach. Such results, in turn, lead to theory (about processes) that is derived from applications of the CA approach.

One critical assumption made in applying the factor analytic method is that conjunction indicates process. Phenomena (e.g., individual differences measurements) that rise and fall together, appear and disappear together, are assumed to indicate common underlying influences affecting the different manifestations (else, why would they covary?). Behaviors that covary (across individual differences) are assumed to indicate the same underlying process.

This assumption of conjunction underlies inferences characteristic of human thinking – concept formation in general. It is the basic assumption of use of correlation, and correlation is at the core of factor analysis. But the use of factor analysis is based on two important additional assumptions, namely: (1) If the covariability that indicates one process is removed mathematically (is partialled out), the remaining covariability (residual) can indicate another process; (2) processes combine additively and "compensatively" to bring about the behavior that is observed and measured. These assumptions are expressed in a simple linear equation of the following form:

$$Y_{ki} = P_{1i} + P_{2i} + \ldots + P_{mi} \qquad (1)$$

Y_{ki} represents the observed score (measure) – an estimate of an effect – for individual i obtained with measurement operations k, and there are $i = 1, \ldots, N$ individuals.

P_{ji} is a factor measurement of individual i on underlying process j, there being m factors (processes), $j = 1, \ldots, m$.

In this equation we see concretely that individuals are assumed to vary reliably in the different processes – P_1, P_2, etc. – and that these processes are assumed to combine additively to produce the observed measurements, Y_{ki}. The compensatory assumption of the model is seen by observing that if one is high on one process, this (to some extent) compensates for being low on another process: If P_{1i} is high in i = Steve, for example, this can "make up" for his being low in P_{2i}. Compensation is seen, also, by observing that the same observed score can be obtained through different combinations of

FACTORS (Processes)

			P1	P2	P3	
MEASUREMENT	V	1	X	O	O	Sum-RT (Sternberg, 1966)
OPERATIONS	A	2	X	O	O	Recency Memory (Murdock, 1962)
	R	3	X	O	O	Primacy Memory (Glanzer-Cunitz, 1966)
	I	4	O	X	O	Vocabulary
	A	5	O	X	O	Analogies (Spearman, 1927)
	B	6	O	X	O	Remote Associations (Mednick, 1956)
	L	7	O	O	X	Power Letter Series (Furneaux, 1952)
	E	8	O	O	X	Matrices (Cattell, 1940)
	S	9	O	O	X	Concept Attainment (Woodcock & Johnson, 1990)

Figure 3.1. Example of simple-structure factor analytic study.

the processes: i = Mary can get the same observed score as Steve by being high on P_2 and low on P_1.

The variables of the factor analytic model can be obtained in many different ways, which is to say the measurement operations can be of different forms. The procedures described for indicating the Sternberg effect indicate one form of measurement operation. Here the Y_{ki} of equation 1 is the sum of reaction times to identify a letter over different lists of letters. Another form of measurement operation is the multiple-choice test, as in classroom examinations. In this case the Y_{ki} score is the number of correct answers (choices judged to be correct) to several questions. Sometimes the measurement operation is simply an item – a stimulus is presented and each of several different response possibilities is assigned a different Y_{ki} score. Regardless of what kind of measurement operations are used, factor analysis is directed at identifying factors (i.e., processes P_{1i}, P_{2i}, etc.) that bring about – can be interpreted as causing – the observed measurements.

Other assumptions of factor analysis are contained within particular models, for there are several factor–analytic models. The one most frequently used in studies of cognitive capabilities is a simple structure model, illustrated in Figure 3.1.

The X's of this figure indicate that a variable is hypothesized to indicate (be related to) the process (symbolized, P_1, P_2, or P_3) of the column in which the X appears; the O's represent the hypothesis that there is only a random (i.e., near zero) relationship between the variable and the process symbolized at the head of a column. Three main hypotheses are represented in this model, namely, that there is:

1. a very short-term memory (STM) process, P_1, that can be seen in the Sternberg effect, Recency Memory (recall of the last few of stimuli – say, letters – presented in a list) and Primacy Memory (recall of the first few stimuli present in a list)
2. a crystallized knowledge (G_c) process, P_2, that can be seen in measures of Vocabulary, Analogies (Aristotle is to Socrates as Sophocles is to . . . ??

Euripides), and Remote Associations (provide a word associated with weddings, prizefighting and bathtubs . . . ?? Ring)
3. a fluid reasoning (G_f) process, P_3, that can be seen in measures of Letter Series (provide the next letter in a series such as $A, C, F, J, O, . . .$?? U), Matrices (for one cell of a matrix, select a symbol that is consistent with variations across the rows and down the columns of the matrix), and Concept Attainment (given instances of a concept and absence of the concept, become aware of the attributes that define the concept and demonstrate this by identifying new instances – e.g., as measured in the Woodcock-Johnson (WJ-R, 1990) battery)

One can say that such a model represents some aspects of human thinking. It is reasonable to suppose that there are separate abilities of short-term memory, crystallized knowledge, and fluid reasoning. Indeed, there are many theories in which the theorist says human thinking is such and so. But such saying does not make it true. It is important in science to have refutable tests of what a theorist says.

The tests for the factor analytic model involve (1) obtaining reliable operational definitions of the variables; (2) finding the multiple relationships among these variables; (3) estimating these relationships in accordance with the specifications of the model – that is, the specification of the right side of equation [1]; (4) checking to see if these estimated relationships are the same (to within chance variability) as the relationships actually obtained: if they are, then one can infer that actual covariabilities came about in a manner consistent with that specified in the model.

It is important in science that models be refutable. The simple-structure factor analytic model is refutable because there may be very little similarity between the relationships it specifies and the relationships actually obtained. For example, the correlation between the scores on Letter Series and Concept Attainment may be quite different from the correlation specified for these two variables in the model of Figure 3.1. If this is found to be the case, then the model is found to provide a very poor fit to the data. On the other hand, the model may very well reproduce the variable intercorrelations, in which case the model can be seen to be a good representation of the data.

If a model provides a good representation of the data, the researcher has evidence that the model is paramorphic to the organization of behavior – that is, *para* meaning alongside or parallel to, and *morphic* referring to the actual shape of the organization. The term *paramorphic* is an important qualifier. In the context of research on cognitive capabilities this qualifier means that it is going too far – beyond the findings – to suggest that the confirmed factor analytic results indicate that human abilities are actually organized in the same manner as specified in the model – that abilities literally are linearly additive, compensatory, based on simple-structure factors. Rather, the confirmed findings say merely that this model is consistent with whatever is the organization of human abilities.

In making this important qualification, and not inferring more than should be inferred, one should not underestimate the value of the evidence. If a factor model provides a good fit to data, then that model is consistent with the true organization insofar as interrelationships among variables can indicate this organization. Factor analytic research also points to an infinity of models that are not consistent with the data, and some of these are, on first consideration, quite plausible. The evidence of what is not consistent is important in reducing the number of possible explanations for observations. The factor-analytic evidence thus suggests what is possible and rules out many otherwise reasonable ideas.

Organization of abilities indicated by factor analysis. Results from a great number of factor analytic studies done in this century add up to suggest a paramorphic organization that has become known as G_f–G_c theory (Cattell, 1957, 1971; Horn, 1968, 1988; Horn & Cattell, 1966). Such results indicate that if, in a substantial and heterogeneous sample of people, a researcher measures a variety of cognitive capabilities sampled to represent a simple structure of the abilities specified in G_f–G_c theory, the results from testing to see if the model fits the intercorrelations will indicate that, indeed, such a model does represent the data. It means, too, that a great number of other, seemingly plausible, models do not provide good approximations to the data.

A theory formed in this way is dependent on, and limited by, the history of research on which it is founded (Sternberg, 1985, p. 67). As Sternberg emphasizes, the factors that emerge to support a theory such as G_f–G_c theory are largely determined by the tasks that are entered into the factor analysis. Rather than choosing tests in accordance with a priori guidelines, tasks were chosen because it was thought they would "work" to indicate the factors. In successive studies over the course of this century tasks were used that were similar to tasks that had been used before. "Tradition," Sternberg points out, "scarcely constitutes an a priori, theoretical basis for choosing tasks that measure intelligence."

This point is important, but one should not ignore the fact that all scientific theory is a product of history and culture (Kuhn, 1970). Indeed, theory should be based on induction – a tradition of observations – as well as deduction, the a priori, theoretical feature that Sternberg emphasizes. The best of scientific theory emerges from an "inductive–deductive spiral" (Cattell, 1957) – induction followed by deduction followed by more induction followed again by deduction and so on.

It is true, too, that the factor analytic research has been deductive in two important ways: (1) Selections of tasks have been designed to test hypotheses about functions; for example, verbal reasoning tasks were selected in the Horn and Cattell (1967) study to test a hypothesis that fluid reasoning (G_f) involves verbal functions – is not simply spatial ability, and is distinctly different from visual processing (G_v); and (2) many of the paradigms, tests, and items that have been studied over this century and that form the basis for G_f–G_c theory were based on a priori hypotheses about the nature of intelligence. The results from factor-analytic research are in this sense a distillation of many theories of intelligence. The results confirm and disconfirm many a priori hypotheses.

Factor analytic evidence provides a basis for what is called structural or organizational theory. Evidence from other kinds of studies (largely group comparison evidence) suggests that the structural organization indicated by factor analytic research is useful for understanding how different abilities relate to age differences and age changes; to variations in central nervous system (CNS) function, to differences between boys and girls, men and women; to differences in education, social, and economic factors; and to variables indicating distinctions between genetic and environmental influences (Horn, 1980, 1989).

In the next section we take a bird's-eye look at historical precursors of G_f–G_c theory, then briefly describe the major concepts of the theory and summarize the structural evidence on which it is based. This is the skeleton for a body of evidence indicating the development of human abilities. That body, particularly in respect to adult development, will be fleshed out in subsequent sections.

Details of organization: Structural theory

Humans display myriad capabilities that are said to indicate intelligence. We do not know precisely how these capacities are organized in neural (and other physiological) structures and through genetic determination and experience. But we do know – from several lines of evidence, as well as from factor-analytic studies – that the capacities fall into separate classes, indicating distinct kinds of intellectual capabilities. It is possible that these separate classes of abilities are organized in accordance with one principle – a principle of general intelligence. But the evidence of most research does not support this hypothesis (although the term *intelligence* is still widely used in a manner suggesting the hypothesis is well supported). The major reason a concept of general intelligence does not provide a sound basis for understanding human cognitive functioning is that different intellectual abilities have different construct validities. Elsewhere, this evidence has been discussed in some detail (Horn, 1985, 1986, 1988, 1989). Without repeating that entire discussion here, we shall point to evidence indicating the different construct validities of different abilities. This will show that different concepts of intelligence are needed – and indicate why scientists are moving away from a theory of general intelligence.

The PMA system

The factor analytic evidence indicates organization at two levels – the level of primary mental abilities and the level of G_f–G_c theory. The latter derives from the former.

Thurstone's (1938, 1947) pioneering research gave us the term *primary mental abilities* (PMA). In studies done in the 1930s and 1940s Thurstone found that a model of no fewer that nine factors was required to describe most of the reliable ID variance obtained with different tests designed to measure important features of intelligence. Careful study of the process features of these factors suggested that they indicate basic abilities of inductive reasoning (I), deductive reasoning (Rs), practical problem reasoning (R), verbal comprehension (V), associative short-term memory (Ma), spatial relations (S), perceptual speed (P), numerical facility (N), and word fluency (Fw).

No fewer than 400 studies (Carroll, 1989) were aimed at replicating Thurstone's findings: Most did. But this research also very much expanded the PMA system. Summaries of this work now indicate (by replicated findings) more than 40 factors among tests – factors of approximately the same level of generality as the factors Thurstone identified as "primary" (Ekstrom, French, & Harman, 1979; French, 1951; French, Ekstrom, & Price, 1963; Guilford, 1967; Hakstian & Cattell, 1974; Horn, 1972). Short descriptions of the best known among these factors are provided in Table 3.1. Some of these factors may be redundant, but the Hakstian-Cattell results indicate that a model of no fewer than 28 factors is needed to describe the variability measured in tests designed to indicate human intelligence.

As evidence of more and more primary abilities accumulated it became increasingly clear that, at this point in history, a system of 28 to 40 primary abilities is too cumbersome to guide most research. We can't deploy the resources needed to build theories of function for more than 28 separate abilities. A rationale was sought for considering smaller numbers of basic cognitive processes. This rationale should accurately take account of the evidence indicating the many factors of the PMA system.

The rationale put forth in accordance with this need for parsimony often stemmed from an armchair. The theorist speculated about the organization among abilities and "thought up" a parsimonious system. Unfortunately, the rationale originated only in the armchair often remained there. The evidence of empirical research was not used. In particular, little use was made of research results such as those of the PMA studies, and no refutable tests of the system were carried out.

Guilford's work (e.g., 1967) in developing a theory called the structure-of-intellect model (SIM) is an important exception to this generalization.

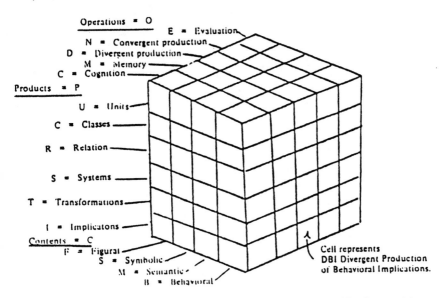

Figure 3.2. Schematic representation of Guilford's structure-of-intellect model.

Guilford based this theory on the results of PMA studies. The theory is displayed in schematic form in Figure 3.2.

The basic idea of Guilford's theory is that each of the many abilities humans display can be described as an expression of one of five separate mental operations – Cognition, Memory, Divergent Production, Convergent Production, Evaluation – operating on one of four separate contents – Figural, Symbolic, Semantic, Behavioral – to produce one of six separate kinds of products – Units, Classes, Relations, Systems, Transformations, Implications. As is seen in the figure, such an organizational system implies that there are 5 × 4 × 6 = 120 separate abilities, one for each block in the figure. The 28-plus abilities indicated by PMA research are, according to the theory, particular exemplars to the model. The model is thus parsimonious only in the number of organizing concepts (operations, contents, products) it requires, not in the number of abilities it specifies.

Although there were many studies of the SIM in the 1960s and 1970s, it is still the case that the implications of the system have not been fully explored in research that provides a sound basis for rejecting or retaining (regarding as tenable) most of its basic hypotheses. The studies designed to test the theory often lacked objectivity (Carroll, 1972; Horn, 1968; Horn & Knapp, 1973, 1974; Humphreys, 1962; Undheim & Horn, 1973). The results overall add up to suggest that some of the three-way combinations of the Guilford system represent empirically based distinctions between established primary

Table 3.1. *First-order (primary) mental abilities*

	Guilford symbol	French symbol	Repli-cated?
Short-term apprehension and retrieval abilities			
Associative memory. When presented with one element of previously associated but otherwise unrelated elements, recall the associated element.	MSR	Ma	Yes
Span memory. Immediately recall a set of elements after one presentation.	MSU	Ms	Yes
Meaningful memory. Immediately recall a set of items that are meaningfully related.	MSR	Mm	?
Chunking memory. Immediately recall elements by categories into which elements can be classified.	MMC		No
Memory for order. Immediately recall the position of an element within a set of elements	MSS		No
Long-term storage and retrieval abilities			
Associational fluency. Produce words similar in meaning to a given word.	DMR	Fa	Yes
Expressional fluency. Produce different ways of saying much the same thing.	DSS	Fe	Yes
Ideational fluency. Produce ideas about a stated condition or object – e.g., a lady holding a baby.	DMU	Fi	Yes
Word fluency. Produce words meeting particular structural requirements – e.g., ending with a particualr suffix.	DMR	Fw	Yes
Originality. Produce "clever" expressions or interpretations – e.g., titles for a story plot.	DMT	O	Yes
Spontaneous flexibility. Produce diverse functions and classifications – e.g., uses for a pencil.	DMC	Xs	Yes
Delayed retrieval. Recall material learned hours before.			Yes
Visualization and spatial orientation abilities			
Visualization. Mentally manipulate forms to "see" how they would look under altered conditions.	CFT	Vz	Yes
Spatial orientation. Visually imagine parts out of place and put them in place – solve jigsaw puzzles.	CFS	S	Yes
Speed of closure. Identify a gestalt when parts of whole of whole are missing.	CFU	Os	Yes
Flexibility of closure. Find a particular figure embedded within distracting figures	NFT	Cf	Yes
Spatial planning. Survey a spatial field and find a path through the field – e.g., pencil mazes.	CFI	Ss	Yes
Figural adaptive flexibility. Try out possible arrangements of elements of visual pattern to find one arrangement that satisfies several conditions.	DFT	Xa	Yes
Length estimation. Estimate lengths or distances between points.		Le	Yes
Figural fluency. Produce different figures using the lines of a stimulus figure.	DFI		No
Seeing illusions. Report illusions of such tests as Muller-Lyer, Sanders, & Poggendorff.	DFS		No
Abilities of listening and hearing			
Listening verbal comprehension. Show understanding of oral communications.			No
Temporal tracking. Demonstrate understanding of sequence of auditory information – e.g., reorder a set of tones.			No
Auditory relations. Show understanding of relations among tones – e.g., identify separate notes of a chord.			No

Table 3.1 (*continued*)

	Guilford symbol	French symbol	Repli-cated?
Discriminate patterns of sounds. Show awareness of differences in different arrangements of tones.			No
Judging rhythms. Identify and continue a beat.			No
Auditory span memory. Immediately recall a set of notes played once.			No
Perception of distorted speech. Demonstrate comprehension of language that has been distorted, e.g., clipped speech.			No
Acculturational knowledge abilities			
Verbal comprehension. Demonstrate understanding of words, sentences and paragraphs.	CMU	V	Yes
Sensitivity to problems. Suggest ways to deal with problems – e.g., improvements for a toaster.	EMI	Sep	Yes
Syllogistic reasoning. Given stated premises draw logically permissible conclusions even when these are nonsensical.	EMR	Rs	Yes
Number facility. Do basic operations of arithmetic quickly and accurately.	NSI	N	Yes
Verbal closure. Show comprehension of words and sentences when parts are omitted.			No
Estimation. Use incomplete information and estimate what is required for problem solution.	CMI		No
Behavioral relations. Judge interaction between people to estimate how one feels about a situation.	CBI		No
Semantic relations: Esoteric Concepts. Demonstrate awareness of analogic relationships among abstruse bits of information.	CMR MR		No
Mechanical knowledge. Demonstrate information about industrial arts – mechanics, electricity, etc.		Mk	?
General information: Demonstrate understanding of science, humanities, social sciences, business.		Vi	
Abilities of reasoning under novel conditions			
Induction. Indicate a principle of relationships among elements.	NSR	I	Yes
General reasoning. Find solutions for problems having an algebraic quality.	CMS	R	Yes
Figural relations. Demonstrate awareness of relationships among figures.	CFR		?
Semantic relations: Common Concepts. Demonstrate awareness of relationships among common pieces of information.	CMR IMR		No
Symbolic classifications. Show which symbol does not belong in a class of several symbols.	CSC		No
Concept formation. Given several examples of a concept, identify new instances.	CFC		No
Speed-of-thinking abilities			
Perceptual speed. Under highly speeded conditions, distinguish similar visual patterns and find instances of a particular pattern.	ESU	P	Yes
Correct decision speed. Speed of finding correct answers to intellectual problems of intermediate difficulty.			No
Writing and printing speed. As quickly as possible, copy printed or cursive letters or words.			No

Source: Eckstrom, French, & Harman (1979).

mental abilities, but many are only logical indications of ways to construct tests, not indications of distinct human abilities. As Humphreys (1962) pointed out, the facets of the Guilford system ". . . are not psychological as defined. They should be useful to the test constructor, [but] they do not need to make a behavioral difference." Distinctions drawn on the basis of different contents or operations or products can be useful, but they are not sharp. The facet of "products," particularly, does not appear to correspond to systematic structural or developmental features of human behavior. On the other hand, the facets of "operations," particularly, and "contents" work better. They point to functions of reasoning (Cognition), short-term apprehension (Memory), retrieval (Divergent Production), and visualization (Figural Content). These are among the functions of modern-day theory, in particular G_f–G_c theory, which is considered next.

G_f–G_c structural theory

Part of the evidence for the G_f–G_c theory derives from studies of how abilities are affected by brain damage and development, particularly in adulthood, but the theory is also based on factor analyses of abilities representing the PMA system. It is a second-order system for the PMA factors, that is, a system of factors among factors. The patterns of intercorrelations that point to the system can be seen in many studies (reviewed in, for example, Carroll, 1989; Horn, 1968, 1976, 1988, 1989; Horn & Donaldson, 1980). The major results are exemplified in the early study of Horn and Cattell (1967), several follow-up studies by these two investigators (e.g., Cattell & Horn, 1978; Hakstian & Cattell, 1978; Horn & Stankov, 1982) and the recent studies of Carroll (1989), Gustaffson (1984), Undheim (1987), and Woodcock (1990). The recent studies, particularly, indicate the generality of the system. Carroll's results stem from 461 separate studies done by almost as many investigators. Woodcock's findings are based on a standardization sample of 6,359 subjects spanning a range from childhood to old age. Gustaffson's sample is Swedish, Undheim's, Norwegian. The results indicate that the PMA system can be organized in terms of nine dimensions that are almost as broad as the sets of abilities people refer to when they use terms such as *intelligence* or *IQ*. Described in capsule form, these abilities are:

> Fluid reasoning (G_f), measured in tasks requiring inductive, deductive, conjunctive, and disjunctive reasoning to arrive at understanding relations among stimuli, comprehend implications, and draw inferences
> Acculturation knowledge (G_c), measured in tasks indicating breadth and depth of the knowledge of the dominant culture
> Quantitative knowledge (G_q), measured in tasks requiring understanding and application of the concepts and skills of mathematics
> Short-term apprehension–retrieval (G_{sm}), also called short-term memory,

measured in a variety of tasks that mainly require one to maintain awareness of, and be able to recall, elements of immediate stimulation – i.e., events of the last minute or so

Fluency of retrieval from long-term storage (G_{lr}), also called long-term memory, measured in tasks that indicate consolidation for storage and mainly require retrieval, through association, of information stored minutes, hours, weeks, and years before

Visual processing (G_v), measured in tasks involving visual closure and constancy, and fluency in "image-ing" the way objects appear in space as they are rotated and flip-flopped in various ways

Auditory processing (G_a), measured in tasks that involve perception of sound patterns under distraction or distortion, maintaining awareness of order and rhythm among sounds, and comprehending elements of groups of sounds, such as chords and the relations among such groups

Processing speed (G_s), although involved in almost all intellectual tasks (Hertzog, 1989), measured most purely in rapid scanning and responding in intellectually simple tasks (in which almost all people would get the right answer if the task were not highly speeded)

Correct decision speed (CDS), measured in quickness in providing answers in tasks that require one to think

Almost all of the abilities of IQ tests and neuropsychological batteries of tests are accounted for by these 9 abilities. In other words, although IQ tests and neuropsychological batteries are not necessarily described as involving these abilities, nevertheless that which is reliably measured in such tests is mainly predicted and accounted for by the 9 factors of G_f–G_c theory. These 9 factors also represent the more than 40 factors of the PMA system in the sense that in a hierarchical system they are higher order organizations of the lower order PMA organizations (Carroll, 1989; Hakstian & Cattell, 1978).

The G_f–G_c system differs from the early PMA system of Thurstone primarily in that each G_f–G_c factor is broader than the similar factor of Thurstone's system: It comprises, and represents, many more elementary abilities. For example, G_c includes the primaries verbal comprehension, deductive reasoning, and numerical facility, as well as knowledge measured in achievement batteries (Woodcock & Johnson, 1990). Other G_f–G_c factors similarly involve several PMA factors.

The component abilities of a G_f–G_c factor are different, which indicates breadth, but these abilities are also similar relative to the abilities of other G_f–G_c factors. The similarity – this conjunction – is responsible for the factor and indicates the common processes of the ability.

Identifying the factor and replicating this finding in different studies help to indicate the distinctiveness of each cognitive function. This distinctiveness is demonstrated, also, by showing that factors are construct independent, showing that the best-weighted linear combination of any set of eight of the factors does not fully predict the reliable covariance among the component abilities of the ninth factor. This evidence shows that each factor measures a function that is not measured in the other factors.

Although construct validity (Campbell & Fiske, 1959; Cronbach, 1987) is indicated by the evidence indicating independence of separate factors, more such evidence is desirable and, indeed, has been adduced. This evidence indicates how the different abilities develop and operate in human personality. It shows that the factors predict different features of important criteria, stem from different sets of determinants – including different sets of genes – and are affected in different ways by influences associated with injuries, child rearing, education, using drugs, and other such practices of life-style.

In general, then, each G_f–G_c factor is broad enough to represent a concept of intelligence, and each involves abilities important in definitions of intelligence, but each is distinct from the others when viewed psychometrically, developmentally, in terms of relations to neurology, in terms of what the ability predicts and what predicts it, and in terms of genetical analyses. Each G_f–G_c factor thus represents a separate concept of intelligence. G_f–G_c theory is in this sense a theory of several intelligences, rather than a theory of intelligence.

In broad outline, this structural theory guides the study of function and development. Such a system guides much current research on the development and expression of cognitive capabilities, especially research on adult humans. The theory also guides research on neurological and genetical correlates of cognitive functioning. In the next section we describe how the concepts of this theory relate to function and development.

Theory of process and development

The evidence from studies of covariability indicates how we can describe the structure of human capability. Structure in this sense is an indication of the things humans can do, and in which some do better than others. Such theory of structure doesn't say much about what causes the abilities or enables them to work or how they relate to learning, genetic determinants, and physiological workings of the body. Theory about this latter is theory of process and development.

Of the nine intelligences described briefly in the preceding section, G_f and G_c most often have been regarded as central to general intelligence (IQ or g). Indeed, G_f and G_c have been discussed as if they are equivalent to each other, as if each indicated the same IQ (Jensen, 1984). Similarly, memory in general and G_{sm} and G_{lr} have been treated as the sine qua non of intelligence. Quick thinking, too, has been regarded as the central feature of intelligence (Eysenck, 1982). But each function is distinct, and no one of them is the essence of all to which people refer when they use the word *intelligence*. In recognizing that these different functions are distinct, one should not assume they are unrelated: A person functions as a whole, not as merely a collection of unrelated parts.

Vulnerable and maintained abilities

As concerns the similarity of functions, the extant evidence – from studies of human development and brain damage, as well as from analyses of structure – suggests that although G_f and G_c often are regarded as indicating the same thing (IQ), G_f is functionally most similar to short-term memory (G_{sm}), not G_c, and G_c is functionally most similar to long-term storage (G_{lr}), not G_f. These functional similarities are expressed in a broad distinction, dating back to the early years of this century (Beeson, 1920), between "vulnerable" and "maintained" abilities (Botwinick, 1977; Matarazzo, 1972).

Prominent among the vulnerable abilities are those of fluid reasoning (G_f), short-term memory (G_{sm}), and processing speed (G_s). These abilities decline first and most with age in adulthood; they are also the abilities most affected and most irreversibly affected by damage to the central nervous system (CNS) in adulthood. These two sets of findings on aging and brain damage lead to a theory that "normal" aging – that is, aging in the absence of identified brain damage – involves an accumulation of CNS injuries over the life course. Each such injury is usually small, but CNS damage is irreversible, so the effects accumulate.

The maintained abilities are well represented by acculturation knowledge (G_c), long-term memory (G_{lr}), and quantitative knowledge (G_q). Although these abilities are affected by brain damage, such as that produced by stroke, they often "spring back" to nearly preinjury levels. These abilities improve, or at least do not decline, throughout most of adulthood. These kinds of findings lead to theory that overdetermination produces hardiness in maintained abilities: A great many associational and neuronal strands become interwoven; if particular strands are lost owing to injury, many others remain to retain the sinew of the abilities. More about this later.

Our strategy for the remainder of the chapter is, first, to describe the major vulnerable and maintained abilities in sufficient detail to enable the reader to understand their basic nature. We then discuss age differences and age changes in these abilities in adulthood. We consider different ideas about the causes of decline and the causes for improvement in abilities, as well as ideas about how to prevent decline and how abilities can be improved.

Major features of vulnerable abilities

Most research on the vulnerability of human intellect has focused on the abilities of fluid reasoning (G_f), short-term memory (G_{sm}), and processing speed (G_s). There is little evidence to indicate the vulnerable features of visual processing (G_v) and auditory processing (G_a).

Fluid reasoning (G_f). Most troublesome to a sanguine view of aging is evidence indicating the vulnerability of G_f. This factor is characterized by reasoning, which is a major feature of concept attainment, as in learning. It is central in almost any definition of human intelligence (Sternberg & Detterman, 1979). Spearman (1927) described the essence of intelligence as the eduction of relations and correlates – in other words, reasoning. These kinds of thoughts lead to a supposition that G_f is the sine qua non of intelligence. It is not pleasant to contemplate that this capability declines with age in adulthood.

If there were a one and only one feature that characterizes all human intellectual capacities, G_f certainly must be regarded as a salient indicator of that feature (Gustaffson, 1984; Hertzog & Schaie, 1986, 1988; Horn, 1988). But there appears to be no such single feature. G_f does not account for – is not correlated with, does not predict – the major proportion of individual differences in all intellectual abilities. It is only one part of the broad conglomerate of all abilities that researchers and laymen alike accept as indicating intelligence. It is an important part.

The tasks that indicate G_f do not so much require one to bring forth knowledge as they require problem solving in the immediate testing situation. Such tasks are said to be "novel." In G_f these novel tasks require one to understand relations, comprehend implications, and draw inferences in inductive, deductive, conjunctive, and disjunctive reasoning. Tasks such as letter series, matrices, concept formation, common word analogies, and analysis synthesis (Woodcock & Johnson, 1990) are measures of G_f reasoning.

The tasks that indicate G_f often were constructed with the aim of reducing the influences of individual differences in education and arriving at a culture-free (culture-fair) measure of intelligence. Such test construction efforts (largely in the 1930s and 1940s) were severely criticized, mainly on grounds that the ideal – a culture-fair test – could not be attained (therefore, one should not attempt to attain it). Efforts to construct culture-fair tests have largely subsided, but in their wake we find good measures of important cognitive capabilities – the measures of G_f. High scores on these measures can be obtained by people of relatively low education and social class. G_f abilities thus are lowly correlated with indicators of acculturation relative to the maintained abilities. G_f correlates about .35 with social class and years of education, for example, whereas the comparable correlation for G_c is .55. Such findings suggest that G_f abilities, more than the maintained abilities, are acquired through personal experience and learning opportunities that are not selectively restricted through the processes of acculturation.

Table 3.2. *Primary ability average intraclass correlations within samples of fraternal (DZ) and identical (MZ) twins*

	MZ	DZ	Dif.	2 Dif.[a]
Crystallized markers				
Knowledge: Social studies	.83	.57	.26	.52
Natural sciences	.80	.64	.16	.32
V: Verbal comprehension	.82	.61	.21	.42
Vocabulary	.84	.60	.24	.48
N: Number facility	.80	.60	.20	.40
Fw: Word fluency	.65	.51	.14	.28
Fe: Expressional fluency	.60	.49	.11	.22
Averages	.76	.58	.18	.37
Fluid markers				
I: Inductive reasoning	.70	.55	.15	.30
S: Spatial reasoning	.64	.40	.24	.48
P: Perceptual speed	.70	.53	.17	.34
N: Number facility	.80	.60	.20	.40
Ma: Associative memory	.53	.39	.14	.28
Averages	.67	.49	.18	.36

[a] Falconer's estimate of broad-sense heritability.
Source: Nichols (1978).

Intuitively, it seems that G_f, more than G_c or the other maintained abilities, should reflect genetic potential. Such a hypothesis was a part of early statements of G_f–G_c theory (e.g., Cattell, 1963; Horn, 1968). The extant evidence, however, does not clearly support this hypothesis (Bock & Kolakowski, 1973; Horn, 1988; Horn, Loehlin, & Willerman, 1979; Jensen, 1983; Kamin, 1974; McArdle, 1986; McArdle, Goldsmith, & Horn, 1981; Nichols, 1978; Plomin, DeFries, & McClearn, 1980; Scarr & McCartney, 1983; Vernon, 1979; Wilson & Matheney, 1983). The Nichols (1978) summary of evidence from twin studies in Table 3.2 illustrates the tenor of the findings. This evidence indicates that the heritabilities of G_f and G_c are about equal; they probably stem from different sets of genetic determiners. But G_f no more reflects genetic potential than does G_c.

Short-term apprehension–retention (G_{sm}). In popular thinking memory is often equated with intelligence: particularly when memory fails, people are likely to worry about loss of intelligence. But G_{sm} is quite separate from G_f and G_c. The distinctions among these abilities are seen in samples of pre-school children (Horn, 1986). The separation is quite clear by adulthood. It means that people with good short-term memories are not necessarily good in reasoning (G_f) or knowledge acquisition (G_c) or even long-term memory (G_{lr}).

The G_{sm} organization unites most of the performances indicating short-term apprehension and memory, working memory, and information processing. Specific indicators include span memory for numbers (as required in dialing a telephone number); span memory for words (remembering names at a party); paired associates recognition memory; serial learning (both primacy and recency); and the slope parameter of the S. Sternberg (1975) paradigm we described earlier. Memory for words measures G_{sm} (rather than G_c) if the words are equally familiar to all respondents (or equally obscure). The Woodcock-Johnson (1990) memory for words tests is defined on this principle.

The indicators G_{sm} have been carefully studied in research on cognitive processing (Craik, 1977; Horn et al., 1981; Hunt, 1980; Hunt, Frost & Lunneborg, 1973; Reese, 1977). This research indicates that G_{sm} involves processes of becoming aware of information, discriminating between different bits of information, retaining such awarenesses and discriminations for short periods of time, and using these awarenesses and discriminations over short periods of time in performing various kinds of tasks.

Processing speed (G_s) and correct decision speed (CDS). Speediness is involved in one way or another in almost all cognitive performances, as Birren (1974), Hertzog (1989), and Salthouse (1985, 1988) have emphasized. Depending on how speediness is measured, however, it relates in different ways to indicators of cognitive capability (Hertzog, 1989; Horn et al., 1981). Consider correct decision speed (CDS) first.

CDS is measured as the complement of the time it takes to produce answers to questions or problems that all subjects attempt. The questions or problems are of the same kind as are used to measure G_f or G_c or other cognitive capabilities. For most people in most such tasks, accuracy must be traded off, as it were, for speediness (Pachella, 1974; Salthouse, 1979, 1985). If one decides to read fast, usually one must expect to be less accurate in comprehending that which is read. But fast readers can be more accurate in comprehension than slow readers. Indeed, ID research indicates a positive correlation between speed of reading and level of comprehension.

One might reason from these observations that, in general, there is likely to be a strong positive correlation between speed of producing solutions to problems – speed of intellect – and the level of difficulty of problems successfully solved – level of intellect. Teachers seem to reason in this manner, for they often measure educational achievement with speeded tests when their aim is to measure level of understanding. Constructors of ability tests often seem to reason in this way, too, for cognitive tests typically are speeded but are presented as measures of level of comprehension. Indeed, it seems to be widely assumed that speed and level are virtually synonymous.

Salthouse (1985) has cautioned that the matter is much more complicated than this popular assumption suggests.

Much empirical evidence suggests that for many kinds of tasks, individual differences in speed and level of comprehension – speed and accuracy – are not highly correlated (Fruchter, 1950, 1953; Cattell, 1957; Hertzog, 1989; Horn et al., 1981; Kantowitz, 1974; Pachella, 1974; Salthouse, 1985). It is not known whether the IDs in being speedy rather than highly accurate stem from preference, from physiological or neurological factors, from a combination of such influences, or from yet other influences. There is evidence, however, that, for whatever reason, older adults relative to younger adults tend to sacrifice speed for accuracy (Hertzog, 1989; Horn et al., 1981; Poon & Fozard, 1978; Salthouse, 1985; Salthouse & Somberg, 1982). Such findings point to the need to carefully distinguish speed from accuracy and level, particularly in studies of development.

Correct decision speed (CDS) and measures of level, obtained by counting the number of correct answers (NC), are sometimes found to be highly correlated because the two kinds of measures are confounded. For example, if CDS is measured as number of problems attempted and NC is the number correct, then people who attempt more problems have a better chance of getting more correct than those who attempt few problems, and CDS and NC will be correlated simply as a function of this chance. Care must be taken to ensure that speed and accuracy, or level, measures are obtained in a manner such that the correlation between them could, in principle, be either high or low (Horn, 1982; Salthouse, 1985). Consider these special precautions.

First, it is important that all subjects of a sample attempt all items on which measures of speed and level are obtained. Otherwise, the measures may reflect only the level of difficulty of the items attempted. Second, the items used to measure level must be different from the items used to measure speed. Otherwise, the two measures will be operationally dependent (Horn, 1979; Humphreys, 1974), and thus correlated. A set of moderately difficult items can be used to measure speed. Items graded for difficulty are needed to measure level. Third, for measures of level, in order to weaken strong task demands (in our culture) to guess and respond quickly, subjects should be taught that some problems do not have solutions (or if they do, no one has found them). They should be taught to abandon a problem if, after expending a reasonable amount of effort, they do not find a solution. Such training gives subjects a basis for abandoning a problem even when there is a good solution but they do not comprehend it. For problems of different levels of difficulty, the measure of level is the average level of difficulty of correct solutions, rather than the number of problems solved (the more usual form of measure). The resulting scores thus do not reflect how fast a subject produces answers; they indicate the level of difficulty with which one successfully copes. This scoring reduces the effects of guessing. Fourth, it is best if the subject must produce the answer, rather than be able to select it from among several choices. This again reduces the effects of guessing.

When CDS and difficulty level are measured with these precautions in tasks that ordinarily indicate G_f (letter series and matrices), the correlation between speed and level is typically only about .20 – between .07 and .26 in three separate studies (Horn et al., 1981). The results thus indicate that when subjects are encouraged to work at their own rate, and task demands for speediness are reduced in measures of level, the quickness with which people solve problems does not have much to do with the level of difficulty of the problems solved. This finding is counter to what seems most often to be assumed.

In contrast to this finding for correct decision speed, the findings for studies of G_s and level measures of G_f suggest that the correlation is rather substantial – about .35 (significantly different from the correlation between CDS and G_f). G_s is a broad factor that is best indicated by simple tasks in which almost all people would get the right answer if the task were not highly speeded. The factor is most closely related to the primary ability described as Perceptual Speed, P: The tasks that measure P are good indicators of G_s. Cross Out in the Woodcock-Johnson (1990) illustrates the measure. The task in this test is to mark as quickly as possible the drawings in a row of drawings that are identical to the first drawing of the row, and to do this for a number of rows. Other indicators include speed of printing, speed of copying, and speed of finding a particular symbol embedded within a collection of other symbols, as if you were asked, for example, to encircle all the letter p's on this page.

We did not predict a relatively high correlation between G_s and G_f. The G_s tasks are simple, seemingly not indicative of what is important in human intelligence. Why would such a simple speediness function be related to G_f reasoning?

Detailed study of the relationship between G_s and G_f, using part correlation techniques (Horn et al., 1981), suggests that G_s involves a capacity (or inclination) for sustaining close attention in tasks that require attentiveness. The tasks that measure G_f reasoning require such attentiveness, as do the simple tasks of G_s speediness. This attentional capacity can be measured in very simple tasks that do not depend on speediness (Botwinick & Storandt, 1974; McDowd, 1986; McDowd & Craik, 1988; Myers, Stankov, & Oliphant, 1989). Measures requiring one to work as slowly as possible, for example, account for most of the relationship between G_s speediness and G_f reasoning, as well as most of the relationship between G_s and G_{sm} memory (Horn et al., 1987). Results such as these suggest it is not speediness, per se, that is central to the relationship between G_s and G_f; instead, the core function is a capacity for sustaining attention. We return to this matter in discussion of correlations between adulthood aging and cognitive performances. But first let us look briefly at G_v, G_a, and the maintained forms of intelligence.

Visual processing (G_v). G_v is a complex set of abilities of fluent visual scanning, WJ-R visual closure, mind's-eye rotation, seeing reversals, visual constancy, and memory for designs and spatial events. The primary abilities that best indicate this broad visualization function are S, spatial orientation (is a depicted figure a flip-flop of another?); C_s, visual closure (see the gestalt of a figure in which parts have been omitted); V_z, visualization (show how cutout parts fit together to depict a particular figure), and C_f, flexibility of closure (find a geometric figure embedded within a set of intersecting lines).

It can be difficult to distinguish G_v from G_f (Humphreys, 1962). To make the distinction, one must measure G_v in tasks where the relationships among visual patterns are clearly manifest, not such that one can infer them by reasoning, and G_f should be measured with reasoning tasks that are not primarily spatial, such as common word analogies and letter series. G_v mainly indicates fluency in perception of patterns, not reasoning to infer them.

Other evidence indicating the construct validity of G_v suggests that it relates to laterality in brain function, field independence, and differences in the developments of males and females.

Considerable evidence has accumulated to suggest that in most right-handed people the primary and principal organizations of visual functions are in the right hemisphere of the brain rather than the left (e.g., Springer & Deutsch, 1981). It is not clear that this distinguishes G_v from G_f, however.

Evidence gathered in several studies by Kosslyn (1987) suggests that within G_v the relationships among visualization abilities and brain functions are complex. The relationships may be understood best in terms of the primary abilities of G_v. With measures similar to those obtained with gestalt closure in the speed-of-closure (C_s) primary ability (described in Table 3.1), Kosslyn found that image generation, encoding and retaining categorical relation representations were better when images were projected into the left hemisphere than when they were projected to the right hemisphere. Also, people with brain damage in the left posterior part of the brain showed deficits in image generation. On the other hand, with tasks similar to the gallows tasks that indicate the flexibility-of-closure (C_f) primary ability (find a figure embedded in a swirl of lines, image inspection) Kosslyn found the right parietal lobe to be implicated. Difficulties in image scanning similar to scanning measured in the spatial relations (S) primary ability also were associated with damage to the right parietal sections of the brain. Subjects with such damage also had difficulty deciding whether two shaded sides of an unfolded cube would be adjacent when the sides were folded to form the cube. This task is similar to a paper-folding task of the visualization (V) primary ability of G_v. Image rotation, measured in tasks similar to those studied by Shepard and Metzler (1971), also was found to be associated with right parietal damage. The Shepard-Metzler measure is reaction time (RT) to decide correctly that a figure in one part of space could be a rotation of a figure in another part of space. (We have no direct correlational evidence showing that such RT measures are a feature of G_v abilities. Studies of the visual abilities of pilot and navigator trainees in the U.S. Air Force (Guilford & Lacy, 1947) suggest that G_v is best measured in tests that are not highly speeded.) Thus, in the main, Kosslyn's findings are consistent with a hypothesis that G_v functions are primarily organized in the right hemisphere of the brain, but closure functions (as in C_c) appear to be mainly organized in the left hemisphere.

The evidence suggesting that G_v is related to the cognitive style concept of field independence is based primarily on the hidden figures test in the work of Witkin and his co-workers (Witkin & Goodenough, 1981). Hidden figures is a good indicator of the C_f primary ability of G_v. The Witkin theory specified that for a variety of reasons some individuals become highly inclined to orient with respect to their own bodies – their own selves. These individuals are said to be "field independent." Other people, the theory states, are most inclined to orient in terms of their surroundings rather than in terms of their own selves. These individuals are said to be "field dependent" (low field independence).

Early in the Witkin research, field independence was measured with rod-and-frame and tilting-room tasks. In the tilting room (as found in amusement parks), field independent people tend to stand upright even though, to align with other objects in the room, they should tilt; but the field dependent people tend to tilt to match the other objects in the room. In the rod-and-frame test, the subject adjusts a rod more and less in accordance with the surrounding field. The tilting-room and rod-and-frame tests thus indicate the extent to which individuals attend primarily to bodily cues or primarily to cues in the field.

The Witkin researchers found that field independence measures obtained with the rod-and-frame and tilting-room tasks correlated about .30 with measures obtained with the hidden figures test. Most of the research that has been done on field independence was based on hidden figures, rather than on tilting-room or rod-and-frame, tests. The results from this research suggest that females and people of low social and economic class score low on hidden figures relative to males and people of high social and economic class.

The link between field independence, as indicated in the tilting-room and rod-and-frame measures, and the attribute measured in hidden figures is thus tenuous, which makes a link to G_v even more tenuous. The results may indicate, mainly, that field independence is a form of visual processing (G_v). The correlations of hidden figures with the male–female dichotomy is not inconsistent with this interpretation. There are research results indicting gender differences in quite a number of G_v visualization functions (Jensen, 1980, for review). Jensen concludes that "the largest and most consistently found sex difference [in cognitive abilities] is for spatial visualization."

Jensen also concludes from his review that the cause for this difference "is still an open question scientifically" (p. 626). Some of the evidence suggests that sex differences in G_v are linked to genetic factors on the XY chromosomes (Bock & Kolakowski, 1973). But Jensen argued that this link "is not as clearly indicated as had been assumed" (p. 27). Fairweather's (1976) results support this caution. Indeed, his analyses cast doubt on any supposition that observed average male–female differences in abilities are indicative of intrinsic differences between the sexes.

Auditory processing (G_a). The G_a function is indicated by any of a wide variety of tasks that require one to be aware of nuances in sounds, perceive sound patterns, hold sound configurations in mind, identify particular sounds amid a swirl of other sounds, and, in general, organize sound percepts (Horn, 1972; Horn & Stankov, 1982; Stankov, 1978; Stankov & Horn, 1980; Woodcock & Johnson, 1990). The function is centrally involved in the comprehension of speech. Tasks that measure the factor include repeated tones (identify the first occurrence of a tone when it occurs several times), tonal series (indicate which tone comes next in an orderly series of tones), cafeteria noise (identify a word amid a din of surrounding noise), and sound blending (from the Woodock-Johnson battery). As in measuring G_v, the G_a abilities are best indicated in tasks in which one does not need to reason to infer auditory patterns but instead can fluently perceive patterns.

Musical abilities and auditory abilities of language comprehension have been studied throughout this century (Carroll, 1962; Drake, 1939; Horn, 1973; Horn & Stankov, 1982; Revesz, 1953; Seashore, Lewis, & Saetveit, 1960; Shuter, 1968; Solomon, Webster, & Curtis, 1960; Stankov & Horn, 1980; Wing, 1955), but only rarely have they been regarded as central features of intelligence. Auditory abilities have not been measured separately to indicate IQ or learning potential. Nevertheless, there is evidence that these abilities are important features of cognitive capability (Stankov, 1986). Hearnshaw (1956) suggests that temporal integration, best measured in auditory tasks, is a central feature of intelligence. In the Atkin et al. (1977) studies, auditory abilities measured in preschool and beginning-school children were more indicative of cognitive performance in the later school years than were commonly used measures of IQ. Stankov (1980) also found that G_a is a substantial indicator of school achievements.

Major features of maintained abilities

All the maintained abilities – crystallized knowledge (G_c), long-term memory (G_{lr}), and quantitative knowledge (G_q) – are readily assumed to be indicative of intelligence. G_c, or even only the verbal comprehension primary ability component, is often treated as if it alone indicates intelligence. But G_{lr}, too, is often cast in this role, particularly when seen in fluent use of language (as in judgments about politicians). A failure in G_{lr} retrieval is likely to be interpreted with concern as a "sign" of one's lack of, or loss of, intelligence.

Acculturation knowledge (G_c). The concept of G_c – breadth and depth of knowledge – is much broader than any operational definition of the concept one can obtain in measurement, as Cattell (1971) has emphasized. Quite fallible estimates, probably more heavily weighted with schoollike information than is ideal, are obtained with measures of knowledge in many areas of scholarship – the humanities, business, history, the social sciences, and the physical sciences – as well as knowledge about avocational aspects of culture – books, movies, music, sports. The Woodcock-Johnson (1990) tests of science, social studies, and humanities are good measures of these abilities. Other indicators can be obtained with tests of vocabulary, esoteric analogies, remote associations, judgment, experience, skills of communication, and understanding of conventions. The measured factor indicates the extent to which an individual has incorporated, through the systematic influences of acculturation, the knowledge and sophistication – the intelligence – of a culture.

Fluency of retrieval from long-term storage (G_{lr}). A person's knowledge system is not static; it is repeatedly restructured throughout life (Broadbent, 1966; Norman, 1979). The network of knowledge that is G_c is rather like a library of books that one repeatedly rearranges as one adds to it. Each rearrangement, as well as each addition, can make the system better and the elements of the system more accessible. In terms of this metaphor, G_{lr} represents the extent to which one can fit a new book into an appropriate section of the library and call up the books from any particular section. It is measured with tests of fluency of retrieval of information – tests that require one to list words similar to a given word, provide interpretations of an event (a man going up a ladder), make up appropriate titles for a story, list uses for an object. It is also indicated by memory retrieval over periods of time longer than a couple of minutes, that is, over hours, weeks, years. Such retrieval indicates consolidation, "making sense out of information," and depth of processing (Craik & Lockart, 1972) – analogous to finding an appropriate section for a book in one's library. It points to processes of encoding information for long-term memory storage that permit ready access to the information through association of one item with another. These associations are not so much correct as they are possible and useful. For example, an association of "teakettle" with "mother" (as items that are "warm") is not necessarily correct, but it can be useful in thinking about both mothers and tea.

The manner in which knowledge is consolidated at the time of acquisition dictates, to some extent, the manner in which it can be retrieved at a later time (e.g., Bower, 1972). This suggests that G_{lr} and G_{sm} should be correlated, as, indeed, they are (approximately .40). But this correlation is well below the internal consistency among the abilities that separately make up G_{lr} and G_{sm}. Thus, although the two functions are related, certain features about the process of retrieving information (G_{lr}) are distinct from the process of initial apprehension and working memory (G_{sm}). Particularly important are consistent findings from several studies showing that in the same samples in which G_{sm} declines with age in adulthood, G_{lr} does not decline and, in some samples, increases.

Quantitative knowledge (G_q). G_q is most often distinguished in educational and vocational guidance and prediction. It is well distinguished in the Woodcock-Johnson (1990) battery. By the time children have reached junior high school in our culture individual differences in a broad range of quantitative understandings and skills can be seen to stand apart from individual differences in G_c, as well as other ability structures. In predictions of various criteria in adulthood, G_q clearly has different construct validity than G_c. Different construct validity is also indicated by gender differences for G_q and G_c.

Differences in G_q averages for samples of males and females have been found repeatedly in this century. On the surface these findings suggest that in our culture gender differences in G_q emerge in early adolescence (Benbow & Stanley, 1983; Jensen, 1980; Maccoby & Jacklin, 1973). Before puberty, there are no particularly large or systematic differences between the averages for boys and girls. If anything, it seems that girls score somewhat higher. But from puberty onward males tend to score higher than females. In mathematical talent searches in late adolescence and early adulthood, the proportions of boys obtaining extremely high scores are substantially larger than the proportions of girls obtaining such scores (e.g., Benbow & Stanley, 1983; Fox, 1976). The content of the problems within which quantitative problems are couched does not seem to account for the difference. When problems deal with cooking, sewing, and other activities more common for girls than for boys, adult males still score somewhat higher (on average) than same-age females. Benbow (1987, 1988) suggests that gender differences in G_q abilities can stem from greater variability of both environmental and biological factors in males.

As we have already mentioned, Fairweather (1976) has done analyses that caution against regarding these findings, or almost any findings of gender differences, as indicative of qualities intrinsic to either sex (see also Boles, 1980; Harris, 1978). Not only are socialization processes within our culture directed at creating gender differences, a point emphasized by Maccoby and Jacklin (1973), but also the samplings of boys and girls are different in studies on which generalizations are based. Boys are absent from school, and drop out of school, more commonly than girls; absentees and dropouts are usually not among the high scorers on quantitative tests. Boys are more likely than girls to sign up for the high-placement courses and high-placement tests that tend to bring them to attention in talent searches. Fairweather works through a line of reasoning from such considerations that leads to a conclusion that reported differences between males and females in cognitive abilities probably are not intrinsic to gender.

Nevertheless, at the surface level of what is seen in average differences, as such, gender differences exist (in G_q and G_v). One should take into account these differences even as one does not assume that they necessarily must occur.

Verbal and nonverbal abilities

The distinction between maintained and vulnerable abilities is sometimes said to be a distinction between "verbal" and "nonverbal" or "performance" abilities. This is not a good way to characterize the distinction, however. The verbal–nonverbal (performance) distinction came into use in response to evidence indicating that a concept of general intelligence does not provide a good basis for describing decline of abilities with age in adulthood and the laterality of organizations of abilities in the left and right hemispheres of the brain. But the verbal–nonverbal distinction does not well characterize the evidence indicating that different abilities are affected in different ways by different influences. In particular, it does not characterize the distinction between abilities that increase and abilities that decrease with age in adulthood. Although many of the abilities that indicate adulthood declines would not be classified as verbal, some would. Similarly, although many of the abilities that increase with age in adulthood can be seen to be verbal, some are "nonverbal."

Picture stories, for example, is a nonverbal test that indicates G_c, and the averages for this ability increase throughout most of adulthood. Common word analogies, on the other hand, and verbal ability in drawing fine distinctions among the meanings of words, are vulnerable abilities that decrease with age in adulthood (Horn & Cattell, 1967; Bromley, 1974). Complex reasoning with novel verbal relations also is a vulnerable ability (probably G_f). It decreases with extended, heavy use of alcohol (Ryan & Butters, 1979; Sharp, Rosenbaum, Goldman, & Whitman, 1977). In general, both vulnerable abilities and maintained abilities can be either verbal or nonverbal.

The Wechsler scales, particularly the Wechsler Adult Intelligence Scale (Wechsler, 1955, 1981), better known as simply the WAIS, are important in the history of research on human abilities. Much of the evidence on vulnerable and maintained cognitive abilities has been based on use of the WAIS. It has been influential, also, in maintaining a distinction between verbal and nonverbal abilities. The following are subtests of the WAIS:

Subtests regarded as verbal	*Subtests regarded as performance*
VO: vocabulary	BD: block design
IN: information	OA: object assembly
CO: comprehension	PC: picture completion
SI: similarities	PA: picture arrangement
AR: arithmetic	CD: digit symbol or coding
DS: digit span	

A score obtained from subtests on the left is said to indicate verbal IQ, here abbreviated VQ; scores for the tests on the right are used to measure what is called performance IQ, abbreviated PQ. A score based on all subtests is said to measure general intelligence, WIQ.

VQ is often discussed as if it is equivalent to G_c, and PQ is often treated as equivalent of G_f. Indeed, there are notable similarities between VQ and G_c, and PQ does resemble G_f (Matarazzo, 1980). But these similarities do not indicate equivalence. There are important differences between G_f and PQ, particularly.

Factoring of the WAIS indicates that vocabulary (VO), information (IN), comprehension (CO), and similarities (SI) form a factor similar to G_c (e.g., Cohen, 1952, 1957; Horn, 1988; Woodcock, 1990). These subtests are part of VQ, but arithmetic (AR) and digit span (DS), which are scored in VQ, are not good indicators of the factor. Also, the factor involves picture arrangement (PA), which in WAIS scoring is a part of PQ, not VQ. Thus, VQ includes more short-term memory than is characteristic of G_c, but it does not include the acculturational knowledge of picture arrangement, which is indicative of G_c.

A second factor prominent in the WAIS subtests is defined primarily by block design (BD), picture arrangement (PA), object assembly (OA), and picture completion (PC), all measures of PQ. The relationship with PC is small, however, and CD, which is scored in PQ, is not at all prominent in the factor. Moreover, digit span (DS), which is scored in VQ, not PQ, is involved in the factor, albeit to a small degree. This factor has been interpreted as indicating G_f (Horn, 1988; Matarazzo, 1980), but it involves visualization to a very considerable extent and some investigators have identified it primarily with G_v (McArdle, 1988; McArdle & Horn, 1983; Woodcock, 1990). Further research is needed to clarify the extent to which it indicates the G_f or G_v factor.

A third factor of the WAIS is indicated primarily by DS, but usually also involves AR and may involve PA and CD (Cohen, 1952, 1957; Horn, 1988). It thus appears to be an underdetermined indicator of G_{sm} but involves G_s as well. Short-term memory is involved in AR arithmetic because the problems are presented orally, so one must hold the elements in immediate awareness while doing the calculations needed to arrive at a correct answer. This factor declines notably with age. This is consistent with much evidence indicating aging decline of G_{sm} and Schaie's (1983) results, particularly, showing aging decline on speeded factors. In one study based on several tests besides the WAIS subtests (Woodcock, 1990), CD was found to relate to the speed of G_s, and AR mainly indicated G_q, not G_{sm}.

The development of human abilities

The intellectual abilities of G_f-G_c theory are learned. This does not dispute a claim that individual differences in abilities result from individual differences in genetic factors. Even if individual differences in an ability were perfectly correlated with genetic factors (a hypothetical that is not near truth for any ability), the ability can result primarily from learning. The evidence for genetic determination would say in this case that the what-is-learned is a function of heredity – and there would have to be equal opportunities for everyone to learn (another hypothetical that is far from reality). It is clear, however, that from an early age onward there are notable individual differences in the efficiency with which people learn different things, the time taken to learn, the amount learned and retained, and thus in level of expression of each of many abilities – in particular the abilities of G_f and G_c. The innate capacities on which different learnings are based mature somewhat independently of learning, even as they provide foundations for learning. The outcomes of learning and maturational influences that unfold throughout development are the abilities we see and measure.

There are individual differences in the rates and asymptotic levels of the maturations and learnings that produce manifested abilities. This is indicated by, among other evidence, the finding of a quasi-simplex pattern of covariances in repeated measures across wide periods of development (Collins, 1991; Collins & Horn, 1991; Humphreys, 1962). This means that over time (age) people change in rank order in level of expression of cognitive abilities. Some of the really smart at one age are relatively less smart when measured at later points in time, and some low-scoring individuals move up to surpass others as development proceeds. The longer the period of time between successive measurements, the lower the correlation between the measures.

Longitudinal, cross-sectional and mixed sampling

Studies designed to indicate typical (average) developmental changes in abilities are of two fundamental kinds: cross-sectional and longitudinal. A few studies are mixtures of these two. It is important to analyze carefully just what can, and cannot, be learned from longitudinal and cross-sectional studies, for the science of human development is largely based on evidence from one or the other. Such analysis is provided in Nesselroade (1990; 1991; Nesselroade & Ford, 1985). Our discussion is based on Nesselroade's analyses.

Bell (1953), Cattell (1950), and Kuhlen (1959) were among the first to study the inferential features of cross-sectional and longitudinal research and to propose methods for improving the basis for inference. The methods they proposed have been modified and improved by a number of investigators. We cannot describe all these variations and improvements in the space of a chapter, desirable though it is to become aware of them. Much of the up-to-date work in this area can be found in Collins and Horn (1991), a collection of papers by people who have developed the methods. Here we outline only the most basic and general features of methods that one must understand in order to comprehend the evidence produced on the development of human abilities.

Longitudinal research is an extension of case study. In case study one individual is observed over and over again, across time. In longitudinal research the sample of one individual is extended to a sample of several individuals, all of whom are observed over and over again. Samples are used in longitudinal research in lieu of the individual of case study because changes for a single individual often are not representative of what happens to people in general and tend to be unreliable.

In most of the longitudinal research of the past, averages were taken when the people of the sample were at different ages, and these averages were compared to provide the basis for inferences about changes that occur within individuals. This will be referred to as "average-comparison longitudinal research."

Rather than take the average for a sample at each age, one can plot each individual's scores over different ages and do analyses on the resulting curves. This will be referred to as "process-pooling longitudinal research." This approach has not been used often in longitudinal research, but it can lead to results quite different from those obtained in average-comparison longitudinal studies.

In cross-sectional research, samples of individuals are studied – again in order to gain representativeness and reliability – but a sample is made up of subsamples of people of different ages. Comparison analysis of the averages for these subsamples is analogous to average-comparison longitudinal research. The cross-sectional averages can be different from the longitudinal averages, however, because people born at different times develop through different periods of history and the different influences of these periods can affect the variable of interest. Differences due to the influences of developing through different histories have come to be called age-cohort differences or simply cohort differences (Schaie, 1965).

Cross-sectional differences thus can indicate age-cohort differences that are quite different from changes that accompany aging. But such differences can also indicate some of the same information about aging as is revealed by longitudinal research. It is important to recognize this because it is tempting to assume that only longitudinal studies can provide a reliable basis on which to base inferences about developmental change – a tempting assumption because we recognize that processes of change must occur within particular people, not across different people. This assumption most logically indicates the need to do process-pooling longitudinal research, however, indicating change within people, not average-comparison longitudinal research.

Cross-sectional studies can reveal the same effects as average–comparison longitudinal studies if age-cohort influences do not operate. If, on average, for example, people wrinkle and turn gray in consequence of aging, not because of the time in this century when they were born, then comparison of cross-sectional average age differences in wrinkles and grayness can indicate the same kinds of changes as are indicated in the subsample averages of longitudinal research. Both cross-sectional and longitudinal results thus can indicate what occurs (on the average) within people.

One can see in this example that although both average-comparison longitudinal research and cross-sectional research can point to the same average change, the results indicate what is typical about groups of individuals, not necessarily the regularities of change within individuals. Neither the cross-sectional study nor the longitudinal study will indicate the truth of change within individuals, namely, that some turned gray, some did not, some wrinkled, some did not. The averages over several individuals (in either case) are not changes within individuals; the change of one individual is averaged with the lack of change in another individual; the moderate change in one individual is averaged with the great change in another, and so forth. The averages in longitudinal research, no less than in cross-sectional research, hide the fact that some people do not become gray with age. The

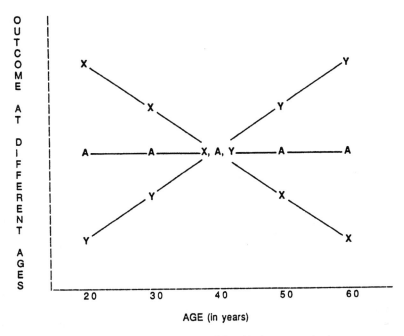

Figure 3.3. Change in two processes, Py and Px, that is not seen in the averages.

conclusion from either kind of study should be of the form "some people" or "most people" or "people on the average" become gray with age.

To see concretely how average-comparison longitudinal research (and cross-sectional research) can fail to reveal change within people one need consider only a simple example such as that depicted in Figure 3.3.

In the figure, a process in one individual is seen to be monotonic ascending (variable Y). The same kind of process in another individual is monotonic descending (variable X). The averages of these two changes is neither ascending nor descending: the averages incorrectly indicate no change within people. Averages thus can be misleading. The Y and X curves in the figure could just as well be for subsamples of subjects as for individuals. Methods of analysis to isolate process changes such as those of Y and X have been developed (as discussed in the collections of articles put together by Cattell, 1966; Collins & Horn, 1991; and Harris, 1963). To understand this chapter, one need not go into the details of this work. It is sufficient to be aware that although results from both kinds of longitudinal research and from cross-sectional research can indicate the same change, they also can provide significantly different information.

We should be aware that information about typical change can be more in error when obtained in longitudinal study than when obtained in cross-sectional research. This is important because it is compelling to suppose, and is often stated in developmental literature, that only longitudinal research can correctly indicate within-person change. But longitudinal analysis of averages can give a more distorted basis for inference about typical change than is provided in cross-sectional research. This can occur if there is systematic dropout in longitudinal research that does not occur in cross-sectional research. The class-reunion effect illustrates such a possibility.

If one were to estimate age changes in income from longitudinal samples of people returning for class reunions, one would be drawn to a conclusion that income increases with age. But this could mainly represent the fact that people who return for reunions have made money and want others to know this, but those who have not made money do not return for reunions. A representative cross-sectional sampling of people 35 to 70 years of age (as found in hospitals and prisons, among the homeless, and on skid row, as well as in money-making occupations) would lead to a better conclusion – which might well be that income, on the average, does not increase with age. This conclusion would be closer to the truth of what happens on the average (in representative samples) than the conclusion based on the longitudinal study.

If variables indicating homelessness, incarceration, profession, and so forth, are obtained in cross-sectioned study, then one can do part correlational analyses to arrive at valid inferences about different changes within different individuals. By statistically removing the influences associated with homelessness and incarceration, for example, one would approximate the class-reunion condition showing that some individuals very much increase their income. By parting out professions that pay well, on the other hand, one would approximate the conditions of no increase in income for the homeless and incarcerated.

This illustrates, too, that age-cohort effects can be studied in cross-sectional studies, for in this instance one would part out variables representing the different influences that define (according to hypothesis) different age-cohorts.

In most of the discussion that follows we refer to results as either longitudinal or cross-sectional, even when they have been obtained in studies in which the two designs are mixed. This convenience is reasonable because in a mixed study one can separately discuss the longitudinal or cross-sectional trends and then discuss comparisons and the extent to which they are convergent.

Age differences indicating different construct validities

If the abilities of G_f, G_c, G_m, G_l, and G_s are all regarded as indicators of g or IQ, then different measures of IQ based on somewhat different combinations of these basic abilities yield quite conflicting and confusing information about the average differences between people of different ages and the average age differences for samples of people followed up in longitudinal study. The vulnerable abilities decline with age from the early twenties onward; the maintained abilities increase throughout most of adulthood. These different developments for vulnerable and maintained abilities are confounded and lost if abilities are clumped together in a single measure of IQ (under assumption that there is one thing called general intelligence).

In the earliest studies of adulthood age changes and differences in cognitive abilities, it was assumed that different abilities indicate the same general intelligence (IQ). It happened that in longitudinal studies, maintained abilities were selected to indicate IQ, while in cross-sectional studies IQ was usually defined in terms of vulnerable abilities. It happened, too, that the times between retests were short in the longitudinal studies, and the sample sizes were small, so conditions were not sufficient to indicate an effect (difference between ages) comparable to the effect found in cross-sectional studies. Not surprisingly, given these conditions and what we now know, it was concluded that longitudinal studies indicated that IQ did not change with age in adulthood, but cross-sectional studies indicated that IQ declined with age, results said to "contradict" each other.

It was reasoned that this "contradiction" resulted because age-cohort influences operated in cross-sectional studies that were not present in longitudinal studies. The age-cohort effect came about (according to this reasoning) because people born earlier in this century attended school for fewer numbers of years than people born later in the century; education enhances intellectual abilities (IQ); therefore, education differences between young and old were responsible for cross-sectional findings showing that younger people score higher on IQ tests than older people. When the same people were followed up in longitudinal study, the reasoning continued, age differences in education were eliminated, and the findings showing that IQ did not decline thus indicated that the cross-sectional results were due to age-cohort differences.

Plausible though this reasoning may seem to be, it is not necessary to explain the results and, indeed, is not a sufficient explanation. Because the abilities analyzed in longitudinal studies were primarily those of G_c, and the averages for these abilities do not decline in cross-sectional studies, there is no contradiction on this account for the findings from longitudinal and cross-sectional studies. Both show "IQ," measured as G_s, to increase with age in adulthood. If allowances are made for the small sample sizes and short periods between testings in longitudinal studies, the results from the two kinds of studies are consistent.

Similarly, when measures of vulnerable abilities were obtained in longitudinal studies (Bayley, 1966; Owens, 1953), and the age range and sample size were sufficient to show a decline of the magnitude indicated by cross-sectional findings, decline was indeed indicated (Horn, 1970; Horn & Donaldson, 1980).

Thus, the finding from both longitudinal and cross-sectional studies is that from young adulthood to old age there is (on the average across many individuals) monotonic decrease in the vulnerable abilities – particularly G_f, G_s, and G_m. Over much of this period, in the same samples of individuals, there are increases in the maintained abilities, G_c and G_{tr}. In very old age these abilities, too, may decline, as the evidence of Schaie and Baltes (1977) suggests.

A refined picture of this general finding is depicted in the results summarized in Figure 3.4. This figure is based on structural equation modeling analyses of abilities selected to represent major factors of G_f–G_c theory in a sample of 215 adult males (McArdle & Horn, 1983). A model for the age differences in the means for both G_f and G_c required a quadratic term, representing a curvilinear relationship. This was true whether or not variations in education were taken into account, but the effect was most pronounced when the cohort differences in the educational levels of people of different ages were not controlled (Fig. 3.4a). This plot indicates that the quadratic curve for G_c turns downward in old age when education is not controlled. The curve is at plateau in the later ages when education is controlled (Fig. 3.4b). These two bits of evidence support the Schaie and Baltes (1977) hypothesis that for G_c there is an age-cohort effect associated with differences in amount of formal education. The downward slope in old age is apparently brought about mainly by people of low formal education. When education is controlled, the downward slope of the curve is reduced to a point where it is no longer statistically significant. On the other hand, the quadratic effect at the young end of the curve for G_f (when education is not controlled) could be a reflection of some of the factors associated with the decline (over the last 10–15 years) of SAT scores in samples of young people. An increase in the influence of television and movies has paralleled a decrease in the influence of books and comics. Abilities associated with reading are probably better represented in the tests that have identified G_c and G_f than are the abilities associated with viewing television and movies (Horn, 1979).

Evidence based on the WAIS: Variability across age. Research with the WAIS has provided a good basis for understanding the similarities and differences in the evidence of cross-sectional, longitudinal, and mixed designs (Schaie, 1973). It also raises important questions about increase with age in individual differences (variance) in major cognitive abilities. Consider the question of variances next.

Besides indicating age differences in ID variances, results from McArdle's

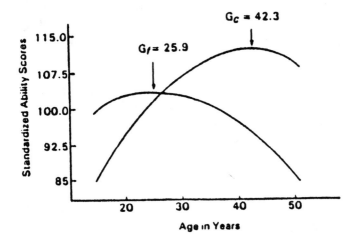

a. Quadratic factor score curves predicted
   from model

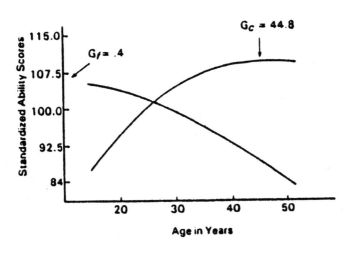

b. Quadratic factor score curves from
   model when education is partialled

Figure 3.4. Age relationship for G_f and G_c.

(1984) work replicate previous studies showing age differences in the mean levels of maintained and vulnerable abilities. The results are based on analyses of cross-sectional data for a sample drawn to match census data for demographic variables such as age and sex. The first two factors of a structural model that well represents these data indicate G_c and G_f, with the

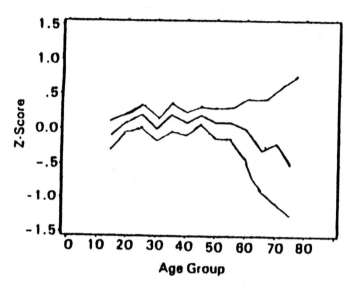

a. Factor I (Gc-like)

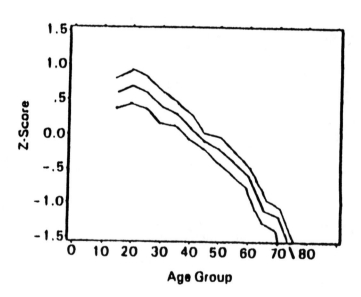

b. Factor II (Gf or Gv)

Figure 3.5. A multiple group factor means and variances for the WAIS as a function of age in a census sample ($n = 2977$).

proviso (considered in describing structure) that factor II might involve G_v. A model that represents age differences for these two factors is shown in Figure 3.5. This model provides a good fit to the data. A model specifying one IQ factor and a single age change curve does not fit the data at all well. These findings summarize results obtained with less sophisticated analyses in many previous studies (as reviewed in Botwinick, 1977, and Matarazzo, 1972).

The middle curve in each of the plots in Figure 3.5 depicts the mean standard score at each age; the two curves on either side of the middle curve represent the variance around the mean at each age. It can be seen that the variances are similar at each age for G_f but that they increase notably for G_c from ages 40 to 75 years.

These results thus indicate that on average, elderly people perform on G_c tests at a level above the average for younger people. This agrees with the common observation that the elderly often are better informed, more knowledgeable, wiser, and more erudite than younger individuals. The wide variances around the mean for G_c indicate that there are notable exceptions to this generalization. Some older individuals score lower on G_c than many younger individuals.

The results for the G_f factor indicate, on the other hand, that in reasoning the youthful usually perform better than the elderly. The nearly constant and small variances around the means in this case indicate that there are not many notable exceptions to the trend showing decline of G_f with age.

The age increase in variance that McArdle found for G_c is consistent with other evidence indicating increase in individual differences with age (Botwinick, 1977; Salthouse, 1985). In research in which number-correct (or percent-correct) scores and level scores are used, reliable and notable age-related increase in variability (for a period from about age 30 to 65 years) has been found for G_c-like abilities, but not for those clearly G_f-like. Also, in several studies of reaction time (RT), aging increase in variance has been found (Hunt, 1980). It is not clear whether these increases mainly stem from increases in time to perceive, time to think about what is perceived, time to react once an appropriate response is formulated, or all three of these processes.

Increase in variability may come about partly because the factors producing intellectual enhancement, on the one hand, and intellectual decline, on the other, accumulate with advancing age, and such factors at one point in development cause such factors at later times. For example, intensive study at a young age can result in enhanced intellectual ability; this enhancement, in turn, can cause further intensive study, which then can cause still more intellectual enhancement. Thus, the smart would get smarter. Similarly, heavy use of alcohol at a young age can cause intellectual decline, and this decline, in turn, can cause further heavy use of alcohol, which then can cause more intellectual decline; thus, the dumb would get dumber.

If factors producing both intellectual decline and intellectual enhancement accumulate more rapidly in some people than in others, then in representative samples of people of different ages, the variance of both vulnerable and maintained abilities should increase along with increase in the average age within samples. Why is such increase in variance seen only in the maintained abilities? Sternberg (1985) and Ackerman (1987, 1989) have put forth evidence that suggests why this result occurs.

On the basis of review of a large body of evidence, Ackerman (1987, 1989) concluded that when people can learn to deal with the complexities of a "consistent task," then variability of performance, both within people and between people, decreases with practice. A consistent task is one in "which the learner can deal with inputs and outputs in an unvarying or consistent manner from one instance to another" (Schneider & Shiffren, 1977). Such consistency is said to indicate automaticity. When RT measures are obtained with consistent tasks, individual differences decrease with increasing practice.

Ackerman points out that consistency is not a function of the task alone. Mainly, it is a function of the complexity of tasks and the capabilities of people. Some subjects may never, as Ackerman puts it, "capture the consistency of a task" because they never master the complexities of the task. In samples that contain such individuals, as well as people who can and do master the task, individual differences will increase as those who can master the task become increasingly more consistent. Thus, for tests with the properties of consistent tasks, if increases in variance are found, they should indicate differences in amounts of practice that can lead some toward consistency. Tests that indicate G_c have these properties. On the other hand, if age increases in variances are not found, the suggestion is that the tasks are not highly practiced – that no individuals have been able to move to a position of automaticity-cum-consistency. This is a way of defining novel tasks – tasks that are not highly practiced by anyone. These are the kinds of tasks that indicate G_f.

The suggestion is that for complex tasks for which abilities in dealing with the task are at asymptote in development, and for tasks that are not highly practiced (people do not reach automaticity), variability due to learning will remain nearly constant over age. For one or the other of these reasons the nearly constant variability over adulthood for G_f seems to fit this case. Ferguson's (1954, 1956) studies suggest that by the time of early adulthood, some abilities (such as those of G_f) are at an asymptote of development. For abilities that are notably developing, however, even if measured with RT, if automaticity can be reached by some and not by others, age increase in variance can be expected. This appears to apply to the abilities of G_c.

More from the WAIS: Two-occasion longitudinal results. Results from two-occasion studies of the WAIS help to summarize the consistency of longitudinal and cross-sectional findings. The principal results are well represented by the work of McArdle (1984), who brought together data from 58 two-occasion repeated-measures longitudinal studies of WAIS verbal (VQ) and performance (PQ). Sample sizes of the separate comparisons ranged from 1 to 300; time between the two testings ranged from 1 hour to 22 years. The averages for each comparison are depicted in Figure 3.6.

Each of the two ends of a line in this figure is a plot of a point representing the age (along the X axis) and average (over the sample) score (along the Y axis) of the percent correct answers (rather than number of correct answers). The length of the line between the two end points indicates the time between testings, expressed in years of age. The slope of the line indicates rise or fall of the sample average. Lines for which the slope is positive depict increased performance over age (time); lines for which the slope is negative indicate decline of performance with age. The figure at the top is for VQ; the one at the bottom is for PQ.

A first look at Figure 3.6 might suggest that there are no dependable aging trends in these longitudinal data. The lines seem to go up and down in a fortuitous manner. There is considerable order in these data, however, as McArdle was able to show. Using mathematical modeling techniques, he held constant the test–retest effect over different amounts of time between testings in analyses of the age change per year. Similarly, he held constant the age change in analyses of the effects of time between testings.

The results of these analyses are consistent with the results summarized in Figure 3.5. When other factors are held constant, the aging slope for VQ changes from positive to negative over the entire age continuum. Most of the consistent part of the negative trend occurs in the period beyond age 60 years. The comparable slope for PQ is persistently negative throughout the age period. A structural equation model for VQ and PQ provides a reasonable fit to the data. If VQ and PQ are combined in a single factor model (to represent the idea of general IQ), the resulting model provides a poor fit to the data. The results are thus quite consistent with those for cross-sectional data.

These findings showing that older adults score higher than younger adults on VQ and other measures of G_c question the reasoning that because older adults usually have had less formal education than younger adults, there should be an age-cohort effect showing older adults scoring lower than younger adults on measures that are particularly enhanced by education. On the other hand, an age-cohort effect, associated with increases in formal education throughout this century, would be expected to be relatively small for PQ and other measures of G_f, but it is precisely on these measures that aging declines are most clearly indicated.

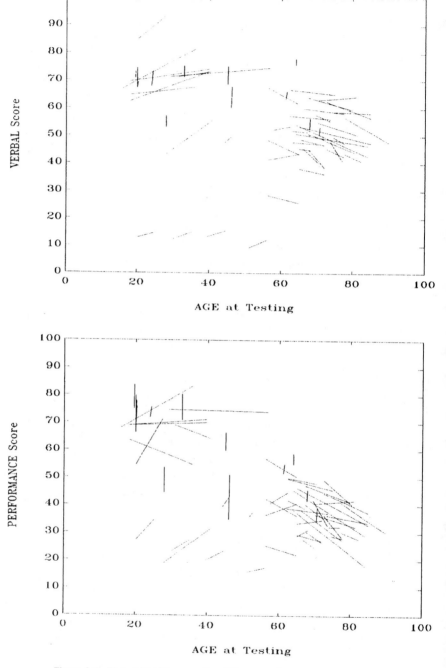

Figure 3.6. Plot of WAIS means from 58 repeated-measures studies.

Component analysis of the aging decline of G_f. The decline of vulnerable abilities over the "vital years of adulthood" is depressing. How should we understand this decline? What are it's features?

The decline of G_f is associated with loss of short-term memory, G_{sm}. Which is the chicken, which is the egg in these declines? What is called "loss of memory" in aging may best be understood as loss of reasoning capacities that support memory – or loss of G_f (Horn et al., 1981). This conclusion comes from studies designed to show, analytically, the particular kinds of cognitive capabilities associated with aging. The results indicate that G_f reasoning predicts much of the variance in measures of encoding novel information (Hultsch, 1971; Mandler, 1967), which is the core of short-term memory. In this sense, then, G_f can be at the base of results obtained with measures of memory. This seems to be particularly the case for encoding done "spontaneously," as in measures of incidental memory. Spontaneously perceiving relationships (in G_f) seems to account for the recall. Similarly, the "forced" encoding directed by explicitly activated metamemory seems to be based on a depth of processing that is G_f reasoning (Botwinick, 1977; Craik, 1977). The abilities of G_f thus seem to account for much of the aging decline of short-term memory.

The important factor here is an interpretation different from that usually given to findings showing relationships between memory and aging or brain damage. Memory loss is important, but it is a reflection of failure to organize information for encoding, and such failure reflects an inability to (spontaneously) comprehend relationships, a capacity that is measured in fluid general reasoning, G_f. These processes of reasoning are similar to those Craik and Lockhart (1972) described as depth of processing.

G_f reasoning also involves capacities for dividing attention, maintaining close attention, and avoiding preoccupation with irrelevancies, each of which relates to memory and intellectual speed and each of which declines with age in adulthood.

The process of keeping focused attention is basic. This elementary capacity is measured in tasks requiring subjects to behave as slowly as possible. The capacity declines with age in adulthood, and such decline largely accounts for aging losses in the parts of G_s speed that are associated with G_f decline. Most of the aging decline of G_s itself is accounted for by this measure of concentration in behaving quite slowly (COS) and a measure of capacities for dividing attention (ATD) (Hertzog, 1989; Horn et al., 1981). When COS and ATD are controlled in G_f, there is control also for the decline of G_s and the part of G_s that is associated with decline of G_f. The part of G_f decline associated with G_s speed thus is accounted for by a decline of capacities for concentration (in slowness and in dividing attention). Thus, it is not the speed per se that declines with age but the attentional capacities that underlie G_f reasoning (Horn et al., 1981).

It has been thought that declines in G_f reasoning might be due to stylistic factors such as inclination to be particularly careful or persistent in ability tasks. It was reasoned that if one is very careful, for example, one would not get as many problems correct as if one were not so careful. The evidence does not support such hypotheses. Care and persistence do increase with age, but when speed in solving problems is not rewarded, care and persistence enable older adults to score higher, not lower, on measures of G_f abilities. Older adults work longer than younger adults before abandoning a difficult problem – a measure of persistence (PRS). Older adults also give fewer incorrect answers to problems attempted (if of nontrivial difficulty), an indication of carefulness (CAR). CAR and PRS are correlated with slowness of performance in timed ability tests. But when care and persistence are controlled in analysis of the aging decline of untimed (level) measures of G_f, the decline is not reduced; it is increased. There is increase in negative slope for curves for G_f when CAR and PRS are controlled. Such findings indicate that carefulness and persistence are qualities that enable older adults to perform better on untimed G_f tasks than they would perform if these qualities were not allowed to operate.

There is considerable overlap in the processes measured in variables representing elementary features of attention, carefulness, and persistence. Many ostensibly different variables measure the same basic intellectual processes. For example, although measures of inspection speediness are operationally independent of measures of concentration on slowness and short-term memory, these variables involve a common process – a form of attentiveness – that is implicated in G_f decline. They do not carry entirely independent variance in accounting for the aging loss of G_f. The same can be said for several other combinations of the variables thought to represent distinct processes.

No combination of elementary process variables has been found to account for all the observed decline in G_f reasoning. The precise proportion of the decline accounted for by different variables varies with the reliabilities of the measures and the extent of variability in the subject sample, but roughly only about half of the aging loss of G_f can be reliably accounted for by variables thus far brought into studies designed to show analytically the elementary processes involved in aging loss of G_f abilities.

On first consideration, a particular set of these results obtained with a measure of inductive reasoning (Horn et al., 1981), a good measure of G_f, may seem to be different from those obtained by Schaie (1983). Schaie found aging declines in inductive reasoning in later adulthood only, whereas Horn et al. (1981) found such change in early as well as later adulthood.

Salthouse (1988) describes a "complexity effect phenomenon" (Salthouse, 1985, for review) that Hertzog (1989) points to as important for understanding the somewhat different results obtained by Schaie (1983) and

Horn et al. (1981) with inductive reasoning measures. The complexity phenomenon is indicated in results showing that processing speed declines with age and this speed is related to increasing complexity of tasks. Complex tasks require greater processing and more solution time. Hertzog (1989) found that complexity was a major feature of the aging decline of G_f. Using these findings, he demonstrated how complexity can account for the differences in the Horn et al. and Schaie results.

The inductive reasoning test used by Schaie, and subsequently by Hertzog (1989), was from the 1948 version of the Primary Mental Abilities battery (Thurstone & Thurstone, 1949). The item difficulties of this test are low relative to other forms of this kind of test. The task is thus of relatively low complexity. Horn's inductive reasoning task, on the other hand, was made quite complex in the most difficult items. His theory predicts that G_f decline is seen largely in loss of ability to resolve complexities. If the capacity for dealing with complexity declines with age in adulthood, Hertzog reasoned, Horn's measures should be more sensitive to age-related decrements than are the measures of the Schaie study, in which case the decline effect will show up more surely along the entire range of adulthood, as in Horn's study, not just in the extremes, as in Schaie's study. Thus, when complexity is taken into account, the results from the Schaie and Horn studies are comparable.

As Hertzog further pointed out, the speed-adjusted curves for G_f reported by Horn [Horn, 1980; Horn et al., 1981] show greater decline in middle age than the speed-adjusted regression equations reported here indicated. His finding, replicating Horn et al. (1981), was that "for test items of high difficulty, the speed with which individuals solve problems may have a low relationship to the probability of correct response" (Hertzog, 1989; p. 649).

Effects of training on vulnerable abilities

There is very little direct evidence of the causes of aging declines in vulnerable abilities. Physiological and neurological factors are involved, but little is known about the causes of the physiological and neurological factors themselves that can cause decline in abilities. Brain damage is known to produce decline in cognitive capabilities and to affect the vulnerable abilities to a greater extent, and more irreversibly, than it affects the maintained abilities. It is good advice to avoid experiences that produce brain damage, such as blows to the head, breathing carbon monoxide, or anoxia, as is brought on by extreme use of alcohol (passing out). There is evidence, also, that life-style factors such as striving to improve one's intellectual capabilities, and practiced use of vulnerable abilities, enhance maintained abilities and may reduce the loss of vulnerable abilities. But the evidence in support of this advice is sketchy and general.

The idea that lack of practice may cause decline of vulnerable abilities (e.g., G_f) is particularly enticing, for it's reasonable to suppose that if this is true, something can be done to reduce or eliminate the decline. Several recent studies of training have derived from this idea (Baltes, 1987; Baltes, Dittman-Kohli, & Kliegl, 1986; Baltes, Sowarka, & Kliegl, 1989; Denney & Heidrich, 1990; Hayslip, 1989a, 1989b; Schaie & Willis, 1986; Schaie, Willis, Hertzog, & Schulenberg, 1987; Stankov & Chen, 1988; Willis & Schaie, 1986).

A major guiding hypothesis in these studies has been that older adults, relative to younger adults, infrequently use G_f reasoning and other vulnerable abilities – have little daily practice in these abilities – and this is why the abilities decline. The thought is, too, that training these abilities can indicate the extent to which older adults retain the "latent competence" to increase G_f performance (Baltes, 1987).

The studies of Schaie and Willis (1986) and Willis and Schaie (1986) are examples of this line of research. In this research, four similar tests were used to measure the inductive reasoning primary ability on a first occasion: PMA Letter Series, ADEPT Letter Series, Word Series, and Number Series. People who scored low on an inductive reasoning test (assumed to have declined) were assigned to a training program in which they were taught pattern description rules of identity, and ways to identify skips and back skips in series problems. Parallel tests were used in follow-up. Analyses were carried out to ensure that these tests measured the same factor on both occasions. Averages for the trained group were compared with averages for two contract groups of individuals, one in which the subjects had scored relatively low in a spatial primary ability test (were assumed to have declined here) and were given a different kind of training thought to help spatial abilities but not inductive reasoning, and one group in which the subjects scored relatively high on both inductive reasoning and spatial ability in the pretest (assumed to have not declined notably). The results indicated that those trained in the skills of induction improved more on the inductive reasoning primary ability than those not trained in these skills.

These results thus indicate that older adults can improve abilities that indicate fluid reasoning. This is not surprising. Much evidence indicates that humans of any age can learn. Also, one should not conclude from this evidence that all the abilities of G_f reasoning were improved by the training. Induction is just one aspect of G_f reasoning. Perhaps all that was taught was how to solve the problems of a particular test, a point Donaldson (1981) made quite convincingly in his critique of this line of research.

G_f reasoning abilities consist of strategies, heuristics, and automatized systems that must be used in dealing with "novel" problems, educing relations, and solving inductive, deductive, and conjunctive reasoning tasks.

These strategies, heuristics, and systems are acquired, over extended periods of development, through individual learnings that ordinarily are not part of the "lesson plan" of acculturation. Some of such learning can be recognized and put into a lesson plan, as in the Willis–Schaie studies. Particular performances thus can be taught. But the full range of G_f capabilities is not thereby taught.

If training in doing the inductive reasoning test of Willis–Schaie were made a part of the curriculum of our schools, this erstwhile G_f ability would become inculcated through acculturation and thus could be expected to relate more to G_c than to G_f. Teaching this test in a particular sample of older people, however, doesn't change the fact that usually this ability is not taught as a part of formal training and thus indicates G_f, not G_c.

An analogy to body building can help in understanding training that improves abilities that ordinarily decline with age in adulthood. People can increase their muscular strength and tone with body-building exercise, just as people can improve their fluid abilities with use and special training of these abilities. Older people can thus improve, just as can younger people. But the fact that older people can increase their muscular strength does not discount evidence showing that older people – in general, on the average – are not as strong as younger people or evidence suggesting that the capacity for muscular strength declines with age. Similarly, evidence that older people can improve fluid abilities does not discount evidence showing that the level of these abilities is lower in older people, on the average, than in younger people, and evidence suggesting that this represents a decline in capacity.

The evidence that an ability can be improved should not, in itself, be interpreted as evidence G_f has been improved, even if the ability is one that ordinarily indicates G_f. The question of whether G_f has been improved by training on a particular ability is a question of transfer and generalization: How much does training on one of the tests indicating G_f transfer to other abilities of G_f?

The evidence of several decades of research (Ackerman, 1989) indicates that transfer is largely a function of similarity: the more similar the trained ability is to another ability, the more transfer there will be to that other ability. This evidence also indicates that the amount of transfer is often depressingly small, even when there appears to be considerable similarity. The results from studies of transfer of training from one G_f ability to improvements on other G_f abilities indicate there is little transfer, particularly over periods of a few months or longer. For example, Baltes et al. (1986) found that training produced a transfer effect only for abilities that were very similar to the trained abilities. There was no transfer to other measures loading high on G_f.

The studies completed thus far have shown that particular abilities can be improved. They have not demonstrated that there is generalized increase in G_f itself.

Frequent use and practice is probably necessary to maintain an ability, one of G_f as well as one of G_c or of the other cognitive capabilities. Decline seen with aging could be due to disuse in patterns of living that have become devoid of intellectual activity. Is that the condition usually seen in adulthood? Future research on life-styles can help us answer this question.

Understanding the stability of maintained abilities

Over the course of childhood and adulthood the many, many elements of information that constitute G_c abilities are interwoven into nodes of knowledge that are further interrelated in networks of many, many associational pathways that enable a person to access and use the knowledge. Underlying this learning and associational overdetermination is neurological overdetermination. In the brain myriad neuroprocessor connections and interconnections among a multitude of neurons form neural networks – functional organizations that support the knowledge system and thinking (Thompson, 1985). Up to a point in such an overdetermined system major features of abilities can be retained even when there is loss within the neural networks and loss of ability elements (as in forgetting). G_c thus can be maintained even when there is brain damage.

The G_c structure contains a vast array of abilities. The breadth of knowledge indicated by this array is highly associated with the extent and quality of acculturation. Through acculturation the abilities appear to be organized in an interwoven, meshlike, knowledge system. If one imagines that each node of this mesh is an element of knowledge, and threads leading to a node are pathways enabling a person to access the element, then it seems that many nodes are created throughout development and many more strands lead to, and are woven into, each node.

The result is a condition of overdetermination. Because many strands lead to each node, one can access a node in a multitude of ways. To access a node, it is not essential to have all the many strands intact. One can lose (as in forgetting) some of these strands and still have enough left to access the information.

This kind of metaphor is used to help explain results showing that the abilities of G_c tend to "spring back" and be maintained following CNS damage such as stroke. Psychological overdetermination of knowledge systems is thought to correspond to neurological overdetermination. The strands leading to nodes of knowledge correspond, in the brain, to links between neurons – neuroprocessor connections. These determine many neural networks and are the functional organizations that support thinking (Thompson, 1985). Up to a point, if aging or brain injury reduce the number of neural strands, this need not show up in loss of G_c abilities – because many neural strands remain to activate the neural network.

There can be irreversible decline in G_c abilities, as Schaie (1983) has emphasized. There is no doubt that in the later stages of Alzheimer's disease, for example, all cognitive functions, including G_c abilities, decline dramatically (and depressingly). It seems that beyond some point, after a critical amount of neural loss, there is sag in the neural networks that support the G_c organization: The gestalts these networks constitute can no longer be activated. The result in behavior is that information formerly available is not obtainable, or can be obtained only with greater effort (by activating more neural strands) or in distorted form, as often is seen in cases of brain damage and brain disease.

Knowledge systems are not static: They are repeatedly restructured throughout each waking moment of life, and perhaps even in unawake moments (Broadbent, 1966; Norman, 1979). The G_c library that one repeatedly enlarges and rearranges becomes more and more useful as one develops it. Each rearrangement, as well as each addition, makes the system better and the elements of the system more accessible. This is the sanguine side of human aging. In some important ways we can become smarter as we age.

Salthouse (1988) extends the network theory we have just outlined. He describes a spreading-activation network and provides a computer simulation of such a network. This is a simulated operational representation of the node and pathway network we have described. Salthouse also describes an integration that links this cognitive theory of structure with possible mechanisms of causal explanation.

Summary

Scientific research on the cognitive capabilities of people is largely based on studies of individual differences (IDs) between people. This research has different methods and involves assumptions different from those of research based on comparisons of average differences between groups of people. The methods of ID research are directed at identifying patterns of covariability. The fundamental assumption of ID research is that such patterns of covariability indicate organizations of functional processes – cognitive capabilities.

Results from a large number of ID studies show that humans have many different cognitive capabilities, a conclusion reached also in common sense. In common sense it is widely believed, however, that these capabilities indicate a single broad ability called intelligence. The evidence of ID research has yet to indicate that there is one organizing principle that unites all intellectual abilities into one intelligence. Rather, the evidence suggests that there are several independent capacities that can be called intelligence.

We are not certain just how many intelligences there are. At present, the evidence points to nine broad organizations of cognitive processes. These are described as organizations of: knowledge inculcated through acculturation (G_c), fluency of retrieval of knowledge (G_{lm}), visualizing capabilities (G_v), auditory capabilities (G_a), quantitative capabilities (G_q), reasoning capabilities (G_f), processes of maintaining immediate awareness (G_{sm}), processes in speed of apprehension (G_s), and processes for quickly arriving at decisions (CDS).

These organizations indicate the structure of intellect. Each is broad enough to represent what has been described as intelligence. Yet people high or low in one of these intelligences are not correspondingly high or low in the others. The intelligences have distinct distributions. They also have distinctly different relationships with other variables. They have different construct validities.

The different cognitive capabilities relate in different ways to age over the life-span. This is seen in different average ability levels at different ages in both longitudinal research, based on repeated measures of the same people, and cross-sectional research, in which people born at different times are compared. The averages for G_f, G_{sm}, G_s, and CDS decrease steadily from the early twenties onward; the averages for G_v and G_a increase into the thirties or early forties and then decrease gradually; the averages for G_c, G_{lm}, and G_q increase into the sixties before decline is indicated.

Abilities that decline early in adulthood are said to be vulnerable. These abilities are adversely and irreversibly affected by brain damage. Abilities that decline late and little in adulthood are said to be maintained. These abilities are initially affected by brain damage but spring back to prior levels as one recovers from the immediate affects of the damage.

Individual differences in G_c increase with age. This appears to reflect the fact that some individuals continue to devote considerable effort to enhancing their cognitive capability after formal schooling ceases, whereas others do less of such work. Individual differences in G_f do not increase with age. This seems to indicate that these abilities reach an asymptote of development in early adulthood.

The aging declines of G_f, G_{sm}, and G_s are related to loss of ability to maintain close attention and divide attention. Loss of these abilities results in loss of ability to comprehend complex relationships. Aging decline of G_f is registered mainly in loss of ability to deal with the most complex of relationships. Loss of abilities in maintaining and dividing attention reduces ability to encode, which is registered in loss of short-term memory and speed of apprehension, as well as reasoning. Aging increases in carefulness and persistence to some extent compensate for these losses.

Training programs have been devised that improve the abilities identified in particular measures of G_f (and other vulnerable abilities). Such training probably has little effect on the total set of abilities of a particular cognitive capability such as G$_f$.

Aging declines of vulnerable abilities appear to result from accumulations of small losses in brain function. These accumulations appear to be related to factors of living that have deleterious effects on the nervous system. For example, abusive use of alcohol seems to have such effects. But little is known precisely about what produces declines and enhancements in cognitive capabilities in adulthood. Research is needed on the different lifestyles people live.

References

Ackerman, P. L. (1987). Individual differences in skill learning: An integration of psychometric and information processing perspectives. *Psychological Bulletin, 102*, 3–27.

Ackerman, P. L. (1989). Individual differences and skill acquisition. In P. L. Ackerman, R. J. Sternberg, & R. Glaser (Eds.), *Learning and individual differences: Advances in theory and research* (pp. 165–217). New York: Freeman.

Atkin, R., Bray, R., Davison, M., Herzberger, S., Humphreys, L. G., & Selzer, V. (1977). Cross-lagged panel analysis of sixteen cognitive measures at four grade levels. *Child Development, 21*, 78–81.

Baltes, P. B. (1987). Theoretical propositions of life-span developmental psychology: On the dynamics between growth and decline. *Developmental Psycholology, 23*, 611–626.

Baltes, P. B., Dittmann-Kohli, F., & Kliegl, R. (1986). Reserve capacity of the elderly in aging-sensitive tests of fluid intelligence: Replication and extension. *Psychology and Aging, 1*, 172–177.

Baltes, P. B., Sowarka, D., & Kliegl, R. (1989). Cognitive training research on fluid intelligence in old age: What can older adults achieve by themselves? *Psychology and Aging, 4*, 217–221.

Bayley, N. (1966). Learning in adulthood: The role of intelligence. In H. J. Lausmeier & C. W. Harris (Eds.), *Analyses of concept learning* (pp. 117–138). New York: Academic Press.

Beeson, M. F. (1920). Intelligence of senescence. *Journal of Applied Psychology, 4*(19), 234.

Bell, R. Q. (1953). Convergence: An accelerated longitudinal approach. *Child Development, 24*, 145–152.

Benbow, C. P. (1987). Possible biological correlates of precocious mathematical reasoning ability. *Trends in Neurosciences, 10*, 17–20.

Benbow, C. P. (1988). Sex differences in mathematical reasoning ability in intellectually talented preadolescents: Their nature, effects, and possible causes. *Behavioral and Brain Sciences, 11*, 169–232.

Benbow, C. P., & Stanley, J. C. (1983). Differential course-taking hypothesis revisited. *American Educational Research Journal, 20*, 469–473.

Birren, J. E. (1974). Psychophysiology and speed of response. *American Psychologist, 29*, 808–815.

Bock, R. D., & Kolakowski, D. (1973). Further evidence of sex-linked major-gene influence on human spatial visualizing ability. *American Journal of Human Genetics, 25*, 1–14.

Boles, D. B. (1980). X-linkage of spatial ability: a critical review. *Child Development, 51*, 625–635.

Botwinick, J. (1977). Aging and intelligence. In J. E. Birren and K. W. Schaie (Eds.), *Handbook of the psychology of aging* (pp. 580–605). New York: Van Nostrand Reinhold.

Botwinick, J., & Storandt, M. (1974). *Memory related functions and age*. Springfield, IL: Thomas.

Bower, G. H. (1972). Mental imagery and associative learning. In L. W. Gregg (Ed.), *Cognition in learning and memory*. New York: Wiley.

Broadbent, D. E. (1966). The well-ordered mind. *American Educational Research Journal, 3*, 281–295.

Bromley, D. B. (1974). *The psychology of human aging* (2nd ed.). London: Penguin.

Campbell, D. T., & Fiske, D. W. (1959). Convergent and discriminant validation by the multitrait-multimethod matrix. *Psychological Bulletin, 56*, 81–105.

Carroll, J. B. (1972). Stalking the wayward factors. *Contemporary Psychology, 17*, 321–324.

Carroll, J. B. (1989). Factor analysis since Spearman: Where do we stand? What do we know? In R. Kanfer, P. L. Ackerman, & R. Cudeck (Eds.), *Abilities, motivation, and methodology: The Minnesota symposium on learning and individual differences* (pp. 43–67). Hillsdale, NJ: Erlbaum.

Cattell, R. B. (1940). A culture free intelligence test. *Journal of Educational Psychology, 31*, 161–180.

Cattell, R. B. (1950). *Personality: A systematic theoretical and factual study*. New York: McGraw-Hill.

Cattell, R. B. (1957). *Personality and motivation structure and measurement*. New York: Harcourt, Brace & World.

Cattell, R. B. (1963). Theory of fluid and crystallized intelligence: A critical experiment. *Journal of Educational Psychology, 54*, 1–22.

Cattell, R. B. (1971). *Abilities: Their structure, growth and action*. Boston: Houghton Mifflin.

Cattell, R. B. (Ed.). (1966). *Handbook of multivariate experimental psychology*. Chicago: Rand McNally.

Cattell, R. B., & Horn, J. L. (1978). A check on the theory of fluid and crystallized intelligence with description of new subtest designs. *Journal of Educational Measurement, 15*, 139–164.

Cohen, J. (1952). A factor-analytically based rationale for the Wechsler-Bellevue. *Journal of Consulting Psychology, 16*, 272–277.

Cohen, J. (1957). The factorial structure of the WAIS between early adulthood and old age. *Journal of Consulting Psychology, 21*, 283–290.

Collins, L. M. (1991). Measurement in longitudinal research. In L. M. Collins & J. L. Horn (Eds.), *Best methods for the analysis of change?* Washington, DC: American Psychological Association.

Collins, L. M., & Horn, J. L. (Eds.). (1991). *Best methods for the analysis of change?* Washington, DC: American Psychological Association.

Craik, F. I. M. (1977). Age differences in human memory. In J. E. Birren & K. W. Schaie (Eds.), *Handbook of the psychology of aging*. New York: Van Nostrand Reinhold.

Craik, F. I. M., & Lockhart, R. S. (1972). Levels of processing: A framework for memory research. *Journal of Verbal Learning and Verbal Behavior, 11*, 671–684.

Cronbach, L. J. (1987). Construct validation after thirty years. In R. Linn (Ed.), *Intelligence: Measurement, theory and public policy*. Urbana: University of Illinois Press.

Denney, N. W., & Heidrich, S. M. (1990). Training effects on Raven's Progressive Matrices in young, middle-aged, and elderly adults. *Psychology and Aging, 5*, 144–145.

Donaldson, G. (1981). Letter to the editor. *Journal of Gerontology, 36*, 634–636.

Drake, R. M. (1939). Factor analysis of music tests. *Psychological Bulletin, 36*, 608–609.

Ekstrom, R. B., French, J. W., & Harman, M. H. (1979). Cognitive factors: Their identification and replication. *Multivariate Behavioral Research Monographs, 79*.

Eysenck, H. J. (1982). *A model for intelligence*. New York: Springer-Verlag.

Fairweather, H. (1976). Sex differences in cognition. *Cognition, 4*, 231–280.

Ferguson, G. A. (1954). On learning and human ability. *Canadian Journal of Psychology, 8*, 95–112.

Ferguson, G. A. (1956). On transfer and the abilities of man. *Canadian Journal of Psychology, 10*, 121–131.

Fox, L. H. (1976). Sex differences in mathematical precocity: Bridging the gap. In D. P.

Keating (Ed.), *Intellectual talent: Research and development* (pp. 183–214). Baltimore: Johns Hopkins University Press.

French, J. W. (1951). The description of aptitude and achievement tests in terms of rotated factors. *Psychometric Monographs, No. 5.*

French, J. W., Eckstrom, R. B., & Price, L. A. (1963). *Manual and kit of reference tests for cognitive factors.* Princeton, NJ: Educational Testing Service.

Fruchter, B. (1950). Error scores as a measure of carefulness. *Journal of Educational Psychology, 41,* 279–291.

Fruchter, B. (1953). Difference in factor content of rights and wrongs scores. *Psychometrika, 18,* 257–263.

Furneaux, W. D. (1952). Some speed, error, and difficulty relationships with a problem solving situation. *Nature, 170,* 3.

Glanzer, M., & Cunitz, A. (1966). Two storage mechanisms in free recall. *Journal of Verbal Learning and Verbal Behavior, 5,* 531–560.

Gleitman, H. (1986). *Psychology* (2nd ed.). New York: Norton.

Guilford, J. P. (1967). *The nature of human intelligence.* New York: McGraw-Hill.

Guilford, J. P., & Lacy, J. I. (Eds.). (1947). *Printed classification tests* (Research Report No. 5). Army Air Forces Aviation Psychology Program.

Gustaffson, J. E. (1984). A unifying model for the structure of intellectual abilities. *Intelligence, 8,* 179–203.

Hakstian, A. R., & Cattell, R. B. (1974). The checking of primary ability structure on a broader basis of performances. *British Journal of Educational Psychology, 44,* 140–154.

Hakstian, A. R., & Cattell, R. B. (1978). Higher stratum ability structure on a basis of twenty primary abilities. *Journal of Educational Psychology, 70,* 657–659.

Harris, C. W. (Ed.). (1963). *Problems in measuring change.* Madison: University of Wisconsin Press.

Harris, L. J. (1978). Sex differences in spatial ability: Possible environmental, genetic, and neurological factors. In Kinsbourne, M. (Ed.), *Asymmetrical functions of the brain* (pp. 337–401). Cambridge: Cambridge University Press.

Hayslip, B. (1989a). Alternative mechanisms for improvements in fluid ability performance among older adults. *Psychology & Aging, 4,* 122–124.

Hayslip, B. (1989b). Fluid ability training with aged people: A past with a future? Special issue: Cognitive aging: Issues in research and application. *Educational Gerontology, 15,* 573–595.

Hearnshaw, L. S. (1956). Temporal integration and behavior. *Bulletin of British Psychological Society, 9,* 1–20.

Hertzog, C. (1989). Influences of cognitive slowing on age differences in intelligence. *Developmental Psychology, 25,* 636–651.

Hertzog, C., & Schaie, K. W. (1986). Stability and change in adult intelligence: 1. Analysis of longitudinal covariance structures. *Psychology and Aging, 1,* 159–171.

Hertzog, C., & Schaie, K. W. (1988). Stability and change in adult intelligence: 2. Simultaneous analysis of longitudinal means and covariance structures. *Psychology and Aging, 3,* 122–130.

Horn, J. L. (1968). Organization of abilities and the development of intelligence. *Psychological Review, 75,* 242–259.

Horn, J. L. (1970). Organization of data on life-span development of human abilities. In L. R. Goulet & P. B. Baltes (Eds.), *Lifespan development in psychology* (pp. 423–466). New York: Academic Press.

Horn, J. L. (1972). The structure of intellect: Primary abilities. In R. M. Dreger (Ed.), *Multivariate personality research* (pp. 451–511). Baton Rouge, LA: Claitor's Publishing Company.

Horn, J. L. (1973). Theory of functions represented among auditory and visual test performances. In J. R. Royce (Ed.), *Contributions of multivariate analysis to psychological theory* (pp. 203–239). New York: Academic Press.

Horn, J. L. (1976). Human abilities: A review of research and theory in the early 1970's. *Annual Review of Psychology, 27,* 437–485.

Horn, J. L. (1979). Trends in the measurement of intelligence. *Intelligence, 3,* 229–240.

Horn, J. L. (1980). Intelligence and age. In R. Tissot (Ed.), *Etats deficitaires cerebraux lies a. l'age. Tire a part due volume Symposium Bel-Air* (pp. 229–260). Geneva, Switzerland: George et Cie S. A. Librairie De L'Université.

Horn, J. L. (1982). The theory of fluid and crystallized intelligence in relation to concepts of cognitive psychology and aging in adulthood. In F. I. M. Craik & S. E. Trehub (Eds.), *Aging and cognitive processes.* Boston: Plenum.

Horn, J. L. (1985). Remodeling old models of intelligence: $G_f - G_c$ theory. In B. B. Wolman (Ed.), *Handbook of intelligence* (pp. 267–300). New York: Wiley.

Horn, J. L. (1986). Intellectual ability concepts. In R. L. Sternberg (Ed.), *Advances in the psychology of human intelligence* (Vol. 3; pp. 35–77). Hillsdale, NJ: Erlbaum.

Horn, J. L. (1988). Thinking about human abilities. In J. R. Nesselroade (Ed.), *Handbook of multivariate psychology* (pp. 645–685). New York: Academic Press.

Horn, J. L. (1989). Cognitive diversity: A framework for learning. In P. L. Ackerman, R. J. Sternberg, & R. Glaser (Eds.), *Learning and individual differences: Advances in theory and research* (pp. 61–114). New York: Freeman.

Horn, J. L., & Cattell, R. B. (1966). Refinement and test of the theory of fluid and crystallized intelligence. *Journal of Educational Psychology, 57,* 253–270.

Horn, J. L., & Cattell, R. B. (1967). Age differences in fluid and crystallized intelligence. *Acta Psychologica, 26,* 107–129.

Horn, J. L., Donaldson, G. (1980). Cognitive development in adulthood. In O. G. Brim & J. Kagan (Eds.), *Constancy and change in human development* (pp. 445–529). Cambridge, MA: Harvard University Press.

Horn, J. L., Donaldson, G., & Engstrom, R. (1981). Apprehension, memory, and fluid intelligence decline in adulthood. *Research on Aging, 3,* 33–84.

Horn, J. L., & Knapp, J. R. (1973). On the subjective character of the empirical base of Guilford's structure-of-intellect model. *Psychological Bulletin, 80,* 33–43.

Horn, J. L., & Knapp, J. R. (1974). Thirty wrongs do not make a right: Reply to Guilford. *Psychological Bulletin, 81,* 502–504.

Horn, J. L., & Stankov, L. (1982). Auditory and visual factors of intelligence. *Intelligence, 6,* 165–185.

Horn, J. M., Loehlin, J. C., & Willerman, L. (1979). Intellectual resemblance among adoptive and biological relatives: The Texas adoption project. *Behavior Genetics, 9,* 177–207.

Hultsch, D. F. (1971). Adult age differences in free classification and free recall. *Developmental Psychology, 4,* 338–342.

Humphreys, L. G. (1962). The organization of human abilities. *American Psychologist, 17,* 475–483.

Humphreys, L. G. (1974). The misleading distinction between aptitude and achievement tests. In D. R. Green (Ed.), *The aptitude achievement distinction* (pp. 35–49). Monterey, CA: CTB/McGraw-Hill.

Hunt, E. (1978). Mechanics of verbal ability. *Psychological Review, 85,* 109–130.

Hunt, E. (1980). Intelligence as an information processing concept. *British Journal of Psychology, 71,* 449–474.

Hunt, E., Frost, N., & Lunneborg, C. (1973). Individual differences in cognition. In G. Bower (Ed.), *The psychology of learning and motivation: Advances in research and theory* (Vol. 7) (pp. 127–139). New York: Academic Press.

Jensen, A. R. (1980). *Bias in mental testing.* New York: Free Press.

Jensen, A. R. (1983). The definition of intelligence and factor-score indeterminacy. *Behavioral and Brain Sciences, 6*(2), 313–315.

Jensen, A. R. (1984). Test validity: g versus the specificity doctrine. *Journal of Social and Biological Structures, 7,* 93–118.

Kamin, L. J. (1974). *The science and politics of IQ.* New York: Wiley.

Kantowitz, B. H. (1974). Double stimulation. In B. H. Kantowitz (Ed.), *Human information processing*. Hillsdale, NJ: Erlbaum.

Kosslyn, S. M. (1987). Seeing and imagining in the cerebral hemispheres: A computational approach. *Psychological Review, 94*(2), 148–175.

Kuhlen, R. G. (1959). Aging and life-adjustment. In J. E. Birren (Ed.), *Handbook of aging and the individual*. Chicago: University of Chicago Press.

Kuhn, T. S. (1970). *The structure of scientific revolutions* (2nd ed.). Chicago: University of Chicago Press.

Maccoby, E. E., & Jacklin, C. N. (1973). Sex differences in intellectual functioning. In *Assessment in a pluralistic society* (pp. 37–55). *Proceedings of the 1972 invitational conference on testing problems.* Princeton, NJ: Educational Testing Service.

Mandler, G. (1967). Verbal learning. In G. Mandler & P. Mussen (Eds.), *New directions in psychology* (Vol. 3, pp. 1–55). New York: Holt.

Matarazzo, J. D. (1972). *Wechsler's measurement and appraisal of adult intelligence* (5th ed.). Baltimore: Williams & Wilkins.

Matarazzo, J. D. (1980). *Wechsler's measurement and appraisal of adult intelligence*. New York: Oxford University Press.

McArdle, J. J. (1984, November). *A dynamic and structural equation model of WAIS abilities.* Presented at the Annual Meeting of the Society of Multivariate Experimental Psychologists, Evanston, IL.

McArdle, J. J. (1986). Latent variable growth within behavior genetic models. *Behavior Genetics, 16*, 163–200.

McArdle, J. J. (1988). Dynamic but structural equation modeling of repeated measures data. In J. R. Nesselroade & R. B. Cattell (Eds.), *Handbook of multivariate experimental psychology* (2nd ed.). New York: Plenum.

McArdle, J. J., Goldsmith, H. H., & Horn, J. L. (1981). Genetic structural equation models of fluid and crystallized intelligence. *Behavior Genetics, 60*, 607–623.

McArdle, J. J., & Horn, J. L. (1983). *Mega-analysis of the WAIS.* National Institute on Aging Grant Number AG04704.

McDowd, J. M. (1986). The effects of age and extended practice on divided attention performance. *Journal of Gerontology, 41*, 764–769.

McDowd, J. M., & Craik, F. I. M. (1988). Effects of aging and task difficulty on divided attention performance. *Journal of Experimental Psychology: Human perception and Performance, 14*, 267–280.

Mednick, S. A. (1956). The associative basis of the creative process. *Psychological Review, 63*, 81–97.

Murdock, B. (1962). The serial position effect of free recall. *Journal of Experimental Psychology, 64*, 482–488.

Myers, B., Stankov, L., & Oliphant, G. (1989). Competing tasks, working memory, and intelligence. *Australian Journal of Psychology, 41*, 1–16.

Nesselroade, J. R. (1990). The warp and the woof of the developmental fabric. In R. Downs, L. Liben, D. S. Palermo (Eds.), *Visions of development, environment and aesthetics: The legacy of Joachim F. Wohlwill*. Hillsdale, NJ: Erlbaum.

Nesselroade, J. R. (1991). Interindividual differences in intraindividual changes. In L. M. Collins & J. L. Horn (Eds.), *Best methods for the analysis of change?* Washington, DC: American Psychological Association.

Nesselroade, J. R., & Ford, D. H. (1985). P-technique comes of age: Multivariate, replicated, single subject designs for research on older adults. *Research on Aging*, 46–80.

Nichols, R. C. (1978) Twin studies of ability, personality and interests. *Homo, 29*, 158–173.

Norman, D. A. (1979). Perception, memory and mental processes. In L. C. Nilsson (Ed.), *Perspectives in memory research*. Hillsdale, NJ: Erlbaum.

Owens, W. A. (1953). Age and mental abilities: A longitudinal study. *Genetic Psychology Monographs, 48*, 3–54.

Pachella, R. G. (1974). The interpretation of reaction time in information processing research.

In B. Kantowitz (Ed.), *Human information processing: Tutorial in performance and cognition* (pp. 41–82). Hillsdale, NJ: Erlbaum.

Pellegrino, J. W., & Glaser, R. (1979). Cognitive correlates and components in the analysis of individual differences. *Intelligence, 3*, 187–214.

Plomin, R., DeFries, J. C., & McClearn, G. E. (1980). *Behavioral genetics.* San Francisco: Freeman.

Poon, L. W., & Fozard, J. L. (1978). Speed of retrieval from LTM in relation to age, familiarity and datedness of information. *Journal of Gerontology, 33*, 711–717.

Reese, H. W. (1977). Measuring development through the lifespan. In L. Montada (Ed.), *Brennpunkle der entwicklungspsychologie.* Stuttgart: Kohlhammer.

Revesz, G. (1953). *Introduction to the psychology of music.* London: Longmans Green.

Ryan, C., & Butters, N. (1979). Further evidence for a continuum-of-impairment encompassing Korsakoff patients and chronic alcoholics. *Alcoholism: Clinical and Experimental Research.*

Salthouse, T. A. (1979). Adult age and the speed-accuracy tradeoff. *Ergonomics, 22*, 811–821.

Salthouse, T. A. (1985). Speed of behavior and its implications for cognition. In J. E. Birren & K. W. Schaie (Eds.), *Handbook of the psychology of aging* (2nd ed., pp. 400–426). New York: Van Nostrand Reinhold.

Salthouse, T. A. (1988). Initiating the formalization of theories of cognitive aging. *Psychology and Aging, 3*, 3–16.

Salthouse, T. A., & Somberg, B. L.(1982). Skilled performance: Effects of adult age and experience on elementary processes. *Journal of Experimental Psychology: General, 111*, 176–207.

Scarr, S., & McCartney, K. (1983). How people make their own environments: A theory of genotype-environment effects. *Child Development, 54*, 424–435.

Schaie, K. W. (1965). A general model for the study of developmental problems. *Psychological Bulletin, 64*, 92–107.

Schaie, K. W. (1973). Methodological problems in descriptive developmental research on adulthood and aging. In J. R. Nesselroade & H. W. Reese (Eds.), *Life-span developmental psychology: Developmental issues.* New York: Academic Press.

Schaie, K. W. (Ed.). (1983). *Longitudinal studies of adult psychological development.* New York: Guilford.

Schaie, K. W., & Baltes, P. B. (1977). Some faith helps see the forest: A final comment on the Horn and Donaldson myth of the Baltes–Schaie position on adult intelligence. *American Psychologist, 32*, 1118–1120.

Schaie, K. W., & Willis, S. L. (1986). Can decline in adult intellectual functioning be reversed? *Developmental Psychology, 22*, 223–232.

Schaie, K. W., Willis, S. L., Hertzog, C., & Schulenberg, J. E. (1987). Effects of cognitive training on primary mental ability structure. *Psychology and Aging, 2*, 233–242.

Schneider, W., & Schiffrin, R. M. (1977). Controlled and automatic human information processing: I. Detection, search and attention. *Psychological Review, 84*, 1–66.

Seashore, C. E., Lewis, D., & Saetvelt, J. C. (1960). *Manual of instruction and interpretations for the Seashore Measures of Musical Talents* (2nd rev. ed.). New York: Psychological Corporation.

Sharp, J. R., Rosenbaum, G., Goldman, M. S., & Whitman, R. D. (1977). Recoverability of psychological functioning following alcohol abuse: Acquisition of meaningful synonyms. *Journal of Consulting Psychology*, 1023–1038.

Shepard, R. N., & Metzler, J. (1971). Mental rotation of three-dimensional objects. *Science, 171*, 701–703.

Shuter, R. (1968). *The psychology of musical ability.* London: Methuen.

Solomon, L. M., Webster, J. C., & Curtis, J. F. (1960). A factorial study of speech perception. *Journal of Speech and Hearing Research*, 101–107.

Spearman, C. (1927). *The abilities of man: Their nature and measurement.* London: Macmillan.

Springer, S. P., & Deutsch, G. (1981). *Left brain, right brain.* San Francisco: Freeman.

Stankov, L. (1978). Fluid and crystallized intelligence and broad perceptual factors among the 11 to 12 year olds. *Journal of Educational Psychology, 70,* 324–334.

Stankov, L. (1980). Ear differences and implied cerebral lateralization on some auditory factors. *Applied Psychological Measurement, 4,* 21–38.

Stankov, L. (1986). Age-related changes in auditory abilities and in a competing task. *Multivariate Behavioral Research, 21,* 65–71.

Stankov, L., & Chen, L. (1988). Can we boost fluid and crystallized intelligence? A structural modelling approach. *Australian Journal of Psychology, 40,* 363–376.

Stankov, L., & Horn, J. L. (1980). Human abilities revealed through auditory tests. *Journal of Educational Psychology, 72,* 21–44.

Sternberg, R. J. (1979). The nature of mental abilities. In *American Psychologist, 34,* 214–230.

Sternberg, R. J. (1985). *Beyond IQ: A triarchic theory of human intelligence.* Cambridge: Cambridge University Press.

Sternberg, R. J., & Detterman, D. K. (Eds.). (1979). *Human Intelligence: Perspectives on its theory and measurement.* Norwood, NJ: Ablex.

Sternberg, S. (1966). High speed scanning in human memory. *Science, 153,* 652–654.

Sternberg, S. (1975). Memory scanning: New findings and current controversies. *Quarterly Journal of Experimental Psychology, 27,* 1–32.

Thompson, R. F. (1985). *The brain.* New York: Freeman.

Thurstone, L. L. (1938). Primary mental abilities. *Psychometric Monographs, No. 1.* Chicago: University of Chicago Press.

Thurstone, L. L. (1947). *Multiple factor analysis.* Chicago: University of Chicago Press.

Thurstone, L. L., & Thurstone, T. G. (1949). *Examiner's manual: SRA Primary Mental Abilities Test* (Form 11–17). Chicago: Science Research Associates.

Undheim, J. O. (1987). The hierarchical organization of cognitive abilities: Restoring general intelligence through the use of Linear Structural Relations (LISREL). *Multivariate Behavioral Research, 22,* 149–171.

Undheim, J. O., & Horn, J. L. (1977). Critical evaluation of Guilford's structure-of-intellect theory. *Intelligence, 1,* 65–81.

Vernon, P. E. (1979). *Intelligence: Heredity and environment.* San Francisco: Freeman.

Wechsler, D. (1955). *Manual for the Wechsler Adult Intelligence Scale.* New York: Psychological Corporation.

Wechsler, D. (1981). *WAIS-R: Wechsler Adult Intelligence Scale–Revised.* New York: Psychological Corporation.

Willis, S. L., & Schaie, K. W. (1986). Training the elderly on the ability factors of spatial orientation and inductive reasoning. *Psychology and Aging, 1,* 239–247.

Wilson, R. S., & Matheny, A. P. (1983). Mental development: Family environment and genetic influences. *Intelligence, 7(2),* 195–215.

Wing, H. D. (1955). Musical aptitude and intelligence. *Education Today, 5,* 1.

Witkin, H. A., & Goodenough, D. R. (1981). *Cognitive studies: Essence and origins.* New York: International Universities Press.

Woodcock, R. W. (1990). Theoretical foundations of the WJ-R measures of cognitive ability. *Journal of Psycho-Educational Assessment.*

Woodcock, R. W., & Johnson, M. B. (1990). *Woodcock-Johnson Psycho-Educational Battery revised.* Allen, TX: DLM Teaching Resources.

4   Beyond the stage debate: Action, structure, and variability in Piagetian theory and research

Thomas R. Bidell and Kurt W. Fischer

Piagetian theory gave the study of cognitive development its first major momentum, and until recently research devoted to extending, testing, and challenging this theory has dominated the literature. Even with the recent decline in the volume of Piaget-oriented research (Beilin, 1983), Piagetian theory remains a topic of keen interest and a rich source of continuing research into the development of children's thinking.

Despite its dominant role in the field, Piagetian theory has engendered continuing controversy. Part of the controversy arises from differences in goals and assumptions between Piaget's own research tradition, dominated by his philosophical interests and unique views on the origin of knowledge, and the mainstream English-language research tradition, based on different epistemological assumptions. Because of this epistemological difference, the most enduring and prolific controversy has been the long-running debate over the validity of Piaget's structural stage theory. Despite the wide-ranging set of hypotheses and predictions offered by Piaget's monumental work, the debate over his stage theory has remained the center of attention for more than a quarter of a century. As a result, many scholars effectively reduce Piaget's perspective to his structural stage theory, and the whole of his theory is considered to stand or fall with the notion of universal stages.

In this chapter we review both Piaget's theory as a whole and the research literature emerging from the debate over stage structure. We argue that the stage debate cannot be resolved as it is typically conceived. The debate needs to be reframed in terms of a broader set of phenomena: the variability in cognitive development that has been demonstrated repeatedly in research. Refocusing on variability shifts attention from the structuralist stage model to the often neglected constructivist aspects of Piagetian theory, which emphasize the role of human action in specific contexts. It also highlights

The work reported in this chapter was supported by grants from the Spencer Foundation, the MacArthur Foundation Network on Early Childhood, the National Institutes of Mental Health, and Harvard University. The authors thank Daniel Bullock, Helen Hand, Catharine Knight, and Michael Westerman for their contributions to the arguments presented.

areas of potential convergence with current topics in cognitive science, including self-regulation, the role of functional processes in development, and the mechanisms by which developmental transitions take place. A focus on variability can therefore lead beyond a fruitless debate to fruitful new directions in research.

Piaget's theory

Piaget based his psychology on a set of assumptions that are antithetical to important parts of the mainstream Western tradition in science. These assumptions often placed him at odds with the psychological traditions of British and American psychology that depend heavily on the Cartesian tradition. As a result, the goals of Piaget's research often diverged in fundamental ways from the goals of researchers working within those traditions. There are two main sources of this divergence. The first involves core conceptions about the nature of knowledge, and the second involves the philosophical motivation of most of his work.

Action, structure, and self-regulation

The key to Piaget's research goals lies in his distinctive epistemological viewpoint – his core conceptions of the nature and origin of knowledge – now often called "constructivism." According to Chapman (1988) this view is based on three interrelated conceptions: (1) the relation between *action* and thought, (2) the construction of cognitive *structure*, and (3) the role of *self-regulation*, or, more abstractly, equilibration in the development of thought. Piaget's basic position was that our knowledge is primarily constructed from our own actions in the process of regulating our interactions with the world (Piaget, 1952). By actively coordinating actions from different situations or contexts, the person stores or "internalizes" actions that can be reused as representations to anticipate actions in other contexts. Representation in the form of internalized action provides our most fundamental knowledge about how the world works because it tells us what we can *do* with the world. In development, internalized actions are coordinated and organized into evolving systems or structures, with each new organizational achievement offering a qualitative advance, or stage, in the general system of thought. Imbalances between existing cognitive structures and the environment lead to the reorganization and extension of the structures to new stages.

Nearly all Piaget's extensive research with children was directed toward the empirical validation of some aspect or corollary of these three ideas. Yet all three ideas differ markedly from standard viewpoints guiding most work in mainstream psychology, whether from a nativist or an empiricist viewpoint. The nativists and the British empiricists have assumed a Cartesian perceptual input model as the origin of knowledge, as opposed to internalized action (Bernstein, 1983; Campbell & Bickhard, 1986; Fischer & Bullock, 1984). The Cartesian model, named for the philosopher Descartes, assumes fundamental divisions or dualisms between aspects of human intelligence. Primary is the assumption that the mind is isolated from the world and from the human body. Therefore, in the Cartesian model, knowledge cannot come from the actions of the body but must either be innate or received from the "outside" by perceptual input. This Cartesian model continues to underlie most contemporary models such as information processing, where memory for perceptual information is the basis of knowledge.

As for structure, the notion is not absent from the Cartesian scientific tradition, but structures have generally been treated as innate, as in the perceptual structures of the Gestalt framework. Piaget, on the other hand, believed they arise from construction of internalized action systems. Finally, although concepts of self-regulation have been a hallmark of contemporary cognitive psychology (Gardner, 1985; Kopp, 1989), Piaget's constructivism remains almost unique among Western developmental theories in linking self-regulation with the construction of knowledge from action (but, for similar non-Cartesian views, see Leontiev, 1978; Vygotsky, 1987).

Genetic epistemology

The second factor contributing to the divergence between Piaget's research goals and those of the mainstream psychological community was his view of his enterprise and the role of psychology within it. Piaget set himself the primary goal of resolving some of the most troubling philosophical dilemmas about the nature and origin of knowledge handed down from 18th- and 19th-century philosophy. Beginning his work during the early part of the 20th century, Piaget shared the widely felt optimism that science offered solutions to philosophy's conundrums. Instead of rejecting philosophy altogether, Piaget attempted to create his own discipline, called "genetic epistemology," which was to be a merger of the science of psychology and the philosophy of knowledge. Within this merger, epistemology was to set the problems and interpret the evidence, which was to be provided by science in the form of "genetic" (developmental) psychology.

This division of labor, in which psychology was assigned a subordinate role, had profound effects on Piaget's research, perhaps the most important being the extremely abstract formulation of Piaget's main research questions. While following preschoolers around or questioning grade school children about the contents of a beaker of liquid, Piaget was attempting to address directly questions like the reasons for particular historical sequences of knowledge in science and mathematics (see Piaget & Garcia, 1989). Because this highly abstract philosophical motivation for his research studies is often not clear in his writings, psychologists concerned with contemporary issues in cognitive development often have difficulty seeing any relevance, or even any sense, in Piaget's theoretical discussions.

Furthermore, genetic epistemology was never widely adopted outside Piaget's home base in Geneva, Switzerland, and therefore remained largely his personal philosophical system. As a result, some of his psychological terms and categories, such as *assimilation, accommodation, equilibration,* and *reflective abstraction,* may make sense within Piaget's system but are often unfamiliar and obtuse from the perspective of non-Genevan frameworks.

Whatever position one may take on the viability of genetic epistemology or its fundamental tenets, it is essential to recognize the role it played in determining the nature and purposes of Piaget's extensive research program. Unless one considers the goals Piaget set for himself, it is difficult to understand his approach to research on intellectual development.

From social to action origins of knowledge

Piaget's psychological research covered more than 60 years from his first studies in Binet's laboratory in 1919 to his death in 1980. In Geneva, he frequently employed a small army of colleagues, graduate students, and assistants to make observations. Four distinct shifts in focus can be discerned in the course of this work: early descriptive research on the structure of child logic, research on the sensorimotor period of infancy, a focus on the genesis of representational thought, and a late period marked by a revived focus on functionalism (Chapman, 1988). The first two periods were marked by a theoretical shift in Piaget's view of the origin of knowledge, from a social perspective-taking model to a model based on constructive action.

Early research on child logic

The early work involved both a *structural description* of a sequence of stages in children's thinking and a *social explanation* for the sequence based on the coordination of perspectives. The main products were a series of descriptive studies, published in five monographs (Piaget, 1954, 1955, 1964, 1965, 1972a). During this period Piaget was looking for evidence in children's speech and social interactions that might support and help to define his intuitions about the organization of thought and how it develops.

This research used two main methods. The first was an observational approach, in which he observed and recorded children's spontaneous conversations during play (Piaget, 1955, 1965). The second approach was an adaptation of Binet and Simon's psychometric tasks – quantitative measures based on pass–fail scoring – to produce what Piaget called a "clinical method" in which children were questioned at length about their reasoning on the test items (Piaget, 1964).

The result of these investigations was a general description of the nature and organization of child thought that presaged much of Piaget's later work, introduced some of his most famous conceptions, and served to define childhood intellectual development as a serious topic on the scientific agenda. Piaget described changes in children's speech patterns as reflecting progressive reorganizations in their thought patterns. For instance, he found that younger preschool children tended to speak in collective monologues, talking past each other without engaging in topical conversation. Somewhat older children began to show evidence of trying to take account of their conversational partner's thoughts; and by age 7 to 8, children engaged in true conversations on a shared topic.

Piaget interpreted these changes as due to gradual development of the ability to understand two perspectives at once. He argued that younger children can understand only one perspective – their own – and he labeled this type of thought "autistic." As children grow older, Piaget argued, they gain in the ability to understand that other people have perspectives, but they still have a hard time considering others' views separately from their own. Thus, their thought remains egocentric, or partly tied to themselves. At 7 to 8 years, children overcome egocentrism by gaining the ability to consider two perspectives at the same time. This allows them to carry on topical conversation because they can consider what the other child has to say while still maintaining their own ideas. This form of thought is thus more socialized and communicative than the earlier forms.

The social process of coordination of perspectives was also considered a major factor leading to the achievement of logical thinking. As children gain the ability to view conversation as a two-way street, so to speak, their thinking begins to show properties of reversibility that Piaget identified as the psychological phenomenon underlying logical thought. Reversibility is the ability to consider a relation simultaneously with its reverse or opposite relation. For instance, when Piaget asked young boys questions based on the logic of classification, such as "How many brothers does your brother have?" they would typically fail to include themselves in their calculations. Piaget argued that to understand adequately a logical category like "brother," a child needs to consider his or her own viewpoint regarding the brother simultaneously with its reverse: the brother's viewpoint regarding him or her.

Evidence of development of reversibility was accumulated in many of Piaget's studies of children's logical (1964), causal (1972), and moral thinking (1965). In each study Piaget found a cross-sectional agewise progression of four stages: (1) consideration of people or objects individually, not in relation with each other (e.g., self or sibling); (2) recognition of relations without reversibility (e.g., recognizing male siblings as brothers without defining "brother" reciprocally); (3) reversible understanding (recognizing one is also a brother to one's brothers); and (4) a formal understanding of relations from all possible perspectives (e.g., recognizing that all brothers must be brothers to their brothers because of the nature of the relationship).

Piaget gradually came to doubt the adequacy of a purely social explanation of these cognitive structures. He increasingly came to view the reversibility of thought as a compensating or regulatory process with strong parallels to the regulatory functions of biological forms of organization. Furthermore, he believed that a social explanation by itself left the role of the individual human agent unaccounted for. Piaget began to pursue the idea that reversible cognitive structures emerge from the individual's own self-regulation of actions. To pursue this part of the explanation, he turned to the study of sensorimotor development during infancy.

his idea: reversability – emerges from self-reg.

Infancy: The origin of knowledge in action

While studying infant development, Piaget reformulated his theory, redefining the notion of structure in terms of internalized action systems based in the biological concept of self-regulation. The resulting description of sensorimotor development in infancy (Piaget, 1951, 1952, 1954) laid a new foundation for his theory by defining representational thinking as the outcome of sensorimotor constructions.

Piaget felt that the hypothesis that knowledge had a perceptual origin, which was shared by both nativist and empiricist branches of the Cartesian tradition, could not adequately account for the tremendous intellectual mobility as well as the organization in reversible thinking. On the one hand, the innate perceptual structures described by the Gestalt psychologists were highly automatized and rigidly circumscribed in their applicability, making them unlikely sources of reversibility. On the other hand, models of perceptual accumulation advanced by learning theorists did not explain how thought was organized.

The alternative view Piaget (1952, 1954) put forth was that action, not perceptual abstraction, is the primary source of information about the world. According to Piaget, perceptual information may be indispensable, but it is limited to relatively static knowledge of configurations in the world. Knowledge of action – what one can do with the world – is much more powerful because it goes beyond configurations to knowledge of process and relation. As one learns about the possible ways of changing and manipulating the world, one gains fundamental knowledge about relations within and between people and objects.

From this perspective, the organizing principle in development is the person's ability to *regulate* her own actions in relation to the environment, including the ability to *reorganize* her actions in order to overcome environmental impediments to her goals. For Piaget, this reorganization of actions seemed a more likely source of reversible thought structures than did perceptual abstractions. Through a case study methodology, using his own three children as subjects, Piaget amassed a wealth of observations in support of his new position: By gradually reorganizing their sensorimotor actions, infants construct a basic understanding of the permanence of objects in space and a rudimentary ability to represent people and objects not immediately present (Uzgiris & Hunt, 1975).

According to Piaget (1952) infants are born with a set of innately organized perceptual and motor abilities in the form of reflexes, broadly conceived. Through efforts at using these reflexes the infant gradually organizes them into independently functioning actions such as looking, grasping, listening, and sucking. Because of the initial independence of the actions, the information about the world that is gained through them is not at first interrelated.

As these newly organized systems of action are applied to people and objects, the infant begins to integrate independent activities like looking and grasping into broader organizations. If infants look at an object, they can also grasp it; if they hear a voice, they can also look for its source. Because some actions now work in unison, they provide some limited cross-referencing of information about the world, which results in an early stage of permanence of objects and spatial organization. For instance, when infants know that whatever they look at can also be grasped, then an object they see disappear behind a cloth can be found by their grasping underneath the cloth. Similarly, an action can be cross-referenced with its opposite, so that an infant knows that an object placed in a container can also be removed. At this stage, however, infants cannot find objects hidden in one location and then rehidden in another location, because that requires further integration of their action systems. Their cross-referencing of information is limited to specific structures and contexts of activity.

This limitation disappears when these activities are further integrated into a broad system of actions and perceptual abilities called the "group of displacements." According to Piaget, infants now interrelate all possible actions on objects in the world. For instance, the actions of hiding and finding are integrated with those of crawling back and forth, so that an infant is able to search systematically in all the possible locations for lost objects. This interrelatedness thus provides the infant with a cross-referencing of information about the world that is so systematic that it resembles the logic of older children and adults while operating only within the realm of actions.

Piaget (1952, 1962) also argued that this system of interrelated activities forms the basis of the representational capacities that develop further in childhood and adolescence. Once the action system is organized systematically, it need no longer operate only to organize direct actions on things in the world. It provides knowledge of the actions that are *possible* in the environment and therefore is the basis for anticipating actions mentally. In this sense actions become internalized and serve as representations of possibilities and relations in the world. For Piaget, cognitive development during childhood was a process of extending and reorganizing the internalized action system constructed during infancy into systems of mental representation and abstract thought.

The development of representation as systems of internalized actions

Subsequent to the infancy studies, all of Piaget's psychological research was directed in one way or another toward assessing and elaborating the implications of his new view of representational thought as internalized action. This huge volume of research may be divided into two major bodies. The first and best known part focused on the implications of the idea of action systems for the development of cognitive structure. The second body of literature focused on the implications of action-based knowledge for mental functioning, including the functional mechanisms for constructing new cognitive structures. This second part is discussed in a later section.

The structure of cognitive activity

Piaget's best-known research is the work on the succession of cognitive stages in various domains such as logic (Inhelder & Piaget, 1969), number (Piaget & Szeminska, 1952), space (Piaget & Inhelder, 1967), time (Piaget, 1971), and physical quantity (Piaget & Inhelder, 1974). Piaget hypothesized that the developmental stages of intelligence he had described earlier could be explained as steps in the gradual reorganization and extension of internalized action systems. He advanced the theory that representational intelligence develops by a process analogous to sensorimotor development during infancy. Through attempts to achieve goals and overcome obstacles in the environment, early internalized actions are gradually integrated until they form an interrelated system. Just as the system of sensorimotor activities allows systematic explorations and reversibility of action, the system of internalized actions allows systematic or logical thinking, a property of which is reversibility.

Piaget referred to the internalized actions that compose such a system as "operations" to distinguish them from the actions of the sensorimotor level. He distinguished three kinds of operations. Preoperations are internalized actions that have not yet been integrated into complete systems and so are not yet true operations. These characterize the long transitional period of development from the end of the sensorimotor stage (at about 2 years) to the achievement of the organized systems of concrete operations (at about 7 years). Concrete operations are so called because, though systematical and reversible, they are limited to specific concrete content, such as a particular arithmetic problem. Gradually, during late childhood, concrete operations themselves are integrated to form a system of formal operations (by about 12 years). In this last stage the internalized actions become fully integrated and thus able to operate on one another – operations on operations – rather than only on concrete contents. The concrete operations that solve a specific logical problem in a specific way can themselves be compared and contrasted with all the possible operations on such a problem. As a result, formal operations allow the subject to think abstractly and hypothetically.

Piaget's research of this period was aimed not simply at describing stages, a task already accomplished by his earlier work, but at evaluating the new *explanation* of stage change embodied in the reformulated theory. This involved the cross-sectional assessment of developmental sequences specifically predicted by the idea of gradually integrated action systems. The famous Piagetian tasks introduced to the clinical interviews at this time were designed to elicit the full range of responses associated with the gradual integration of internalized actions in a particular domain. Children's cognitive abilities were assessed in terms of how they performed with these materials and how they justified what they did.

As an example, consider the research on classification. Children were asked to sort and classify concrete objects such as blocks, beans, or flowers. Piaget placed their performances and justifications into a sequence based on the internalized actions of putting things together. Piaget argued that children must integrate two types of putting-together: those based on *similarity* and those based on *belonging*. For example, a baby can be grouped with an adult based on similarity (they are both people), or it can be grouped with a cradle based on belonging (babies go with cradles). In logical classification, similarity defines relations among the parts, and belonging defines relations between the parts and the whole.

There are four main stages in the integration of relations of similarity and belonging. In stage 1 (preoperations) children can represent putting-together only one action at a time. In classifying objects they tend to switch between pairing based on similarity and pairing based on belonging. At times children form a series of independent pairings of similar objects like two triangles, two squares, and so forth. At other times children notice a pattern in the objects, such as a house, and group the objects on the basis of belonging to that pattern. Because pairings are not integrated, children cannot refer to other pairings when seeking a criterion for membership and are forced to switch between criteria.

During stage 2 (still preoperations but in transition to concrete operations) children have partially integrated the two types of actions. Information about the two types can be partly cross-referenced, so that children can create groupings that simultaneously involve relations of similarity between the parts and relations of belonging to the group. Because of this cross-referencing, children can refer to other pairings for the criteria of belonging. Thus children can construct groups consisting of only triangles or only blue blocks, because a pair of triangles (or blue blocks) formed by similarity can be simultaneously considered as a group to which other triangles (or blue blocks) can belong. However, at stage 2 these subsystems of internalized actions have not yet been integrated with one another, and so the groupings formed remain independent and nonexhaustive: The pile of triangles may contain some blue blocks (triangles), and the pile of blue blocks may contain some (blue) triangles.

Stage 3 (concrete operations) sees the integration of the subsystems and thus the systematic cross-referencing of information about similarity and belonging. Children at this point can classify exhaustively because they simultaneously refer to different subsystems of similarity and belonging. This enables them to determine, for instance, that the triangles among the blue blocks are triangles and blue at the same time. The subsystems themselves are classified with respect to both similarity and belonging, with the result that the classes are fully systematic and exhaustive – that is, completely logical. Children can therefore build a classification matrix that coordinates a dimension of shape and a dimension of color.

The classification abilities of stage 3, while exhaustive, are confined to concrete situations. Children of this stage cannot reason propositionally about classes and relations. Although Piaget did not specifically study classification beyond stage 3, he argued that the generalization of classification principles to propositional or hypothetical reasoning comes at stage 4 (formal operations). At this point, operations of classification are integrated not only among themselves but with other kinds of operations to form a system of propositional logic. Children at this stage can reason about the abstract form of the relations of similarity and belonging as in the proposition, "If A belongs to subclass B', then A must belong to the class B of which B' is a subclass."

The research on stage structure documented similar sequences of internalization of action in a number of other intellectual abilities, conservation being one of the best known. Conservation, the ability to understand that a quantity does not change when its perceptual configuration is altered, is essential to an understanding of stability and regularity in the world – indispensable elements of scientific reasoning. Developmental sequences of conservation include domains such as number, length, area, and weight. In each of these cases and many more, Piaget sought to establish descriptive evidence for his theory of development as a sequence of reorganizations of internalized action systems, such as stretching and compressing, emptying and filling.

Structure, holism, and organism

The action-system conception was strongly holistic and closely tied to the organismic approach to development (Reese & Overton, 1970). As the research on intellectual development continued, Piaget increasingly described development in terms of pervasive, cross-domain systems of thought despite the domain-specific nature of his actual research. He seemed to feel that an organism-wide integration or equilibrium of action systems, termed the structure-of-the-whole, or *structure d'ensemble*, was required to account for the consistency of logical thinking across so many contents and circumstances. On the one hand, he recognized age gaps, called *décalage*, between the same type of structural acquisition in different domains, and did not explicitly predict perfect age synchrony across domains (Chapman, 1988; Gelman & Baillargeon, 1983). But on the other hand, he persisted in describing childhood thought in terms of an organism-wide logic that implied relatively tight temporal synchrony in operational acquisitions across domains (Broughton, 1981; Fischer & Canfield, 1986).

The domain-general view was reinforced by cognitive universalism. Piaget's work increasingly focused on properties of action systems general to the person across contexts and systematically deemphasized the effects of particular contexts, even while he maintained that social factors are indispensable in explaining cognitive development (Piaget, 1960). This led to the explicit prediction that the three stages of operational thinking would be culturally universal and the implicit prediction of age synchrony in the acquisition of stages across cultures. These predictions have been strongly contested and have found only mixed empirical support. Children in all cultures do seem to acquire some form of concrete reasoning during the childhood years (White, 1970) and some form of abstract reasoning abilities in adolescence (Gladwin, 1970; Scribner, 1977). Yet the specifically *formal-operational*, abstract mode of reasoning seems to be characteristic mostly of Western-style, schooled cultures (Greenfield, 1976). The specific tasks Piaget designed to tap reasoning skills are acquired at very different ages and rates in many other cultures. And although abstract thinking appears to emerge after concrete thinking in all cultures, the order of acquisition Piaget found for specific tasks – such as conservation of number before substance – can be different in other cultures (Price-Williams, 1981).

Piaget's focus on domain-general knowledge and cultural universalism stands in sharp contrast to the implications of his argument that knowledge is constructed from actions in the environment. Such constructive activities must take place in specific contexts in relation to particular tasks. Knowledge derived from such activities should reflect the particular ways in which the activities are organized to meet contextual demands (Fischer, 1980; Rogoff, 1990; Rogoff & Lave, 1984; Zimmerman, 1989). This apparent conflict between the implied context specificity of constructivism and the domain-general universalism of Piaget's structural stage model was never resolved within Piaget's theory. (In his final writings, however, he acknowledged it as an issue and suggested there might be ways to resolve it [Inhelder & Piaget, 1980; Piaget, 1987].) It remains a fundamental problem in contemporary cognitive developmental theory. A later section of this chapter returns to this problem and suggests some possible resolutions based on contemporary developments in neo-Piagetian psychology.

The role of action in the development of intellectual functioning

Although the work on the structure of development of logical thinking has received by far the largest share of attention, Piaget also completed a sizable body of developmental research on the functioning of intelligence. In this research Piaget's goal was to apply the idea of action-based knowledge to the way thinking works or functions, with less focus on how it is organized (Gallagher & Reid, 1981). Piaget's functionally oriented research includes two large bodies of work. The first is a series of studies dealing with three traditional areas of intellectual functioning: perception, memory, and mental imagery. The second body addresses questions about the mechanisms by which knowledge may be constructed out of action.

Perception, memory, and mental imagery

Piaget believed that actions not only form the basis of logical thought but also play a crucial role in all aspects of human cognitive functioning. Intelligence requires both mobility and stability in order to operate effectively. That is, thought must be capable of representing both *states* of reality and the *transformations* by which the states come about and are altered (Piaget, 1977; Piaget & Inhelder, 1971). The representation of states gives thought a stable field on which to operate, and the representation of transformations affords an understanding of changes and relations in the world. Internalized actions or operations of thought provide the basis for knowledge about transformations (operative knowledge), whereas such cognitive functions as perception, memory, and mental imagery furnish information about the states of things (figurative knowledge).

To a large extent the development of such functions as perception, memory, and mental imagery is based on automatized actions. All actions have as an outcome some state, and so automatized internalized actions can be used as objects of thought to index potential outcomes or states of

Cartesian Model

Perceptual Development   Conceptual Development

Piagetian Constructivist Model

Track 1: Perceptual Development

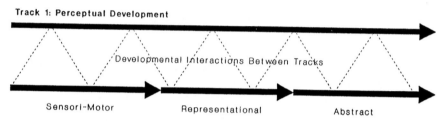

Developmental Interactions Between Tracks

Sensori-Motor   Representational   Abstract

Track 2: Conceptual Development

Figure 4.1. Piaget's two-track model of perceptual and conceptual development compared with the Cartesian one-track model.

reality. Memory, imagery, and even perception are, therefore, less basic to intelligence than is action. For example, mental images are formed this way. Whereas some of the contents of images are related to perceptual information, the structure of mental images derives from automatized acts of mental imitation. The pattern of ocular movements needed to organize information about an object, say, a table, is automatized and organizes that information internally, in the absence of the table. Then cross-referencing of such internalized, automatized actions occurs through the action system. With the development of concrete operational thinking, the basis for automatized actions becomes increasingly mobile, resulting in dynamic and even reversible images (Piaget & Inhelder, 1971).

Piaget's work on perceptual development reflects his epistemological stance that higher forms of knowledge are derived more from action than from perception (Piaget, 1969). Rather than the single line of development from perception to conception presupposed within the Cartesian tradition, Piaget proposed a two-track model in which perception and conception develop independently but in growing interrelation (Figure 4.1). The conceptual track, the development of the internalized action system, is constantly informed by the perceptual track but not determined by it. Perception gradually comes under the influence and domination of the system of internalized action. The action system, through its mobility, provides for increasing exploratory capacity and active regulation of perceptual functions, correcting misleading information from more static, highly automatized, gestaltlike structures present from infancy (Elkind, 1975; Fischer & Bidell, 1991; Vurpillot, 1976).

Construction mechanisms

In Piaget's late career a substantial, and often unrecognized, body of research work was devoted to questions about the mechanisms by which cognitive structures emerge and change (Piaget, 1976, 1978). Although this work was highly general and oriented toward the issue of stage transition rather than specific acquisitions, it nevertheless opened an important research direction dealing with the constructive relation between action and thought. According to this model of *reflective abstraction,* knowledge is constructed by thinking about, or reflecting upon, actions in specific situations. When children encounter obstacles to their goals, they reflect upon current courses of action and represent possibilities for alternative actions. They then integrate the representations of possible actions to achieve a more extensive system of internalized actions or thoughts.

One set of studies tested the most general prediction of the reflective abstraction model (Piaget, 1976). If new understandings derive from actions, then the actions involved in a given task should appear developmentally before the conceptualization of those actions. Piaget found this developmental order to hold true consistently across a wide range of tasks. For instance, with a movement problem such as using a sling to throw a ball or stone, there was a consistent gap of several years between the age of successful performance and the age of accurate conceptualization of the problem. Similar performance–concept gaps were found for a range of games and problem-solving tasks such as the Tower of Hanoi.

In the second set of studies Piaget went on to explore some of the functional dynamics involved in the construction of knowledge from action (Piaget, 1978). In these studies Piaget posed problems that could not be solved by direct action. These tasks required children to reconceptualize their actions in the immediate situation in order to solve the problem. Again there was a developmental relation between action and understanding on these tasks. In young children, problem solving was action-oriented and conceptualizations served only to rationalize their actual performance. In somewhat older children there was a give-and-take between action and conceptualization. Now the child's concepts, while derived from their actions, also helped to inform their actions by providing partial plans, which were then extended through further action. In late childhood, conceptualization led and guided actions, and children were able to develop systematic plans in advance based on a generalized understanding of the kinds of activities involved in the problem.

In addition to the studies already discussed, Piaget conducted a number of further studies on the mechanisms of cognitive acquisition, which we will mention but lack the space to describe. These included investigations of the role of contradictions between anticipations and feedback in the construction of new structures of internalized actions (Piaget, 1980), as well as studies of the developmental relations between mental comparisons or correspondences and mental transformations (Piaget, 1979). Finally, the general line of research on constructive mechanisms inspired recent research on problem solving by students of Inhelder and Piaget known as the "strategy group." Their studies examine children's informal theories and mental models of problem situations, as well as the relation between procedural routines and these theories or models (Ackermann-Valladao, 1980; Karmiloff-Smith, 1979; Karmiloff-Smith & Inhelder, 1974; Kilcher & Robert, 1977).

Summary: Ambiguities of Piagetian theory

We have traced the outlines of Piaget's research on intellectual development from his early descriptions of cognitive structures and social bases through his reformulation of the theory in terms of the reorganization of internalized action systems via organic self-regulation. We saw how the notion of action-based knowledge became a central theme not only for his structural research on cognitive stages but also for his wide-ranging research on intellectual functioning, including memory, perception, and mental imagery. We also examined the theory and research on construction of cognitive abilities through internalization and integration of action systems.

Within the corpus of the theory there remains an unresolved tension between a structuralist emphasis on cross-domain, universal stages and Piaget's functionalist emphasis on the construction of knowledge from action. Often the two themes appear to be confounded in research. For instance, many times Piaget took evidence for structural stages as a confirmation of the theory of internalization of action, without designing research to test that assumption directly. Furthermore, when he did attempt to test the theory of action-based knowledge, he simply adapted the same cross-sectional methodology he had used throughout the structural research. Only very late in his career did he and his colleagues turn to truly functional research on problem solving, carried out by the strategy group.

Furthermore, because of his primary interest in epistemological and historical questions, Piaget did not attempt to control or manipulate various factors such as testing conditions, learning history, or cultural background. And because of these very general goals, he accepted generalized cross-sectional *group* age criteria that often masked important *individual* differences in developmental sequences.

The stage debate: Structure and variation in Piagetian theory

The theoretical and methodological ambiguities in Piaget's work left many researchers skeptical about his central claims. Piaget's own reliance on stage descriptions encouraged a focus on the predictions of the stage model, and in the wake of this debate questions about self-regulation and the origin of knowledge in action have been generally neglected.

In the debate over the validity and interpretation of stages, one large volume of research offers evidence contradictory to predictions of stage theory, while another large volume tends to substantiate it. Taken together, the results suggest that the challengers and the defenders are both partly right. In general, large-scale developments from preconcrete to concrete and then to abstract thinking have been remarkably replicable, showing the order and the approximate ages reported by Piaget. In particular, however, there is a great deal more variation in cognitive development than Piaget's stage theory either predicts or explains. The central role of this variation in developmental phenomena is perhaps the most important lesson to be drawn from the lengthy debate over Piaget's stage theory.

The focus on structure

Initial interest in Piaget's first books was submerged in the United States by the hegemony of behaviorism during the 1930s and 1940s. Current psychological interest in Piagetian theory dates more directly from the late 1950s and early 1960s when the cognitive revolution rekindled a widespread interest in intellectual development (Gardner, 1985). The renewed interest focused almost exclusively on the structural or stage aspects of his work. In addition to Piaget's own structural bent, this trend may have been encouraged by Flavell's (1963) early interpretive book that made the stage theory accessible to a wide range of researchers, and it was probably also partly due to the character of the emerging cognitive paradigm. On one hand, self-regulation had been a feature of that paradigm from its inception (Miller, Galanter, & Pribram, 1960), and although the concept holds a different status within Piaget's framework, it was not a hotly contested proposition. On the other hand, the hypothesis of the origin of knowledge in action was largely ignored by cognitivists because it lay so far outside the epistemological tradition of learning theory, from which cognitive science was emerging. The question of structure, however, was being rediscovered by cognitive science (e.g., Mandler, 1963), and Piaget's proposals about structure provided a testable set of questions for researchers to debate.

Within the experimental, learning-theory traditions of American and British psychology, which emphasized environmental factors in explaining acquisition, there was much cause for skepticism about Piaget's organismic structuralism (Fischer & Silvern, 1985). Are the stages Piaget described really universal? Do they cut across domains of knowledge as the structure-of-the-whole seems to imply? Do the various cognitive abilities associated with the stages emerge at the ages Piaget reported? Are the developmental sequences he described invariant across individuals and cultures? Such questions dominated the research on Piagetian theory.

Developmental variability

results vary depending on how tasks-presented

In the debate over these questions researchers manipulated a number of environmental factors, including assessment condition, learning history, and cultural background. Not surprisingly, they found variability in children's cognitive development, and it fell into three broad categories: variability in *age* of acquisition of specific skills, *relative synchrony* of structurally similar acquisitions in different domains, and *sequence* of a given set of acquisitions across different domains or cultural backgrounds.

In each of the three categories, when relevant conditions are manipulated, results vary as a function of the manipulation. Conditions like those used by Piaget usually produce results similar to those he reported. Conditions different from his usually produce results that vary from his. The following sections examine this pattern of variability in representative research from each of the three categories.

Variability in age of acquisition

Piaget argued that cognitive structures must be built hierarchically, in stages, and therefore must appear at periodic intervals during development. Specifically, he predicted three major transitions during childhood: from sensorimotor intelligence to preoperational representational abilities at about 18 months, from preoperations to concrete operations at about 7 years, and from concrete operations to formal operations at around 12 years. He recognized that these ages were approximate, that individuals would vary from group norms, and that *décalage* or time gaps occurred between acquisitions in differing domains that seemed structurally similar. Despite all these qualifications, Piaget's research relied on the mean age of acquisition to index development. The problems he posed should have led him instead to construct direct tests of within-individual stage sequences with longitudinal designs or Guttman-scale techniques (Wohlwill, 1973). When a group of children on average responded preoperationally to a task like conservation of substance at age 5 and then concrete operationally at age 7, these data were taken as evidence that individual children acquire concrete operations after preoperations in these tasks.

Piaget's reliance on mean age has encouraged acceptance of this questionable tendency among other cognitive-developmental researchers, even those questioning his theory. For example, researchers demonstrate substantial variation in age of acquisition (usually downward to younger ages) and then conclude that Piaget's stage sequence has been disconfirmed.

The tacit acceptance of the indirect age criterion over more direct tests of sequential ordering has led to a prolific and, at times, confusing debate in the literature as to whether children acquire abilities at the ages Piaget reported. By manipulating factors such as task structure, familiarity of task materials, practice, and social support, researchers have demonstrated wide variability in the age of acquisition for a number of Piagetian tasks (Fischer & Bidell, in press; Flavell, 1982). Some manipulations have produced older ages of acquisition, some younger, and some ages that approximate Piaget's results. The most widely cited studies of age variation have been those in which age of acquisition has been moved downward (e.g., Bryant & Trabasso, 1971; Donaldson, 1978; Gelman & Gallistel, 1978). Typical is Gelman's (1972) study of number conservation, in which she manipulated task complexity to achieve conservation judgment from children much younger than expected.

The standard number conservation task involves two parallel rows of 8 to 10 objects placed in one-to-one correspondence. One row is then transformed, usually by extending the items to make it longer. To show conservation, the child must indicate that the rows remain equal in number and justify that conclusion in terms of logical necessity – the rows *must* remain equal. Piaget and Szeminska (1952) reported this skill at about 6 to 7 years of age.

In Gelman's (1972) study, task complexity was manipulated in two ways. First, the number of counters in each row was reduced to as few as two or three. Second, the method of assessing conservation was altered substantially. After children initially judged the two rows to be equal, one row was transformed surreptitiously either by adding more counters or by simply rearranging the counters already there. Then, children who showed more surprise at viewing the enlarged set than the transformed set were scored as number conservers; there was no need for explicit judgment and justification. Under these conditions children as young as 3 years were coded as conserving number.

Following up on Gelman's and similar studies, other researchers have shown that changes in task complexity can move age of acquisition upward again, even with tasks like Gelman's (Cooper, 1984; Fischer & Canfield, 1986). For instance, Silverman and Briga (1981) argued that children in Gelman's study might simply be counting rather than applying conservation reasoning. When they altered the task to preclude counting, by covering part of the transformed array, 3-year-old children no longer showed conservation-like responses. Similarly, Halford and Boyle (1985) used a number conservation task in which the transformed array was configured in ways that were difficult to count. Under these circumstances too, 3-year-olds failed to conserve number; but 6- to 7-year-olds did show conservation.

Age of acquisition has also been adjusted downward by manipulating the amount of practice children have with conservation tasks. Training studies typify this kind of manipulation (for reviews, see Beilin, 1978; Field, 1987; Halford, 1982). Various techniques have been used to teach conservation responses to children who fail to demonstrate them in pretests; children were then retested on a new conservation problem. In a number of studies, children as young as 4 or even 3 years of age have been trained to produce appropriate conservation responses under some circumstances (Halford, 1989). At the same time, this literature shows that effectiveness of training is constrained by various factors that require explanation, including task complexity, content, the complexity of the training, the age of the child, and the developmental status of the child. Some sort of developmental explanation seems to be required by findings that training is more effective if the children are older (Beilin, 1965; Murray, 1968), have higher mental ages (Sigel, Roeper, & Hooper, 1966), or already show some progress in concrete operations (Inhelder, Sinclair, and Bovet, 1974).

Age of acquisition also varies in types of tasks other than conservation (Gelman & Baillargeon, 1983; Halford, 1989). One is class inclusion tasks, in which children must simultaneously consider (1) relations among subclasses (e.g., daisies and tulips) and (2) relations between subclasses and the superordinate class (e.g., daisies and flowers) (Halford, 1982; Winer, 1980). Preoperational children who can handle only one set of these relations at a time typically focus on the subclass comparison alone and cannot understand that there must be more flowers than either daisies or tulips – missing the part–whole relation of inclusion.

Again, age of acquisition varies both upward and downward depending on assessment conditions. Researchers using tasks similar to Piaget's have reported approximately similar ages of acquisition (Elkind, 1964; Wohlwill, 1968). Winer's (1980) review reported more studies showing later than earlier ages. Yet challenges to Piaget's stage of concrete operations have come mainly from those citing earlier ages of acquisition (Donaldson, 1978; Gelman & Baillargeon, 1983; Markman, 1978; Smith, 1979) associated with conditions such as high socioeconomic status of the children, weakening of scoring criteria, and reduction of task complexity (Halford, 1989).

Most of the dramatic reductions in age of acquisition once again come from reductions in task complexity. In a typical study McGarrigle, Grieve, and Hughes (1978) attempted to use a familiar situation and, in doing so, greatly reduced task complexity. They showed children a picture in which a teddy bear had to climb a set of six steps, four red and two white. Cues marked the two groups: a chair at the end of the red steps and a table at the end of the white ones. The investigators asked the children, "Are there more red steps to go to the chair, or more steps to go to the table?" Under these conditions a majority of the 4-year-old subjects gave class-inclusion responses. By providing cues (the chair and table) to support the representation of the aspects of the problem and by using everyday terminology, the authors seem to have reduced the complexity of the task. An important question to be considered later is whether such reductions in task complexity fundamentally change the nature of the task, thereby requiring a different, developmentally earlier skill (Halford, 1989).

In short, Piaget's ages for abilities at each of his stages represent rough central tendencies in a range of both upward and downward variation, not fixed landmarks. This variation is not random but is closely related to both organismic and environmental factors, the manipulation of which has a powerful effect on age of acquisition.

Variability in synchrony of acquisitions across contexts and domains

Another focus of the debate over Piaget's structural theory involves the stability of cognitive stages across contexts and domains. As already noted, Piaget's conception of the structure-of-the-whole implies a system of logic that pervades the entire mind at each stage. Many researchers have taken this "hard stage" (Kohlberg, Levine, & Hewer, 1983) version of the theory to mean that children should perform at precisely the same logical stage on each task they encounter, regardless of the situational context or the content domain of the task.

Such strong synchrony is seldom empirically supported. The research literature shows a high degree of variability in the cognitive stage an individual exhibits on structurally equivalent tasks from one context to another and across domains (Feldman, 1980; Fischer, 1980; Flavell, 1982). For both context and domain, variation in cognitive stage appears to be affected by a range of environmental and organismic variables, in the same way that age of acquisition is affected. We prefer to use the term *level* rather than *stage* to reflect this fact of variation.

In terms of context, an individual's cognitive level varies widely depending on the degree of contextual support immediately available (Rogoff, 1982). When the context provides support for high-level functioning, such as familiarity of settings and materials and modeling or prompting of key components of performance, individuals exhibit much higher levels of cognitive performance than under less supportive circumstances (Fischer &

Bullock, in press). A given child's cognitive level will vary from high to low over a period of a few minutes depending on the degree of support. Children, adolescents, and young adults have all shown consistently higher developmental levels under high-support conditions than they showed spontaneously for the same content domain. Domains in which this has been shown include concepts of social roles like nice and mean (Fischer, Hand, Watson, Van Parys, & Tucker, 1984); reflective judgment (Kitchener & Fischer, 1990); and concepts of honesty and kindness (Lamborn & Fischer, 1988).

Similar variation is found across content domains. Numerous studies covering a wide range of Piagetian tasks have consistently produced notoriously low correlations either among Piagetian tasks or between those tasks and other cognitive measures such as school achievement (Gelman & Baillargeon, 1983; Jamison, 1977). In general there is a high degree of variability and a low degree of synchrony across theoretically equivalent tasks in different domains.

The high degree of variability across both contexts and domains clearly disconfirms the strong version of the structural unity hypothesis as just described. A common alternative view among contemporary theorists is that cognitive structure is organized within specific domains rather than as a systemwide logic (Feldman, 1980; Flavell, 1982), although some theorists have argued that such variability brings the whole idea of cognitive structure into question (e.g., Brainerd, 1978).

Other theorists have argued that the existence of variability does not indicate the absence of broader organizing principles: More limited, local forms of cross-contextual or cross-domain organization can be detected if the proper methods are used. Fischer and Bullock (1981) have argued that although "point synchrony" (same-level acquisitions occurring at exactly the same time) is almost never found, there is good evidence for "interval synchrony" (same-level acquisitions occurring within a narrow time frame), especially when the degree of environmental support is controlled. When support is not controlled, the factors producing variability in performance lead naturally to widely variable performance. When degree of support is held constant, the upper limit on children's performance across contexts or domains can show substantial consistency.

A reasonable interpretation of the evidence seems to be that neither absolute structure nor absolute variability reigns over cognitive development. Although Piaget's structure-of-the-whole clearly does not exist in the strong sense, some cross-domain organization seems to exist, as evidenced in the human ability to think and act consistently from one situation to another. Instead of being imposed by an underlying abstract logic, such organization seems to be constructed by a specific real-time process of generalization from one context to another (Fischer & Farrar, 1987; Rogoff, 1990).

X Cognitive organization from generalization

the stages appear to be in order w/ considerable variation in appearance

Variability in sequence of acquisitions

Even more basic than the question of synchrony is the question of whether Piaget's developmental sequences remain invariant across individuals and groups. Once again, the evidence gives rise to conflicting interpretations. On one side, evidence of variation in specific developmental sequences has been taken as evidence against the notion of hierarchically constructed stages (Brainerd, 1978; Gelman & Baillargeon, 1983). On the other side, a large number of studies have supported general predictions of long-term Piagetian stage sequences (Case, 1985; Fischer, 1980; Halford, 1989).

An examination of the evidence shows a familiar pattern: High variability occurs in developmental sequences but is neither random nor absolute. The number and order of steps in developmental sequences tend to vary as a function of such factors as learning history, cultural background, and content domain. In addition, the variability in steps appears to be contingent on the level of analysis at which the sequence is examined. Developmental sequences tend to appear mainly at two levels of analysis: (1) large-scale sequences covering several years at a stretch, relatively independent of domain, and (2) small-scale sequences found within particular domains (Fischer & Bullock, 1984; Flavell, 1972). Large-scale sequences appear to be invariant. Children do not, for instance, exhibit concrete operational performances across a wide range of tasks, and then years later begin to exhibit preoperational performance on these tasks. On the other hand, small-scale sequences have often been found to vary (Dodwell, 1960; Kofsky, 1966; Lunzer, 1960).

Typically, variation in small-scale sequences is associated with variation in context or assessment conditions. For instance, Kofsky (1966) constructed an 11-step developmental sequence for classification based on Inhelder and Piaget's (1969) research and tested it using scalogram analysis. Kofky's sequence, while following a logical progression, drew on an assortment of different tasks and materials to evaluate each step. The results showed weak scalability with several nonstandard mini-sequences.

Other sources of variation in small-scale sequences include cultural background, learning history, and learning style. Price-Williams, Gordon, and Ramierez (1969), for instance, examined the order of acquisition of conservation of number and substance, in two Mexican villages. The villages were comparable in most ways except that in one village the children participated in pottery making at an early age. Children of the pottery-making families tended to acquire conservation of substance (tested with clay) before conservation of number, while non-pottery-making children showed the opposite tendency.

Furthermore, some recent work has shown that when factors such as learning style or treatment group are controlled, task sequences that scale poorly can be resolved into alternative, group-specific sequences that scale well. For instance, Knight found that a sequence of six reading-related tasks scaled badly when tested on a sample of poor readers in first to third grade (Knight, 1982; Fischer & Knight, 1990). But when she used a scaling technique that could detect alternative sequences (Krus, 1977; Kuleck & Fischer, 1989), she found that subsamples of poor readers showed different, well-ordered sequences. Research methods should allow detection of alternative sequences instead of forcing all children either to fit or not to fit one sequence. Even research on synchrony benefits from more careful testing of sequences: A recent study of development of perspective taking found that careful assessment of sequences showed much more synchrony across perspective-taking domains than had been found in previous research (Rose, 1990).

These patterns of variation in developmental sequences suggest that both sides of the debate over Piagetian theory are partly right. Very large-scale, long-term developmental sequences appear to be invariant, as Piaget predicted. However, short-term sequences show high variability as a function of such factors as domain, cultural background, learning style, and diagnostic group.

Conclusion: The centrality of variation Variation exists in cog devel.

Perhaps the most important lesson from the debate over Piaget's stage theory is the central role of variability itself in cognitive development. The overriding pattern of intellectual development is not the existence of structural development or its absence but the *variability* present in structural development. In each area we have reviewed – age of acquisition, synchrony of acquisitions, and sequence of acquisitions – developmental variability has been the basic finding allowing arguments for and against Piaget's propositions. Despite this omnipresence of variability, both sides in the debate have treated it as a background issue. In their interpretations of the evidence, both sides have tended to ignore the developmental variation that forms the basis of the debate and to focus on the particular meaning of a particular variation vis-à-vis their own position. In so doing, they have ignored the central phenomenon itself – variability that follows naturally from the basis of intelligence in contextualized action.

The dilemma of developmental variation

The backgrounding of developmental variability has thus given rise to a basic dilemma in the research influenced by Piaget's stage framework. Because each theoretical position focuses on only a small part of the relevant variability, no single framework can adequately interpret all the data. Thus, instead of being a legitimate competition among theories, the debate over stage theory has shown the failure of all involved to account systematically for the central phenomenon of the field: developmental variability.

Meaningful comparisons among studies of development require attempts at systematic manipulation of major factors related to the dependent variables. As long as the manipulation of these key covariates is nonsystematic, each piece of research remains self-contained and incommensurable with other pieces that manipulate the covariates in different ways or manipulate entirely different covariates. For example, a study that simplifies a task and then finds a lower age of acquisition has manipulated task complexity in only one direction. To conclude that Piagetian predictions are disconfirmed is misleading because the opposite manipulation has not been included for comparison. Whenever a given manipulation produces an early age of acquisition in one study, another study, with a new manipulation, can counter with a later age. The result is a perpetual seesaw.

If this methodological shortcoming is not recognized, it leads to a number of intractable problems for researchers trying to make sense out of development. For instance, if differing degrees of environmental support produce different cognitive levels, ages of acquisition, or developmental sequences, what degree of support is "right" to evaluate these phenomena? One is forced to ask which is the right cultural context producing the right developmental sequence, or which is the right degree of practice or training to determine cognitive level or age of acquisition (Fischer & Bidell, 1991).

A good example of this problem is the McGarrigle et al. (1978) version of the class inclusion task described earlier. McGarrigle had hoped to facilitate children's performance by posing the part–whole problem in terms of the familiar context of climbing two sections (the parts) of a stairway (the whole) and by providing visual cues to which children could refer. But the alteration of the task makes it unclear whether class inclusion is still being assessed at all. Since the part–whole comparison was framed in terms of the relative distance involved in climbing the stairs, the early age of acquisition McGarrigle reported may be due to children solving the task by a simple length comparison (Halford, 1989). McGarrigle's subjects may have treated his task as a class inclusion problem, or they may have treated it as a length comparison, or perhaps some took it each way. Because only one task manipulation was used it is impossible to determine the source of the effect. In studies of this kind, there is no good way to interpret the results.

Instead of clarifying the question, such evidence only continues a debate that cannot be resolved unless the terms of the argument are changed. Focus on a particular variation or on unidirectional descriptions of variability will perpetuate the seesaw effect in the debate. Without a systematic approach to developmental variability, which grows naturally from a focus on the basis of intelligence in action, researchers inadvertently sustain an irreconcilable debate over the meaning of developmental phenomena.

Beyond the dilemma: Foregrounding developmental variation

If researchers are to address the problem of developmental variability, they must foreground the phenomenon for direct analysis and develop theoretical and methodological tools adequate to describing, measuring, and controlling it. Only by analyzing the dimensions of developmental variability will it be possible to construct a comprehensive theory of development. The dynamic hypothesis that cognition is formed from actions in contexts leads naturally toward a focus on variability, and it has led us to the use and construction of methods to investigate it (Fischer, 1980; Fogel & Thelen, 1987). Three of the most useful methodological tools for analyzing variability are developmental scaling, the developmental range, and maps of alternative developmental pathways.

Developmental scaling

One of the main methodological problems contributing to a nonsystematic approach to variability is the inadequate, extremely gross scales of measurement that have traditionally been used to gauge developmental change. To get an idea of the nature of this problem, imagine trying to measure the weekly changes in the depth of snow in your backyard during the winter, using a yardstick with no inch markings but only feet. The depth of the snow could vary tremendously – say, from 0 to 8 inches – but a graph of your results measured in feet would show only a flat line. The crudeness of the scale would force you to lump all the change into one static category: less than a foot.

A similar problem exists with traditional Piagetian stages. Piaget's stages mark off the course of cognitive development in the crudest fashion, dividing the reorganization into units that can cover 3 to 5 years per stage. In practice, Piaget described a few smaller substages for each of the large stages of preoperational, concrete operational, and formal operational intelligence, but these substages were not done consistently from one study to the next, and there was no clear basis for defining them (Droz & Rahmy, 1974). It was difficult to use them as part of a measuring instrument.

A crude measuring instrument makes it hard to detect variability and encourages misinterpretations of the variability that comes to light. For instance, if the only measure of change during the childhood period is the distinction between preoperational and concrete operational thinking, then factors like contextual support or task complexity have to move performance a whole stage – the equivalent of about 5 years – if their effects are to be detected. When manipulations are strong enough to produce such a large effect, the use of only two huge categories can obscure the phenomenon of variability, just as variation in snow depth can be obscured by measuring it in categorical terms (less than or more than a foot). In the face of such a static description of development, it is highly tempting to conclude that an individual simply is concrete operational and that any variations detected are due to either measurement error or performance limitations unrelated to the true underlying competence. As a result, researchers ignore the flexibility in behavior that occurs under a range of differing organismic and environmental conditions.

For these reasons it is important to devise more sensitive scales for measuring changes in developmental performance and to use them to measure developmental variation. A focus on actions in contexts, with its concomitant emphasis on variability, has led us to use more sensitive scales (Fischer & Canfield, 1986). And some other neo-Piagetian researchers have also been devising such scales, especially Case (1985) and Siegler (1981). Table 4.1 contrasts a scale designed to measure developmental changes in middle-class American children's understanding of mean and nice social interactions based on neo-Piagetian skill theory with the traditional Piagetian

Table 4.1. *Piagetian stages compared with a skill theory sequence in social interactions*

Piagetian stage	Skill level	Step	Skill
Preoperations	*Rp*1: single representational skills	1	*Active agent*: A person performs at least one behavior fitting a social-interaction category of mean or nice.
		2	*Behavioral category*: A person performs at least two behaviors fitting a category of mean or nice.
		3	*Shifting behavioral categories*: One person performs at least two behaviors fitting the category "nice," as in step 2, and then a second person performs at least two behaviors fitting the category "mean."
	*Rp*2: representational mappings	4a	*Combination of opposite categories in a single person*: One person performs concurrent behaviors fitting two categories, such as "nice" and "mean."
		4b	*One-dimensional social influence*: The mean behaviors of one person produce reciprocal mean behaviors in a second person. The same contingency can occur for nice behaviors.

Table 4.1 (*continued*)

Piagetian stage	Skill level	Step	Skill
		5	*One-dimensional social influence with three people behaving in similar ways*: Same as step 4b, but with three people interacting reciprocally in a mean way (or a nice way).
		6	*Shifting one-dimensional social influence*: The nice behaviors of one person produce reciprocal nice behaviors in a second person. Then, in a separate story, the mean behaviors of a third person produce reciprocal mean behaviors in the second person. (Or a reciprocal mean interaction can occur first, and then a reciprocal nice interaction.)
		7	*One-dimensional social influence with three people behaving in opposite ways*: The nice behaviors of one person and the mean behaviors of a second person produce reciprocal nice and mean behaviors in a third person.
Concrete Operations	*Rp*3: representational systems	8	*Two-dimensional social influence*: Two people interact in ways fitting opposite categories, such as that the first one acts both nice and mean and the second one responds with reciprocal behaviors in the same categories.
		9 –	*Two-dimensional social influence with three people*: Same as step 8, but with three people interacting reciprocally according to opposite categories.
	*Rp*4/A1: single abstract skills	10	*Single abstract control structure integrating opposite social behaviors*: Two interactions involving opposite behaviors (as in step 8) coordinated in terms of an abstract control structure, such as that intentions matter more than actions.
		11	*Shifting abstract control structures, each integrating opposite social behaviors*: First, two interactions involving opposite behaviors are coordinated in terms of one control structure, such as intention (as in step 10). Then two interactions involving opposite behaviors are responsibility: What matters is whether people take responsibility for the harm they do.

stages that would apply to the same period of development (Fischer, Shaver, & Carnochan, 1990).

A comparison of these two scales shows that where the Piagetian stage framework divides the entire period of childhood into only two giant reorganizations, the skill theory framework distinguishes four levels and 11 steps in the construction of social interactions during this period. Each step in the sequence involves only a small reorganization of the skills needed to understand mean and nice social interactions. In addition, the theory and method allow discrimination of even more steps when a more detailed scale is needed. The result is a fine-grained measuring tool sensitive to small variations in children's behavior.

The use of a scale sensitive to small developmental steps helps to move research in cognitive development beyond the dilemma created by stage theory by reframing the debate in terms of *processes* instead of categories. Instead of asking whether or not children have "really" reached the concrete operational stage in the domain of mean and nice interaction, researchers can ask more analytic questions: What are the particular sequences of reorganizations children go through in this domain? How do children move from one step to another? Do different children show different pathways, different orderings of the tasks used to assess the sequence? Similarly, instead of debating which of the many possible assessment conditions is the "right" one for measuring concrete operational performance, the debate can focus on *how* changes in environmental conditions affect the level of children's cognitive skills.

For example, in McGarrigle's (1978) classification study already cited, the structure of the task was changed in order to achieve a better assessment of the logical ability to classify. An alternative approach would be to use developmental scaling to understand where McGarrigle's task as well as Piaget's fit in a developmental sequence of classification skills. Fischer and Roberts (1989), for instance, have constructed a 12-step sequence of classification skills for the period between 1 and 7 years of age: Each step represents a small reorganization of classification skills moving toward the skill of classifying objects in a three-dimensional matrix. McGarrigle's task could be analyzed in a smilar manner. Then, instead of debating whether or not this particular task variation is the best assessment of classification skills, researchers could ask what specific kind of classification skill this particular task demands and what its relation might be to earlier and later classification skills.

The developmental range

Another important tool for describing and analyzing developmental variation is the developmental range (Lamborn & Fischer, 1988). Because developmental level varies, an individual child's cognitive level is not simply a point on a developmental scale, even for a narrowly defined domain. An individual's cognitive skills for a given task actually span a potentially wide interval of levels. The developmental range is a tool for describing this span of abilities and the individual variation an individual can show within this span in relation to specific environmental conditions.

As previously discussed, if cognitive abilities are viewed only in the long term, they can seem to be fixed categories of thought imposed on various types of contents. On the other hand, if they are viewed as actions adapted to specific contexts – a more short-term view – attention is directed to the concrete processes by which cognitive skills are used and formed. From this shorter-term perspective, the level of organization of cognitive skills is flexibly affected by the many environmental and organismic factors indicated earlier, including the class of factors we have called "environmental support." Children and adults show systematic variation in cognitive levels with differing degrees of support, and the upper and lower limits of this variation delineate what is called the "developmental range." It is similar to Vygotsky's (1978; Wertsch, 1985) concept of the zone of proximal development, but it offers a specific set of methodological and conceptual tools for measuring and analyzing the effects of contextual support.

Table 4.2 illustrates the developmental range in relation to a given developmental sequence of skills. Three levels of performance can be distinguished for any individual performing a given task, depending on the degree of environmental support available. The *functional* level is the highest level of performance the child exhibits when carrying out a task spontaneously, with no special help from other people. Some behaviors will be at lower steps than the functional level (the earliest steps in Table 4.2), but the functional level represents the limit of performance under spontaneous conditions. When children receive support, such as modeling, instruction, or familiarization with the task, they can move to a higher level of performance, called the *optimal* level, which is the upper limit on performance they can generally sustain in that domain. The gap between functional and optimal level is typically large, as shown in Table 4.2.

In some cases performance moves to an even higher level called the *scaffolded* level (Bruner, 1982; Wood, 1980). Here the degree of social support goes beyond modeling or instruction to actual coparticipation in the task by an adult or more knowledgeable peer (Foreman & Kraker, 1985). With another person performing part of the task, the duo can produce a level much higher than the child can sustain even at his or her optimal level; but, of course, the child cannot yet sustain this level in the absence of the other person's direct participation.

Like developmental scaling, the developmental range can help reframe the debate over Piagetian stage theory by refocusing attention away from

Table 4.2. *Developmental range of a skill under varying social support conditions*

Developmental sequence (step)	Performance levels	Social support
1		
2		
3		
4	Functional	None
5		
6	Optimal	Modelling, instruction, etc.
7		
8	Scaffolded	Direct participation
9		
10		
11		
12		

[handwritten: below functional/node level]

fixed stages and toward developmental variability. The fact that the same child, adolescent, or adult shows consistently different levels of the same tasks under different support conditions makes it necessary to stop treating the individual as having a single stage of knowledge. If the person's level varies so routinely, then surely variation must be included in research. Also, the strong effects of support lead researchers to ask questions about the ways in which social support affects the construction and use of cognitive skills. *[handwritten: we need to study how social support (or lack of) affects cog devel]*

Maps of alternative developmental pathways

Another form of variation we have described is in developmental pathway. Individuals' cognitive-developmental pathways are the particular sequence of skills they acquire for a given domain in the environmental context where they live, especially the social context. Different people can show different pathways, and one individual can show distinct pathways in different domains. If researchers are to incorporate variability into their explanatory frameworks, they must devise tools for characterizing differences in developmental pathways as a function of contextual differences. One such tool is the map of developmental pathways.

Perhaps because Piaget described the course of cognitive development in very abstract terms, focusing on only a few general stages, he did not deal much with cross-cultural variability. For him there seemed to be a single, universal pathway culminating in the formal abstraction of the Western scientist (Gardner, 1973). Although Piaget (1967) eventually acknowledged

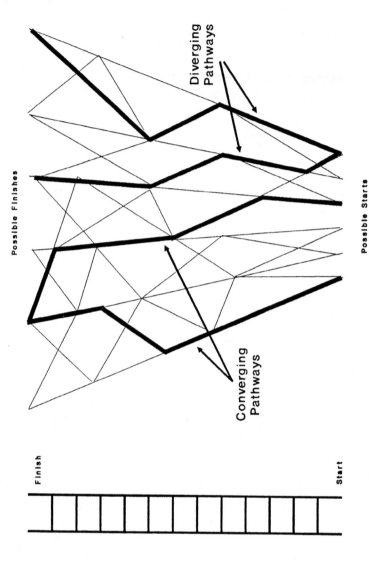

Figure 4.2. Two metaphors for conceptualizing developmental pathways.

this shortcoming and suggested that other cultures may have different developmental outcomes (Greenfield, 1976; Piaget, 1972), he never specifically adjusted his theory to take such alternatives into account.

The mapping of developmental pathways is a tool for detecting and describing variations in the number, kind, and sequence of skills. In Figure 4.2 the traditional Piagetian model of the developmental pathway is depicted in terms of its underlying metaphor – a ladder. In contrast, the context-sensitive model of diverse pathways is depicted in terms of a web of constructive generalizations (Bidell & Fischer, in press).

The traditional metaphor of the ladder of development suggests a single generalized pathway that everyone must follow. However, the metaphor of the web suggests that instead of being imposed by general structures, developmental pathways are constructed and can be influenced in different directions by both organismic and contextual factors. (Similarly, evolutionary theorist Stephen J. Gould has used a "bush" metaphor to describe the multidirectionality of alternate evolutionary pathways.) A web is constructed by first establishing a few strands in some particular place, and then extending those strands to new but nearby points that offer possible support. Therefore, the particular direction and ultimate shape of a given pathway within a web is a joint function of the constructive activity of the web builder and the type of environment in which it is built.

Figure 4.2 depicts an idealized version of a web of development, representing many possible pathways that might be followed by different children constructing their knowledge in different environments. The darkened lines indicate two kinds of potential relations between developmental pathways: convergent and divergent development. In convergent development children begin at different points in development – say, two different expectations about schemas for stories (Michaels, 1981). Through constructive activity in similar contexts, such as educational settings, such children can wind up at very similar points in development, for instance, with similar literacy skills. In divergent development, on the other hand, children can begin at the same point and pursue different pathways of development toward differing developmental outcomes, as when boys and girls start out showing few differences in dealing with gender roles at 3 years of age and end up years later with large differences in their understanding and relation to gender (Fischer et al., 1984; Gilligan & Attanucci, 1988).

Alternative developmental pathways can also be traced for different subgroups of children within a population, as illustrated by the study of reading development cited earlier (Fischer & Knight, 1990). Poor readers in first to third grade were found to follow different developmental pathways from those of normal readers in acquiring a set of reading-related skills. When the standard metaphor of the developmental ladder is used, as in Figure 4.3, children are compared only in terms of relative progress or delay on a single

Reading Production

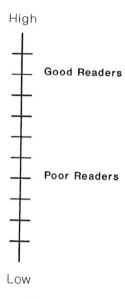

Figure 4.3. The conventional ladder metaphor applied to assessment of reading production skills.

progression from low to high performance on a single task or criterion – in this case, reading production. As long as only a single pathway is considered, there seems only one remedial choice: to work to speed up the apparently delayed group.

Figure 4.4, however, shows an alternative method of comparison based on the constructive web metaphor. In this instance, instead of comparing each group in terms of achievement on a single task or criterion, the groups are compared in terms of the developmental pathways they take through a series of tasks. For each group, the order of acquisition for six reading tasks was tested using a statistical technique called "partially ordered scaling," which is based on the logic of Guttman scaling (Krus, 1977; Kuleck & Fischer, 1989) but allows more than one task sequence. In the figure, tasks acquired first are shown at the top of the sequence, and later acquisitions are shown below them. A line between two tasks means the ordering is statistically reliable, and tasks that are parallel but have no lines between them are acquired at about the same time.

A comparison of the two developmental pathways shows that the poor readers are not simply delayed with respect to a universal sequence of acquisitions, but actually follow *different* pathways in acquiring these skills, one of which is shown in the figure. Normal readers all showed one common

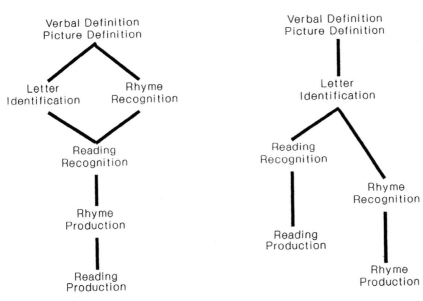

Figure 4.4. Alternative developmental pathway maps for reading skills in two diagnostic groups.

very helpful distinctions for remediation

pathway, but poor readers showed three different pathways, all different from the normal one. This map of alternative pathways suggests a different remedial educational strategy. Instead of attempting to speed up development in poor readers, teachers can think in terms of helping to channel children following divergent pathways into pathways that converge on the goal of competent reading. By providing environmental support, teachers can channel development, building bridges from the known to the unknown instead of providing frustrating repetitive encounters with the unknown (Rogoff, 1990).

From this perspective, the tool of mapping alternative developmental pathways is especially important for the study of cognitive development among working-class children and children of color. Against the backdrop of a developmental ladder based on white, middle-class norms, children from these social groups are frequently seen as exhibiting "deficits" in development. Within the developmental web metaphor it is possible to view developmental differences as alternative pathways instead of deficits. An important direction for future research will be to describe the webs of divergent and convergent developmental pathways in differing sociocultural groups in order better to understand and address the educational needs of diverse segments of human communities (Bidell & Fischer, in press).

Conclusion: Toward structural and functional unity

At the start of the chapter we noted the tension between Piaget's abstract structuralist stage theory and his constructivist view of knowledge as the product of self-regulated functional activity in specific contexts. We have also described the intractable debate generated by research directed at the notion of stage abstracted from considerations of specific contexts and activities, and have pointed to the phenomenon of variability as the key to resolving that debate.

Foregrounding developmental variability naturally brings into play questions of developmental contexts and mechanisms. Variability is a characteristic of real activities and processes and can only be excluded or backgrounded by an act of abstraction. Questions about the structural aspects of cognitive development in real people and situations imply questions about the functional aspects, and vice versa. For instance, it is hard to think about the role of varying contexts in shaping particular (structural) developmental sequences without raising questions about the functional mechanisms by which people naturally incorporate context into the organization of their cognitive activities.

For these reasons, a refocus on variability in cognitive development also entails a refocus within Piagetian theory, away from abstract structuralism and toward the constructivist elements of the theory. Researchers who examine the functional aspects of Piagetian theory may be surprised to find a number of connections with contemporary theories of cognitive development. In particular, the central notion of self-regulated action is closely related to contemporary concepts of the role of *control* in the organization and processing of information (Case, 1985; Fischer, 1980). At least one neo-Piagetian theory of cognitive development describes developmental mechanisms in terms of the organization of control structures to govern activity in specific contexts (Fischer, 1980).

However, despite its constructivist elements focusing on activity in context, Piagetian constructivism retains a primary focus on individual psychological processes and neglects social processes. To make effective use of constructivism, contemporary research needs to treat activities in *social* context, taking advantage of the increasingly articulated descriptions of the social context of development currently available (Leontiev, 1978; Rogoff, 1990; Wertsch, 1985; Westerman, in press). Neither an individual nor a social-contextual perspective alone can adequately account for variability in cognitive development. Instead, theoretical accounts of developmental variability must provide tools to describe the mechanisms by which persons-

(handwritten top margin: ✱ Knowl through actions / in context ⟹ overarching stages (less well defined))

in-context (Fischer & Farrar, 1987) regulate and reorganize themselves and their world.

(handwritten: ✱ the dilemma w/ Piaget: Stages are abstract / knowledge acquisition is constructivist / built / an Self-regulation w/in context (actions))

References

Ackermann-Valladao, E. (1980). Etudes de relations entre procedures et attribution de signification aux instruments, dans une tache de construction de chemins. *Archives de Psychologie, 48*, 59–93.

Beilin, H. (1965). Learning and operational convergence in logical thought development. *Journal of Experimental Child Psychology, 2*, 317–339.

Beilin, H. (1978). Inducing conservation through training. In G. Steiner (Ed.), *Psychology of the twentieth century: Piaget and beyond* (Vol. 7). Zurich: Kindler.

Beilin, H. (1983). The new functionalism and Piaget's program. In E. K. Scholnick (Ed.), *New trends in conceptual representation: Challenges to Piaget's theory?* Hillsdale, NJ: Erlbaum.

Bernstein, R. J. (1983). *Beyond objectivism and relativism: Science, hermeneutics, and praxis.* Philadelphia: University of Pennsylvania Press.

Bidell, T. R., & Fischer, K. W. (1989). Commentary on G. S. Halford, Reflections on 25 years of Piagetian Cognitive Developmental Psychology, 1963–1988. *Human Development, 32*, 363–368.

Bidell, T. R., & Fischer, K. W. (in press). Cognitive development in educational contexts: Implications of skill theory. In A. Demetriou, M. Shayer, & A. Efklides (Eds.), *Modern theories of cognitive development go to school.* London: Routledge & Kegan Paul.

Brainerd, C. J. (1978) The stage question in cognitive development. *The Behavioral and Brain Sciences, 2*, 173–213.

Broughton, J. M. (1981) Piaget's structural developmental psychology, III. Function and the problem of knowledge. *Human Development, 24*, 257–285.

Bruner, J. S. (1982). The organization of action and the nature of adult-infant transaction. In M. Cranach & R. Harre (Eds.), *The analysis of action.* Cambridge: Cambridge University Press.

Bryant, P. E., & Trabasso, T. (1971). Transitive inferences and memory in young children. *Nature, 232*, 78–96.

Bullinger, A., & Chatillon, J.-F. (1983). Recent theory and research of the Genevan school. In P. H. Mussen (Ed.), *Handbook of child psychology. Vol. 3: Cognitive development* (J. H. Flavell & E. M. Markman, Eds., pp. 231–262). New York: Wiley.

Campbell, R. L., & Bickhard, M. H. (1986). *Knowing levels and developmental stages.* Basel, Switzerland: Karger.

Case, R. (1985). *Intellectual development: Birth to adulthood.* New York: Academic Press.

Chapman, M. (1988). *Constructive evolution: Origins and development of Piaget's thought.* Cambridge: Cambridge University Press.

Cooper, R. G., Jr. (1984). Early number development: Discovering number space with addition and subtraction. In C. Sophian (Ed.), *Origins of cognitive skills.* Hillsdale, NJ: Erlbaum.

Dasen, P. (1972). Cross-cultural Piagetian research: A summary. *Journal of Cross-Cultural Psychology, 3*, 23–39.

Dodwell, P. C. (1960). Children's understanding of number and related concepts. *Canadian Journal of Psychology, 14*, 191–205.

Donaldson, M. (1978). *Children's minds.* New York: Norton.

Droz, R., & Rahmy, M. (1974). *Lire Piaget.* Brussels: Psychologie et Sciences Humaines/ Dessart.

Elkind, D. (1964). Discrimination, seriation, and numeration of size and dimensional differences in young children: Piaget replication study VI. *Journal of Genetic Psychology, 104*, 275–296.

Elkind, D. (1975). Perceptual development in children. *American Scientist*, 63, 533–541.

Feldman, D. H. (1980). *Beyond universals in cognitive development*. Norwood, NJ: Ablex.

Field, D. (1987). A review of preschool conservation training: An analysis of analyses. *Developmental Review*, 7, 210–251.

Fischer, K. W. (1980). A theory of cognitive development: The control and construction of hierarchies of skills. *Psychological Review*, 87, 477–531.

Fischer, K. W., & Bidell, T. R. (1991). Constraining nativist inferences about cognitive capacities. In S. Carey & R. Gelman (Eds.), *Structural constraints on knowledge in cognitive development*. Hillsdale, NJ: Erlbaum.

Fischer, K. W., & Bullock, D. (1981). Patterns of data: Sequence, synchrony, and constraint in cognitive development. In K. W. Fischer (Ed.), *Cognitive development* (pp. 69–78). New Directions for Child Development, no. 12. San Francisco: Jossey-Bass.

Fischer, K. W., & Bullock, D. (1984). Cognitive development in school-age children: Conclusions and new directions. In W. A. Collins (Ed.), *The years from six to twelve: Cognitive development during middle childhood* (pp. 70–146). Washington, DC: National Academy Press.

Fischer, K. W., & Bullock, D. (in press). The failure of competence: How context contributes directly to skill. In R. Wozniak & K. W. Fischer (Eds.), *Specific environments: Thinking in contexts*. Jean Piaget Society Series on Knowledge and Development. Hillsdale, NJ: Erlbaum.

Fischer, K. W., & Canfield, R. L. (1986). The ambiguity of stage and structure in behavior: Person and environment in the development of psychological structures. In I. Levin (Ed.), *Stage and structure: Reopening the debate* (pp. 246–267). New York: Plenum.

Fischer, K. W., & Farrar, M. J. (1987). Generalizations about generalization: How a theory of skill development explains both generality and specificity. *International Journal of Psychology*, 22, 643–677.

Fischer, K. W., Hand, H. H., Watson, M. W., Van Parys, M., & Tucker, J. (1984). Putting the child into socialization: The development of social categories in preschool children. In L. Katz (Ed.), *Current topics in early childhood education* (Vol. 5, pp. 27–72). Norwood, NJ: Ablex.

Fischer, K. W., & Knight, C. C. (1990). Cognitive development in real children: Levels and variations. In B. Presseisen (Ed.), *Styles of learning and thinking: Interaction in the classroom*. National Education Association.

Fischer, K. W., & Pipp, S. L. (1984). Processes of cognitive development: Optimal level and skill acquisition. In R. J. Sternberg (Ed.), *Mechanisms of cognitive development* (pp. 45–80). New York: Freeman.

Fischer, K. W., & Roberts, R. J., Jr. (1989). The development of classification skills in the preschool years: Developmental level and errors. Unpublished manuscript. Cambridge, MA: Cognitive Development Laboratory Report, Harvard University.

Fischer, K. W., Shaver, P., & Carnochan, P. (1990). How emotions develop and how they organize development. *Cognition and Emotion*, 4, 81–127.

Fischer, K. W., & Silvern, L. (1985). Stages and individual differences in cognitive development. *Annual Review of Psychology*, 36, 613–648.

Flavell, J. H. (1963). *The developmental psychology of Jean Piaget*. Princeton, NJ: Van Nostrand.

Flavell, J. H. (1971). Stage-related properties of cognitive development. *Cognitive Psychology*, 2, 421–453.

Flavell, J. H. (1972). An analysis of cognitive developmental sequences. *Genetic Psychology Monographs*, 86, 279–350.

Flavell, J. H. (1982). On cognitive development. *Child Development*, 53, 1–10.

Fogel, A., & Thelen, E. (1987). Development of early expressive and communicative action: Reinterpreting the evidence from a dynamic systems perspective. *Developmental Psychology*, 23, 747–761.

Foreman, E., & Kraker, M. J. (1985). The social origins of logic: The contributions of Piaget and Vygotsky. In M. W. Berkowitz (Ed.), *New directions for child development: Vol. 23. Peer conflict and psychological growth*. San Francisco: Jossey-Bass.

Gallagher, J. M., & Reid, D. K. (1981). *The learning theory of Piaget and Inhelder*. Monterey, CA: Brooks/Cole.

Gardner, H. (1973). *The quest for mind*. New York: Knopf.

Gardner, H. (1985). *The mind's new science: A history of the cognitive revolution*. New York: Basic Books.

Gelman, R. (1972). Logical capacity of very young children: Number invariance rules. *Child Development, 43*, 75–90.

Gelman, R., & Baillargeon, R. (1983). A review of some Piagetian concepts. In P. H. Mussen (Ed.), *Handbook of child psychology. Vol 3: Cognitive development* (J. H. Flavell & E. M. Markman, Eds., pp. 167–230). New York: Wiley.

Gelman, R., & Gallistel, C. R. (1978). *The child's understanding of number*. Cambridge, MA: Harvard University Press.

Gilligan, C., & Attanucci, J. (1988). Two moral orientations: Gender differences and similarities. *Merrill-Palmer Quarterly*.

Gladwin, T. (1970). *East is a big bird: Navigation and logic on Puluwat atoll*. Cambridge, MA: Harvard University Press.

Greenfield, P. M. (1976). Cross-cultural research and Piagetian theory: Paradox & progress. In K. Riegel & J. Meacham (Eds.), *The developing individual in a changing world*. The Hague: Mouton.

Halford, G. S. (1982). *The development of thought*. Hillsdale, NJ: Erlbaum.

Halford, G. S. (1989). Reflections on 25 years of Piagetian cognitive psychology, 1963–1988. *Human Development, 32*, 325–357.

Halford, G. S., & Boyle, F. M. (1985). Do young children understand conservation of number? *Child Development, 56*, 165–176.

Hooper, F. H., Goldman, J. A., Storck, P. A., & Burke, A. M. (1971). Stage sequence and correspondence in Piagetian theory: A review of the middle childhood period. *Research relating to children*, Bulletin 28. Urbana, IL: Educational Resources Information Center.

Inhelder, B., & Piaget, J. (1969). *The early growth of logic in the child*. (E. A. Lunzer & D. Papert, Trans.). New York: Norton. (Original work published 1959)

Inhelder, B., & Piaget, J. (1980). Procedures and structures. In D. R. Olsen (Ed.), *The social foundations of language and thought*. New York: Norton.

Inhelder, B., Sinclair, H., & Bovet, M. (1974). *Learning and the development of cognition*. Cambridge, MA: Harvard University Press.

Jamison, W. (1977). Developmental interrelations among concrete operational tasks: An investigation of Piaget's stage concept. *Journal of Experimental Child Psychology, 24*, 235–253.

Kagan, J. (1982). *Psychological research on the human infant: An evaluative summary*. New York: W. T. Grant Foundation.

Karmiloff-Smith, A. (1979). Problem solving procedures in the construction and representation of closed railway circuits. *Archives de Psychologie, 67*, 37–59.

Karmiloff-Smith, A., & Inhelder, B. (1974). If you want to get ahead, get a theory. *Cognition, 3*, 195–212.

Kilcher, H., & Robert, M. (1977). Procedures d'actions lors de construction de ponts et d'escaliers. *Archives de Psychologie, 45*, 53–83.

Kitchener, K. S., & Fischer, K. W. (1990). A skill approach to the development of reflective thinking. In D. Kuhn (Ed.), *Developmental perspectives on teaching and learning thinking skills. Contributions to human development* (Vol. 21, no. 4, pp. 48–62). Basel, Switzerland: Karger.

Knight, C. C. (1982). Hierarchical relationships among components of reading abilities of beginning readers. *Dissertation Abstracts International, 43*, 403A.

Kofsky, E. (1966). A scalogram study of classificatory development. *Child Development, 37*, 191–204.

Kohlberg, L., Levine, C., & Hewer, A. (1983). *Moral stages: A current formulation and a response to critics.* New York: Karger.

Kopp, C. B. (1989). Regulation of distress and negative emotions: A developmental view. *Developmental Psychology, 25*, 343–354.

Krus, D. J. (1977). Order analysis: An inferential model of dimensional analysis and scaling. *Educational and Psychological Measurement, 37*, 587–601.

Kuleck, W., & Fischer, K. W. (1989). *Partially ordered scaling of items.* Cambridge, MA: Cognitive Development Laboratory Report, Harvard University.

Lamborn, S. D., & Fischer, K. W. (1988). Optimal and functional levels in cognitive development: The individual's developmental range. *Newsletter of the International Society for the Study of Behavioral Development* (no. 2, Serial No. 14), 3–4.

Leontiev, A. N. (1978). *Activity, consciousness, and personality* (M. J. Hall, Trans.). Englewood Cliffs, NJ: Prentice-Hall. (Original work published 1975)

Lunzer, E. A. (1960). Some points of Piagetian theory in the light of experimental criticism. *Journal of Child Psychology and Psychiatry, 1*, 191–202.

Mandler, G. (1963). From association to structure. *Psychological Review, 69*, 415–427.

Markman, E. M. (1978). Empirical versus logical solutions to part–whole comparison problems concerning classes and collections. *Child Development, 49*, 168–177.

McGarrigle, J., Grieve, R., & Hughes, M. (1978). Interpreting inclusion: A contribution to the study of the child's cognitive and linguisitic development. *Journal of Experimental Child Psychology, 28*, 528–550.

Michaels, S. (1981). "Sharing time": Children's narrative styles and differential access to literacy. *Language in Society, 10*, 423–442.

Miller, G. A., Galanter, E., & Pribram, K. (1960). *Plans an the structure of behavior.* New York: Holt, Rinehart & Winston.

Murray, F. B. (1968). Cognitive conflict and reversibility training in the acquisition of length conservation. *Journal of Educational Psychology, 59*, 82–87.

Piaget, J. (1951). *Play, dreams, and imitation in childhood* (C. Gattegno & F. M. Hodgson, Trans.). New York: Harcourt Brace. (Original work published 1946)

Piaget, J. (1952). *The origins of intelligence in children* (M. Cook, Trans.). New York: International Universities Press. (Original work published 1936)

Piaget, J. (1954). *The construction of reality in the child* (M. Cook, Trans.). New York: Basic Books. (Original work published 1937)

Piaget, J. (1955). *The language and thought of the child* (M. Gabain, Trans.). Cleveland: Meridian. (Original work published 1923)

Piaget, J. (1960). *The psychology of intelligence* (M. Piercy & D. E. Berlyne, Trans.). Totowa, NJ: Littlefield, Adams. (Original work published 1947)

Piaget, J. (1964). *Judgement and reasoning in the child* (M. Warden, Trans.). Paterson, NJ: Littlefield, Adams. (Original work published 1924)

Piaget, J. (1965). *The moral judgement of the child* (M. Gabain, Trans.). New York: Free Press. (Original work published 1932)

Piaget, J. (1967). Review of *Studies in cognitive growth* by J. S. Bruner, R. P. Olver, & P. M. Greenfield. *Contemporary Psychology, 12*, 532–535.

Piaget, J. (1969). *The mechanisms of perception* (G. N. Seagrim, Trans.). New York: Basic Books. (Original work published 1961)

Piaget, J. (1971). *The child's conception of time* (A. J. Pomerans, Trans.). New York: Ballantine. (Original work published 1946)

Piaget, J. (1972a). *The child's conception of the world* (J. Tomlinson & A. Tomlinson, Trans.). Totowa, NJ: Littlefield, Adams. (Original work published 1926)

Piaget, J. (1972b). Intellectual evolution from adolescence to adulthood. *Human Development, 15*, 1–12.

Piaget, J. (1976). *The grasp of consciousness* (S. Wedgewood, Trans.). Cambridge, MA: Harvard University Press. (Original work published 1974)

Piaget, J. (1977). The role of action in the development of thinking (H. Furth, Trans.). In W. Overton & J. M. Gallagher (Eds.), *Knowledge & development: Vol. 1. Advances in research and theory*. New York: Plenum.

Piaget, J. (1978). *Success and understanding* (A. J. Pomerans, Trans.). London: Routledge & Kegan Paul. (Original work published 1974)

Piaget, J. (1979). Correspondences and transformations. (L. DiLisio, Trans.). In F. B. Murray (Ed.), *The impact of Piagetian theory on psychology, psychiatry, philosophy, and education*. Baltimore: University Park Press.

Piaget, J. (1980). *Experiments in contradiction*. (D. Coltman, Trans.). Chicago: University of Chicago Press.

Piaget, J. (1987). *Possibility and necessity* (2 Vols.; H. Feider, Trans.). Minneapolis: University of Minnesota Press. (Original work published 1981 and 1983)

Piaget, J., & Garcia, R. (1989). *Psychogenesis and the history of science* (H. Feider, Trans.). New York: Columbia University Press. (Original work published 1983)

Piaget, J., & Inhelder, B. (1967). *The child's conception of space* (F. J. Langdon and J. L. Lunzer, Trans.). New York: Norton. (Original work published 1948)

Piaget, J., & Inhelder, B. (1971). *Mental imagery in the child: A study of the development of imaginal representation* (P. A. Chilton, Trans.). New York: Basic Books. (Original work published 1966)

Piaget, J., & Inhelder, B. (1974). *The child's construction of quantities: Conservation and atomism* (A. J. Pomerans, Trans.). London: Routledge & Kegan Paul. (Original work published 1941)

Piaget, J., & Szeminska, A. (1952). *The child's conception of number* (C. Gattegno & F. M. Hodgson, Trans.). London: Routledge & Kegan Paul. (Original work published 1941)

Price-Williams, D. (1981). Concrete and formal operations. In R. H., Munroe, R. L. Munroe, & B. B. Whiting (Eds.), *Handbook of cross-cultural human development*. New York: Garland STPM Press.

Price-Williams, D., Gordon, W., & Ramirez, M., III. (1969). Skill and conservation: a study of pottery making children. *Developmental Psychology, 1*, 769.

Reese, H. W., & Overton, W. F. (1970). Models of development and theories of development. In L. R. Goulet & P. B. Baltes (Eds.), *Life-span developmental psychology: Research and theory*. New York: Academic Press.

Rogoff, B. (1982). Integrating context and cognitive development. In M. E. Lamb & A. L. Brown (Eds.), *Advances in developmental psychology* (Vol. 2). Hillsdale, NJ: Erlbaum.

Rogoff, B. (1990). *Apprenticeship in thinking: Cognitive development in social context*. New York: Oxford University Press.

Rogoff, B., & Lave, J. (Eds.). (1984). *Everyday cognition: Its development in social context*. Cambridge, MA: Harvard University Press.

Rose, S. P. (1990). *Levels and variations in measures of perspective-taking*. Unpublished doctoral dissertation, University of Denver, Denver, Colorado.

Scribner, S. (1977). Modes of thinking and ways of speaking: Culture and logic reconsidered. In P. N. Johnson-Laird & P. C. Wason (Eds.), *Thinking: Readings in cognitive science*. Cambridge: Cambridge University Press.

Siegler, R. S. (1981). Developmental sequences within and between concepts. *Monographs of the Society for Research in Child Development, 46*(2, Serial No. 189).

Sigel, I., Roeper, A., & Hooper, F. H. (1966). A training procedure for acquisition of Piaget's conservation of quantity: A pilot study and its replication. *British Journal of Educational Psychology, 36*, 301–311.

Silverman, I. W., & Briga, J. (1981). By what process do young children solve small number conservation problems? *Journal of Experimental Child Psychology, 32*, 115–126.

Smith, C. L. (1979). Children's undestanding of natural language hierarchies. *Journal of Experimental Child Psychology, 27*, 437–458.

Uzgiris, I. C., & Hunt, J. McV. (1975). *Assessment in infancy: Ordinal scales of psychological development.* Urbana: University of Illinois Press.

Vurpillot, E. (1976). *The visual world of the child* (W. E. C. Gillham, Trans.). New York: International Universities Press. (Original work published 1972)

Vygotsky, L. S. (1978). *Mind in society: The development of higher psychological processes* (M. Cole, V. John-Steiner, S. Scribner, & Ellen Souberman, Trans.). Cambridge, MA: Harvard University Press.

Vygotsky, L. S. (1987). Thinking and speech. In R. W. Rieber & A. S. Carton (Eds.), *The collected works of L. S. Vygotsky. Vol. 1: Problems of general psychology* (N. Minick, Trans.). New York: Plenum. (Original work published 1934)

Wertsch, J. V. (1985). *Vygotsky and the social formation of mind.* Cambridge, MA: Harvard University Press.

Westerman, M. A. (in press). Coordination of maternal directives with preschoolers' behavior in compliance problem and healthy dyads. *Developmental Psychology.*

White, S. H. (1970). Some general outlines of the matrix of developmental changes between five and seven years. *Bulletin of the Orton Society, 20*, 41–57.

Winer, G. A. (1980). Class-inclusion reasoning in children: A review of the empirical literature. *Child Development, 51*, 309–328.

Wohlwill, J. F. (1968). Response to class-inclusion questions for verbally and pictorially presented items. *Child Development, 39*, 449–465.

Wohlwill, J. F. (1973). *The study of behavioral development.* New York: Academic Press.

Wood, D. J. (1980). Teaching the young child: Some relationships between social interaction, language, and thought. In D. R. Olsen (Ed.), *The social foundations of language and thought.* New York: Norton.

Zimmerman, B. J. (1989). A social cognitive view of self-regulated academic learning. *Journal of Educational Psychology, 81*, 329–339.

Some decline in elderly –
more related to educ'l levels
& environment

5 The study of adult cognition from a Piagetian perspective

stage after formal –
dilectical

also it
occup
ed
social

James A. Blackburn and Diane E. Papalia

training did help

Although Piaget's theory of cognitive development is generally assumed to provide a comprehensive account of cognitive functioning from infancy through adolescence, culminating in the stage of formal operations, its applicability to changes in cognitive functioning during adulthood and old age is at present equivocal at best. Piaget himself indicated that the adult years are not a time of meaningful cognitive change. He (Piaget, 1972) suggested that formal operations may be reached at different times by different adolescents, depending on their progressively differentiating aptitudes and particular professional specialization. Piaget regarded this differentiation as nonqualitative in nature, and consequently he did not suggest the development of a stage beyond formal thought. On the other hand, others have postulated an additional qualitatively unique stage of development during adulthood, dilectical operation. (See Labouvie-Vief, Chapter 7 in this volume.) Therefore, it may be that although Piaget's interpretations captured a rich variety of performances during childhood, he failed to represent adequately the thought and emotions of mature people (Riegel, 1973).

In this chapter, we survey the current status of the literature on cognitive functioning during adulthood and old age as measured by various Piagetian tasks. We review the age-difference Piagetian research assessing both concrete and formal abilities. We examine various intervention (training) techniques that have been employed to improve task performance among the elderly. Then, we discuss general issues related to the extension of Piagetian research to the later portions of the life-span, such as the role of individual difference factors as well as task and other methodological factors. Fianlly, we offer an evaluation of the Piagetian model for the study of cognition in adulthood.

Studies of concrete tasks

There has been considerable research addressing cognitive task performance in adulthood and old age on a variety of conservation tasks. These abilities,

141

according to Piaget's theory, come into a person's cognitive repertoire during the early elementary school years. Once established, they are expected to remain stable. Thus, an assessment of their "fate" in adults and the elderly is intriguing especially if such abilities are found lacking.

Conservation is the awareness that two stimuli that are equal (for example, in length, weight, amount, or volume) remain equal in the face of perceptual alteration, so long as nothing has been added to, or taken away from, either stimulus. For example, in a weight-conservation task the participants are asked if two clay balls weigh the same. Once they agree they weigh the same, one ball is altered perceptually, perhaps reshaped into a log or a pancake. After this alteration, participants are asked if the two pieces of clay weigh the same or if one weighs more. Then, they must justify their answers. In general, research from the 1960s and 1970s indicated that although young adults and the middle-aged performed quite well on conservation tasks, many noninstitutionalized, healthy elderly people demonstrated lower than optimal levels of task performance. Much of this research found that the level of performance of elderly adults seemed comparable to that of young children (Eisner, 1973; Graves, 1972; Kominski & Coppenger, 1968; Papalia, 1972; Kennedy, & Sheehan, 1973a; Papalia, Salverson, & True, 1973b; Rubin, Attewell, Tierney, & Tumulo, 1973; Sanders, Laurendeau, & Bergeron, 1966; Storck, Looft, & Hooper, 1972). In other words, a sizable number of healthy elders demonstrated nonconservation and "justified" their responses in a manner similar to the ways young children do (saying, for example, that two clay balls no longer weigh the same because "one is longer now").

Other research looked at Piagetian conservation task performance in clinical samples of older adults (e.g., Ajuriaguerra & Angelergues, 1960; Ajuriaguerra, Boehme, Richard, Sinclair, & Tissot, 1967; Ajuriaguerra & Hécaen, 1960; Ajuriaguerra, Muller, & Tissot, 1960; Ajuriaguerra, Rey-Belley-Muller, & Tissot, 1964; Ajuriaguerra, Richard, Rodriquez, & Tissot, 1966; Sinclair-de-Zwart, Ajuriaguerra, Boehme, & Tissot, 1966). These studies generally found a significant deterioration within the groups of older adults, not only in conservation concepts but also in object permanence (the awareness that an object continues to exist even when out of sight) and the concept of time.

Several studies conducted during the 1970s and 1980s (Chance, Overcast, & Dollinger, 1978; Graves, 1972; Papalia et al., 1973a,b; Rubin, 1973; Papalia-Finlay, Blackburn, Davis, Dellmann, & Roberts, 1980) looked at education as one correlate of task performance. Initial research reported a moderate relationship between educational level and task performance. In addition, Chance et al. (1978) and Papalia et al. (1980) found almost perfect performance on a variety of conservation tasks. Participants in both of these studies were highly educated and socioeconomically privileged. Thus, something about educational attainment appears to influence conservation performance in later life, although what this is, is unclear.

Research has also examined the effects of gender (e.g., Denney, 1980; Gallagher & Reid, 1978; Papalia, 1972; Papalia et al., 1973a; Rubin, 1973), levels of intelligence (e.g., Clayton & Overton, 1973; Eisner, 1973; Hornblum & Overton, 1976), and institutionalization (e.g., Clayton & Overton, 1973; Rubin, 1973, 1976; Selzer & Denney, 1980). The evidence on gender differences is unequivocal and reveals that these differences in conservation are minimal, regardless of age. On the other hand, the effects of intelligence levels and institutionalization are less clear. Although Hornblum and Overton (1976) found that nonconservers and partial conservers generally had lower mean intelligence than did the conservers, this finding was not statistically significant. Eisner (1973) also reported that a sample of elderly men who were moderate to severely brain damaged performed less well than healthy elderly men on a variety of conservation tasks. This evidence is scanty, but it does suggest that intellectual intactness would appear to be necessary for adequate conservation performance.

The results of the research on the effects of institutionalization on conservation are also inconclusive. Seltzer and Denney (1980) reported no significant effect of institutionalization on conservation of substance, weight, and volume among a sample of elderly adults. Rubin (1973b), however, reported that a sample of institutionalized males performed significantly less well than noninstitutionalized males on a variety of conservation tasks. But it should be kept in mind that although relatively high levels of conservation performance have been reported among samples of noninstitutionalized older adults (e.g., Chance et al., 1978; Papalia et al., 1980), other research has demonstrated low levels of performance (e.g., Papalia et al., 1973) in *noninstitutionalized* elders. Although it is difficult to draw clear-cut conclusions about conservation performance among the elderly, given the current status of the literature, it appears that at least *some* elders fail at least *some* of these tasks. On the other hand, conservation ability seems largely intact for healthy young and middle-aged adults.

Studies of classification

A number of studies have assessed classification abilities. Classification, or the capacity to sort stimuli, involves tasks in which subjects are instructed to categorize or to sort objects that can be unidimensional or multidimensional, meaningful or meaningless. According to Denney (1974b), "classification is said to be based on *complementary criteria* if the items share some interrelationship either in the subject's past experience or in the experimental situation or based on *similarity criteria* if the items are similar perceptually or functionally" (p. 41). The research reviewed by Denney (1974b) indicated that children tend to sort by using complementary criteria; adults, by using similarity criteria; and the elderly, by using complementary criteria. According to Denney, these differences are due to the lack of educational and occupational pressure to categorize in a particular way, rather than to an underlying loss of ability to classify by similarity criteria. In fact, Denney points out that it may be more "natural" to use complementary criteria to classify, and that classification by use of similarity criteria arises from the demands of formal education and occupation.

When given a free classification situation (e.g., Denney & Lennon, 1972; Denney, 1974a), elderly subjects tend to classify by arranging stimuli in complex designs, whereas young and middle-aged adults classify by similarity. Denney (1974b) argues that this shift is not the result of age-related neural disintegration but is due, rather, to isolation from occupational and educational experience. The significance of such age differences remains unclear, however.

Research has also examined age differences in performance on class inclusion and multiple classification in middle-aged and elderly subjects (e.g., Denney & Cornelius, 1975; Papalia & Bielby, 1974; Storck, Looft, & Hooper, 1972). The results of these studies also indicate that middle-aged adults perform significantly better on both types of tasks compared to the elderly. Again, however, there is little evidence that these age differences reflect actual cognitive disorganization or deterioration. Although these abilities probably peak during adulthood rather than childhood, as would be predicted based on theory, their status in adulthood and old age may be related to differences in health, education, and intelligence.

Considerable age-difference research indicates that young and middle-aged adults outperform the elderly at a variety of Piagetian concrete logical reasoning tasks; however, this apparent regression may be due not to neurological decrement but to occupational, educational, and social factors, as well as to the inherent design problems associated with age-difference research. We take up these issues in the final section of this chapter.

Training studies

Several training studies have been conducted in an attempt to address the possibility of regression being related to environmental factors. The rationale behind such studies is that if intervention improves performance, something in the environment must be affecting performance negatively before training. These interventions can be as simple as providing positive feedback or as complex as rule-based training. Rubin (1976) extended an earlier life-span study by including a continuous quantity training procedure identical to that of Brainerd (1972) and by introducing an extinction procedure. The rationale for the extinction procedure was to extend the earlier investigations of life-span conservation, countersuggestive to the typical quantitative invariance paradigm (e.g., Brainerd, 1972). According to Piaget, conservation, once attained, should not be subject to regression. In addition, the strength and stability of the conservation response should increase with the length of time it has been in the cognitive system. Thus, greater resistance to extinction would be expected among older conservers. The extinction procedure involved giving all participants who produced 12 correct responses on the posttests a subsequent battery of the sample problems with procedural modifications designed to extinguish conservation judgments. The experimenter used a glass identical in size and shape to the standard glasses, but equipped with a 2-cm false bottom. In general, the young adult sample was the most resistant to extinction.

The middle-aged group was more resistant to extinction than either the grade-two children, grade-five children, or institutionalized elderly, and the elderly were more resistant than grade-two and grade-five children. No significant differences were found between the institutionalized and noninstitutionalized elderly subjects. Finally, the extinction response of the noninstitutionalized elderly did not differ significantly from those of the middle-aged sample.

Hornblum and Overton (1976) – who studied the hypothesis that the elderly maintain the ability to solve Piagetian conservation problems and will, in fact, conserve when and if the strategies necessary to conserve are activated – proposed to activate these strategies using a training procedure. In their initial assessment, area and volume conservation abilities were measured in elderly subjects. Those elderly who failed to conserve on at least two tasks included in the initial assessment were provided feedback training, and subsequent performance on a posttest was assessed. Training consisted of a 20-trial procedure that entailed informing participants of the correctness or incorrectness of their responses.

Results indicated that the trained subjects performed significantly better on all near transfer tasks (area conservation) and on four of the five far transfer tasks (volume conservation), suggesting a generalized rather than a specific effect on performance. Interestingly, the control group's performance improved from the pretest to posttest on some of the tasks. This finding may indicate improvement due to practice effects or to self-generation of problem-solving strategies.

Perhaps the most striking result, however, is the ease with which training effects were established. This would suggest the activation of a preexisting cognitive structure – not the creation of a new structures. In addition, training effects persisted during a 6-week posttest period given to a subsample of the subjects.

Denney (1974a) attempted to replicate her earlier findings that the elderly tend to classify geometric objects in a manner similar to young children, and then to provide training (modeling) to those subjects who did not group according to complete similarity. Modeling consisted of having the subjects classify objects by size and shape, following the trainer. Of the 214 subjects aged 35 to 95 years involved in the study, 24 did not initially group according to complete similarity. All of the 24 subjects were nursing-home residents, and they were randomly assigned to the modeling condition or the no-contact control condition. The results indicate greater improvement in the modeling than in the control condition at the first posttest, which occurred immediately after training. When a second posttest with a new set of materials was given immediately after the first, however, the relationship between improvement and the experimental condition was not significant. It would appear that training by means of modeling does not generalize to the classifying of objects beyond those actually used in training. However, caution in generalizing these results is indicated, given the institutionalized nature of the elderly sample being trained.

From the review of the few training studies that have been conducted using Piagetian tasks, training appears to be quite effective even when it consists of fairly simple and brief procedures. But an important unanswered question is, How durable are the training effects over time? All of the training studies using Piagetian tasks have only posttested the subjects immediately or very shortly after training. Thus, no long-term follow-up data have been reported.

Characteristics of formal operational thought

To date there have been only a few studies of formal reasoning during the adult and aging years. As Inhelder and Piaget (1958) point out, however, "this general form of equilibrium (formal operation) can be conceived of as final in the sense that it is not modified during the lifespan of the individual" (Rybash, Hoyer, & Roodin, 1986, p. 19). Thus, the stage of formal operations is of critical importance in the study of cognitive functioning during the adult and aging years because it represents the final stage in the Piagetian cognitive developmental sequence and reflects Piaget's concept of mature cognition. From Piaget's perspective, formal thought does not involve specific behavior, but represents a generalized explicit or implicit *orientation* toward problem solving. The current review addresses not only the characteristics and structures of formal operational thought, but also the results of the research as it relates to formal reasoning among adult populations.

Characteristics and structure of formal operational thought

Hypotheticodeductive reasoning is closely related to the reversal of the roles of reality and possibility, and marks the transition to formal thought. Inhelder and Piaget state that "deduction no longer refers directly to perceived realities but to hypothetical statements – i.e., it refers to propositions which are formulations of hypotheses or which postulate facts or events independently of whether or not they actually occur. Thus, the deductive process consists of linking these assumptions and drawing out the necessary consequences even when their validity, from the standpoint of experimental verification, is only provisional" (Inhelder & Piaget, 1958, p. 251). The elements of such thought are propositions – conceptual rather than physical entities. The content-independence of reasoning in terms of propositions allows one to deduce conclusions from provisionally valid premises (hypotheses) rather than exclusively from facts that have been empirically verified. Brainerd (1978) points out, however, that for deduction to be fully utilized, one must have some way of verifying premises. Thus, the necessity for inductive reasoning exists as well.

Brainerd (1978) also characterizes hypotheticodeductive thought as reasoning that "extends beyond the boundaries of both perception and memory" (p. 205). This view leads to an emphasis on the possible rather than the real, and implies that there are two senses in which this is true (Flavell, 1977); that is, the initial hypothesized theory represents only one of many possible ones, and the empirical reality predicted from or deduced from the theory is itself only a possibility. The return to perception or to memory occurs only when one verifies a theory by seeing whether the existing reality is consistent with the theory, that is, is the predicted one.

The eight concrete operational groupings (four for classes and four for relation) form the structure underlying concrete thought. There are two structural counterparts at the formal level: the combinatorial system of 16 binary propositional operations, and the INRC (identity, negation, reciprocity, correlation) group. These represent *hypothesized* structures inferred from the protocols set forth by Inhelder and Piaget (1958). There is also a logical structure to each of these. The combinatorial system is described by a lattice structure and the four transformations of the INRC group. Psychological behaviors are used to infer the existence of these logical structures.

The 16 elements of the lattice are obtained by taking four binary propositional statements (of conjunction and negation) in all possible combinations. This structure reflects the mental processes of generating hypotheses and arriving at conclusions by deductive reasoning. Note that the combinatorial system provides a *structure* for formal operations as well as a function for the formal thinker in certain problem situations.

For any one of the 16 elements of the combinatorial system there exists an INRC group that relates that propositional combination to others of the system (Brainerd, 1978; Seggie, 1978). The INRC group exhibits the new integrative character of negation and reciprocity, the two reversible operations that functioned independently before this operational period. (This does not apply for the natural number domain.) Also included in this mathematical group are the operations of identity and correlation. The INRC group models cognition in that it describes the ability to "discriminate various direct and opposing operations and to assess their effects vis-à-vis one another" (Flavell, 1963, p. 218). This is the essence of the "systemness" of the INRC group. This model serves as a guiding conceptual framework within which certain types of problems are approached.

Let us examine the adolescent's combinatorial operations and the INRC groups somewhat more closely in order to see what is meant here. The essential difference between adolescent and middle childhood reasoning, and the one most relevant to the lattice structure, is that the adolescent possesses a technique for generating all the possible combinations of variables in any given problem situation. In any four-variable problem (e.g., A, B, C, D) there are 16 distinct possible combinations of the four variables or letters (i.e., AB, AC, AD, etc.). It is this set of all possible combinations that forms a lattice.

For example, in the chemical task the participant is asked to combine four different chemicals and an activating solution to produce a red color. The participant must be able to produce all possible combinations along with the activating solution that will yield the red color. Thus, formal operational thought involves a process of determining all possibilities, then all the actualities, and then the causal structure these actualities imply. As we have noted, adolescent cognition is said also to have an INRC group as well as a lattice structure. Piaget believed that the adolescent's behavior in certain problem situations manifests itself as a mathematical group whose elements consist of four transformations – identity, negation, reciprocal, and correlative – that make up the INRC group. The four transformations of the INRC group can be defined in the following manner: (1) Identity is the "null" transformation and changes nothing in the proposition on which it is performed; (2) negation changes everything in the proposition on which it bears (negation is the inverse operation); (3) reciprocal is a different kind of reversible operational that has the same effect as negation but does it by compensating for an effect by introducing an equal but opposite countereffect; and (4) correlative is simply defined as the product of negation and reciprocal. The formal operational adolescent, besides being able to identify all four, also sees that all the operations are interrelated.

As Seggie (1978) notes, however, many studies indicate that adolescents do not reason logically with the competence that Piaget attributes to them. Lunzer (1965) points to the tenuous connection between the two formal structures in terms of psychological reality, and Flavell (1977) anticipates that Inhelder and Piaget's model will ultimately prove inadequate to any attempts to comprehensively describe formal thought. The model remains, however, a useful starting point for formal operational thought research.

General replication studies

A number of studies of volume conservation, often considered to be an index of formal reasoning, have noted sizable percentages of nonconserving adult subjects (e.g., Elkind, 1962; Graves, 1972; Papalia, 1972; Storck, 1975). Investigations that examine volume conservation performance among elderly adults have typically found that these subjects pass the volume conservation task far less frequently than they do the concrete conservation measures (Eisner, 1973; Papalia, 1972; Papalia, Salverson, & True, 1973b; Storck, Looft, & Hooper, 1972).

Overton and Clayton (1972) compared the performance of four groups of adult women (college coeds, 60- to 69-year-old women, 70- to 79-year-old women, and 70- to 79-year-old women residing in a nursing home) on two measures of formal reasoning: the pendulum task and a derived card-sorting task (an alternative form of the pendulum task). In the pendulum task, the participant has to determine which one or combination of relevant variables (i.e., length, velocity, or weight) affects the arc of the pendulum. Both tasks require the subject to isolate relevant variables in order to solve the problem. A significant age effect on these measures was found: The older women were less successful at solving both formal reasoning tasks. An earlier-appearing concrete logical ability, transitive inference, showed no such age effect. Transitive inference is the most difficult ordering skill, requiring subjects to do part of the ordering "in their heads." In addition to examining the status of formal operational thought, Overton and Clayton also studied the relationship between traditional intelligence measures (the *Raven Progressive Matrices Test* [RPMT] and the verbal subtest of the WAIS) and logical reasoning. For the entire sample, there was a significant overall relationship between the measure of fluid intelligence (RPMT) and both formal operational tasks. This finding reflects a possible relationship between fluid measures of intelligence and formal operational abilities. Comparisons of the oldest age group's place of residence revealed no effect due to institutionalization.

Replications relevant to proportionality

The proportionality scheme typically has been approached in terms of the concept of ratio, although this raises certain questions. One question involves the extent to which ratio and proportion concepts demand the same intellectual ability. Lovell and Butterworth (1966) factor analytically identified a general intellectual ability underlying proportion tasks. They concluded that ratio tasks depend less on this general factor than do proportion tasks.

A second question concerns the format in which tasks are presented or the mode in which subjects' responses are generated. It is possible to present proportion tasks in a concrete manner, as did Lunzer and Pumfrey (1966). They found that the (concrete) rods tasks were much simpler for 6- to 15-year-olds than Inhelder and Piaget's balance task. Steffe and Parr (1968) concluded that children solve many proportionalities presented to them in the form of pictorial data by visual inspection. Items not conducive to such a solution were difficult for fourth- through sixth-graders. Karplus, Karplus, and Wollman (1974) found similar results for the paper clips task.

The metric component of proportion appears to be the aspect of the proportionality scheme that develops during the onset of formal operations. Inhelder and Piaget's (1958) results concerning the proportionality scheme continue to be replicated, if metric proportionality is implied as the criterion for formal level functioning. Karplus and Peterson (1970) and Karplus and Karplus (1972) report that far fewer than half of their eighth-grade subjects used a strategy involving metric proportionality. Their attachment of the "preoperational, concrete, and formal" labels to response types is as yet unsubstantiated, but their results are clearly in the direction of Inhelder and Piaget's results.

Noelting's (1978) work delineates stages in the acquisition of the ability to compare ratios. The abilities attributed to the formal period include dealing with ratios in which two corresponding terms are multiples of each other (e.g., $1:3$ versus $2:5$), and dealing with any arbitrary ratios. The formal strategies include some type of quantification in computational terms (i.e., use of common denominator or percentage). Noelting notes that whereas some tasks involve only concrete data, others involve simplification, equivalence, and retention of constructed data and eventual operation on these data. Tasks that constitute formal reasoning involve comparisons of two derived quantities (ratios) rather than perceptual (visual) comparison of two ratios that involve some common element.

Capon and Kuhn (1979) found that only 32% of adult female shoppers in a supermarket were able to use a proportional reasoning strategy to determine the correct choice when the size ratio involved was a simple one (i.e., $2:3$). Their results support Noelting's finding that there are various levels at which the proportionality scheme can be manifested.

It seems fair to conclude, based on the research reviewed, that there exists significant variability in the level of logical reasoning among adults. Blackburn (1984), however, examined the effects of age, sex, and curriculum on the cognitive performance of 20 college students and 20 college-educated elderly persons. Subjects were given a battery of formal operational tasks that required the use of proportionality abilities, as well as a combinational system. The results revealed a *lack* of significant age differences in any of the measures of formal reasoning. Gender and curriculum were found to be, however, significant predictors of cognitive performance among both cohort groups.

Replications relevant to the probability scheme

Although the probability scheme is linked closely with the scheme of proportionality, it has been directed specifically to the probability scheme and the concept of chance (e.g., Chapman, 1975; Tomlinson-Keasey & Campbell, 1977).

Brainerd (1978) contends that evidence is available to indicate that proportionality and probability are not related. Piaget and Inhelder (1975) indicate that performance is enhanced when memory and language demands are alleviated. Brainerd is not referring, however, to the same performance criteria as Piaget and Inhelder (1975). The tasks may be similar, but the responses involving judgments based on ratios are qualitatively different from responses involving quantification of probability. Lovell (1972) also emphasizes that "metrical proportion in nongeometrical form" and "quantitative probability" (p. 171) are not acquired until the junior high school years. Thus, the replication research remains reconcilable to Piaget and Inhelder's original findings.

Although most of the research on the probability scheme has focused on children's performances, Hawley and Kelley (1973) found a relationship between performances on chemical combinations, *Nassefat's Probability Test*, and *Conservation of Volume Test* with performance on fluid and crystallized intelligence tasks in males aged 25 to 75 years. Interestingly, results of the study indicated that for the high educational males, all correlations between age and Piagetian task performance were nonsignificant. This finding suggests the possible influence of education rather than chronological age on formal reasoning abilities.

Combinatorial reasoning

Empirical evidence suggests that the combinatorial scheme develops at ages 12–16. Although this places acquisition within Inhelder and Piaget's age range for formal operational thought – because the studies were not designed to measure simultaneously combinatorial reasoning and performance on other formal tasks – they lack independent measure of cognitive level. Age remains, therefore, as the only indicator of the level of development.

Studies of the elderly have found that combinatorial reasoning is significantly more difficult for them than other formal tasks (Chap & Sinnott, 1975; Muhs, Papalia, & Hooper, 1976; Storck, 1975). As reported earlier in this chapter, however, Blackburn (1984) did not find support for age differences in difficulty levels within his sample of college-educated young adults and elderly people. Again, education and curriculum may be better predictors of performance than chronological age.

This description of formal operations and review of the literature on formal operations provide a background for the consideration of two main points that are of concern here. It is evident, first of all, that the literature does not establish a relationship between Piaget's theory and formal operation among the elderly, in part because the theory emphasizes development from infancy to adolescence. Second, the literature suggests that formal operational thought is not universal. Issues relating to cognitive development during adulthood and aging have been the focus of a number of recent studies, which have discussed what transpires after the development of adolescent reasoning (e.g., Blackburn, 1984; Papalia, 1972; Papalia et al., 1973b; Sanders et al., 1966; Sanders, Storck, Looft, & Hooper, 1972).

A number of studies have dealt with the importance of experiential factors in the development of formal reasoning beyond adolescence. Blackburn (1984), Flavell (1971), Furth and Youniss (1971), Graves (1972), Piaget (1972), and Sabatini (1979) have emphasized the role of specific experiences, education, and environmental stimulation in bringing about formal operativity. This, in turn, leads to a widening diversity of behavior. In fact, Flavell (1970, 1977) suggests that experiential factors are the *only* really interesting ones in adulthood.

It would appear, therefore, that the attainment of formal operations may be more dependent on environmental experiences than is the case at the earlier developmental levels. Clearly, the exploration of formal operational capacities across the life-span is a viable area for future research, theory, and speculation (Hooper & Sheehan, 1977; Papalia & Bielby, 1974).

The question of universality has been examined by Flavell (1977), who suggests that not everyone may be capable of formal thought, and that the higher the level of development, the less likely is its universal attainment. Neimark (1975) provides a possible reason for this, noting that whereas earlier stages of development are, in effect, forced on a person through those cultural demands described by Bruner (1959), the formal stage represents a "refinement of advanced civilization" and, as such, is not imposed on everyone. This position receives some support from cross-cultural studies, which have shown a recurrent lack of attainment of formal thought within non-Western civilizations (Dasen, 1977; Neimark, 1975). Even in Western cultures, moreover, there appears to be a significant age delay and a lower level of performance on formal tasks, when compared to the predictions of Piaget's theory (Brainerd, 1978; Elkind, 1962; Lovell, 1961; Neimark, 1979; Papalia, 1972). These results suggest that formal thought, as described by Inhelder and Piaget (1958), may not be universally attained, and that where it is attained, acquisition only begins during early adolescence and continues into adulthood.

Related to this is the question of the pervasiveness of formal thought. Theory would appear to predict the emergence of a generalized ability, available for use in and applicable to all situations. Piaget (1972) also suggested, however, that its use may be more *content-specific* than previously thought, and Inhelder has noted that "both adolescents and adults are far from reasoning formally all the time. The attainment of a cognitive stage merely means that the individual becomes capable of behaving in a certain way which was impossible before" (Inhelder, pp. 125–6, in Tanner & Inhelder, 1960). Smedslund (1963) concurs with this position, and suggests that each developmental level describes the optimal performance that can occur during that stage.

The possible specificity of formal operational thought and analysis of the formal operational tasks used by Inhelder and Piaget (1958) also suggest that the instructions used may be a crucial element in determining success on these tasks. For example, an awareness and understanding of the formula for ratio in Smedslund's (1963) study and of volume in Lunzer's (1965) study would seem to be facilitated by, if not to require, formal instruction. Evidence supporting this view was reported by Papalia (1972) and Blackburn (1984). Both studies found a nonsignificant correlation between years of formal schooling and success on Piagetian tasks, but the correlation values increased with higher-level tasks. In addition, Papalia, Salverson, and True (1973b) found that educational attainment was related to performance on *all* the Piagetian tasks administered to a sample of elderly individuals. This finding seems to provide further evidence for the importance of formal instruction, at least at the higher levels of logical thought development. Denney and Cornelius (1975) note, however, that this may reflect the importance of other factors closely related to education (i.e., occupation, social class, memory, and motivation).

Issues in the study of adult cognition using a Piagetian model

There is considerable evidence of differences favoring young and middle-aged adults over the elderly on a variety of Piagetian logical operations tasks. This section considers the factors that affect task performance, and examines some methodological issues involved in the use of Piagetian measures. It also offers suggestions about the direction of future research and, finally, evaluates the usefulness of the Piagetian model for the study of adult cognition.

Specific Piagetian tasks

Research indicates that the particular task used in the study influences our ability to reach conclusions about the status of "Piagetian" abilities among adults and the elderly. On conservation and classification tasks, young and middle-aged adults typically perform quite well, while many elderly demonstrate less than optimal task performance.

There is considerably more variability in performance on formal operations tasks at all adult age levels. A significant proportion of adolescents and adults fail such tasks as volume conservation, proportionality, and combinatorial reasoning, implying that not all adults attain the ability to think formally. Elderly adults generally perform even lower on these formal operations measures than do younger adults, with combinatorial reasoning being significantly more difficult than other formal tasks for the aged. It should be noted, however, that there have been relatively few studies employing formal reasoning measures with adults and the elderly, and that not all formal measures have been used with these age groups.

Individual difference factors

A number of studies indicate that Piagetian task performance among the elderly may be influenced by education and related experiential factors. Thus, in the area of conservation early research reported a moderate correlation between educational attainment and performance, while studies involving educationally, economically, and socially "elite" groups found almost perfect performance on these measures.

The attainment of formal operations appears to be more influenced by experiential factors such as education than are the earlier-developing stages abilities. Thus, while the attainment of these earlier stages may constitute a cultural "requirement," formal operations may be considered as a "refinement of advanced civilization" (Bruner, 1959), and, as such, that is neither required of nor attained by everyone. Blackburn's (1984) finding in the lack of significant age differences between college students and college-educated elderly on a battery of formal measures strongly supports such a position. Significant effects of college curriculum have also been observed, with natural and physical science majors performing at higher levels than social science and humanities majors (Blackburn, 1984).

Gender differences appear to have a minimum effect on earlier-appearing abilities (i.e., conservation). Differences in formal reasoning tend, however, to favor males on a variety of tasks.

Studies assessing the impact of institutionalization have reported differing results, with a number of these studies finding no difference in performance between institutionalized and noninstitutionalized samples. However, studies comparing institutional and noninstitutional samples report poorer performance by the clinical groups (e.g., chronic organic brain syndrome patients) on a variety of tasks including conservation, object permanence, and time concepts.

Methodological issues

Although cross-sectional studies of Piagetian performance, particularly those that employ concrete tasks, suggest that these concepts deteriorate at least among some elderly individuals, one must be cautious in reaching this conclusion. Caution is also recommended concerning those studies involving formal operations, because it would appear that a sizable proportion of adults may never attain these skills. Longitudinal studies are required in order to prove that a particular cognitive ability (either concrete or formal) that was once present actually deteriorates with age. Moreover, the use of cross-sectional data-collection methods tend to confound age differences with cohort effects; that is, the data may reflect the effects of cohort differences rather than true age changes.

Questions may also be raised concerning the appropriateness of using Piagetian tasks that were developed for use with children in studies of adults and the elderly. Are these tasks equally motivating for all ages? Do answers reminiscent of childlike responses signify the same thing for old people as they do for children? Although some elderly may "justify" nonconservation responses by offering prelogical explanations (e.g., "that clay weighs more now because it is longer"), others "fail" such tasks because they may misinterpret or overcomplicate task demands, or because they are responding to the tasks in a reality-oriented way. For example, when an elderly woman was given the traditional conservation of surface area tasks using the same number of cows and barns arranged differently on two fields, her response to the question of whether the cows on the two fields would have the same amount of grass to eat was that "no two fields ever grow grass the same way" (Roberts, Papalia-Finlay, Davis, Blackburn, & Dellman, 1982, p. 190). This type of response reflects a greater complexity in thinking and a more reality-based orientation, rather than the inability to conserve. Future research in this area should attempt to develop and employ flexible clinical methods as part of the assessment procedure in order to determine the precise meanings behind a particular response, as in Piaget's original clinical method. Such an approach would allow for differentiation between a true lack of ability to solve the task, and "failures" due to misinterpretation of task demands or other extraneous factor.

Interpretations of task performance

Perhaps the most intriguing findings in the Piagetian literature of adulthood and aging involves the age difference in performance found on a number of concrete operations tasks. Several explanations have been offered in the attempt to account for the relatively poor performance of elderly individuals on these tasks. As just indicated, methodological concerns may cloud the interpretation of these findings. Other factors that may be involved include neurological decrement and isolation from various experiences.

In a theoretical analysis of logical functioning among the elderly, Hooper, Fitzgerald, and Papalia (1971) predicted that Piagetian abilities would deteriorate as a result of the neurological decrement involved in the aging process. This conclusion was based on the putative similarity in task demands between Piagetian tasks and those fluid intelligence measures which decline during adulthood and old age. Perhaps the most persuasive evidence in support of this interpretation is the hierarchical nature of performance on Piagetian tasks. Thus Papalia (1972) noted that substance, weight, and volume conservation appeared to disintegrate in the reverse of their order of acquisition, a finding that implies an orderliness to decline from the most complex to the least complex tasks.

One useful and intriguing area of future research would involve the relationship between task performance and nearness to death (i.e., terminal drop). It is possible that at least some of the elderly subjects who fail cognitive tasks may be demonstrating a drop in performance prior to death. The apparent orderliness of cognitive decline would appear to support this.

A competing hypothesis is that the low levels of performance are actually due to occupational, social, and educational differences rather than neurological factors. We have noted the relationship between educational attainment and performance. Isolation from various stimulating educational, social, and occupational experiences during old age may well contribute to the lowered levels of performance in the elderly. One source of evidence that favors an experiential interpretation is the success of cognitive training studies. The ease with which training effects in the area of conservation were established by Hornblum and Overton (1976) in a brief 20-trial practice-with-feedback session for training, implies that training may reactivate pre-existing cognitive structures that were not manifest in pretraining performance. This suggests that the lack of stimulation in the environment of the elderly may be an important determinant of cognitive performance. Further research is required to determine which aspects of the environment support the maintenance of Piagetian cognitive abilities in adulthood and aging and which ones promote or encourage deterioration. Related to this is the work of Papalia-Finlay, Blackburn, Davis, Dellmann, and Roberts (1980–1), who found almost perfect conservation performance in a sample of highly educated, healthy elderly women who had adequate income, satisfying leisure activities, and positive attitudes about aging.

Evaluation of the Piagetian model for the study of adult cognition

We have suggested some of the limitations in the use of Piagetian assessment indices with adults and the elderly. This section considers the appropriateness of the Piagetian model for the study of adult cognition.

Piagetian theory defines formal operations as the apex of cognitive development. Piaget's emphasis on the evolution of logical-mathematical thought structures implies, however, a rather limited view of cognition, particularly as it relates to adulthood and aging. Although formal operations generates solutions based on logical analyses, this may represent a realistic approach to cognition for the mature adult who must deal with the pragmatics and ambiguities of daily life. Piaget's model provides few useful insights into how adults solve "real life" personal problems. The intellectual demands of adulthood involve, in many instances, practical problems that require a capacity to accept contradiction, uncertainty, and the relative and changing nature of knowledge. These traits provide the basis for what has come to be known as "postformal thought."

Mature thought involves personalized reasoning and the use of experience to demonstrate wisdom or sound judgment in the attempt to resolve the meaningful but ambiguous problems of everyday life (Dixon & Baltes, 1986). The study of wisdom and of the related dimensions of postformal thought may, in this sense, provide an appropriate and fruitful direction in the study of adult cognition.

References

Ajuriaguerra, J. de, & Angelergues, R. (1960). Les apraxies; variétés cliniques et lateralisation lésionnelle. *Revue neurologique, 102*, 566–594.

Ajuriaguerra, J. de, Boehme, M., Richard, J., Sinclair, H., & Tissot, R. (1967). Désintégration des notions de temps dans les démences désintératives du grand age. *Encéphale, 5*, 438–485.

Ajuriaguerra, J. de, & Hécaen, H. (1960). *Le cortex cérébral*. Paris: Masson.

Ajuriaguerra, J. de, Muller, M., & Tissot, R. (1960). A propos de quelques problèmes posés par l'apraxie dans les démences. *Encéphale, 5*, 375–401.

Ajuriaguerra, J. de, Rey-Belley-Muller, M., & Tissot, R. (1964). A propos de quelques problèmes posés par le déficit opératoire des vieillards atteints de démence désintégrative en début d'évolution. *Cortex, 1*, 103–132, 232–256.

Ajuriaguerra, J. de, Richard, J., Rodriquez, R., & Tissot, R. (1966). Quelques aspects de la désintégration des praxies ideomatricas dans les démences du grand age. *Le cortex cérébral, 2*, 438–462.

Annett, M. (1959). The classification of instances of four common class concepts by children and adults. *British Journal of Educational Psychology, 29*, 223–236.

Blackburn, J. A. (1984). The influence of personality, curriculum, and memory correlates on formal reasoning in young adults and elderly persons. *Journal of Gerontology, 39*, 207–209.

Brainerd, C. J. (1972). Reinforcement and reversibility in quantity conservation acquisition. *Psychonomic Science, 27*, 114–116.

Brainerd, C. J. (1978). *Piaget's theory of intelligence*. Englewood Cliffs, NJ: Prentice-Hall.

Bruner, J. S. (1959). A psychologist's viewpoint. [Review of *The growth of logical thinking*]. *British Journal of Psychology, 50*, 363–370.

Capon, N., & Kuhn, D. (1979). Logical reasoning in the supermarket: Adult females' use of proportional reasoning strategy in an everyday context. *Developmental Psychology, 15*(4), 450–452.

Chance, J., Overcast, T., & Dollinger, S. J. (1978). Aging and cognitive regression: Contrary findings. *Journal of Psychology, 98*, 177–183.

Chap, J., & Sinnott, J. (1975). *Performance of old persons on Piaget's tasks.* Unpublished manuscript, the Catholic University of America, Washington, DC.

Chapman, R. H. (1975). The development of children's understanding of proportions. *Child Development, 46,* 141–148.

Clayton, V., & Overton, W. F. (1973). *The role of formal operational thought in the aging process.* Paper presented at the meeting of the Gerontological Society, Miami, FL. (Cited in Papalia & Bielby, 1974, and Hooper & Sheehan, 1977, as Overton & Clayton, unpublished manuscript, 1972.)

Dasen, P. R. (1977). *Piagetian psychology: Cross-cultural contributions.* New York: Wiley.

Denney, N. W. (1974a). Classification abilities in the elderly. *Journal of Gerontology, 29,* 309–314.

Denney, N. W. (1974b). Evidence for developmental changes in categorization criteria for children and adults. *Human Development, 17,* 41–53.

Denney, N. W. (1980). The effect of manipulation of peripheral, noncognitive variables on problem-solving performance of the elderly. *Human Development, 23,* 268–277.

Denney, N. W., & Cornelius, S. W. (1975). Class inclusion and multiple classification in middle and old age. *Developmental Psychology, 11,* 521–522.

Denney, N. W., & Lennon, M. L. (1972). Classification: A comparison of middle and old age. *Developmental Psychology, 7,* 210–213.

Dixon, R. A., & Baltes, R. B. (1986). Toward life-span research in the functions and pragmatics of intelligence. In J. R. Sternberg & R. K. Wagner (Eds.), *Practical intelligence: Nature and origins of competence in the everyday world* (pp. 203–234). New York: Cambridge University Press.

Eisner, D. (1973). *The effect of chronic brain syndrome upon concrete and formal operations in elderly men.* Unpublished manuscript. (Cited in Papalia & Bielby, 1974.)

Elkind, D. (1962). Quantity conceptions in college students. *Journal of Social Psychology, 57,* 459–465.

Flavell, J. H. (1963). *The developmental psychology of Jean Piaget.* Princeton, NJ: Van Nostrand.

Flavell, J. H. (1970). Cognitive changes in adulthood. In L. R. Goulet & P. B. Baltes (Eds.), *Life-span developmental psychology* (pp. 247–253). New York: Academic Press.

Flavell, J. H. (1971). Stage-related properties of cognitive development. *Cognitive Psychology, 2,* 421–453.

Flavell, J. H. (1977). *Cognitive development.* Englewood Cliffs, NJ: Prentice-Hall.

Furth, E. G., & Youniss, J. (1971). Formal operation and language: A comparison of deaf and hearing adolescents. *International Journal of Psychology, 6,* 49–64.

Gallagher, J. McC., & Reid, D. K. (1978). An empirical test of judgments and explanations in Piagetian-type problems of conservation of continuous quantity. *Journal of Perceptual and Motor Skills, 46,* 363–368.

Graves, A. J. (1972). Attainment of conservation of mass, weight, and volume in minimally educated adults. *Developmental Psychology, 1,* 223.

Hawley, I., & Kelly, F. (1973, November). *Formal operations as a function of age, education and fluid and crystallized intelligence.* Paper presented at the Annual Meeting of the Gerontological Society, Miami, FL.

Hiemark, E. D. (1975). Intellectual development during adolescence. In F. D. Horowitz (Ed.), *Review of child development research* (Vol. 4, pp. 541–594). Chicago: University of Chicago Press.

Hooper, F. H., Fitzgerald, J., & Papalia, D. E. (1971). Piagetian theory and the aging process: Extensions and speculations. *Aging and Human Development, 2,* 3–20.

Hooper, F. H., & Sheehan, N. W. (1977). Logical concept attainment during the aging years: Issues in the neo-Piagetian literature. In W. F. Overton & J. M. Gallagher (Eds.), *Knowledge and development: Vol. 1. Advances in research and theory* (pp. 205–253). New York: Plenum.

Hornblum, J. N., & Overton, W. F. (1976). Area and volume conservation among the elderly: Assessment and training. *Developmental Psychology, 12,* 68–74.

Inhelder, B., & Piaget, J. (1958). *The growth of logical thinking from childhood to adolescence.* New York: Basic Books.

Karplus, E. F., Karplus, R., & Wollman, W. (1974). Intellectual development beyond elementary school. IV. Ratio: The influence of cognitive style. *School Science and Mathematics, 74,* 476–482.

Karplus, R., & Karplus, E. F. (1972). Intellectual development beyond elementary school. III. Ratio: A longitudinal study. *School Science and Mathematics, 72,* 735–742.

Karplus, R., & Peterson, R. (1970). Intellectual development beyond elementary school. II. Ration: A survey. *School Science and Mathematics, 70,* 813–820.

Kominski, C., & Coppinger, N. (1968). *The Müller-Lyer illusion and Piaget's test for the conservation of space in a group of older institutionalized veterans.* Unpublished manuscript.

Lovell, K. (1961). A follow-up study of Inhelder and Piaget's *The growth of logical thinking. British Journal of Psychology, 52,* 143–153.

Lovell, K. (1972). Intellectual growth and understanding mathematics. *Journal for Research in Mathematics Education, 3,* 164–182.

Lovell, K., & Butterworth, L. B. (1966). Abilities underlying the understanding of proportionality. *Mathematics Teaching, 35,* 5–9.

Lunzer, E. A. (1965). Problems of formal reasoning in test simulations. In P. H. Mussen (Ed.), European research in cognitive development (pp. 19–46). *Monographs of the Society for Research in Child Development, 30*(2, Whole No. 100).

Lunzer, E. A., & Pumfrey, P. D. (1966). Understanding personality. *Mathematics Teaching, 34,* 7–12.

Muhs, P., Papalia, D., & Hooper, F. (1976). *An initial analysis of cognitive functioning across the life-span: Final research report.* University of Wisconsin Agricultural Experiment Research Project (Hatch) No. 142–1857. Madison, WI: Child and Family Studies Program.

Neimark, E. D. (1975). Intellectual development during adolescence. In F. D. Horowitz (Ed.), *Review of child development research* (Vol. 4, pp. 541–595). Chicago: University of Chicago Press.

Neimark, E. D. (1979). Current status of formal operations research. *Human Development, 32,* 60–67.

Noelting, G. (1978). *Constructivism as a model for cognitive development and (eventually) learning. The development of proportional reasoning in the child and adolescent.* Unpublished manuscript.

Overton, W., & Clayton, V. (1972). *The role of formal operational thought in the aging process.* Unpublished manuscript, State University of New York, Buffalo.

Papalia, D. E. (1972). The status of several conservation abilities across the life-span. *Human Development, 15,* 229–243.

Papalia, D. E., & Bielby, D.D.V. (1974). Cognitive functioning in middle and old age adults: A review of research based on Piaget's theory. *Human Development, 17,* 424–443.

Papalia, D. E., Kennedy, E., & Sheehan, N. (1973a). Conservation of space in non-institutionalized old people. *Journal of Psychology, 84,* 75–79.

Papalia, D. E., Salverson, S., & True, M. (1973b). An evaluation of quantity conservation performance during old age. *International Journal of Aging and Human Development, 4,* 103–109.

Papalia-Finlay, D., Blackburn, J., Davis, E., Dellmann, M., & Roberts, P. (1980). Training cognitive functioning in the elderly – inability to replicate previous findings. *International Journal of Aging and Human Development, 12,* 111–117.

Piaget, J. (1972). Intellectual evolution from adolescence to adulthood. *Human Development, 15,* 1–12.

Piaget, J., & Inhelder, B. (1958). *The origin of the idea of chance in children.* (L. Leake, P.

Burrell, & H. D. Fishbein, Trans.). New York: Norton. (Original work published 1951.)

Riegel, K. (1973). Dialectic operations: The final period of cognitive development. *Human Development, 16,* 346–370.

Roberts, P., Papilia-Finlay, D., Davis, E., Blackburn, J. A., & Dellmann, M. (1982). No two fields ever grow grass the same way: Assessment of conservation abilities in the elderly. *International Journal of Aging and Human Development, 15,* 185–195.

Rubin, K. [H.] (1973). Egocentrism in childhood: A unitary construct? *Child Development, 44,* 102–110.

Rubin, K. H. (1976). Extinction of conservation: A life-span investigation. *Developmental Psychology, 12,* 51–56.

Rubin, K. H., Attewell, P., Tierney, M., & Tumulo, P. (1973). The development of spatial egocentrism and conservation across the life-span. *Developmental Psychology, 9,* 432.

Rybash, J. M., Hoyer, W. J., & Roodin, P. A. (1986). *Adult cognition and aging: Developmental changes in processing, knowing and thinking.* New York: Pergamon Press.

Sabatini, P. (1979). *Age and professional specialization in formal reasoning.* Unpublished dissertation, Wayne State University, Detroit.

Sanders, S., Laurendeau, M., & Bergeron, J. (1966). Aging and the concept of space: The conservation of surfaces. *Journal of Gerontology, 21,* 281–286.

Seggie, J. L. (1978). Formal operational thought. In J. A. Keats, K. F. Collis, & G. S. Halford (Eds.), *Cognitive development: Research based on a neo-Piagetian approach.* New York: Wiley.

Selzer, S. C., & Denney, N. W. (1980). Conservation abilities in middle-aged and elderly adults. *International Journal of Aging and Human Development, 11,* 135–146.

Sinclair-de-Zwart, H., Ajuriaguerra, J. de, Boehme, M., & Tissot, R. (1966). Quelques aspects de la désintégration des notions de temps a travers des épreuves morphosyntaxiques de langage et a travers des épreuves opératoires chez des vieillards atteints de dégénérative. *Bulletin de Psychologie, 247,* 8–12, 745–751.

Smedslund, J. (1963). The concept of correlation in adults. *Scandinavian Journal of Psychology, 4,* 165–173.

Steffe, L. P., & Parr, R. B. (1968). *The development of the concepts of ratio and fraction in the fourth, fifth and sixth years of elementary school.* (Technical Report No. 49). Madison: Wisconsin Research and Development Center for Cognitive Learning, March.

Storck, P. A. (1975). *The status of logical thought: Stability or regression?* Paper presented at the Society for Research in Child Development Biennial Meeting, Denver.

Storck, P. A., Looft, W. R., & Hooper, F. H. (1972). Interrelationships among Piagetian tasks and traditional measures of cognitive abilities in mature and aged adults. *Journal of Gerontology, 27,* 461–465.

Tanner, J. M., & Inhelder, B. (Eds.). (1960). *Discussion on child development* (Vol. 4). New York: International University Press.

Tomlinson-Keasey, C., & Campbell, T. (1977). *Formal operational assessments.* Unpublished test battery, University of California, Riverside.

6   Neo-Piagetian theories of child development

Robbie Case

I. Classical theories of intellectual development and their philosophic underpinnings

Classical theories of intellectual development may be divided into three broad categories, as a function of the assumptions they make regarding human knowledge.

Theories based on British empiricism

In the first category are theories whose roots lie in the writings of the British philosophers Locke and Hume. According to these authors, the process of knowledge acquisition is one in which the sensory organs first detect stimuli in the external world, and the mind then detects the customary patterns or "conjunctions" in these stimuli. Because Locke and Hume located the source of human knowledge in the empirical world, their position is often referred to as *empiricist*. Developmental psychologists who have accepted the empiricist view have tended to see the study of intellectual development as one whose object is to chart the child's increasing ability to discriminate or encode various classes of empirical stimuli (perceptual learning), to induce the correlations or associations among them (cognitive learning), and to access and use the resultant knowledge in other contexts or situations (transfer).

A wide range of theories have resulted from pursuing these objectives, including Gibson's (1969) theory of perceptual learning, behaviorist and neobehaviorist theories of cognitive learning (e.g., Gagné, 1968; Kendler, 1963), and the more recent information-processing theories, including those that draw their inspiration from classical psychometrics (Sternberg, 1984), as well as those inspired by classical learning theory (Klahr & Wallace, 1976; Rumelhart & McLelland, 1987; Siegler & Jenkins, 1989). While they differ

This chapter was prepared with support provided by the Spencer Foundation, whose assistance is gratefully acknowledged. I am indebted to Marc Lewis and Robert Sternberg for comments on an earlier draft.

161

in many respects, these theories share fundamental assumptions about knowledge and the knowing process. As a result, they also share a general view of knowledge acquisition in young children and in the scientific community.[1] Finally, they are united in their view that cumulative learning and development are essentially equivalent.

Theories based on Continental rationalism

The second class of theories are those with their roots in the writings of Continental philosophers such as Decartes and Kant. In reaction to Locke and Hume, Kant suggested that knowledge is acquired by a process in which order is imposed on sensory data by the human faculty of reason, not merely detected in these data. Because he located the source of human knowledge in the activity of human reason, Kant's position is often referred to as a *rationalist* one. Developmental psychologists who have accepted the rationalist positon have tended to assume that the study of intellectual development should entail an elucidation of the order-imposing framework (structure) with which children's minds come equipped at birth, and any changes that may take place in this structure with age. Once again, a reasonably wide variety of theories have been premised on these assumptions, including the biological-recapitulationist theory of J. M. Baldwin, the constructivist theory of Jean Piaget, and the nativist theory of Noam Chomsky. More recent theories in this tradition include the neo-nativist theories of Carey (1985) and Spelke (1988), and certain of the neo-Piagetian theories reviewed in this chapter.

Once again, in spite of their considerable differences, the foregoing theories share a number of assumptions. One particularly important assumption is that development does not take place by a process that is equivalent to cumulative learning. Cumulative learning is presumed to lead to a growing body of "data," "facts," or "empirical generalizations." By contrast, development is presumed to lead to a restructuring of the rational framework by means of which facts are gathered and interpreted. This is presumed to be true both for young children and for the scientific community, both of whom are seen as being engaged in essentially the same endeavor, namely, constructing a model of the world around them.

Theories based on social and historical analyses

The third category of developmental theory has its roots in the writings of Hegel and Marx. According to these authors, knowledge and thought always evolve in a *social* and *historical context*, and cannot be understood without reference to the dynamic tensions that are inherent in that context. For this reason, their view of knowledge is often referred to as a *sociohistoric* one. Psychologists who have accepted this view have tended to assume that the study of intellectual development should entail an elucidation of the social and physical contexts in which human cultures find themselves, the social and intellectual tools they have developed over the years for coping with these contexts, and the social institutions by means of which these tools are passed on from one generation to the next. The theories of Vygotsky (1962) and Bruner (1966, 1989) are the best-known examples in this tradition, although the more recent writings of Cole and Scribner (1974), Olson (1986a), and Lave (1988) belong in the same general category.

Theorists in the sociohistoric tradition also offer a distinctive view of not just the young child's intellectual competences and practices but those of the scientific community as well. Also, they are much more likely to search for universal laws in the relationship between a culture's institutions and the linguistic or intellectual patterns of its members than between such internally referenced variables as "learning" or "development" (McDermott, 1990).

Dialogue among the three traditions

In recent years, there has been a growing spirit of dialogue among the three major developmental traditions, and a sense that the assumptions that underlie their efforts must somehow be integrated. At the same time, however, the particular forms of integration that have been proposed continue to bear the stamp of one particular tradition or another: normally the one that the individual proposing the integration has inherited.

Perhaps nowhere is this trend more apparent than in the rationalist tradition, where an unbroken line may be traced from the earliest writings of James Mark Baldwin (1894), through the more widely known work of Jean Piaget (1962, 1970), to the work of contemporary neo-Piagetian theorists. A detailed chronicle of this progression has been presented elsewhere (Case, 1985, chs. 2–4). For the purpose of the present chapter, what is important is the most recent events that have taken place, as the classical Piagetian theory that was described in Chapters 4 and 5 has been subjected to critiques by scholars from the other two traditions.

II.   The origins of neo-Piagetian theory

Essential elements of the classical Piagetian system

As the preceding two chapters have made clear, Piaget's view of child development was primarily a rationalist one, notwithstanding the sociohistoric influences. In effect, Piaget viewed the child as a young scientist, constructing ever more powerful theories of the world, as a result of applying a set of logical structures of increasing generality and power. Beginning with his wartime lectures, and continuing for the next 15 or 20 years, Piaget attempted to specify the nature of these logical structures, as well as the processes by which they are acquired and the knowledge of the world to which they give rise. By and large, these structures were construed as systems of internal operations, which remain invariant in the face of considerable differences in surface content and cultural milieu, and which have an underlying coherence and stability. The formalism Piaget used to represent these systems was drawn from symbolic logic, and the operational systems themselves were said to result from "logico-mathematical experience," that is, the experience of reflecting on one's own mental operations, and abstracting the underlying logical and mathematical structure these operations entail.

Piaget's theory had a number of important strengths that made it attractive to investigators in all three of the classical developmental traditions. One of its strengths was its vision of young children as active constructors and testers of their own knowledge. This view seemed much more congruent with the actual behavior of young children than that provided by the empiricist model of a "blank slate" on which empirical data were simply "written." Another strength was the theory's broad and coherent view of young children, which had a high degree of heuristic and explanatory power. Among the data to whose discovery the theory led (and for which it also provided a coherent and parsimonious explanation), were the following: (1) Many sequences of intellectual development – particularly those dealing with the concepts enumerated by Kant as being fundamental to human reason, namely, time, space, quantity, and causality – appear to be universal, both within and across cultures. (2) Children cannot solve a wide variety of problems in these domains, often ones that appear quite elementary and even trivial to adults, until a surprisingly late age. (3) Training children to solve these problems is a difficult endeavor, when it is possible at all. (4) A wide range of these problems appear to be solved spontaneously (i.e., without formal training) during middle childhood.

Critiques of the classic Piagetian system

After its importation to North America (Flavell, 1963; Hunt, 1961), Piaget's theory received a good deal of attention, and induced a flurry of controversy. A good deal of this controversy resulted not from the specifics of the theory but from the underlying assumptions about knowledge on which it was based, and the general type of research to which these assumptions gave rise. As empiricists were quick to point out, Piaget's theory was both formulated and presented in a way that made it difficult to test in any straightforward empirical fashion (Brainerd, 1978; Flavell, 1963). Moreover, to the extent that it *could* be tested, it revealed data that were not easily reconciled with its underlying claims. These data included (1) the local success of many short-term training studies on Piagetian tasks, that is, successes that exerted an impact on one class of task without affecting any other task that was supposed to be "structurally related" (Gelman, 1969); (2) the apparent "unevenness" of children's intellectual development when measured across different tasks, contexts, or domains (Beilin, 1971); and (3) individual differences in the order of task acquisition, which gave rise to low correlations among tasks that were supposedly dependent on the same underlying structure (Pinard & Laurendeau, 1969). Note that all three data raise questions about the same aspect of the Piagetian system, namely, the hypothesis that there are general logical structures, which are relatively insensitive to environmental or contextual factors, and which emerge as a result of the operation of a set of endogenous or "autoregulative" processes. It was to the hypothesis that such structures exist and determine the nature of children's learning that empiricist scholars had the strongest objection.

The problems pointed out by empiricists were not the only ones with which Piagetian theory had to contend. Even scholars who accepted the basic assumptions about knowledge and its acquisition on which Piaget's theory had been premised expressed dissatisfaction with certain aspects of the theory – aspects that seemed unclear, incomplete, or inconsistent. Of particular concern were (1) the absence of a detailed treatment of stage transition, that is, the mechanism by which children replace early forms of logico-mathematical structure with more powerful ones (Pascual-Leone, 1969); (2) the absence of any account of individual differences in the developmental process (Pascual-Leone, 1969); and (3) the absence of any treatment of factors such as affect or perception in influencing the direction of children's thought (Beilin, 1971; Pascual-Leone, 1969).[2] On purely rational grounds, it seemed clear that these lacunae in the theory would have to be filled in, if a fully satisfactory account of development was to be provided.

A final group of problems was pointed out by investigators in the socio-historical tradition. One was that the theory provided no explanation for differences in the rate or terminal level of children's performance on Piagetian tasks between Western and non-Western cultures (Dasen, 1972). Another was that the theory provided no means of describing the alternative forms of reasoning such cultures appear to apply to these tasks in adulthood (Bruner, 1966; Greenfield, 1966). The theory also failed to provide a satisfactory means of characterizing new intellectual structures that might emerge in the life of a culture, during particular historical epochs (Keating, 1980; Olson, 1986b). Finally, the theory provided no explanation of developmental changes in thinking that take place within a particular culture, as a result of differential exposure to such institutions as formal schooling (Bruner, 1966; Cole & Scribner 1974; Olson, 1986a). In general, then, when seen from a sociohistorical perspective, the view of development that Piaget's theory painted was too universal, too static, and too focused on the individual rather than on the cultural institutions in which the individual's life is embedded.

Response of neo-Piagetian theorists

Neo-Piagetian theory was born in response to these three general categories of criticism, that is, to the criticisms raised by empiricist, rationalist, and sociohistoric scholars. What neo-Piagetian theorists attempted was (1) to *preserve* those aspects of Piagetian theory which give it its breadth, coherence, and explanatory power; (2) to *develop* further those aspects of the theory that seemed incomplete; and (3) to *alter* those aspects of the theory that made it difficult to operationalize empirically or suggested that a growing child is insensitive to its physical or cultural environment.

Different neo-Piagetian theorists, of course, made different decisions regarding which elements of Piaget's theory to retain, which to develop further, and which to alter. (See Biggs & Collis, 1982; Case, 1978, 1985; Fischer, 1980; Fischer & Ferrar, 1988; Halford, 1982, 1988; Demetriou & Efklides, 1988; Mounoud, 1986; Pascual-Leone, 1970, 1988a.) Nevertheless, there was a good deal of commonality in the general directions they pursued. Thus, after 20 years of further writing and research, it is now possible to specify a set of postulates on which neo-Piagetian theorists are generally agreed.

III. Core postulates of neo-Piagetian theory

A. Postulates retained from the classic Piagetian system

The following traditional Piagetian postulates have been retained by most neo-Piagetian theorists in developing more modern systems of their own:

1. Importance of children's cognitive structures. Children do not simply "observe" the world around them and note its regularities. Rather, they actively assimilate the world to their existing cognitive structures.

2. Role of child's own activity in creating such structures. Children's cognitive structures at any age are not merely a product of their empirical experience. They are a product of the children's attempts to organize that experience in a coherent fashion.

3. Universal sequence of structural levels. Three or four general levels of cognitive structure can be identified in children's intellectual development. Although different neo-Piagetian theorists label and analyze these structures somewhat differently, they all agree there is a preliminary stage in which sensorimotor structures predominate, followed by two or three further stages in which children's intellectual structures become increasingly symbolic and abstract.

4. Hierarchical inclusion of earlier structures in later ones. The increasingly abstract structures of later stages build on, and yet transform, those of earlier stages. Thus, for example, the higher-order conservation concepts possessed by elementary school children, although they are qualitatively different from those possessed by infants (Mounoud & Bower, 1974; Starkey, Spelke, & Gelman, 1983), are not unrelated to them. Rather, they are based on these concepts and constitute a higher-order "reworking" of them.

5. Characteristic ages for acquisition of structures at different levels. The final assumption that has been retained from Piaget's theory is that a characteristic age range may be identified for the acquisition of structures at any of the major levels specified by the theory, providing that subjects are exposed to what might be termed an "optimal environment."

B. Postulates that extend the classic Piagetian system

1. Development and learning distinguished. In the classic Piagetian system, development is said to involve a transformation or "accommodation" of a child's existing structural framework, while learning is said to involve the assimilation of new content to an existing structural framework. Virtually all neo-Piagetian theorists have maintained some sort of distinction of this sort and have sought to explicate in greater detail the processes that underlie each form of change. Thus, for example, Fischer (1980) has distinguished the process of "intercoordination," which is subject to very strong developmental constraints, and which can lead to a major change in children's level of cognitive functioning, from processes such as differentiation, refocusing, and chaining, which are not subject to such strong developmental constraints, and which lead to a greater degree of elaboration or complexity within an existing cognitive level.

Pascual-Leone (1969, 1988a) has focused on the different ways in which attention is involved in these two general classes of transformation. When they are engaged in major structural reorganization, Pascual-Leone suggests, children must actively inhibit the application of a current logical structure while bringing a new set of schemes to full activation by mental effort and coordinating them. (This is called LM-learning.) In the second type of structural change, children may repeatedly apply an existing logical structure to a variety of situations, thus causing the existing structure to differentiate and incorporate new "cues" in its releasing component. (This is called LC-learning.)   LC = assim.

Finally, in the context of my own system (Case, 1985), a distinction is made between processes such as problem solving and exploration, on the one hand – which lead to the intercoordination of new structures via the active and effortful mediation of attention – and processes such as consolidation and automization, on the other, which lead to the formation of stronger associations or cues among existing structural units. It is suggested that – in stage transition – the initial change in a child's structure for dealing with a situation normally occurs via one of the first two processes, but that change continues to take place via one of the second two processes after a new structure is formed, as the child attempts to determine the range of situations to which it can be applied. The net result of engaging in these two categories of activity is a smoothly functioning new structure, which has a wide range of applicability and takes a minimum of attention to activate. Once this sort of automatic functioning is attained, the stage is set for further episodes of problem solving or exploration – which may be socially mediated or independent – and for further stage (or substage) transitions.

To the reader who is unfamiliar with neo-Piagetian theory, these various distinctions may seem rather complicated and hard to follow. It is hoped, however, that the details of the various proposals will not obscure the following simple points; (1) All the proposals take off from Piaget's original distinction between development and learning in some fashion (see also Halford, 1982; Mounoud, 1986); (2) all the proposals use this distinction in some fashion to provide a more detailed account of the stage transition process; and (3) although the various proposals are different, they are not incompatible but are complementary (see Case, 1988a, for an elaboration of this point).

2. *Developmental restructuring presumed local in nature.* A second neo-Piagetian notion that involves an extension of the classic Piagetian position is actually one on which Piaget's position evolved over the years. In his best-known work, which was done in his middle years, Piaget spoke of the processes of structural transformation as though they operated on the entire system of structures in the child's repertoire (the structure-of-the-whole). In his later work, however, he preferred the notion that such processes operate on one particular class or subgroup of such structures at a time, in a dynamic fashion (Piaget, 1985). It is this latter position that has been adopted by neo-Piagetian theorists. Thus, whether they characterize the process of

development as one that entails the intercoordination of lower-level skills (Fischer,1980), attentional (LM) learning (Pascual-Leone, 1988a), or problem solving and exploration (Case, 1985), all contemporary neo-Piagetian theorists are explicit that the processes driving these activities act on one local structure or set of structures at a time, not on the child's entire structural repertoire. They also all provide specific examples, worked out in considerable detail, of how these processes actually take place as the child encounters particular sets of experiences and reflects on them.

There is an important corollary to this position. As long as development is seen as occurring in the structure-of-the-whole, then the expectation is that individual children should be at the same level of functioning across the entire range of tasks one might care to expose them to. Once one sees structural change as taking place in a more local and focused fashion, however, it becomes possible to understand how a child might be at quite different levels, in different structural domains. Thus, the existence of *décalage* poses a much less serious theoretical problem in the context of neo-Piagetian theory than in the classical Piagetian system.[3]

3. Cyclic recapitulation of structural sequences hypothesized. A third notion of Piaget's that neo-Piagetian theorists have attempted to extend is the idea that there is a cyclic recursion through substages at each general stage or level of development. Once again, although this notion does exist within the classic Piagetian system (where it goes by the name of "vertical displacement" or "vertical *décalage*"), it is relatively undeveloped. In the context of most neo-Piagetian theories, however, the notion has been considerably strengthened, and is stated in a much more stringent form. The more modern assertion is that there is a progression through exactly the same *number* of structural steps at each major stage, and that these steps are traversed in exactly the same *sequence* (Biggs & Collis, 1982; Case 1978, 1985; Fischer, 1980; Mounoud, 1986).

4. Affective and cognitive structures related. There is a final assumption in this group on which there is increasing, although not yet universal, agreement among neo-Piagetian theorists. This is that children's affective development and their cognitive development are closely intertwined. In particular, it is assumed that the complexity of children's socioemotional structures – that is, structures that evolve in the context of interaction with significant others such as the primary caretaker – are subject to the same general developmental constraints as all other structures, and thus follow the same epigenetic timetable. Piaget (1981) made this same general assumption.[4] What distinguishes the work of neo-Piagetian theorists, however, is their attempt to provide a more detailed model of socioemotional functioning, and its role in the overall developmental process.

C. Postulates that alter the classic Piagetian system

[handwritten: CHANGED]

The final group of neo-Piagetian postulates require a genuine alteration, rather than a simple extension, of the classic Piagetian system.

1. Cognitive structures redefined. In most neo-Piagetian systems, children's cognitive structures are not defined or described in terms that involve symbolic logic. Rather, they are defined in terms of their form, their complexity, and their levels of hierarchical integration. Because children's structures are defined in this more general fashion, it becomes possible to suggest that the constraints they entail apply across a broader range of children's behavior. Thus, for example, children's motor activity and their language also become targets for structural analysis (Body, 1977; Johnson, Fabian, & Pascual-Leone, 1989; Reid, in press; Todor, 1979).

[handwritten margin note: Extend stages; broader + more domains]

2. Shifting upper limit on complexity of cognitive structures postulated. There is a potential contradiction between two groups of postulates mentioned so far; namely, those dealing with generality and those dealing with specificity. On the one hand, the new forms of structural analysis that have been proposed are more broadly applicable than Piaget's, and thus more general. They also yield very similar age norms to those that Piaget proposed across a wider range of domains. On the other hand, the processes of structural transformation are held to apply more locally, and thus to yield considerable unevenness or "displacement" in children's measured level of development. How can development simultaneously be more general and more specific than Piaget's system implies? Stated differently, if the processes of structural transformation are of genuinely local applicability, why is there any typical age of acquisition across different sorts of cognitive structure at all?

The answer to this question is that a distinction is made in neo-Piagetian theory between the general processes that *constrain* and *potentiate* development and the more specific processes of structural acquisition that operate *within* these general constraints and potentials. Although the processes of structural transformation mentioned so far do operate quite locally, and thus do give rise to considerable variation in measured developmental level, there is an upper limit to the amount of this variation which is possible. Following the lead of Pascual-Leone (1969) or McLaughlin (1963), most neo-Piagetian theorists assume that this upper limit is closely linked to the size of children's attentional capacity, or "working memory."[5] They also assume that a lower limit is set by the fact that certain aspects of children's experience are virtually universal (e.g., exposure to some form of caretaker, to some form of language, to some form of motor opportunity, and to some form of cultural training). It is these upper and lower "boundary conditions," then, and not the environmentally sensitive stage transition

[handwritten margin note: Consider variability w/in structures; w/an upper limit]

processes themselves, that neo-Piagetian theorists believe constrain the ages at which certain prototypic structures are characteristically observed.

3. Role of maturation in determining upper limit hypothesized. A third postulate in this group is that specifiable biological factors regulate the gradual shift in this upper limit with age. Although different theorists have modeled these biological factors in different fashions, their proposals are by and large complementary, and quite unified in the overall view they provide. (See, for example, Case, 1985, ch. 17, in press[b]; Fischer, 1987; Mounoud, 1986; Pascual-Leone, 1974, 1989a,b.)

4. Importance of individual differences stressed. A fourth postulate is that individual differences must be taken into account, both in modeling the process of structural transformation (Pascual-Leone, 1974) and in modeling the ease with which different subjects can apply their existing structures within particular domains (Case & Griffin, 1990; Demetriou, 1988).[6] As a result, different individuals may often follow different developmental "micro-pathways" (Fischer & Knight, in press; Hoppe-Graff, 1989).

5. Content of high-level structures asserted to be cultural in origin. Finally, because children's structures are no longer defined in terms that are logical or mathematical in nature (see postulate C-1), the structures of Western logical and mathematical thought lose their primacy in the context of neo-Piagetian theory. This shift in conceptualization has a number of rather far-reaching consequences. One implication is that the formal structures of Western science and mathematics (e.g., those structures that involve the partitioning of the world into variables, which can then be systematically manipulated and controlled), can be seen as cultural inventions, not as universals. Another implication is that other structures, such as those involved in the visual arts or in social analysis, can be seen as playing a role in the development of high-level Western thought that is just as important as that played by structures of a logical and mathematical nature. A third implication is that sociocultural processes and institutions can be seen as playing a vital role in promoting children's intellectual development, at all stages. Finally, a fourth implication is that there may be high-level intellectual structures in non-Western cultures that are different from, yet every bit as sophisticated as, those structures that have evolved in the West.

D. Other postulates

All neo-Piagetian theorists include at least some further element from Piaget's system in their own theories, and import other elements from elsewhere. Beyond those elements just mentioned, however, different neo-

Piagetian theories begin to diverge considerably, in accordance with the theoretical predilections of their developers, and the nature of the Piagetian problems that they have tackled most directly.

A detailed presentation of these differences is available elsewhere. (See Case, 1988a; Demetriou, 1988.) Just to give a flavor of their nature, however, it is perhaps worthwhile to mention that certain neo-Piagetian theorists have attempted to preserve and elaborate on Piaget's notions of conflict and equilibration (cf. Pascual-Leone, 1988a), while others have emphasized the search for consistency and reflexive abstraction (Halford, 1988), and still others have emphasized the notions of differentiation and coordination (Case, 1988b). Taking off from these different points in the classic Piagetian system, each of the above theorists has worked out a detailed set of postulates concerning the nature of children's cognitive structures at different ages, and the way in which those structures are transformed as children move from one stage or level in their development to the next.

IV. Examining the structure of a particular behavioral sequence

Unlike empiricist theory, which normally remains quite close to the empirical data from which it is induced, neo-Piagetian theory has retained a property that reflects its rationalist origin, namely, its formulation in terms that are quite general and remote from the empirical data on how children actually behave on particular cognitive tasks. At the same time, however, all neo-Piagetian theorists have conducted extremely detailed analyses of empirical tasks, and of the way in which their general theories may be applied to them. Before proceeding, we should examine some of the behaviors that children can actually exhibit in particular task situations, and give at least some general indication of how these behaviors might be analyzed from a neo-Piagetian perspective.

Stages in children's mastery of the art of drawing

The behavioral sequence that will be analyzed has to do with children's acquisition of the art of drawing. In order to analyze the developmental changes that are observed in this domain, the particular neo-Piagetian theory I employ is the one I myself have developed (Case, 1985; in press[a]). In applying this theory, however, I shall try to emphasize those aspects of its position with which other neo-Piagetian theorists are in greatest agreement. In addition, because of limited space, I use a modified form of general-structural analysis suggested by another neo-Piagetian theorist (Fisher, 1980), rather than the more detailed form of problem-solving analysis I myself have developed.

A – Control Structure for Moving Eyes to Point X from point Y, in pursuit of Moving Object

PROBLEM SITUATION	OBJECTIVE
Interesting object moving out of view, in direction (x).	Return pattern of stimulation to its original focal state.

STRATEGY
1 Move head and eyes from
  Y toward X, probably using
  peripheral input from the
  block as a guide.

B – Control Structure for Moving Hand to Point X, from initial point Y

PROBLEM SITUATION	OBJECTIVE
Small object within reach at position X.	Make contact with object with hand.

STRATEGY
1 Move arm from current
  position (Y) to (X), using
  original visual input as a
  guide.

Figure 6.1.

Competences that develop during the first few months of life. In order to draw, children need some sort of tool, such as a pencil or crayon. In the context of most neo-Piagetian theories, children's first understanding of such tools would be presumed to develop during the sensorimotor stage, that is, during the period from 4 to 20 months. Before this stage, infants would be seen as assembling and consolidating the structures that will be the "building blocks" for the sensorimotor period: for example, structures for controlling the movement of their hands, or for tracking moving objects with their eyes. The content of these control structures might be represented as shown in Figure 6.1.

The letters A and B in the bottom left-hand panel of Figure 6.2 stand for such elementary control structures. What the figure indicates is that although infants can activate either one of these sorts of structure at this age in isolation (i.e., A or B) they can not as yet activate both structures at the same time, owing to their limited attentional capacity or *working memory*.

Competences that develop during infancy (4–20 months). The capability of integrating two discrete control structures emerges during the age range from 4 to 8 months, as children's working memory expands from one to two

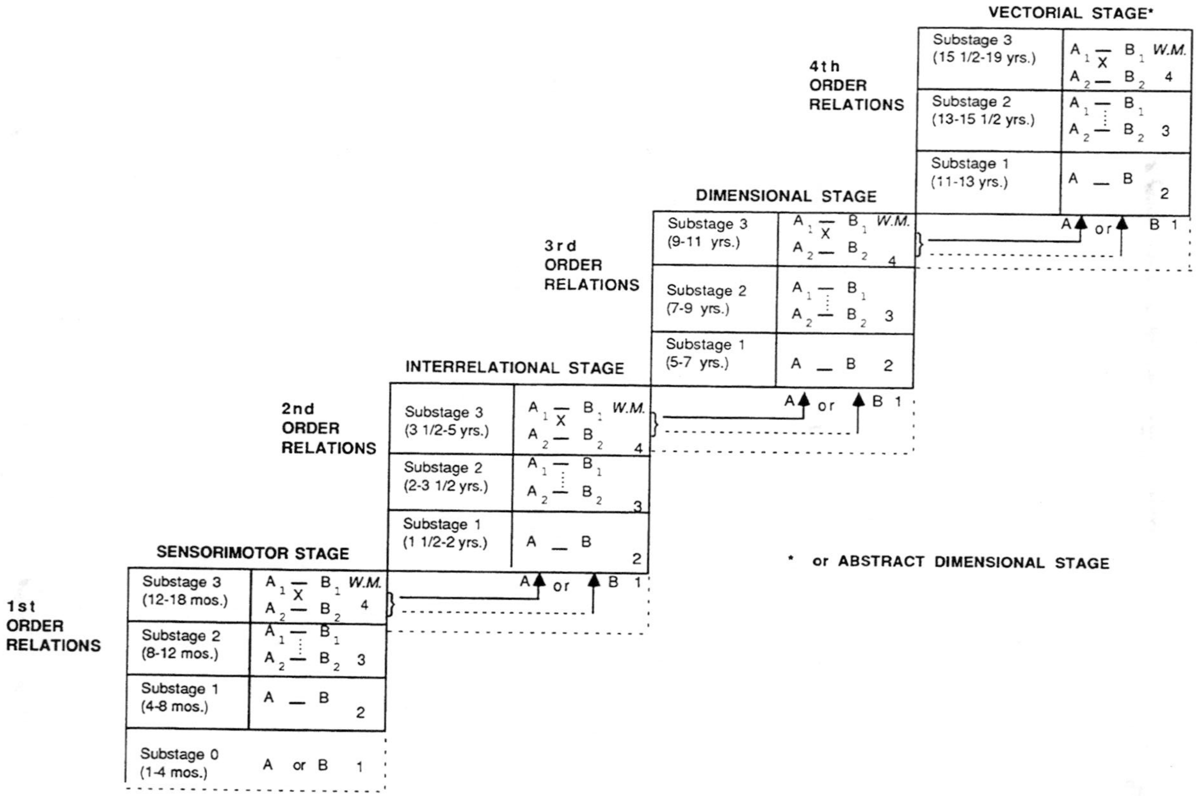

VECTORIAL STAGE*

Substage 3 (15 1/2-19 yrs.)	$A_1 \overline{\underset{\times}{}} B_1$ _W.M._ $A_2 \overline{} B_2$	4
Substage 2 (13-15 1/2 yrs.)	$A_1 \overline{} B_1$ $A_2 \overline{} B_2$	3
Substage 1 (11-13 yrs.)	$A \overline{} B$	2
	A or B	1

4th ORDER RELATIONS

DIMENSIONAL STAGE

Substage 3 (9-11 yrs.)	$A_1 \overline{\underset{\times}{}} B_1$ _W.M._ $A_2 \overline{} B_2$	4
Substage 2 (7-9 yrs.)	$A_1 \overline{} B_1$ $A_2 \overline{} B_2$	3
Substage 1 (5-7 yrs.)	$A \overline{} B$	2
	A or B	1

3rd ORDER RELATIONS

INTERRELATIONAL STAGE

Substage 3 (3 1/2-5 yrs.)	$A_1 \overline{\underset{\times}{}} B_1$ _W.M._ $A_2 \overline{} B_2$	4
Substage 2 (2-3 1/2 yrs.)	$A_1 \overline{} B_1$ $A_2 \overline{} B_2$	3
Substage 1 (1 1/2-2 yrs.)	$A \overline{} B$	2
	A or B	1

2nd ORDER RELATIONS

SENSORIMOTOR STAGE

Substage 3 (12-18 mos.)	$A_1 \overline{\underset{\times}{}} B_1$ _W.M._ $A_2 \overline{} B_2$	4
Substage 2 (8-12 mos.)	$A_1 \overline{} B_1$ $A_2 \overline{} B_2$	3
Substage 1 (4-8 mos.)	$A \overline{} B$	2
Substage 0 (1-4 mos.)	A or B	1

1st ORDER RELATIONS

* or ABSTRACT DIMENSIONAL STAGE

Figure 6.2.

units. This change is symbolized in the panel above the one just mentioned by the notation A – B. Note that the line between A and B stands for the particular form of relationship that the child apprehends and generates. With an object such as a crayon, this understanding would be a very elementary one, namely, that the visual properties of the object (A) can be manipulated (–), by reaching out the hand and grabbing the object (B). If they were allowed to play with such objects over time, children would build up a representation of the particular visual and tactile properties which each particular object exhibits (e.g., A crayon is a brightly colored object that fits in the grip and tastes wonderful).

Although such representations would be acquired quite rapidly during the age range from 4 to 8 months because both their elements could be attended to simultaneously, it is important to realize that these "conjoint representations" would not incorporate any explicit information about the consequences that can result when a second object such as a piece of paper is available. This sort of information should first become available to the infant at the second substage of the sensorimotor period, that is, at the age of 8 to 12 months. At this point, as a result of a further expansion in working memory, infants should become capable of focusing on a second action – reaction pair $(A_2 - B_2)$ at the same time as a first pair $(A_1 - B_1)$ is generated. This capability is symbolized in the figure as follows:

$$A_1 - B_2$$

$$\vdots$$

$$A_2 - B_2$$

In the case of drawing, the first action–reaction pair might be thought of as involving a particular action of the hand, and the reaction of crayon that this action generates. The second two elements might be thought of as involving essentially the same hand action and the re-action of the paper against which the crayon comes to rest.

Although infants can control two action–reaction pairs during the second substage of the sensorimotor period, this does not permit them to form a very *detailed* or *explicit* notion of the relationship between the two objects toward which their actions are directed. In effect, infants merely learn that the action of moving their hand down can have two interesting effects: one on the crayon and one on the object against which the crayon comes to rest. Thus, a favorite activity for children at this stage is simply treating a table as a "drum" and a crayon as a "drumstick."

As infants' working memory expands still further, during the age range from 13 to 20 months, they become capable of coordinating two action–

reaction pairs that are quite separate and of linking them in real time. This capability is represented in the figure as

$$A_1 - B_1$$
$$\times$$
$$A_2 - B_2$$

One can think of this capability as permitting children to pay attention to the particular action they execute on the pencil (e.g., lateral movement: B_1), and the reaction of a crayon (A_1), at the same time as they focus on the movement of pencil tip across the paper (B_2), and the visual pattern this generates (A_2). As a result of applying (and reversing) actions of this sort, infants come to recognize that a crayon is more than a brightly colored object (a substage 1 insight). They also come to realize that it is more than a small object that can be brought into contact with other objects with interesting results (a substage 2 insight). Rather, they see a crayon as a device capable of producing a delightful set of patterns on a flat surface when moved across it. This "relational" insight (i.e., this insight concerning the relation between pencil and paper) results from possessing a fully consolidated and "reversible" system of sensorimotor operations.

Developments during early childhood (2–5 years). At about the age of 2 years, a qualitative change begins to take place. Although children still love scribbling on pieces of paper and observing the results, they now become more interested in producing different kinds of scribbles (Kellog & O'Dell, 1967). They also become capable, if asked, of copying a particular *sort* of line, for example, a straight one, or a wavy one. Within the context of neo-Piagetian theory, this change may be presumed to result from the coordination of children's structures for controlling the relationship between a marker and a paper, with their structures for controlling the relationship between any given object, such as a line, and the edge of the paper on which it is placed. Because two relations are involved, each one of which can be manipulated on its own at the end of the sensorimotor stage, this new stage is called the *inter*relational stage in my theoretical system.[7]

During this second stage, children become sensitive to the interrelations that are present around them in a wide variety of domains, including language, family interaction, and spatial cognition. In the domain of drawing, their continued development reveals itself as follows: At substage 1 (as already mentioned), toddlers become capable of exerting control over a pencil such that it generates a particular type of line on a paper (A – B). At substage 2, they develop the capability of putting two different sorts of lines together, in a global fashion. For example, they may draw a curved line going up ($A_1 - B_1$), followed by another curved line coming back ($A_2 - B_2$), with the whole thus forming a sort of circle. Alternatively, they may draw a straight line going up ($A_1 - B_1$) and a straight line going sideways ($A_2 - B_2$), with the whole forming a sort of primitive cross. Finally, toward the end of the substage, children become capable of elaborating on and improving these early combinations, to form more integrated shapes that can clearly be recognized as objects such as "suns" (a circle with straight lines radiating from it) or "people" (a circle with dots in the middle, and straight lines radiating out at the sides to form arms and legs) (Kellogg & O'Dell, 1967). Once again, these systems may be symbolized in the abbreviated format indicated in Figure 6.1, namely,

$$A_1 - B_2$$
$$\times$$
$$A_2 - B_2$$

Developments during middle childhood (5–10 years). As at the end of the preceding stage, the child's interrelational structures, once consolidated, come to form the basic elements out of which the structures at the next stage are constructed. A clear shift in the quality of children's drawings is evident around 6 years, as they move into the third stage (Dennis, 1992). Two major changes take place at this time. First, the human figure is represented more accurately and in more detail. In contrast to the undifferentiated, global figure of the 4-year-old, the 6-year-old figure is composed of integrated but differentiated body parts, including a head, a trunk, arms, and legs. Second, and more important, the human figure is placed in the context of a number of surrounding objects, in such a fashion that the relationship of any one of these objects to the others corresponds to their spatial relationship in the real world. Because the sky is high up in the real world, for example, it now appears above all the other objects. Because the ground is underneath people's feet, it now appears below the other objects, and touching them. In effect, the 4-year-old's drawing has been differentiated into two elements, a figure (A) and a background (B), each of which requires that a system of relations be integrated. Moreover, the two systems have been coordinated such that, for the first time, a spatially unambiguous "scene" results (Dennis, in press).

By 8 years, and again by 10 years, two further developments occur that are less dramatic but important nonetheless: Typically, 8-year-olds differentiate between the foreground scene and a background scene, and introduce a number of (Western) artistic conventions for indicating which is which. These include drawing the background figure or figures on a second ground line higher up on the page, making the background scene smaller than the foreground figures, and occluding background figures with foreground figures. If the background is empty, they may also bring the sky right down to the ground line around the foreground figures, so that it appears to form a backdrop for them. If the main figure and surrounding objects that form the foreground scene are symbolized as $A_1 - B_1$, and the background figure and surrounding objects are symbolized as $A_2 - B_2$, then the structure of the overall picture may once again be symbolized as

$$A_1 - B_2$$
$$\vdots$$
$$A_2 - B_2$$

Finally, at the 10-year-old level children's pictures take on a more integrated quality, often because the 10-year-old artist introduces a "middle ground" as well as a foreground and background, and thus draws a picture in which space appears to have a more continuous quality. With this "integrating device" included, the overall structure of children's drawings may be represented as

$$A_1 - B_1$$
$$\times$$
$$A_2 - B_2$$

What this form of notation is meant to convey is that, just as 2-year-olds assembled the actions they could generate into a coherent form, so that they could monitor the on-line use of a tool such as a pencil, and just as 4-year-olds assembled their interrelational operations into a coherent form, so that they could use a pencil to make an integrated figure such as a human being or a sun, 10-year-olds now assemble their dimensional operations so they can arrange figures into a coherent scene, which has the same integrated quality on the page as do scenes in the three-dimensional world.

Developments during late childhood and adolescence (11–18 years). As children move into the fourth stage, they once again become capable of apprehending and drawing relationships at a higher level. In Dennis's (1992) work, the relationship that was investigated was the "point of view" someone takes when looking at a scene – not from the perspective of the artist but from the perspective of another scene. To determine children's capabilities in this regard, Dennis asked children to draw her a picture of a mother looking out the window of her house and watching her son playing peekaboo in the park across the street. The proviso she added was that from where the mother was standing, she could only see her son's face, because he was peeking out at her from behind a tree.

As she had expected, Dennis found that most 10-year-olds drew each scene that she had described in an integrated manner. The most frequent way they did so, however, was by drawing one three-dimensional scene on

Figure 6.3.

the right (e.g., a mother looking out her house window) and the other one on the left (e.g., a boy peeking out from behind a tree), with a street going straight up the middle. (See Figure 6.3.) What the children did not seem able to do was to *integrate* their depiction of the two scenes so that – within the higher-order framework thus created – (1) the boy and mother would be looking at each other, not at the artist, that is, so that there would an abstract "corridor" or "line of sight" between the mother's face and the boy's, and (2) the corresponding line of sight between the mother's face and the boy's body would be obscured (by the presence of a tree).

By the late teens, these two requirements no longer pose a problem, and adolescents or young adults can draw a scene in which the artist's point of view is differentiated from, and coordinated with, the point of view of the figures who are depicted. The result is that their overall pictures thus once again assume a unified quality. The two most common ways in which the "scene within the scene" was rendered in Dennis's study were either by taking the view of the mother, and drawing her from behind, looking out a window at the scene in which her child is playing peekaboo; or taking the point of view of the child, and drawing him from behind, peering around the tree and looking at the scene formed by the house with his mother visible in the window. (See Dennis, 1992, for illustration.)

Requirements for stage transition

What general factors are involved in propelling the child from one stage in the foregoing sequence to the next? As was implied by postulate C–5 in the preceding section, one factor is the availability of models of drawing in general, and of Western perspective drawing in particular. Because the forms by which space is represented are constructions that took our culture centuries of highly focused activity to perfect (Gombrich, 1968), one would not expect children to pass through this sequence without any external support or challenge. In fact, increasingly as children near the upper levels of the hierarchy, one would expect some form of direct instruction to be helpful, and perhaps necessary for the underlying changes in insight and operational capability to take place (Case, 1985, ch. 18).

A second factor is motivational. Because the structures symbolized by the letters A, B, and so forth, all have some form of goal as a component, it is necessary for children actively to set themselves appropriate goals if the developmental sequence is to proceed in the fashion indicated. This, in turn, requires that an appropriate affective state be present and directed toward, rather than away from, this goal. Different neo-Piagetian theorists have modeled these affective requirements differently. All agree, however, that they must be taken into account (Case, Hurst, Hayward, & Lewis, 1988; Fischer, 1989; Pascual-Lèone, 1988a,b). The empirical data also back this assertion up, since children's drawing performance is known to decay under a variety of emotion-provoking conditions, such as when there is symbolic equivalence between an object being drawn and a real-world object about which the child is anxious (Kroeber, 1990).

A third factor is the availability of sufficient opportunity to practice their existing structures, under the stimulus these motivational factors produce. Opportunity for practice is necessary not only to ensure that consolidation of complex structures occurs at substage 3, but to ensure sufficient automization of simpler structures, without which functional working memory growth would not keep pace with the more biologically regulated changes in working memory that most neo-Piagetian theorists presume (Case, 1985; Fischer & Pipp, 1984; Pascual-Leone, 1970).

A fourth factor is the internal equivalent of the third. For practice to be effective, children must be capable of some form of structural learning, which enables them to recruit new structures into their available repertoire and integrate them with existing ones. As has already been mentioned (postulate B–1), different theorists model this process in different but complementary fashions.

The final factor is a controversial one, or at least one that might not be accepted outside the neo-Piagetian school. This is the necessity for a biologically regulated set of changes as well. Different theorists disagree on the precise nature of these changes, but there is general agreement that some form of biological change is needed if children are to make the major stage transitions at the normal time, and to show continued working memory growth within each stage after they have done so. The necessity for biological change – in order to coordinate all the elements of the increasingly complex structures that have been described – does not imply that no acceleration of children's perspective drawing can be produced by purely didactic means. Indeed, certain neo-Piagetian theorists have specified in some detail what conditions are necessary for such acceleration to take place (Case, 1985, ch. 18; Pascual-Leone & Smith, 1969). What it does mean, however, is that any attempt to produce such an acceleration must take into account a set of very real biological constraints, and operate within them.

biological constraints & abil's

Summary

What the foregoing "neo-Piagetian" analysis suggests is that children progress through four general stages in their understanding and mastery of the conventions of Western perspective drawing. During the first stage, they come to understand that the act of drawing entails the control of the action of a tool, such as a crayon, as it moves across a flat surface such as a piece of paper. During the second stage, they come to understand that drawing involves the careful arrangement of certain particular marks on a paper in relationship to other marks and the background that the page provides. During the third stage they come to understand that the manner in which the objects are arranged on a page relative to each other is also critical, if the overall picture is to have the qualities of a three-dimensional "scene." Finally, by the end of the fourth stage, children understand that a drawing can also depict a particular "point of view" by the way in which two or more such scenes are coordinated with one another.[8]

needed factors:

Progression through this four-stage sequence depends on exposure to a particular (Western) culture on the one hand, and the natural operation of certain biologically regulated processes on the other, particularly those relating to the growth of working memory. Progression also depends on the presence of socioemotional reactions that will make the goal of drawing a valued one, and (particularly at higher stages) on the availability of explicit instruction. Provided these boundary conditions are met, however, children *[maybe]* will progress through the recursive process indicated in Figure 6.1 in this domain, as in all others. That is to say, they will first differentiate, then integrate, and finally consolidate their existing structures before coordinating them with other well-consolidated structures and moving on to the structures of the next stage.

Reevaluating the force of the classic Piagetian critique

At the beginning of this chapter, I pointed out that neo-Piagetian theory was born in response to the criticisms that were leveled at classical Piagetian theory from two rival philosophic traditions. A third sort of criticism was influential as well, namely, the one that developed within the rationalist tradition itself. The goal that neo-Piagetian theorists implicitly set themselves was to create a new body of theory that would preserve the strengths of the classical Piagetian position but introduce whatever extensions or modifications seemed necessary, in order to eliminate the weaknesses that the various criticisms of the classical position had highlighted.

Now that the general principles of neo-Piagetian theory have been described, and an example has been provided of how these principles might be applied to the analysis of a particular behavioral sequence, it seems worthwhile to return to this original goal, and to examine the extent to which it has been met.

Preserving the strengths of the classic Piagetian position

Although the classic Piagetian position had a number of strengths, the two that were most generally acknowledged were (1) that it offered a vision of young children as active constructors of their own knowledge and (2) that it brought to light a large number of previously unrecognized facts about young children's development and explained them in a coherent fashion.

The way in which neo-Piagetian theorists have attempted to preserve the original power of the classic Piagetian position is by preserving its core postulates, and basing their own explanatory frameworks on them. Five general postulates that appear to have been preserved by virtually all neo-Piagetian theorists were listed at the beginning of the section in this chapter entitled "Core Postulates of Neo-Piagetian Theory." These postulates formed an implicit part of the analysis of children's drawing that was presented, where they assumed the following more particular form:

1. Importance of children's cognitive structures. Children do not simply "observe" the form that is present in the drawing of those around them. Rather, they assimilate that form to their own internal structures.

2. Role of child's own activity in creating such structures. The cognitive structures to which children assimilate their drawing are not normally a direct function of their empirical experience. Rather, they are a product of children's own attempts to organize the experience in the most sophisticated fashion of which they are capable.

3. Four structural levels distinguished. A sequence of four different "stages" or "levels" can be identified in children's drawing, which result from the application of underlying structures that have different forms and degrees of complexity. These structures lead to the four different ways of understanding drawing that were summarized at the end of the section entitled "Examining the Structure of a Particular Behavioral Sequence."

4. Hierarchical inclusion of earlier structures in later ones. Higher-order drawing structures build on, and transform, the structures of earlier levels. Thus, for any given achievement at one stage (e.g., imitating the line drawn by an adult), it is always possible to indicate two precursor insights at the previous stage from which this achievement has been constructed (e.g., understanding how to make a mark with a pencil or crayon, and understanding the spatial relationship between a straight line and the edge of a paper).

5. Characteristic age of acquisition. This recursive process takes place according to a timetable that is subject to general biological limits. Thus, for any particular level of organization in children's drawing (e.g., drawing with a baseline) there will be an age before which this form is unlikely to emerge, even in an environment rich in opportunities for exploring the properties of the drawing act.

Although neo-Piagetian theory is different from classical Piagetian theory in its particulars, then, it highlights and provides an explanation for the same general set of developmental phenomena, and does so in the same general fashion.

Eliminating the weaknesses in the classic Piagetian system

Response to the classic empiricist critique

The first criticism empiricist scholars raised with regard to the classic Piagetian system was that it was difficult to operationalize and tie to empirical data in a hypotheticodeductive fashion (Brainerd, 1978; Flavell, 1963). Neo-Piagetian theorists have tried to alleviate this problem in two ways. The first is by avoiding the use of symbolic logic in their characterization of children's cognitive structures (postulate C–1 in the section on core postulates). The second is by providing more precise "process" characterizations of the process by which new structures are acquired and used (postulate B–1). The developmental descriptions to which these changes have led are still rather abstract. Nevertheless, with the aid of intervening models of a more task-specific variety, neo-Piagetian theorists have managed to generate and test a wide variety of empirical predictions. In fact, virtually all the modified postulates outlined in this chapter's core-postulate section have been evaluated in the context of some sort of hypotheticodeductive experiment. The following are some illustrations.

1. There have been many demonstrations that the new way of defining structural levels can lead to correct predictions regarding the sequence of developmental attainments on novel tasks. The tasks that have been developed have included the sort of perspective problems described in this chapter's section examining a particular behavioral sequence (Dennis, 1992), as well as tasks that evaluate children's motor capabilities (Dennis, 1992; Todor, 1979), their language (Body, 1977; Case & McKeough, 1990; Johnson, Fabian, & Pascual-Leone, 1989; Johnson & Pascual-Leone, in press), and their social behavior (Bruchkowsky, 1992; Fischer et al., 1984). Novel tasks of a more classic logicomathematical nature have also been designed, and the conformity of their acquisition sequence to the new structural descriptions has been evaluated (Case, 1972; Halford, 1982; Pascual-Leone & Smith, 1969).

2. Most of the foregoing studies have not only predicted the *sequence* in which novel tasks will be passed, they have also predicted the *absolute age* at which they will be passed, as a result of assumptions about the upper bounds of children's performance (postulate C–2). The role of working memory has received particular attention, with investigators designing new measures of this construct and predicting the absolute level of attainment children will exhibit at different ages (Burtis, 1982; Case, 1972, 1985, ch. 14; Parkinson, 1969, 1975; Pascual-Leone, 1970).

The new working memory measures have also been related to children's performance of a variety of more complex tasks, including the sort of drawing tasks described in the section on a particular behavioral sequence. (See Dennis, 1992; Morra, Moizo, & Scopessi, 1988.) Most of the studies have used cross-sectional designs, and have correlated working memory size and structural attainment within age cohorts, partialling out any residual age effects statistically (e.g., Case, 1985; Groenwig, 1983; McKeough, in press). Longitudinal studies have also been conducted, however, and the parallel in the developmental course of the two sorts of measures established (Goodman, 1979; Leitner, 1990; Lewis, 1989). Finally, studies have been designed in which children of the same age but different working memory capacities are selected for training, and predictions regarding their learning tested (Case, 1974; Daneman & Case, 1981; Scardamalia, 1977; Watson, 1984, cited in Case, 1985, ch. 14).

3. For obvious reasons, the neurological–maturational factors that have been postulated have not been investigated as thoroughly or directly. However, recent investigations by neuropsychologists have produced strong evidence that certain aspects of working memory are localized in the frontal lobes (Goldman-Rakic, 1989), and that developments in these areas are linked to increases in performance on Piagetian tasks (Diamond, 1991).

Neo-Piagetian researchers have also provided *in*direct evidence for some sort of maturational implication in working memory growth, by showing that children's functional working memory increases in response to practice in a fashion that is directly proportional to the speed of their processing (Case, Kurland, & Goldberg, 1978), but reaches different asymptotes at different ages, under conditions of maximum practice (Kurland, 1981). The changes that take place on working memory measures have also been related to the known neurological data on maturation of the frontal lobes in an analytic fashion (Case, in press[b]; Pascual-Leone, 1974, 1988). Finally, one or two specific predictions have been generated and tested regarding the existence of certain frontal EEG patterns that may be associated with certain levels of cognitive functioning (Fischer, 1987; Menna, 1989; Pascual-Leone, 1990).

4. The way in which individual differences (postulate C–4) have been examined has depended on the particular theory in which their action has been explicated. In Pascual-Leone's theory, the cognitive style of field independence versus dependence is hypothesized to be strongly related to certain sorts of developmental changes. This hypothesis has been evaluated in a number of fashions. In an early study, Pascual-Leone predicted the complete factorial pattern in a battery of some 40 tests of cognitive style, cognitive development, and IQ subtests, with considerable success (Pascual-Leone, 1969). In subsequent studies, he and his colleagues predicted different patterns of performance on cognitive-developmental tasks, both before and after learning, as a function of this variable, as well as the relationship of this variable to measures of working memory, mental effort, and learning (e.g., Case & Globerson, 1974; Globerson, 1983, 1985; Globerson, Weinstein, & Sharabany, in press; Goodman, 1971; Parkinson, 1969). Within other neo-Piagetian frameworks, different individual difference variables have been isolated, and tested using an equally wide range of methodologies. For example, Demetriou and Efklides (1988) have used a variety of analytic techniques that combine developmental and individual analysis, including factor analysis and Rasch scaling. Fischer (1989), Fischer and Knight (in press), and Hoppe-Graff (1989) have used the individual difference variables highlighted in their own theories to predict different paths through the same microdevelopmental hierarchy, by individuals with different characteristics. Lautrey, DeRiboupierre, and Rieben (1987) have examined differences in "digital" versus "analogic" processing styles.

5. The impact of culture on children's cognition (postulate C–5), like the impact of maturational variables, has not been investigated as extensively as one might wish (see Dasen & DeRibeaupierre, 1988). Nevertheless, it, too, has received at least some scrutiny, with predictions being made regarding the constancy of working memory growth across cultures, and variability in skill or strategy acquisition (Bentley, Kvalsvig, & Miller, 1990; Case, 1975;

Miller & Pascual-Leone, 1981; Miller, Pascual-Leone, Campbell, & Juckes, 1989). More recent work has also examined different patterns of development with regard to more specific structural systems in different cultures, and has tried to link these differences to different social and institutional factors (Case & Fiati, 1992; Shayer, Demetriou, & Pervez, 1987).

The foregoing studies have gone a considerable way toward answering the charge leveled against classical Piagetian theory in regard to the difficulty of testing its assertions empirically via hypothetico-deductive experiments. As will, we hope, have been apparent, an attempt has also been made to meet the more substantive empirical criticism, namely, that Piagetian theory provides a view of the young child's thought that is too monolithic and too insensitive to influences from its external environment. Postulates about external influence and learning now figure directly in neo-Piagetian theory (see postulates B–1, B–2, B–4, and C–5), as do postulates regarding developmental variability (postulate B–2). All these general postulates were explicit in this chapter's analysis of children's drawing, where it was asserted (1) that children would not learn about this aspect of the world at all, if they were not exposed to some form of model in the world around them, (2) that practice would also be necessary both to consolidate children's structures at the end of any stage and to produce the automization of children's basic operations that would permit working memory to reach its full potential, and (3) that development to the higher stages is contingent on some form of direct instruction as well.

Although no detail was provided as to how this instruction might be presented, this is also a problem to which neo-Piagetian theorists have also given explicit attention (see Case, 1985, ch. 18; Case & Griffin, 1990; Case & Sandieson, 1987; Pascual-Leone, Goodman, Ammon, & Subelman, 1978). The attention paid to this latter class of variables is important because it underscores a point that may not have been noticed in the rather lengthy account that has been presented of basic neo-Piagetian "postulates." This is that many of the new postulates that have been introduced into the classical tradition have been taken directly from one of the other two traditions (e.g., Gagné, 1967; Hull, 1945; Vygotsky, 1962). Although these postulates have taken on a new significance in the context of neo-Piagetian theory, they still carry some of their old implications, and motivate experimenters to pursue similar problems.

To say neo-Piagetian theory has been responsive to the classic empiricist critique is not to say it can as yet meet all the criteria that its critics would like. As Flavell (1984) has pointed out, for example, there are still serious problems in defining the units of working memory, and in determining how many of them are necessary to execute any given cognitive strategy. In addition, the battle as to whether development can be reduced to cumulative learning is by no means over, notwithstanding the attempt of neo-Piagetian theorists to define each sort of factor in a more precise fashion. (See, for example, Chi & Rees, 1983; Klahr, 1988; Rumelhart & McLelland, 1987.) Notwithstanding the continuing debate between the two traditions, however, it seems clear that neo-Piagetian theory has come a considerable distance in responding to both the methodological and the substantive aspects of the empiricist critique.

Response to the rationalist critique

The second critique of Piagetian theory was one that developed within the rationalist camp itself. This critique held that the theory was incomplete because it provided too global an account of how children moved from one form of structure to another, and because it took no account of individual differences or nonrational factors in this process.

Whether or not neo-Piagetian theories present a more *accurate* picture of stage transition than the classical theory is, of course, open to question. That they present a more detailed view, however, is difficult to dispute. As was indicated in discussing neo-Piagetian models of development and learning (see postulate B–1), virtually all neo-Piagetian theories offer a more detailed model of the process by which structural transformation takes place, and the reason that this process is subject to more severe developmental constraints than is the process of learning. As was mentioned in connection with postulate B–1, the particular nature of this further detail varies considerably, depending on the particular neo-Piagetian system one considers and the predilections of the theorist who has constructed it. My own system, for example, has emphasized children's exploration and problem solving, and the way in which this leads to new executive control structures. In other accounts, the emphasis has been on other factors, such as the way in which the internal consistency of a new system is checked (Halford, 1982), the step-by-step process by which new units are first differentiated from each other, then concatenated, and then intercoordinated (Fischer, 1980), or the dynamic interplay of perceptual, affective, and cognitive factors as this process takes place (Pascual-Leone, 1988a). Common to all these accounts, however, is a concern with going beyond the classic Piagetian account of stage transition, both by specifying a greater number of structural "steps," and by providing a better model of the process by which each step is realized. In fact, in many cases, it was the author's desire to provide such a model that was the motivation for devising the new theory in the first place. A similar set of points could be made for the neo-Piagetian treatment of individual differences (see postulate C–3),[9] and for its treatment of affect. (See postulate C–4.)

Response to the sociohistorical critique

The *sociohistorical* critique of Piaget's theory was that it painted a picture of children's development that was too universal, too focused on the individual rather than on society, and too closed to the processes of cultural change. How does the new body of theory that has been summarized fare in response to this sort of criticism?

In the set of postulates that have been added to neo-Piagetian theory, this response was reflected in three different ways. It was reflected, first, in the theory's suggestion that the actual *content* to which children's thinking is applied (e.g., systems for perspective drawing) is cultural in nature (postulate C–5). Because this system varies across cultures – or, within any culture such as our own, across time – one would not expect 10-year-olds' drawings to look alike in all cultures, or even to look the same in our culture now as they did in the Middle Ages.

The neo-Piagetian response to the sociohistorical critique is reflected, second, in the suggestion that social processes in general, and institutional processes such as schooling in particular, play as important a role as more endogenous processes in promoting transition to higher levels of thought. (See postulate C–5.) Because certain individuals go to art school and others do not, for example, one would expect large differences in the paintings they produce.

Finally, the response is reflected in the neo-Piagetian specification of a recursive process within stages (postulate B–3) within which repeated cycles of conflict and conflict resolution may be expected. These "dialectical cycles" provide another point of contact between the two traditionally opposed views of the developmental process, since they parallel the form of change that certain sociohistorical theorists (especially those influenced by Hegel) have proposed for social change (Case, 1988b).

As it incorporates notions such as those mentioned above, neo-Piagetian theory appears to be moving in a direction that makes it much more congruent with the classical sociohistorical position: namely, that children only attain their full intellectual power once they have reconstructed the intellectual systems that are their cultural inheritance, and taken their place at the living tip of their culture. This appears to be a particularly important area of growth for neo-Piagetian theory, and one directly related to the theme of the present volume, since new intellectual developments in the history of a culture are almost always contributed by adults – in the course of their own further intellectual development during adulthood.

Application of neo-Piagetian theory to the study of adult development

The object of the present volume is to build a bridge between studies of child development and of adult development. It therefore seems worthwhile to conclude by mentioning several attempts that have already been made by neo-Piagetian theorists to extend their theories to the adult years. Six closely related suggestions that have been proposed are as follows:

1. The first suggestion is that there may be further structural levels in adulthood (Case, 1978, 1988a,b; Demetriou, 1988; Fischer, Kenny, & Pipp, 1990; Kitchener & Fischer, 1988).

2. The second suggestion is that a recurrent structural cycle may be present within each level, of the same sort illustrated in Figure 6.1 (Case, 1978, 1988b, 1989; Fischer & Knight, in press).

3. A third suggestion is that movement within and across such cycles may continue to be a function of the recursive differentiation, coordination, and integration of existing structures (Case, 1985; Fischer, 1980; and Pascual-Leone, 1986, 1988b).

4. A fourth suggestion is that this process of recursive differentiation and integration may extend to affective processes as well, and that affective factors may play an increasingly important role in human development during the adult years (Case, 1989, in press; Pascual-Leone, 1986, 1988a).

5. A fifth suggestion is that there may be a *decrement* in the power of working memory about the age of 35 to 40, and that this decrement – somewhat paradoxically – may play the role of maturational potentiator that was formerly played by *increases* in the power of working memory. The sort of decrement that has been hypothesized is in the power of working memory to prevent irrelevant intrusion into its contents or into its processes (Pascual-Leone, 1986). The effect of this proposed decrement is that of expanding the potential range of structures that may be integrated (Pascual-Leone, 1988b).

6. When coupled with the rich and complex repertoire of previously existing structures and the active exercise of will, the final suggestion has been that the new potential of the middle-age cognitive system may be to permit individuals to overcome the blind spots and "defenses" of their youth, and to gain a new form of "wisdom" that was not possible in their earlier years (Pascual-Leone, 1988b).[10]

As may be apparent from the foregoing set of postulates, neo-Piagetian theory is continuing to evolve, in the same sort of dynamic historical context in which it had its original inception. That is to say, it is continuing to evolve in a context that is sensitive to internal tensions stemming from gaps in the view of development it currently presents, as well as external tensions stemming from alternative conceptions of the knowing process that are being advanced within the other major philosophic and developmental traditions. While the theoretical structure that is emerging in the Piagetian tradition is a relatively complex one, the same may be said for the process of development itself. This, in and of itself, should not count as a strike against the new systems. The dilemma that neo-Piagetian theorists continue to face, however, is one they originally confronted at the beginning of their endeavor – namely, deciding which postulates of their system are essential to explain the established empirical phenomena of child and adult development, and are thus worthy of preservation; which postulates are incomplete and must be further developed; and what sorts of new postulates need to be added to account for phenomena that have only recently been discovered. Finally, of course, an additional dilemma is how to ensure that the entire process remains "progressive" (Lakatos, 1962), that is, that it continues to proceed in a fashion that preserves the simplicity and explanatory power of the original core theory, while guiding the search for new data and conceptual insights along productive pathways and permitting successful predictions about at least some of these new phenomena to be ventured.

Notes

1 Knowledge is normally assumed to be acquired in the scientific community by a process that includes (1) observation of empirical phenomena, (2) formulation of tentative generalizations about these phenomena, (3) formulation of models to explain the generalizations, (4) generation of new predictions that follow from the model, and (5) testing the predictions via empirical experiment. As will be seen, this characterization is challenged by the other traditions, or at least it is assumed to be a very limited aspect of the overall process.

2 The absence of such an account is, of course, quite common in the rationalist tradition, where it is Descartes's *cogito* that often defines the *sum*.

3 This notion is present in the classical Piagetian system, where it goes by the name of horizontal "unevenness" or "displacement" (*décalage*). Rather than simply giving the phenomenon a label, however, most neo-Piagetian theorists have treated it as an essential characteristic of development, whose presence is explained by their models of learning and stage transition.

4 In Piaget's system, affect and cognition were seen as indissociable. Some theorists (e.g., Fischer, Shaver, & Carnochan, 1990) have followed Piaget in this regard, whereas others (e.g., Case et al., 1988; Pascual-Leone, 1969) have taken a different tack and assumed that affect and cognition are generated by different though closely linked systems.

5 The one theorist who appears to demur is Mounoud (1986), who favors an account of the upper limit based on representational format. While acknowledging the possible role of attentional capacity, Fischer (1980) also has his own distinctive view of it (see Fischer & Pipp, 1984).

6 In Demetriou's theory, these are referred to as *specific structural systems*. My own work suggests that a powerful set of *central conceptual structures* underlies these systems and can be seen to play a vital organizing role (Case, 1992).

7 Other theorists preserve the classic Piagetian terms, such as the representational stage, the stage of one-way functions, or the preoperational stage.

8 A variety of other higher-order capabilities also emerge during this stage, as a result of the capability of coordinating one scene with another (Case & Berg, 1990).

9 This feature is more central to certain theories than to others. (See especially Demetriou & Efklides, 1988; Pascual-Leone, 1969, 1988a.)

10 For tests of some of these suggestions, see Demetriou & Efklides, 1988; Fischer & Knight, in press; Jedrzkiewicz, 1986; Kitchener & Fischer, 1988.

References

Baldwin, J. M. (1894). *The development of the child and of the race.* New York: Macmillan. (Reprinted by Augustus M. Kelley, 1968.)

Beilin, H. (1971). Developmental stages and developmental processes. In D. R. Green, M. P. Ford, & G. B. Flamer (Eds.), *Measurement and Piaget.* New York: McGraw-Hill.

Bentley, A. M., Kralsvig, J., & Miller, R. (1990). The cognitive consequences of poverty. A neo-Piagetian study with Zulu children. *Applied Cognitive Psychology, 4,* 451–459.

Biggs, J., & Collis, K. (1982). *Evaluating the quality of learning: The SOLO taxonomy.* New York: Academic Press.

Body, B. (1977). Language development and cognitive development: A neo-Piagetian interpretation of before and after. Unpublished doctoral dissertation, University of California, Berkeley.

Brainerd, C. J. (1978). The stage question in cognitive-development theory. *The Behavioral and Brain Sciences, 1,* 173–182.

Bruchkowsky, M. (1992). The development of empathic cognition in early and middle childhood. In R. Case (Ed.), *The mind's staircase: Exploring the structural underpinnings of human thought and knowledge,* pp. 153–170. Hillsdale, NJ: Erlbaum.

Bruner, J. S. (1966). On cognitive growth. In J. S. Bruner, R. Oliver, & P. M. Greenfield (Eds.), *Studies in cognitive growth* (pp. 1–67). New York: Wiley.

Bruner, J. S. (1989). Culture and human development: A new look. Address to SRCD, Kansas City.

Burtis, P. J. (1982). Capacity increase and chunking in the development of short-term memory. *Journal of Experimental Child Psychology, 34,* 387–413.

Carey, S. (1985). *Conceptual change in childhood.* Cambridge, MA: MIT Press.

Case, R. (1972). Validation of a neo-Piagetian mental capacity construct. *Journal of Experimental Child Psychology, 14,* 278–302.

Case, R. (1974). Structures and strictures: Some functional limitations on the course of cognitive growth. *Cognitive Psychology, 6,* 544–573.

Case, R. (1975). Social-class differences in intellectual development: A neo-Piagetian investigation. *Canadian Journal of Behavioral Science, 7,* 244–261.

Case, R. (1978). Intellectual development from birth to adulthood: A neo-Piagetian interpretation. In R. S. Siegler (Ed.), *Children's thinking: What develops?* Hillsdale, NJ: Erlbaum, pp. 37–72.

Case, R. (1985). *Intellectual development: Birth to adulthood.* Orlando, FL: Academic Press.

Case, R. (1988a). Neo-Piagetian theory: Retrospect and prospect. In A. Demetriou (Ed.), *The neo-Piagetian theories of cognitive development: Toward an integration.* Amsterdam: North-Holland.

Case, R. (1988b). Dialectical cycles in the development of creative intelligence. *Journal of Social and Biological Structures, 11,* 71–76.

Case, R. (1989, June). *Situating the development of outstanding achievement in the adult life cycle.* Paper presented at the annual meeting of the Jean Piaget Society, Philadelphia.

Case, R. (1992). *The mind's staircase: Exploring the conceptual underpinnings of children's thought and knowledge.* Hillsdale, NJ: Erlbaum.

Case, R. (in press). The role of frontal lobe maturation in regulating development of the executive function. *Brain and Cognition.*

Case, R., & Berg, R. (1990). A pilot investigation of the development of drawing skill during early and late adolescence. Unpublished manuscript. Centre for Educational Research at Stanford, Stanford University.

Case, R., & Globerson, T. (1974). Field independence and mental capacity. *Child Development, 45,* 772–778.

Case, R., & Griffin, S. (1990). Child cognitive development: The role of central conceptual structures in the development of scientific and social thought. In C. A. Hauert (Ed.), *Advances in psychology: Developmental psychology.* New York: North-Holland Elsevier.

Case, R., Hurst, P., Hayward, S., & Lewis, M. (1988). Toward a neo-Piagetian theory of cognitive and emotional development. *Developmental Review, 8*, 1–51.

Case, R., Kurland, M., & Goldberg, J. (1978). Operational efficiency and the growth of short term memory. *Journal of Experimental Child Psychology, 33*, 386–404.

Case, R., & McKeough, A. (1990). Schooling and the development of central conceptual structures: An example from the domain of children's narrative. *International Journal of Educational Psychology, 8*, 835–855.

Case, R., & Sandieson, R. (1987). *General developmental constraints on the acquisition of special procedures (and vice versa)*. Paper presented at American Educational Research Association, Washington, DC.

Chi, M. T. H., & Rees, E. R. D. (1983). A learning framework for development. *Contributions to Human Development, 9*, 71–107.

Cole, M., & Scribner, S. (1974). *Culture and thought*. New York: Wiley.

Daneman, M., & Case, R. (1981). Syntactic form, semantic complexity and short term memory as factors affecting children's ability to acquire new linguistic structures. *Developmental Psychology, 17*, 367–377.

Dasen, P. (1972). Cross-cultural Piagetian research. A summary. *Journal of Cross-Cultural Psychology, 17*, 367–378.

Dasen, P., & DeRibeaupierre, A. (1988). Neo-Piagetian theories: Cross cultural and differential perspectives. In A. Demetriou (Ed.), *The neo-Piagetian theories of cognitive development: Toward an integration*. New York: North-Holland Elsevier.

Demetriou, A. (1988). *The neo-Piagetian theories of intelligence: Toward an integration*. Amsterdam: North-Holland.

Demetriou, A., & Efklides, A. (1988). Experiential structuralism and neo-Piagetian theories: Toward an integration. In A. Demetriou (Ed.), *The neo-Piagetian theories of intelligence: Toward an integration*. Amsterdam: North-Holland.

Dennis, S. (1992). Stage and structure in the development of children's spatial representations. In R. Case (Ed.), *The mind's staircase: Exploring the conceptual underpinnings of human thought and knowledge*, pp. 229–245. Hillsdale, NJ: Erlbaum.

Diamond, A. (1991). Neuropsychological insights into the meaning of object concept development. In S. Carey & R. Gelman (Eds.), *The epigenesis of mind: Essays on biology and knowledge* (pp. 67–110). Hillsdale, NJ: Erlbaum.

Fiati, T. (1992). Cross-cultural variation in the structure of children's thought: A comparison of children's numerical, social and spatial development in four different educational and ecological environments. In R. Case (Ed.), *The mind's staircase: Exploring the conceptual underpinnings of children's thought and knowledge*, pp. 315–342. Hillsdale, NJ: Erlbaum.

Fischer, K. W. (1980). A theory of cognitive development: The control and construction of hierarchies of skills. *Psychological Review, 87*, 477–531.

Fischer, K. W. (1987). Relations between brain and cognitive development. *Child Development, 58*, 623–633.

Fischer, K. W. (1989, July). *Individual differences in developmental sequence and the effects of personal import*. Paper presented in the symposium on the challenges and constraints of structuralism at the biennial meetings of the International Society for the Study of Behavioral Development, Jyvaskyla, Finland.

Fischer, K. W., & Canfield, R. L. (1986). The ambiguity of stage and structure in behavior: Person and environment in the development of psychology structure. In I. Levin (Ed.), *Stage and structure: Reopening the debate* (pp. 246–267). New York: Plenum.

Fischer, K. W., et al. (1984). Putting the child into socialization: The development of social categories in the preschool years. In L. Katz (Ed.), *Current topics in early childhood education, 5*, 27–72. Norwood, NJ: Ablex.

Fischer, K. W., & Ferrar, M. J. (1988). Generalizations about generalization: How a theory of skill development explains both generality and specificity. *International Journal of Psychology*.

Fischer, K. W., Kenny, S. L., & Pipp, S. L. (1990). How cognitive processes and environmental conditions organize discontinuities in the development of abstractions. In C. N. Alexander, E. J. Langer, & R. M. Oetzel (Eds.), *Higher stages of development* (pp. 162–187). New York: Oxford University Press.

Fischer, K. W., & Knight, C. (in press), Cognitive development in real children: Levels and variations. In B. Presseisen (Ed.), *The at-risk student and thinking: Perspectives from research*. Washington, DC: National Education Association.

Fischer, K. W., & Pipp, S. (1984). Processes of cognitive development: Optimal level and skill acquisition. In R. Sternberg (Ed.), *Mechanisms of cognitive development*. New York: Freeman.

Fischer, K. W., Shaver, P. R., & Carnochan, P. (1990). How emotions develop and how they organize development. *Cognition and Emotion, 4*, 81–127.

Flavell, J. H. (1963). *The developmental psychology of Jean Piaget*. Princeton, NJ: Van Nostrand.

Flavell, J. H. (1984). Discussion. In R. J. Sternberg (Ed.), *Mechanisms of cognitive development* (pp. 188–209). New York: Freeman.

Gagné, R. M. (1968). Contributions of learning to human development. *Psychological Review, 75*, 177–191.

Gelman, R. (1969). Conservation acquisition: A problem of learning to attend to relevant attributes. *Journal of Experimental Child Psychology, 7*, 167–187.

Gibson, E. (1969). *Perceptual development*. New York: Appleton-Century-Crofts.

Globerson T. (1983). Mental capacity and cognitive functioning: Developmental and social class differences. *Developmental Psychology, 19*, 225–250.

Globerson, T. (1985). Field dependence/independence and mental capacity: A developmental approach. *Developmental Review, 5*, 261–273.

Globerson, T., Weinstein, E., & Sharabany, R. (in press). Teasing out cognitive development from cognitive style: A training study. *Developmental Psychology*.

Goldman-Rakic, P. (1989, June). *Working memory and the frontal lobes*. Paper presented at the Toronto General Hospital.

Gombrich, E. (1968). *Art and illusion*. London: Phaedon.

Goodman, D. R. (1971). *Cognitive-style factors and linguistic performance with ambiguous sentences*. Unpublished master's thesis, York University, Toronto.

Goodman, D. [R.] (1979). *Stage transition and the developmental trace of constructive operations: An investigation of a neo-Piagetian theory of cognitive growth*. Unpublished doctoral dissertation, York University, Toronto.

Greenfield, P. M. (1966). On culture and conservation. In J. S. Bruner, R. Oliver, & P. M. Greenfield (Eds.), *Studies in cognitive growth* (pp. 1–67). New York: Wiley.

Groenwig, G. (1983). *The development of comprehension: Some linguistic and cognitive determinants of sentence verification*. Unpublished doctoral dissertation, University of Toronto.

Halford, G. S. (1982). *The development of thought*. Hillsdale, NJ: Erlbaum.

Halford, G. S. (1988). A structure mapping approach to cognitive development. In A. Demetriou (Ed.), *The neo-Piagetian theories of cognitive development: Toward an integration*. Amsterdam: North-Holland.

Hoppe-Graff, S. (1989, July). *The process of development as construction: Evidence from pretend play*. Paper presented in the symposium on challenges and constraints of structuralism at the biennial meetings of the International Society for the Study of Behavioral Development, Jyvaskyla, Finland.

Hull, C. (1943). *Principles of behavior*. New York: Appleton-Century-Crofts.

Hunt, J. M. (1961). *Intelligence and experience*. New York: Ronald.

Jedrzkiewicz, J. A. (1986). *Adult development and mental effort: A neo-Piagetian experimental analysis*. Unpublished master's thesis. York University.

Johnson, J., Fabian, V., & Pascual-Leone, J. (1989). Quantitative hardware stages that constrain language development. *Human Development, 32*, 245–271.

Johnson, J., & Pascual-Leone, J. (in press). Developmental levels of processing in metaphor interpretation. *Journal of Experimental Child Psychology*.

Keating, D. P. (1980). Thinking processes in adolescence In. J. Adelson (Ed.), *Handbook of adolescent psychology*, pp. 211–246. New York: Wiley.

Kellog, R., & O'Dell, S. (1967). *The psychology of children's art*. San Diego, CA: CRM.

Kendler, T. S. (1963). Development of mediating responses in children. In J. C. Wright & K. Kagan (Eds.), Basic cognitive process in children. *Monographs of the Society for Research in Child Development, 28*(2), 33–48.

Kitchener, K. W., & Fischer, K. W. (1988). A skill approach to the development of reflective thinking. In D. Kuhn (Ed.), *Developmental perspectives on teaching and learning thinking skills*. Contributions to Human Development. Basel. Switzerland: Karger.

Klahr, D. (1988). Information processing approaches to cognitive development. *Annals of Psychology*.

Klahr, D., & Wallace, J. G. (1976). *Cognitive development: An information processing view*. Hillsdale, NJ: Erlbaum.

Kroeber, C. (1990). *The effect of emotional arousal on drawing ability*. Unpublished master's thesis, University of Toronto.

Kurland, D. M. (1981). *The effect of massive practice on children's operational efficiency and short term memory span*. Unpublished master's thesis, University of Toronto.

Lakatos, I. (1962). Falsification and the methodology of scientific research programmes. In I. Lakatos & A. Musgrave (Eds.), *Criticism and the growth of knowledge*. Cambridge: Cambridge University Press.

Lautrey, J., DeRibaupierre, A., & Rieben, L. (1987). Operational development and individual differences. In E. DeCorte, H. Lodewighs, R. Parmentier, T. P. Span (Eds.) *Learning and instruction*. Oxford: Pergamon Press.

Lave, J. (1988). *Cognition and practice*. Cambridge: Cambridge University Press.

Leitner, K. L. (1990). *Cognitive and affective development in the second year of life: A neo-Piagetian and object relations perspective*. Unpublished doctoral dissertation, University of Toronto.

Lewis, M. D. (1989). *Cognition–emotion interactions in infancy: The development of individual differences*. Unpublished doctoral dissertation, University of Toronto.

McDermott, R. (1990). The acquisition of a child by a learning disability. In J. Lave & S. Chaiklin (Eds.), *People in action*. Cambridge: Cambridge University Press.

McKeough, A. (1992). A neo-structural analysis of children's narrative, and its development. In R. Case (Ed.), *The mind's staircase: Exploring the structural underpinnings of human thought and knowledge*, pp. 171–188. Hillsdale, NJ: Erlbaum.

McLaughlin, G. H. (1963). Psychologic: A possible alternative to Piaget's formulation. *British Journal of Educational Psychology, 33*, 61–67.

Menna, R. (1989). *Working memory development: An E.E.G. investigation*. Unpublished master's thesis, University of Toronto.

Miller, M. S., & Pascual-Leone, J. (1981). *Disconfirming Jensen experimentally: Intellectual versus executive-structural deficiency in underperforming low SES children*. Paper presented at the Society for Research in Child Development, Boston.

Miller, R., Pascual-Leone, J., Campbell, C., & Juckes, T. (1989). Learning and development: A neo-Piagetian cross-cultural analysis. *International Journal of Psychology, 24*, 293–313.

Morra, S., Moizo, C., & Scopesi, A. M. (1988). Working memory (or the M-operator) and the planning of children's drawing. *Journal of Experimental Child Psychology, 46*, 41–73.

Mounoud, P. (1986). Similarities between developmental sequences at different age periods. In I. Levin (Ed.), *Stage and structure: Reopening the debate*. Norwood, NJ: Ablex.

Mounoud, P., & Bower, T. G. H. (1974). Conservation of weight in infants. *Cognition, 3*, 29–40.

Olson, D. R. (1986a). Interpreting text and interpreting narrative: The effects of literacy on hermeneutics and epistemology. *Visible Language, 20*, 302–317.

Olson, D. R. (1986b). Mining the human sciences: Some relations between humanities and epistemology. *Interchange*, 119–171.

Parkinson, G. M. (1961). *Adaptive flexibility, field dependence, and two Piagetian tasks as independent variables in mirror tracking experiments.* Unpublished honors thesis, University of British Columbia, Vancouver, Canada.

Parkinson, G. M. (1969). *The recognition of messages from visual compound stimuli: A test of a quantitative developmental model.* Unpublished master's thesis, York University, Toronto.

Parkinson, G. M., (1975). *The limits of learning: A quantitative investigation of intelligence.* Unpublished doctoral dissertation, York University, Toronto.

Pascual-Leone, J. (1969). *Cognitive development and cognitive style: A general psychological integration.* Unpublished doctoral dissertation, University of Geneva, Switzerland.

Pascual-Leone, J. (1970). A mathematical model for the transition rule in Piaget's development stages. *Acta Psychologica, 32*, 301–345.

Pascual-Leone, J. (1974). *A neo-Piagetian process-structural model of Witkin's psychological differentiation.* Paper presented at the symposium on cross-cultural studies of psychological differentiation in the meetings of the International Association for Cross Cultural Psychology, Kingston, Ontario, Canada.

Pascual-Leone, J. (1986). Reflections on life span intelligence, consciousness, and ego development. In. C. N. Alexander, E. J. Langer, & R. M. Oetter (Eds.), *Higher stages of development: Adult growth beyond formal operations.* New York: Oxford University Press.

Pascual-Leone, J. (1988a). Organismic processes for neo-Piagetian theories: A dialectical causal account of cognitive development. In A. Demetriou (Ed.), *The neo-Piagetian theories of cognitive development: Toward an integration.* Amsterdam: North-Holland.

Pascual-Leone, J. (1988b). *An essay on wisdom: Toward organismic processes that make it possible.* Unpublished manuscript, Youk University, Toronto.

Pascual-Leone, J. (1989). An organismic process model of Witkin's field-dependence–independence. In T. Globerson & T. Zelniker (Eds.), *Cognitive style and cognitive development.* Norwood, NJ: Ablex.

Pascual-Leone, J., Goodman, D., Ammon, P., & Subelman, I. (1978). Piagetian theory and neo-Piagetian analysis as psychological guides in education. In J. Gallagher & J. Easley (Eds.), *Knowledge and development* (Vol. 2). New York: Plenum.

Pascual-Leone, J., Hamstra, N., Benson, N., Khan, I., & England, R. (1990). The P300 event-related potential and mental capacity. Paper presented at the Fourth International Symposium on Evoked Potentials, Toronto.

Pascual-Leone, J., & Smith, J. (1969). The encoding and decoding of symbols by children. *Journal of Experimental Child Psychology, 8*, 328–355.

Piaget, J. (1962). *Play, dreams, and imitation in childhood* [*La formation du symbole*]. New York: Norton.

Piaget, J. (1970). *Science of education and the psychology of the child.* New York: Orion Press.

Piaget, J. (1981). *Intelligence and affectivity: their relationship during child development.* Palo Alto, CA: Annual Review Monographs.

Piaget, J. (1985). *The equilibration of cognitive structures: The central problem of intellectual development.* Chicago: University of Chicago Press.

Pinard, A., & Laurendeau, M. (1969). "Stage" in Piaget's cognitive-developmental theory: Exegesis of a concept. In D. Elkind & J. H. Flavell, *Studies in cognitive development.* New York: Oxford University Press.

Reid, D. (in press). Horizontal and vertical structure: Stages and substages in the development of children's motor functioning. In R. Case (Ed.), *The mind's staircase: Exploring the structural underpinnings of human thought and knowledge.* Hillsdale, NJ: Erlbaum.

Rumelhart, D. E., & McLelland, J. C. (1987). Learning the past tenses of English verbs:

Implicit rules or parallel distributed processing? In B. MacWhinney, *Mechanisms of Language Acquisition.* Hillsdale, NJ: LEA.

Scardamalia, M. (1977). Information-processing capacity and the problem of horizontal décalage: A demonstration using combinatorial reasoning tasks. *Child Development, 48,* 28–37.

Shayer, M., Demetriou, A., & Pervez, M. (1988). The structure and scaling of concrete operational thought: Three studies in four countries. *Genetic, Social, and General Psychology Monographs, 114,* 307–376.

Siegler, R. S., & Jenkins, E. A. (1989). *How children discover new strategies.* Hillsdale, NJ: Erlbaum.

Spelke, E. S. (1988). Where perceiving ends and thinking begins: The apprehension of objects in infancy. In A. Yonas (Ed.), *Perceptual development in infancy: Minnesota symposia in child psychology,* pp. 197–234. Hillsdale, NJ: Erlbaum.

Starkey, P. D., Spelke, E. S., & Gelman, R. (1983). Detection of intermodal numerical correspondence by human infants. *Science, 222,* 179–181.

Sternberg, R. J. (1984). Mechanism of cognitive development: A componential approach. In R. J. Sternberg (Ed.), *Mechanisms of cognitive development* (pp. 163–186). San Francisco: Freeman.

Todor, J. (1979). Developmental differences in motor task integration: A test of Pascual-Leone's theory of constructive operators. *Journal of Experimental Child Psychology, 28,* 314–322.

Vygotsky, L. S. (1962). *Thought and language.* Cambridge, MA: MIT Press. (Original work published in Russian in 1934.)

balanced dualism emerges - adulthood

7   A neo-Piagetian perspective on adult cognitive development

Gisela Labouvie-Vief

Once Piaget's theory of cognitive development had been popularized in America, it quickly effected no less than a revolution in the study of childhood cognition. It was inevitable that sooner or later, researchers would begin to wonder if and how the theory applied to the more general domain of life-span development. In a first attempt to extend Piaget's theory and its methods to areas other than childhood, it soon became apparent, however, that many assumptions of the theory needed to be reevaluated.

Some assumptions of Piaget's theory that required revision are not unique to the field of adulthood. The assumption that development may be less coherent across domains and more dependent on context was quickly adopted by adult developmentalists as well. But additionally an entirely new set of problems arose for adult developmentalists. Piaget had constructed his tasks with an infallible intuition for what "seemed to work" for children: His tasks were engaging and compelling for that age group but appeared to hold much less interest and much less face validity for people considerably older. Hence it quickly appeared that if Piaget's theory worked at all for adults, it did so less literally and less concretely than had been suggested at the first stage of Piagetian inquiry.

One possible recommendation to be derived from this only partially successful attempt to extend Piagetian theory and method is to abandon the search for universal stages altogether (see Gardner, 1985; Miller, 1983), and criticisms of stage theories like Piaget's certainly have become commonplace enough. But not all writers on the issue have agreed that we ought to exchange his broad vision of a unified process of development for one that reduces all individual variability to variations in content or context. Rather, a growing body of work reflects the conviction that a structurally oriented – albeit more contextually open – theory *can* offer an important avenue to understanding adulthood.

Recently, many writers on the subject have felt we should hold fast to the search of a coherent and inclusive theory of the life course, and that one way to do so is to turn to a reexamination of Piaget's kind of project. The primary goal now was not to offer a more or less literal translation of the

197

theory and its methods from childhood and adolescence to later life stages. Rather, it was a more critical one: to attempt to separate the wheat of the theory from the chaff, and to preserve the former while discarding the latter.

As a result of this specific interest of researchers on adulthood processes, the term *neo-Piagetian* when applied to the study of adulthood takes on a meaning somewhat different from childhood studies. On the one hand, there has been much interest in identifying core issues of Piaget's theoretical approach and in sorting out which of them should and can continue to guide our vision of a theory of the life course. On the other hand, there has been equal interest in attempting to define avenues that are less useful for a theory of the total life-span and that should hence be abandoned or transformed. The ultimate hope is, then, that out of this process of critique and deconstruction it will be possible to reconstruct a more comprehensive theory of mature cognitive behavior and its evolution over the life course.

This chapter attempts to present an overview and to integrate these various attempts. The first section briefly summarizes the scope of Piaget's theoretical program and is followed by discussion of why his program has failed for investigations of adulthood. The second section of the chapter is empirically oriented, summarizing research stimulated by the neo-Piagetian perspective on adult cognition.

The Piagetian perspective: Goals and critiques

The vision of Piaget's program

It is useful to begin this discussion with a question: Why has Piaget's theory, despite all the criticism it has evoked, continued to fascinate theoreticians and researchers? The answer, I believe, is that the theory represents a major intellectual movement of this century. Since the beginning of philosophy, our intellectual tradition has upheld a particular ideal of human nature – one in which criteria of mature conduct are severed and dissociated from organic forms. In contrast, Piaget asserts a view of the human organism and its mental equipment as part and parcel of the organismic and biological world.

The assertion that our mature capacities are part of the organismic world may sound rather obvious at first blush. Nevertheless, on the background of past views of the mind it is, in fact, a quite revolutionary view. Its uniqueness is best appreciated if it is compared to past views of the mind. (For discussion, see Labouvie-Vief, 1990.) Those views rose with the birth of Greek philosophy when over several centuries a new way of speaking about such concepts as self, mind, and reality evolved, culminating in the writings of Plato in the fourth century B.C.

To the pre-Platonic thinker, reality was permeated with magical, mythic, and organismic aspects (Collingwood, 1945; Frankfort & Frankfort, 1946; Onians, 1954; Simon, 1978; Whyte, 1948). There was no sense of individuals' being separate from their instincts, from sacred processes, or from others in an interpersonal matrix. More logical forms of knowing only gradually began to grow out of those mythic forms and found an early culmination in Plato's concept of the mature person controlled by reason. For the language of a mythic, bodily self Plato substituted a language of a self primarily identified no longer with its bodily processes and concrete actions, but now as a mental agent different from its bodily manifestations. The new language was that of a self who was the author of concrete actions, of a psychological causal agent who was at their center and was responsible for them. Thus, the new selves were abstract rather than concrete, oriented toward thought rather than toward the imaginative and mythic. They also were no longer fused with their interpersonal context but were aware of themselves as somewhat separate, individuated entities.

All these differentiations were of extraordinary importance in the process of cultural evolution, but they remained, in essence, dualistic (Cassirer, 1946). The new concept of the mind was based on such opposition as mind versus body, self versus system, objective truth versus subjective inclination, and so forth. Thinking was described in terms of thinker-independent processes rather than being primarily understood as a human activity. This "objectivist" view of the mind (Lakoff, 1987) was further elaborated in the classical philosophies of 17th- and 18th-century Europe, and it persisted – albeit in altered and more complex forms – well into the current century.

In contrast, this century has seen a thorough revision of that objectivist view. Many philosophers and cognitive scientists (e.g., Bruner, 1986; Habermas, 1984; Lakoff, 1987) have begun to emphasize that thinking is permeated with bodily, mythic, and communal dimensions. Piaget's theory occupies a key position in that movement because it, too, squarely proposes a more integrated view of the human organism and its capacities.

The attempt to integrate the two poles of knowing is apparent in several propositions basic to the Piagetian program. First and foremost, Piaget proposes that the organic realm is the very ground out of which more abstract mental capacities evolve. The continuity between the organic and the mental is assured, according to Piaget, because every adapted act is based on a balance of assimilation and accommodation. Assimilation tends to preserve the existing inner form, whereas accommodation tends to modify actions according to the demands of the outer world.

Much of Piaget's work has carefully charted how, early in infancy, intelligence is closely identified with this organic ground. Instincts and hereditary reflexes form organic adaptations from which later, more complex forms of intelligence evolve. These organic forms soon become extended cognitively, empowering behavior with a greater degree of foresight and planning.

As detailed in Chapters 4 and 5, the bulk of Piaget's work has traced the development of formal and scientific forms of thought. At the core of Piaget's program, however, is the belief that these forms of thinking reflect pervasive reorganizations in the way the individual structures reality, generally. Thus, Piaget (1965; see also Labouvie-Vief & Lawrence, 1985; Youniss, 1980) proposes that it is impossible to separate levels of intellectual understanding from ways of relating. The child's cognitive immaturity and the adult's sophistication create an imbalance that is not only cognitive but social as well. Because of that imbalance, relations between children and adults are asymmetrical and reflect the power differential between the two age groups. In the child's eyes, parents are all-powerful; their rules are seen as unalterable and as representing something akin to universal order. Piaget calls that asymmetrical relationship a "unilateral relation of constraint." He states that reason proper cannot develop in such a relationship. This is because reason implies a reciprocal relationship wherein individuals are equal in power and exchange their views without social coercion. This ideal is not possible, however, in the relationship between children and adults. Instead, in the interaction between children and adults, understanding "is imposed from without [and] it leads to a calculation of [individual] interests or remains subordinated to ideas of authority and external rules" (Piaget, 1965, p. 280). Piaget, following Kant, calls this orientation to rules and knowing "heteronomous."

In adolescence, Piaget claims, these unilateral relationships of constraint give way to ones of reciprocal exchanges and cooperation. A good example of such exchanges is that of a peer group. In such a relationship, rules are no longer understood as coming from some outside authority. Rather, they are created from within the group: Ideally, Piaget says, they are being co-constructed cooperatively among a group of individuals equal in power. In such a setting, there is "continuous comparison, . . . opposition . . . , discussion, and mutual control" (Piaget, 1965, p. 393), placing on each individual a system of checks and balances that modulates subjectivity and caprice of any one member of the group. The new orientation to knowing is "autonomous," based on the recognition of both one's own individuality and that of other members in the group.

Thus, for Piaget, increasing levels of cognitive development involve also a restructuring of power relations. Indeed, cognitive development implies that processes of decision making are decoupled from conventional structures of authority and, instead, subordinated under processes accessible to every individual. In this way, a more lasting equilibrium of rationally motivated laws is substituted for the coercive quasi equilibrium of social power and convention.

Finally, Piaget (1981) also asserts that mental operations are continuous with the emotional and imaginative realms. Thus he rejects a reductionism

she claims Piaget linked mental operations w/ emot & imaginative — really?

that would claim that emotions are the cause of cognitions – or alternatively, that would make cognitions the cause of emotions. Instead, Piaget thinks of the two rather as two sides of the same coin: Cognition provides the structure, while emotions provide the dynamics and energy. As the individual develops, the two codevelop in essential interdependence.

In this way, affective experience develops along with cognitive development, creating feelings that become more differentiated and more internalized. First, affect is dictated by inborn affective reactions, which, however, soon become modified with increasing mastery over the world. The toddler's mastery of language and symbol adds increasing stability and internality to feelings. Emotions related to norms, morality, and one's evolving will are soon added. Finally, in adolescence, "feelings for other people are overlaid by feelings for collective ideals. Parallel to this is the elaboration of personality where the individual assigns himself a role and goals in social life" (Piaget, 1981, p. 14).

Critiques of Piaget's program

Piaget's various proposals imply a sweeping view of the nature of mental experience. As already noted, the major criticisms of child developmentalists have focused on the notion that this sweeping view is overly general and imprecise. Adult developmentalists have joined that criticism, but also have added criticisms of a more general kind. Believing that the basic vision implied in Piaget's theory is valid – if perhaps excessively unified – here the question has been to explain why Piaget's vision of the mature organism has been less fruitful for postadolescent periods of the life-span than it has been for earlier life stages.

In a sense, a major tenet that appears to hold together these various critiques is not that Piaget's theory has gone too far in emphasizing a uniform process of development, but rather that he has stopped short of carrying the vision of an organismic cognitive program into adulthood. Overall, Piaget retains an objectivist bias according to which mental experience is the master organizer of all other forms of organic experience. Thus, in his theory mature reality is objective, judgment is rational, and communal processes are strongly idealized.

This objectivism emerges as something of a paradox because, as we have noted, the theory was based on the basic assumption that mental life could be explained as a form of biological life. In the abstract, that assumption is evident in many aspects of the theory, especially in Piaget's discussions of the assimilation–accommodation balance (Piaget, 1962), of the relations between concept and action (Piaget 1976, 1980), and of the process of equilibration (see Moessinger, 1978). In its empirical implementation, however, Piaget's theory is successively slanted toward a form of mentalism that becomes dissociated from its organic base.

Riegel (1973) has commented on this slant and argued that in Piaget's theory, development is represented as a successive alienation of the individual from a rich organismic base. But Piaget, argues Riegel, is primarily interested in showing how people overcome their organismic limitations by embracing the power of logical concepts. Thus, mature thinking is described primarily in terms of the noncontradictory thinking of formal operations. The theory's organismic focus becomes progressively weakened as the individual grows to maturity: Whereas we are confronted with children who are emoting, playing, symbolizing, and struggling with issues of authority, Piaget's adolescent is described almost exclusively in terms of idealized structures of mathematical and scientific thinking. But this offers only a partial account of mature thought, which needs to embrace contradiction and tension as well. Arguing that change and contradiction rather than rest and equilibrium drive development forward, Riegel suggests that adults need to evolve a "dialectical" form of thought – one that accepts contradiction and change rather than one that is merely oriented toward resolving contradictions.

Turner (1973; see also Labouvie-Vief, Hakim-Larson, DeVoe, & Schoeberlein, 1989), too, has discussed this bias toward formalism, noting that Piaget's theory is almost exclusively concerned with the mechanisms by which the individual relates to collective and arbitrary *signs*, in contrast to more private and individual *symbols*. Werner (e.g., Werner & Kaplan, 1963) has similarly discussed cognitive development as the ability to forgo more state-dependent, organic, and private modes of experience for ones that are abstract and collective. This adaptation to a collective language happens as we successively dissociate inner meanings from impersonal outer ones. Thus, meaning systems that originate in the organismic, the sensorimotor, the figurative, the dynamic, and the personal gradually are displaced by ones that are abstract, conceptual, stable, conventional, and impersonal. Indeed, we assume that the former are characteristic of immature thought.

Piaget incorporates that bias in a manner that is profound: In general, increasing development is equated with a decrease in a playful, symbolic, imaginative, assimilating, animistic, and individualizing attitude. These inner processes are pathologized and compared to childish, autistic forms of thought and behavior (Labouvie-Vief, Hakim-Larson, DeVoe, & Schoeberlein, 1989; Piaget, 1955; Watkins, 1986).

Piaget's bias toward the world of imagination is matched by his neglect of interpersonal processes of attachment and love. The Piagetian infant is equipped, to be sure, with organic reflexive adaptations. But one dimension of those adaptations is almost completely left out: those adaptations –

studied by ethologists and psychoanalysts – that are oriented not toward impersonal objects but toward the maintenance of social bonds. For Piaget, such interpersonal adaptations do not constitute part of the individual's organicity, but instead are reduced to advances in cognitive development. Thus, for example, Piaget's description of the infant is one of an individual interacting with an impersonal world of objects rather than a reality that is primarily social. Piaget (1981) asserts that with the acquisition of the object concept, the infant is able to develop an attachment to the caretaker. Social bonding is not assumed to be a major variable in development from the outset, only to be transformed with advances in cognitive development (see Piaget, 1965, 1981). Rather, it is caused by the emergence of new cognitive structures. Thus, here we have a basic conception of the human being as an egocentric and isolated entity who can only break out of that isolation and construct a social network through the means of logical operations.

Much literature on the subject (see Neumann, 1973; Werner & Kaplan, 1963) has pointed out that the success of early development is, in large part, based on that very dissociation. The adaptive advantage of this process of dissociation and hierarchization in early development is the acquisition of culturally relevant symbols and language systems. These systems permit the novice adult to categorize experience in a stable and reliable manner. But what is an advantage in early development may turn into a hazard later on. In accordance with that view, researchers in the adulthood area have concentrated on recovering the dimensions lost to Piaget's description of the mature organism – the subjective and intuitive, the interpersonal, and the imaginative.

With respect to the first dimension, for example, researchers have pointed out that a complete model of human reasoning cannot be based on the hypothetico-deductive method only (Kahnemann & Tversky, 1984, Kitchener & Kitchener, 1981; Koplowitz, 1984; Labouvie-Vief, 1980, 1982a). The latter method is best suited to processes of inference that take place within a well-structured, preexisting system. In that case, a model that separates the knower from the process of knowing is sufficient. Even so, thinking cannot reach true objectivity, because it remains embedded in implicit epistemic and metaphysical assumptions about reality, assumptions that – though tacit – carry over into one's thinking. These assumptions cannot be penetrated with a model that excludes processes of self and history from thinking (Broughton, 1980; Edelstein & Noam, 1982; Labouvie-Vief, 1982a; Wood, 1983). Thus, the mature adult needs to evolve more powerful cognitive structures through which these assumptions can be examined so that a fuller level of objective and critical analysis can be reached.

Mature thinking also needs to give up the dualism between objective-rational thinking and those forms of thought that are considered less rational. For example, the philosopher Imre Lakatos has pointed out that if thinking is to extend beyond already established formal structures – that is, if it is to be creative and produce genuine novelty – it is necessary to give up the equation of advanced thinking with rational–deductive processes. Rather, the thinker needs to become increasingly open to nonrational processes such as conjectures, intuitions, the mythical. Of course, these eventually need to be subjected to rational analysis; but because they do not *originate* from rational processes, Lakatos proposes that formal thinking must be followed by a more complex, "postformal" form of thought that embraces the rational and the nonrational with equal facility (see also Hoyer, Rybash, & Roodin, 1989).

These limitations also have implications for the interpersonal realm. Kohlberg (1969, 1984) was the first to expand on these limitations when he pointed out that Piaget's simple differentiation between heteronomy and autonomy is too binary. Kohlberg agrees that adolescents' ability to think abstractly enables them to construct an abstract third-person perspective. Thus, their values can embrace abstract ideals rather than merely reflect the more local dynamics of concrete dyadic social exchanges. Nevertheless, this move to higher abstraction is not an all-or-none matter, since adolescent moral judgment remains constrained by the conventional value systems. Eventually, these systems need to be restructured and subsumed under more universal, postconventional perspectives.

Finally, these changes also have implications for the realms of self and emotional processes. For example, Labouvie-Vief (e.g., Labouvie-Vief et al., 1989) has argued that in the emotional arena, too, Piaget stresses the individual's ability to relate to the collective rather than what is "merely" personal and symbolic. More generally, many cognitive-developmental theories of self-development (for review, see Damon & Hart, 1982; Harter, 1983), taking their lead from Piaget and G. H. Mead (1934), have described how the self becomes increasingly invested in the objectified and idealized categories of the "Me." Yet, in evolving this perspective, one also needs to mask much of his or her inner life with an overlay of inhibitions, guilt, and shame concerning those impulses and aspects of self that do not have a place in public language. To disinhibit those repressed response systems so as to evolve a more adequate and complex language for them may be a major task of development after adolescence.

In sum, then, I suggest that many recent critiques of Piaget's theory have come about because the Piagetian brand of organicism has remained much too idealistic. Thus, his account of cognitive development is well suited to understanding the rudiments of deductive scientific thinking, as well as the adolescent's ability to step into a Platonic world and to embrace ideal and ideology. Piaget, however, has not addressed the dark side of these idealistic strivings – the youthful penchant toward an unbridled, dissociative mentalism and the difficulty of integrating the tensions between mind and body, autonomy and dependence, reason and feeling. These integrations, I suggest, remain as the major developmental milestone of adult development.

Investigations of adult cognitive structure

Early research

Although theoretical argument has been fairly prolific in the area of cognitive-developmental dimensions of adulthood, research is still somewhat sparse. Nevertheless, a growing body of evidence suggests that important cognitive developments do continue well beyond the period of formal operations.

In the attempt to provide empirical evidence for such movements, the work of several individuals has been seminal. Riegel's (1973) notion of the emergence of dialectical operations in adulthood has inspired several authors to describe such dialectical, multilevel modes of thinking. Riegel's work has remained rather abstract, however, and many empirical approaches took their impetus from Perry's (1968) influential study of the reasoning of Harvard undergraduates about issues they faced in the day-to-day problems of academic study. A similar study has since been done with women (Clinchy & Zimmerman, 1981; see also Belenky, Clinchy, Goldberger, & Tarule, 1986). Both studies found youths to be profoundly confused about the lack of certainty typical of most programs of study. Searching for safe techniques of how to tell "right" theories from "wrong" ones, or how to do a course assignment correctly, they displayed a striking inability to formulate a general and autonomous standard by which such judgments could be made. Instead, they attempted to reiterate what they thought teachers thought correct, only to find out that teachers, in turn, thought poorly of such attempts, judging them to lack independence.

These students appeared to possess a concept of "logic" or "rationality" that was entirely antagonistic to their own sense of autonomy; they operated on the basis of sharp polarizations of what they felt to be "objective" (i.e., a matter of factual evidence) and what, in turn, they felt to be "subjective" (i.e., a matter of opinions and assumptions), and they saw as their task the pursuit of the former and the avoidance of the latter. With that conceptual background, their notions of the "rational" became highly context-bound. Only eventually did these students learn that "truth" and "objectivity" were a matter not of a particular argument or content but, rather, of a general abstract argument structure that could accommodate many opinions and subjective beliefs.

Perry thus argued that formal thinking makes the individual uniquely vulnerable to an emphasis on product rather than process, stasis rather than change. This rigidity is loosened as the youth moves into a position of contextual relativism. Now the individual rejects the notion of any one certain truth and asserts instead that truth is inherently relative to a context. Eventually, this fairly radical relativism is integrated in a final position of "commitment in relativism": in the midst of multiple logical choices, the individual now accepts the need for an integration that is ultimately subjective.

Another major influence of research in this field has been the work of Kohlberg and his colleagues and students. As detailed by Turiel (1974; see also Gilligan & Murphy, 1979), in moral development, too, research suggested that as individuals moved out of the conventional law-and-order orientation of stage 4, they entered a period of subjectivism and relativism. Now they emphasized that it was impossible to make a moral choice that was generally and rationally justified, claiming instead that one "can pick and choose obligations, which are defined by particular societies, but one has no principle for choice." Unlike Perry, however, Kohlberg argued that this emphasis on relativism was followed by a new search for objectivity – a search for rationally justified, universal ethical principles valid for every human being.

The notion that a stage of contextual relativism follows one of the certainty of formal operations has influenced most subsequent work, but most authors have sided with Kohlberg in searching for a final stage that goes beyond a merely subjective synthesis and strives for some higher-order integration. Just how to describe this most mature level of cognitive functioning depends, however, on what aspect of Perry's work is further developed. On one hand, this work suggests that the youth's ability to conceptualize is still limited by a single system perspective (Commons, Richards, & Kuhn, 1982; Fischer, Hand, & Russell, 1984; Labouvie-Vief, 1982a), and that a more complex multiple system perspective remains to be developed thereafter. On the other hand, Perry also focused on some more general epistemological consequences of that cognitive shift. Young college students with their cognitive limitation also remain dependent on, and vulnerable to, authorities who need to give them conceptual guidance and define truth for them. In contrast, movement beyond the stage of dualism also brings with it a restructuring of the relationship between authority and self as the self is understood to be a full participant in the process of knowing.

Systematic thinking

An example of the first approach is the work of Commons and colleagues (e.g., Commons, Armon, Richards, & Schrader, 1989; Commons et al., 1982). These authors presented undergraduates and graduate students with a series of problems, each comprising a set of asymmetric relations. For example, one story read:

In Madras, India, V. P. Vanktesh, a man of habit and variable income, has a favorite restaurant. Although his tastes never vary, the food he can afford does. Of the three foods the restaurant serves he prefers, curry, birani, and alu paratha, in that order. Also, he likes curry better than alu paratha, and anything better than nothing. When V. P. has more money he buys two dishes, except it is not known whether he would choose the curry over both the birani and the alu paratha. He likes the combination of curry and birani better than curry and alu paratha, and he also likes curry and alu paratha better than birani and alu paratha, and birani and alu paratha better than curry and birani. Although a temperate man, at festivals, given the means, he has all three dishes instead of any single dish or pair.

This task requires that the individual compare several such stories and indicate which one violates a common ordering relationship. All of the stories can be described in terms of a transitive ordering sequence with two items tied (curry vs. birani + alu paratha). This particular story, however, also involves a violation of transitivity (birani + alu paratha is liked both more and less than curry + birani and curry + alu paratha). To detect this violation is no easy matter, since the individual must find out which one of many possible ways of describing the stories will yield systematic results. He or she must therefore construct an exhaustive representation that holds across the stories, a task that requires constructing possible representations for any one story and then cross-checking and intercoordinating those so as to arrive at the correct representation.

As Commons and his colleagues demonstrate, formal thinkers are able to abstract order relations in a systematic manner, but the entire system is not regarded as a single entity having characteristic properties that can be systematically compared to other systems. Thus, the individual merely attempts to show that single elements or two-element order relations map from one of the stories to another, but no full representations of all order relations are constructed. In contrast, systematic thinkers do attempt to construct full representations of each story. However, cognition remains focused merely on intrasystem analysis. There is no attempt at intersystem comparisons, a requirement for successful solution. The metasystematic thinker finally realizes that because a multiplicity of comparison systems could be used, the "correct" system is one that yields isomorphic transformations across systems. Aware that no language unique to any one of the systems can provide solutions, this individual constructs a common, overarching system by reciprocal assimilation.

In the work of Commons and his colleagues, a progression from formal to metasystematic reasoning was found in a comparison between undergraduate and graduate students. There was some evidence, as well, that this progression was dependent on prior acquisition of Piagetian formal thinking. This work is exemplary for its fine-grained theoretical analysis of progressive task features. Still, it is echoed by that of other authors, who also note that the hallmark of mature adult thinking is the ability to move from intrasystem thinking to the ability to construct coordinations and transformative relationships between abstract systems (e.g., Fischer et al., 1984; Gilligan & Murphy, 1979; Koplowitz, 1984; Labouvie-Vief, 1982a; Sinnott, 1984, 1989). Though based on a somewhat more global qualitative analysis, this work suggests a similar picture.

Following up on Riegel's (1973) work, Basseches (1984), for example, outlined a series of 24 schemata that are thought to characterize the move from formal to metasystematic thinking. These schemata are based on the thesis that formal thinking, because it focuses on propositions, not systems, as objects of thought, is static and closed. In contrast, metasystematic thought is dialectical, as it focuses not on static propositions but on relationships among and transformations of entire systems. Consequently, Basseches proposes schemata dealing with the ability to conceptualize motion, contradiction, relationship, transformation, and relativism. There is evidence that these schemata show progressions along an age–education continuum (Basseches, 1984), and also that they to some extent seem to parallel Perry's scheme (Benack & Basseches, 1989). However, the exact sequential nature of the various schemas is still rather unclear (Irwin & Scheese, 1989).

Other authors also have suggested that adulthood brings an enhanced ability to think dialectically (e.g., Kramer, 1983, 1989; Ozer & Reich, 1987; Reich, 1990; Sinnott, 1984, 1989). Kramer (1983, 1989), for example, proposes that thinking from adolescence to mature adulthood develops from a dualistic and absolutistic, through a relativistic, to a dialectical level. This work also is notable for including a broad span of ages, ranging from young to old adults. For example, in a comparison of young, middle-aged, and elderly adults, Kramer and Woodruff (1986) found older adults to display the highest level of relativistic and dialectical thinking. There also was some evidence that Piagetian formal thinking was prerequisite but not sufficient for dialectical thinking, but that relativistic thinking actually was necessary but not sufficient for formal operations. In a second study (Kramer, Melchior, & Levine, 1989), both middle-aged and older adults showed somewhat higher level of relativistic thinking than adolescents and young adults. Thinking level, however, was mediated by variation in content: subjects tended to perform more poorly on material constructed to be relevant for their own age group.

Knowing and the self

Much of the work just discussed has concentrated on relatively abstract features of the coordination between systems. These abstract features have been fleshed out in the work of other authors, who suggest that the inability to coordinate systems brings specific limitations for the way in which youth comprehend reality. Broughton (1980, 1982), following up on that notion as well as the work of J. M. Baldwin and Kohlberg, suggests that adolescence brings, at best, a divided and then dualistic world picture. That picture is characterized by realism and a separation of knower from known: Truth is assumed to reside in some objective perspective of an idealized "generalized other." Scientific laws of cause and effect are opposed to a subjective world of belief and purpose. Broughton found that adolescents tend to construct epistemologies that are sharply dualistic and disconnected. In turn, more mature individuals move to an understanding of these categories as dialectically and interactively related. Hence, the mature knower comes to understand knowledge as an active, social transformation of reality through a process of critical inquiry that is historically situated (see also Labouvie-Vief & Lawrence, 1985).

Kitchener and King (1981; see also King, Kitchener, Wood, & Davison 1989; Kitchener & Brenner, 1990; Kitchener, King, Wood, & Davison, 1989) have offered a detailed account of how individuals come to coordinate such categories as objectivity and subjectivity. These authors also carry futher Perry's contention that the mark of mature rationality is a return to a new, if more educated, form of subjectivism. Rather, they suggest that from this more abstract form of subjectivism, the individual again begins to search for a set of "objective" criteria.

Kitchener and King (1981) presented high school students, undergraduates, and graduate students with a series of open-ended problems asking them to make decisions about such controversial issues as whether to believe in a scientific or a religious account of creation. Results were charted in terms of a seven-stage progression of criteria by which individuals justified their judgments.

The lowest stages are characterized by the belief that there is an objective and knowable reality. But just how that reality is known becomes successively more problematic at stages to follow. At first merely intuitive and known to the self, knowledge becomes more assumptive and uncertain. From there, the individual moves into a position of radical relativism in which the possibility of absolute knowledge is completely denied, and reality is ascertained to be a matter of subjective and personal knowledge only. The position of radical relativism confronts the individual, however, with the limits of subjectivism, and initiates a research for revised criteria of objectivity. Criteria of rational inquiry now become more procedural, involving an open-ended process of critical inquiry and evaluation.

The work of Kitchener and King represents one of the most detailed efforts thus far to translate notions of postformal development into a coherent research program. Their original sample consisted of a group of high school juniors, college juniors, and advanced graduate students with mean ages ranging from 16 to 28. This sample was followed up in waves separated by 3-year intervals, resulting most recently in 9-year longitudinal data. Overall, this research demonstrates progressive development of reflective thinking at least into middle age (the highest age level sampled thus far in that research).

An important aspect of Kitchener and King's work is revealed by a comparison with the work of Perry. Both research programs reveal that to reach genuine objectivity, the knower needs to bring the self into the process of knowing. This inclusion happens as he or she moves from a definition of knowledge as something outer and knower-independent to something that is mediated by subjective processes. For Perry, however, the ultimate integration remains purely subjective:

> Reason reveals relations within any given context; it can also compare one context with another on the basis of metacontexts established for this purpose. But there is a limit. In the end, reason itself remains reflexively relativistic, a property which turns reason back upon reason's own findings. In even the farthest reaches then reason will leave the thinker with several legitimate contexts and no way of choosing among them – no way at least that he can justify through reason alone. If he is still to honor reason he must now also transcend it; he must affirm his own position from within himself in full awareness that reason can never completely justify him or assure him. (Perry, 1968, pp. 135–136)

For Kitchener and King, however, the further development of reason involves a fuller dialectic. Realizing the limits of a purely outer concept of what is "objective," their knower relocates truth criteria not in the purely personal but, rather, into the interpersonal sphere. Thus, he or she realizes that truth is not immanent in some outer authority but is embedded in a social process that requires the cooperation between autonomous individuals.

Overall, we may relate this work back to Piaget's proposal that objective thinking requires an integration between purely formal aspects and interpersonal processes. The studies just reviewed might concur with that assertion, but with a significant amendment. Just as Piaget's description of formal thinking may have set the apex of cognitive development too low, so his discussion of an adolescent community of critical thinkers cooperatively engaged in the coconstruction of knowledge has remained far too idealistic. Indeed, more recent work suggests that such a vision of objectivity remains entirely out of reach of the adolescent's conceptual abilities and that, indeed, it remains a rather lofty ideal for most adults.

This work, therefore, has implications for modern discussions about the nature of mature reason. Beyond these implications, it may also help highlight the cognitive roots of some major psychological differences between adolescents and adults. Labouvie-Vief (1982a), for example, has argued that the adolescent understanding of truth as certain and computable may be a significant factor in her or his defense structure. Because that structure is based on a dualism of objective and subjective processes, it does not involve a mechanism by which such defensive cognitive distortions can be analyzed and, therefore, corrected. In turn, the movement to a model of knowledge that is more historically situated may bring a more integrated structure that, by analyzing its own subjectivity, provides a more powerful device for self-regulation and correction (see also Edelstein & Noam, 1982; Wood, 1983).

How such distortions are gradually corrected was the subject of a study by Blanchard-Fields (1986, 1989), who, following up on a study by Kuhn, Pennington, and Leadbeater (1983), presented adolescents, college students, and middle-aged adults with problems requiring the coordination of information from two discrepant accounts of the same event. Blanchard-Fields showed that with increasing age, there was a better ability to differentiate an event from one's interpretation of it. That awareness also brings the ability to render more balanced, less biased versions of the opposing accounts.

In a somewhat related fashion, Kitchener (1983) proposes that the adult evolves a unique mode of cognitive regulation. Not concerned merely with the enactment of cognition, or with the monitoring of its success and failure (i.e., metacognition), that mode of "epistemic cognition" is concerned with the very conditions of knowing (its limits, certainty, etc.) themselves.

Other authors also propose that the type of cognitive monitoring changes in adulthood. Pascual-Leone (1984), for example, also suggests that mature adulthood brings an awareness of and concern with the transcendental conditions of knowledge. On an empirical level, a similar progression of epistemological levels was found in a study by Adams, Labouvie-Vief, Hakim-Larson, DeVoe, and Hayden (1988). Using a think-aloud procedure, subjects from preadolescence to midlife responded to logical problems. A developmental progression was evident in the metalanguage individuals used to represent the problems and to monitor problem-solution strategies. At first, there was virtually no metalanguage and no evidence of self-monitoring. Individuals reacted with little reflective awareness and were entirely literal in their approach. They thought of problem solutions as being inherent in the text rather than emanating from their own thought processes, as when they rationalized their solutions by pointing to the text and saying, "It says so right here!" At a somewhat more mature level, individuals possessed a metalanguage for logical strategies, although they still did not admit ambiguity and interpretation in that language. Thus, when realizing ambiguities they responded with invigorated efforts to monitor their behavior in the apparent hope of thus reducing ambiguity. In contrast, at the most mature levels individuals realized that because the truth value of a conclusion depends on how one interprets premises, ambiguity in principle cannot be eliminated. These individuals were explicit in their recognition that problem solution requires an active thinker who not only monitors the deductive application of rules, but who also selects and interprets the premises on which those rules are to operate.

As a consequence of such advanced epistemological understanding, the mature adult often may be less concerned with solving problems than with finding them. That notion has been propagated by Arlin (1975, 1984, 1989), who also rejects the idea that adult thinking achieves a final equilibrium with formal operational, problem-solving thought. Instead, Arlin proposes a fifth, problem-finding stage in which mental activity is characterized by creative thought, the formulation of generic problems, the isolation and resolution of ill-defined problems, and processes of scientific progressive thought. Arlin has obtained evidence to suggest a sequential relationship between problem solving and problem finding, and proposes that creative thought, the envisioning of new questions, and the discovery of new heuristics are unique and emergent aspects of adult cognition (Sinnott, 1984; Wood, 1983).

Self and collective

The research already discussed relates cognition back to the self in relation to a the broader social group, or collective. Thus, it echoes the long-standing view that conceptual processes ought to bear profoundly on values and the organization of the self (e.g., Haan, 1977; Harvey, Hunt, & Schroeder, 1961), thereby providing a link with the work of Kohlberg. Indeed, until his death Kohlberg maintained an active interest in the postformal "movement," serving as a mentor to many of the individuals working in this area.

A major assumption underlying Kohlberg's (1984) theory of moral development is that the development of moral and ethical judgments from youth to mature adulthood is defined by the changing relationship of the individual to his or her social milieu. Unlike Piaget, Kohlberg suggests that the movement from "heteronomy" to "autonomy" is not a binary progression achieved in the single step from concrete to formal operations. Rather, the movement happens stepwise through a gradually widening social radius, as the individual is able to evolve standards that ground moral judgment in a more and more abstract relationship between self and some "other" or reference group (see also Cook-Greuter, 1990; Selman, 1980).

At the *preconventional* level, that other is purely personal, and rules and standards are mediated by the most intimate concrete dyadic exchanges. Adolescence brings the ability to function on the basis of a more abstract, interpersonal or systemic "other" – an abstract third person perspective that mediates group and then social system rules and norms. This abstract perspective permits the emergence of a more group-dependent and social system–dependent *conventional* morality. The task of adulthood, however, is to evolve a more autonomous value system that transcends the merely local and reaches toward the universal in a third, *postconventional* level. Indeed, although by far not all adults move to this postconventional level of reasoning, Kohlberg and his co-workers claim there is definitive evidence that moral development continues into at least the 20s and 30s (Colby, Kohlberg, Gibbs, & Lieberman, 1983).

Kohlberg has addressed himself most explicitly to morality, but his theory has a much broader sweep and in fact involves an implicit theory of evolving self-structures around which values and emotions are organized. These implications have been worked out by a group of subsequent researchers for both childhood (e.g., Damon & Hart, 1982; Selman, 1980) and adulthood.

In his book *The evolving self*, Kegan (1982) discussed the implications of a cognitive-developmental perspective for a theory of self. For Kegan, increasing cognitive development has the result that the individual gradually differentiates from a primary attachment relationship that provides an original holding matrix within which all cognitive and organic activity is regulated. Eventually, he or she acquires the ability for more autonomous self-regulation. Before the conventional level, children can control impulses but still lack in their ability for social coordination. The strength of the conventional level is that a more genuinely shared reality, based on the coordination of social perspectives, emerges. However, the self remains fused with an interpersonal and then institutional matrix, and the ability to experience distinctness and an individuated self remains limited. That capacity to maintain a more autonomous sense of selfhood emerges at the final stage, when self and other can be understood as entities that transcend interpersonal and institutional meanings. Thus, both a more authentic sense of selfhood and a deeper capacity for intimacy can result.

Armon (1984, 1989) has applied Kohlberg's notions to conceptions of what constitutes a good or ethical life and work. In her study, preconventional thought is focused around merely individual interests and desires, while conventional thinking becomes organized around such goals as socially beneficial work, positive interpersonal experiences, financial security, and social utility. For the postconventional individual, the potential conflict between social commitment and self-fulfillment is heightened and the individual aims at balancing responsibility to self with that to society.

Armon has provided data to show continued development in adulthood. Overall, from preadolescence to later adulthood, the data indicate positive and decelerating rates of change, although some change continues into late adulthood. Her postconventional stages are achieved only by individuals over the age of 30 and parallel Kohlbergian moral judgment stages.

Fowler (1981) also has applied Kohlbergian (as well as Eriksonian) notions to another domain – that of faith and religious values. Fowler argues that the preconventional individual has a magical and concrete conception of God. At the conventional level, the orientation is based on acceptance of cultural values with only little critical evaluation: Religion now is oriented toward maintaining dogma and interpersonal validation. In contrast, the postconventional individual becomes critical of conventional religion and evolves a perspective in which conventional religious frameworks form separate though equivalent paths toward more universal spiritual goals.

Another theory proposing a broad reorganization of the self in relation to the social collective is Loevinger's (1976; Loevinger & Wessler, 1978) model of ego development. Loevinger proposed that the impulsiveness of the child gives way to a conventional model in which one's own subjective inner life is suppressed and subordinated to social norms. The mature individual, however, evolves a more flexible language in which the conflicts between impulse and norm, self and society, or inner and outer, are first acknowledged and then integrated within more self-chosen standards. Cognitive complexity thus replaces a youthful language of self-regulation preoccupied with physical, mental, or emotional control, good–bad dichotomies, and little or no tolerance of intrapersonal or interpersonal conflict. The developmental significance of Loevinger's conception and measure has been demonstrated in age-related trends in both cross-sectional and longitudinal samples (e.g., Cook-Greuter, 1990; Hauser, 1976; Redmore & Loevinger, 1979). Ego development is also a good index of such dimensions of developmental complexity as moral development and empathy (see Loevinger, 1979) and intellectual development, as discussed later in this chapter.

Processing of organismic information

As Kohlberg has suggested throughout his career, one implication of the research just discussed is that the individual is able to construct a perspective increasingly aimed at the universal and general aspects of the human condition. Although few would disagree that this search for universal, transcendent aspects of life and human nature constitutes the essence of mature adult functioning, Kohlberg's specific formulation of that search has been criticized. Kohlberg's approach to morality has remained primarily guided by a search for rational universal principles, mirroring Piaget's predominant concern with formal and paradigmatic modes of cognition.

One specific limiting consequence of the rationalist bias is that these theories do not deal very well with the organismic constraints on development. As already noted, Piaget's theory does not fully incorporate, for example, the importance of interpersonal attachments and connectedness in development (see also Gilligan, 1982). As a result, the child is often described in pejorative terms as egocentric. Indeed, in Piaget's work there is little consideration of the fact that nonegocentric forms of morality do emerge well before the advent of complex cognitive operations, or that morality may constitute a primary emotional requirement of the human condition (see, e.g., Hoffman, 1978).

The limits of a purely rational account of development may become particularly important in adulthood. The outer orientation of the rationalist account of development may be primarily adaptive for the acquisitive tasks of youth, but in mature adulthood, criteria for what is adaptive may shift (Labouvie-Vief, Hakim-Larson, DeVoe, & Schoeberlein, 1989). To become a competent member of the collective, the youth needs to be able to dissociate impersonal, abstract, and collective meanings from more concrete and personal meanings that carry a great deal of organismic significance. The focus is on the development of a strong ego and on the containment of instinctual processes. Hence, the individual evolves a "vertical" cognitive organization in which mental processes are understood to control or superordinate more organismic aspects of life. For the mature adult, however, it becomes evident that these mental ideals and objective structures are themselves symbolic of the subjective conditions of life. Hence, the individual learns to see through and beyond the "objective" to encode underlying conditions of human subjectivity. As a consequence, an epistemological shift is necessitated in which the organismic and inner dimensions are successively upgraded, permitting the individual to evolve a lateral or dialogic structure between rational and nonrational ways of processing.

In our own research, we have applied that notion of an epistemological shift to an examination of how individuals of different ages process information. This work follows up on the earlier view that middle and later adulthood bring a turn inward (e.g., Neugarten, 1968), and expands on that view by adding that such an inward turn brings specific cognitive consequences. For the young adult, information is seen as an outer given that one attempts to reproduce with a minimum of infusion of one's own self. Hence, young adults are apt to have a literal, text-dependent bias. In contrast, middle and older adults relate to text in a more interpretive and psychological mode. As the individual realizes that information is not independent of an interpreter – a self who reads and who infuses herself or himself into a text – the individual turns more to the landscape of human motivations and intentions that determines how texts are generated and interpreted. Hence, these adults may become experts at the processing of information relating to subjective processes and inner dynamics. Although this processing style will result in deficits in tasks requiring more objective and formal ways of processing, it may be an advantage in ones that specifically require more psychological ones.

This shift from a more text-dependent mode to a more interpretive and subjective one was shown in a series of studies about individuals' rendition and interpretation of narratives (Adams, 1986; Adams, Labouvie-Vief, Hobart, & Dorosz, 1990; Jepson & Labouvie-Vief, in press). That research suggests that adolescents and college students in reading text primarily attend to the structure of actions and events depicted in the text. For mature or elderly adults, however, the primary interest is not in the action-event structure but, rather, in what it reveals about underlying aspects of the human condition. To that extent, the mature adult's interest in text becomes more abstract and symbolic: A narrative does not refer to the concrete here and now of protagonists and their actions but, rather, is taken as indicative of human actions in general.

On the basis of this and similar evidence, Jepson and Labouvie-Vief (in press) suggest that adulthood may bring a return of symbolic processing. On that view, mature adulthood brings a symbolic processing style that emerges in a uniquely adult form. In contrast to Piaget, who held that symbolic ways of processing, along with their tendency to animism, are immature, Jepson and Labouvie-Vief (in press) propose that these ways of processing also may show a developmental line. For example, as argued by the Nobel laureate of biochemistry Monod (1971), vitalism always has constituted a major alternative to determinism for scientists. In turn, a loss of sense of being related to nature is often blamed for our current ecological crises.

The adaptive function of that symbolic shift forms the cornerstone of Jung's (see Whitmont, 1969) theory of adult development. Like Piaget's theory, Jung's is also structured around the opposition of sign and symbol. Unlike Piaget, however, Jung argues that human experience always remains intimately tied to the symbolic. For him, mature adulthood brings the ability not merely to live out these symbols but also to enrich them with rational understanding. Indeed, Jung believes that out of the dialogue between the rational sign and the nonrational symbolic individuals can activate the "transcendental function" that constitutes an essential dynamic force for continued development in later life.

The adult's need for mythic and symbolic forms of experience is also the topic of the famed essay by Thomas Mann (1978) on "Freud and the future." In that essay, Mann argues that mythic thinking, far from constituting an immature and childish form, is a uniquely adult form of meaning making: It represents the need to see one's individual life in terms of patterns that can be experienced as universal and necessary, thus grounding individual biography in the broad and typical patterns that underlie myths.

That a return of the symbolic and mythic may be one of the critical features of adult cognition has also been suggested by Fowler (1981), who has argued that the basic contrast between knowing on the basis of reason and of faith is resolved by stage 4 individuals in a demythologizing mode. A person may be motivated to show that faith and myth can be reduced to structures of reason – a motivation that also dominated the philosophy of the Enlightenment era. In contrast, postconventional religion is less concerned with reinterpreting myth in the light of reason. This level of thinking involves an integration in which "symbolic power is reunited with conceptual meanings" (p. 197) – a "second naivete" (Ricoeur, 1970) or "emancipated innocence" (Chinen, 1989), in which one opens to the nonrational in a way that is not precritical but, rather, postcritical.

The work cited so far involves rather complex epistemological arguments about the "natural epistemologies" (Broughton, 1980) of individuals. However, such naive epistemologies are rather directly expressed in individuals' cognitions about the regulation of their organismic processes. For this reason, my collaborators and I turned to a cognitive-developmental investigation of how individuals reorganize their understanding of the regulation of emotional processes over the life-span.

That processes of emotional regulation are organized by an underlying dimension of cognitive complexity is by now well accepted in the area of child development. Following Piaget (1981), many researchers (e.g., Harris, 1983; Harter, 1983; Kegan, 1982; Selman, 1980) have proposed that as the cognitive system evolves, so does the individual's emotional repertoire. Specifically, that repertoire could be said to evolve along two epistemological dimensions.

The first of these is a mind–body dimension. Younger or less mature individuals express emotions externally in terms of actions, physical processes, and their concrete social consequences. This physicalistic, impulsive language is replaced in older or more mature individuals by an understanding of emotions as inner, cognitive or "mental" processes that are symbolic and that emanate from one's memories, wishes, and other inner states. Similarly, processes of coping and defense also come to be more dominated by more complex intellectual and interpretive processes (Donaldson & Westerman, 1986; Harris, 1983; Harter, 1983; Selman, 1980).

Second, the standards or norms by which the individual references and regulates his or her behavior also become more complex. The young child depends for the regulation of behavior on the identification with concrete reference persons such as parents and, later, peers. By adolescence, a somewhat more autonomous self emerges that no longer needs such direct supervision but that has internalized more abstract, conventional, and collective standards (e.g., Kegan, 1982; Kohlberg, 1969; Saarni, 1984).

By adolescence, therefore, individuals master a set of rules permitting them to regulate behavior in accordance with cultural dictates. That outward movement, however, carries with it certain disadvantages as well: In the process of adaptation to outer reality, the youth needs to be able to dissociate impersonal, abstract, and collective meanings from more concrete and personal ones that carry a great deal of organismic significance. In contrast to the outward movement, adulthood may bring a compensatory movement inward. A focus on inner dynamics, on private experience, and on rich organismic experience and emotive content now comes to the fore.

We investigated this process of reconnection in a large-scale research project on the development of self-regulation in adulthood. We interviewed 100 individuals, ranging in age from 10 to 77, about their experience of four prototypical emotional states, and the responses were coded in terms of a four-level coding scheme (Labouvie-Vief, DeVoe, & Bulka, 1989; Labouvie-Vief, Hakim-Larson, DeVoe, & Schoeberlein, 1989). The hypothesis was that from early adolescence to later life, there would be a progression of emotion language from a *presystemic*, body-oriented, and egocentric language to an *intrasystemic* language focusing on mental and normative standards. Next, individuals would evolve a language attempting to integrate the dualisms of mind–body and self–other at an *intersystemic* level, and a few would go on to integrate these dualisms at an *integrated* level.

Our data showed this progression from adolescence to middle adulthood. Younger individuals, or adults with less advanced ego development, used a language of emotions that was almost entirely devoid of felt sense. Feelings were described not in terms of inner feedback but in terms of an outer conventional language (e.g., "Things were bottled up"). Formal and technical processes and distant, static terms were used as descriptors (e.g., "Your blood pressure rises"). In addition, feelings were described in terms of how one *should* feel: External rules and standards of conduct rather than the felt experience characterized people's expression of emotions (e.g., "I was really scared, because I knew that if I didn't play good, that they'd tease me about it").

Our mature adults – those around middle adulthood – gave evidence of a significantly reorganized emotion language. Feelings were described in terms of a vivid felt process (e.g., "My heart felt like bursting" or "I felt a rush of energy"). Their language was inner and personal rather than outer and technical. Metaphors became dynamic, dealing not with static states but with process and transformation. At the same time, individuals began to differentiate an inner realm of emotional experience from an outer realm of convention. The conflict between these realms was acknowledged, and the individual was concerned with accepting impulses and thoughts that had previously seemed too overwhelming to accept.

This progression in how individuals describe their emotions was paralleled by the control strategies mentioned. The young person or less mature adult often controlled emotions through active metacognitive strategies such as forgetting, ignoring, and redirecting one's thoughts. The primary end of emotion control appeared to be repression of emotional tension and freedom from emotional conflict. The individual also looked to others to affirm the self's feelings. These controls contrasted with the language of the mature adult who was open to acknowledging periods of intense inner conflict and rumination. Aware that emotions have a lawful regularity of their own that may oppose our concepts about them, these people evolved means of control that allowed more full acknowledgment of their emotional experience. For example, realizing that "you can't paper your emotions over," individuals often made an effort to examine their felt experience rather than inhibiting it under a layer of shoulds and oughts. Emotions were accepted as motivating energy to assist the self in either acting on or accepting the prevailing situation. Others were no longer blamed for the self's emotional state but were viewed as part of a more complex system of interaction and communication.

At different parts of the life-span, this research also suggests, emotional experience is organized by quite different causes. For example, the experience of stress was found to change along an ego-level dimension (Labouvie-Vief et al., 1987). The preconformist individual's experience of stress related to blocking of egocentric impulses and a sense of powerlessness vis-à-vis others who are viewed as overpowering and whose demands and commands are seen as thwarting the self. Conformist individuals experience stress because of their need for approval and belongingness and adherence to norms and conventions. In contrast, postconformist individuals' experience of stress is tied to a more individuated sense of self that accepts conflicts between inner and outer demands. More recently, a similar analysis was also applied to the causes individuals give for emotional experience (DeVoe & Labouvie-Vief, 1990).

Developmental interrelationships

The assumption is often implicit in much of the cited work that the various cognitive-developmental models of adulthood map out a relatively unified process. It is certainly true that most of the approaches discussed in this chapter have common roots in the structural developmental assumptions of Piaget and Kohlberg, and there has been much cross-fertilization among researchers in this new field. And as this new field is defining its directions, a number of more specific questions are emerging.

An overarching question emerging in the new field is that of in just what sense the various approaches I have discussed are developmental. Certainly, all of the research involves speculations about the sequential nature of the various stages, but evidence relating to this claim is extremely sparse. Most available studies to date are of a cross-sectional nature and strong methods to examine assumptions about the sequential nature of the competences studied have therefore rarely been applied (see, however, Armon, 1984; King et al., 1989). That lack is particularly limiting in the postadolescent period, where change appears to become decoupled from the parameter of age. In our own research on emotional understanding (Labouvie-Vief, DeVoe, & Bulka, 1989), for example, results indicated that when charted along age as a parameter, and when using overall level of emotional understanding scores, this developmental pattern is curvilinear, appearing to abate in adulthood. Indeed, when the adolescent age groups were excluded from the analysis, linear and quadratic affects of age disappeared. When ego level and verbal ability were used as independent markers of developmental maturity, however, the relationship to levels of emotional understanding remained linear.

These results suggest that development in adulthood is not best indexed by age (see also Labouvie-Vief et al., 1987), but that other indicators of developmental maturity become more meaningful when studying adult development. Armon's (1984) analysis of her stages of ethical reasoning also showed similar conclusions. Such findings have important methodological implications for the study of adulthood. They suggest that even more than is true in the period of childhood, age-comparative strategies are a poor method by which to search for adult developmental change. Rather, developmental assessments of adults need to be theory-driven and based on strong indices of developmental complexity.

A second important question raised by this body of work is that of whether the various "postformal" competences we have discussed do, indeed, form a unitary competence, or whether they are domain-specific. As far as the empirical literature is concerned, there is strong evidence that many cognitive-developmental measures of progressive adult development may indeed indicate a general dimension of cognitive complexity – however, not necessarily of the formal but, rather, of the practical type. With respect to ego level, for example, a high association with verbal ability has been reported widely in research dealing with subjects of different ages (see Hauser, 1976), including adult groups (e.g., Blanchard-Fields, 1986; Kitchener & Brenner, in press; Kitchener & King, 1981; Kitchener et al., 1989; Labouvie-Vief, Hakim-Larson, DeVoe, & Shoeberlein, S., 1989). These correlations are not restricted to ego level but appear to extend to other cognitive-developmental measures, more generally. Thus, Kitchener and King (1981; see also King et al., 1989) and Kitchener et al. (1989), using a measure of reflective judgment, reported correlations ranging from .54 to .79; Blanchard-Fields obtained correlations between her measure of socio-relational reasoning and verbal ability ranging from .40 to .60. Moral judgment scores also have been found to show similarly strong and significant relationships with measures of verbal ability (e.g., Rest, 1985). Finally, similarly in our own research we have consistently obtained high correlations between verbal ability and cognitive-emotional maturity. Thus, all of these measures may tap versions of a relatively coherent dimension of cognitive complexity. However, that conclusion needs to remain tentative at this time, since research evidence still is somewhat sparse.

Another question raised by this body of work is that of just how the various approaches truly are *post*formal in the sense of having a logical, temporal, or even statistical dependence on the achievement of formal thinking. Commons et al. (1982) established some degree of dependence on formal thinking, as did Kramer and Woodruff (1986). The latter authors also provide evidence that dialectical but not relativistic thinking is dependent on formal operations.

Boutilier and Chandler (1990) also suggest that at least some of the measures map separate domains that are parallel to, rather than dependent on, formal thought. These authors demonstrated that at least some aspects of system thinking – those generally associated with a "general systems approach" – appear to develop in tandem with, or as alternate routes to, formal thinking. These findings are also congruent with those of Reich and Ozer (1990; Reich, 1990) who examined the development of thinking in terms of complementarity – thinking that requires the capacity to coordinate non-compatible theories or belief systems. Many of the forms of thinking discussed in this chapter would seem to fall into this category, involving as they do the coordination of such categories as mind and body, objectivity and subjectivity, self and society, reason and emotion, and so forth. Reich and Ozer propose that the development of this form of thought requires sufficient levels of formal reasoning as a prerequisite, although achievement of formal reasoning is not a sufficient condition of complementarity thinking. If that assumption is correct, it may well be correct to refer to many of the competences we have discussed as postformal. In that case, however, the term *postformal* may not imply a progression in formal complexity. Instead, it could mean that for some individuals, formal thinking forms a base from which thought branches out into more nonformal domains.

The latter possibility raises another question: What are the dynamics that may drive developmental processes in adulthood? As Flavell (1970) suggests – and his interpretation is congruent with the data just discussed – the strong morphological growth component that directs early development may carry less variance in adulthood, where factors related to individualized experience may carry more weight. That this may be so has long been suggested by psychometric research suggesting that intellectual functions become more differentiated in early adulthood (e.g., Baltes, 1987).

Flavell's argument may be particularly valid for some cognitive components that are not strongly tied to maturational changes in adulthood. Nevertheless, there certainly is strong evidence as well that maturational changes relevant to cognitive performance may continue into adulthood (see, e.g., Salthouse, 1985). But because maturational changes in childhood often are indicative of growth, whereas those in adulthood suggest decline, a paradox emerges: How is one to reconcile the dual claims of growth and decline in adulthood? Pascual-Leone (1984) has argued that the dynamics of progressive adult development may exactly be driven by such decline processes. In childhood, argues Pascual-Leone, the emergence of new competences is directed by gradual growth of processing resources. Later development, however, may be driven by underlying regressive changes in processing resources that nevertheless prompt new functional reorganizations. Specifically, the individual may become more concerned with transcendental thinking in part as a response to certain cognitive losses.

Labouvie-Vief (1981, 1982b; Labouvie-Vief & Schell, 1982) has suggested a somewhat similar argument, although she has noted that such trade-offs between regressive and progressive changes are by no means unique to adulthood. Rather, she has reviewed evidence to show that changes suggesting loss often go along with changes that are termed growth at a higher level of complexity, and that such trade-off relationships are ubiquitous in childhood as well (see also Baltes, 1987).

In addition to those mechanisms, it is possible that a structural developmental model, when extended into adulthood, needs to be particularly attentive to how mechanisms of cultural development affect those of individual development. I have argued throughout this chapter, for example, that the very process of child development is, in part, culturally driven in an attempt to socialize youth to acquire a cultural symbol system. Thus, the epistemological development of a culture provides a gradient that regulates and canalizes growth early in life. In later life, however, development mechanisms may shift over to more individuated ones. Thus, as Helson and Wink (1987) note, the notion of "maturity" increasingly comes to stress self-chosen, long-term motives. Indeed, the goals of the highest states may often conflict with the compliance needed for adjustment to a surrounding social reality, and as a result later development may place much greater emphasis on maturity of ego functioning than do earlier phases of the life-span.

Discussion and conclusion

In this chapter, I have summarized research and theory that has attempted to apply core assumptions of the Piagetian program of development to the study of adulthood. Out of these efforts appears to be emerging a fairly coherent body of findings and propositions about the study of adult adaptations. Congruent with the Piagetian program, these studies have addressed cognitive changes in the broadest sense of the word *cognition*, encompassing not only relatively formal aspects of reasoning, but extending to such areas as self, values, emotions, and coping processes.

Despite the diversity of these domains, the various endeavors are held together by a common assumption. According to that assumption, a major organizing feature of adult cognition is the ability to move beyond conventional forms of thinking, and the attempt to identify more transcendent and permanent dimensions of life. In that move, thought is less and less considered a purely objective, impersonal, and rational activity. Instead, it embraces dimensions that are subjective, interpersonal, and nonrational. By establishing a dialogue with those dimensions, thinking becomes rebalanced into a more genuinely organismic structure.

The research here discussed adopts Piaget's proposition that the developing individual's cognitive efforts can best be understood by examining the epistemological perspective underlying each stage of development. Like a philosopher, the individual attempts to evolve a coherent perspective on reality. The work reviewed here, however, extends that proposal by adding that adolescents evolve an epistemological position that is only a preliminary stage to mature cognitive functioning. Much as Piaget's theory has retained many objectivist assumptions, so the adolescent's world picture, too, retains an objectivist epistemology that is oriented toward an outer definition of reality. As a consequence, adulthood requires an epistemological transformation that restores the dissociations resulting from objectivism. As the individual restores the subjective, the communal, and the symbolic to his or her world picture, early-life dualisms are healed: Now subjective and objective, individual and community, self and other, reason and emotion, mind and body all partake in genuine interaction.

Whereas the research reviewed here provides a theoretical extension of the Piagetian program, a major task for future research will be to specify just how these studies extend Piaget's program in an empirical sense. Certainly, the assumption, borrowed from Piaget, that cognitive developments serve as important pacemakers of diverse developmental domains has proved extremely fertile. Nevertheless, despite that common intellectual heritage, it is not clear that these domains all address a unitary form of development. Nor is it clear that the different domains all can be said to extend Piaget's sequence of development in a sequential manner. As we have seen, it is likely that at least some studies may have addressed accomplishments that parallel rather than extend those described by Piaget himself. To trace the continuity of the various competences addressed in the study of adulthood with those studied at earlier parts of the life span remains, then, an area of much needed research.

References

Adams, C. (1986). *Qualitative changes in text memory from adolescence to mature adulthood.* Unpublished doctoral dissertation, Wayne State University, Detroit.

Adams, C., Labouvie-Vief, G., Hakim-Larson, J., DeVoe, M., & Hayden, M. (1988). Modes of thinking and problem solving: Developmental transitions from preadolescence to middle adulthood. Unpublished manuscript, University of Michigan, Ann Arbor.

Adams, C., Labouvie-Vief, G., & Hobart, C. J., & Dorosz, M. (1990). Adult age group differences in story recall style. *Journal of Gerontology, 25*, 17–27.

Arlin, P. K. (1975). Cognitive development in adulthood: A fifth stage? *Developmental Psychology, 11*, 602–606.

Arlin, P. [K.] (1984). Adolescent and adult thought: A structural interpretation. In M. L. Commons, F. A. Richards, & C. Armon (Eds.), *Beyond formal operations: Late adolescent and adult cognitive development* (pp. 258–271). New York: Praeger.

Arlin, P. [K.] (1989). Problem solving and problem finding in young artists and scientists. In M. L. Commons, J. D. Sinnott, F. A. Richards, & C. Armon (Eds.), *Adult development: Vol.*

1. Comparisons and applications of developmental models (pp. 197–216). New York: Praeger.

Armon, C. (1984). Ideals of the good life and moral judgment: Ethical reasoning across the life span. In M. L. Commons, F. A. Richards, & C. Armon, *Beyond formal operations* (pp. 357–380). New York: Praeger.

Armon, C. (1989). Individuality and autonomy in adult ethical reasoning. In M. L. Commons, J. D. Sinnott, F. A. Richards, & C. Armon (Eds.), *Adult development: Vol. 1. Comparisons and applications of developmental models* (pp. 179–196). New York: Praeger.

Baltes, P. B. (1987). Theoretical propositions of life-span developmental psychology: On the dynamics between growth and decline. *Developmental Psychology, 23*, 611–626.

Basseches, M. A. (1984). Dialectical thinking as a metasystematic form of cognitive organization. In M. L. Commons, F. A. Richards, & C. Armon (Eds.), *Beyond formal operations*. New York: Praeger.

Basseches, M. A. (1989). Dialectical thinking as an organized whole. In M. L. Commons, J. D. Sinnott, F. A. Richards, & C. Armon (Eds.), *Adult development: Vol. 1. Comparisons and applications of developmental models* (pp. 161–178). New York: Praeger.

Belenky, M. F., Clinchy, B. M., Goldberger, N. R., & Tarule, J. M. (1986). *Women's ways of knowing*. New York: Basic Books.

Benack, S., & Basseches, M. A. (1989). Dialectical thinking and relativistic epistemology: Their relation in adult development. In M. L. Commons, J. D. Sinnott, F. A. Richards, & C. Armon (Eds.), *Adult development: Vol. 1. Comparisons and applications of developmental models* (pp. 95–109). New York: Praeger.

Blanchard-Fields, F. (1986). Reasoning on social dilemmas varying in emotional saliency: An adult developmental perspective. *Psychology and Aging, 1*, 325–333.

Blanchard-Fields, F. (1989). Postformal reasoning in a socioemotional context. In M. L. Commons, J. D. Sinnott, F. A. Richards, & C. Armon (Eds.), *Adult development: Vol. 1. Comparisons and applications of developmental models* (pp. 73–93). New York: Praeger.

Boutilier, R. G., & Chandler, M. J. (in press). The development of systemic reasoning. *Human Development*.

Broughton, J. M. (1980). Genetic metaphysics: The developmental psychology of mind–body concepts. In R. W. Rieber (Ed.), *Body and mind* (pp. 177–221). New York: Academic Press.

Broughton, J. M. (1982). Genetic logic and the developmental psychology of philosophical concepts. In J. M. Broughton & D. J. Freeman-Moir (Eds.), *The cognitive developmental psychology of James Mark Baldwin* (pp. 219–276). Norwood, NJ: Ablex.

Bruner, J. (1986). *Actual minds, possible worlds*. Cambridge, MA: Harvard University Press.

Cassirer, E. (1946). *Language and myth* (pp. 32–33). New York: Harper & Brothers. (Reprinted 1953, New York: Dover Publications.)

Chinen, A. B. (1989). *In the ever after: Fairy tales and the second half of life*. Wilmette, IL: Chiron.

Clinchy, B., & Zimmerman, C. (1981). Epistemology and agency in the development of undergraduate women. In P. Perun (Ed.), *The undergraduate woman: Issues in educational equity*. Boston: D. C. Heath.

Colby, A., Kohlberg, L., Gibbs, J., & Lieberman, M. (1983). A longitudinal study of moral development. *Monographs of the Society for Research in Child Development, 49*, (2, Serial No. 206).

Collingwood, R. G. (1945). *The idea of nature*. Oxford: Clarendon Press.

Commons, M. L., Armon, C., Richards, F. A., & Schrader, D. E. (1989). A multidomain study of adult development. In M. L. Commons, J. D. Sinnott, F. A. Richards, & C. Armon (Eds.), *Adult development: Vol. 1. Comparisons and applications of developmental models* (pp. 33–56). New York: Praeger.

Commons, M. L., Richards, F. A., & Armon, C. (1984). *Beyond formal operations*. New York: Praeger.

Commons, M. L., Richards, F. A., & Kuhn, D. (1982). Systematic, metasystematic, and cross-paradigmatic reasoning: A case for stages of reasoning beyond Piaget's stage of formal operations. *Child Development, 53*, 1058–1068.

Cook-Greuter, S. (1990). Maps for living: Ego development theory from symbiosis to conscious universal embeddedness. In M. L. Commons, J. D. Sinnott, F. A. Richards, & C. Armon (Eds.), *Adult development: Vol. 2. The development of adult thinking and perception.* New York: Praeger.

Damon, W., & Hart, D. (1982). The development of self-understanding from infancy through adolescence. *Child Development, 53*, 841–864.

DeVoe, M. R., & Labouvie-Vief, G. (1990, August). An adult developmental analysis of causes of emotions. *Paper presented at the annual meeting of the American Psychological Association.* Boston.

Donaldson, S. K., & Westerman, M. A. (1986). Development of children's understanding of ambivalence and causal theories of emotions. *Developmental Psychology, 22*, 655–662.

Edelstein, W., & Noam, G. (1982). Regulatory structures of the self and postformal stages in adulthood. *Human Development, 25*, 407–422.

Erikson, E. (1978). Reflections on Dr. Borg's life cycle. In E. Erikson (Ed.), *Adulthood* (pp. 1–31). New York: Norton.

Fischer, K. W., Hand, H. H., & Russell, S. (1984). The development of abstractions in adolescence and adulthood. In M. L. Commons, F. A. Richards, & C. Armon, Eds., *Beyond formal operations* (pp. 43–72). New York: Praeger.

Flavell, J. H. (1970). Cognitive changes in adulthood. In L. R. Goulet & P. B. Baltes (Eds.), *Life span developmental psychology: Theory and research.* New York: Academic Press.

Fowler, J. W. (1981). *Stages of faith: The psychology of human development and the quest for meaning.* San Francisco: Harper & Row.

Frankfort, H., & Frankfort, H. A. (1946). *Before philosophy: The intellectual adventure of ancient man.* Baltimore: Penguin.

Gardner, H. (1985). *Frames of mind.* New York: Basic Books.

Gilligan, C. (1982). *In a different voice.* Cambridge, MA: Harvard University Press.

Gilligan, C., & Murphy, J. M. (1979). Development form adolescence to adulthood: The philosopher and the dilemma of fact. In D. Kuhn (Ed.), *Intellectual development beyond childhood* (pp. 85–99). New York: Jossey-Bass.

Haan, N. (1977). *Coping and defending: Processes of self-environment organization.* New York: Academic Press.

Habermas, J. (1984). *The theory of communicative action: Vol. 1. Reason and the rationalization of society.* Boston: Beacon.

Harris, P. L. (1983). Children's understanding of the link between situation and emotion. *Journal of Experimental Psychology, 36*, 490–509.

Harter, S. (1983). Developmental perspectives on the self system. In E. M. Hetherington (Ed.), *Handbook of child psychology* (Vol. 4, pp. 275–385). New York: Wiley.

Harvey, O. J., Hunt, D. E., & Schroder, H. M. (1961). *Conceptual systems and personality organization.* New York: Wiley.

Hauser, S. T. (1976). Loevinger's model and measure of ego development: A critical review. *Psychological Bulletin, 83*, 928–955.

Helson, R., & Wink, P. (1987). Two conceptions of maturity in the findings of a longitudinal study. *Journal of Personality and Social Psychology, 53*, 531–541.

Hoffman, M. L. (1978). Toward a theory of empathic arousal and development. In M. Lewis & L. A. Rosenblum (Eds.), *The development of affect* (pp. 227–256). New York: Plenum.

Hoyer, W. J., Rybash, J. M., & Roodin, P. A. (1989). Cognitive change as a function of knowledge access. In M. L. Commons, J. D. Sinnott, F. A. Richards, & C. Armon (Eds.), *Adult development: Vol. 1. Comparisons and applications of developmental models* (pp. 293–305). New York: Praeger.

Irwin, R. R., & Scheese, R. L. (1989). Problems in the proposal for a "stage" of dialectical thinking. In M. L. Commons, J. D. Sinnott, F. A. Richards, & C. Armon (Eds.), *Adult development: Vol. 1. Comparisons and applications of developmental models* (pp. 113–132). New York: Praeger.

Jepson, K., & Labouvie-Vief, G. (in press). Symbolic processing in the elderly. In J. Sinnott & R. West (Eds.), *Everyday memory*. Hillsdale, NJ: Erlbaum.

Kahnemann, D., & Tversky, A. (1984). Choices, values, and frames. *American Psychologist, 39*, 341–350.

Kegan, J. (1982). *The evolving self*. Cambridge, MA: Harvard University Press.

King, P. M., Kitchener, K. S., Wood, P. K., & Davison, M. L. (1989). Relationships across developmental domains: A longitudinal study of intellectual, moral, and ego development. In M. L. Commons, J. D. Sinnott, F. A. Richards, & C. Armon (Eds.), *Adult development: Vol. 1. Comparisons and applications of developmental models* (pp. 57–72). New York: Praeger.

Kitchener, K. S. (1983). Cognition, metacognition, and epistemic cognition. *Human Development, 26*, 222–232.

Kitchener, K. S., & Brenner, H. G. (1990). Wisdom and reflective judgment: Knowing in the face of uncertainty. In R. Sternberg (Ed.), *Wisdom: Its nature, origin, and development* (pp. 212–229). Cambridge: Cambridge University Press.

Kitchener, K. S., & King, P. M. (1981). Reflective judgement: Concepts of justification and their relationship to age and education. *Journal of Applied Developmental Psychology, 2*, 89–116.

Kitchener, K. S., King, P. M., Wood, P. K., & Davison, M. L. (1989). Consistency and sequentiality in the development of reflective judgment: a six year longitudinal study. *Journal of Applied Developmental Psychology, 10*, 73–95.

Kitchener, K. S., & Kitchener, R. F. (1981). The development of natural rationality: Can formal operations account for it? In J. A. Meacham & N. R. Santilli (Eds.), *Social development in youth: Structure and content. Contributions to Human Development*. (Vol. 5, pp. 160–181). Basel: Karger.

Kohlberg, L. (1969). Stage and sequence: The cognitive-developmental approach to socialization. In D. A. Goslin (Ed.), *Handbook of socialization theory and research* (pp. 347–480). Chicago: Rand McNally.

Kohlberg, L. (1984). *Essays on moral development: Vol. 2. The psychology of moral development*. San Francisco: Harper & Row.

Koplowitz, H. (1984). A projection beyond Piaget's formal operations stage: A general systems and a unitary stage. In M. L. Commons, F. A. Richards, & C. Armon (Eds.), *Beyond formal operations* (pp. 272–295). New York: Praeger.

Kramer, D. A. (1983). Post-formal operations? A need for further conceptualization. *Human Development, 26*, 91–105.

Kramer, D. A. (1989). Development of an awareness of contradiction across the life span and the question of post-formal operations. In M. L. Commons, J. D. Sinnott, F. A. Richards, & C. Armon (Eds.), *Adult development: Vol. 1. Comparisons and applications of developmental models* (pp. 133–160). New York: Praeger.

Kramer, D. A., Melchior, J., & Levine, C. B. (1989). Age relevance of content material and relativistic and dialectical reasoning from adolescence through old age. Unpublished manuscript, Rutgers University, New Brunswick, NJ.

Kramer, D. [A.], & Woodruff, D. (1986). Relativistic and dialectical thought in three adult age-groups. *Human Development, 29*, 280–290.

Kuhn, D., Pennington, N., & Leadbeater, B. (1983). Adult thinking in developmental perspective. In P. B. Baltes & O. G. Brim, Jr. (Eds.), *Life-span development and behavior* (Vol. 5, pp. 158–195). New York: Academic Press.

Labouvie-Vief, G. (1980). Beyond formal operations: Uses and limits of pure logic in life span development. *Human Development, 23*, 141–161.

Labouvie-Vief, G. (1981). Re-active and pro-active aspects of constructivism: Growth and aging in life span perspective. In R. M. Lerner & N. A. Busch-Rossnagel (Eds.),

Individuals as producers of their development: A life-span perspective. New York: Academic Press.

Labouvie-Vief, G. (1982a). Dynamic development and mature autonomy. *Human Development, 25,* 161–191.

Labouvie-Vief, G. (1982b). Growth and aging in life span perspective. *Human Development, 25,* 65–88.

Labouvie-Vief, G. (1990). Wisdom as integrated thought: Historical and developmental perspectives. In R. J. Sternberg (Ed.), *Wisdom: Its nature, origins, and development.* Cambridge: Cambridge University Press.

Labouvie-Vief, G., DeVoe, M., & Bulka, D. (1989). Speaking about feelings: Conceptions of emotion across the life span. *Psychology and Aging, 4,* 425–437.

Labouvie-Vief, G., Hakim-Larson, J., DeVoe, M., & Schoeberlein, S. (1989). Emotions and self-regulation: A life span view. *Human Development, 32,* 279–299.

Labouvie-Vief, G., Hakim-Larson, J., & Hobart, C. J. (1987). Age, ego level, and the life-span development of coping and defense processes. *Psychology and Aging, 2,* 286–293.

Labouvie-Vief, G., & Lawrence, R. (1985). Object knowledge, personal knowledge, and processes of equilibration in adult cognition. *Human Development, 28,* 25–39.

Labouvie-Vief, G., & Schell, D. (1982). Learning and memory in later life: A developmental perspective. In B. Wolman & G. Stricker (Eds.), *Handbook of developmental psychology.* Englewood Cliffs, NJ: Prentice Hall.

Lakoff, G. (1987). *Women, fire, and dangerous things.* Chicago: University of Chicago Press.

Loevinger, J. (1976). *Ego development.* San Francisco: Jossey-Bass.

Loevinger, J. (1979). Construct validity of the sentence completion test of ego development. *Applied Psychological Measurement, 3,* 281–311.

Loevinger, J., & Wessler, R. (1978). *Measuring ego development.* San Francisco: Jossey-Bass.

Mann, T. (1978). Freud und die Zukunft. In T. Kurzke (Ed.), *Thomas Mann: Essays, Band 3* (pp. 173–192). Frankfurt: Fischer.

Mead, G. H. (1934). *Mind, self, and society.* Chicago: University of Chicago Press.

Miller, P. H. (1983) *Theories of developmental psychology.* San Francisco: Freeman.

Moessinger, P. (1978) Piaget on equilibration. *Human Development, 21,* 255–267.

Monod, J. (1971). *Chance and necessity: An essay on the natural philosophy of modern biology.* New York: Knopf.

Neugarten, B. L. (1968). The awareness of middle age. In B. L. Neugarten (Ed.), *Middle age and aging* (pp. 93–98). Chicago: University of Chicago Press.

Neumann, E. (1973). *The origins and history of consciousness.* Princeton, NJ: Princeton University Press.

Olson, D. R. (1977). From utterance to text: The bias of language in speech and writing. *Harvard Educational Review, 47,* 257–281.

Onians, R. B. (1954). *The origins of European thought: About the body, the mind, the soul, world, time, and fate.* Cambridge: Cambridge University Press.

Ozer, F. K., & Reich, K. H. (1987). The challenge of competing explanations: The development of thinking in terms of complementarity of "theories." *Human Development, 30,* 178–186.

Pascual-Leone, J. (1984). Attentional, dialectic, and mental effort: Towards an organismic theory of life stages. In M. L. Commons, F. A. Richards, & C. Armon (Eds.), *Beyond formal operations* (pp. 182–215). New York: Praeger.

Perry, W. G. (1968). *Forms of intellectual and ethical development in the college years.* New York: Holt, Rinehart, & Winston.

Piaget, J. (1955). *The language and thought of the child.* New York: New American Library.

Piaget, J. (1962). *Play, dreams, and imitation in childhood.* New York: Norton.

Piaget, J. (1965). *The moral judgment of the child.* New York: Free Press.

Piaget, J. (1971). *Biology and knowledge.* Chicago: University of Chicago Press.

Piaget, J. (1976). *The grasp of consciousness: Action and concept in the young child.* Cambridge, MA: Harvard University Press.

Piaget, J. (1980). *Experiments in contradiction.* Chicago: University of Chicago Press.

Piaget, J. (1981). *Intelligence and affectivity: Their relationship during child development.* Palo Alto, CA: Annual Reviews.

Redmore, C. D., & Loevinger, J. (1979). Ego development in adolescence: Longitudinal studies. *Journal of Youth and Adolescence, 8,* 129–134.

Reich, K. H. (1990, May). *Commonalities and differences of Piagetian operations and complementarity reasoning: A conceptual model and its support by empirical data.* Paper presented at the 1990 meeting of the Jean Piaget Society. Philadelphia.

Reich, K. H., & Ozer, F. (1990). Konkret-operatorisches, formal-operatorisches and komplementaeres Denken, Begriffs- und Theorienentwicklung: Welche Beziehungen? Unpublished manuscript, University of Fribourg, Switzerland.

Rest, J. (1985). *Manual for the Defining Issues Test.* Unpublished manuscript, Center for the Study of Ethical Development, University of Minnesota, Minneapolis.

Ricoeur, P. (1970). *Freud and philosophy: An essay on interpretation.* New Haven, CT: Yale University Press.

Riegel, K. F. (1973). Dialectical operations: The final period of cognitive development. *Human Development, 16,* 346–370.

Saarni, C. (1984). An observational study of children's attempts to monitor their expressive behavior. *Child Development, 55,* 1504–1513.

Salthouse, T. (1985). *A theory of cognitive aging.* Amsterdam: North-Holland.

Selman, R. L. (1980). *The growth of interpersonal understanding.* New York: Academic Press.

Simon, B. (1978). *Mind and madness in ancient Greece.* Ithaca, NY: Cornell University Press.

Sinnott, J. D. (1984). Postformal reasoning: The relativistic stage. In M. L. Commons, F. A. Richards, & C. Armon (Eds.), *Beyond formal operations* (pp. 298–325). New York: Praeger.

Sinnott, J. D. (1989). Life span relativistic post-formal thought: Methodology and data from everyday problem solving. In M. L. Commons, J. D. Sinnott, F. A. Richards, & C. Armon (Eds.), *Adult development: Vol. 1. Comparisons and applications of developmental models* (pp. 239–278). New York: Praeger.

Turiel, E. (1974). Conflict and transition in adolescent moral development. *Child Development, 45,* 14–29.

Turner, T. (1973). Piaget's structuralism. *American Anthropologist. 75,* 351–373.

Watkins, M. (1986). *Invisible guests: The development of imaginal dialogues.* Hillsdale, NJ: Analytic Press.

Werner, H., & Kaplan, B. (1963). *Symbol formation.* New York: Wiley.

Whitmont, E. C. (1969). *The symbolic quest: basic concepts of analytical psychology.* Princeton, NJ: Princeton University Press.

Whyte, L. L. (1948). *The next development in man.* New York: Holt.

Wood, P. K. (1983). Inquiring systems and problem structure: Implications for cognitive development. *Human Development, 26,* 249–265.

Youniss, J. (1980). *Parents and peers in social development.* Chicago: University of Chicago Press.

8 The information-processing perspective on cognitive development in childhood and adolescence

Robert Kail and Jeffrey Bisanz

Introduction

The status of the information-processing approach in the study of intellectual development has changed markedly over the years. In the 1960s and 1970s, information processing was touted by proponents as a conceptual and methodological framework that had exceptional potential for enabling substantive advances in our understanding of cognitive development (Klahr, 1976; Klahr & Wallace, 1976; Simon, 1962). At the same time, skeptics viewed information processing as inherently adevelopmental, suffocatingly mechanistic, and fundamentally misleading in its characterization of human cognition and its development (e.g., Brown, 1982). These criticisms were viewed by proponents as being the result of misconceptions about the true nature of information processing. Consequently, in the early 1980s, reviews of the field focused on (1) describing basic concepts and methods of information processing as used to explore cognitive development, (2) speculating about the potential of this approach for understanding cognitive development, and (3) dispelling misconceptions about the approach that might interfere with its productive use (Kail & Bisanz, 1982a,b; Siegler, 1983).

As we enter the 1990s, the information-processing perspective pervades the study of cognitive development, at least in the sense that the majority of researchers use some concepts, methods, and interpretations that carry an information-processing flavor. Information processing is best characterized as a family of theories, concepts, and methods, and the diversity of members within this family is considerable. The combination of pervasiveness and diversity makes defining the perspective extremely difficult. Consequently, our approach is not to summarize or sample the entire range of developmental research done under the banner of information processing but,

Preparation of this chapter was made possible, in part, by grants to the first author from the National Institute of Child Health and Human Development, and to the second author from the Natural Sciences and Engineering Research Council of Canada. We thank Monique Senechal and Alice Yu for their helpful comments on a previous draft.

229

rather, to describe instances of information-processing research that illustrate the distinct contributions of the approach.

We begin, in the next section, by outlining some of the core assumptions of information-processing research on cognitive development, in an effort to provide a broad characterization of the perspective. The central feature, we argue, is a commitment to a particular way of describing and explaining cognitive activity. Then we examine three programs of research in some detail in order to illustrate common features of information-processing research in cognitive development and to provide a basis for an analysis, in the following section, of some emerging trends. Finally, we examine some directions for future inquiry.

Characteristics of information-processing approaches

Several assumptions prevail in information-processing research and define a commonly shared, if minimal, view of this perspective. We begin with assumptions about human cognition generally, and then we turn to an assumption about development. Finally, we contrast information-processing explanations briefly with those of other approaches to highlight differences and similarities.

Core assumptions

1. Cognitive phenomena can be described and explained in terms of mental processes and representations that intervene between observable stimuli and responses. Information processing is primarily an approach to understanding cognition, which might be defined in its broadest sense as consisting of psychological acts of knowing. The fundamental notion is that acts of knowing are best understood in terms of mental mechanisms and representations. More specifically, information-processing theorists assume that *information* is represented internally and manipulated in real time by mental *processes*. Researchers seek to determine what types of information are represented, how information is coded, and how it is organized. They also seek to identify specific processes and how they are organized in a coherent, functional system. In principle, research should lead to theories about an *architecture of cognition* that can be used to explain regularities in human performance on a wide variety of cognitive tasks (e.g., Anderson, 1983; Klahr, 1989; Newell, 1988).

Characterizing human thought in terms of internal codes and processes is strikingly similar to describing the way in which computers process information, and the similarity is not at all accidental. Newell, Shaw, and Simon (1958) were among the first to note that humans and computers engage in many similar activities: They must interpret symbolic information, perform operations on the interpreted information, and emit a response. Thus humans, like computers, can be considered as symbol manipulators.

This insight led to the view that computer-based concepts can be used to represent important characteristics of human thought, that knowledge of computer operations can be used as a source of hypotheses about cognition, and that computer programs can be used as a medium for representing theories about human cognition (cf. Kail & Bisanz, 1982b; Palmer & Kimchee, 1986). Thus, information-processing psychologists can use computer programs to describe and, to some extent, test their theories about human cognition and its development (e.g., Ashcraft, 1987; Rabinowitz, Grant, & Dingley, 1987), much as other psychologists have used verbal, logical, or mathematical languages for description.

2. *A relatively small number of elementary processes underlie all cognitive activity.* Information-processing psychologists contend that, in principle, acts of knowing can be decomposed into distinct, component processes, which themselves can be decomposed even further. As a result, cognitive activities can be analyzed at many levels. For example, reading might be considered as a single process at one level of analysis, but at another level it might be viewed in terms of such components as decoding and comprehension. These components, in turn, might be decomposed into even more fine-grained operations, such as specific memory-manipulation processes.

Years ago Newell and Simon (1972) wrote that "it is one of the foundation stones of computer science that a relatively small set of elementary processes suffices to produce the full generality of information processing" (p. 29). For example, the central processing unit (CPU) for most microcomputers enables users to analyze large data sets with complex statistical methods, to use electronic mail, and to write chapters, but it contains only several dozen basic instructions. Similarly, information-processing psychologists assume that the number of fundamental processes underlying human cognition is relatively small. There is little agreement as to the exact number or nature of these fundamental processes (Palmer & Kimchee, 1986), but the ability and desire to identify them are important goals of information-processing research.

3. *Individual processes operate in concert.* The elementary operations of a computer become useful only when they are combined with other operations to form routines that may, in turn, be combined with other routines to form higher-order programs. The same is assumed to be true of human cognition, according to the information-processing view. A critical goal of research is to understand how fundamental processes are combined and organized to produce performance on different tasks. Moreover, it generally is assumed that higher levels of organization may have emergent properties that are qualitatively different than the properties of lower-level operations (Palmer & Kimchee, 1986).

A comparison of assumptions 2 and 3 is instructive. Assumption 2 implies that searching for more microscopic components is essential. Assumption 3, however, should make it clear that this sort of reductionism is not sufficient for a complete information-processing analysis. Instead, it is essential to identify both elementary processes and the ways in which they are organized to understand performance (Kail & Bisanz, 1982b).

4. Cognitive development occurs by means of self-modification. Information-processing theories consist of descriptions of how a system of processes and information codes interact over time to account for observed performance. That is, the primary focus is on internal factors rather than external, environmental factors. Similarly, when information-processing psychologists seek to explain how cognitive systems change, they focus on internal factors. The mechanisms that enable development to occur are assumed to be internal to the system itself, rather than imposed by the environment, and hence development is construed as self-modification. This orientation does not deny the importance of environmental events for cognitive change, but it represents the view that "whatever the form of the external environment, the information-processing system itself must ultimately encode, store, index and process that environment" (Klahr, 1989, p. 138). Some proposed mechanisms of self-modification are described in a later section of this chapter.

Information-processing explanations

These assumptions are shared by a large number of theories that vary widely in the phenomena investigated, the level of analysis used, and the properties of cognition proposed and tested. This diversity often makes information processing appear to be a fragmented framework, but this appearance is deceiving. At the core of information-processing research is a shared view of how psychological activities are best understood. The commitment to this shared view provides a common ground for diverse theories and research.

As noted in assumption 1, information-processing psychologists seek to explain relations between observable stimuli (input) and observable responses (output) by describing activities that intervene between input and output. They proceed by developing models of cognitive activity on various tasks with the belief that these models will converge in a way that reveals characteristics of a general architecture of cognition. The components of these models consist of internal representations of information and of processes that operate over real time on these representations. A complete model of cognition for a certain task would incorporate specific mechanisms for all cognitive activities that underlie performance, including perceptual mechanisms for encoding information, processes for manipulating and storing information, processes for selecting and retrieving stored information, and processes that decide among alternative actions. Also important in a complete model would be specification of the ways in which information is organized, sequenced, and represented internally. Researchers interested in learning and development have the additional goals of (1) describing changes in information processing that take place over time and (2) identifying characteristics of the system and its environment that both enable and constrain change.

This approach differs in fundamental ways from other approaches in psychology (Palmer & Kimchee, 1986). Information-processing descriptions are not *phenomenological* in nature, because they are not limited to conscious experience and do not rely on principles of conscious experience for explanation. Nor are they *physical* in nature because they do not invoke material causes, such as biochemical reactions or neural firings, as primary explanations. Information-processing theories may be constructed in ways that correspond to phenomenological and physical theories, and they may be constrained by compelling evidence or concepts that arise from phenomenological or physical approaches, but the emphasis on cognitive processes and representations is fundamentally different from these other approaches.

Information processing is similar to many other nonphenomenological and nonphysical approaches in that it can be characterized as an effort to map relations between input (stimuli) and output (responses), but the way in which the mapping function is described varies considerably (Palmer & Kimchee, 1986). In classic differential or psychometric theories, the approach is to identify *abilities* that vary among individuals and that determine how individuals respond differentially to input. In other approaches theorists have attempte to described relations between input and output in terms of logical formalisms (Inhelder & Piaget, 1958), mathematical information theory (Garner, 1962), and probability theory (e.g., Edwards, 1965), among others. Traditional learning theorists describe input–output relations in terms of associative links that are modified according to principles of learning, and contextual theorists rely heavily on the organization of environmental characteristics in their explanations. From an information-processing view, these approaches are all similar in that they fail to specify *how* the mapping function between input and output is realized over real time. Only in information processing is there an attempt to specify how stimuli are manipulated and transformed, in sequence, to produce a particular response.

This fundamental difference does not imply that these other approaches are irrelevant to information processing. Indeed, insights, findings, and concepts can be generated with these approaches that constrain information-processing theories or that could be incorporated into information-processing theories (Palmer & Kimchee, 1986). For example, psychometric theories and findings have contributed prominently to information-processing research on individual difference in cognition (e.g., Hunt, Lunneborg, & Lewis, 1975; Pellegrino & Glaser, 1979).

Information-processing research on cognitive development

As already discussed, the core of information-processing research is a shared view of how psychological activities are best described and explained, and it is this view that provides a common ground for information-processing theories and research. This general approach has resulted in a multitude of productive research programs on a wide variety of topics, including perception, problem solving, language, and motor control. In the present section, we describe three of these research programs with the goal of illustrating some important characteristics of information processing as a framework for cognitive-developmental research.

The first program of research concerns how children add mentally, as well as how their performance changes with development. In this research, a major goal is to develop an integrative and detailed model of performance on one task. Information-processing research often is designed to explore regularities across tasks, however. This more general aim is exemplified in the second program of research, where the focus is on developmental changes in speed of specific elementary processes and where the goal is to identify a pervasive characteristic of cognitive development. The third program of research, which concerns identification of general processes that underlie reading skill, illustrates how an information-processing approach often can be used to study individual differences among children as well as developmental change.

The development of mental arithmetic

Competence in arithmetic is an important ingredient in a large number of everyday tasks faced by adults in many cultures, and in most societies the acquisition of arithmetic skill is an important objective in the early years of schooling. Competence in arithmetic is also an appealing focus for research because it has implications both for theories of cognitive development and for improved instruction.

A large amount of empirical work has been focused on how children solve arithmetic problems (e.g., Fuson, in press). Recently a number of information-processing theories of children's solutions to simple arithmetic problems have been proposed (Ashcraft, 1982, 1987, 1990; Siegler, 1989; Siegler & Jenkins, 1989; Siegler & Shrager, 1984). Many elements of these theories are complementary as well as overlapping; consequently, research in this area seems to be converging on a relatively unified explanation of these phenomena (Bisanz & LeFevre, 1990). For present purposes we focus primarily on Siegler's theory (1986, 1989; Siegler & Shrager, 1984), and especially on his explanation of performance and changes therein.

A performance model. In Siegler's model, solution of addition problems proceeds according to the steps illustrated in Figure 8.1. An individual begins by encoding the problem and then attempting to retrieve an answer directly from a knowledge base consisting of stored facts. These facts are represented mentally in terms of associations between problems (e.g., 2 + 5) and candidate answers (6, 7, 8, etc.), associations that vary in strength. Retrieval is assumed to be probabilistic, so that even weakly associated answers will be retrieved sometimes. If the associative strength ($Act\ [A_n]$) between the retrieved answer and the problem exceeds a preset *confidence criterion* (c), then the answer is stated. If this associative strength does not exceed the confidence criterion, then retrieval is attempted again. This retrieval cycle continues until one of two outcomes occurs. If an answer finally is retrieved that has an associative strength exceeding the confidence criterion, then this answer is stated. Alternatively, if the number of retrieval attempts exceeds a certain limit (*max*), then retrieval is abandoned and a backup procedure is selected to solve the problem. Backup procedures are slower than retrieval and typically involve counting (counting fingers or counting without an external referent). Evidence for their existence comes from observations (Siegler & Shrager, 1984) and from self-reports (Siegler, 1987).

The general process illustrated in Figure 8.1 is assumed to be developmentally invariant. The knowledge of arithmetic facts, however, is the key for understanding how retrieval or backup procedures are selected. As noted, knowledge of arithmetic is represented in terms of associative strengths between problems and possible answers. Siegler estimated these associative strengths by analyzing the performance of 4-year-old children who were required to answer simple addition problems relatively quickly and without the use of overt backup procedures (Siegler & Shrager, 1984). For example, children responded to "4 + 5" with "9" on 18% of all trials, and with "7" on 9% of all trials. Siegler assumed that the probabilities with which various answers are elicited are related directly to underlying associative strengths. Thus, for 4-year-olds, the associative strength between "4 + 5" and "9" is assumed to be stronger than between "4 + 5" and "7."

Associations between a problem and its candidate answers vary considerably. For example, 4-year-olds responded to 5 + 1 with 6 on 71% of all trials, but no other answer was elicited on more than 7% of trials. Given the assumption that recall probabilities reflect associative strengths, then such a pattern represents a *peaked* distribution of associative strengths. Problems with peaked distributions have been learned well in the sense that they are strongly associated with one answer. Problems that have been learned

"2 + 5 = ?"

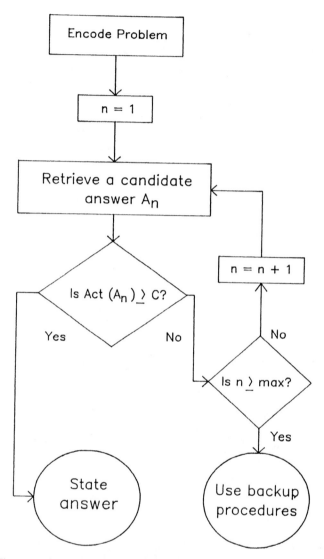

Figure 8.1. A simplified model of mental arithmetic processes, based on Siegler and Shrager (1984). The number of retrieval attempts is indexed by *n*, and *max* represents an upper limit on this number. $Act(A_n)$ refers to the activation level of the candidate answer retrieved on attempt *n*, and *C* refers to the confidence criterion for accepting a retrieved answer.

poorly should have different distributional patterns. As examples, the problem 5 + 2 elicited 5, 6, and 7 on 18%, 27%, and 25% of all trials, respectively, and the problem 4 + 5 elicited six answers with frequencies from 9% to a maximum of only 18%. Problems such as these appear to be associated weakly with several answers and strongly with none. They have distributions of associative strengths that are relatively *flat*, rather than peaked.

In Siegler's model, whether an individual uses retrieval or a backup procedure is determined jointly by the general solution process outlined in Figure 8.1 and by the distribution of associative strengths for the presented problem. Given a confidence criterion of .2, for example, children presented with the problem 5 + 1 would be very likely to retrieve and state the correct answer without a backup procedure. On 5 + 2, however, the same children would be about equally likely to use retrieval (usually obtaining 6 or 7) as they would to use a backup procedure. On 4 + 5, the children would use backup procedures.

This model accounts for a variety of empirical data, including solution latencies, patterns in error data, and correlations among accuracy rates, latencies, and use of retrieval and backup procedures (Siegler & Shrager, 1984). Consider the correlation of .91 between error rates and use of backup procedures (Siegler & Robinson, 1982). According to the model, both error rates and use of backup procedures are determined by the distribution of associative strengths. Thus, the high correlation between these two measures is explained by the assumption that they have a common cause, the peakedness of distributions. If this interpretation is correct, then two otherwise nonobvious relations should be obtained: (1) Use of backup procedures should be highly correlated with *errors on retrieval trials*, not just with total errors, because the distribution of associations directly determines both of these variables, and (2) use of backup procedures should be correlated less strongly with *errors on backup trials*, because the latter presumably depend on other factors (e.g., miscounting). In fact, this pattern was supported: The first correlation was .92 and the second was .38. Thus, the model not only accounts for the high correlation between total errors and use of backup procedures, it also provides an insight about how two components of total errors, errors on retrieval trials and errors on backup trials, differ in relation to the use of backup procedures.

To test their proposal, Siegler and Shrager (1984) formulated the model in a set of algebraic equations and simulated performance on a computer. The outcomes of these simulations were compared with observed data from an independent study. Correlations between predicted and observed values for the complete set of 25 simple addition problems were substantial for solution latencies ($r = .83$), error rates (.77), and the incidence with which backup procedures were used (.87). The performance model is impressive in its consistency with observed data.

Development. Given a model of how simple arithmetic problems are solved, the next step is to describe how a system might change to account for age-related changes in performance. Retrieval generally becomes more common, and counting-based procedures less common, as children progress through school (Ashcraft, 1982; Ashcraft & Fierman, 1982; Siegler, 1987). However, this shift occurs at different times for different problems, so that a child may use retrieval primarily for some problems but backup strategies primarily for others.

In their account of development in simple arithmetic, Siegler and Shrager (1984) postulate a learning mechanism that strengthens associations between problems and responses. In everyday experiences, a child's answers to problems are frequently confirmed or disconfirmed by parents, teachers, peers, self-discovery, or other sources of feedback, so that some answers "grow" in associative strength relative to others. In Siegler and Shrager's model, the associative strength between a problem and an answer increases every time the child responds with that answer. Associations with false answers increase as well, although the rate of increase is less than for correct answers. Thus, this learning mechanism results in increasing peakedness in the distributions of associative strengths, which in turn influence the probabilities of selecting backup procedures, latencies, and accuracy rates.

With this learning mechanism, exposure to problems is a critical factor in the acquisition of arithmetic skill. Children do not experience all simple addition problems equally often. Problems with smaller addends are presented by parents and in textbooks more often than problems with larger addends (Hamann & Ashcraft, 1986; Siegler & Shrager, 1984). Given the learning mechanism just described, problems that are presented more frequently to younger children are more likely to be "learned" earlier, in the sense of establishing problem–answer associations.

Siegler and Shrager (1984) tested the hypothesis that this learning mechanism, in combination with the performance model, could generate developmental outcomes similar to the results seen in children. They assumed an initial state consisting of (1) the process model depicted in Figure 8.1 and (2) a naive knowledge base, in which all the associative strengths for problem–answer combinations were near zero. Siegler and Shrager then simulated development by implementing the learning mechanism and by exposing the system to problems according to the frequencies with which these problems are presented to children. After a large number of trials, the patterns of peakedness for the simulated knowledge base became remarkably similar to what had been expected. Moreover, correlations between children's behavior and the model's performance were high ($rs > .8$) for the frequency of errors, for solution times, and for the frequency with which backup procedures were used.

Thus, a model of performance, when augmented with simple assumptions about a learning mechanism and about the ways in which the domain-specific environmental stimuli are encountered and processed, can be used to explore hypotheses about the nature of development. The extent to which the simulation mimicked data obtained with children is impressive, and it is consistent with the view that the assumptions and hypotheses represented in the model are at least reasonable and deserving of closer examination.

Summary. Siegler's work on the development of mental arithmetic exemplifies the information-processing perspective in many ways. The goal is *not* to describe a child's phenomenological sense of solving a problem, nor is it to describe the physiological substrates of performance. Instead, Siegler has attempted to account for observed behaviors by proposing that a relatively small set of processes operates in certain ways on internal representations of knowledge. In this case, the retrieval cycle (Figure 8.1) includes the relevant processes, and children's knowledge of arithmetic facts is represented by the associative strengths that are acquired over the course of development. Performance (the selection of solution procedures) is determined by how these processes and knowledge representations interact while the child is attempting to solve a problem. The environment, and particularly the frequency with which a child experiences certain types of problems, has an important influence on development, but this influence is mediated by the way in which information is processed.

This program of research has helped to highlight a number of important questions about the nature of development. One such question is whether the general architecture proposed by Siegler, with a relatively simple retrieval cycle operating on a knowledge base represented by associative strengths, is applicable to domains other than simple arithmetic. The degree to which models of performance and development are *domain specific* has become an exceedingly important issue in developmental research over the past 10 years, in part because of the need to understand why a child's success in one domain does or does not transfer to other domains. Another question of broad interest is the degree to which developmental changes in performance can be understood in terms of components that change (e.g., the representations of addition facts) and other components that are *developmentally invariant* (e.g., the retrieval cycle). The focus in developmental research typically is on components that change, but identification of developmentally invariant characteristics of information-processing systems have important implications for theories of development.

A third issue highlighted in Siegler's work is the importance of identifying characteristics of environmental experience that contribute to development, as well as how the influence of these characteristics is mediated. In his own work, Siegler has focused on frequency of exposure to certain problems, but other characteristics doubtlessly are involved (e.g., the type of contingent reinforcement a child receives, and the effect of the child's behavior in determining the selection of problems by parents and teachers). Similarly, the research by Siegler and others on arithmetic has helped to identify a variety of questions about retrieval, about learning mechanisms, and about interactions among different kinds of knowledge (e.g., Ashcraft, 1987; Bisanz & LeFevre, 1990) that are central to building a thorough understanding of cognitive development.

Developmental change in processing speed

For processes ranging from memory scanning to mental rotation to name retrieval to analogical reasoning, the typical outcome is the same: Children need more time to execute processes than do adults (e.g., Bisanz, Danner, & Resnick, 1979; Kail, Pellegrino, & Carter, 1980; Keating & Bobbitt, 1978; Sternberg & Rifkin, 1979). For example, Bisanz et al. (1979) measured name retrieval time with a task in which subjects determined whether pairs of pictures were identical physically or in name. Subjects judged name similarity more slowly than physical similarity, and the difference was used to estimate the time needed to retrieve the name of the stimulus. Retrieval times for 8-, 10-, 12-, and 19-year-olds were 282, 210, 142, and 115 ms, respectively. Thus, 8-year-olds needed more than twice the time needed by adults to retrieve names.

Developmental changes in speed of processing seem to be implicated in at least three major cognitive developmental phenomena. First, speed of processing appears to be an important factor in aging. Specifically, processing speed often is slower among the elderly, and this change may well be responsible for declines in performance in a number of cognitive domains (Salthouse & Kail, 1983). Second, typical accounts of cognitive development during adolescence emphasize the emergence of powerful reasoning skills associated with formal operational thought (Keating, 1979). These skills may emerge in adolescence because basic cognitive processes become functionally mature (i.e., achieving adultlike speeds), thus allowing mental resources to be allocated entirely to the "higher" processes typified by formal thought (Kail et al., 1980). Third, the impact of processing speed is not limited to performance on tasks with an obvious speeded component: Whenever there is external control on the pacing of responses, or, more generally, on the number of activities to be completed in a given period of time, quality of performance may suffer because processing was too slow for all task components to be completed (e.g., Hulme, Thomson, Muir, & Lawrence, 1984).

Two hypotheses about changes in processing speed. Changes with age in processing speed can be explained in two general ways. One hypothesis is that these differences reflect changes that are specific to particular processes, tasks, or domains. For example, age differences in processing speed may reflect acquisition, with increasing age, of more efficient strategies for task solution (e.g., Chi, 1977). Similarly, age differences in processing speed might reflect the fact that knowledge in specified domains becomes more elaborate (Roth, 1983), providing multiple paths by which the information can be accessed more rapidly (Anderson, 1983).

A second hypothesis is that age differences in processing speed are due to widespread change that is independent of specific domains. For example, in information-processing theories, performance on many cognitive tasks is believed to require processing resources or attention (Shiffrin & Dumais, 1981). Increasing resources typically increases speed of processing, even when all other factors are held constant (Anderson, 1983). Hence, age-related increases in the amount of processing resources could produce age-related increases in processing speed.

These two hypotheses can be distringuished by comparing developmental functions for different cognitive processes. If performance on different speeded tasks is limited by a common central mechanism, then the same pattern of growth in processing speed is expected for all tasks. Specifically, if some central mechanism changes monotonically with age, and if the function that relates decreases in processing time to changes in this central mechanism has the same form for two or more processes, the form of the growth function should be the same for those processes (Kail, 1986).

In contrast, if performance on different speeded tasks reflects the acquisition of distinct task-specific skills, there is no necessary relation between developmental change in speeds of various processes. That is, assume that change in processing speed reflects the acquisition of task-specific knowledge. Presumably the events (e.g., specific experiences, maturational changes) that produce increased speed for one process are independent of those events that yield increases in speed of a second process. Because the events that facilitate the two processes are independent, there is no necessary relation between developmental change in the speeds of these processes.

In fact, performance on many speeded tasks yields the same pattern of development: Processing time decreases steadily in middle childhood and continues to do so in late childhood and early adolescence, but more slowly. This common pattern of developmental change in speeded performance is consistent with the view that some central mechanism is responsible for age differences in speeded performance. To provide a stronger test of the proposed common limiting mechanism, Kail (1986, 1988, 1991) conducted experiments in which subjects were tested on several different tasks. Typically, 8- through 21-year-olds were tested, thereby providing ample data to determine the precise shape of the developmental function for processing speed on each task.

For example, Kail (1988) reported the results for five different tasks. The

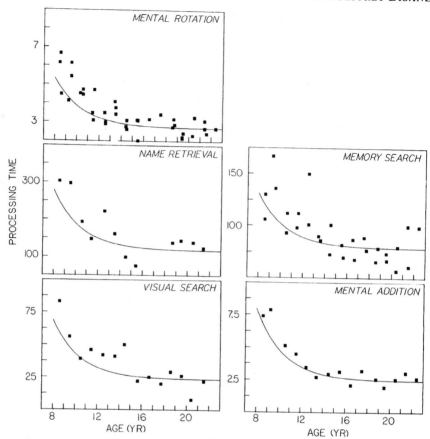

Figure 8.2. Developmental functions for rates of mental rotation (data from Kail [1986, Experiments 1 and 2] and from Kail [1988, Experiment. 2]), name retrieval (from Kail [1986, Experiment 1]), memory search (from Kail [1988, Experiments 1 and 2]), visual search (from Kail [1988, Experiment 1]), and mental addition (from Kail [1988, Experiment 2]). Rate of mental rotation is estimated by the slope of the function relating response time (RT) to the orientation of the stimulus. Name retrieval is estimated by the difference between times for name and physical matching. Visual search is estimated by the slope of the function relating RT to the size of the search set. Memory search is estimated by the slope of the function relating RT to the size of the study set. Retrieval of sums on the mental addition task is estimated from the slope of the function relating RT to the sum squared. The solid line depicts values derived from an exponential function in which the decay parameter, c, is the same for all five tasks.

name retrieval task was taken from Bisanz et al. (1979), already described. In a mental rotation task (from Kail et al., 1980), subjects judged whether stimuli presented in different orientations were letters or mirror images of letters. On a visual search task, subjects studied a single digit, then were shown a set of 1–5 digits. The subject's task was to determine whether the set of digits included the study digit. On a memory search task, subjects first studied 1–5 digits. Then they were shown a single digit and asked to judge whether that digit was a member of the set they had studied previously. Finally, in a mental addition task, subjects quickly determined the accuracy of simple sums.

Means for each measure of processing time and each age group are presented in Figure 8.2. Processing time clearly declined with increasing age on every task, but the question of particular interest is whether the rate of decrease is highly similar across tasks. Similar rates of change would be consistent with the view that a central mechanism is involved, whereas dissimilar rates would be consistent with the hypothesis that task-specific processes are responsible. To answer this question, the data from each of the five tasks were fitted to an exponential function of the form

$$y = a + be^{-cx} \tag{1}$$

where a represents asymptotic processing time, e is the base of natural logarithms, $a + b$ is the intercept (for $x = 0$, $e^{-cx} = 1$), x is age, and c is a "decay" parameter that indicates how rapidly the function approaches a. The key result was that the data for each task were described extremely well by the exponential function when c, the parameter representing rate of change with development, was the same for all five tasks. Thus, the times needed to execute mental rotation, name retrieval, memory search, visual search, and mental addition seem to decline with age at the same rate. This outcome, of course, is the pattern of results expected from the assumption that some mechanism common to all of these processes limits the speed with which they can be executed.

In the most recent experiment in this series, Kail (1991) provided further evidence that a common, general mechanism is responsible for developmental change in speed of processing. The predicted common rate of developmental change was assessed by testing $7\frac{1}{2}$- to 21-year-olds on six tasks: simple response time, in which subjects released a button upon detection of a visual stimulus; tapping, in which they pressed a button as rapidly as possible; a pegboard task, in which they moved pegs from one side of a board to the other; the coding task from the Wechsler Intelligence Scale for Children, in which subjects placed various lines in different geometric figures according to a specified code (e.g., a horizontal line within triangles); and two tasks used previously, mental addition and name retrieval.

Age-related differences in performance times for these six tasks was well described by equation 1 with c set to .334, the value obtained in the earlier study (Kail, 1988). Thus, for a large number of speeded tasks, developmental change is exponential and occurs at a common rate. This pattern would be expected if performance on all of the speeded tasks is limited by some common component that is itself developing. As already mentioned, limited processing resources is a prime candidate.

Summary. Kail's focus on specific elementary processes is characteristic of many information-processing investigations, but his approach differs from Siegler's in many respects. Whereas Siegler focused on a single task (mental arithmetic), Kail examined performance on several tasks. Whereas Siegler sought to develop a comprehensive and relatively complex model of both the processes and the representations underlying performance, Kail used simpler analyses limited primarily to particular elementary processes. Whereas Siegler sought to describe development in terms of explicit and specific changes in his model, Kail's research implicates a general mechanism that needs to be better understood and that has not been incorporated very explicitly in existing models. The differences between these two lines of research represent the diversity of approaches within the information-processing perspective.

Although Kail's research involves processing speed on relatively simple tasks, the implications are much broader and address a fundamental issue in developmental psychology, namely, the extent to which mechanisms of development are general or domain specific. Kail's evidence in favor of a general mechanism is inconsistent with other research that points to domain-specific developmental change (e.g., Chi, 1977). The task for researchers is to identify these mechanisms with greater precision, to determine which are general and which are domain specific, and to discover how both types of mechanisms interact in the course of development.

Contextual effects on word recognition

Teachers and parents commonly observe that children, when they read, often use a variety of cues to understand the text. They might use accompanying pictures, for example, to infer the meaning of a sentence. Similarly, when young readers do not immediately recognize a word, they often use contextual cues to help identify a word. Consider, for example, a child who is trying to read the sentence "The dog ran after the cat" but who is not familiar with the last word, *cat*. The child might use his or her knowledge of dogs to infer that the last word is *cat*.

Context need not affect word recognition and comprehension in the same manner or to the same degree. In comprehending text, skilled readers apparently use contextual cues more effectively than less skilled readers in comprehension of text (Stanovich, 1980). To determine whether similar ability differences in use of context were found in identification of individual words, West and Stanovich (1978, Experiment 1) tested 9- and 11-year-olds, and adults on a sentence priming task. Subjects read aloud a sentence in

Table 8.1. *Mean times (in ms) to read words as a function of grade level and context condition*

	Context		
Grade	Congruous	None	Incongruous
Fourth	555	594	633
Sixth	478	512	546
College	394	425	425

Note: Times are estimated from Figure 1 of West and Stanovich (1978).

which the final word was omitted. After the incomplete sentence was read, the last word appeared and the subject read it aloud as quickly as possible. In the *congruous-context* condition, the last word was semantically consistent with the incomplete sentence (e.g., "The dog ran after the . . . *cat*"). In the *incongruous-context* condition, the last word was inconsistent with the preceding sentence (e.g., "The girl sat on the . . . *cat*"). In the *neutral* condition, only the word *the* preceded the last word (e.g., "the . . . *cat*").

If context affects word recognition, then the last word in the congruous-context condition should be read faster than in the neutral condition. This effect of contextual facilitation would be consistent with the idea that readers use previous information in a sentence in a way that speeds up word recognition. Latencies in the incongruous-context condition should be slower than in the neutral condition, representing contextual interference, because contextual cues from the sentence might result in expectations that do not match the last word and thus interfere with reading it. Regarding differences between skilled and less skilled readers, the critical prediction is that contextual facilitation (and perhaps contextual interference) should be minimal for younger children but more pronounced in older children and, especially, adults.

Mean latencies are presented in Table 8.1. Congruous-context latencies were less than neutral latencies at all age levels, indicating that sentence context cues facilitated word recognition, as expected. However, contextual facilitation did *not* increase with age; in fact, the effect diminished slightly (not significantly) between 9 and 11 years. Moreover, the amount of contextual facilitation was related negatively to performance on a standardized test of reading ability. That is, better readers showed less facilitation. Finally, notice that contextual interference occurred for 9- and 11-year-olds, but not for adults. These results, as well as others (e.g., West, Stanovich, Feeman, & Cunningham, 1983), are inconsistent with the hypothesis that skilled readers use contextual information more effectively to recognize words than less skilled readers.

In summary, the results imply that (1) context cues can influence word recognition but (2) better readers generally are, if anything, *less* influenced by context cues than less skilled readers. Thus, the relation between individual differences and use of contextual information appears to be different for word recognition than for comprehension, where better readers benefit from contextual information more than poorer readers (Stanovich, 1980).

The interactive-compensatory model. A focus on underlying processes led to the distinction between comprehension and word recognition, and subsequently to disconfirmation of a common hypothesis about individual differences in use of context during reading. Considering reading as a single, holistic process would never have led to the insights that motivated the research. Being analytic in this fashion, however, is only part of the approach that information-processing researchers attempt to take. The complementary component is to be synthetic, to put the pieces back together in some form that can account for the data and provide a basis for additional insights and hypotheses. In the present case, information-processing researchers are compelled to identify a model of reading, or at least characteristics of such a model, that incorporate new findings and lead to a more coherent picture of reading.

Stanovich's (1980, 1984) synthesis is an interactive-compensatory model of reading. The basic notion is that reading consists of various component processes, and that these components interact with each other in the course of reading. For example, comprehension processes may be influenced by the output of word-recognition processes, and, at the same time, word recognition may be influenced by the output of comprehension processes. This view can be contrasted with two other common models: *top-down* models, in which higher levels of processing (e.g., comprehension) can influence lower levels (e.g., word recognition) but not vice versa; and *bottom-up* models, in which higher levels cannot do anything until supplied with information from lower levels. Stanovich proposed that information from one process can compensate for insufficient information from another. More specifically, if word recognition does not provide sufficient information about the identity of a word, then the output of other processes will be used in a compensatory manner.

To gain an understanding of this view, consider how the results in Table 8.1 might reflect the operation of an interactive-compensatory model (Stanovich, 1980; West & Stanovich, 1978). Many cognitive psychologists assume that for a symbol or word to be identified, a representation in memory that corresponds to that symbol or word must be activated (Neely, 1977). Activation may occur by means of *automatic* or *controlled* processes. (See Schneider & Shiffrin, 1977.) Automatic processes generally are conceived as being fast or obligatory, in the sense that they are initiated without voluntary control. Also, they require little or no allocation of attentional resources, which are assumed to be limited in supply. Controlled processes, in contrast, are considered to be more voluntary and slower, and they require limited attentional capacity. Posner and Snyder (1975) argued that automatic processing can result in excitation but not inhibition of internal representations, whereas controlled processing can have either result.

In West and Stanovich's (1978) experiment, then, a pertinent question is whether contextual cues influence word recognition by means of automatic or controlled processes. Children showed both contextual facilitation and contextual interference, results consistent with the view that controlled processes are involved. Adults showed only contextual facilitation, which implies that automatic processes are involved. Thus, the data in Table 8.1 can be interpreted as showing that word recognition processes become more automatic with development.

Now consider the conclusion that word recognition is affected by context more in less skilled readers than in skilled readers. Stanovich claims that contextual effects occur via automatic *and* controlled processes. For highly skilled readers, automatic word-recognition processes alone are sufficient to identify words; no compensatory information from controlled processes is necessary. Consequently, they should show contextual facilitation but little or no contextual interference, a pattern consistent with Stanovich's data. In less skilled readers, automatic word recognition is slower and so they are more likely to invoke controlled processes that can provide supplemental information relevant to recognition of the word. Consequently, less skilled readers should show both contextual facilitation and interference, again a result consistent with Stanovich's data. Stanovich (e.g., 1984) proposed, moreover, that the benefits of compensation come at a cost: Because less skilled readers must allocate some of their limited attentional capacity to word recognition, less capacity remains for comprehension processes that demand attention. As a consequence, less skilled readers are less likely to understand what they have read. Thus poorly developed word-recognition processes could, over time, contribute to attenuated development of comprehension skills, even though word recognition and comprehension involve different processes (Perfetti & Lesgold, 1979).

Summary and implications. Stanovich's work on word recognition illustrates many information-processing investigations but differs from the foregoing examples in two respects. First, the level of analysis is more general. The interactive-compensatory model is not nearly as detailed and integrative as Siegler and Shrager's (1984) model of mental arithmetic, and the identification and measurement of processes is not as precise as in Kail's (1988) work on processing speed. Nevertheless, Stanovich's findings have important implications for our understanding of reading, and they constrain the kinds of more specific theories that can be developed. (For a recent discussion of word recognition processes in the context of advances in cognitive science, see Stanovich, 1990.) Second, the concern with individual differences contrasts sharply with the previous examples. Many developmental researchers seek to identify and understand universal developmental changes, and in doing so they ignore or average across individual differences. This time-tested approach has considerable utility, but it can obscure potentially important insights that may be obtained by examining individual differences. For example, ignoring individual differences makes it impossible to distinguish alternative developmental paths or to identify important parallels between common developmental changes and some kinds of individual differences. Stanovich's research not only provides insights for understanding development, it has important implications for identifying the cognitive bases of reading disability (Stanovich, 1988).

Characteristics of contemporary research

These examples illustrate two characteristics of contemporary information-processing research. First, information-processing research shares a common view of how cognitive phenomena are to be described and explained. In each case, researchers seek to identify or measure processes or representations that intervene between stimuli and behavior and that, together with stimuli, determine behavior. Moreover, in all of the examples, researchers have tried to identify possible sources of developmental change. In Siegler's work, development reflects interactions among a developmentally invariant retrieval system, a changing representation of factual knowledge, a simple learning mechanism, and experience in the environment. Kail's work implicates a central, common mechanism or constraint that limits processing speed on a variety of tasks and that changes in a lawful fashion with increasing age. Stanovich's research indicates that increasing automaticity may underlie development of a skill. None of these theories could be considered as complete information-processing accounts of performance and development, but they all provide insights about the architecture of cognition and its development.

Second, information-processing research is quite diverse. The level of analysis varies from relatively fine-grained (e.g., measurement of fairly elementary processes in Kail's research) to coarse-grained (e.g., Stanovich's word recognition and comprehension processes), and the focus of study includes performance on tasks that appear to have direct correspondence to daily activities (e.g., mental arithmetic and reading) as well as to others that have been developed primarily for laboratory investigation (e.g., the mental rotation task). The diversity evident in these examples is a testimony to the flexibility of information-processing methods and concepts. We know of no other approach that can be adapted for use on such a wide range of cognitive activities.

Trends in the information-processing perspective

As we noted at the outset, information-processing research in developmental psychology has evolved considerably since its first appearance in the 1960s. This section describes three trends that seem to typify the approach in the early 1990s.

Generality

In years past, information-processing research was criticized for an apparent preoccupation with specific tasks (e.g., Breslow, 1981). The concern was that, given a seemingly inherent focus on task-related details, information-processing theories could never attain a level of generality that would make them applicable across a broad range of cognitive activities. In our view, this argument was a result of confusing the potential of the information-processing perspective with characteristics of existing programs of research (Kail & Bisanz, 1982a,b). As information processing was emerging, the focus indeed was on performance on circumscribed, specific tasks. With a few exceptions (e.g., Newell & Simon, 1972), the goal of producing theories with high levels of generality was sacrificed, temporarily, in favor of exploring new methods and attempting to gain precision.

Generality is now a major goal in information-processing research, and the influence of this goal is evident in two ways. First, researchers are addressing issues and developing theories that have very broad implications for understanding cognition and development. All three of the research programs described here exemplify this trend. Kail's research, for example, involves a comparison of parameters estimated in many different tasks in an effort to identify similarities that reflect a pervasive developmental mechanism. Similarly, Stanovich's notion of interactive and compensatory processing is potentially applicable to any cognitive activity influenced by both higher- and lower-level processes, a description that probably characterizes many complex mental activities.

Siegler's model was developed to account for performance on a very specific task, but it too is applicable to performance in several domains. Consider, for example, reading single words. When children or adults read words, they typically either pronounce the word quickly, if it is familiar, or they sound the word out, if it is not familiar. The first alternative has the character of retrieving a pronunciation code, much as addition sums are retrieved. It would be reasonable to propose that retrieval of pronunciation codes depends on a retrieval cycle and on the distribution of associative strengths between the printed word and many possible pronunciations. The second alternative is a slower and more constructive process, similar to using a counting-based calculation procedure in addition. In fact, Siegler's general has been elaborated along these lines to investigate and understand reading (Siegler, 1988a), as well as to study subtraction (Siegler & Shrager, 1984), multiplication (Siegler, 1988b), reasoning on balance-scale problems (Siegler & Taraban, 1986), spelling (Siegler, 1986), and telling time (Siegler & McGilly, 1989).

Second, the quest for greater generality is reflected in the ever-increasing range of domains in which information-processing analyses are used. Early in its development, information-processing research was limited largely to a narrow set of laboratory tasks. This focus is still important, as shown in Kail's research, but information processing has attempted to encompass a broader range of tasks. Tasks assessing academic skills have been studied intensively, illustrated here in work by Siegler on arithmetic and work on reading by Stanovich. These and other sustained programs of research contribute to an emerging science of academic assessment and instruction, as well as to cognitive and developmental theory. In addition, there is a growing literature in which children's developing social skills are studied from an information-processing perspective (e.g., Dodge, 1983). More recently, some developmental theorists have begun the task of integrating cognition, affect, and motivation (Case, Hayward, Lewis, & Hurst, 1988; Wallace, Klahr, & Bluff, 1987), a problem that must be solved for a full understanding of developmental change. Collectively, these new lines of research suggest that information processing might provide a unifying framework for a large number of diverse lines of developmental research.

Precision

One common characteristic of information-processing research is a commitment to increasing levels of precision. A principle that guides many information-processing psychologists is that we should be able to derive specific predictions concerning children's performance. These predictions may take the form of statements of the relative difficulty of problems, as in Siegler's work on arithmetic, or expected values of latency parameters, as in Kail's work on developmental functions. In these and other cases, the typical aim is to assess, quantitatively, the degree of fit between the predictions derived from the model and the actual results.

A potential problem, particularly as theories become more complex, is that predictions cannot always be derived in a straightforward manner. When theories contain many components that may interact with one another, predictions about performance may not be obvious. Consequently, for many information-processing psychologists the aim is to be able to write a computer program producing output that is indistinguishable from human performance (Klahr, 1989). Recall, for example, that Siegler and Shrager (1984) used a computer simulation to show the sufficiency of the network of associative strengths in combination with the learning mechanism. To the extent that the computer program mimics human performance, then we can claim, at a minimum, that our understanding is sufficient; that is, our theory about human performance is at least coherent and complete enough to produce humanlike responses (Newell & Simon, 1972). If a theory contains inconsistencies or ambiguities, then a program that is intended to represent that theory will fail in a disturbingly obvious way: The program will crash or it will produce bizarre outputs (cf. Ashcraft, 1987). Not all information-processing research involves this level of precision, but it is becoming more common and is the goal of many.

Just because a theory is sufficient does not mean it is correct, of course. The apparent similarity between the output of the simulation and human behavior may be spurious because, for example, the measures of human behavior are not sufficiently sensitive. Alternatively, a more valid but as yet unformulated theory may exist that yields the same output. The sufficiency criterion is important, however, because it constrains theorists to synthesize their assumptions and hypotheses in a working model so that specific predictions can be made and tested.

Mechanisms of development

Developmental psychologists who use an information-processing perspective have an additional rationale for improving theoretical precision. It is often argued that developmental psychologists should be especially concerned with understanding the mechanisms that underlie developmental change, but in fact theorizing of this sort is scarce (Banks, 1987; Klahr, 1989). Klahr (1989) has argued persuasively that the root of the problem is the lack of precision in the way theories have been formulated. If, for example, development is viewed as a series of states connected by transitions (Siegel, Bisanz, & Bisanz, 1983), then an understanding of transition mechanisms must rely on precise descriptions of the states. Many developmental psychologists now share this view.

As the number of precise state descriptions has increased, attention has turned to mechanisms of change. Hypotheses about specific mechanisms are still quite speculative, but some consensus is beginning to emerge about the general functions and characteristics of developmental mechanisms. This section briefly describes some ways in which information-processing researchers are approaching the problem of identifying mechanisms of development.

Change in procedures and rules. As children develop they solve problems in different ways, a change easily cast in terms of more sophisticated "mental software." For example, in reasoning about scientific concepts, adolescents typically use more sophisticated rules than children do (Siegler, 1976). Similarly, in trying to remember information, adolescents use more powerful mnemonics than do younger children (Kail, 1990). Of course, these insights about development are not unique to the information-processing view. Where information processing has made a distinct contribution is in explaining how changes in rules and procedures could be represented mentally. Given an explicit theory of this sort, it is possible to describe the nature of cognitive change. Consider the following, simplified example. Suppose children just learning to add sometimes use the following rule:

Rule 1: If the goal is to add (1 + 2), then count 1 finger, followed by 2 fingers, and say the result.

Suppose that children also have

Rule 2: If the goal is to add (3 + 4), then count 3 fingers, followed by 4 fingers, and say the result.

A generalized version of these results would replace the constants such as (2 + 3) and (3 + 4) with variables, producing a new, generalized rule:

Rule 3: If the goal is to add two numbers, m and n, then count m fingers, followed by n fingers, and say the result.

Generalization is thought to occur because new rules are compared to existing rules. If a new rule differs from an existing rule only in the constants included in the conditions, then a more general rule is created by replacing the constants with variables (Anderson, 1983).

Of course, sometimes children learn rules that are too general and they must learn appropriate boundary conditions. *Discrimination* refers to the process by which more specific conditions are associated with rules. Continuing the examples with simple addition, children might attempt to apply Rule 3 to problems like 8 + 11 and 6 + 7. On discovering that they lack enough fingers for these problems, the situations associated with successful use of Rule 3 are compared with those associated with unsuccessful use. The result is a narrowing of the conditions that elicit Rule 3:

Rule 4: If the goal is to add two numbers, m and n, each of which is less than 6, then count m fingers, followed by n fingers, and say the result.

For changes such as generalization and discrimination to occur, self-modification processes are necessary that examine existing rules and their output, that examine the adequacy of the outputs, and that modify existing rules. Most information-processing theorists assume that the human cognitive system comes equipped with many or most of the basic processes for self-modification. For years, researchers could only speculate on the fundamental question of the precise nature of these processes (Kail & Bisanz, 1982b; Klahr & Wallace, 1976; Sternberg, 1984). Recently, however, some specific and sophisticated hypotheses have been advanced about the nature of self-modification processes, and the sufficiency of these hypotheses has been tested preliminarily with computer simulations (see Klahr, Langley, & Neches, 1987). Although a full account of this work is beyond the scope of this chapter, it is important to note that significant work on the identification of self-modification processes has been done.

Development caused by change in mental effort. Many cognitive tasks require some degree of *mental effort*, particularly when people first perform them. For example, when given addition problems that adults solve with ease, young children typically answer more slowly and seem to concentrate harder. Children's processing is effortful and deliberate; adults' processing is relatively effortless and automatic.

Evidence for automatic and effortless processing comes from studies of dual-task performance. Latencies for two tasks are recorded when each is performed alone and when they are performed concurrently. If both tasks require mental effort, then latencies during concurrent performance of the tasks should be greater than latencies when the tasks are performed alone: The difference shows that mental effort must be divided between the tasks rather than allocated entirely to a single task.

A study by Birch (1978) illustrates this approach and the impact of practice on mental effort. Two groups of 8-year-olds were tested on two tasks: a tracking task, in which subjects used a knob to center a cursor on a target; and a matching task, in which subjects judged whether words were from the same category. Subjects in one group performed the tasks individually, then immediately performed them concurrently. Tracking by this group was 54% less accurate when the tasks were performed concurrently, and matching was 57% less accurate. The second group was given several practice sessions on the individual tasks, then performed the tasks concurrently. Here performance declined by 32% on the tracking task and 25% on the matching task. Concurrent performance was substantially better following lengthy practice on the tasks individually, which is consistent with the view that practice reduces the mental effort required for the individual tasks.

In this study, intensive training produced differences in the mental effort needed by different groups of 8-year-olds. However, the more typical case is that because age is usually correlated with experience, the mental effort required for most tasks should decline with increased age.

Mental resources have been implicated as a developmental mechanism in a second way. With age children can complete more complicated cognitive

Table 8.2. M *values at different developmental levels*

Age (years)	M value
3–4	$e + 1$
5–6	$e + 2$
7–8	$e + 3$
9–10	$e + 4$
11–12	$e + 5$
13–14	$e + 6$
15–16	$e + 7$

Note: The value of e is constant across tasks and refers to the processing capacity necessary for storing the task instructions and a general strategy for solving the task. Table derived from Case (1972).

tasks – those that apparently are more demanding in terms of the resources needed for performance. One straightforward explanation of this change would be that the total pool of processing resources increases as children develop. Elaborating this basic idea, Pascual-Leone (1970) proposed that cognitive change was regulated by a central computing space, denoted M, that increased systematically with age. As shown in Table 8.2, M-space is related to Piaget's stages of development and increases by one unit biennially. In Pascual-Leone's (1970) theory, increased processing represents a change in a fundamental parameter in the cognitive system. Consequently, systematic age differences in performance are expected on all resource-demanding tasks. In fact, as noted earlier, speed of processing on many tasks changes with age at the same rate, consistent with the notion that some basic parameter of the information-processing system is changing with development.

This view resembles traditional stage theories of development, which were often criticized for their monolithic view of development. That is, the expectation was that development should consist of a steady progression toward more successful performance, with considerable consistency across tasks. These views were often unable to account for the fact that children sometimes solved tasks successfully at younger ages than those expected by the theories, or that performance on some tasks would improve more quickly with age than performance on other tasks that should have been equally demanding. Such observations are not necessarily inconsistent with theories based on changes in processing resources, however. To the contrary, variability in performance across tasks can be explained in a principled manner. Whenever performance on a task reflects effortful use of a strategy, a common rate of developmental change is expected, reflecting reliance on limited processing resources. However, repeated practice means that task performance is more likely to be automatic and thus less constrained by limited resources (Case, 1985; Case et al., 1988). (See a set of articles in the February 1989 issue of the *Journal of Experimental Child Psychology* for assessments of the strengths and weaknesses of resource-based theories as explanation of cognitive development.)

Summary. Developmental psychologists have had a *latent* interest in mechanisms of development, but more precise statements have had to await conceptual and methodological advances in describing states in the course of development. In recent years, however, information-processing psychologists have proposed a number of possible mechanisms for developmental change, mechanisms that can explain the age-related march toward greater cognitive skill.

Epilogue

We began by describing some of the core characteristics of information-processing approaches in the study of cognitive development and went on to describe three research programs that illustrate the scope and nature of contemporary investigations. Finally, we identified a few of the trends in information-processing research that have emerged over the past decade. If an approach is to be judged according to its record for generating new insights, new methods, and productive lines of inquiry, then information processing has fared well in developmental research in the three decades since some of its tenets were first outlined by Simon (1962).

The utility of the information-processing perspective in the 1990s will depend largely on the degree to which researchers are able to make significant advances in increasing both the generality of theories and the breadth of their application. In its early days, information-processing research seemed, if anything, too oriented toward developing mini-theories of performance on very specific, circumscribed tasks (Breslow, 1981; Kail & Bisanz, 1982b). In recent years the trend has been toward integrating results and mini-theories across tasks (e.g., Siegler, 1986), so that genuine progress can be made toward identifying a general architecture of cognition that has the potential for unifying concepts and theories and for defining central questions and issues. Similarly, researchers have continued to apply information-processing concepts and methods to an ever-widening array of activities. Research on social development and on academic skills would have fallen outside the purview of information processing 15 years ago. Today, in contrast, research on these topics and others is growing rapidly (e.g., Dodge, Pettit, McClaskey, & Brown, 1986; Siegler & Jenkins, 1989). We expect these trends to continue in the future.

The viability of information-processing research on cognitive development also will depend on how well traditional issues of development can be explored. For example, the issue of whether abilities, skills, and concepts are general or domain specific is critical for understanding how knowledge is organized and how it develops (e.g., Keil, 1984). Information-processing concepts and methods seem to be quite appropriate for addressing this issue. Kail's (1986, 1988) research on developmental functions for specific processes illustrates one way in which this central issue can be addressed productively (see also Siegler, 1989). As another example, concepts such as *differentiation, hierarchic integration, assimilation,* and *accommodation* have a long and important history in developmental psychology (e.g., Siegel, Bisanz, & Bisanz, 1983), but precise and operational interpretations of such concepts have been elusive (Klahr, 1976). If we are to understand development better, concepts such as these need to be replaced or reinterpreted in ways more conducive to operationalization and research. Contemporary theories about mechanisms of development have considerable potential in this regard (e.g., Neches, Langley, & Klahr, 1987). We expect that information-processing research on mechanisms of development, as well as on other traditional issues of learning or development, will and must increase over the next decade.

We anticipate one other change in the next decade that will complement the trends we described. As mentioned earlier, information-processing researchers assume that explanations of self-modification must center ultimately on internal cognitive mechanisms rather than on external factors such as features of the environment. This assumption, a central component of information-processing approaches, will not wane. We expect, however, that researchers will find they need increasingly to analyze and carefully to describe important features in children's environments, and to incorporate these features explicitly in models of development. The need for this change has become evident in recent research on the acquisition of skills in specific domains. For example, to account for developmental change in arithmetic performance, investigators have found it necessary to identify how frequently different arithmetic facts are presented to children (Ashcraft, 1987; Siegler & Shrager, 1984). The ways in which environmental experience is characterized and indexed in these studies have tended to be relatively crude, but the effects on explanatory power have been striking. As contextual and ecological research provides new insights and data (see Chapters 12 and 13 in this volume), information-processing researchers will have a better basis for describing external variables and how they interact with internal factors in development. Indeed, it is reasonable to predict that a productive rapprochement might occur between contextual and information-processing researchers, in much the same way that some differential and information-processing researchers managed to find a common ground (Pellegrino & Glaser, 1979).

In summary, we anticipate that information-processing research on cognitive development over the next ten years will converge toward increasingly general theories about the architecture of cognition and about how cognitive change occurs. At the same time, a wider variety of cognitive and social behaviors will be subjected to information-processing investigations, and more attention will be given to the role and influence of the environment. We expect considerable progress in defining important developmental issues and problems and, like Klahr (1989), we look forward to a time when "we will no longer talk of 'approaches' to our problems, but rather, of their solutions" (p. 178).

References

Anderson, J. R. (1983). *The architecture of cognition*. Cambridge, MA: Harvard University Press.

Ashcraft, M. H. (1982). The development of mental arithmetic: A chronometric approach. *Developmental Review, 2*, 213–236.

Ashcraft, M. H. (1987). Children's knowledge of simple arithmetic: A developmental model and simulation. In J. Bisanz, C. Brainerd, & R. Kail (Eds.), *Formal methods in developmental psychology: Progress in cognitive development research* (pp. 302–338). New York: Springer-Verlag.

Ashcraft, M. H. (1990). Strategic processing in children's mental arithmetic: A review and proposal. In D. Bjorklund (Ed.), *Children's strategies: Contemporary views of cognitive development*. Hillsdale, NJ: Erlbaum.

Ashcraft, M. H., & Fierman, B. A. (1982). Mental addition in third, fourth, and sixth graders. *Journal of Experimental Child Psychology, 33*, 216–234.

Banks, M. S. (1987). Mechanisms of visual development: An example of computational models. In J. Bisanz, C. Brainerd, & R. Kail (Eds.), *Formal methods in developmental psychology: Progress in cognitive development research* (pp. 339–371). New York: Springer-Verlag.

Birch, L. L. (1978). Baseline differences, attention, and age differences in time-sharing performance. *Journal of Experimental Child Psychology, 25*, 505–513.

Bisanz, J., Danner, F., & Resnick, L. B. (1979). Changes with age in measures of processing efficiency. *Child Development, 50*, 132–141.

Bisanz, J., & LeFevre, J. (1990). Strategic and nonstrategic processing in the development of mathematical cognition. In D. Bjorklund (Ed.), *Children's strategies: Contemporary views of cognitive development* (pp. 213–244). Hillsdale, NJ: Erlbaum.

Breslow, L. (1981). Reevaluation of the literature on the development of transitive inferences. *Psychological Bulletin, 89*, 325–351.

Brown, A. L. (1982). Learning and development: The problems of compatibility, access, and induction. *Human Development, 25*, 89–115.

Case, R. (1972). Validation of a neo-Piagetian mental capacity construct. *Journal of Experimental Child Psychology, 14*, 287–302.

Case, R. (1985). *Intellectual development: Birth to adulthood*. New York: Academic Press.

Case, R., Hayward, S., Lewis, M., & Hurst, P. (1988). Toward a neo-Piagetian theory of cognitive and emotional development. *Developmental Review, 8*, 1–51.

Chi, M. T. H. (1977). Age differences in speed of processing. *Developmental Psychology, 13*, 543–544.

Dodge, K. A. (1983). A social information processing model of social competence in children. In M. Perlmutter (Ed.), *The Minnesota Symposia on Child Psychology* (Vol. 17, pp. 77–125). Hillsdale, NJ: Erlbaum.

Dodge, K. A., Pettit, G. S., McClaskey, C. L., & Brown, M. M. (1986). Social competence in children. *Monographs of the Society for Research in Child Development, 51*(2, Serial No. 213).

Edwards, W. (1965). Optimal strategies for seeking information: Models for statistics, choice RT, and human information processing. *Journal of Mathematical Psychology, 2*, 312–329.

Fuson, K. C. (in press). Research on whole number addition and subtraction. In D. Grouws (Ed.), *Handbook of research on mathematics teaching and learning*. New York: Macmillan.

Garner, W. R. (1962). *Uncertainty and structure as psychological concepts*. New York: Wiley.

Hamann, M. S., & Ashcraft, M. H. (1986). Textbook presentations of the basic arithmetic facts. *Cognition and Instruction, 3*, 173–192.

Hulme, C., Thomson, N., Muir, C., & Lawrence, A. (1984). Speech rate and the development of short-term memory span. *Journal of Experimental Child Psychology, 38*, 241–253.

Hunt, E. B., Lunneborg, C. E., & Lewis, J. (1975). What does it mean to be high verbal? *Cognitive Psychology, 7*, 194–227.

Inhelder, B., & Piaget, J. (1958). *The growth of logical thinking*. New York: Basic Books.

Kail, R. (1986). Sources of age differences in speed of processing. *Child Development, 57*, 969–987.

Kail, R. (1988). Developmental functions for speeds of cognitive processes. *Journal of Experimental Child Psychology, 45*, 339–364.

Kail, R. (1990). *Development of memory in children* (3rd ed.). New York: Freeman.

Kail, R. (1991). Processing time declines exponentially with age during childhood and adolescence. *Developmental Psychology, 27*, 259–266.

Kail, R., & Bisanz, J. (1982a). Cognitive development: An information-processing perspective. In R. Vasta (Ed.), *Strategies and techniques of child study* (pp. 209–244). New York: Academic Press.

Kail, R., & Bisanz, J. (1982b). Information processing and cognitive development. In H. W. Reese (Ed.), *Advances in child development and behavior* (Vol. 17, pp. 45–81). New York: Academic Press.

Kail, R., Pellegrino, J., & Carter, P. (1980). Developmental change in mental rotation. *Journal of Experimental Child Psychology, 29*, 102–116.

Keating, D. P. (1979). Adolescent thinking. In J. Adelson (Ed.), *Handbook of adolescence*. New York: Wiley.

Keating, D. P., & Bobbitt, B. L. (1978). Individual and developmental differences in cognitive processing components of mental ability. *Child Development, 49*, 155–169.

Keil, F. C. (1984). Mechanisms of cognitive development and the structure of knowledge. In R. J. Sternberg (Ed.), *Mechanisms of cognitive development* (pp. 81–99). New York: Freeman.

Klahr, D. (1976). Steps toward the simulation of intellectual development. In L. B. Resnick (Ed.), *The nature of intelligence* (pp. 99–133). Hillsdale, NJ: Erlbaum.

Klahr, D. (1989). Information-processing perspectives. In R. Vasta (Ed.), *Annals of child development* (Vol. 6, pp. 133–185). Greenwich, CT: JAI Press.

Klahr, D., Langley, P., & Neches, R. (Eds.). (1987). *Production system models of learning and development*. Cambridge, MA: MIT Press.

Klahr, D., & Wallace, J. G. (1976). *Cognitive development: An information processing view*. Hillsdale, NJ: Erlbaum.

Neches, R., Langley, P., & Klahr, D. (1987). Learning, development, and production systems. In D. Klahr, P. Langley, & R. Neches (Eds.), *Production system models of learning and development* (pp. 1–53). Cambridge, MA: MIT Press.

Neely, J. H. (1977). Semantic priming and retrieval from lexical memory: Roles of inhibitionless spreading activation and limited-capacity attention. *Journal of Experimental Psychology: General, 106*, 226–254.

Newell, A. (1988). Putting it all together. In D. Klahr & K. Kotovsky (Eds.), *Complex information processing: The impact of Herbert A. Simon* (pp. 399–440). Hillsdale, NJ: Erlbaum.

Newell, A., Shaw, J. G., & Simon, H. A. (1958). Elements of a theory of human problem solving. *Psychological Review, 65*, 151–166.

Newell, A., & Simon, H. A. (1972). *Human problem solving*. Englewood Cliffs, NJ: Prentice-Hall.

Palmer, S. E., & Kimchee, R. (1986). The information processing approach to cognition. In T. J. Knapp & L. C. Robertson (Eds.), *Approaches to cognition: Contrasts and controversies* (pp. 37–77). Hillsdale, NJ: Erlbaum.

Pascual-Leone, J. (1970). A mathematical model for the transition rule in Piaget's developmental stages. *Acta Psychologica, 32*, 301–345.

Pellegrino, J. W., & Glaser, R. (1979). Cognitive correlates and components in the analysis of individual differences. *Intelligence, 3*, 187–214.

Pellegrino, J. W., & Kail, R. (1982). Process analyses of spatial aptitude. In R. J. Sternberg (Ed.), *Advances in the psychology of human intelligence* (Vol. 1, pp. 311–365).

Perfetti, C. A., & Lesgold, A. M. (1979). Coding and comprehension in skilled reading and implications for reading instruction. In L. B. Resnick & P. A. Weaver (Eds.), *Theory and practice of early reading* (Vol. 1, pp. 57–85). Hillsdale, NJ: Erlbaum.

Posner, M. I., & Snyder, C. R. R. (1975). Attention and cognitive control. In R. L. Solso (Ed.), *Information processing and cognition* (pp. 55–85). Hillsdale, NJ: Erlbaum.

Rabinowitz, F. M., Grant, M. J., & Dingley, H. L. (1987). Computer simulation, cognition, and development: An introduction. In J. Bisanz, C. J. Brainerd, & R. Kail (Eds.), *Formal methods in developmental psychology: Progress in cognitive development research*. New York: Springer-Verlag.

Roth, C. (1983). Factors affecting developmental change in the speed of processing. *Journal of Experimental Child Psychology, 35*, 509–528.

Salthouse, T. A., & Kail, R. (1983). Memory development throughout the life span: The role of processing rate. In P. B. Baltes & O. G. Brim (Eds.), *Life-span development and behavior* (Vol. 5). New York: Academic Press.

Schneider, W., & Shiffrin, R. M. (1977). Controlled and automatic human information processing: I. Detection, search, and attention. *Psychological Review, 84*, 1–66.

Shiffrin, R. M., & Dumais, S. T. (1981). The development of automatism. In J. R. Anderson (Ed.), *Cognitive skills and their acquisition* (pp. 111–140). Hillsdale, NJ: Erlbaum.

Siegel, A. W., Bisanz, J., & Bisanz, G. L. (1983). Developmental analysis: A strategy for the study of psychological change. In D. Kuhn & J. A. Meacham (Eds.), *On the development of developmental psychology* (pp. 53–80). Basel, Switzerland: Karger.

Siegler, R. S. (1976). Three aspects of cognitive development. *Cognitive Psychology, 8*, 481–520.

Siegler, R. S. (1983). Information processing approaches to development. In P. H. Mussen (Ed.), *Carmichael's manual of child psychology*. New York: Wiley.

Siegler, R. S. (1986). Unities in strategy choice across domains. In M. Perlmutter (Ed.), *Minnesota Symposium on Child Development* (Vol. 19, pp. 1–48). Hillsdale, NJ: Erlbaum.

Siegler, R. S. (1987). The perils of averaging data over strategies: An example from children's addition. *Journal of Experimental Psychology: General, 116*, 250–264.

Siegler, R. S. (1988a). Individual differences in strategy choices: Good students, not-so-good students, and perfectionists. *Child Development, 59*, 833–851.

Siegler, R. S. (1988b). Strategy choice procedures and the development of multiplication skill. *Journal of Experimental Psychology: General, 117*, 258–275.

Siegler, R. S. (1989). How domain-general and domain-specific knowledge interact to produce strategy choices. *Merrill-Palmer Quarterly, 35*, 1–26.

Siegler, R. S., & Jenkins, E. (1989). *How children discover new strategies*. Hillsdale, NJ: Erlbaum.

Siegler, R. S., & McGilly, K. (1989). Strategy choices in children's time telling. In I. Levin & D. Zakay (Eds.), *Time and human cognition: A life-span perspective* (pp. 181–218). New York: North-Holland.

Siegler, R. S., & Robinson, M. (1982). The development of numerical understandings. In H.

Reese & L. P. Lipsett (Eds.), *Advances in child development and behavior* (Vol. 16, pp. 241–312). New York: Academic Press.

Siegler, R. S., & Shrager, J. (1984). Strategy choices in addition and subtraction: How do children know what to do? In C. Sophian (Ed.), *Origins of cognitive skills* (pp. 229–293). Hillsdale, NJ: Erlbaum.

Siegler, R. S., & Taraban, R. (1986). Conditions of applicability of a strategy choice model. *Cognitive Development, 1,* 31–51.

Simon, H. A. (1962). An information processing theory of intellectual development. *Monographs of the Society for Research in Child Development, 27*(2, Serial No. 82).

Stanovich, K. E. (1980). Toward an interactive-compensatory model of individual differences in the development of reading fluency. *Reading Research Quarterly, 16,* 32–71.

Stanovich, K. E. (1984). The interactive-compensatory model of reading: A confluence of developmental, experimental, and educational psychology. *Remedial and Special Education, 5*(3), 11–19.

Stanovich, K. E. (1988). Concepts in developmental theories of reading skill: Cognitive resources, automaticity, and modularity. *Developmental Review, 10,* 72–100.

Stanovich, K. E. (1990). Explaining the differences between the dyslexic and the garden-variety poor reader: The phonological-core variable-difference model. *Journal of Learning Disabilities, 21,* 590–612.

Sternberg, R. J. (Ed.). (1984). *Mechanisms of cognitive development.* New York: Freeman.

Sternberg, R. J., & Rifkin, B. (1979). The development of analogical reasoning processes. *Journal of Experimental Child Psychology, 27,* 195–232.

Wallace, I., Klahr, D., & Bluff, K. (1987). A self-modifying production system model of cognitive development. In D. Klahr, P. Langley, & R. Neches (Eds.), *Production system models of learning and development* (pp. 359–435). Cambridge, MA: MIT.

West, R. F., & Stanovich, K. E. (1978). Automatic contextual facilitation in readers of three ages. *Child Development, 49,* 717–727.

West, R. F., Stanovich, K. E., Feeman, D., & Cunningham, A. (1983). The effect of sentence context on word recognition in second- and sixth-grade children. *Reading Research Quarterly, 19,* 6–15.

9 The information-processing perspective on cognitive aging

Timothy A. Salthouse

Although there are frequent references to "information-processing theory," the information-processing perspective is best characterized as a broad conceptual framework rather than a specific theory. That is, there is no single unified information-processing theory, but instead, a large number of distinct theories postulate different relations among different concepts to account for different phenomena. A common characteristic of virtually all information-processing theories, however, is an emphasis on the analysis of the fundamental processes or components presumed to be responsible for human performance. That is, a major goal of the information-processing approach has been to attempt to specify the identity and sequence of representations and transformations responsible for converting input into output, or stimulus patterns into responses representing decisions.

The information-processing approach has been enthusiastically adopted by many researchers in the area of cognitive aging because of the potential it seems to offer for allowing detailed analysis of the age-related differences observed in many measures of cognitive functioning. The goals of this chapter are to describe how the information-processing perspective has been applied to the field of aging and cognition and briefly to review some of the results of that research.

The organization of the chapter is as follows: First, a broad overview of the information-processing perspective is presented in the context of a "meta modal model" of human information processing. Next, examples of research relevant to several proposed localizations of adult age differences in cognition are discussed. Finally, the chapter concludes with a brief discussion of the advantages and disadvantages of the information-processing approach for explaining age-related differences in cognitive functioning.

A "meta modal model" of human information processing

As just noted, the goal of researchers in the information-processing perspective has been to try to understand how cognitive tasks are performed by specifying the nature of the cognitive representations used during the task,

261

and the identity and sequence of mental processes presumed to operate on those representations. Speculations about the knowledge structures and the cognitive processes involved in a particular cognitive task are typically expressed in the form of a model of how that task is performed. Because many different tasks have been subjected to information-processing analyses, and because there are sometimes several alternative models for the same task, the number of distinguishable information-processing models is quite large. Nevertheless, a few general features are common to many models. These commonalities are portrayed in the schematic model illustrated in Figure 9.1. This is referred to as a "modal model" because it is designed to represent a sort of central tendency of many different models, and it is termed "meta" because it is at a higher level of abstraction than models proposed to account for performance in specific tasks.

Knowledge in this model, and in many current information-processing models, is represented by a collection of interconnected knowledge units. Each circle in the top portion of Figure 9.1 can be considered to correspond to a concept, or whatever the smallest unit of knowledge might be. Knowledge units are assumed to have two types of connections. Long-term or relatively permanent connections are represented in the diagram by dotted lines, and short-term connections, indicating what is currently active in consciousness, are represented by solid lines. Short-term connections can be either portions of the long-term network that are currently active or temporary connections between previously unrelated knowledge units.

The organization of knowledge is represented by the pattern of interconnections among knowledge units. For example, the cluster of units in the upper right of the diagram may represent different types of animals that are all related to one another but that are not directly related to pieces of furniture (represented in the top middle of the diagram) or to colors (corresponding to the units in the lower left cluster in the diagram).

Process models of cognitive tasks frequently involve three distinct types of entities, as illustrated in the bottom portion of the diagram. These are processing components (represented by the boxes labeled C_1, C_2, and C_3), an executive processor (portrayed by the circle and the bidirectional arrows connecting it to the individual components), and one or more kinds of processing resources (indicated by the amorphous entity channeling its contents to the processing components).

Processing components are hypothesized to correspond to the mental operations that receive stimulus input and transform it in various ways to allow the production of a response. Each processing component is assumed to represent a single cognitive operation or transformation, and can vary with respect to efficiency (duration) or effectiveness (probability of successful execution).

The executive processor is frequently postulated to be responsible for

KNOWLEDGE

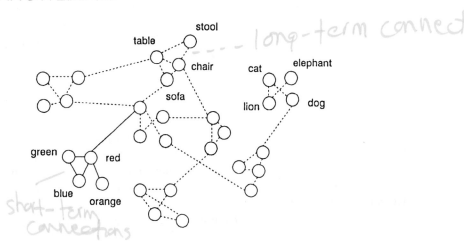

PROCESSING

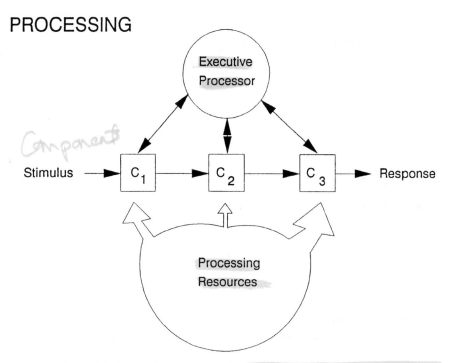

Figure 9.1. Schematic illustration of typical assumptions concerning knowledge structure (*top*) and types of processing determinants (*bottom*) in information-processing models of cognition.

selecting which particular processing components are used to perform a task (i.e., the task strategy), and also to supervise the execution of those components. It can be considered to function somewhat like a manager in that it is hypothesized to be responsible for coordinating, scheduling, and monitoring the various components of the processing system.

Processing resources are postulated to be something necessary for the effective operation of most processing components, and something that exists in limited quantities. The exact nature of processing resources is not yet known, but two of the most popular metaphors for processing resources consider them to be roughly analogous either to energy or to space (Salthouse, 1988). In the energy metaphor, resources are assumed to function like a fuel needed for the execution of most processing operations. According to the space metaphor, many processing operations compete for access to the same limited-capacity region or workspace where cognitive operations can be executed. With both conceptualizations, however, the fundamental assumption is that just a few relatively general, but finite, entities influence many aspects of cognitive performance.

Although not originally proposed to account for individual differences, the information-processing perspective has been attractive to developmental researchers at all portions of the life-span because it offers a rich assortment of theoretical concepts that might be useful in understanding age-related differences in cognition. For example, individual differences might be associated with variations in the intactness or organization of the knowledge system, in the efficiency or effectiveness of specific processing components, in the availability or effectiveness of alternative strategies, or in the quantity of available processing resources. The challenge to many researchers interested in aging and cognition has therefore been to specify which aspect of information processing is most affected by increased age. Some results of these efforts are described in the next section.

Isolating the impairment

Age-related declines in cognitive functioning have been found in many measures of intelligence test performance, and in a variety of miscellaneous cognitive tasks (e.g., for general reviews, see Birren & Schaie, 1985; Charness, 1985; and Salthouse, 1982). Information-processing researchers, in attempting to specify what is responsible for these robust age differences, have used a wide range of procedures to compare adults of different ages in measures intended to reflect the functioning of different aspects of information processing. Because the success of these attempts depends on the extent to which the procedures truly assess the relevant aspect of processing, the following review describes the rationale underlying these comparisons and reports the major results obtained from them. This should put the reader in a better position to evaluate the validity of the conclusions reached from the results of those manipulations. It should be noted at the outset, however, that the review is necessarily quite selective because the relevant research literature is far too extensive to allow an exhaustive review in a single chapter.

Knowledge representation

Several findings have been interpreted as indicating that there are few or no structural alterations across most of the adult years in how information is represented in long-term memory. Among the evidence leading to this conclusion is the absence of age-related declines on scores in general information or vocabulary tests from psychometric intelligence batteries. The fact that with increased age there is no decrease, and sometimes even an increase, in measures of accumulated knowledge seems to suggest that there is no appreciable loss in the number of, or interconnections among, nodes in the associative network assumed to correspond to the individual's knowledge system.

Studies of word associations are another source of evidence suggesting that information in longer-term memory remains intact with increased age. The task for the research participant in these studies is simply to say the first word that comes to mind when presented with a stimulus word. It has been assumed that the pattern of associations produced by an individual reflects the organization of information within his or her long-term memory. For example, a response of "girl" to the stimulus word "boy" would suggest that these two concepts are closely related to each other in memory. Conversely, the absence of responses such as "chair" or "elephant" to the stimulus word "boy" can be interpreted as indicating that these particular concepts are probably not closely related in memory.

Word associates can be analyzed in terms of the type of associate (e.g., same class as in "boy"–"girl," instrumental as in "car"–"drive," etc.), and in terms of the commonality of the associates (e.g., 60% of the respondents might say "girl" to the stimulus word "boy," and 10% of them might say "male"). Several studies have revealed that young and old adults do not differ in either the type or the commonality of associates produced in word association tasks (e.g., Burke & Peters, 1986; Lovelace & Cooley, 1982; Scialfa & Margolis, 1986). The implication of these results is that the organization of concepts in the associative network of long-term information appears to be similar for young and old adults.

Very few methods are available within the information-processing perspective to evaluate properties of short-term representations of information. However, one indirect technique used in several studies with adults of different ages is based on what is referred to as the "priming paradigm."

There are many variants of the basic paradigm, but most involve presenting a word or a sentence followed within a fraction of a second by a target word to which a decision is to be made as rapidly as possible. The nature of the decision can be simple, such as deciding whether the string of letters forms a word, or complex, as when the task is to determine whether the word is a member of a particular category or is implied by the preceding sentence.

The priming phenomenon is evident in faster decisions to the target word when the preceding word or sentence is related to that word compared to when the preceding context is unrelated. For example, the time to decide that "nurse" is a word is generally faster if it is immediately preceded by the word "doctor" than if it is preceded by the word "train." The prevailing interpretation of this phenomenon is that the related word causes some type of energy or activation to flow or spread from its node in the associative network to all closely connected nodes. Decisions to the target words are postulated to be facilitated because the corresponding knowledge node is already partially activated or primed by the prior presentation of the related material.

Two points concerning the priming phenomenon are important in the current context. The first is that the existence of priming can be interpreted as reflecting a type of short-term representation because partial activation of the knowledge units is analogous to an internal representation, and the representation is temporary because the activation gradually dissipates over time. The second relevant point is that several studies have reported that similar magnitudes of priming effects are evident in both young and old adults (e.g., Balota & Duchek, 1988; Bowles & Poon, 1985, 1988; Burke, White, & Diaz, 1987; Burke & Yee, 1984; Howard, 1983; Howard, Heisey, & Shaw, 1986; Howard, McAndrews, & Lasaga, 1981; Howard, Shaw, & Heisey, 1986). The absence of age differences in the beneficial effects on decision time from the presentation of a related word therefore suggests that certain aspects of short-term representations do not change with increased age. Unfortunately, little is currently known about other aspects of these temporary representations, or about possible age-related influences on them. Most information-processing researchers working in the field of aging probably agree that there are few or no age-related differences in the organization, quantity, or quality of long-term knowledge representations, but there are still questions about the influence of age-related factors on properties of short-term or temporary representations of information in memory.

Component effectiveness or efficiency

By far the greatest amount of age-comparative research conducted within the information-processing perspective has attempted to investigate age-related effects on the efficiency or effectiveness of different processing components. Because models of specific task performance are often represented by flow charts with arrows connecting boxes corresponding to hypothesized components, these efforts are sometimes facetiously characterized as attempting to explain age-related cognitive deficits by determining "which box is broken."

One of the most extensively investigated processing components is the one responsible for the mental operation of information retrieval. A relatively large number of studies have used a variety of different procedures to try to isolate contributions of retrieval processes to performance in memory tasks, and then have attempted to determine the influence of adult age on these processes. For example, a popular way to investigate the retrieval component has involved contrasting performance in recognition tests, in which the remembered items are selected from a set of presented alternatives, with that in recall tests, in which the remembered information must be generated by the research participant. The assumption has been that recognition and recall tests are similar except that much more retrieval is required in recall than in recognition because the individual must locate the relevant information in memory rather than simply selecting it from among a set of alternatives. A discovery that the magnitude of the age differences is often greater in recall tests of memory than in recognition tests has therefore led to the inference that deficient retrieval processes may be responsible for some of the memory impairments associated with increased age (e.g., Schonfield & Robertson, 1966).

The retrieval-deficit interpretation has received broad acceptance, although most researchers also realize that across-task comparisons of this type are meaningful only to the extent that the measures being contrasted do not differ except with respect to the critical process – in this case, retrieval. There has been some debate as to whether this criterion is satisfied in recognition-recall comparisons. In particular, there is controversy regarding the role of retrieval processes in recognition tests, and concerning the possibility that recall and recognition tests might differ in the amount, as well as the type, of required processing.

Another procedure used to investigate age differences in retrieval processes relies on what are known as "implicit" tests of memory. These are assessments of memory for previously presented information obtained without deliberate recollection on the part of the research participant. One technique that has been used to assess memory in this implicit, and presumably retrieval-independent, fashion involves two distinct phases. In the first phase, a list of words is presented under the guise of obtaining ratings on some dimension such as pleasantness or category membership. In the second phase, versions of these and other words are presented with several letters missing, and the research participants are instructed to fill in the missing letters to produce the first word that comes to mind. Memory is demonstrated in this situation by higher probabilities of completing the letter strings with the target words when those words had been previously presented, compared to when the target words had not been presented earlier in the experimental situation.

Implicit memory assessments are most useful in making inference about the influence of age on retrieval processes when the results from them are contrasted with the results from otherwise comparable explicit memory assessments. A method used by several researchers to obtain explicit assessments of memory in this same type of situation involves instructing a different group of research participants to treat the incomplete words as cues to remember as many of the previously presented words as possible. Because both the presentation materials and the test materials are identical in the implicit ("complete the words with any word that comes to mind") and explicit ("use the word fragments as cues to remember words presented earlier") assessments, the critical difference is presumably the involvement of conscious recollection or deliberate retrieval in the explicit assessment. The discovery that young and old adults are nearly equivalent in implicit assessments, but that young adults are superior to older adults with explicit assessments (e.g., Chiarello & Hoyer, 1988; Light & Singh, 1987, Experiment 2), has therefore been interpreted as supporting the existence of a retrieval deficit on the part of older adults.

Results from the recognition–recall and implicit–explicit contrasts, as well as those from several other investigative procedures, are consistent with the existence of a retrieval deficit. It is therefore probably reasonable to conclude that there is an age-related impairment in the processing component concerned with the retrieval of information from memory. However, it is important to note that it cannot yet be concluded that difficulties in retrieval are the only, or even the primary, cause of age differences in memory. The reason is that it is possible that comparisons of other components of memory would also reveal age-related differences. In fact, many researchers have argued that age-related impairments are just as pronounced in measures of encoding proficiency as they are in measures of retrieval effectiveness.

Processing components are also postulated to vary with respect to the efficiency of the relevant operations, and much research has been conducted attempting to determine whether there are adult age differences in the duration of particular processing components. One component in which age-related influences on efficiency have been extensively investigated is that postulated to be responsible for mentally rotating visual stimuli. A procedure introduced by Shepard and his colleagues (e.g., Cooper & Shepard, 1973; Shepard & Metzler, 1971) provides a means of estimating the duration of these mental rotation processes. The procedure consists of the presentation of two stimuli (e.g., letters or geometric figures) at varying orientations relative to one another, with the research participant instructed to decide as rapidly as possible whether the two stimuli are identical except for orientation, or whether one stimulus is a mirror image of the other.

A consistent finding across many studies is that decision time in this task is a linear function of the angular discrepancy in orientation between the two stimuli. These results have been interpreted in the context of a model with components postulated to be responsible for stimulus encoding, mental rotation, and decision and response. The intercept parameter of the linear function is assumed to correspond to the duration of encoding, as well as decision and response processes, whereas the slope of the function has been interpreted as an estimate of the rate at which the stimuli are mentally rotated.

At least six studies have reported that older adults have larger slopes, and by inference slower rates of mental rotation, than young adults have (e.g., Berg, Hertzog, & Hunt, 1982; Cerella, Poon, & Fozard, 1981; Clarkson-Smith & Halpern, 1983; Gaylord & Marsh, 1975; Jacewicz & Hartley, 1987; Puglisi & Morrell, 1986). These results therefore suggest that the efficiency of the component concerned with mental rotation declines with increased age. It should be pointed out, however, that most of these studies have also found older adults to be slower than young adults in the intercept parameter of the linear functions relating decision time to angular discrepancy. This implies that there are age-related differences in the duration of components concerned either with encoding processes or with decision and response processes, in addition to those inferred to exist in the component concerned with mental rotation.

Many more examples of age-comparative research on processing components could be provided because, as mentioned earlier, a major focus of information-processing researchers interested in aging has been to compare adults of different ages in measures of the efficiency or effectiveness of particular processing components. However, there has also been interest in investigating possible age differences in presumably more general aspects of processing that may be partially responsible for differences in the efficiency or effectiveness of specific processing components. The two most frequently mentioned general mechanisms – executive processes and processing resources – are discussed in the next two sections.

Executive processes

Although it is clearly conceivable that age-related differences in executive processes could either magnify or minimize the consequences of differences in particular components, there has been relatively little research contrasting adults of different ages in measures of executive functioning. A major reason why there has not been more research of this type is undoubtedly the difficulty of assessing the operation of executive processes independent of the efficiency of processing components.

Because one of the functions presumed to be performed by the executive processor is the selection of optimal strategies, research investigating strategy usage by young and old adults is relevant to the issue of possible age differences in executive processes. Several studies have examined the strategies used by young and old adults in free recall memory tasks, in which a list of items is presented and the research participant is allowed to recall the items in any order he or she chooses. Because accuracy of recall generally declines as the interval between presentation and test of the items lengthens, an effective strategy in free recall tasks is to report the most recently presented items first. If recall begins with the earlier items, then the later-presented items are frequently forgotten, and consequently the overall level of recall with often be relatively low. If, instead, recall begins with the most available items, which are usually those presented at the end of the list, then overall recall is likely to be relatively high. Comparing young and old adults with respect to the tendency to recall items from the end of the list at the beginning of their recall is therefore one means of examining strategy usage in adults of different ages. Few or no age-related differences in this behavior have been found in two different studies (e.g., Parkinson, Lindholm, & Inman, 1982; Wright, 1982), despite substantially higher levels of recall by young adults than by older adults in both studies.

Analyses of serial position functions relating probability of recall to serial position of the items during presentation are also relevant to the question of strategy usage because the early (primacy) and late (recency) segments of the function are often assumed to be at least partially attributable to strategic variables. That is, recall for early input items is postulated to be high because those items receive the greatest concentration of rehearsals, and recall for late input items is hypothesized to be high because those items are often recalled first. People who do not follow this strategy of more rehearsals of initial items and early recall of late items would be expected to have serial position functions without elevated primacy (initial items), and recency (late items), segments. However, comparisons of young and old adults have generally revealed that the two groups have qualitatively similar recall functions, although the functions for young adults tend to be uniformly higher than those of older adults (e.g., Arenberg, 1976; Parkinson et al., 1982; Salthouse, 1980). The recall-order and serial-position results therefore both suggest that young and old adults do not differ with respect to the tendency to use effective memory strategies.

Results from an experiment by Sanders, Murphy, Schmitt, and Walsh (1980) imply a somewhat different conclusion about the relation between age and strategy usage. These researchers requested the participants in their study to say aloud whatever they were thinking of during the presentation of the words that were to be remembered. Later analyses of the taped records of these verbalizations revealed that older adults rehearsed the words in categories or groups less frequently than did young adults. Categorical or elaborative rehearsal has often been found to lead to better recall than mere repetition of the items. In this particular study, then, it appears as if older adults may have been impaired relative to young adults in some type of executive process because they were less likely to use the most effective rehearsal strategies.

The discrepancy in outcomes concerning age differences in strategy usage within the same type of free recall task is unfortunately mirrored in analyses of other tasks. That is, some studies report no age differences in measures of the type of strategy used (e.g., Salthouse, 1987b; Salthouse & Prill, 1987), while others report that older adults use less effective strategies than young adults (e.g., Hartley & Anderson, 1986).

Another aspect of executive functioning that has been investigated in adults of different ages concerns the accuracy of monitoring the status of information in memory. For example, accuracy of monitoring can be assessed by asking the research participant to rate how likely it is that he or she will be able to remember items in a memory test. These ratings can be generated when the items are initially presented, or produced immediately before attempting the test of recall or recognition. Furthermore, the information to be recalled either can be material presented in the context of the experimental situation or can be based on previously learned historical, or general, knowledge.

Young and old adults have been compared in various combinations of these procedures, and in most cases the two groups were found to be similar in their memory monitoring accuracy (e.g., Butterfield, Nelson, & Peck, 1988; Lachman, Lachman, & Thronesberry, 1979; Lovelace & Marsh, 1985; Perlmutter, 1978; Rabinowitz, Ackerman, Craik, & Hinchley, 1982; Shaw & Craik, 1989). The apparent implication is that there are few or no age differences in the effectiveness of at least some monitoring functions carried out by the executive processor.

The research results concerning age-related effects on executive processes are rather equivocal. Evidence based on analyses of age differences in strategy use is mixed, and young and old adults do not appear to differ in the accuracy of monitoring certain cognitive processes. Very few executive processes have yet been investigated, however, and it is probably premature at this time to evaluate the contribution of this aspect of information processing to the age differences in cognitive functioning.

Processing resources

The idea that age-related differences in cognitive performance might be partially attributable to reductions in the quantity of some type of general-purpose processing resources is also relatively new, and like the executive processes interpretation, has not yet received extensive investigation. Two sets of observations appear to have contributed to the recent interest in the processing resource interpretation of cognitive aging phenomena. One is the pattern, reported in many studies designed to investigate age differences in specific processing components, for age-related effects to be evident in nearly every component examined. This is apparent in the research discussed earlier in connection with the memory retrieval and mental rotation components because in both cases evidence is available suggesting that other processing components (e.g., stimulus encoding) are also affected by increased age. The empirical results suggesting that age-related differences may not be easily localized in a single component have led a number of researchers to consider the possibility that a few relatively general factors may be responsible for many of the cognitive performance differences observed between young and old adults.

The second set of observations inspiring interest in the processing resources interpretation relates to the frequently noted tendency for the magnitude of the age differences in performance of cognitive tasks to increase with increases in the apparent complexity, or hypothesized processing demands, of the taks. For example, many of the contrasts intended to isolate the contribution of specific processes also appear to differ with respect to the overall processing requirements in the task. The results of these studies may therefore be as consistent with an interpretation postulating a general impairment, such as a limitation in the quantity of processing resources, as they are with interpretations proposing deficits in specific processes. The contrast between recognition performance and recall performance is a good example of this phenomenon because the recognition tests that exhibit the smallest age differences also seem to require less total processing than most recall tests.

More convincing evidence that it is *how much* processing – not necessarily *what type* of processing – that influences the magnitude of age differences in cognitive performance comes from studies in which experimental manipulations are designed to vary the number of repetitions of the same processing operations. The rationale is that if the processing demands are increased by increasing the number of times the same operation is performed, then it is unlikely that qualitative differences in the form of the introduction of new age-sensitive processing components can account for changes in the relation between age and performance. Instead, it seems more reasonable to postulate that there is greater reliance on a limited number of common or general entities that diminish in certain quantitative respects with increased age. The findings in several studies that age differences in decision time or decision accuracy increase with additional premises in reasoning problems (Salthouse, Legg, Palmon, & Mitchell, 1990; Salthouse, Mitchell,

Skovronek, & Babcock, 1989), with additional elements in geometric analogy problems (e.g., Salthouse, 1987a, 1988), with additional stimulus frames in mental synthesis problems (Salthouse, 1987a, 1988; Salthouse & Mitchell, 1989), and with additional folds in paper-folding problems (Salthouse, 1988; Salthouse et al., 1989), therefore appear more consistent with quantitative, than with qualitative, age-related differences.

An important assumption of the processing resource interpretation is that age differences favoring young adults are expected in measures of nearly every processing component that requires processing resources for its successful execution. That is, as long as effectiveness or efficiency of the component is dependent on processing resources, then if there is a decrease with age in the quantity of resources, older adults should be less proficient in the execution of those processes than young adults. (This expectation must be qualified somewhat because it is possible that the resource requirements of a component are still within the diminished capabilities of older adults.) Unfortunately, the assumption of age differences in all resource-dependent components has proven to be extremely difficult to test because of the lack of suitable techniques for assessing the degree to which processing components are dependent on processing resources. It is clearly circular to claim, as has sometimes been done, that the resource demands are great because the age differences are large, and that the age differences are large because of the great resource demands.

Another approach to investigating age differences in processing resources essentially ignores variations in the extent to which processes or tasks may depend on processing resources, and simply examines the relation between the performance of young adults and the performance of older adults across a number of different performance measures. This is a very gross type of analysis because measures of performance from different tasks almost certainly vary in a number of respects in addition to the presumed dependence on processing resources. Nevertheless, the existence of a systematic relation between the performance of young adults and the performance of older adults would suggest that the differences between the two groups may be more quantitative than qualitative. That is, if the performance of older adults across a variety of different tasks can be accurately predicted from the general relation between the performances of young and old adults, regardless of the specific processing components involved in the tasks, then the bases for the age differences are more likely to be quantitative in nature (i.e., related to how much processing is required) than they are to be qualitative in nature (i.e., dependent on which particular type of processing is required).

A number of analyses have revealed that there are orderly, and often linear, relations between measures of performance from young and old adults (e.g., Cerella, 1985; Salthouse, 1985). Most of the analyses have been conducted with temporal measures such as reaction time, but similar relations have also been reported for a variety of accuracy measures (e.g., Brinley, 1965; Salthouse, 1987b, 1988; Salthouse et al., 1989). Following the reasoning outlined above, these results can be considered as support for quantitative interpretations of the age-related cognitive differences, such as that based on the notion of a reduction with age in the quantity of available processing resources.

Although some of the recent results are encouraging to proponents of the processing-resource version of the information-processing perspective, it is still too early to reach a definite conclusion regarding its contribution to age differences in cognition. One concern is that there has been considerable variability across different combinations of tasks in the specific parameters of the functions relating the performance of young and old adults. It is unclear whether this variation is attributable to variability in the sampling of research participants or in the sampling of cognitive measures, or whether it might reflect the operation of as yet unidentified qualitative factors. It is also not yet known whether statistically significant improvements in prediction of older adult performance from young adult performance would be obtained if qualitative variables were introduced into the prediction equations.

Summary and evaluation of the information-processing approach

The results of research applying the information-processing perspective to intellectual or cognitive differences in adulthood can be succinctly summarized as follows. Currently available research suggests that there appear to be small to nonexistent age differences in the amount and organization of information stored in long-term memory, but fairly pronounced age-related declines have been found in the effectiveness or efficiency of many processing components. It is not known at the present time whether the differences at the level of processing components are the causes, or merely consequences, of age differences in more general executive processes or in the quantity of some type of processing resources.

Although definitive localizations of the adult age differences in cognition are not yet possible, it should be apparent from the preceding pages that a primary characteristic of the information-processing perspective is an emphasis on the processes responsible for producing particular behavior, and not simply the quality or quantity of the behavior itself. This analytical focus on processes as opposed to just on products has led to quite refined descriptions of the nature of age-related differences in cognitive performance. The great precision in specifying the locus of age-related differences in cognitive functioning is undoubtedly the major advantage of the information-processing approach to developmental research.

Perhaps the most important limitation of information-processing research today is that there is still relatively little evidence concerning the validity of the proposed analytical models. Although there is generally moderate to strong support for the models within the context of specific tasks, there is seldom much independent evidence for the validity of the models, or of the hypothesized components, outside that relatively narrow context. Two types of research evidence would be particularly useful in this connection: (1) evidence that measures of the same component derived from different tasks have at least moderate correlations with each other and (2) evidence that both the identity and the effectiveness or efficiency of the components remain invariant when the same basic task is performed in different situations or contexts.

A second limitation of the information-processing perspective is that questions can be raised regarding the extent to which description or localization is equivalent to explanation. That is, it is sometimes argued that description, even if quite precise and refined, merely addresses the issue of *what* the age differences are, and does not directly provide an answer to the question of *why* these differences originate. The boundary between description and explanation is not always clear, however, and few would doubt that the task of explanation is much easier when the descriptions of what is to be explained are precise rather than vague.

In summary, the information-processing perspective provides an extremely rich set of theoretical concepts and mechanistic models that can be applied to the analysis and, one hopes, to the understanding of intellectual development. Many issues are still unresolved, but the emphasis on analysis has been, and seems likely to continue to be, an extremely powerful heuristic in motivating and guiding developmental research.

References

Arenberg, D. (1976). The effects of input condition on free recall in young and old adults. *Journal of Gerontology, 31*, 551–555.

Balota, D. A., & Duchek, J. M. (1988). Age-related differences in lexical access, spreading activation, and simple pronunciation. *Psychology and Aging, 3*, 84–93.

Berg, C., Hertzog, C., & Hunt, E. (1982). Age differences in the speed of mental rotation. *Developmental Psychology, 18*, 95–107.

Birren, J. E., & Schaie, K. W. (Eds.). (1985). *Handbook of the psychology of aging*. New York: Van Nostrand Reinhold.

Bowles, N. L., & Poon, L. W. (1985). Aging and retrieval of words in semantic memory. *Journal of Gerontology, 40*, 71–77.

Bowles, N. L., & Poon, L. W. (1988). Age and context effects in lexical decision: An age by context interaction. *Experimental Aging Research, 14*, 201–205.

Brinley, J. F. (1965). Cognitive sets, speed and accuracy of performance in the elderly. In A. T. Welford & J. E. Birren (Eds.), *Behavior, aging and the nervous system* (pp. 114–149). Springfield, IL: Charles C. Thomas.

Burke, D. M., & Peters, L. (1986). Word associations in old age: Evidence for consistency in semantic encoding during adulthood. *Psychology and Aging, 1*, 283–292.

276 TIMOTHY A. SALTHOUSE

Burke, D. M., White, H., & Diaz, D. L. (1987). Semantic priming in young and older adults: Evidence for age constancy in automatic and attentional processes. *Journal of Experimental Psychology: Human Perception and Performance, 13*, 79–88.
Burke, D. M., & Yee, P. L. (1984). Semantic priming during sentence processing by young and older adults. *Developmental Psychology, 20*, 903–910.
Butterfield, E. C., Nelson, T. O., & Peck, V. (1988). Developmental aspects of the feeling of knowing. *Developmental Psychology, 24*, 654–663.
Cerella, J. (1985). Information processing rates in the elderly. *Psychological Bulletin, 98*, 67–83.
Cerella, J., Poon, L. W., & Fozard, J. L. (1981). Mental rotation and age reconsidered. *Journal of Gerontology, 36*, 620–624.
Charness, N., (Ed.). (1985). *Aging and human performance*. Chichester, England: Wiley.
Chiarello, C., & Hoyer, W. J. (1988). Adult age differences in implicit and explicit memory: Time course and encoding effects. *Psychology and Aging, 3*, 358–366.
Clarkson-Smith, L., & Halpern, D. F. (1983). Can age-related deficits in spatial memory be attenuated through the use of verbal coding? *Experimental Aging Research, 9*, 179–184.
Cooper, L. A., & Shepard, R. (1973). Chronometric studies of the rotation of mental images. In W. G. Chase (Ed.), *Visual information processing* (pp. 76–176). New York: Academic Press.
Gaylord, S. A., & Marsh, G. R. (1976). Age differences in the speed of a spatial cognitive process. *Journal of Gerontology, 30*, 674–678.
Hartley, A. A., & Anderson, J. W. (1986). Instruction, induction, generation, and evaluation of strategies for solving search problems. *Journal of Gerontology, 41*, 650–658.
Howard, D. V. (1983). The effects of aging and degree of association on the semantic priming of lexical decisions. *Experimental Aging Research, 9*, 145–151.
Howard, D. V., Heisey, J. G., & Shaw, R. J. (1986). Aging and the priming of newly learned associations. *Developmental Psychology, 22*, 78–85.
Howard, D. V., McAndrews, M. P., & Lasaga, M. I. (1981). Semantic priming of lexical decisions in young and old adults. *Journal of Gerontology, 36*, 707–714.
Howard, D. V., Shaw, R. J., & Heisey, J. G. (1986). Aging and the time course of semantic activation. *Journal of Gerontology, 41*, 195–203.
Jacewicz, M. M., & Hartley, A. A. (1987). Age differences in the speed of cognitive operations: Resolution of inconsistent findings. *Journal of Gerontology, 42*, 86–88.
Lachman, J. L., Lachman, R., & Thronesberry, C. (1979). Metamemory through the adult life span. *Developmental Psychology, 15*, 543–551.
Light, L. L., & Singh, A. (1987). Implicit and explicit memory in young and older adults. *Journal of Experimental Psychology: Learning, Memory and Cognition, 13*, 531–541.
Lovelace, E. A., & Cooley, S. (1982). Free association of older adults to single words and conceptually related word triads. *Journal of Gerontology, 37*, 432–437.
Lovelace, E. A., & Marsh, G. R. (1985). Prediction and evaluation of memory performance by young and old adults. *Journal of Gerontology, 40*, 192–197.
Parkinson, S. R., Lindholm, J. M., & Inman, V. W. (1982). An analysis of age differences in immediate recall. *Journal of Gerontology, 37*, 425–431.
Perlmutter, M. (1978). What is memory aging the aging of? *Developmental Psychology, 14*, 330–345.
Puglisi, J. T., & Morrell, R. W. (1986). Age-related slowing in mental rotation of three-dimensional objects. *Experimental Aging Research, 12*, 217–220.
Rabinowitz, J. C., Ackerman, B. P., Craik, F. I. M., & Hinchley, J. L. (1982). Aging and metamemory: The roles of relatedness and imagery. *Journal of Gerontology, 37*, 688–695.
Salthouse, T. A. (1980). Age and memory: Strategies for localizing the loss. In L. W. Poon, J. L. Fozard, L. Cermak, D. Arenberg, & L. W. Thompson (Eds.), *New directions in memory and aging* (pp. 47–65). Hillsdale, NJ: Erlbaum.
Salthouse, T. A. (1982). *Adult cognition: An experimental psychology of human aging*. New York: Springer-Verlag.

Salthouse, T. A. (1985). Speed of behavior and its implications for cognition. In J. E. Birren & K. W. Schaie (Eds.), *Handbook of the psychology of aging* (pp. 400–426). New York: Van Nostrand Reinhold.

Salthouse, T. A. (1987a). Adult age differences in integrative spatial ability. *Psychology and Aging, 2,* 254–260.

Salthouse, T. A. (1987b). The role of representations in age differences in analogical reasoning. *Psychology and Aging, 2,* 357–362.

Salthouse, T. A. (1988). The role of processing resources in cognitive aging. In M. L. Howe & C. J. Brainerd (Eds.), *Cognitive development in adulthood* (pp. 185–239). New York: Springer-Verlag.

Salthouse, T. A., Legg, S. E., Palmon, R., & Mitchell, D. R. D. (1990). Memory factors in age-related differences in simple reasoning. *Psychology and Aging, 5,* 9–15.

Salthouse, T. A., & Mitchell, D. R. D. (1989). Structural and operational capacities in integrative spatial ability. *Psychology and Aging, 4,* 18–25.

Salthouse, T. A., Mitchell, D. R. D., Skovronek, E., & Babcock, R. L. (1989). Effects of adult age and working memory on reasoning and spatial abilities. *Journal of Experimental Psychology: Learning, Memory and Cognition, 15,* 507–516.

Salthouse, T. A., & Prill, K. A. (1987). Inferences about age impairments in inferential reasoning. *Psychology and Aging, 2,* 43–51.

Sanders, R. E., Murphy, M. D., Schmitt, F. A., & Walsh, K. K. (1980). Age differences in free recall rehearsal strategies. *Journal of Gerontology, 35,* 550–558.

Schonfield, A. E. D., & Robertson, E. A. (1966). Memory storage and aging. *Canadian Journal of Psychology, 20,* 228–236.

Scialfa, C. T., & Margolis, R. B. (1986). Age differences in the commonality of free associations. *Experimental Aging Research, 12,* 95–98.

Shaw, R. J., & Craik, F. I. M. (1989). Age differences in predictions and performance on a cued recall task. *Psychology and Aging, 4,* 131–135.

Shepard, R. N., & Metzler, J. (1971). Mental rotation of three-dimensional objects. *Science, 171,* 701–703.

Wright, R. E. (1982). Adult age similarities in free recall output order and strategies. *Journal of Gerontology, 37,* 76–79.

10 Integrating learning into a theory of intellectual development

Richard L. Canfield and Stephen J. Ceci

> Both learning and development must be incorporated in integral ways in the more complete and successful theory of human information processing that will emerge at a later stage in the development of our science.
> (Newell & Simon, 1972, p. 8)

Despite calls for the integration of learning and development, from many quarters, over the past twenty years little has actually been accomplished in this regard. Therefore, it is a pleasure to contribute to an integrative volume that brings together diverse perspectives on the growth, maintenance, and decline of intellectual functions, as it provides us with an opportunity to reconcile learning and development perspectives. In this chapter we describe the learning approach to intellectual development, but we find ourselves compelled at the outset of this enterprise to state a caveat. Although each of us has studied learning and has endorsed its centrality as a developmental process (Canfield & Haith, 1991; Chi & Ceci, 1987), neither of us considers himself strictly a "learning" psychologist. In the service of our particular identities, and in the hope of promoting conceptual integration, we do not present the learning approach as a comprehensive theory of intellectual development. Rather, we begin by outlining some of the historical and philosophical roots of the learning approach and describe the current learning perspective as "resurgent learning theory." We then describe the current approach in relation to traditional learning theory, noting that it has evolved by incorporating (or reinstantiating) mentalistic constructs and by identifying the site of intellectual change as the amount and organization of content knowledge. Research demonstrating powerful effects of the knowledge base on memory processing is reviewed in support of the learning hypothesis. Limitations associated with resurgent learning theory are then discussed, and it is concluded that the approach suffers from a lack of generality, owing to its exclusive focus on content knowledge. Other sources of developmental

Portions of this research were made possible through grants F31MH03983 and R03MH45298 to R. L. Canfield and 5 K04 HD00801-03 to S. J. Ceci.

278

change, such as maturation of the frontal cortex and organism-guided learning, are presented as posing challenges to the current learning formulation. Finally, we present a simple scheme for understanding relations between learning and development where change mechanisms traditionally associated with learning theories are seen as a proper subset of the entire set of mechanisms producing intellectual development.

Learning versus development: A brief historical backdrop

One of the most enigmatic issues in the history of psychology is the explanation of intellectual change over time. One tradition in psychology has struggled to understand change by categorizing it according to the size of the change, its time scale, the population affected, and its relation to maturation. Within this tradition, an enduring division for classifying types of change is the distinction between learning and development. A second tradition remains more dubious regarding the utility of a concept of "development" as distinct from the accumulation of learning experiences or memory traces. Instead, scientists in this tradition see learning as the source of virtually all intellectual change.

As a result of these two traditions competing for explanatory adequacy, considerable energy has been devoted to defining the terms *learning* and *development*. Unfortunately, the definitional approach has tended to reinforce preexisting metatheoretical commitments rather than to provide conceptual integration (Baer, 1970; Inhelder, Sinclair, & Bovet, 1974; Liben, 1987; Skinner, 1974). Given the lack of progress in defining the terms, we strongly suspect that the learning-versus-development debate represents one of the many conundrums that plague us in our attempt to explain cognitive growth.[1]

Using a more descriptive approach, it is evident that scientists generally understand both learning and development as involving change. Learning is associated with relatively small, day-to-day accumulations of skills and knowledge (Siegler & Shipley, 1987), whereas development refers to something more profound and somewhat independent of learning. Development refers to some form of *growth*, resulting in increased *capacity* to learn (Brown & Reeve, 1987). This increase in capacity is usually tied to some underlying maturational change – although the mix of nature and nurture varies substantially from one theory to the next (Gesell, 1928; Piaget, 1970; Skinner, 1974; Vygotsky, 1962). In addition, development is often conceived to involve global or radical psychological changes and to be more lasting than learning. For example, one can learn and then forget how to tie a sheep shank knot, but once one has acquired the requisite fine motor control and memory for sequences of actions, the *capacity* to learn to tie a sheep shank is a permanent acquisition.

Given these modal differences between the notions of learning and development, it is important to see how those researchers taking a learning perspective have approached the study of age differences in intellectual ability. Although there have been several dominant learning theories proposed over the last century or so, each has its roots in the philosophy of empiricism. This philosophy, solidified by the writings of David Hume (1958), held that all knowledge is built from raw sense data; thus, the infant's mind is a tabula rasa, or blank slate, devoid of innate ideas and waiting for experience to give it form and meaning. The concept of innate structure (e.g., Kant, 1965), or readiness, was explicitly rejected.

The psychological theories of the 19th and 20th centuries that were spawned by empiricism relied on mechanisms of learning as the cause of age-related cognitive changes. Skinner's operant learning theory was founded on mechanisms proposed by the doctrines of empiricism and associationism, namely, associations between molecular behaviors and their consequences, and the accumulation of complex chains of responses. For example, when Bijou and Baer applied Skinner's operant learning theory to the study of development, they began with a definition of development as "progressive changes in the way an organism's behavior interacts with the environment" (Bijou & Baer, 1961, p. 1). Their behaviorist agenda called for a discovery of the causes of these progressive changes and the mechanisms used to explain development were the familiar learning mechanisms of *reinforcement, punishment, extinction, generalization,* and *discrimination.* Development was held to be an accumulation of learning experiences, a result of environmental contingencies that activated the various learning mechanisms in a particular context.

Although development was seen to be caused by the basic learning mechanisms, change is not guaranteed by the application of any given procedure: Timing is important. For Bijou and Baer, the "right" time was not an age or a maturational level but, rather, a point in the child's sequence of learning experiences. Thus, the strong form of this argument is that age is irrelevant to the study of development (Baer, 1970). Baer argued that development can be wholly accounted for by the number and ordering of an individual's learning experiences, and nothing besides the sequencing of learning experiences differentiates learning from development.

In addition to reducing development to the ordered accumulation of specific learning experiences, the antimentalistic stance of this version of learning theory commanded that the only site of behavioral change was the individual's overt behavioral repertoire. That is, evidence for learning was a change in the probability of a specific observed response.

Behavioristic learning theory has been repeatedly criticized by scientists of development (Brown, 1982; Chomsky, 1959; Goldman-Rakic, 1986; Inhelder et al., 1974; Liben, 1987). One of the most persistent critiques stems from the antimentalistic stance toward cognition. For example, Chomsky (1959) noted that Skinner's theory failed to account for the distinction between competence and performance, and Goldman-Rakic (1986), among others, has criticized S-R psychology for utilizing an "empty-organism" metaphor that envisions an individual devoid of intentions, cognitive structures and processes, maturational schedules, and even a central nervous system.

As a result of learning theorists' own questions regarding the site of behavioral change and what is learned (Greeno, 1980; Lachman, Lachman, & Butterfield, 1979), as well as developments in ethology (Garcia, Clarke, & Hankins, 1973), linguistics (Chomsky, 1959), and developmental psychology (Piaget, 1954), the theory went through a major reorganization. In short, the learning approach ran head-on into the cognitive revolution.

A resurgent learning approach

Today students of cognitive development often express the view that cognitive (i.e., mentalistic) orientations to learning and development such as connectionism and information processing have much in common with traditional learning approaches (Fodor & Pylyshyn, 1988; Holyoak, 1987; Lachman et al., 1979; Lachter & Bever, 1988). In addition, some universal novice theories of development suggest that cognitive and learning perspectives are simply different levels of discourse, one fully mappable on to the other (Brown, 1982; Skinner, 1987). Historically, empiricist learning approaches were also "cognitive" in that they strove to explain knowledge acquisition and thought processes via some notion of association or connection between perceptions, situations, thoughts, and behaviors (Murphy & Kovach, 1972). Seen in this light, antimentalism as definitional of a learning approach was a positivistic detour in the history of thought on the topic.

It is our view that the learning approach, at least with regard to its account of intellectual development, survived the cognitive onslaught of the 1960s and 1970s through a combination of "incorporation" and "retrenchment." Concerning the former (incorporation of some mentalistic aspects), learning theorists revised their view of the *what* of learning from a change in the probability of a specific response to a change in a state of knowledge, and finally to changes in the amount and organization of knowledge (Greeno, 1980). According to several prominent researchers whom we view as "resurgent learning theorists," intellectual development is seen as a matter of learning mechanisms operating on an inferred construct. The inferred construct is a cognitive entity, an organized knowledge base such as a schema, script, frame, or production (Chi & Rees, 1983; Klahr & Wallace, 1976; Minsky, 1975; Rumelhart & Norman, 1978). In this system learning proceeds via some "accretion" mechanism for the accumulation facts and information in memory, and via an associative mechanism that leads to interconnections between elements of an (inferred) knowledge base. In addition, some form of "tuning" of the knowledge structure is needed so that it applies to reality with a functional amount of generality and specificity. Finally, "restructuring" of the knowledge base is hypothesized to occur when new conceptual categories are needed or when old structures cannot be adapted to meet a present need. The incorporation of mentalistic concepts by learning theories is often billed as a radical shift in scientific theory, sometimes approaching the magnitude of a Kuhnian paradigm shift (Lachman et al., 1979). As discussed in the next section, however, we feel that such a view hides enduring continuities between the two approaches. (See also Beilin, 1983.)

Schemata and schema change

The most profound "incorporation" of mentalistic constructs by the learning approach has been its importation of schema models of memory organization. The concept of a schema has its historical roots in Kant's philosophy and was brought into modern psychology via the writings of Bartlett (1932), although the latter drew on the neurologist Sir Henry Head's depiction of a schema more than on Kant's. In the modern formulation (e.g., Brown, 1978; Chi & Rees, 1983; Rumelhart & Norman, 1978) schemata are seen as organized memory structures that specify the interrelationships among events and concepts that constitute a person's internal model of a situation. For example, an infant's schema of the human face may specify spatial relations between initially separate images of the features of a face and results in an organized whole. Because eyes, mouth, nose, and hairline regularly co-occur in a fairly predictable manner, they provide a basis on which to build a schema. This process of building up a schema from experience is often termed "induction." Induction requires the person to build up a data base of experiences and then extract patterns of co-occurrence and predictive relations among the elements (i.e., associative links). Once primitive schemata are "up and running," other forms of learning such as tuning and restructuring can take place. As can be seen, these three processes of accretion, tuning, and restructuring characterize the learning approaches just discussed.

Accretion as a mechanism of intellectual development

Accretion is the relatively simple mode of learning wherein we accumulate new information. For example, when children are first learning about animals, exposure to an animal picture book or a visit to a zoo provides them with many new exemplars for their animal schemata. Similarly for episodic memories, children will accumulate information about school, restaurants, baby sitters, and the like, which will make up sets of information and constitute the children's schemata for such situations. Accretion refers to the accumulation of the data or facts that the memory system has available for organization and reorganization. Accretion is accomplished via operant and classical conditioning as well as by associations between stimuli. Learning through accretion is greatly facilitated by the existence of an appropriate set of schemata.

Tuning existing schemata

Schemata are generalized memory structures. They do not record all of experience as that would be costly and likely dysfunctional; rather, schemata are an abstraction from the details of experience, they capture its *structure* and *regularity*. Abstraction carries with it an inevitable cost – when the normally useless details of an exemplar or experience are not attended to, the schema fills in those details with default values or assumptions about what the details must have been. This power to generalize also carries with it an important liability – something Bruner and Postman (1949) called the "problem of incongruity." Sometimes our assumptions turn out to be false or incomplete in some important way. When an existing schema is incongruous with the demands of a given situation, then either the schema must be modified or a new one must be constructed.

Tuning is the set of processes that describes how schemata are modified. Several kinds of tuning have been described by Rumelhart and Norman (1978); however, for our present purposes all can be characterized as processes of constraint satisfaction. When our knowledge structures meet novel situations, there is always some degree of mismatch between incoming information and existing memories. If the mismatch is large enough to hinder behavioral success, then we must work to resolve the conflict. For example, when a child learns about goldfish, a knowledge structure is built that may also apply more generally to other varieties of fish (salmon, bass, grouper). The variables in her goldfish schema (has fins, swims upright, eyes on either side of head) actually apply more broadly to other varieties of fish. The mismatch of perceptual features between trout, pike, and goldfish may cause her to generalize variables concerning length-to-girth ratios, skin color, and size. Alternatively, when she confronts examples of flounders, halibut, and sole, she will need to tune her budding fish schema to specialize its application. In this case, she has likely overgeneralized the features "swims upright" and "has eyes on either side of head." Such everyday experiences lead to subtle but important changes in existing schemata, improving their fit to the constraints of a situation or set of concepts.

It is interesting to note the relationship between tuning processes and the traditional learning mechanisms. When tuning takes the form of specialization, it appears little different from the traditional function played by discrimination. Similarly, another process of tuning is generalization – and here both the name and the function remain unchanged. What has changed in resurgent learning theory is that these processes are now assumed to take place with respect to a mental structure, namely, aspects of the knowledge base that are not available to direct observation. It should not be forgotten that basic laws of association (contiguity, reinforcement, extinction, discrimination, and generalization) were important to empiricist philosophy beginning with Aristotle. What has been at issue more than the laws of association are the entities to be associated. Over the centuries the elements of association have varied widely (e.g., primary sensory qualities, secondary sensory qualities, thoughts, reflexes, overt behaviors, stimuli and responses, responses and responses, stimuli and stimuli), whereas the laws of association have been relatively unchanged since the time of Pavlov (Hilgard & Bower, 1975).

Creating new schemata

Traditional learning theories relied solely on small, incremental changes in behaviors to explain growth; resurgent theorists recognize a need for large-scale changes in cognitive structures. For example, when existing memory structures are inadequate to satisfy the constraints imposed by a new context, then new structures must be built. If learning could only occur as a result of accretion or tuning, then new conceptual categories could not be created. For example, without the capacity to create new schemata, our hypothetical child might never comprehend whales as members of a nonfish category.

There are two general mechanisms for creating new schemata: patterned generation (or analogy), and schema induction (Chi & Rees, 1983; Rumelhart & Norman, 1978). Patterned generation occurs when one uses an existing schema to generate new ones. For example, a whale schema could be generated by analogy with a bat schema. Both are atypical exemplars of mammals that are highly similar to another group in their habits (in this example, similar to fish and birds). A second way to create a new schema is the way we create our initial schema – through the identification of co-occurrence information and the extraction of predictive relations – that is, induction. Even as adults we use induction to create new schemata. In the study of some new domain of politics or economics one may learn a broad set of facts corresponding to the political and economic activities of countries around the world. For example, the recent events in Iran, Panama, and the Philippines have made it possible to induce a category representing short, ruthless, despotic rulers (i.e., the Shah, Manuel Noriega, and Ferdinand Marcos). Such a category would be built on information such as the rulers' positions as generals of their respective militaries, an ability to embezzle billions of dollars from their respective treasuries, murderous social controls, and suspiciously close ties to the U.S. government before being overthrown. The construction of such a category requires the effort to accumulate and remember facts surrounding these events, and further, to relate these facts in order to extract co-occurrence relations between initially separate events. Compared to analogy, induction is exceedingly difficult.[2] In the future, it may be possible to refer to a leader as a "Noriega" and much will have been said. Induction takes time and effort.

When possible, induction is supported by analogy in at least two ways. First, soon after a new schema is induced, it is quickly related to other schemata in order to generate useful analogies which can then be used to schematize new sets of data, as would be possible with our hypothetical Noriega example. Second, even when the hard work of induction is accomplished by a single talented person, the communication of that insight to others is often expedited through the use of analogy. Much of our success at education depends on the use of analogies for quickly communicating ideas that originally required the tedious work of induction by one or more individuals.

Whether comprehension requires only small schema changes, such as tuning, or wholly new schemata through restructuring depends on the generality of a given knowledge structure. Perhaps one of the thorniest and most enduring issues facing developmentalists has to do with the presumed specificity versus generality of cognition. Historically, this issue was first raised in the context of the debate over transfer of learning that was waged at the turn of the century between Edward Thorndike and Charles Judd. Thorndike attacked the belief that learning one discipline helps children think more rationally in another discipline (e.g., learning Latin fosters learning English; similarly, learning chess was promoted as a means of fostering greater transfer to other subjects). Therefore, learning how to think in one area was thought to lead to facilitation in learning in other areas because of the presumed ubiquity of transfer. Thorndike (Thorndike & Woodworth, 1901), using a simple perceptual discrimination paradigm, showed that subjects were not adept at transferring their ability to estimate the area of particular shapes to new shapes, despite similarities in the parameters of the old and new shapes. On the other hand, Judd (1908) demonstrated that transfer was indeed possible. He asked fifth- and sixth-graders to throw darts at a target submerged under 12 inches of water until they improved at hitting it. Half of these children were initially taught the laws of refraction. Following success at hitting the submerged target, Judd raised its level to only 4 inches beneath the water surface. Those children who had been taught the laws of refraction transferred this learning to the new situation and as a result outperformed the children who did not learn these laws.

Since this debate, the issue has become broader, and it now addresses the question, How general is learning? Entire volumes have been written on this topic, and it would take us well beyond the confines of this chapter to review that literature in any degree of detail (see, for example, the 1989 special issue of the *Merrill Palmer Quarterly*, entitled *Children's cognitive and social-cognitive development: Domain specificity and generality*). But at its root the following generalization can be abstracted: With few exceptions following Watson, learning psychologists have argued that nothing as general as a new mode of reasoning or a pervasive logical capacity emerges simultaneously and is immediately applied to all intellectual challenges. Instead, general abilities result from gradually acquiring specific knowledge one domain at a time. More recent hybrid theories struggle with these opposing views (Fischer, 1980; Siegler, 1981).

Retrenchment and effects of the knowledge base

In addition to incorporating some mentalism using the schema formulation, another way the learning approach has survived and distinguished itself from cognitive approaches is through a form of "retrenchment" that has rarely been made explicit, namely, by placing the site of developmental change in the knowledge base as opposed to other inferred cognitive loci such as increases in short-term or long-term memory capacity, processing speed, or mode of representation (Chi & Rees, 1983). In this view, an increase in memory capacity or processing speed is because of the facilitating effect of an elaborate, well-organized knowledge base in a particular domain rather than because of some independent, maturationally induced increase in speed, capacity, or style.

As for past formulations of the learning approach, the processes that regulate growth of the knowledge base and thus intellectual development in children are considered to be identical to the processes that regulate learning in adults. The central difference between children and adults is postulated to be a relatively short learning history for children. That is, children are unable to learn as well as adults because they are universal novices (Brown & DeLoache, 1978).

The most common paradigm for demonstrating the effects of knowledge base is the expert–novice contrast. A task domain is identified in which reliable individual and developmental differences exist in the amount of knowledge subjects possess, and in the degree of its organization. Subjects in a subgroup are known to be experts in this task domain, whether it is picking winners at a racetrack (Ceci & Liker, 1986), classifying new exemplars as to their family of dinosaurs (Chi, Hutchinson, & Robin, 1989), or understanding soccer strategy (Schneider, Korkel, & Weinert, 1989). When such experts are compared to persons who lack extensive domain-relevant knowledge, they are found to outperform them at a wide range of cognitive tasks tied to that domain, such as the amount of information they can recall in that domain, their reading comprehension level in that domain, and their ability to form new concepts in that domain.

In general, the literature on expert–novice contrasts makes a persuasive case for the importance of the content and structure of the knowledge base because experts excel over novices even when the latter are chronologically older or have higher IQs. This formulation is consistent with the learning approach of Bijou and Baer, that is, resurgent learning theory views age as irrelevant to development. For example, in the expertise literature, a classic test of age irrelevance was undertaken by Chi, who studied children and adult chess players. She used a powerful age X expert–novice design to tease apart the contributions of knowledge base and age on various memory tasks incidental to the game of chess. Chi designed tests of immediate and delayed recall of chess positions and administered them to adult chess novices and child chess experts. As a control, she measured memory for digits. Her findings showed that subjects with a more elaborate knowledge base were better able to recall the locations of chess pieces seen briefly on a board on a single trial, stored information in larger chunks, and required fewer trials to memorize a board configuration – independent of age. However, in the domain of memory for digits, where adults were presumed to have more elaborate knowledge, there was a large age effect. In this domain, the older subjects had longer memory spans and formed larger chunks. Thus, by varying age and knowledge base independently, Chi showed that memory processing is linked to expertise as opposed to being inexorably tied to age.

Studies that have reversed the normally occurring correlation between age and knowledge suggest it is the latter that plays a causative role in development. On those occasions when young children are more knowledgeable about items to be remembered than older children – for example, if the materials are cartoon characters that are more familiar to the younger children – their memory performance for these materials has been shown to be superior (Lindberg, 1980). Importantly, such knowledge effects can work in reverse as well. If an elaborate knowledge base leads to the generation of false inferences, then whenever younger children have more knowledge about the characters than older children they will be more likely to make false inferences (Ceci, Caves, & Howe, 1981). In this latter study it was shown that how knowledge is organized influences the level of false inferences. Young children's knowledge base contained certain implicational relations that were not true of older children's knowledge base (e.g., if someone is handsome, then he must also be smart and brave). Age differences in memory for a script involving highly familiar characters were due largely to differences in the way the children structured their knowledge.

Another study supports a principle of ability irrelevance. Ceci and Liker (1986) studied racetrack handicappers. Two groups of men were identified who attended the races practically every day of their adult lives. One group was referred to as experts because of their knowledge and skill at handicapping races, while the other group was referred to as nonexperts. Despite an equivalent amount of experience at the track, it was demonstrated that low-IQ men who were rated as experts were far more complex in the way they thought about the racing variables than were high-IQ men who were nonexperts. Experts took into consideration more variables *interactively* than did nonexperts, and it was this factor that was shown to be responsible for their superior skill. Thus, in this study the type of knowledge one possesses and the manner in which it is organized was shown to be instrumental in determining expertise; IQ was unrelated to this form of interactive reasoning.

It is important to restate here that the measures of intellectual growth used by those in the learning camp are usually measures of memory processing. The implicit and sometimes explicit assumption is that what develops is memory and that the most appropriate index of intellectual growth is the structure, capacity, or efficiency of one's memory. Only recently have researchers tried to account for nonmemorial forms of intellectual growth, such as text comprehension (Schneider et al., 1989), metaphor appreciation (Keil, 1984), and animism (e.g., Berzonsky, 1971). With some exceptions this new line of research has been congruent with the resurgent learning perspective: In general, cognitive outcomes (be they metaphorical reasoning, text processes, animism, or the traditional memory measures) are tied to accumulation of rote, declarative knowledge, and the manner in which this knowledge is proceduralized (i.e., the addition of qualifiers, deleting rules, etc.), structured, and restructured. These and other results have led Chi to argue that the development of expertise in the form of an elaborate knowledge base is the primary cause of intellectual development rather than a growth in memory capacity, processing speed, or ability to deal with abstractions: "Clearly, the knowledge-base differences between younger and older children are enormous . . . but, as demonstrated in Section IV, C, when researchers have equated for age differences in knowledge, previously observed age differences in memory are often attenuated, if not abolished" (Chi & Ceci, 1987, p. 112).

The effect of knowledge on mental processing may be even more fundamental than the cognitive outcomes already discussed. Take, for example, the most basic indicant of processing efficiency – the speed with which one can recognize or encode an overlearned lexical item. Ordinarily, age trends in this type of encoding are quite pronounced; 12-year-olds require approximately half the processing time (i.e., the item's presentation duration before the onset of a "mask" – a string of densely packed letters and digits that eliminates afterimages) to identify an alphanumeric stimulus as do 8-year-olds. But the average 12-year-old also possesses more knowledge about such stimuli, and a richer organization of this knowledge. For example, even though both age groups have no difficulty recognizing a digit (say "49"), older children's representation of it is far more elaborate than younger children's, including greater or less than, odd or even, multiples, divisors, concepts of roots, cardinality, and so forth. If one were to exert controls on how much one knows about the stimuli to be processed, developmental and individual differences may turn out to be explained by the size and structure of the child's knowledge base rather than by maturational factors per se. There is some preliminary evidence for this position as far as individual differences in encoding speed is concerned (Ceci & Cornelius, 1989), though clearly much more research is needed. In particular, the hypothesis that simple accretion and organization are responsible for driving the developmental engine is still a leading concern for resurgent learning theory. The alternative hypothesis that views knowledge and organization as a result of some more profound developmental process would see these outcomes as similar to the puffs of smoke that result from processes that drive an engine, but which themselves have no causal role in its propulsion. In this regard, developmental researchers need to determine whether differences in knowledge base explain development, or are themselves explained by it. For now, at least, learning theorists have proposed an alternative to maturational accounts of development that is undaunted by the demonstration of age differences even on very basic forms of mentation, such as the above encoding example.

Challenges to resurgent learning theory

The learning approach has contributed to an understanding of the effects of content knowledge on cognitive processing and has been a primary cause for the revision of Piagetian theory. Developmentalists from a wide range of perspectives now believe that horizontal *décalage* is the rule in development rather than the exception as proposed by Piaget (Case, Marini, McKeough, Dennis, & Goldberg, 1986; Fischer, 1980; Siegler, 1981). Proponents of organismic theories have been motivated by the work of resurgent learning theorists to incorporate the fact of domain specificity. In addition to the successes of resurgent learning theory, significant challenges lay ahead. The following discussion addresses two challenges we believe to be central: incorporation of maturational mechanisms, and increased focus on the organism's role in guiding learning.

Maturation and development at the extremes

Research on learning has shown that amount and organization of content knowledge has profound effects on memory performance; however, it has become equally clear that developmental change occurs on many fronts – not only with respect to content knowledge. In fact, a central criticism of the learning approach is that it is too narrowly focused on postinfantile and presenescent development. Developmentalists who work at the extremes of the life-span are forced to consider a broader range of change mechanisms than just accretion, tuning, and restructuring. If we look at infants, for example, we see qualitative shifts and maturationally based upper limits on information processing that are not easily explained by standard learning mechanisms.

Recent research with nonhuman primates and human infants suggests one way that maturation works. Goldman-Rakic (1987), using a combination of methods including behavioral, electromicroscopic, and lesion studies, has found that a specific region of the prefrontal cortex mediates the ability to perform spatial memory tasks such as delayed response or Piaget's A not B object permanence task (Diamond & Goldman-Rakic, 1986). The delayed response task, which is formally equivalent to Piaget's task, involves three components. First comes a cue period where the subject watches the experimenter place a desired object in one of two wells, placing identical covers over each well. Second, a delay is imposed by placing an opaque screen between the subject and the wells. Finally, there is a response phase where the screen is removed after a delay of 1 or more seconds. At this time the subject is allowed a single reach to retrieve the object. In rhesus monkeys, the ability to retrieve the object correctly with the first reach is dependent on age and the length of the delay. At minimal delays of 2–5 seconds, 2-month-old infant monkeys make the A not B error. At 4 months of age, infants make errors only when the delays are 10 seconds or longer. A similar developmental shift occurring between 2 and 4 months is seen in other tasks that require the coordination of spatial information over a delay (Goldman-Rakic, 1987).[3] Coincident with the period when performance on the delayed response task emerges and develops is the period of excess synaptic density in the principal sulcus, the region that mediates performance on these tasks (Goldman-Rakic, 1987). In rhesus monkeys synaptic density in the cortex increases until 4 months of age, and the period from 2 to 4 months is when the density exceeds adult levels. Goldman-Rakic believes these findings "suggest that a critical mass of cortical synapses is important for the emergence of this cognitive function, and that fully mature capacity may depend upon the elimination of excess synapses that occurs during adolescence and young adulthood" (Goldman-Rakic, 1987, p. 601).

For another example of maturation in the domain of visual information processing, Held has discovered that stereoscopic vision develops through the segregation of neural input from the eyes to form ocular dominance columns. This segregation leads to the formation of cells sensitive to binocular disparity. The growth of columnar organization seems to occur very rapidly, often over a period of 1 or 2 weeks (Held, 1985; Shimojo, Bauer, O'Connell, & Held, 1986).

It is not that such developments are impervious to learning; it is instead that they require more than accretion, tuning, and restructuring of content knowledge to explain. Without positing the growth of neural processes under maturational control, it is hard to understand the pervasiveness of such changes. Thus, the kinds of developments studied by Goldman-Rakic, Held, and others (e.g., Newport, 1980) requires reference to change mechanisms not included in the learning psychologist's tool kit.

Organism-guided learning

It is important to recognize that the learning approach shares a central assumption with most other developmental theories, that is, change and growth result from conflict. Resurgent learning theory, Piagetian theory, and, of course, psychoanalytic theory postulate that internal conflicts arising from competing representations of a situation lead to psychological change. However, learning and development approaches tend to focus on different causes underlying the conflict. Learning theory tends to focus on the environment as the originator of the conflict. Learners are seen as blindly moving about in the world, being confronted with difficulties that force them to alter their cognitive structures. This situation does exist, but it is not the only context for learning and intellectual change. When the environment is responsible for initiating conflict, the organism can be likened to a passive machine, rather than an active subject capable of producing conditions favorable for learning and change.

Recent advances in the integration of learning theory and information processing in "expert systems" research has moved away from this view. Glaser (1990) speaks of learning as the result of conscious mental activity in the face of failure, as opposed to a more passive change. In commenting on an intelligent tutoring system, he notes: "The learning process is driven by detection and explanation of failures . . . After detecting a failure . . . the student has to generate possible repairs by reasoning about the additional domain knowledge that, if available, might have prevented the failure. She or he then articulates the nature of the specific question to the system" (p. 34).

Thus, expert systems research has gone beyond the use of traditional learning mechanisms to account for change, and in particular has incorporated metacognitive awareness as a critical ingredient for the student who has reached an impasse.

What has been less a concern for learning theorists like Glaser is the role of expectancies as a primary source of conflict and cognitive growth. Recent research with human infants shows they not only detect and react to conflicts but can actively produce the conditions that result in conflict and change. In fact, recent research has supported the view that expectations are both a result of learning and a foundation for future learning.

Learning and the development of expectations

Since the early 1970s, research on animal and machine learning has resulted in widespread agreement that what is produced in learning is an *expectation*. But as Bolles (1972) observed, this is not a novel insight. Tolman (1932, 1949) placed expectancies at the center of his theory by arguing that animals don't just learn responses, they learn something about the predictive relations between events in the environment. In other words, animals learn expectancies that allow them to predict outcomes that bode them well or ill.

Tolman's ideas were out of step with the antimentalism of his time. But in the past two decades, the field of animal learning has seen an explosion of research and theory that supports and refines the expectancy approach (Bolles, 1972; Hulse, Fowler, & Honig, 1978; Rescorla & Wagner, 1972; Roitblat, Bever, & Terrace, 1982). A central facet of this approach is that organisms do not simply wait for environmental information to impinge upon them but, rather, actively engage in searching for information that will test existing knowledge structures. This more active view of learning reveals that schemata should be conceptualized as future-oriented, similar to what Neisser (1976) has argued with the concept of "anticipatory schemata." The future-oriented component provides an important pathway for schema change besides environmentally produced or bottom-up conflict, namely, expectancy-guided learning.

Research on expectations. Traditional research programs focus on the retrospective function of memory. People and animals are exposed to information and some time later asked to recall or recognize what that information was. What receives less attention is that memory is generally used as a prospective device – especially in everyday contexts. We try to predict the behavior of an erratic driver as we cross the street, or we estimate how long a task will take as we schedule our day (Ceci & Bronfenbrenner, 1985). Memory, when viewed from a functional perspective, derives much of its adaptive value from providing us with a representation of past experience that enables us to cope successfully with an uncertain future (Rovee-Collier & Hayne, 1987). Expectations provide an organism with a way to exercise internal control over behavior but still have the action adapted to prevailing circumstances. Internal control is necessary for guiding behavior toward a goal when environmental circumstances vary.

Recent studies have revealed that expectancies are not only used by adults, they exist early in ontogeny. In one study of expectancies, infants were shown a sequence of pictures that flashed left and right of visual center. Evidence for expectations would be found if infants are able to encode the regularity of the picture sequence, and then use the representation to guide their looking in anticipation of the next picture onset. That is, after some experience with the sequence, they may begin to look in the direction of the next picture before it actually appears.

The investigation involved 48 three-month-old infants who were shown one of four sequences of pictures. Three sequences varied in spatiotemporal complexity but were predictable – 1/1 (L-R symmetric alternation), 2/1 (L-L-R or R-R-L asymmetric alternation), 3/1 (L-L-L-R or R-R-R-L asymmetric alternation) – and the fourth was unpredictable. Each picture was separated by a 1-second no-stimulus interval. As the babies watched the pictures their eye movements were captured on videotape, which was later played back in slow motion to reveal two measures of visual activity that were taken as evidence of expectation: (1) anticipatory eye movements to future picture locations and (2) reduced saccadic latencies to fixate pictures.

Results from this study showed that babies only 3 months old could quickly form expectations for future pictures in the three predictable sequences (Canfield & Haith, 1991). They reliably shifted fixation to the next picture location during no-stimulus intervals. In addition to anticipatory fixations, infants tended to react more quickly to pictures when they appeared in a predictable manner. By contrast, infants who saw an unpredictable sequence had generally longer saccadic latencies and comparatively few anticipatory shifts during the no-stimulus interval (Canfield & Haith, 1991).

Although young infants are often thought of as rather passive creatures who react only to sources of stimulation, this study reveals that even young infants are motivated to develop expectations for events that occur in their visual environment. A rather surprising aspect of their learning is that it occurred very rapidly. Infants viewed the picture sequences for only 2 minutes, yet this was sufficient time for them to demonstrate an expectancy for the recurrent regularity. Thus, even with a *very* limited knowledge base, infants only 3 months old produced their first anticipation after an average of only 8 L-R alternations in condition 1/1.

Possibly, what we see in these babies is an example of a more general principle – expectancies provide an important avenue for schema change. As a schema for the regularity of picture presentations was being built, infants may have been using anticipation to test the adequacy of their mental model. It is important to note that testing the adequacy of a mental model is not a form of conflict that originates in the environment, it is tuning and reorganization guided by the individual's current cognitive state. Anticipatory behaviors can serve as hypotheses about the accuracy of the schema being built. As such, expectations are essential self-regulative strategies, necessary for efficient learning because they allow one to monitor the applicability of their emerging rules (Glaser & Bassok, 1989; Roberts, Aman, & Canfield, 1989).

Another, more subtle issue is at stake here. Recent neural models of learning have also recognized the importance of expectations. A central problem of learning is how to develop a cognitive code flexible enough to learn new facts, yet rigid enough that old memories are not overwritten by incoming information. Grossberg (1980) has termed this the "stability/ plasticity dilemma" and presents it as a challenge to all theories of learning and memory. It is now known that any learning theory that relies solely on feed-forward (bottom-up) computations is, in principle, unable to correct coding errors without some sort of homunculus that knows a priori whether an error has in fact occurred (Grossberg, 1982). One way of correcting such errors without a homunculus is to combine feed-forward signals with feed-back (top-down) computations to create a resonant state whereby these representations compete for activation (Grossberg, 1982). An obvious role for the top-down feedback is the psychological notion of an "expectancy."

Given the wealth of evidence documenting important effects of maturation and the organism's role in guiding learning, it is apparent there is a more complex pattern of data to explain than is currently attempted by the learning perspective. At this time it is farfetched to maintain that intellectual development across the life-span can be adequately explained as a consequence of increasing (or decreasing) content knowledge. This situation has led us to view learning mechanisms as a proper subset (a crucial set in themselves) of the developmental mechanisms responsible for cognitive growth. As such, accretion, tuning, and restructuring join other mechanisms, such as genetic scheduling, myelination, synaptogenesis, and ecology, to foster intellectual growth. The next section expands on this view.

Development and learning: A set–proper subset relation

As many writers have noted, conceptions of learning and development traditionally reside in opposing camps (Inhelder et al., 1974; Liben, 1987). In our attempt to promote theoretical integration, we strive to view development and learning not as antagonistic processes but, rather, as having a set–proper subset relation. "Learning" is a concept that cannot be defined to universal satisfaction, and the same can be said of "development."

Fortunately, we do not require a universally agreed-upon definition in order to make scientific progress. What we seek to understand is the various causes of relatively long-lasting changes in behavior. In particular, we seek to discover the general principles and mechanisms that underlie these changes. If we can accomplish this task, then learning and development will be two of the phenomena explained (Staddon, 1983). For the present, it will suffice to say that learning represents a class of mechanisms that directly and indirectly cause changes in mental content, organization, competence, and performance. Learning is one kind of intellectual development that coexists and interacts with other kinds of intellectual development.

"Development" – more specifically, intellectual development – subsumes a broad set of change mechanisms, of which learning is a subset. Other known causes of change include cell proliferation, arborization and myelination, genetic scheduling, hormone and neurotransmitter production, as well as the everyday aspects of life ecology that affect opportunities for exposure to information-rich environments, such as the onset of self-produced locomotion, values of the peer culture, and formal schooling (Campos, Svejda, Campos, & Bertenthal, 1982; Goldman-Rakic, 1986; Siegler, 1989). Thus, we understand the term "development" to refer to a multiplicity of change mechanisms, all influencing, and some being influenced by, changes in the structure and function of the brain and its associated behavioral capacities.

This conceptualization of the relation between learning and development may help resolve conflicts between scientists who study intellectual change from different perspectives. In addition, it adds a perspective to traditional conceptual battles. If learning is a proper subset of development, then it becomes impossible to claim that learning mechanisms can account for all changes in intellectual function across age, as some have done (e.g., Baer, 1970). On the other hand, such a view discourages the reduction of all development to maturational change. Developmental psychologists have often been criticized by themselves and others for setting out to study change but failing to specify plausible mechanisms to account for the change. The result is often superficial statements regarding normative age differences (Baer, 1970; Flavell, 1984; Siegler, 1989). One implication of our view is that statements about age or maturational differences are vacuous with respect to questions of development because all such statements must eventually be rendered in terms of plausible change mechanisms.

Finally, there is an added benefit to the set–proper subset conception: It focuses on classes of mechanisms that cause mental change but avoids specific theory-dependent concerns regarding the kinds of changes that may count as examples of "true development" as opposed to "mere learning." We prefer to focus on understanding change and leave as an empirical question the age periods and content domains where one class of mechanisms may dominate others.

Conclusion

Concepts of learning and development have long been treated as opposing ways of studying intellectual development, in spite of continued reminders of the need for integration. Much of the rift between these opposing views originates from historically distinct methods, goals, and questions endemic to each particular arena of research. In addition, it appears that a focus on particular age periods has a profound effect on theory development. We believe it is not coincidental that the proponents of a learning approach have concentrated on middle childhood through middle adulthood (e.g., Chi, 1978), whereas proponents of a developmental approach study behavioral change during periods of rapid qualitative shifts in abilities during infancy (e.g., Piaget, 1954) and senescence (e.g., Horn, 1982; Schaie, 1979). Those working at the developmental extremes know only too well the limitation in accounting for change solely in terms of accretion, tuning, and restructuring of content knowledge. Behavioral change during periods of biologically programmed growth and decline involves a conspiracy of forces that compete and cooperate to produce new structures in behavior. Learning is certainly one of those forces, but its contribution waxes and wanes across the life-span, playing a leading role during the years of greatest biological stability.

Learning is only one mechanism of change that influences intellectual development. Still, the learning approach has made unique contributions to the study of mechanisms of cognitive growth. It has been successful in utilizing the language of schemata and schema change as concrete ways of representing cognitive structure and development. It proposes that intellectual development proceeds as a result of the construction of a rich, well-organized knowledge base that, in turn, is responsible for increasing speed, capacity, and accessibility of knowledge. In addition, the learning approach promises to pay off handsomely in the development of educational technologies that efficiently promote the construction of a large, flexible knowledge base for creative thinking and problem solving (Glaser, 1990; Glaser & Bassok, 1989).

The future role of the learning approach in a comprehensive theory of intellectual development depends in part on its further ability to incorporate useful concepts developed by other approaches. Just as learning theory was invigorated through meeting the challenges of the cognitive revolution, it now faces the challenge of accounting for organism-guided learning and development at the extremes. How successfully it meets those challenges will determine the part it plays.

Notes

1 Other conundrums have been discussed recently by Sternberg (1989) and Sternberg & Okagaki (1990).

Kant, I. (1965) *Critique of pure reason* (N. K. Smith, Trans.). New York: Macmillan. (Original work published in 1781.)

Keil, F. (1984). Mechanisms in cognitive development and the structure of knowledge. In R. J. Sternberg (Ed.), *Mechanisms in cognitive development*. New York: Freeman.

Klahr, D., & Wallace, J. G. (1976). *Cognitive development: An information processing view.* Hillsdale, NJ: LEA.

Lachman, R., Lachman, J. L., & Butterfield, E. C. (1979). *Cognitive psychology and information processing.* Hillsdale, NJ: LEA.

Lachter, J., & Bever, T. G. (1988). The relation between linguistic structure and associative theories of language learning: A constructive critique of some connectionist learning models. *Cognition, 28,* 195–247.

Liben, L. (1987). *Learning and development: Conflict or congruence?* Hillsdale, NJ: LEA.

Lindberg, M. (1980). Is knowledge base development a necessary or sufficient condition for memory development? *Journal of Experimental Child Psychology, 30,* 401–410.

Minsky, M. A. (1975). A framework for representing knowledge. In P. Winston (Ed.), *The psychology of computer vision.* New York: McGraw-Hill.

Murphy, G., & Kovach, J. K. (1972). *Historical introduction to modern psychology* (3rd ed.). New York: Harcourt Brace Jovanovich.

Neisser, U. (1976). *Cognition and reality.* San Francisco: Freeman.

Newell, A., & Simon, H. (1972). *Human problem solving.* Englewood Cliffs, NJ: Prentice-Hall.

Newport, E. (1980). Constraints on structure: Evidence from American sign language and language learning. In W. Collins, (Ed.), *Minnesota Symposium on Child Development.* Hillsdale, NJ: LEA.

Piaget, J. (1954). *The construction of reality in the child.* (M. Cook, Trans.). New York: Basic Books. (Original work published in 1950.)

Piaget, J. (1970). *Genetic epistemology* (E. Duckworth, Trans.). New York: Norton.

Rescorla, R. A., & Wagner, A. R. (1972). A theory of Pavlovian conditioning: Variations in the effectivess of reinforcement and nonreinforcement. In A. Black & W. R. Prokasy (Eds.), *Classical conditioning II.* New York: Appleton-Century-Crofts.

Roberts, R. J., Jr., Aman, Christine J., & Canfield, R. L. (1989, April). *Developmental differences in learning a new skill: The role of self-imposed constraints.* Paper presented at the meetings of the Society for Research in Child Development, Kansas City, MO.

Roitblat, H. L., Bever, T. G., & Terrace, H. S. (Eds.). (1982). *Animal cognition.* Hillsdale, NJ: LEA.

Rovee-Collier, C., & Hayne, H. (1987). Reactivation of infant memory: Implications for cognitive development. In L. Lipsitt & C. Rovee-Collier (Eds.), *Advances in child behavior and development.* New York: Academic Press.

Rumelhart, D. E., & Norman, D. A. (1978). Accretion, tuning and restructuring: Three modes of learning. In J. Cotton & R. Klatzky (Eds.), *Semantic factors in cognition.* Hillsdale, NJ: LEA.

Schaie, K. W. (1979). The primary mental abilities in adulthood: An exploration in the development of psychometric intelligence. In P. B. Baltes & O. G. Brim, Jr. (Eds.), *Development and behavior* (Vol. 2, pp. 67–115). New York: Academic Press.

Schneider, W., Korkel, J., & Weinert, F. (1989). Expert knowledge and general abilities and text processing. In W. Schneider & F. Weinert (Eds.), *Interactions among aptitudes, strategies, and knowledge in cognitive performance.* New York: Springer-Verlag.

Shimojo, S., Bauer, J., Jr., O'Connell, K. M., & Held, R. (1986). Pre-stereoptic binocular vision in infants. *Vision Research, 26,* 501–510.

Siegler, R. S. (1981). Developmental sequences within and between concepts. *Monographs of the Society for Research in Child Development, 81* (Serial No. 189).

Siegler, R. S. (1989). Mechanisms of cognitive development. *Annual Review of Psychology, 40,* 353–379.

Siegler, R. S., & Shipley, C. (1987). The role of learning in children's strategy choices. In L. Liben (Ed.), *Learning and development: Conflict or congruence?* Hillsdale, NJ: LEA.

Skinner, B. F. (1974). *About behaviorism.* New York: Knopf.

Skinner, B. F. (1987). *Upon further reflection.* Englewood Cliffs, NJ: Prentice-Hall.

Staddon, J. E. R. (1983). *Adaptive behavior and learning.* Cambridge: Cambridge University Press.

Sternberg, R. J. (1989). Domain-generality versus domain-specificity: The life and impending death of a false dichotomy. *Merrill-Palmer Quarterly, 35,* 115–130.

Sternberg, R. J., & Okagaki, L. (1989). Continuity and discontinuity in intellectual development are not a matter of "either-or." *Human Development, 32,* 158–166.

Thorndike, E. L., & Woodworth, R. S. (1901). The influence of improvement in one's mental function upon efficiency of other functions. *Psychological Review, 3,* 247–384.

Tolman, E. C. (1932). *Purposive behavior in animals and men.* New York: Appleton-Century-Crofts.

Tolman, E. C. (1949). There is more than one kind of learning. *Psychological Review, 56,* 144–155.

Vygotsky, L. S. (1962). *Thought and language* (E. Hanfmann & G. Vakar, Trans.). Cambridge, MA: MIT Press. (Original work published in Russian in 1934.)

11   The learning perspective: Adulthood

Neil Charness and Sherrie Bieman-Copland

Intellectual development in adulthood: A learning perspective

How does aging affect intelligence? In the mid-1970s, the answer to such a question would have been clear: Intellectual decline with aging is inevitable. The outstanding growth in aging research since then, however, has clearly shown that the questions and answers are not nearly so simple. First, there are a variety of ways to look at intellectual development, as the diverse chapters of this volume make evident. Second, intelligence is an extremely complex construct, and its manifestation in behavior is influenced by many processes. For the purposes of this chapter, we view intelligence as a set of skills, or expertise (e.g. Charness, 1988), that enables its possessors to be more effective problem solvers, and intellectual development as the process by which people become more competent over time, a sort of novice-to-expert transition.

Central to this framework is the concept of learning. In this chapter, we define learning very generally as the process that enables organisms to respond differently, usually more adaptively, to familiar environmental events. The more optimal learning experiences one is exposed to, the farther along the novice-to-expert continuum one will move. It should be emphasized, however, that experience is a necessary but not sufficient condition for achieving expert levels of performance. Few reach expert levels, and many do not even reach modest competence in the many domains of intellectual performance humans have developed.

In this chapter, we are specifically interested in how age influences this novice-to-expert transition. Age is correlated, albeit imperfectly, with experience. Although cognitive-aging researchers are frequently hard-pressed to enumerate favorable aspects of aging, the one they most often cite is the wealth of knowledge older adults ought to possess by virtue of their lifetime of experience. Nonetheless, a great deal of research also shows

This work was supported by grants from the Natural Sciences and Engineering Research Council of Canada, NSERC A0790, to the first author, and an NSERC postgraduate scholarship to the second author.

that older adults are less competent than younger ones at many intellectual tasks. The paradox of older adults' having more knowledge but often performing less well can be clarified by considering an analogy to another information-processing system: the computer. Computer performance is determined by both its hardware and its software. The human information-processing system can also be partitioned in that way.

For humans, hardware means the relatively invariant features of the information-processing system, such as working memory capacity measured in chunks, asymptotic speed of elementary information processes, and the rate at which information is transferred from working memory to long-term memory (learning rate). All these features are conceived as being genetically transmitted through the constraints of brain architecture. There is reasonable evidence to indicate that the neural substrate supporting cognition declines in an accelerating rate beyond the age of 50 or 60 (Bondareff, 1985). From a hardware-oriented perspective, therefore, it is sound to conclude that there is substantial cognitive loss in late adulthood and that such loss accelerates with increasing age (e.g., Salthouse, 1985a). However, a more complete picture emerges when we also consider software changes.

Software for humans means the malleable features of the information-processing system, such as the contents of long-term memory (knowledge base) and the programs that manipulate this information (problem-solving strategies, mnemonic techniques, metaknowledge). In other words, software is the information that cultures transmit to their members (e.g., through formal education), and that individuals acquire through their own experience. Older adults, by their mere survival to old age, are virtually guaranteed to have built up a huge knowledge base. A key focus of this chapter is on how older adults use their knowledge base to maintain intellectual competence. For older adults, the axiom "Knowledge is power" seems especially fitting. (See Feigenbaum, 1989, for further elaboration.)

Older adults do suffer from the declines in cognitive architecture supporting information processing; however, on specific tasks they can sometimes compensate for those declines via the extensive task-specific knowledge they have acquired. Unfortunately, the most usual pattern in late adulthood is one that results not in increasing adaptivity but in a diminishing ability to cope with environmental challenges. A consistent finding is that on various performance measures older adults perform worse than younger ones, even when the problem-solving tasks have been biased in favor of older adults (e.g., Denney & Pearce, 1989). A frequent explanation for such age-related declines stresses disuse – a "use it or lose it" argument that emphasizes older adults' lack of cognitively challenging opportunities. Recent studies of architects show, however, that you can use it (spatial reasoning) daily and still lose it (Salthouse, Babcock, Skovronek, Mitchell, & Palmon, 1990). Further, access to knowledge, as measured by reaction time experiments, also shows older adults to be consistently slower than younger adults (e.g., Cerella, 1990; Salthouse, 1985a,b). Thus, adult performance on any task may reflect the unique trade-offs between possession of a rich knowledge base and the diminishing ability to activate old knowledge and acquire new knowledge.

On the more practical side, we would like to emphasize the significance of creating a better understanding of learning in older adults. It has been well documented that late adulthood is marked by many declines in physiological functioning; likewise, many life changes occur, such as retirement, relocation, and death of a spouse. Such life changes require substantial adaptation so that functional independence can be maintained. Learning is the key to such adaptation and, in turn, to independence. Although age-related declines in learning ability are most frequently emphasized, one should never lose sight of the fact that there is considerable plasticity in human physiology. What needs to be documented is how best to enhance the learning, specifically of older adults, so as to provide maximal impact on their functional capabilities. Those who work with older adults want practical advice; we want to emphasize that the key to effective intervention strategies is developing a sound theoretical understanding of learning in older adults.

Within this theoretical and practical framework are a number of topics we shall consider in more depth. First, we provide a brief overview of past research in learning and aging. This research has furnished good general descriptions of how young and old adults differ in learning performance; however, much still needs to be gleaned about why these differences occur. We also examine the learning process itself more thoroughly. Learning conditions can vary on a number of dimensions. We want to clarify the types of learning that older adults have difficulty with and those that seem relatively unimpaired by aging. We also discuss in greater detail the role experience and increased knowledge play in learning. Specifically, we outline the advantages as well as what we speculate are concomitant disadvantages of having a large knowledge base. Finally, we look at research in one of the more promising areas of learning and aging: the training area. The goal of this research is to focus directly on older learners and develop a better understanding of the conditions under which they show the greatest increases in performance.

Traditional approaches to learning and aging

A major criticism of research into learning and aging is that it has been largely atheoretical. Too often, research is geared toward documenting age-related differences in performance on various tasks; however, when explanations of the age-related differences are offered, they are also task- or paradigm-oriented, which leads to a circularity in thinking from which it is difficult to break (e.g., old people have learning problems because they have problems on learning tests). This situation has made it difficult to move beyond a descriptive level of scientific inquiry, but we must have such progression if we are to develop effective interventions.

To provide a context for the remainder of the chapter, we briefly review the traditional approaches to learning in aging research. (For comprehensive overviews, see Craik, 1977; Kausler, 1982.) Early work investigating the relationship between learning and age followed an associationist tradition, frequently emphasizing verbal learning. Specifically, young and old adults most often were compared on paired-associate and list-learning tasks. Generally, older adults were found to learn less effectively than their younger counterparts, regardless of how learning was operationalized (i.e., rate of improvement over trials, trials-to-criterion, or quantity of recall after a fixed learning interval). Pacing was considered to be an important variable. Age differences increased with decreases in the anticipation interval (i.e., exposure to the stimulus word alone) but remained constant with changes in study interval (i.e., exposure to the pair of words) (Monge & Hultsch, 1971). Likewise, it was found that the age gap would persist, though narrow, under self-paced versus experimenter-paced conditions (e.g., Canestrari, 1963).

Later studies attempted to attribute such age-related decline to organizational and mediational strategy differences between young and old. For instance, older adults do not spontaneously use categorical information to cue recall (Hultsch, 1975). Their performance is enhanced considerably when cues are provided by the experimenter, but only when the cues are categorical; their performance, unlike that of young adults, does not improve with alphabetic cues (Smith, 1977). Other work indicated that imagery was a potent mediator for young adults but rarely was used spontaneously by older adults (Hulicka & Grossman, 1967). At the same time, it was shown that the elderly could gain from instruction in mnemonic techniques based on mental imagery, such as the method of loci (linking images associated with words to a predefined sequence of spatial locations), yet they would fail to apply the newly learned technique unless specifically instructed to do so (Robertson-Tschabo, Hausmann, & Arenberg, 1976).

Another approach, depth of processing, emphasized that for both young and old adults, how they process the material to be learned is probably more important than how long they do it (i.e., quality over quantity of processing: Craik & Lockhart, 1972; Craik & Tulving, 1975). Most recently, Craik and his colleagues (Craik, 1986; Craik, Byrd, & Swanson, 1987) have been emphasizing the importance of contextual support for the elderly. They argue that when mental operations are driven by the task or materials, age differences are reduced or eliminated; on the other hand, if the individual must initiate or organize such operations in a conscious, controlled, and effortful manner, age differences are magnified. In our lab, we have found parameter estimation (i.e., quantifying learning differences between young and old adults), to be a useful enterprise. For example, on a complex learning task, learning to use a computer, we have found that older adults require about twice as much time as younger ones to complete an experimental session that is self-paced (Zandri & Charness, 1989).

In short, these early studies were concerned with the conditions under which learning was helped or hindered by such variables as familiarity, study time, pacing, retrieval conditions, and instructions. As we emphasized earlier, one problem with this rather descriptive approach is its inability to generate firm guidelines to those working in applied concerns, such as education. How do you structure a course to facilitate learning by older adults? How much additional time should you allow older workers to spend on a training program? How should it be paced?

Dimensions of learning

How, then, do we come to understand adult learning in a way that will facilitate intervention with older learners? To begin, we feel that distinguishing dimensions of learning that vary from one learning situation to another is a useful exercise. Significant features we examine are the temporal duration, the degree of intentionality, and the degree of directness of its assessment. Of particular interest here is how variations in each dimension influence the learning performance of old and young adults.

The time dimension

We want first to characterize learning processes associated with different time scales. Here we are following up on an observation of Langley and Simon (1981):

Adaptation takes place on several different time scales. On the shortest time scale, each problem that the environment presents to the organism challenges its adaptive capacity; that is to say, problem solving and other performance skills are the most immediate adaptive mechanisms. On the longest time scale, the biological evolution of the genotype is the adaptive mechanism. Between the rapid processes of problem solving and the slow processes of evolution lie learning processes that gradually bring about improvements in the organism's performance programs on an intermediate time scale. (p. 362)

We see learning itself as occurring over a range of time scales. A rough but useful partitioning of types of learning along the time dimension is given in Table 11.1. The first type, priming, is the most rapid but also the most ephemeral type of learning. Usually, priming is measured in the lexical

Table 11.1. *Dimensions of learning*

Type	Time to establish	Duration	Example
Priming	ms–seconds	seconds	Repetition priming
Chunking	s–minutes	years	Learning your phone number
Metaknowledge	minutes–hours	years	Strategies for learning

decision task, where subjects must decide as quickly as possible whether a set of letters forms a word. When the prior trial contains a related word (e.g., the word "nurse" precedes the word "doctor"), response time is quicker than when "doctor" is preceded by "book." The advantage in response time for the related word is called "priming." Another example, repetition priming, would be the learning that results in a faster second naming or reading of an identical word. Such facilitation lasts longer than associative priming, sometimes for days, even in older adults (Mitchell, Brown, & Murphy, 1990). Priming represents frequency-based strengthening of preexisting knowledge structures (e.g., Anderson, 1982, 1983).

A second form of learning, chunking, allows more lasting reorganization of knowledge in such a way that the learner begins to recognize what were formerly complex stimuli as single units. Such learning spans multiple seconds to minutes depending on the complexity of the chunking. Simon (1974) suggested 5–10 seconds as an estimate of the time to establish a new chunk through rote memorization. The outcome of this type of learning is clearly evident in reading. The skilled monolingual reader of English sees as a unitized entity the word "learning" but not the word *mélangé*, whereas for the skilled monolingual reader of French the reverse is true.

Finally, there is the form of learning that induces elaborate interconnections between knowledge structures or schemas that contain complex arrays of perceptual and cognitive information. Here we refer both to learning general rules and procedures that enhance cognitive performance (e.g., learning strategies), and to learning about your learning system. (See Klahr, Langley, & Neches, 1987, for one approach to simulating these processes.) The result of this type of learning is often referred to as metacognition, metamemory, or metaknowledge. Such learning takes multiple minutes or hours of task-specific experience. This type of learning is essential for developing expertise in a performance area. Individuals who have become skilled in digit recall (e.g., can repeat back sequences of over 100 digits) do so through chunking the large series into smaller familiar units, then holding these within a highly structured retrieval hierarchy until recall is required (Chase & Ericsson, 1981). In the domain of physics, skilled problem solvers classify new problems via a hierarchy of physics principles such as conservation of energy and conservation of motion. Relevant equations for solving such problems are then evoked. Novices, however, tend to classify problems based on surface features such as whether there is a spring present in the problem description. They then consider all the equations relevant to such problems, leading to inefficient problem solving (Chi, Feltovich, & Glaser, 1981; Chi, Glaser, & Rees, 1982). Adults, but not children, seem to be able to predict how well they will do on a learning task (Flavell & Wellman, 1977), and to apply strategies to learning tasks.

Comparisons of young and old learners on tasks that span this time dimension have shown varying patterns. Older adults appear relatively unimpaired on the shortest duration learning (i.e., priming). They show benefits comparable to those of young adults from recent exposure to various stimuli (e.g., Light & Albertson, 1989). Older adults show their greatest and most consistent difficulties with chunking. This is the form of learning, briefly summarized in the preceding section, that has attracted the most research effort. (For recent reviews of this research, see Hultsch & Dixon, 1990; Poon, 1985.) At the other extreme – that is, metaknowledge formation and expression – the evidence concerning age-related differences in learning behavior is more equivocal, although specific deficits among older adults have been shown in prediction accuracy (Bruce, Coyne, & Botwinick, 1982), use of rehearsal strategy (Murphy, Sanders, Gabriesheski, & Schmitt, 1981), and strategy selection (Brigham & Pressley, 1988). Clearly, more research effort is required in this area, especially considering its proven importance in expert performance.

Any discussion of learning is incomplete without considering that it is balanced by forgetting. We have little to say about forgetting, except to discuss general problems of accessing information from a large database. In general, the literature has shown older adults to forget information at about the same rate as young adults. This finding holds whether the tests are direct ones for very recently acquired visual or verbal information (e.g., Charness, 1981; Wickelgren, 1975; but see Poon & Fozard, 1980, for an exception) or indirect tests of longer term retention for skills after a month's layoff (e.g., Charness & Campbell, 1988; Salthouse & Somberg, 1982).

The incidental–intentional dimension

Another important dimension to learning is how it is accomplished. We can distinguish between effortful–intentional processes and automatic–incidental ones (e.g., Hasher & Zacks, 1979). Effortful processes are those employed by someone who is aware that he or she is to be tested later for the information. It is the mode of learning that characterizes a good deal of our formal educational process. It has also been termed "rote learning," or memorizing. Automatic processes are those that are engaged simply by attending to the task environment; in other words, they are rehearsal-independent. Most learning that takes place outside the laboratory and the school is an automatic by-product of comprehending environmental events. Most people do not attempt to memorize the information in a commercial, or a novel, or a television show. Yet, by virtue of the mostly effortless processes engaged in reading and listening, people typically remember the gist of the information that was processed.

Not enough is known yet to provide hard-and-fast generalizations about incidental learning and age effects. Generally, age trends appear to be roughly the same across incidental and intentional learning, although the nature of the orienting task and the retrieval requirements plays an important role in performance (e.g., Perlmutter, 1978, 1979). Herzog and Rodgers (1989) investigated incidental learning with a large ($N = 1,463$) representative sample. They tested incidental memory for questions asked earlier in the interview, using both recognition and recall procedures, and found age-related linear decline with both performance measures ($r = -.29$ for recall, $r = -.39$ for recognition). Likewise, Kausler and his colleagues have shown that, in the laboratory, memory for performed activities is largely rehearsal-independent, and that predictable age differences emerge when this type of memory is assessed through either recall or recognition (Kausler & Hakami, 1983).

Practice studies also provide a fair amount of data about adult incidental learning. Studies involving multiple trials in a reaction time paradigm invariably show that people become faster and more accurate through repetition of operations. As has been pointed out (Charness, 1989), much of the initial age-related deficit shown by old adults compared to young ones disappears when the old adult groups practice for as little as 3 minutes per year of age difference. That is, a 65-year-old adult who practices a typical reaction time task for 2 hours will perform at the same level as the 25-year-old does on the first few trials.

Although there is a substantial literature in educational psychology about how to teach effectively, and how students learn effectively in the classroom (e.g., Glaser & Bassok, 1989), there is little knowledge about self-taught, and even less about automatically acquired, skills. It is tacitly assumed that infants do not try to learn intentionally. Farther along the life-span it is rarely assumed that one ever learns unintentionally. The burgeoning interest in incidental learning suggests that a significant change of focus is evolving.

The direct–indirect performance dimension

As many theorists have pointed out, if someone fails to demonstrate learning, it may be a problem with the performance test rather than the individual's learning. In recent years this distinction has led to the differentiation of implicit and explicit memory (Schacter, 1987), or what has come to be termed "direct and indirect" (Richardson-Klavehn & Bjork, 1988) measures of memory. Direct measures are those that tap intentional memory, such as asking someone to memorize a list of items, and then testing recall. Indirect measures are those that tap incidental memory for prior events. An example would be asking someone to read aloud a set of words. Later a word from the set is flashed quickly and the person is asked to identify the word. To the extent that their recognition threshold is lower for previously seen words than for new words, you have demonstrated memory for the earlier words in an indirect test. In this case it is presumed that the person does not try consciously to recall the earlier words; rather, by dint of having seen them earlier, the person's recognition threshold has been changed.

Traditional approaches to learning have always used direct tests of memory. The consistent finding has been that older adults perform at a lower level. When indirect measures of learning performance are used, age-related differences are greatly reduced or even insignificant (Howard, 1988; Light & Albertson, 1989; Mitchell et al., 1990). From an intervention viewpoint, however, it is difficult to know how to make use of such a dissociation. Older adults experience difficulty only when intentional retrieval is required, yet the only way one can experience memory failure is when one perceives an inability to recall willfully some prior event. Therefore, it should not be surprising to find that when we examine age differences in memory complaints, older adults report more memory problems (see Perlmutter, 1978); moreover, it is clear that what older adults are most concerned about is direct tests of memory that occur everyday, such as recall of names for faces, and recall of facts or past episodes (Hultsch, Hertzog, & Dixon, 1987).

The role of experience in learning

Comparisons of novices and experts in various domains have shown that experience is a major determinant of task performance. In other words, we can accurately predict an individual's performance on a task from the amount of practice or learning experience the individual has had with the task. The importance of domain-specific experience holds true even at the earliest part of the life-span (Chi, 1978). Interestingly, it has been suggested that many of the difficulties older adults experience in laboratory tasks, such as those utilized in traditional studies of learning and aging, arise because they have less current, relevant experience with such tasks. (See Gillund & Perlmutter, 1988, for a recent overview.) Older adults who have experience on related cognitive and perceptual–motor tasks will often outperform unpracticed younger adults (e.g., Murrell & Humphries, 1978; Murrell, Powesland, & Forsaith, 1962).

What does experience provide the learner? There are a number of possibilities. First, experience can provide knowledge in the form of efficient procedures for learning. Instructing someone with a mnemonic, such as the method of loci, or pegword schemes, can vastly increase their ability to memorize new items. There would be no contest between a young, uninstructed adult and one of Kliegl, Smith, and Baltes's (1989) trained older adults in a serial word recall task, if the pacing were kept slow. One critical issue that hasn't been addressed is whether young and old adults are comparable in generating effective mnemonic techniques, such as the ones adopted spontaneously by Chase and Ericsson's (1981) digit-memorizing subject, SF.

Second, experience can provide knowledge in the form of new vocabulary, or rapid access to normatively poorly known lexical items (e.g., older cohorts would be more familiar with words such as "doily," "parasol," "poultice"). Assume that the task is to memorize lists of such normatively difficult items, or to read them. An old adult can expect to perform better if he or she is quite familiar with those items, compared to a young adult who is not (e.g., Barrett & Wright, 1981; Hultsch & Dixon, 1983; Poon & Fozard, 1978).

Third, learning increases the speed and efficiency of the underlying components of performance, especially in typical laboratory learning tasks. These underlying components consist of basic cognitive processes such as perceptual search, pattern recognition, and movement initiation. For younger adults the increased speed in processing with extensive practice is impressive; younger adults trained on digit-learning tasks can recall 50+ digit strings presented at the standard pace of 1 second per digit (Chase & Ericsson, 1981, 1982). Older adults have also been trained to become skilled at recalling digit strings of comparable length, but only under self-paced conditions (Kliegl, Smith, & Baltes, 1986). The learning of older adults appears more constrained by hardware limitations than that of younger adults. Therefore, if we are interested in a more complete picture of age-related differences in learning processes, we should also compare older and younger adults under self-paced learning conditions.

Laboratory learning tasks have been intentionally designed to reduce the amount of domain-specific knowledge the subject can utilize in performance; they are by design controlled, artificial, and irrelevant in order to create a situation where all subjects are, in essence, novices. Only the resources available to novices (so-called weak methods) can be used in performing such tasks. Performance on these tasks reflects an early or initial stage in learning, where age-related differences in performance are largest. Such age-related differences arise because young adults have advantages in the raw materials of performance; they are superior in the domain of basic cognitive processing, speed of elementary information processes (Chase, 1978), the "mechanics" of intelligence (Hunt, 1978). In addition, young adults appear to be "more advanced" novices. They seem more apt at transferring relevant knowledge from other domains to the novel task at hand. Although this knowledge is not as potent as domain-specific knowledge, it does give younger adults an initial advantage.

The age-insensitive nature of expert performance is of great interest because older experts can maintain high overall levels of performance even though the tasks being performed demand basic cognitive processes on which age-related declines have been documented. The reliance on domain-specific knowledge in such tasks somehow insulates tha older expert against deterioration in performance. Lehman (1953) demonstrated that peak performance for many human endeavors is seen in the decade of the 30s. (See the recent review by Simonton, 1988.) When a task depends heavily on knowledge, and speed of processing is not a significant constraint, peak performance can appear significantly later. An example in a highly competitive area is correspondence-chess world champions. In correspondence (postal) chess, players are permitted 3 days to deliberate each move. The mean age when a world championship is first won is about 46. This peak age is much later than that for tournament chess (age 30), where deliberation averages 3 minutes per move (Charness & Bosman, in press). Thus, older experts can still be world champions. When speed is a constraining factor, as in athletics, peak ages are generally in the 20s (Schulz & Curnow, 1988).

Disadvantages of knowledge

We now offer some admittedly speculative hypotheses for looking at learning in adulthood that deal with the tension between gains and losses. Generally, it is believed that learning is good and that more learning is better. We want to show the "dark side" of the knowledge acquisition function. The principles we are espousing can be summarized as "A lot of learning can be a dangerous thing."

We come to this paradoxical conclusion from two routes – one theoretical, one empirical. The empirical route derives from work on the "fan effect" and on "proactive inhibition." The theoretical route derives from consideration of database systems. Ideally, a database should be organized to promote efficient retrieval and efficient modification (adding new items and deleting old ones), two goals that are usually mutually exclusive (Severance, 1974). Unlike artificial databases, which carefully specify fields for incoming information, the human database fails to have the benefit of prespecified string length for entry of new information, and prespecified categories for indexing. People don't have the luxury of specifying how the environment serves up the next potential entry. Further, the size of the human database (long-term memory) is thought to be virtually unlimited.

In computer databases, the general result is that when organizing a database to promote efficient retrieval, time to access any item tends to increase with the logarithm of the number of entries. With extremely large databases – and some have put the human long-term memory system's capacity in the billion-bits range (Landauer, 1986) – this can lead to a significant retrieval time. Human retrieval rates, as measured in tasks such as lexical decision, and fixation times for individual words, are in the range of several hundred milliseconds (ms).

Although certain sound principles of aging can predict many phenomena, focusing solely on hardware declines – for example, slowing (Birren, Woods, & Williams, 1980; Salthouse, 1985a,b), working memory decline, and the like – we focus on broad information activation and retrieval principles in the spirit of Anderson's (1988) rational analysis of cognition, as well as Lachman and Lachman's (1980) attempt to look at knowledge retrieval efficiency in young versus older adults. We can illustrate the potential negative aspects of lifetime learning with three principles:

1. The more *related* information you possess, the slower your access will be to any part of that knowledge base if the information is not categorized hierarchically.
2. The more information you possess, the more likely that your attention will be captured by environmental events that automatically activate information in your knowledge base.
3. The more information you possess, the slower you will be to add a new piece of information to your database.

The first principle – slower access to related information – has been the focus of research (with young adults) into the "fan effect" (Anderson, 1983). A recent conference paper has shown that the fan effect also holds for older adults (Zacks, Radvansky, Hasher, & Gerard, 1990). The fan effect refers to the slowing in verification time associated with a concept that is linked to more than one sentence. For instance, you are slower to verify that you have seen the sentence "The lawyer was in the park" when you also have memorized the sentence "The lawyer was at the concert" than when it was the only sentence referring to "lawyer." Such slowing associated with interconnecting constructs has given rise to speculation about the *paradox of the expert.* How is it that those with enormous knowledge bases can access any records faster than a novice can? One possibility is that knowledge is organized in the expert in hierarchies (see Chi et al., 1981, 1982, for physics knowledge). Another possibility is that people do not always retrieve the answer to the question, but base their response on a plausibility judgment. They compute the answer (Reder, 1988).

Another example of how having more information can hurt retrieval is the part-list cuing effect, where having some information present during retrieval blocks the retrieval of related information (Roediger & Neely, 1982), although this may be mitigated when information to be remembered is highly interrelated (Watkins, Schwartz, & Lane, 1984). Diary studies show that older people are more likely to report such retrieval blocks, that is, tip-of-the-tongue experiences, than are younger ones (Burke, Worthley, & Martin, 1988). Similarly, picture naming is less accurate in older adults (Albert, Heller, & Milberg, 1988).

The second principle – the more you know, the more likely that some of it will match the current situation – has been discussed as "distractibility" (Layton, 1975) or "inability to focus attention" (Plude & Hoyer, 1985; Rabbitt, 1965), and more recently as "inhibition failure" (Hasher & Zacks, 1988; McDowd & Oseas, 1990). Older adults show *more* Stroop interference than younger ones (Comalli, Wapner, & Werner, 1962). In the Stroop task, people must name the color of the ink that words are printed in. Some words are themselves color names (incongruent items) and hence interfere with the person's ability to say the ink color, in part because word naming is faster than color naming. Thus, when the word "green" is printed in red ink, people are very slow to say red, far slower than saying red when the red-colored word item is "book." Older adults are even more hurt by these incongruent stimuli than young adults. In a non-aging context Britton and Tesser (1982) have shown that experts are *slower* to process a secondary task event when the primary one engages their domain-related knowledge store. In short, the more you know, the more likely it is that past knowledge will be primed by a current event. If you have to select from a large set of competing associations, processing will be slowed.

The third principle – the more you know, the slower you add new information – falls out of the venerable work on proactive inhibition. Early, classic experiments, reviewed by Underwood (1957), showed that the more lists of similar items you had memorized, the worse you performed with a new list. Indexing new information into a small net takes less time than indexing it into a large net, since the length of the index itself will grow with the number of items in the network. Again, hierarchical organization can delay such results for a while, and even accelerate learning relative to systems possessing less information in a less well organized form. But, inevitably, in fully developed knowledge systems, speed will decline. The other disadvantage to having more information in a system is that it may conflict with later information that must be learned. Winocur and Moscovitch (1983) found older adults to be even more affected by negative transfer than young adults were.

When you put all these principles together, you find that lifelong learning can overload the system in interesting ways. Our assumption is that older adults have incidentally acquired an enormous amount of information. Although this is a plausible assumption, there are few direct tests. One area where information is available is in standardized tests of "crystallized" intelligence (Horn, 1982), such as vocabulary and information tests. A not infrequent result, when you test the vocabulary ability of opportunistic samples of younger and older adults, is that the old are either equal to or superior to the young group. Unfortunately, because groups are not randomly selected from the population, it is not clear whether this is due to sampling problems or to a real growth in vocabulary.

Miller and Gildea (1987) suggest that high school graduates have a vocabulary of about 80,000 words, if you assume that words found in dictionaries account for half the vocabulary, with proper names, places, and idiomatic expressions accounting for the other half. Estimates for college graduates are about 50,000 to 120,000 words from dictionary experiments (e.g., Oldfield, 1963). Again, expanding for proper names and places, the real vocabulary may be in the range of 200,000 words. Children in the early years learn about 10 words per day (Miller & Gildea, 1987). If you accept Miller and Gildea's assumption that words are acquired through high school at the rate of about 5,000 per year, a 20-year-old will be expected to have 100,000 entries, and a 70-year-old, about 350,000 entries.

Linear extrapolation is somewhat risky for vocabulary because we can assume that frequent words will be added quickly but rare ones much less easily. Miller and Gildea (1987) point out that for every million words read, there are probably only 50,000 distinct word types. A power law acquisition function seems more reasonable, given standard chunking mechanisms and a skewed frequency distribution of items (Newell & Rosenbloom, 1981). But even if you assume that the 70-year-old has only double the number of items in memory, accessing any one of them would be expected to take longer. Unfortunately, little is known about the organization of words in memory. Some dispute the idea of lexical units at all (Seidenberg & McClelland, 1989) but others maintain that they are needed (Besner, Twilley, McCann, & Seergobin, 1990).

Assume for the moment that lexical information is accessed via an Elementary Perceiver and Memorizer (EPAM)-like discrimination structure (see Feigenbaum & Simon, 1984; Richman & Simon, 1989). That is, for a word to access its meaning, it must be recognized from its component letters by sorting through a treelike structure of tests of letters. Assume that the root node leads to 10 subnodes, and each of these to 10 daughter subnodes, and so on, until the bottom of the tree is reached, with the leaf nodes containing the word entries with associated links to their meaning. Assume that the time to execute all tests at a node (to see which subnode to follow next) takes 40 ms. (You could use other rates; we are relying here on the Sternberg memory-scanning rate of 40 ms per item as an estimate of the minimal time for an elementary information process. See Card, Moran, & Newell, 1983, for other estimates of the cognitive processor's cycle time.) A high school student's 100,000 lexical entries could be accessed via $\log_{10}(100,000) = 5$ tests, meaning an access time of $5 \times 40 = 200$ ms, a figure fairly close to Just and Carpenter's (1980) average eye-movement fixation time for reading a word. The 70-year-old's assumed 200,000 lexical entries will need 5.3 tests on average, or 212 ms to access an entry.

Thus, even without assuming age-related changes in hardware, such as slowing in information-processing speed, a 6% slowing is predicted by virtue of the larger database alone. Of course, reaction time studies usually show a much greater difference between young and old. For instance, Cerella's (1985) meta-analysis of young versus old reaction time plots yielded slopes in the range of 1.2 to 2.0. See Cerella (1990) for a succinct discussion of different models of slowing.

Advantages of knowledge

Although we have argued that the increasing knowledge base that is associated with age can result in some slowing of information processing, we are far from concluding that knowledge acquisition is maladaptive. In fact, the predicted 6% slowing is negligible in the context of the large gains in performance that accompany increasing expertise. For example, younger and older adults under optimal training conditions have been observed to increase digit span performance by up to an order of magnitude (Chase & Ericsson, 1981, 1982; Kliegl, Smith, & Baltes, 1989). When we refer to optimal training we mean training where two types of knowledge acquisition are enhanced, namely, domain-specific knowledge and executive knowledge. The second type of knowledge is frequently referred to in the literature as "metacognition" or "metamemory."

Such knowledge helps control or direct one's knowledge base to important aspects of a task so as to maximize performance. For example, we know that experts represent a problem space differently than novices (Chi et al., 1981). Novices tend to focus on surface features of a problem, whereas experts consider information not directly stated but implied by the problem (Chi et al., 1982). Because of their representational superiority, experts may also be able to generate multiple representations for a problem. Multiple representations allow one to generate a solution through converging operations and offer a person a better means to monitor and evaluate solutions. This ability to monitor and evaluate ongoing cognitive processing is also an important function of the executive or metaknowledge system. (For a more complete discussion, see Sternberg, 1988.)

We would like to argue that a better understanding of the commonly reported differences between young and old adults on memory tasks may be related to quantitative or qualitative differences in the knowledge that these individuals bring to bear on memory tasks such as list learning. It seems unlikely that older adults are at a disadvantage when it comes to relevant domain-specific knowledge (i.e., knowledge of words); if anything, older adults may be at an advantage. Rather, we speculate that differences in cognitive performance may relate to differences in representation or utilization of executive or metaknowledge.

Let us consider some of the reported research that would support such a hypothesis. First, several studies have been done comparing older and younger adults on performance prediction on laboratory-type memory tasks (Bruce et al., 1982; Murphy et al., 1981; Lovelace & Marsh, 1985; Rabinowitz, Ackerman, Craik, & Hinchley, 1982; Shaw & Craik, 1989) In all of these studies no age-related differences in performance prediction were found, despite consistent differences in memory performance. Generally, older adults tended to overpredict performance, whereas younger adults were either accurate or underestimated how well they would perform on memory tasks. This higher congruence for younger adults between predicted and actual performance on such novel tasks may result in better allocation of cognitive resources by the younger subjects. Although both groups are novices on these types of tasks, young adults appear to be "more advanced" novices.

More direct support for such a hypothesis comes from the study by Murphy et al. (1981). In a second experiment, they equated task difficulty across subjects by manipulating list length for each subject based on initial memory spans. With increasing task difficulty older adults demonstrated declines in performance while the younger subjects did not. Moreover, older adults spent less time studying the more difficult lists than the younger adults did. Later, task demands were changed so that the older adults were forced to study the more difficult lists for the same amount of time as the younger subjects had used. Under such conditions their performance increased to the level demonstrated by the young adults. By substituting external monitoring guides for the older subjects' internal executive knowledge, age-related performance differences were attenuated.

It may be that older adults are less effective at learning about their own learning processes. That is, they may have more difficulty altering strategies in response to feedback from previous or ongoing cognitive processing. Brigham and Pressley (1988) compared young and old subjects on a vocabulary learning task in which subjects utilized two different strategies to learn the meaning of novel words. The two strategies differed in their effectiveness on vocabulary learning. Before the learning experience, there were no age-related differences in strategy preference. However, after the learning experience the young adults showed almost unanimous preference for the more effective strategy, whereas no change was observed in the preference of older adults.

The question of most interest now is, Why do such age-related differences in monitoring and performance evaluation arise? Using the hardware–software heuristic already described, we can suggest two possible explanations. First, the older adults fail to monitor ongoing performance results because of limitations in working memory, a simple hardware explanation. Second, older adults may not possess as extensive an executive knowledge base because of cohort differences such as education, and recency of exposure to intentional learning situations. That is, we may be able to show that the metaknowledge of older and younger adults is quantitatively or qualitatively different.

Developing new skills

The advantages of having a large knowledge base are most evident in skilled performance. But most studies are cross-sectional, meaning that they examine currently skilled and unskilled people rather than track one person over time as she or he acquires skill. One of the more promising areas of research in aging and learning is the training study area. Here the goal is to assess the conditions under which older adults improve their performance. The range of tasks explored has been impressive, spanning classical conditioning (e.g., Woodruff-Pak & Thompson, 1988) and simple perceptual motor (e.g., Salthouse & Somberg, 1982) through to memorizing digits (Kliegl, Smith, & Baltes, 1989), face-name and list learning (Yesavage, Sheikh, Friedman, & Tanke, 1990), and even intelligence test performance (e.g., Willis & Schaie, 1986).

Handwriting

Interest in adult learning is not a recent phenomenon. Thorndike (1928) reported research findings on adult learning in numerous domains such as wrong-hand writing, typing, and learning a logical language system (Esperanto). In terms of today's standards his older adults would be considered middle-aged (i.e., mean age = 41 years), but despite this limitation some interesting findings emerged. We performed secondary analyses on raw data reported by Thorndike on wrong-hand writing. These data were particularly interesting because they contained measures that allowed learning to be analyzed while controlling for speed–accuracy trade-off confounds.

Thorndike had 33 subjects (age range 20–57) perform a prepractice writing task with both their dominant and nondominant hands. He obtained measures of speed (number of letters written in 10 minutes) as well as a quality measure (*Thorndike Handwriting Scale*) on four prepractice trials. Subjects then engaged in 30 half-hour practice sessions of wrong-hand writing of material different from the test material. Following practice, the same measures of speed and quality were obtained. The correlations between the various measures are shown in Table 11.2.

Table 11.2. *Thorndike's handwriting study*

	Age	Dspeed	Dqual	Ispeed	Iqual	Fspeed
Dspeed	−.48*					
Dqual	−.19	−.15				
Ispeed	−.22	.38*	−.13			
Iqual	.04	.01	.12	−.04		
Fspeed	−.67*	.66*	−.06	.51*	.05	
Fqual	−.05	−.16	.32	.04	.52*	−.30

Age = age in years
Dspeed = dominant (normal) hand writing speed in words per 10 min
Dqual = dominant-hand writing quality (Thorndike's scale)
Ispeed = initial speed (before practice) of nondominant hand
Iqual = initial quality of nondominant hand
Fspeed = final speed of nondominant hand (after practice)
Fqual = final quality of nondominant hand (after practice)
Note: * $p < .05$

From these data it is clear that there are substantial and significant correlations between age and dominant-hand writing speed as well as between age and nondominant-hand writing speed after 15 hours of practice. Furthermore, the correlation between nondominant-hand writing speed before and after practice is significant, whereas the relationship between age and nondominant-hand writing speed before practice is negligible. Therefore, it is possible that the negative relationship between age and nondominant-hand writing speed after practice arises because of the speeded nature of the task and has little to do with differences in learning per se. But the partial correlation between age and nondominant-hand writing speed, controlling for an underlying speed factor (i.e., nondominant-hand writing speed before practice, and dominant-hand writing speed) remains significant ($r = -.56$). Likewise, it does not appear that speed–accuracy trade-offs can totally account for the decrease in learning with increasing age.

In a multiple regression analysis, age still accounts for a significant amount of variance in nondominant-hand writing speed after nondominant-hand writing quality (after practice) and the two speed measures have been entered into the equation. Together, these four variables account for 72% of the variance in nondominant-hand writing speed after practice. Thus, there appears to be more to the story of adult learning than older adults learn at a slower pace or that older adults tend to favor accuracy over speed in performance. Differences exist between the two groups in learning processes, even when university-aged students are compared to middle-aged adults.

Thorndike's wrong-hand writing task has limitations in terms of understanding age-related learning differences, largely because of its perceptual–motor nature. It would seem that domain-specific knowledge has little influence on the performance of such a task; however, as indicated previously, the ability to use such knowledge in performance may insulate older adults from typically reported declines with age. For example, handwriting speed in adulthood shows some dependence on what type of job niche one occupies. LaRiviere and Simonson (1965) found that those in clerical positions showed little age-related change in speed of copying random digits but that both those in blue-collar positions and those in executive positions did show age-related decline.

Mental arithmetic

Charness and Campbell (1988) showed how simple practice could result in remarkable gains in efficiency for the task of squaring two digit numbers mentally (e.g., what is 84 × 84?). As expected, there were highly significant age group ($N = 16$) effects, with older adults taking twice as much time as younger ones, and middle-aged adults about 1.5 times as long. Gains in speed and accuracy for all groups with practice were equally impressive. Everyone virtually halved their response times and their errors within six sessions. Improvements were achieved at a number of levels. First, the time to carry out basic practiced arithmetic operations, such as 8 × 80, diminished significantly (about 33% averaged across operation type). This was attributed to strengthening of preexisting knowledge. Second, major gains occurred for the sequencing of steps of the instructed algorithm. About two-thirds of the speed-up in the task as a whole (e.g., answering 9,604 to the problem 98 × 98), was attributable to faster access to the next step in the procedure and faster access to the results of previous steps. This change fits with Anderson's (1982, 1983) notion of knowledge compilation and proceduralization.

More impressive was the fact that with six sessions of practice, older adults were as fast and accurate as were young adults at their first session. Because time to do each component step of the algorithm was measured, as well as the time to do an entire problem, a ratio measure was derived: the mean sum of individual components to the mean time to do a complete problem. The ratio measure for the older adults at session 6 equaled that for the young adults at session 1, suggesting that when the two groups were at equivalent molar performance levels, they were doing the task the same way. In other words, they were quantitatively and qualitatively the same following practice for the older group.

Further analysis by Campbell and Charness (1990) suggests that this conclusion may be too strong. The errors that were committed at different levels of practice seemed to vary between age groups. Older adults had more trouble eliminating working memory errors than younger adults, but both groups were equally successful at eliminating long-term memory retrieval errors. This result is consistent with the idea that hardware sets limits on learning efficiency, and that working memory is a significant locus of age effects. A parallel finding occurs in reasoning tasks where retaining accurate information is critical to performance (Salthouse, Legg, Palmon, & Mitchell, 1990). Still, a software factor such as practice with a task can be far more influential for overall performance levels.

What this study and others such as Salthouse and Somberg (1982) show is that knowledge acquisition can be a powerful factor in predicting performance, often overriding any initial differences between young and old when they are novices at a task. Knowledge acquired through task-specific practice can compensate for minor differences in hardware efficiency. We should stress that we are not implying that asymptotic performance levels will be the same for young and old after extensive practice. We would be forced to predict that younger adults who are equally practiced at a task should do better. Even a small edge in hardware should make a difference. (See Charness & Bosman, 1990, for a more complete discussion.)

Memorizing words

A strong endorsement for that perspective is afforded by data from Kliegl, Smith, and Baltes (1989). In the first experiment they trained younger ($N = 4$) and older ($N = 20$) adults for up to 26 sessions to improve their ability to do serial recall of nouns. All groups were trained in the same way, to use the method of loci and imagery to link words to a fixed sequence of 40 Berlin landmarks to retain order information. People were pretested at 10 s and 4 s per word, and posttested at these same rates, as well as at a self-paced rate.

There were several noteworthy results. Although the groups were not significantly different in serial recall at pretest (though the old, $M = 2.35$, were nominally worse than young, $M = 3.65$), they split apart at posttest. The best older adults never equaled the performance of the best younger adults, particularly at fast presentation rates. In fact, there was almost no overlap between the groups at posttest. Nonetheless, the groups easily tripled (old) or sextupled (young) their performance. Older subjects took about twice as long in the self-paced training than did younger ones.

In the second experiment 18 younger and 19 older adults were trained to 50% accuracy at individually tailored presentation rates (starting at 20 s per word) and both pre- and posttested at presentation rates of 20, 15, 10, 5, 3, and 1 s per word. The groups did differ at pretest, with the young superior to the old ($M = 5.8$ vs. $M = 2.7$ words recalled in the correct serial position). At posttest the gap between young and old increased, particularly with the slower presentation rates. At 1 word per s there were no real age differences. Here again, both groups at posttest tripled or quadrupled their performance at the slower presentation rates (20 s–5 s rates). In short, practice made for prodigious spans, but also widened the gap between young and old. The two groups were clearly going to different asymptotes in performance. So, although there is marked plasticity in behavior for both age groups, the young learn more effectively.

An important feature of this project was that when pacing of items was very rapid, the old were unable to capitalize on their new mnemonic techniques. Speed of encoding was also a factor for the young. The point at which it limited performance came sooner for the old, illustrating the limits to trade-off between software and hardware.

Conclusions

Intellectual development in infancy can be seen as a revolutionary process. In adulthood, it is more likely that intellectual prowess represents evolutionary change, the accretion of new building blocks of knowledge. When older adults are capable of outstanding performance at difficult tasks, it is usually because of the highly specialized knowledge base they have assembled for those tasks via extensive task-related experience. Most human endeavors demand such a knowledge base for expert performance by young and old alike. Because it takes hundreds to thousands of hours to acquire high levels of skill, most inexperienced young adults are unlikely to compete with experienced older ones in semantically rich domains.

Yet, older adults are at the same time more vulnerable than less skilled younger adults when a new task demands the assembly of a new performance program. They are less able to organize and store new information; they are slower to access old information; and they may be less able to avoid accessing related but irrelevant information. Intentional learning slows down as adults age. Some slowing may be due to the problems that accrue from a large knowledge base. Most slowing is more than likely attributable to deterioration of the cognitive architecture supporting learning. What happens to incidental learning is not yet totally clear, although it, too, appears to decline. On the other hand, priming and other indirect memory tasks show less age-related decline than intentional learning tasks. Thus, a complex picture is unfolding about learning in adulthood.

There are techniques for estimating the size of a knowledge base, such as the lexicon (Oldfield, 1963). What has yet to be accomplished is putting together estimates of size, and measures of performance, such as naming and lexical decision. More important, estimates of the time to acquire a new lexical entry as a function of vocabulary size are missing. Is there really a "snowball" effect in knowledge acquisition, where the more you know, the easier it is to add new knowledge? Or do the "fan effect" and proactive inhibition make it more difficult to add to the knowledge store? Further, what role does hardware (maturational decline) play in these issues?

Last but not least, practical issues abound. How do you structure learning opportunities to maximize acquisition for older adults in intentional situations such as job training or rehabilitation? Can you facilitate incidental learning? How can you add to the repertoire of metacognitive tools responsible for learning and problem solving? Sometimes it appears that older adults are better left to their own devices rather than given explicit instruction (Baltes, Sowarka, & Kliegl, 1989). What is the role of knowledge acquisition in producing wisdom (e.g., Smith & Baltes, 1990)? Determining the trade-offs between size of the knowledge base and an older adult's efficiency in accessing and adding to it presents a challenging agenda for research in adult intellectual performance.

References

Albert, M. S., Heller, H. S., & Milberg, W. (1988). Changes in naming ability with age. *Psychology and Aging*, *3*, 173–178.

Anderson, J. R. (1982). Acquisition of cognitive skill. *Psychological Review*, *89*, 369–406.

Anderson, J. R. (1983). *The architecture of cognition*. Cambridge, MA: Harvard University Press.

Anderson, J. R. (1988, August 17–19). The place of cognitive architectures in a rational analysis. *Program of the Tenth Annual Conference of the Cognitive Science Society*, Montreal, Canada (pp. 1–10.). Hillsdale, NJ: Erlbaum.

Baltes, P. B., Sowarka, D., & Kliegl, R. (1989). Cognitive training research on fluid intelligence in old age: What can older adults achieve by themselves? *Psychology and Aging*, *4*, 217–221.

Barrett, T. R., & Wright, M. (1981). Age-related facilitation in recall following semantic processing. *Journal of Gerontology*, *36*, 194–199.

Besner, D., Twilley, L., McCann, R. S., & Seergobin, K. (1990). On the association between connectionism and data: Are a few words necessary? *Psychological Review*, *97*, 432–446.

Birren, J. E., Woods, A. M., & Williams, M. V. (1980). Behavioral slowing with aging: Causes, organization, and consequences. In L. W. Poon (Ed.), *Aging in the 1980s: Psychological issues*. Washington, DC: American Psychological Association.

Bondareff, W. (1985). The neural basis of aging. In J. E. Birren & K. W. Schaie (Eds.), *Handbook of the psychology of aging* (2nd ed., pp. 95–112). New York: Van Nostrand Reinhold.

Brigham, M. C., & Pressley, M. (1988). Cognitive monitoring and strategy choice in younger and older adults. *Psychology and Aging*, *3*, 249–257.

Britton, B. K., & Tesser, A. (1982). Effects of prior knowledge on use of cognitive capacity in three complex cognitive tasks. *Journal of Verbal Learning and Verbal Behavior*, *21*, 421–436.

Bruce, P. R., Coyne, A. C., & Botwinick, J. (1982). Adult age differences in metamemory. *Journal of Gerontology*, *37*, 354–357.

Burke, D., Worthley, J., & Martin, J. (1988). I'll never forget what's-her-name: Aging and tip of the tongue experiences in everyday life. In M. M. Gruneberg, P. E. Morris, & R. N. Sykes (Eds.), *Practical aspects of memory: Current research and issues* (Vol. 2, pp. 113–118). New York: Wiley.

Campbell, J. I. D., & Charness, N. (1990). Age-related declines in working-memory skills: Evidence from a complex calculation task. *Developmental Psychology, 26*, 879–888.

Canestrari, R. E., Jr. (1963). Paced and self-paced learning in young and elderly adults. *Journal of Gerontology, 18*, 165–168.

Card, S. K., Moran, T. P. & Newell, A. (1983). *The psychology of human–computer interaction.* Hillsdale, NJ: Erlbaum.

Cerella, J. (1985). Information processing rates in the elderly. *Psychological Bulletin, 98*, 67–83.

Cerella, J. (1990). Aging and information-processing rate. In J. E. Birren & K. W. Schaie (Eds.), *Handbook of the psychology of aging* (3rd ed., pp. 201–221). San Diego: Academic Press.

Charness, N. (1981). Visual short-term memory and aging in chess players. *Journal of Gerontology, 36*, 615–619.

Charness, N. (1988). Expertise in chess, music, and physics: A cognitive perspective. In L. K. Obler & D. A. Fein (Eds.), *The exceptional brain: The neuropsychology of talent and special abilities.* New York: Guilford Press.

Charness, N. (1989). Age and expertise: Responding to Talland's challenge. In L. W. Poon, D. C. Rubin, & B. A. Wilson (Eds.), *Everyday cognition in adulthood and late life* (pp. 437–456). Cambridge: Cambridge University Press.

Charness, N., & Bosman, E. A. (1990). Expertise and aging: Life in the lab. In T. H. Hess (Ed.), *Aging and cognition: Knowledge organization and utilization* (pp. 343–385). Elsevier Science Publishers.

Charness, N., & Campbell, J. I. D. (1988). Acquiring skill at mental calculation in adulthood: A task decomposition. *Journal of Experimental Psychology: General, 117*, 115–129.

Chase, W. G. (1978). Elementary information processes. In W. K. Estes (Ed.), *Handbook of learning and cognitive processes* (Vol. 5, pp. 19–90). Hillsdale, NJ: Erlbaum.

Chase, W. G., & Ericsson, K. A. (1981). Skilled memory. In J. R. Anderson (Ed.), *Cognitive skills and their acquisition* (pp. 141–189). Hillsdale, NJ: Erlbaum.

Chase, W. G., & Ericsson, K. A. (1982). Skill and working memory. In G. H. Bower (Ed.), *The psychology of learning and motivation* (Vol. 16, pp. 2–58). New York: Academic Press.

Chi, M. T. H. (1978). Knowledge structures and memory development. In R. S. Siegler (Ed.), *Children's thinking: What develops?* (pp. 73–96) Hillsdale, NJ: Erlbaum.

Chi, M. T. H., Feltovich, P. J., & Glaser, R. (1981). Categorization and representation of physics problems by experts and novices. *Cognitive Science, 5*, 121–152.

Chi, M. T. H., Glaser, R., & Rees, E. (1982). Expertise in problem solving. In R.J. Sternberg (Ed.), *Advances in the psychology of human intelligence* (pp. 7–75). Hillsdale, NJ: Erlbaum.

Comalli, P. E., Wapner, S., & Werner, H. (1962). Interference effects of Stroop color-word test in childhood, adulthood and aging. *Journal of Genetic Psychology, 100*, 47–53.

Craik, F. I. M. (1977). Age differences in human memory. In J. E. Birren & K. W. Schaie (Eds.), *Handbook of the psychology of aging* (pp. 384–420). New York: Van Nostrand Reinhold.

Craik, F. I. M. (1986). A functional account of age differences in memory. In F. Klix & H. Hagendorf (Eds.), *Human memory and cognitive capabilities: Mechanisms and performances* (pp. 409–422). Amsterdam: North-Holland.

Craik, F. I. M., Byrd, M., & Swanson, J. M. (1987). Patterns of memory loss in three elderly samples. *Psychology and Aging, 2*, 79–86.

Craik, F. I. M., & Lockhart, R. S. (1972). Levels of processing: A framework for memory research. *Journal of Verbal Learning and Verbal Behavior, 11*, 671–684.

Craik, F. I. M., & Tulving, E. (1975). Depth of processing and the retention of words in episodic memory. *Journal of Experimental Psychology: General, 104*, 268–294.

Denney, N. W., & Pearce, K. A. (1989). A developmental study of practical problem solving in adults. *Psychology and Aging, 4*, 438–442.

Feigenbaum, E. A. (1989). What hath Simon wrought? In D. Klahr & K. Kotovsky (Eds.), *Complex information processing: The impact of Herbert A. Simon* (pp. 165–182). Hillsdale, NJ: Erlbaum.

Feigenbaum, E. A., & Simon, H. A. (1984). EPAM-like models of recognition and learning. *Cognitive Science, 8*, 305–336.

Flavell, J. H., & Wellman, H. M. (1977). Metamemory. In R. V. Kail, Jr. & J. W. Hagen, (Eds.), *Perspectives on the development of memory and cognition* (pp. 3–34). Hillsdale, NJ: Erlbaum.

Gillund, G., & Perlmutter, M. (1988). Episodic memory and knowledge interactions across adulthood. In L. L. Light & D. M. Burke (Eds.), *Language, memory, and aging* (pp. 191–208). Cambridge: Cambridge University Press.

Glaser, R., & Bassok, M. (1989). Learning theory and the study of instruction. *Annual Review of Psychology, 40*, 631–666.

Hasher, L., & Zacks, R. T. (1979). Automatic and effortful processes in memory. *Journal of Experimental Psychology: General, 108*, 356–388.

Hasher, L., & Zacks, R. T. (1988). Working memory, comprehension, and aging: A review and a new view. In G. H. Bower (Ed.), *The psychology of learning and motivation* (Vol. 22, pp. 193–225). San Diego: Academic Press.

Herzog, A. R., & Rodgers, W. L. (1989). Age differences in memory performance and memory ratings as measured in a sample survey. *Psychology and Aging, 4*, 173–182.

Horn, J. L. (1982). The theory of fluid and crystallized intelligence in relation to concepts of cognitive psychology and aging in adulthood. In F. I. M. Craik & S. Trehub (Eds.), *Aging and cognitive processes* (pp. 237–278). New York: Plenum.

Howard, D. (1988). Implicit and explicit assessment of cognitive aging. In M. L. Howe & C. J. Brainerd (Eds.), *Cognitive development in adulthood: Progress in cognitive development research* (pp. 3–37). New York: Springer-Verlag.

Hulicka, I. M., & Grossman, J. L. (1967). Age group comparisons for the use of mediators in paired-associate learning. *Journal of Gerontology, 22*, 46–51.

Hultsch, D. F. (1975). Adult age differences in retrieval: Trace-dependent and cue-dependent forgetting. *Developmental Psychology, 11*, 197–201.

Hultsch, D. F., & Dixon, R. A. (1983). The role of pre-experimental knowledge in text processing in adulthood. *Experimental Aging Research, 9*, 17–22.

Hultsch, D. F., & Dixon, R. A. (1990). Memory and learning and aging. In J. E. Birren & K. W. Schaie (Eds.), *Handbook of the psychology of aging* (3rd ed., pp. 258–274). San Diego: Academic Press.

Hultsch, D. F., Hertzog, C., & Dixon, R. A. (1987). Age differences in metamemory: Resolving inconsistencies. *Canadian Journal of Psychology, 41*, 193–208.

Hunt, E. (1978). Mechanics of verbal ability. *Psychological Review, 85*, 109–130.

Just, M. A., & Carpenter, P. A. (1980). A theory of reading: From eye fixations to comprehension. *Psychological Review, 87*, 329–354.

Kausler, D. H. (1982). *Experimental psychology and human aging.* New York: Wiley.

Kausler, D. H., & Hakami, M. K. (1983). Memory for activities: Adult age differences and intentionality. *Developmental Psychology, 19*, 889–894.

Klahr, D., Langley, P., & Neches, R. (Eds.). (1987). *Production system models of learning and development.* Cambridge, MA: MIT Press.

Kliegl, R., Smith, J., & Baltes, P. B. (1986). Testing-the-limits, expertise, and memory in adulthood and old age. In F. Klix & H. Hagendorf (Eds.), *Human memory and cognitive capabilities: Mechanisms and performances* (pp. 395–407). Amsterdam: North-Holland.

Kliegl, R., Smith, J., & Baltes, P. B. (1989). Testing-the-limits and the study of adult age differences in cognitive plasticity of a mnemonic skill. *Developmental Psychology, 25*, 247–256.

Lachman, J. L., & Lachman, R. (1980). Age and the actualization of world knowledge. In L. W. Poon, J. L. Fozard, L. S. Cermak, D. Arenberg, & L. W. Thompson (Eds.), *New directions in memory and aging* (pp. 285–311). Hillsdale, NJ: Erlbaum.

Landauer, T. K. (1986). How much do people remember? Some estimates of the quantity of learned information in long-term memory. *Cognitive Science*, *10*, 477–493.

Langley, P., & Simon, H. A. (1981). The central role of learning in cognition. In J. R. Anderson (Ed.), *Cognitive skills and their acquisition* (pp. 361–380). Hillsdale, NJ: Erlbaum.

LaRiviere, J. E., & Simonson, E. (1965). The effect of age and occupation on speed of writing. *Journal of Gerontology*, *20*, 415–416.

Layton, B. (1975). Perceptual noise and aging. *Psychological Bulletin*, *82*, 875–883.

Lehman, H. C. (1953). *Age and achievement*. Princeton, NJ: Princeton University Press.

Light, L. L., & Albertson, S. A. (1989). Direct and indirect tests of memory for category exemplars in young and older adults. *Psychology and Aging*, *4*, 487–492.

Lovelace, E. A., & Marsh, G. R. (1985). Prediction and evaluation of memory performance by young and old adults. *Journal of Gerontology*, *40*, 192–197.

McDowd, J. M., & Oseas, D. M. (1990). *Aging, inhibitory processes, and negative priming.* Poster presented at the 1990 Cognitive Aging Conference, Atlanta.

Miller, G. A., & Gildea, P. M. (1987). How children learn words. *Scientific American*, *257*, 94–99.

Mitchell, D. B., Brown, A. S., & Murphy, D. R. (1990). Dissociations between procedural and episodic memory: Effects of time and aging. *Psychology and Aging*, *5*, 264–276.

Monge, R. H., & Hultsch, D. F. (1971). Paired-associate learning as a function of adult age and the length of the anticipation and inspection intervals. *Journal of Gerontology*, *26*, 157–162.

Murphy, M. D., Sanders, R. E., Gabriesheski, A. S., & Schmitt, F. A. (1981). Metamemory in the aged. *Journal of Gerontology*, *36*, 185–193.

Murrell, H., & Humphries, S. (1978). Age, experience and short term memory. In M. M. Gruneberg, P. E. Morris, & R. N. Sykes (Eds.), *Practical aspects of memory.* London: Academic Press.

Murrell, K. F. H., Powesland, P. F., & Forsaith, B. (1962). A study of pillar-drilling in relation to age. *Occupational Psychology*, *36*, 45–52.

Newell, A., & Rosenbloom, P. S. (1981). Mechanisms of skill acquisition and the power law of practice. In J. R. Anderson (Ed.), *Cognitive skills and their acquisition* (pp. 1–55). Hillsdale, NJ: Erlbaum.

Oldfield, R. C. (1963). Individual vocabulary and semantic currency: A preliminary study. *British Journal of Social and Clinical Psychology*, *2*, 122–130.

Perlmutter, M. (1978). What is memory aging the aging of? *Developmental Psychology*, *14*, 330–345.

Perlmutter, M. (1979). Age differences in adults' free recall, cued recall, and recognition. *Journal of Gerontology*, *34*, 533–539.

Plude, D. J., & Hoyer, W. J. (1985). Attention and performance: Identifying and localizing age deficits. In N. Charness (Ed.), *Aging and human performance* (pp. 47–99). New York: Wiley.

Poon, L. W. (1985). Differences in human memory with aging: Nature, causes, and clinical implications. In J. E. Birren & K. W. Schaie (Eds.), *Handbook of the psychology of aging* (2nd ed., pp. 427–462). New York: Van Nostrand Reinhold.

Poon, L. W., & Fozard, J. L. (1978). Speed of retrieval from long-term memory in relation to age, familiarity and datedness of information. *Journal of Gerontology*, *5*, 711–717.

Poon, L. W., & Fozard, J. L. (1980). Age and word frequency effects in continuous recognition memory. *Journal of Gerontology*, *35*, 77–86.

Rabbitt, P. M. A. (1965). An age-decrement in the ability to ignore irrelevant information. *Journal of Gerontology*, *20*, 233–238.

Rabinowitz, J., Ackerman, B. P., Craik, F. I. M., & Hinchley, J. L. (1982). Aging and metamemory: The roles of relatedness and imagery. *Journal of Gerontology*, *37*, 688–695.

Reder. L. M. (1988). Strategic control of retrieval strategies. In G. H. Bower (Ed.), *The psychology of learning and motivation* (Vol. 22, pp. 227–259). San Diego: Academic Press.

Richardson-Klavehn, A., & Bjork, R. A. (1988). Measures of memory. *Annual Review of Psychology, 39,* 475–543.

Richman, H. B., & Simon, H. A. (1989). Context effects in letter perception: Comparison of two theories. *Psychological Review, 96,* 417–432.

Robertson-Tschabo, E. A., Hausmann, C. P., & Arenberg, D. (1976). A classical mnemonic for older learners: A trip that works! *Educational Gerontology, 1,* 215–226.

Roediger, H. L., III, & Neely, J. H. (1982). Retrieval blocks in episodic and semantic memory. *Canadian Journal of Psychology, 36,* 213–242.

Salthouse, T. A. (1985a). *A theory of cognitive aging.* Amsterdam: Elsevier Science Publishers.

Salthouse, T. A. (1985b). Speed of behavior and its implications for cognition. In J. E. Birren & K. W. Schaie (Eds.), *Handbook of the psychology of aging* (2nd ed., pp. 400–426). New York: Van Nostrand Reinhold.

Salthouse, T. A., Babcock, R. L., Skovronek, E., Mitchell, D. R. D., & Palmon, R. (1990). Age and experience effects in spatial visualization. *Developmental Psychology, 26,* 128–136.

Salthouse, T. A., Legg, S., Palmon, R., & Mitchell, D. (1990). Memory factors in age-related differences in simple reasoning. *Psychology and Aging, 5,* 9–15.

Salthouse, T. A., & Somberg, B. L. (1982). Skilled performance: Effects of adult age and experience on elementary processes. *Journal of Experimental Psychology: General, 111,* 176–207.

Schacter, D. L. (1987). Implicit memory: History and current status. *Journal of Experimental Psychology: Learning, Memory, and Cognition, 13,* 501–518.

Schulz, R., & Curnow, C. (1988). Peak performance and age among superathletes: Track and field, swimming, baseball, tennis, and golf. *Journal of Gerontology: Psychological Sciences, 43,* 113–120.

Seidenberg, M. S., & McClelland, J. L. (1989). A distributed, developmental model of word recognition and naming. *Psychological Review, 96,* 523–568.

Severance, D. G. (1974). Identifier search mechanisms: A survey and generalized model. *Computing Surveys, 6,* 175–194.

Shaw, R. J., & Craik, F. I. M. (1989). Age differences in prediction and performance on a ‧cued recall task. *Psychology and Aging, 4,* 131–135.

Simon, H. A. (1974). How big is a chunk? *Science, 183,* 482–488.

Simonton, D. K. (1988). Age and outstanding achievement: What do we know after a century of research? *Psychological Bulletin, 104,* 251–267.

Smith, A. D. (1977). Adult age differences in cued recall. *Developmental Psychology, 13,* 326–331.

Smith, J., & Baltes, P. B. (1990). A study of wisdom-related knowledge: Age/cohort differences in responses to life-planning problems. *Developmental Psychology, 26,* 494–505.

Sternberg, R. J. (1988). *The triarchic mind.* New York: Viking.

Thorndike, E. L. (1928). *Adult learning.* New York: Macmillan.

Underwood, B. J. (1957). Interference and forgetting. *Psychological Review, 64,* 49–60.

Watkins, M. J., Schwartz, D. R., & Lane, D. M. (1984). Does part-set cueing test for memory organization? Evidence from reconstruction of chess positions. *Canadian Journal of Psychology, 38,* 498–503.

Wickelgren, W. A. (1975). Age and storage dynamics in continuous recognition memory. *Developmental Psychology, 11,* 165–169.

Willis, S. L., & Schaie, K. W. (1986). Training the elderly on the ability factors of spatial orientation and inductive reasoning. *Psychology and Aging, 1,* 239–247.

Winocur, G., & Moscovitch, M. (1983). Paired-associate learning in institutionalized and noninstitutionalized old people: An analysis of interference and context effects. *Journal of Gerontology, 38,* 455–464.

Woodruff-Pak, D. S., & Thompson, R. F. (1988). Classical conditioning of the eyeblink response in the delay paradigm in adults aged 18–83. *Psychology and Aging, 3*, 219–229.

Yesavage, J. A., Sheikh, J. I., Friedman, L., & Tanke, E. (1990). Learning mnemonics: Roles of aging and subtle cognitive impairment. *Psychology and Aging, 5*, 133–137.

Zacks, R. T., Radvansky, G. A., Hasher, L., & Gerard, L. (1990). *Age-related differences in retrieval interference: The fan effect in younger and older adults.* Paper presented at the Cognitive Aging Conference, Atlanta.

Zandri, E., & Charness, N. (1989). Training older and younger adults to use software. *Educational Gerontology, 15*, 615–631.

12   A sociocultural approach to
intellectual development

James V. Wertsch and Bonnie G. Kanner

A sociocultural approach to intellectual development begins with the assumption that an account of human mental functioning must consider how this functioning is situated in cultural, historical, and institutional contexts. In contrast to focusing on forms of mental functioning that are thought to exist across contexts, researchers using a sociocultural approach are concerned with how mental functioning reflects and creates the specific settings in which it occurs. For example, such researchers might be concerned with how intellectual development in contemporary U.S. settings differs from that in contemporary Japan. Or they might focus on differences between children's intellectual development in the United States today and a century ago or on differences between the intellectual development that occurs at home and at school.

As authors such as Toulmin (1980) have noted, the claim that sociocultural situatedness must play a central role in psychology dates back at least to Wundt (1916). Recently, scholars from disciplines such as cultural anthropology, linguistic anthropology, cross-cultural psychology, and developmental psychology have been at the forefront of a resurgence of interest in these issues. They have variously referred to a "sociohistorical" approach (Cole, 1988), to a "cultural-historical" approach (Cole, 1990b), to a "socio-cultural" approach (Rogoff, 1990; Wertsch, 1991), and to "cultural psychology" (Berry, 1985; Cole, 1990a; Price-Williams, 1979, 1980; Shweder, 1989) to describe the area of inquiry in which they are working. Important differences separate the various authors' treatments of these issues. However, in this chapter we focus on what unites them and sets them apart from treatments based on other views rather than on what separates them.

An essential characteristic of sociocultural approaches is that they "delve

The research and writing of this chapter were supported by a grant from the Spencer Foundation to the first author and by a grant from the Literacies Institute to the second author. The statements made and the views expressed are solely the responsibility of the authors.

328

into the contextual behavior of psychological processes" (Price-Williams, 1979, p. 14). Instead of attempting to provide accounts of individuals or mental processes as if they exist in a cultural, historical, and institutional vacuum, such approaches begin with the assumption that context must be built into a theoretical framework at the most fundamental level. Scholars adopting various perspectives on this issue differ on what they see as relevant contexts and how they describe these contexts, but they agree on the importance of incorporating some notion of context into the theoretical and empirical research they pursue.

A second, related characteristic of sociocultural approaches is their focus on how different contexts create and reflect different forms of mental functioning. This does not mean that a sociocultural approach to intellectual development must entail a rejection of universal or general factors. Indeed, many investigators pursuing such an approach agree on the importance of recognizing universals and the role they play in any comprehensive account of mental functioning. But researchers also tend to believe that the universalism now so dominant in psychology makes it extremely difficult to deal in a serious, theoretically motivated way with how mental functioning reflects and constitutes specific sociocultural contexts.

Thus, instead of assuming that universals provide a basic explanatory core to which sociocultural processes and "factors" can be appended, sociocultural approaches begin by considering cultural, historical, and institutional situatedness. In such a view "cultural traditions and social practices regulate, express, transform and permute the human psyche, resulting less in psychic unity for humankind than in ethnic divergences in mind, self, and emotion" (Shweder, 1989, p. 1).

In what follows we draw selectively on various authors and schools of thought as we outline a sociocultural approach to mind. Above all, however, our analysis is grounded in the writings of the Soviet psychologist, pedagogue, and semiotician L. S. Vygotsky (1896–1934). Our use of Vygotsky's ideas to provide an integrative focus for our chapter is motivated by the fact that he is a figure who has had a major influence on many present-day practitioners of a sociocultural approach. For example, he is specifically recognized by several of the authors whom we have cited so far as having a pivotal influence on their thinking. After our presentation of a theoretical perspective, we shall move to a review of empirical research, much of it contemporary, that bears on the theoretical framework we shall have presented.

Three themes

The theoretical framework we outline is grounded in three basic themes: (1) a reliance on a genetic or developmental analysis, (2) a claim that higher mental functioning in the individual has its origins in social life, and (3) a claim' that human action, on both the social and the individual plane, is mediated by tools and signs. All three themes derive from writings by Vygotsky (1977, 1978, 1981a,b,c, 1987). In actuality, they are closely intertwined, and much of their power comes from the ways they presuppose one another. For this reason it is somewhat artificial to isolate them, but we do so, at least to start with, for the sake of clarity of presentation.

Genetic analysis

Genetic analysis in this approach is motivated by the assumption that one can understand many aspects of mental functioning only if one understands their origin and the transitions they have undergone. Like theorists such as Piaget (1970) and Werner (1948; Werner & Kaplan, 1963), Vygotsky placed genetic analysis at the very foundation of the study of mind. This is reflected in his frequent use of Blonskii's (1921) assertation that "behavior can be understood only as the history of behavior." According to Vygotsky:

> To encompass in research the process of a given thing's development in all its phases and changes – from birth to death – fundamentally means to discover its nature, its essence, for "it is only in movement that a body shows what it is." Thus, the historical [that is, in the broadest sense of "history"] study of behavior is not an auxiliary aspect of theoretical study, but rather forms its very base. (Vygotsky, 1978, pp. 64–65)

In a nutshell, the claim here is that in order to understand any aspect of human mental functioning we must understand its origins and the transitions it has undergone. In this view, attempts to unpack the nature of mental processes by analyzing only the static products of development will often be misleading. Instead of correctly identifying various aspects of these processes as emerging from the genetic transformation they have undergone, such attempts will often focus on the appearance of "fossilized" forms of behavior (Vygotsky, 1978).

Social origins of mental functioning in the individual

The second theme in the sociocultural approach we outline is the claim that a great deal of the mental functioning in the individual has its origins in social life. The fact that "origins" are mentioned in the formulation of this theme reflects its close relationship with the genetic analysis we have just presented.

In Vygotsky's writings the most general statement about the social origins of individual mental functioning can be found in his "general genetic law of cultural development":

Any function in the child's cultural development appears twice, or on two planes. First it appears on the social plane, and then on the psychological plane. First it appears between people as an interpsychological category, and then within the child as an intrapsychological category. This is equally true with regard to voluntary attention, logical memory, the formation of concepts, and the development of volition [and] it goes without saying that internalization transforms the process itself and changes its structure and functions. Social relations or relations among people genetically underlie all higher functions and their relationships. (1981b, p. 163)

The general genetic law of cultural development entails several claims that are not widely shared in contemporary psychology, at least in the West. First, it makes a much stronger claim than simply that mental functioning in the individual derives from participation in social life. This genetic law assumes that the specific structures and processes of intramental functioning can be traced to their genetic precursors on the intermental plane. Even though this point is seldom explicitly argued in contemporary research literature on intellectual development, cases can be found where authors have implicitly made assumptions quite similar to Vygotsky's. For example, the term *self-interrogation* as used by Brown, Campione, and Barclay (1979) reflects the assumption that important insights can be gained into intramental functioning by examining how it is structured along the lines of processes that are first and foremost social.

In Vygotsky's view the relationship between intermental and intramental functioning is quite strong:

[Higher mental functions'] composition, genetic structure, and means of action [forms of mediation] – in a word, their whole nature – is social. Even when we turn to mental [internal] processes, their nature remains quasi-social. In their own private sphere, human beings retain the functions of social interaction. (Vygotsky, 1981b, p. 164)

His statement on this issue does not assume that higher mental functioning (e.g., logical memory, thinking–reasoning, voluntary attention) in the individual is a direct and simple copy of socially organized processes; the point he makes in his formulation of the general genetic law of cultural development about the transformations involved in internalization warns against any such view. But his statement does mean there is a close connection, grounded in genetic transitions, between the specific structures and processes of intermental functioning, on the one hand, and intramental functioning, on the other. This, in turn, implies that different forms of intermental functioning give rise to related differences in the forms of intramental functioning.

A second claim entailed in the general genetic law of cultural development concerns the definition of higher mental functions. The definition involved here is quite different from what psychologists usually have in mind when they speak of mental functions. Specifically, it assumes that the notion of a mental function can properly be applied to social as well as individual forms of activity. In this view it is appropriate to predicate of dyads and other groups terms such as *think* and *remember*. As Middleton (1987) has noted, this point was being made by Bartlett (1932) in England at the same time as Vygotsky was producing his writings, and it is one that has recently received a great deal more attention in psychology and related disciplines (cf. Resnick, Levine, & Behrend, in press).

As an example of the kinds of phenomena Vygotsky had in mind, consider the following case from Tharp and Gallimore (1988):

A 6-year-old child has lost a toy and asks her father for help. The father asks where she last saw the toy; the child says "I can't remember." He asks a series of questions – did you have it in your room? Outside? Next door? To each question, the child answers "no." When he says "in the car?," she says "I think so" and goes to retrieve the toy. (p. 14)

In such cases one cannot answer the question "Who did the remembering?" by pointing to an individual. Instead, the dyad as a system carried out the function of remembering on the intermental plane. This point has been made in connection with other aspects of mental functioning, such as problem solving, as well (cf. Wertsch, McNamee, McLane, & Budwig, 1980).

An instance when Vygotsky's general claim about the social origins of higher mental functioning in the individual surfaces most clearly is in the "zone of proximal development." This zone is defined as the distance between a child's *"actual developmental level as determined by independent problem solving"* and the higher level of *"potential development as determined through problem solving under adult guidance or in collaboration with more capable peers"* (Vygotsky, 1978, p. 86).

Vygotsky examined the implications of the zone of proximal development in connection with two main issues: (1) the assessment of intelligence and (2) the organization of instruction. With regard to the former he argued that measuring the level of potential development is just as important as measuring the actual developmental level. He illustrated this point as follows:

Imagine that we have examined two children and have determined that the mental age of both is seven years. This means that both children solve tasks accessible to seven-year-olds. However, when we attempt to push these children further in carrying out the tests, there turns out to be an essential difference between them. With the help of leading questions, examples, and demonstrations, one of them easily solves test items taken from two years above the child's level of [actual] development. The other solves test items that are only a half-year above, his or her level of [actual] development. (1960, pp. 446–447)

Given this set of circumstances, Vygotsky proceeded to ask, "Is the mental development of these two children the same?" (1956, p. 447), and he argued that in an essential sense they are not:

From the point of view of their independent activity they are equivalent, but from the point of view of their mediated potential development they are sharply different. That which the child turns out to be able to do with the help of an adult points us towards the zone of the child's proximal development. This means that with the help of this method, we can take stock not only of today's completed process of development, not only the cycles that are already concluded and done, not only the processes of maturation that are completed; we can also take stock of processes that are now in the state of coming into being, that are only ripening, or only developing. (1956, pp. 447–448)

The second set of implications deriving from the notion of the zone of proximal development concerns instruction. As with assessment, the issue is one of the relationship between the intermental and intramental functioning outlined in the general genetic law of cultural development. In Vygotsky's view, "instruction creates the zone of proximal development" (1934, p. 450). This is not to say that when children collaborate with an adult, their level of potential development can be arbitrarily high. The inherent tension between learning, or instruction, and development that characterizes ontogenesis cautions against any such view. Vygotsky argued that a child can operate "only within certain limits that are strictly fixed by the state of the child's development and intellectual possibilities" (1934, p. 219). Hence the zone of proximal development is jointly fixed by the child's level of development and the form of instruction involved; it is a property of neither the child nor the intermental functioning alone.

When considering specific forms of instruction, Vygotsky focused on how intermental functioning can be structured so that it will maximize the growth of intramental functioning: "*Instruction is good only when it proceeds ahead of development. Then it awakens and rouses to life an entire set of functions which are in the stage of maturing, which lie in the zone of proximal development.* It is in this way that instruction plays an extremely important role in development" (1934, p. 222).

Mediation

The third general theme that runs throughout a Vygotskian formulation of a sociocultural approach is the claim that higher mental functioning is mediated by tools (or "technical tools") and signs (or "psychological tools"). Vygotsky's main contribution came in connection with the latter. His lifelong interest in the complex processes of human semiotic activity (i.e., activity involving signs as mediational means) made it possible for him to bring great sophistication to the task of outlining the role of sign systems, such as human language, in intermental and intramental functioning.

In his studies of mediational means Vygotsky's primary focus was on human language, but he recognized that many other phenomena deserve consideration as well. In his view, "the following can serve as examples of psychological tools and their complex systems: languages; various systems for counting; mnemonic techniques; algebraic symbol systems; works of art; writing; schemes, diagrams, maps, and mechanical drawings; all sorts of conventional signs; and so on" (1981a, p. 137).

In Vygotsky's view, an essential point to be kept in mind about mediational means is that their incorporation into human action does not simply facilitate, or make more efficient, a form of action that could otherwise exist. Instead, "by being included in the process of behavior, the psychological tool alters the entire flow and structure of mental functions. It does this by determining the structure of a new instrumental act, just as a technical tool alters the process of a natural adaptation by determining the form of labor operations" (Vygotsky, 1981a, p. 137).

In the Vygotskyian approach, mediational means are viewed as being essentially social, in two basic senses. First, they are the products of sociocultural history. Mediational means are neither invented by each individual nor discovered in the individual's independent interation with nature. Furthermore, they are not inherited in the form of some kind of universal, innate competence. Instead, the means that mediate mental functioning exist as part of a sociocultural context, and individuals "appropriate" (A. N. Leont'ev, 1959) them.

The second sense in which Vygotsky viewed psychological tools as social concerns the more "localized" social phenomena of face-to-face communication and social interaction. This second sense in which mediational means are social was central to Vygotsky's understanding of signs, or psychological tools, a fact reflected in such statements as "A sign is always originally a means used for social purposes, a means of influencing others, and only later becomes a means of influencing oneself" (Vygotsky, 1981b, p. 157). In a similar vein he said of language, the most important mediational means in his approach, that "the primary function of speech, both for the adult and for the child, is the function of communication, social contact, influencing surrounding individuals" (1934, p. 45).

Vygotsky employed these ideas about the social origins and social nature of mediational means in dealing with several issues. One of these is the internalization of speech. In Vygotsky's view, one fundamental mechanism that gives rise to intramental functioning is the transition from social to inner speech. The development of inner speech obviously does not mean that speech used for social, communicative purposes disappears. Instead, it reflects the appearance of a new, self-regulative speech function that has become differentiated from speech directed to others.

A fundamental method for studying this developmental transition involves examining the overt speech directed to oneself manifested by many children before this speech "goes underground" (Vygotsky, 1987) to form inner speech. Vygotsky carried out much of his research on this issue in response to Piaget's (1926) analyses of "egocentric speech." In contrast to Piaget, who viewed such speech as reflecting mental egocentricity and hence as simply dying out with age, Vygotsky proposed that this speech form manifests the transition from intermental to intramental functioning. Indeed, in Vygotsky's view, it is precisely because the same general mediational means (i.e., language) are used on both the intermental and intramental plane that the transition from the former to the latter is possible.

Contemporary empirical research

Since the early 1970s, a great deal of empirical research on intellectual development has grown out of sociocultural approaches to intellectual development. In some instances this research was directly inspired by Vygotsky's theoretical claims, and in others it was motivated primarily by alternative theoretical perspectives or by practical issues. Virtually all investigators have employed a genetic method, and the specific focus of most research has been on the social origins of individual mental functioning. For this reason, such research is the main concern in the first major section of our review. Vygotsky's claims about the mediational role of sign systems has received less attention to date, but it is increasingly recognized as needing more detailed investigation. It is the topic of the second major section of our review.

Contemporary research on the social origins of intellectual development

Our review of the research on the social origins of intramental functioning is organized in terms of the distinction between adult–child and child–child interaction. Most contemporary researchers proceeding from Vygotskian assumptions (e.g., Palincsar, 1987; Palincsar & Brown, 1984; Rogoff, Ellis, & Gardner, 1984; Tharp & Gallimore, 1988; Wertsch et al., 1980) have examined the impact of adult–child (parent–child or teacher–child) interactions on children's development. For this reason, we begin by reviewing studies that examine how parent–child and teacher–child interactions influence various aspects of children's intellectual development. From Rogoff's (1986, 1990) notion of *guided participation* – in which the interaction between an adult's understanding of a child's readiness level and a child's willingness and provision of feedback facilitates development – to Newman, Griffin, and Cole's (1989) concept of *appropriation* – in which adults, by interacting with children, assess the children's level of understanding and use that understanding to provide further information to the child – all the studies cited entail elaborations of the concept of zone of proximal development.

After reviewing studies of adult–child interaction, we shall turn to literature addressing the role of child–child interaction in intellectual development. Recently, several studies have focused on the effects of interaction in which one child is more expert than the other (e.g., Tharp & Gallimore, 1988). Other studies have compared the effects of adult–child and child–child interactions on the development of skills and knowledge (e.g., Gauvain & Rogoff, 1989; Radziszewska & Rogoff, 1988). Most of this research tends to treat child–child interactions as mimicking, perhaps poorly, the interactions between adults and children that facilitate development.

As Damon (1984) points out, however, adult–child and child–child interaction may make *unique* and *complementary* contributions to children's intellectual development. In his view, adult–child interaction is necessary for the child's development of new knowledge and existing social rules and institutions. In contrast, child–child interactions "can provide a forum for discovery learning [and] can introduce children to the process of generating ideas and solutions with equals" (p. 335).

Damon's (1984) arguments concerning the difference between adult–child and child–child interaction are grounded in the ideas of Piaget, the theorist most often juxtaposed to Vygotsky in discussions of the social origins of intellectual development. Piaget (1932) distinguished between adult–child interaction, in which an adult authority figure controls the goals and course of an activity, and *peer* interactions, in which negotiation and persuasion among equals leads to the elaboration of children's understanding of how to generate and coordinate the goals of an activity. In contrast to adult–child interaction, the benefits of peer interaction are posited to result from the need to elaborate understanding in the face of challenges from equals.

Because of Piaget's important role in the discussion of these issues, we discuss a few studies (e.g., Forman, 1987; Forman & Cazden, 1985) that examine the collaborative aspects of child–child interactions. These particular studies, however, do not derive from the Piagetian assumption that child–child interactions provoke disturbances in the individual that he or she then resolves alone. Instead, they proceed from the assumption that child–child interactions facilitate development by enabling children to carry out aspects of tasks together that they could not perform alone, and which they rarely get the chance to perform with adults.

Throughout our review, we use the term *child–child* rather than *peer* when speaking of children's interactions. We do so because the notion of peers implies interactants of equal status. Although equal status is often assumed, most investigations of child–child interaction have not determined whether it actually is present in the interactional settings they study. Indeed, an extensive research literature indicates that even when age-mates participate in interaction, they generate social hierarchies as early as pre-school age (see Kanner, 1989, for a discussion). Thus, our use of *child–child* indicates only that the interactions occur among children.

Adult–child interaction. Over the past decade or so, a variety of studies have examined the role of parent–child interaction in intellectual development. For example, Wertsch and his colleagues (Wertsch, 1979; Wertsch & Hickmann, 1987; Wertsch, et al., 1980; Wertsch, Minick, & Arns, 1984; Wertsch & Sammarco, 1985) and Wood and his colleagues (Wood, Bruner, & Ross, 1976; Wood & Middleton, 1975) have investigated the development of problem-solving strategies for tasks requiring the construction of an object in accordance with a model, and investigators such as Ninio and Bruner (1978) have examined the role of mother–child interaction in the development of early literacy skills. These studies concentrate on the process whereby mothers calibrate their expectancies and requirements of children "microgenetically" (Wertsch, 1985) over the course of a task and across age groups.

Wertsch et al. (1980) presented a puzzle task to parent–child dyads, with the children ranging from toddlerhood to preschool age. Based on analyses of videotaped data, the authors reported that mothers tailored their interactions with their children so that the youngest children (who rarely understood the goal of the task) received the most direct and repeated help, whereas the eldest children tended to get more indirect questions and suggestions and, in general, received less help. The authors' focus on the "adult–child dyad as a problem solving system" is grounded in Vygotsky's claim that mental functioning occurs on the intermental as well as the intramental plane, and one aim of the study was to document how the transition from the former to the latter occurs.

A landmark study conducted by Ninio and Bruner (1978) demonstrated a sequence of interactions through the preschool years that prepares middle-class children for literacy. In this inquiry, the authors catalogued the shifts in parental attempts to "scaffold" their children's participation in reading bedtime stories before the children had attained literacy. At first, parents were found to engage their children in the interaction by asking them to label objects depicted in pictures, often supplying the answer but asking for confirmation (e.g., "It's a ball, right?") in the case of children with limited vocabularies. The authors found that parents "up the ante" when children begin to master labeling, by asking them to carry out tasks such as finding an object or providing its proper name rather than a "baby" term. Later, parents begin to ask children questions about what has already happened in the story or what will come next.

Throughout the process of scaffolding, the authors report, objects and events in stories were related to children's own possessions and experiences.

As a result of the carefully modulated interactions during story reading, parents were found to enable children to enter the process of telling and reading stories long before they were able to do so on their own. Again, a form of intermental functioning is viewed as occurring before children are able to take over a task on the intramental plane, and the transition from inter- to intramental functioning is viewed as a basic mechanism for intellectual development.

A study by Rogoff, Ellis, and Gardner (1984) provides another example of how parents regulate their interactions with their children on the basis of the shifting skill level of the latter. The tasks in this study consisted of home-based and school-based organization tasks, in which 6- and 9-year-old children participated in dyads with mothers. The investigators predicted that mothers would treat both age groups fairly similarly when carrying out the kitchen task, since both age groups would have had some exposure to family chores. In contrast, they predicted that during the school task, mothers would be more directive with the younger children, given the recency of their entry into school. These predictions were borne out, indicating that parents can adjust their task demands depending on the requirements of particular tasks as well as on the age of the child involved.

In addition to studies involving parent–child interaction in the zone of proximal development, a variety of studies have been conducted over the past decade on teacher–child interaction in the classroom. Some of the most interesting and successful of these have been carried out by Palincsar and Brown under the heading of "reciprocal teaching" (Brown & Palincsar, 1982; Palincsar, 1987; Palincsar & Brown, 1984, 1988). These researchers have sought to articulate the zone of proximal development in the case of low-achieving students as they master various reading skills. In particular, they were concerned with promoting children's reading comprehension by enhancing the strategic skills of *summarizing, questioning, clarifying,* and *predicting.*

In a major study, Palincsar and Brown (1984) organized and observed reciprocal teaching procedures as carried out by classroom teachers with poor seventh-grade readers. The procedure called for a teacher to work with a small group of students during the actual reading of stories for 20 half-hour sessions over 20 days. During the initial phases the teacher explicitly labeled the four strategies of summarizing, questioning, clarifying, and predicting and then called on students to provide the information needed for each strategy. When students provided only partial information or no response, the teacher rephrased or elaborated their attempts, or offered an answer and had the student model it. This enabled students who at first could not contribute to be brought into the interaction and participate in a successful completion of the task. It also required students to be active participants in the task.

As students learned to provide appropriate information to teacher prompts, they were given increased responsibility for carrying out the various strategies themselves. Specifically, they were required to pose strategic questions to their fellow students, asking them to summarize, question, clarify, and predict. This amounted to a gradual shift from "other-regulation" (Wertsch, 1979) on the part of the teacher to self-regulation on the part of the student, in which students were expected to make a transition from this kind of scripted intermental process to intramental functioning.

Palincsar and Brown reported significant and robust gains in the students' scores on standardized tests of comprehension, and strong maintenance over time and generalization of these skills to other tasks. Their results demonstrate that if adult–child interaction is organized in a way that promotes children's active participation in, and reflection on, the strategic skills required to carry out a task, it can produce major gains. These results are especially striking because they were obtained with a group of students who have traditionally been considered to have great difficulties in making and maintaining gains in reading skills.

Another set of investigations of how classroom interaction provides the social foundations for individual mental functioning has been carried out by Tharp and Gallimore (1988). In this case the studies examine the impact of implementing Vygotskian principles in classrooms with native Hawaiians and with minority groups in California and Arizona. The classrooms were structured such that children move through various "activity centers" during a day. At the primary center, small groups of same-ability children met with the teacher for approximately 20 minutes. During this period they focused on developing literacy skills, using materials from various areas of the curriculum (especially reading and science).

The student populations in the studies conducted by Tharp and Gallimore contained many children whose early childhood experiences had not focused extensively on the kinds of preliteracy activities that seem most closely tied to success in reading in school (cf. Ninio & Bruner, 1978). They did, however, bring other forms of knowledge to the tasks they confronted in the classroom. With this in mind, the procedure employed by Tharp and Gallimore called on teachers to use children's existing knowledge as a foundation for building bridges to the kind of intellectual skills required in the classroom. Thus, in the early grades of the program, children were drawn into the interaction by talking about their own experiences, often with the aid of concrete objects, and were then led to relate their personal experiences to those depicted in texts. Whether they were learning how to recognize words or how to formulate an inferential question, students were constantly encouraged to relate their activities to the content to their previous knowledge and experience. Tasks were structured such that children participated at a level appropriate for them and were gradually brought by the teacher to focus on the goal and central points of the lessons.

As in the Palincsar and Brown study, the procedure used by Tharp and

Gallimore assumed that intellectual processes appear first on the intermental and then on the intramental plane. Furthermore, it was grounded in the idea that desired intramental outcomes can be obtained by organizing inter- mental functioning in certain ways. Both of these studies see at least three key points as important in creating forms of social interaction that will enhance the individual's intellectual functioning. First, it is essential for teachers to come into contact with and assess students' existing level of knowledge. This involves recognizing students' "situation definitions" (Wertsch, 1984) and seeking to create some level of "intersubjectivity" (Rogoff, 1990; Wertsch, 1985) between teacher and student. Second, teacher–student interaction must be organized so that students are required to participate actively in carrying out strategic activities. This is an essential aspect of Rogoff's studies of guided participation: Active participation must be enhanced, but it must be guided or organized in accordance with certain principles. Finally, there must be some mechanism for ensuring that the transition from intermental to intramental functioning is encouraged at the appropriate points.

The overall picture is one of a constantly changing process of attaining intersubjectivity, ensuring active participation, and handing over increased strategic responsibilities to children. The effectiveness of these principles is reflected in the fact that, like Palincsar and Brown, Tharp and Gallimore report that students participating in their curriculum score significantly higher on standardized tests than children from similar populations in public schools. Again, such results are particularly impressive because they were obtained with groups who typically have great difficulty in succeeding in school.

In contrast to the success reported in the studies by Palincsar and Brown and by Tharp and Gallimore, other authors have recently examined some of the reasons why teacher–child interaction in classrooms often fails to produce the desired results. The work of Newman, Griffin, and Cole (1989) is particularly important in this connection. These authors provided two interesting examples in which interaction involving adults and low-achieving children failed to lead to the students' mastery of skills or content.

In the first example, Newman et al. described a series of math lessons taught to a fourth-grade class divided into five ability groups. The lessons involved learning to do long division. To develop the intended skills, students must know the strategy of making successive approximations. Newman et al. reported that different facilities with basic number-facts underriding long division did not account for why most children in the high-achieving groups mastered long division while many in the low-achieving groups did not. Indeed, they argue that focusing on number facts will not foster the mastery of long division even though teacher–student interactions in the low- achieving group centered on these facts.

On the basis of several analyses, the authors found that although children in the high-achieving groups had not fully mastered the multiplication table, they could succeed interactively with the teacher in solving a problem. This was because they conveyed to the teacher that they understood the steps involved, even though they could not supply the specific answer. In contrast, children in low-achieving groups tended to be silent if they did not know a number fact. As a result, the teacher was often left with no means of assessing the child's understanding and had to focus on the first steps of the task and not its more complex aspects.

This pattern of interaction produced a situation in which students in the low-achieving groups spent the least amount of time on the very aspects of the task that would have conveyed the overall logic of successive approximations and the most amount of time learning to supply relatively simple content. In contrast, the high-achieving groups spent the most time learning to generate successive approximations. To no one's surprise, the authors report that few in the low-achieving groups mastered long division. What these findings indicate is that despite teachers' efforts to convey the basics of a task in interaction with children, their inability to assess children's starting points and the children's inability to provide teachers with hints result in interactions that do not lead to eventual mastery on the part of the children.

In another example provided by Newman et al. (1989), a teacher carried out a unit of instruction with her class on six different groups of Native Americans. For each group, information about how they obtained food, their style of government, and their family arrangements was provided to the students in a number of formats, including narratives, role playing, same–different games, worksheets, and the like. The authors reported that low-achieving children scored higher as a group than did high achievers after one lesson, but that by the end of the unit, high achievers has resumed their expected higher level of understanding. They found that, like high achievers, low achievers initially made mistakes *within* categories of information (e.g., types of food gathering). Unlike high achievers, however, low-achieving children also produced mistakes *across* categories (e.g., type of family instead of type of food gathering).

What Newman et al. gleaned from this pattern was that high achievers had mastered the hidden task requirement of placing information into mutually exclusive categories, whereas low achievers had not. Their investigation demonstrates that not all children bring the same set of expectations and readiness to a task, and that teachers can be hard put to assess children's readiness and engage them effectively in interaction.

Child–child interaction. Rogoff and her colleagues (Ellis & Rogoff, 1986; Gauvain & Rogoff, 1989; Radziszewska & Rogoff, 1988) have compared the effects of adult–child and child–child interactions on children's development of planning and organizational skills. In the study by Ellis and Rogoff (1986), adult and 9-year-old participants aided 6-year-olds' learning of an organization task. The investigators report that adult teachers were more likely to provide explicit rationales for why certain categories should be used to organize each task than were the 9-year-old helpers. In contrast to the adults, few of the 9-year-olds broke the tasks into subgoals for the learners, and teachers failed to provide explicit redirection when a learner made an error.

In a related study, Radziszewska and Rogoff (1988) examined the impact of adult–child and child–child interactions on 9-year-old children's development of planning skills. The task consisted of presenting the dyads with a set of imaginary errands to be run in a town represented on a map. The authors reported that relative to child–child dyads, adult–child dyads were characterized by more sophisticated planning strategies, greater involvement of children in these strategies, and more communication within the dyads. Furthermore, children who had participated in the adult–child interactions subsequently demonstrated more sophisticated planning strategies in intramental functioning.

Although these results appear to indicate that children benefit more from adult–child than from child–child interactions when learning planning strategies, another study, by Gauvain and Rogoff (1989), indicates that the picture is a bit more complex. In this study, 5-year-olds worked in dyads with adults or with age-mates to plan routes through a model grocery store. The authors found that when dyads (adult–child *or* child–child) shared the responsibility for generating the plan, the children showed greater use of advanced planning when performing a later task alone. The authors concluded that coordinated interactions rather than independent functioning appears to facilitate the development of planning strategies. Gauvain and Rogoff (1989) pointed out that their task had *no single* correct answer or best way of being carried out. In the other tasks, however, a single, correct goal could be identified. It would seem, therefore, that child–child interaction can be as conducive to learning as adult–child coordinations when a specific goal is not prespecified. But the results of these studies suggest that when a particular strategy must be learned, adults are better skilled than children at structuring the task for a novice.

An additional example of child–child interaction that mimics adult–child interaction can be found in the writings of Tharp and Gallimore (1988). In their instructional program, children were actively encouraged to work together to carry out tasks at the activity centers, and the authors documented that children alternated between teacher and learner roles with each other. The switching of roles with domain expertise enabled children to learn the skills of organization and evaluation of tasks as well as relevant content.

In contrast to focusing on how child–child interaction fares when it mimics adult–child interaction, a few investigators have examined more reciprocal interactions among children (Forman & Cazden, 1985; Newman, Griffin, & Cole, 1989). Forman and Cazden (1985) had fourth- and seventh-grade students work in pairs to perform a "shadows" task, which consisted of matching three-dimensional shapes to projected shadows of two-dimensional shapes on a screen. She reported that some of the dyads worked collaboratively, shifting roles in the task from tester to evaluator. Forman argued that, especially when operating as a dyad, the children developed analytic skills they did not demonstrate individually. That is, intermental functioning in such cases seems to produce a result whose whole is greater than the sum of its parts.

The claim that child–child interaction can lead to "joint discovery" has also been examined by Newman, Griffin, and Cole (1989). The authors generated a task in which fifth-graders were given four liquids and asked which paired combinations would generate a certain color. From an adult perspective, the most efficient means to accomplish this task is systematically to pair the liquids to generate the six possible combinations. The authors found that the children did not start with this strategy. Instead, they tended simply to pick up the nearest liquid and combine it with others. When the students checked to see if they had completed the task, they *then* "discovered" the need to avoid repetitions or deletions of pairs, and some dyads sequenced the pairs of liquids in orders approximating those expected by the adults. The essential point here is that children discovered the strategy in a collaborative manner, working together to verify that they had completed the task.

Studies such as these suggest that child–child interaction can enable children to articulate their reasoning, reformulate their understanding, and generate new strategies that they might not create on their own. Furthermore, such studies indicate that child–child interaction may be qualitatively different from adult–child interaction in its organization and in the intramental results it can be expected to produce.

The idea that different forms of intermental functioning will be associated with different intramental outcomes is an essential implication of Vygotsky's general genetic law of cultural development. It is an assumption that is only now beginning to be explored, however. Claims such as those put forth by Damon (1984) about the different products that might result from different forms of social interaction are suggestive and provide an interesting possibility for future research.

Contemporary research on the role of mediational means

In contrast to the issue of how social interaction plays a role in intellectual development, the role of mediational means has until now received relatively little attention in Western research literature. As Cole (1990a) and Wertsch (1985, 1991) have argued, however, claims about mediational means play an essential, even primary, role in a Vygotskian sociocultural approach. One reason for their importance is that they provide a concrete mechanism for specifying how sociocultural setting is linked to the intellectual development of the individual. It is by mastering the varieties of mediational means – especially the varieties of language in a range of cultural, historical, and institutional contexts – that children's mental functioning emerges in this view.

One reason for the relative dearth of research on how mediational means are tied to intellectual development is that intellectual development tends to be studied in one set of disciplines (e.g., developmental and instructional psychology), whereas socioculturally situated language use tends to be studied in others (e.g., sociolinguistics and linguistic anthropology). The result is that quite different theoretical frameworks and methodologies are often employed to address the two sides of the issue and cross-fertilization has therefore been slow in coming. Only quite recently have investigators begun to search for ways to combine the research foci involved. For example, Ochs (1988) and Ochs and Schieffelin (1984) have recently undertaken this interdisciplinary task in their study of "language socialization."

A principal forum for addressing this kind of issue has been ethnographic studies of language use in schools, homes, and communities. In a seminal work on the topic, Heath (1983) wrote about the language variants used in three communities, all of which fed into a mainstream school. She documented in detail the multiple aspects of family and social life in each community, and how these social interactions generate different "ways with words" that result in children's being differentially prepared to engage in literacy practices in school.

In one community, children did not participate regularly in reading activities involving books or magazines, but there were many contexts in which storytelling took place. Through listening to and interacting with adults and children, the children in this community learned that a "good" story contains elaborations and exaggerations to entertain listeners. Repetition and suspense are important in such stories, whereas strict accuracy and coherence around a central theme are less so. In the second community, children were exposed to picture books, Bible stories, and adults' stories from toddlerhood on. From these interactions children learned to stick to "the facts," not to embellish their account, and to end with a moral. Embellishments or exaggerations were treated as "lying" or stretching the truth and were actively discouraged. In the third, middle-class community, children were exposed to storybooks from early toddlerhood and were led by adults to relate events and objects in the stories to their everyday experiences. Children were read many different types of stories, including fairy tales and stories about animals, and thus learned that stories could be about real events or fantasies.

The children from these three communities entered schools that based their literacy program on assumptions compatible with the preliterate activities occurring in the homes of middle-class children. As a result, when children from the second community were asked to draw inferences from a story or to predict future events, they found themselves being asked to do what at home would be termed "lying," and therefore they resisted carrying out these tasks. They could, however, report plot lines and details quite well. Children from the first community had difficulty seeing book stories as closed texts that could be recounted without reference to one's own experience. Furthermore, their attempts at embellishment and elaboration were interpreted by teachers as getting offtrack or making things up. These children experienced great difficulty acquiring reading, and by the later grades, where their skill at metaphor and hyperbole could have been exploited, were already so far behind that they could not invoke these skills appropriately. Not surprisingly, children from middle-class homes tended to be in the top reading groups and made the smoothest progress in learning to read.

Heath's (1983) documentation of the clash of language variants in teacher–student interactions suggests that many children "fail" not because they function poorly in some absolute sense, but because teachers' lack of awareness of different language variants can greatly impede their abilities to engage children in interactions that lead to the development of skills valued in the classroom. This same general point has been made by authors such as Gee (1988). On the basis of detailed transcriptions of recordings of children's stories, he concluded that what *appears* confusing and unconnected orally to a teacher can be organized in tightly ordered prose when *written down*. This suggests it is the highly difficult task of understanding spoken language presented in forms with which one is unfamiliar that makes the teachers' task so difficult.

The idea that mismatches of language variants can impede teacher–student interactions even in nonacademic activities has been demonstrated by Michaels (1981) and Gee (1988). Michaels (1981) studied the activity of "sharing time" in elementary schools – a period when children are given the opportunity to talk individually about an event or possession that interests them. She documented that with children whose understanding of story-telling differs from that of their teacher, the teacher often has difficulty following the thread of the child's story. Instead of being able to augment what the child has said or offer an evaluation, the teacher often ends up interrupting the child to encourage her or him to "just tell one thing" or to stay on track or not make things up. Of course, these interruptions disrupt the organization of children's stories and tend to result in their being terminated prematurely or becoming muddled to the point where the teacher produces the end for the student.

Building on the ideas of M. M. Bakhtin (1981, 1984, 1986; Voloshinov, 1973), Wertsch (1991) has argued that the notion of a "social language" can profitably be employed to organize our understanding of the findings of such authors as Heath, Gee, and Michaels. In Bakhtin's view, the meaning of an utterance derives in large part from our knowledge of the "voice" producing it. Because voices of individuals and of the groups that individuals represent are culturally, historically, and institutionally situated, this approach links the meaning of individuals' participating in intermental functioning with specific sociocultural settings. This view of social languages as mediational means in a Vygotskian sociocultural approach provides a way to account for how intellectual development in the individual is inherently linked with sociocultural context.

Conclusion

The approach outlined in this chapter argues for the need to approach intellectual development from the perspective of how it is situated in sociocultural context. Indeed, many essential aspects of intellectual functioning are viewed as being constituted by the sociocultural setting in which development occurs.

The theoretical orientation for the sociocultural approach we have outlined draws on several sources, all of which have their roots in the writings of Vygotsky. We outlined three central themes in his writings that have come to guide a great deal of contemporary research on intellectual development.

First, virtually all of this research employs some version of genetic analysis.

Second, claims about the social origins of individual mental functioning have been quite productive in giving rise to new empirical research questions. Vygotsky's general genetic law of cultural development and his account of the zone of proximal development have suggested that the study of intellectual development can be greatly enhanced by considering how mental functioning may occur on the intermental as well as the intramental plane, and how the former kind of functioning structures the latter.

Third, Vygotsky's theme about the importance of mediational means in shaping intellectual development has until quite recently received relatively little attention, but it may play a pivotal role in organizing an overall picture in which the other themes will be most productively developed. This is so because a study of mediational means such as social languages provides a major mechanism for linking individual mental functioning both to its intermental precursors and to the cultural, historical, and institutional settings in which it occurs. This overall linkage contrasts with many studies of the social origins of individual mental functioning that tend to stop at the intermental level and say little about how this is, in turn, situated socioculturally. Recent studies in such disciplines as sociolinguistics and the ethnography of speaking bear on these issues and highlight the need for much more interdisciplinary collaboration. Indeed, a key to the entire sociocultural approach we have outlined is to formulate principled links between kinds of phenomena and disciplines that are all too often considered in isolation in contempoary research.

References

Bakhtin, M. M. (1981). *The dialogic imagination: Four essays by M. M. Bakhtin* (M. Holquist, Ed.; C. Emerson & M. Holquist, Trans.). Austin: University of Texas Press.

Bakhtin, M. M. (1984). *Problems of Doestoevsky's poetics* (C. Emerson, Ed. & Trans.). Minneapolis: University of Minnesota Press.

Bakhtin, M. M. (1986). *Speech genres and other late essays* (C. Emerson & M. Holquist, Eds.; V. W. McGee, Trans.). Austin: University of Texas Press.

Bartlett, F. C. (1932). *Remembering: A study in experimental and social psychology.* Cambridge: Cambridge University Press.

Berry, J. W. (1985). Cultural psychology and ethnic psychology: A comparative analysis. In I. Reyes & Y. Poortinga (Eds.), *From a different perspective: Studies of behavior across cultures.* Lisse: Swets & Zeitlinger.

Blonskii, P. P. (1921). *Ocherki po nauchnoi psikhologii* [Essays in scientific psychology]. Moscow: Gosudarstvennoe Izdtel' stvo.

Brown, A. L., Campione, J. C., & Barclay, C. R. (1979). Training self-checking routines for estimating test readiness: Generalization from list learning to prose recall. *Child Development, 50,* 501–512.

Brown, A. L., & Palincsar, A. S. (1982). Inducing strategic learning from texts by means of informed, self-control training. *Topics in Learning and Learning Disabilities, 2*(1), 1–17.

Cole, M. (1988). Cross-cultural research in the sociohistorical tradition. *Human Development, 31,* 136–151.

Cole, M. (1990a). Cultural psychology: A once and future discipline? In J. Berman (Ed.), *Nebraska Symposium on Motivation: Cross-cultural perspectives* (Vol. 37). Lincoln: University of Nebraska Press.

Cole, M. (1990b). *Cultural psychology: Some general principles and a concrete example.* Paper presented in May at the Second International Congress of Activity Theory, Lahti, Finland.

Damon, W. (1984). Peer education: The untapped potential. *Journal of Applied Developmental Psychology, 5,* 331–343.

Ellis, S., & Rogoff, B. (1986). Problem solving in children's management of instruction. In E. Mueller & C. Cooper (Eds.), *Process and outcome in peer relationships.* Orlando, FL: Academic Press.

Forman, E. (1987). Learning through peer interaction: A Vygotskian perspective. *Genetic Epistemologist, 15,* 6–15.

Forman, E., & Cazden, C. (1985). Exploring Vygotskian perspectives in education: The cognitive value of peer interaction. In J. V. Wertsch (Ed.), *Culture, communication, and cognition: Vygotskian perspectives* (pp. 323–347). Cambridge: Cambridge University Press.

Gauvain, M., & B. Rogoff (1989). Collaborative problem solving and children's planning skills. *Developmental Psychology, 25,* 139–151.

Gee, J. P. (1988). *Literacy, linguistics, and ideology: An overview.* Unpublished paper, Department of Linguistics, University of Southern California, Los Angeles.

Heath, S. B. (1983). *Ways with words: Language, life, and work in communities and classrooms.* Cambridge: Cambridge University Press.

Kanner, B. G. (1989). *When are peers not peers: Implications for investigating the effects of peer interactions on conceptual development.* Paper presented at the 19th Symposium of the Jean Piaget Society, Philadelphia.

Leont'ev, A. N. (1959). *Problemy razvitiya psikhiki* [Problems in the development of mind]. Moscow: Moscow University Press. (Published in English as *Problems in the development of mind.* [Moscow: Progress Publishers, 1981].)

Michaels, S. (1981). "Sharing time": Children's narrative style and differential access to literacy. *Language in Society, 10,* 423–442.

Middleton, D. (1987). Some issues and approaches. *The Quarterly Newsletter of Comparative Human Cognition* (special issue devoted to collective memory and remembering), *9*(1).

Newman, D., Griffin, P., & Cole, M. (1989). *The construction zone: Working for cognitive change in school.* Cambridge: Cambridge University Press.

Ninio, A., & Bruner, J. S. (1978). The achievement and antecedents of labelling. *Journal of Child Language, 5,* 1–16.

Ochs, E. (1988). *Culture and language development: Language acquisition and language socialization in a Samoan village.* Cambridge: Cambridge University Press.

Ochs, E., & Schieffelen, B. B. (1984). Language acquisition and socialization. In R. A. Shweder & R. A. LeVine (Eds.), *Culture theory: Essays on mind, self and emotion.* Cambridge: Cambridge University Press.

Palincsar, A. S. (1987). *An apprenticeship approach to the instruction of comprehension skills.* Paper presented at the symposium "Perspectives on Expert Learning: An Integrative Examination of Theoretical and Empirical Issues," American Education Research Association.

Palincsar, A. S., & Brown, A. L. (1984). Reciprocal teaching of comprehension-fostering and comprehension-monitoring activities. *Cognition and Instruction, 1*(2), 117–175.

Palincsar, A. S., & Brown, A. L. (1988). Teaching and practicing thinking skills to promote comprehension in the context of group problem solving. *RASE, 9*(1), 53–59.

Piaget, J. (1926). *The language and thought of the child.* New York: Harcourt Brace.

Piaget, J. (1932). *The moral judgement of the child.* New York: Free Press.

Piaget, J. (1970). *Genetic epistemology* (E. Duckworth, Trans.). New York: Columbia University Press.

Price-Williams, D. (1979). Modes of thought in cross-cultural psychology: A historical review. In A. J. Marsella, R. G. Tharp, & T. J. Ciborowski (Eds.), *Perspectives in cross-cultural psychology.* New York: Academic Press.

Price-Williams, D. (1980). Toward the idea of a cultural psychology: A superordinate theme for study. *Journal of Cross-cultural Psychology, 11,* 75–89.

Radziszewska, B., & Rogoff, B. (1988). Influence of adult and peer collaborators on children's planning skills. *Developmental Psychology, 24,* 840–848.

Resnick, L. B., Levine, J. M., & Behrend, S. (Eds.). (in press). *Perspectives on socially shared cognition.* Washington, DC: American Psychological Association.

Rogoff, B. (1986). Adult assistance of children's learning. In T. E. Raphael (Ed.), *The contexts of school based literacy.* New York: Random House.

Rogoff, B. (1990). *Apprenticeship in thinking: Cognitive development in social context.* New York: Oxford University Press.

Rogoff, B., Ellis, S., & Gardner, W. (1984). Adjustment to adult–child instruction according to child's age and task. *Developmental Psychology, 20,* 193–199.

Shweder, R. (1989). Cultural psychology: What is it? In J. W. Stigler, R. A. Shweder, & G. Herdt (Eds.), *Cultural psychology: Essays on comparative human development.* Cambridge: Cambridge University Press.

Tharp, R. G., & Gallimore, R. (1988). *Rousing minds to life: Teaching, learning, and schooling in social context.* Cambridge: Cambridge University Press.

Toulmin, S. (1980). Toward reintegration: An agenda for psychology's second century. In

R. A. Kasschau & F. S. Kessel (Eds.), *Psychology and society: In search of symbiosis*. New York: Holt, Rinehart & Winston.

Voloshinov, V. N. (1973). *Marxism and the philosophy of language* (L. Matejka & I. R. Titunik, Trans.). New York: Seminar Press.

Vygotsky, L. S. (1934). *Myshlenie i rech': Psikhologicheskie issledovaniya* [Thinking and speech: Psychological investigations]. Moscow: Gosudarstvennoe Sotsial'no-Ekonomicheskoe Izdatel'stvo.

Vygotsky, L. S. (1956). *Izbrannye psikhologicheskie issledovaniya* [Selected psychological investigations]. Moscow: Izdatel'stvo Akademii Pedagogicheskikh Nauk SSSR.

Vygotsky, L. S. (1960). *Razvitie vysshykh psikhicheskikh functsii* [The development of higher mental functions]. Moscow: Izdatel'stvo Akademii Pedagogicheskikh Nauk.

Vygotsky, L. S. (1977). Iz tet'ryadei L. S. Vygotskogo [From the notebooks of L. S. Vygotsky]. *Vestnik Moskovskogo Universiteta: Scriya psikhologii* (Moscow University record: Psychology series), *15*, 89–95.

Vygotsky, L. S. (1978). *Mind in society: The development of higher psychological processes*, M. Cole, V. John-Steiner, S. Scribner, & E. Souberman (Eds.). Cambridge, MA: Harvard University Press.

Vygotsky, L. S. (1981a). The instrumental method in psychology. In J. V. Wertsch (Ed.), *The concept of activity in Soviet psychology*. Armonk, NY: Sharpe.

Vygotsky, L. S. (1981b). The genesis of higher mental functions. In J. V. Wertsch (Ed.), *The concept of activity in Soviet psychology*. Armonk, NY: Sharpe.

Vygotsky, L. S. (1981c). The development of higher forms of attention in childhood. In J. V. Wertsch (Ed.), *The concept of activity in Soviet psychology*. Armonk, NY: Sharpe.

Vygotsky, L. S. (1987). *Thinking and speech* (N. Minick, Ed. & Trans.). New York: Plenum.

Werner, H. (1948). *Comparative psychology of mental development*. New York: International Universities Press.

Werner, H., & B. Kaplan (1963). *Symbol formation: An organismic developmental approach to language and the expression of thought*. New York: Wiley.

Wertsch, J. V. (1979). From social interaction to higher psychological processes: A clarification and application of Vygotsky's theory. *Human Development, 22*, 1–22.

Wertsch, J. V. (1984). The zone of proximal development: Some conceptual issues. In B. Rogoff & J. V. Wertsch (Eds.), *Children's learning in the "zone of proximal development,"* New directions for child development, no. 23. San Francisco: Jossey-Bass.

Wertsch, J. V. (1985). *Vygotsky and the social formation of mind*. Cambridge, MA: Harvard University Press.

Wertsch, J. V. (1991). *Voices of the mind: A sociocultural approach to mediated action*. Cambridge, MA: Harvard University Press.

Wertsch, J. V., & Hickmann, M. (1987). A microgenetic analysis of problem-solving in social interaction. In M. Hickmann (Ed.), *Social and functional approaches to language and thought*. New York: Academic Press.

Wertsch, J. V., McNamee, G. D., McLane, J. G., & Budwig, N. A. (1980). The adult–child dyad as a problem solving system. *Child Development, 51*, 1215–1221.

Wertsch, J. V., Minick, N., & Arns, F. J. (1984). The creation of context in joint problem-solving. In B. Rogoff & J. Lave (Eds.), *Everyday cognition: Its development in social context*. Cambridge, MA: Harvard University Press.

Wertsch, J. V., & Sammarco, J. G. (1985). Social precursors to individual functioning: The problem of units of analysis. In R. A. Hinde & A. N. Perret-Clermont (Eds.), *Interindividual relations and cognitive development*. Oxford: Oxford University Press.

Wood, D., Bruner, J. S., & Ross, G. (1976). The role of tutoring in problem solving. *Journal of Child Psychology and Psychiatry, 17*, 89–100.

Wood, D., & Middleton, D. (1975). A study of assisted problem-solving. *British Journal of Psychology, 66*, 181–191.

Wundt, W. (1916). *Elements of folk psychology*. London: Allen & Unwin.

13   Contextual approaches to
         adult intellectual development

handwritten annotation: least affected areas of expertise vocabulary

Roger A. Dixon

In many research areas of psychology – and the study of adult cognitive development is no exception – one frequently encounters the term *contextualism*. In these appearances, it is linked variously to terms such as *contextual models*, *contextual theories*, or *contextual approaches*. Although there are differences among scientific models, theories, and approaches, for the present purposes we treat them as though they are roughly synonymous. In the title of this chapter, I use the milder of these expressions, namely, *contextual approaches*. For many observers this term involves less commitment to specific metatheoretical positions. Instead, it emphasizes the dual activities of psychological theory and research, coordinated activities that may lead in multiple theoretical directions. From this perspective, contextualism is considered less a particular model of psychology than a rubric for a family of "approaches." These approaches are related in that they sample from a common pool of theoretical and methodological tenets.

Suggesting that contextualism – at least as the term is used in contemporary psychology – is less a systematic model than a family of theories and methods does not exempt one from analyzing its meanings and, especially, the uses to which it is put. Indeed, it encourages such an analysis, one goal of which is to identify the common features of this family of theories. This is in fact possible, for scientific families have family resemblances in the same way siblings do, a point made by the influential philosopher Wittgenstein (see Chapman & Dixon, 1987). In the case of scientific families, they share not biological but intellectual genotypic and phenotypic features. These shared characteristics take the form of related research questions, hypotheses, research designs, interpretive inclinations, and analytic techniques. I begin this chapter by describing some of these characteristics of contextual

My work on this chapter, and the research summarized in it, were supported by grants from the Natural Sciences and Engineering Research Council of Canada and the Network of Centres of Excellence (Canadian Aging Research Network). I thank Ingrid Friesen and David Kurzman, who contributed significantly to the studies summarized in this chapter. I would also like to express my appreciation to Cynthia Berg and Robert Sternberg for their helpful comments on an earlier version of this chapter.

350

approaches. After this, I consider the application of contextual issues in the general area of intellectual development in adulthood. The focus is on cognitive compensation as an exemplar of adaptive cognitive aging in context. I subsequently describe recent theory and research on one form of such compensation, namely, the use of human cognitive aids, or collaborative cognition.

Features of contextual approaches

If contextualism has an extensive network of meanings and implications, what are some of the common features of the network? Since the turn of the century, contextualism has been entertained and embraced by some psychologists and ignored or dismissed by others. This is not unusual, for no family of theories – no model or metatheory in psychology – has been endorsed by all psychologists. In the past two decades, however, there seems to have been a growing concern with contextual issues in several areas of psychology. As testimony to this, in a recent collection of essays, developmental, cognitive, personality, and social psychologists were provided with a forum in which to discuss the relevance and application of contextualism in their areas of specialization (see Rosnow & Georgoudi, 1986). For various reasons, life-span developmental psychology – and perhaps especially the study of adult development and aging – is frequently associated with contextual approaches (e.g., Baltes, 1987). One reason for this association is that numerous principles frequently allied with contextualism have natural applications to the study of life-span human development. For example, the life-span development of a given process is portrayed as a lifelong set of dynamic phenomena influenced by multiple historical, cultural, ecological, biological, and other psychological factors (Lerner, 1986). Therefore, human development is influenced by multiple contexts – which is something of a truism, unless it is taken as seriously as it seems to be by many developmental and contextual psychologists (e.g., Baltes, 1987; Baltes, Reese, & Lipsitt, 1980; Bronfenbrenner, 1979; Lerner, 1986). These psychologists often point to the evidence that intellectual development in adulthood is related to the historical context in which individuals are born and raised (Schaie, 1983, 1990).

Specific features of various contextual approaches have been reviewed extensively elsewhere (e.g., in Rosnow & Georgoudi, 1986), so in this chapter I simply summarize these reviews with the purpose of setting the stage for an examination of contextual approaches to intellectual development in adulthood. Psychologists advocating a contextual approach to the study of development descend from a variety of historically prominent figures. Three sets of these intellectual ancestors are especially notable. First are the contextual pragmatic psychologists such as William James

(1842–1910), John Dewey (1859–1952), and George Herbert Mead (1863–1931), all of whom were enormously influential early psychologists and educators. They are remembered for, among other things, integrating pragmatic philosophy (or the philosophy of the practical, as opposed to the ideal), perspectives on evolution and development (such as the theory associated with Charles Darwin), and psychological issues (e.g., Wiener, 1949). Second, it is important to remember the related group of early functional psychologists, such as James Rowland Angell (1869–1949), Harvey Carr (1873–1954), and James Mark Baldwin (1861–1934). One of the goals of these authors was the development of a psychology in which cognition was viewed as useful, adaptive, and functional. For this reason, their major focus was on mental operations in practical living conditions, as well as on dynamic portrayals of these essentially adaptive activities. A third set of intellectual influences is dialectical – and especially Soviet – psychology. Examples include Lev Vygotsky (1894–1934), Alexander Luria (1902–1977), and Klaus Riegel (1925–1977), psychologists who emphasized the historical and contextual embeddedness of all psychological functioning. As such, they have been instrumental in the growing research area of cross-cultural developmental psychology.

Analyses of the linkage of these figures to contemporary contextual psychology are available in several sources (e.g., Dixon & Lerner, in press). In general, contextual approaches are characterized by the metaphor of the changing event (Pepper, 1970); that is, the life course is represented as being a series of changing events or activities. These events are viewed as being embedded in multiple changing contexts. Events occur on multiple levels, including biological, psychological, ecological, and sociohistorical. Events or activities at any one of these levels may affect developmental processes at any other level. Of most relevance to life-span developmental psychology, events or activities at any level may play some role in psychological development (e.g., Bronfenbrenner, 1979; Lerner, 1986; Riegel, 1976). For example, historical events such as earthquakes and economic changes have been linked to long-term psychological change (see McCluskey & Reese, 1984). In sum, the dual contextual emphases on (1) multiple levels of interrelated change and (2) practical or functional psychological activity are represented in contemporary contextual approaches to psychology. Each emphasis has many implications for theory and research – implications that are sampled by specific approaches.

In addition to these foci, however, most historical and contemporary contextualists seem to emphasize a number of key issues. I highlight the ones that are especially relevant to the study of intellectual development in adulthood. Before doing this, however, two caveats are in order. First, these issues are not intended to distinguish contextualism completely from other approaches to intellectual development. Indeed, some overlap may be found in a number of these issues for the learning (Charness & Bieman-Copland, this volume), neo-Piagetian (Labouvie-Vief, this volume) and information-processing (Salthouse, this volume) perspectives. Second, specific contextual theories or research programs do not necessarily adopt all of the contextual emphases in this network of issues (see Wertsch & Kanner, this volume). In practice, however, contextual theories and empirical research programs use these emphases (1) to construct the logical framework and research questions of their studies, (2) to inform their selection of methods, including designs and measures, and (3) to interpret the results and offer suggestions for future research. These major features of the theory and practice of contextualism in the study of psychological development are described in the sections that follow. To a greater or lesser extent, such principles are necessary but not sufficient for contextual theory.

Multidimensionality of constructs

As do many psychologists, contextualists emphasize the multidimensionality of numerous complex constructs. Several theories of intelligence (e.g., Gardner, 1983; Sternberg, 1984) and theories of intellectual development in adulthood (e.g., Baltes, Dittmann-Kohli, & Dixon, 1984; Berg & Sternberg, 1985; Sternberg & Berg, 1987) are both multidimensional and have contextual characteristics. It is important to note that these theories are continuous with theories that do not adopt contextual principles but that are also multidimensional (e.g., Horn, 1982, this volume). Horn's theory of crystallized and fluid intelligence is similar in many respects to the more contextual-oriented pragmatics and mechanics orientation of Baltes et al. (1984). Although both have two major dimensions of intelligence, the latter orientation makes explicit connections to recent work on cognitive skills, which include such practical aspects as wisdom (e.g., Baltes, 1987; Baltes & Smith, 1990; Dixon & Baltes, 1986).

Multidimensionality of constructs is important for contextual theories of intelligence for it emphasizes that (1) there are multiple aspects of intelligence, (2) these aspects may be both independent and interrelated, and (3) some of these aspects may include quite practical and functional forms of intelligence. In addition, identifying separate but related dimensions of constructs allows for the analysis of differential trajectories of change across dimensions of a single construct. This ramification is central to the next major feature.

Multidirectionality of change

If there are multiple dimensions of constructs, then there may be individual differences in performance on each of these dimensions at one point in time. Numerous theories of intelligence have addressed this important issue.

Contextual approaches to intellectual development focus, as well, on the individual differences that occur in the trajectory of change of any one of these dimensions across the life-span. The description of such individual differences in development is an important goal of contextual researchers. For explanation, contextual researchers might consider unique life histories of events and activities, as well as specific constellations of sociohistorical and educational experiences.

In research on intellectual development in adulthood, an important issue is the extent to which there is decline in functioning with advancing age (e.g., Botwinick, 1977; Schaie, 1983). This feature of contextualism relates to the decline issue in that some dimensions of intelligence may not decline as rapidly or inevitably as others. For example, whereas crystallized intelligence (or the pragmatics of intelligence) may be maintained into late life, fluid intelligence (or the mechanics of intelligence) may show more of the classic decline pattern (Baltes et al., 1984). The multidirectionality of change is evident when multiple aspects (or dimensions) of intelligence are considered independently.

Ecological representativeness

The importance of examining practical and adaptive aspects of psychological functioning was emphasized by early contextual philosophers and functional psychologists. In many contemporary contextual approaches this issue continues to guide some theoretical and empirical work. One way in which this interest is manifested in contemporary research in intellectual aging is encapsulated in the term *ecological representativeness*. At its most basic, the notion is to investigate the extent to which it is necessary to incorporate research on ecologically relevant forms of cognitive activity into theories of life-span intellectual development. It is a thorny theoretical problem to decide what forms of cognitve activity are in fact "ecologically relevant," and it is a complicated methodological problem to devise unique ways to measure those forms.

Frequently, researchers focus on the ecological representativeness of tasks. The extent to which the tasks presented to adults represent the cognitive activities of daily living is of concern to some researchers who have been influenced by contextual thinking. *Represent* is perhaps the key word. On the one hand, it is apparent that the tasks presented to adults do not have to be exactly the same tasks – have exactly the same surface structure – that they encounter in everyday life. It has not been demonstrated that such a strict criterion of ecological representativeness purchases much theoretical understanding. On the other hand, it is possible that a complete understanding of cognitive changes in adulthood cannot be accomplished without serious attention to the processes and conditions represented in activities in which people engage in the course of adapting to everyday cognitive demands, or solving problems in professional or leisure pursuits (Ceci & Liker, 1986; Charness, 1989).

As Schaie (1987) points out, competent performance in different cognitive situations may require unique combinations of intellectual abilities. If intelligence reflects cognitive adaptation, then shifting some attention to adaptation to nonacademic environments may be useful. In some research, practical intelligence has been indicated by performance on tasks involving everyday activities (e.g., Cavanaugh, Kramer, Sinott, Camp, & Markley, 1985; Willis & Schaie, 1986). This point about the usefulness of investigating ecologically representative processes and conditions leads to the fourth major feature of contextualism in practice, and that is an explicit consideration of the role of experience in cognitive aging.

The role of experience

If cognitive testing were done primarily with academic tasks, then educational experience might be the primary experiential contributor to individual differences in performance. If cognitive adaptation to nonacademic environments is investigated, then nonacademic (even specialized) experience may play a critical role in predicting performance (e.g., Ceci & Liker, 1986; Scribner, 1986). This is of no small concern to researchers in cognitive aging (e.g., Charness, 1989; Salthouse, 1987). Whereas most intelligence tests are somewhat academic in nature (Labouvie-Vief, 1985; Willis & Schaie, 1986), most cognitively demanding activities in which mature adults engage are not oriented to formal educational demands. Of course, as was alluded to in the preceding section, this lack of similarity in surface structure of tasks does not necessarily invalidate standardized intelligence testing. Nevertheless, familiarity with test item content and testing procedures may be associated with performance (Cornelius, 1984).

Researchers interested in intellectual aging have begun to investigate the role that experience or practice with particular tasks plays in age-related performance differences (e.g., Denney, 1982; Willis, 1985). For example, in the problem-solving literature, there is some evidence that performance on everyday (experience-related) problem-solving tasks increases with advancing age, whereas performance on traditional problem-solving tasks declines (e.g., Cornelius & Caspi, 1987). More generally, considerable evidence pertaining to the role experience plays in cognitive performance has accumulated. When experience is considered – for example, when domains of cognitive functioning in which adults of many ages have considerable practice or expertise – older adults are not necessarily inferior performers. Hence, a critical issue is the extent to which observed individual differences reflect (1) age (or cohort) effects and (2) experience effects (Salthouse,

1987). If they reflect to a significant extent experience effects, then the exceptions to the classic decline pattern of intellectual aging may be even more numerous and, more important, theoretically coherent.

One additional implication of the role of experience in intellectual aging is noteworthy. As mentioned, if tested in domains in which they have a lifetime of practice and experience, older adults may perform at a level that indicates some maintenance of skill. Is it possible to engineer such experience in unfamiliar domains (Denney, 1982; Kliegl & Baltes, 1987)? Although the evidence is mixed, there is some suggestion that if older adults are given experience in domains in which they have little if any practice, they may improve their performance markedly (e.g., Baltes & Willis, 1982), though not to the same level and with the same robustness as younger adults (Kliegl, Smith, & Baltes, 1990). Such findings would indicate some plasticity, which is the fifth emphasis of contextual psychology I mention.

Developmental plasticity   — improvement may be possible

If differences in experience play a role in observed age differences in performance on intelligence tests, then experimentally manipulating pertinent experience should result in attenuated age differences. For intelligence test performance, providing educational experiences – for example, training in ability-specific skills or sheer practice – for older adults may result in attenuated age differences. The existence of developmental plasticity – or at least improvement on intelligence tests – on the part of older adults can be demonstrated (Baltes & Willis, 1982; Willis, 1985). That age-related decline in performance can be at least temporarily reversed suggests that the classic aging decline pattern may reflect more age-related performance differences than competence differences (Kliegl & Baltes, 1987). That is, some older adults may have considerable capacity for further learning in both (1) areas of current expertise and (2) areas of former (or even no) expertise, such as fluid intelligence tests. This is consistent with the notion incorporated into contextual approaches that the human organism is a constructive, active agent interacting with a constructive, active environment (see Rosnow & Georgoudi, 1986). Plasticity is an issue of considerable importance to contextual approaches (Baltes, 1987; Lerner, 1984).

Summary

These five features of contextualism are neither exhaustive nor exclusive. I have selected them because of their relevance to intellectual aging, and more complete accounts of the theoretical assumptions of contextualism may be found elsewhere. The five features also do not distinguish completely this approach from other approaches to intelligence. These features are, however, a family of emphases that typify much contextual work in cognitive aging. Specific research projects, of course, would not be addressed to all of these issues, but there are programmatic research projects devoted to a variety of combinations of them.

It is important to note that contextual approaches to intellectual development in adulthood do not normally attempt to sever their methodological and theoretical connections to neighboring models or theories. For example, research on the cognitive or affective contexts of intellectual performance may be conducted with contextual issues in mind, but using appropriate experimental or psychometric techniques (e.g., Cornelius & Caspi, 1987; Lachman, 1983). This borrowing from neighboring approaches may not be so common in contextual work in intellectual development in children (Wertsch & Kanner, this volume). As it has been applied thus far, contextualism offers less a new theory of adult intellectual development than a new set of questions, issues, and emphases. In the next section we consider what is known about intellectual aging and how contextualism can supplement this knowledge.

Contextualism and cognitive aging

As might be expected from the foregoing discussion of the five features of contextualism, two of the prominent issues in cognitive aging continue to be (1) the extent to which there are exceptions to the rule of aging-related decline and (2) the degree of theoretical coherence available for interpreting these exceptions. The fact of considerable decline in many aspects of cognition is clear (e.g., Botwinick, 1977; Craik, 1977; Hultsch & Dixon, 1990; Schaie, 1990). Indeed, this fact has been called the "classic aging" or "general decrement" pattern. Some empirical and anecdotal evidence regarding exceptions to this pattern have been accumulating. What are the conditions under which exceptions can be observed?

First, because of multidimensionality, not all aspects of cognition "age" alike. Some performance levels are maintained at a relatively high level even on psychometric tests until relatively late in life (Perlmutter, 1988; Schaie, 1983). Especially likely to be maintained until late life is performance on crystallized intelligence tests (particularly vocabulary ability). Possibly because of continued experience with words and their meanings, and because of low demands typically placed in such tasks on processes that undergo aging-related decline (e.g., these tasks are typically not performed under time pressure), older adults perform at a relatively high level (see Salthouse, 1988). Shifting the focus from standardized vocabulary tests to the contextual issue of ecological relevance is, in this instance, instructive.

Other aspects of cognitive performance may not "age" (read: decline) for the same reasons that vocabulary ability may be spared. That is, experience or continued practice with them may support their continued efficient expression into late life. Thus, processes and activities that involve one's expertise may also be spared, barring significant pathological change. Research in this area has provided some empirical examples of maintenance of performance (e.g., Charness, 1989; Salthouse, 1987). These empirical examples lend some indirect credence to the often mentioned anecdotal cases of older people who are outstanding diplomats, social problem-solvers, wise personal advice givers, productive executives, accomplished musicians, creative writers, and active scientists (Perlmutter, 1988). I address this question again in a subsequent section.

For now, it is sufficient to report that numerous authors have chosen to emphasize either the absence or late onset of decline (e.g., Schaie, 1983) or even the potentially progressive nature of some seeming age-decrements (e.g., Labouvie-Vief, 1985). The discussion of relative gains and losses is one example of this (Baltes, 1987; Uttal & Perlmutter, 1989). According to this discussion, it is conceivable that gains in some aspects of intelligence may "compensate" for decrements in others. Unfortunately, although an appreciation of the dynamic relationship between gains and losses in intellectual aging is critical, relatively little theoretical and empirical work has been directed at this developing relationship and the compensation that it may, in select cases, imply. In this section I describe further this notion of compensation and present some research on its potential role in cognitive aging.

Compensation in intellectual aging

The concept of compensation is frequently used by researchers associated with contextual approaches to research on intellectual aging (e.g., Baltes, 1987). Indeed, this concept is related to each of the five features of contextualism already described. As is consistent with a contextual view of development (Dixon & Baltes, 1986; Lerner, 1986), a key focus is on the changing (and interactive) relationship between developing (or aging) skills and changing contextual demands. As we shall see, deficits occur both (1) when a person's skill declines as a function of advancing age, and (2) when a person's skill is actually maintained but the demands of the context have increased substantially. As a potentially adaptive response, compensation may occur in either case. With respect to the five features I have sketched, compensation relies on both a multidimensional representation of intelligence and the premise that multiple directions of intellectual change are possible. Simply put, the principle is that some aspects of intelligence may decline while other, spared aspects may serve to compensate for this decline. In addition, an expectation is that experience and practice in particular skill domains are often (but not necessarily) associated with the tendency to compensate (e.g., Salthouse, 1987).

selective optimization w/ compensation — SOC

According to Bäckman and Dixon (in press), the basic principle of compensation is as follows: Compensation can be inferred when an objective or perceived mismatch (usually a deficit) between accessible skills and contextual demands is counterbalanced by utilization of a latent skill (or component thereof) or acquisition of a new skill (or component thereof), such that performance levels are maintained or even surpass "normal" levels of proficiency. Further elaboration of this definition, including a review of theories of compensation (Bäckman & Dixon, in press) and its application to cognitive aging (Dixon & Bäckman, in press) is available elsewhere. Several potential compensatory mechanisms in cognitive aging have been described in the literature. Although this is a relatively new literature, there are even some conceptual treatments regarding how they are acquired and deployed in adulthood.

One of these treatments is offered in several publications by Baltes (Baltes, 1987; Baltes & Baltes, 1990; Baltes et al., 1984), who uses the expression *selective optimization with compensation* (SOC). This term refers to the process whereby adult age-related decrements in the mechanics of intelligence – for instance, reasoning and other fluid intelligence indicators – are compensated by age-related gains in the pragmatics of intelligence, which is the context-related application of the mechanics of intelligence. Baltes (1987) describes SOC as follows: Cognitive aging is characterized by gains (e.g., growth in specialized procedural and declarative knowledge systems) as well as losses (e.g., reduction in reserve capacity for high levels of fluid functioning).

Compensation can occur through (1) channeling one's efforts into a select number of domains or (2) developing substitutable mechanisms. The increased selection and reduction of domains of activity are referred to as "selective optimization." The assumption is that it is more likely that aging individuals can perform at high levels when a reduced – and tailored – number of domains must be supported by continued practice. Although it is an appealing perspective, research support is not yet available. Observers (e.g., Uttal & Perlmutter, 1989) have suggested ways in which these issues could be addressed empirically.

The second way in which compensation can occur, developing a substitutable mechanism, is the focus of a methodologically sophisticated model of compensation. Following Charness (1979, 1981, 1989), Salthouse (1987) elucidated the molar equivalence–molecular decomposition (ME–MD) strategy for investigating the relationship between experience and aging. Salthouse began the explication of this model by noting the discrepancy in performance by older adults between laboratory settings (in which they typically perform poorly) and real-life contexts (in which some older adults perform some tasks at a competent, if not expert, level). He argued that it was critical to investigate the extent to which this lab–life discrepancy for older adults is attributable to a parallel discrepancy between tasks that are unpracticed versus practiced or unfamiliar versus familiar. If it is a question of experience with the content or procedures of a task, then observed age effects may reflect as much experience differences as true aging differences. This conclusion is consistent with the principles of contextualism already outlined.

The ME–MD strategy has been used to examine empirically the aging of such experience-related, cognitively complex skills as chess, bridge, and typing (Charness, 1989). It begins with the assumption that the successful performance of a cognitive skill is accomplished via a finite set of molecular components. Performance of even relatively simple psychomotor skills, such as typing, depends on the effective functioning of such molecular skills as finger tapping and eye–hand coordination. Molar equivalence refers to the requirement that the correlation between age and the molar skill performance be close to zero. For example, in examining compensation in typing, Salthouse (1984) ensured that there were no systematic age differences in performance by younger and older professional typists. In the absence of such age differences, the research task becomes one of identifying age-related differences in the molecular components of the molar skill. Some molecular components of complex cognitive skills – for example, those similar to fluid intelligence measures – typically decline with advancing age. If the molar skill is being maintained into old age at a high level despite the fact that some molecular components of that skill are declining, then there may be alternative molecular components supporting the molar performance. Molecular decomposition refers to the identification of specific molecular components of the molar skill. Given that the sample of younger and older adults perform at an equivalent level on the molar skill, the ME–MD strategy allows the researcher to identify the extent to which the subjects are relying on the same (or different) molecular components.

According to this model, compensation occurs when there is an age-related decline in the components typically used to perform the molar skill and a counterbalancing increase in at least one substitutable component. This substitution is illustrated in Figure 13.1. As seen in the figure, although the typical molecular components are declining with advancing age, an age-related increase in the compensatory mechanism allows the molar competency to be maintained into late life.

The ME–MD strategy represents an important step forward in research and theory in compensation and intellectual aging. Indeed, it opens up the possibility of investigating empirically the extent to which this form of compensation actually occurs in a variety of domains of intellectual aging. This research can contribute directly to the conceptual treatments of compensation (e.g., Bäckman & Dixon, in press; Baltes, 1987; Gillund & Perlmutter, 1988). In addition, the debate about the potential role of experience in intellectual aging can now be sharpened; there is a conceptual

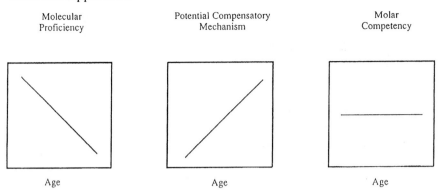

Figure 13.1. The molar equivalence–molecular decomposition strategy for compensation research of Salthouse (1987) and Charness (1989).

difference between experience contributing (1) to the maintenance of typical molecular components and (2) to the emergence of new compensatory mechanisms (Bäckman & Dixon, in press). This difference between the two contributions of experience is important even if both of them result in continued skilled performance. Taken together, the Baltes (1987) and the Salthouse (1987) approaches widen our conceptual understanding of, and the empirical possibilities for investigating, compensation in intellectual aging.

Bäckman and Dixon (in press) reviewed these and other approaches, commenting specifically on the current state of research on the origins, mechanisms, and forms of compensation. Although not addressing contextual approaches to cognitive aging explicitly, the issues they identified point to the critical ways in which compensation is a concept of considerable importance to this area. If compensation was confined to just the Baltes (1987) SOC or Salthouse (1987) ME–MD models, it would still be an important concept to contextually oriented cognitive aging researchers. The more detailed consideration of the origins, mechanisms, and forms of compensation, however, reveals just how contextual a concept it is.

As described earlier, the researcher interested in investigating compensation must begin by attending to the relationship between the psychological skills of an individual and the performance demands of the context. An inherent and key focus is on the changing (and interactive) relationship between developing (or aging) skills (and components thereof) and changing contextual demands. It is worth underscoring that compensation is not required exclusively when skills decline and the contextual demands remain unchanged (as is implied in Figure 13.1). It may also be required under a number of other possible combinations of changes in skills and demands across the life course. It is possible, for example, that some older adults may maintain a high level of performance on an intellectually challenging skill (e.g., in their profession or hobbies) but, because of changes in the context of performance, still experience a deficit vis-à-vis their expected performance level. Changes in the context of performance that may increase demands on older individuals include technological advances in a profession and improved competition in a leisure activity. With aging, shifting ratios of contextual demands, contextual support, and cognitive skills create a variety of opportunities for compensation to occur, as well as a variety of potential forms of compensation (Bäckman, 1989).

As both Baltes (1987) and Salthouse (1987) pointed out, there is more than one mechanism of compensation. Bäckman and Dixon (in press) described two categories for these mechanisms. The most common definition is compensation as substitution, the category that is the target of the ME–MD procedure. Although the contextual demands and one's expected level of performance remain at parallel levels across time, a need for compensation arises by a decline in a skill (or in the molecular components thereof). The associated mechanism of compensation involves an increase in a substitutable skill (or substitutable components). Compensation is achieved when the overall performance again matches the level of environmental demand and one's expectations.

The second mechanism of compensation is less frequently included in treatments of the concept, and may be more controversial, but may have particular relevance in normal successful aging. Although the contextual demands and expected performance remain at parallel levels across time, the skill may either decline or fail to increase at the same pace as the contextual demands. Compensation in this case could involve decreasing one's expected level of performance, whatever the contextual demands. In this way, a personally satisfactory, although not objectively maintained, degree of match between contextual demands and performance is attained (Bäckman & Dixon, in press).

Both mechanisms – but perhaps especially the second – reveal another important contextually related aspect of compensation. In intellectual aging, processes of compensation may involve at least some degree of assessment or initial awareness of complex interactions among one's own skill level, one's own expected level of performance, and contextual demands. It also suggests the importance of considering the extent to which aging adults may be aware of the shifting relation between skills and demands, and the need and availability of compensatory mechanisms.

Awareness and compensation with cognitive aids

To what extent are young and old adults knowledgeable about the operation of cognitive processes, and to what degree are they aware of their own cognitive functioning? Knowledge and awareness of cognition are known generally as "metacognition." It is evident from the metacognition literature that older adults are knowledgeable about cognitive processes such as memory (e.g., Hultsch, Hertzog, & Dixon, 1987). They are often also aware of their own declining cognitive resources (e.g., Cavanaugh, 1989; Dixon, 1989; Gilewski & Zelinski, 1986; Lachman, 1983). Indeed, older adults frequently evaluate themselves as cognitively less competent than (1) younger adults are and (2) they themselves were when they were younger (e.g., Cornelius & Caspi, 1986). Some older adults who are knowledgeable about cognitive processes, and who perceive their own cognitive skills as in decline, may more carefully monitor their everyday cognitive performance, and produce strategies designed to maintain a relatively high level of functioning. Such older adults are potential compensators; they stand in contrast to the older adult who may perceive the experienced decline as inevitable and uncontrollable and hence reduce their expectations and effort, thereby limiting their performance (Lachman, Steinberg, & Trotter, 1987).

Perhaps the simplest form of compensation available to older adults who are experiencing difficulty in everyday remembering tasks is the use of memory aids. Specifically, older adults might compensate for memory deficits by using strategies that either improve the efficiency with which their memory functions or relieve them of some memory demands while not sacrificing memory performance. In this way, use of memory aids contributes to continued cognitive adaptation to the contexts of life. Whereas relatively internal memory mnemonic techniques (such as method of loci or rhyming) are examples of the first alternative, use of physical or external memory aids (such as writing notes in a calendar or leaving something in an obvious place) is an example of the second.

Research has indicated the breadth of normal older adults' capacity to acquire and use internal mnemonics (see Yesavage, Lapp, & Sheikh, 1989). For example, Kliegl and Baltes (1987) trained older adults in the method of loci; these adults were able to recall an impressive number of words and digits using this system. The paradigm these researchers employed allows for virtually complete control over the growing expertise and any possible compensatory mechanisms that might be used. Despite this obvious experimental benefit, the mnemonic systems actually trained may be somewhat domain-specific. Such specificity may limit their usefulness, at least to typical older adults in everyday memory problems. Using external memory aids, on the other hand, requires little training, and such use is generalizable to a variety of real-world memory tasks.

Some research has been directed at discovering the extent to which younger and older adults report using internal mnemonics or external aids in everyday life. Harris's (1980) study of memory aids revealed that in his two groups (university students and housewives) external memory aids (such as shopping lists, timers, and address books) were more frequently used than internal memory aids. Two early studies of memory aid use in adults of all ages (Dixon & Hultsch, 1983; Perlmutter, 1978) found no reliable age differences for scales combining internal and external aids. The former study, however, described two nonsignificant trends: (1) Older adults reported more use of external memory aids than younger adults, and (2) younger adults reported more use of internal mnemonics than older adults. Cavanaugh, Grady, and Perlmutter (1983) reported similar results, and interpreted them in terms of compensation, an interpretation consistent with that of Dixon and Hultsch (1983). Dobbs and Rule (1987), however, found that the reported use of memory aids is greatest in middle age (age 40–49 years), and the older adults in their sample actually reported less frequent use. Similarly, Hultsch et al. (1987) found (in one of two samples) evidence that use of memory strategies was greatest for 50-year-olds, and declined thereafter.

Results such as those of Dobbs and Rule (1987) and Hultsch et al. (1987) could render problematic a straightforward compensation interpretation. Indeed, Dobbs and Rule suggested that the context of middle age encourages the use of external memory aids more than does the context of old age. In a recent study, Loewen, Shaw, and Craik (1990) found significant age effects in the same direction as the nonsignificant trends observed by Dixon and Hultsch (1983). As Loewen et al. point out, if there is indeed a shift with advancing age toward the use of external memory aids, it may be due to compensatory efforts or to changes in the contextual demands on memory. That is, younger adults (especially the student sample in Loewen et al., 1990) require more frequently than older adults the use of internal encoding strategies. Older adults, on the other hand, may actually avoid the use of such strategies, either because they are difficult to acquire and implement or because they are less effective for the memory-demanding situations of their lives. Although Loewen et al. suggest further research to disentangle the two interpretations – that is, aging-related compensation and life-style memory demands – it is possible to argue that both alternatives involve compensation, at least as we have defined it above (Bäckman & Dixon, in press). In any event, both alternatives reflect contextual considerations in cognitive aging.

External aids are concrete, practical, easy to learn and use, and efficient. For memory problems, old adults report using them frequently, and in some studies more frequently than younger adults. Memory plays a role in a variety of laboratory and everyday problems. As this memory load may become increasingly taxing with aging (Rabbitt, 1977; Salthouse, Legg, Palmon, & Mitchell, 1990), it is fitting that older adults use physical aids and reminders. One frequently used form of external memory and problem-solving aids has been largely ignored in the aging literature. This form is simply other people; teachers, colleagues, friends, spouses, even strangers are often asked to help solve a perplexing cognitive problem. Questions such as the following are designed to elicit assistance from an external (human) aid: (1) asking teachers for assistance in understanding the logic behind a complicated problem, (2) asking colleagues to demonstrate how they solved an analogous problem, (3) asking friends for advice about child rearing or gardening, (4) asking a spouse to help you remember to make a phone call in the morning, and (5) asking a stranger for assistance in finding a location or reading a roadmap.

In each of these cases, one is seeking to use an external aid to solve a problem, whether a memory or logical problem. In the child development literature, the role of tutors, teachers, and colleagues has been studied more frequently than in the aging literature. In part, this research has employed Vygotsky's notion of the zone of proximal development. In the social cognition literature, there is a long tradition of research on the role of collaborators in solving a variety of cognitive problems. In the next section, I describe the rationale for studying this phenomenon in intellectual aging. Subsequently, I describe briefly two related research projects on this topic.

Cognitive performance in a group context

A contextual approach to intellectual development?

I have indicated that some research suggests that one typical means of compensating for individual-level cognitive decrement could be through the use of problem-solving or memory aids. Such aids can include mnemonic devices or external aids. In whatever form, they serve (1) to reduce the cognitive complexity or demands of remembering and reasoning problems and (2) to increase the probability of successful performance. Such aids can be static and passive in the sense of calendars or notes to oneself, or they can be active and dynamic in the sense of other people (e.g., asking a spouse to remind one of an impending appointment). In a recent set of studies I have explored the extent to which one important variety of external cognitive aids could be other people (e.g., friends, family members, colleagues). This research is directed at the extent to which older adults use other people to compensate for age-related decrements in cognitive functioning.

To what extent is the study of cognitive performance in social settings an example of a contextual approach to intellectual aging? To answer this question, one might begin by comparing the characteristics of studies of collaborative intellectual performance with the features of contextualism described earlier in the chapter. I am suggesting that such studies may be consistent with a contextual approach at a general theoretical level. For example, they focus on (1) one typical context of cognitive performance in everyday life (in social or group settings); (2) cognitive adaptation, at least in the sense of the use of strategies and aids; and (3) the use of such aids as potential compensatory mechanisms. Let us now turn to the question of the procedural consistency of such studies. The five features of contextual approaches I identified earlier can be considered.

It bears emphasis that a contextual study of collaborative cognition and aging would not necessarily employ tasks and procedures unique to contextualism. Rather, the researcher would seek tasks in which individuals could combine their cognitive resources with those of other individuals (e.g., using interpersonal cues and aids). In principle, this could include virtually all tasks and tests of multidimensional theories of intelligence (e.g., Horn, 1982). In this way, then, tasks and procedures would not have to be designed uniquely for contextual collaborative studies (although they might have to be tailored for group administration). Unlike in other legitimate approaches to contextual study of intellectual aging (e.g., Cornelius & Caspi, 1987; Denney & Pearce, 1989), there would be no need to develop specifically practical intelligence, everyday problem-solving, or social cognition tasks. From this perspective, it is actually beneficial for some work to be done using tasks for which there is a great deal of information about performance by individual young and old adults. Thus, the tasks could be adapted from batteries previously used in cognitive aging research. Tasks of interest would include simple free recall of digits (forward and backward), recall of common nouns, remembering complex personal narratives, solving logical and practical problems, and remembering world facts. With few exceptions, these are tasks in which groups of older individuals – whether in intelligence tests or cognitive experiments – have typically performed worse than groups of younger individuals. Because of this age-related expected deficit, it may be possible to observe compensation through the use of human cognitive aids.

Thus, one point of overlap is that the tasks may indeed parallel those used by theorists proposing multidimensional theories of intelligence. Among the multiple cognitive tasks it would help to employ both fluid and crystallized tasks. It is not necessary, however, to represent thoroughly and explicitly these domains. A second point of overlap is that although age-related decrements are observed on most of these tasks, for some of them some maintenance or even improvement may be observed. For example, performance on world information memory may improve with advancing age (Camp, 1989). Having tasks that vary in the extent to which age decrements are commonly observed provides a variety of opportunities for compensatory behaviors to emerge.

Third, the tasks need not be exceptionally ecologically representative; they need not be typical for practical intelligence or practical problem-solving tasks (Demming & Pressey, 1957; Denney & Pearce, 1989; Willis & Schaie, 1986), although these, too, would be of interest. I have been involved in some studies where the tasks have included story recall as well as storytelling, problem solving, and autobiographical memory, but where there has been no deliberate effort to transport the surface structure of real-world tasks into the laboratory. It is also not necessary to move testing immediately into the real world.

Fourth, if typical intelligence tasks can be used – and if it is, in fact, beneficial to begin with such tasks – to what extent is the role of experience incorporated into these studies? The most immediate answer must be that domain-specific experience or knowledge plays no greater a role in these studies than in scores of other cognitive aging studies. Indeed, no manipulation, or even consideration, of prior knowledge of the content or procedures involved in the tasks is necessarily attempted. Although domain-specific experience is not involved in my own recent studies, an important – and often neglected – aspect of everyday cognitive experience certainly is. For example, in a collaborative story-recall study (Gould, Trevithick, & Dixon, 1991) we did not consider the extent to which our adults had prior experience with the content of the stories, but adults obviously have a great deal of experience collaborating with other people in remembering personal narratives, a common activity among family members and friends. Such experience may not be manipulated in a collaborative cognition study, but it would be important to allow it to emerge and to explicitly measure its influence. In this way, the ecological relevance of collaborative cognition studies is not so much in the characteristics of the tasks themselves as in the context of performance.

The fifth major feature of contextual approaches is plasticity. In the sense of changes across trials, plasticity may certainly be an active concern of collaborative cognition studies. Age and group differences in adjustments and strategy use would be of interest. In the sense of training, however, plasticity plays a minimal role in the design of most collaborative cognition studies. In a later section, however, I mention at least one way in which individual cognitive training may be an important model for some collaborative work to pursue.

Collaboration in cognitive tasks

We have seen that the investigation of collaborative or group cognition can be an example of contextual research in intellectual aging. In this section, I describe (1) how such work is conducted and (2) some highlights of recent results. Although a growing emphasis in such areas as developmental, social and cognitive psychology, social cognition in adulthood and aging has been underexplored (Roodin & Rybash, 1985). Among the major ways to conceptualize social cognition are the following: It is cognition in social situations or directed at solving social or life problems. Whereas the second kind of social cognition has received some attention in aging research (e.g., Denney & Pearce, 1989), the first has received little empirical attention (Scribner, 1984). Both may be approached from a contextual perspective. The first, however, often involves research on collaborative or group performance.

Collaborative cognition – one form of social cognition as defined here – involves individual and group performance of standard laboratory cognitive tasks. Two issues are of equivalent concern, namely, the quantity or level of performance and the quality or style of performance. In this paradigm, one would investigate not only the level at which various ages and group compositions perform, but also the way in which they achieve their performance levels. The latter aspect involves social intelligence, or the skill at recognizing and using the preferences and resources of other people.

There is indeed a large literature on group psychology, one that is far beyond the range of the current chapter (see McGrath, 1984; Paulus, 1989; Shaw, 1976; Steiner, 1972). According to this literature, groups are defined in terms of dynamic social (occasionally goal-directed) interactions, involving two or more individuals who are mutually influential. In the literature on group psychology, there is a long tradition of studying groups charged with engaging in productive cognitive behavior, for example, reaching decisions, solving problems, and remembering information (e.g., Bales & Strodtbeck, 1951; Middleton & Edwards, 1990a; Paulus, 1989; Williams & Sternberg, 1988). Critical issues in this literature have included (1) whether the productivity of the group exceeds that of individuals, (2) whether the productivity of the group exceeds that of the same number of individuals working independently, (3) the relations between group size and productivity, and (4) the dynamics through which group members assemble their resources and allocate their efforts (e.g., Hill, 1982; Steiner, 1972).

Tasks that are similar to those of intelligence tests, cognitive batteries, or everyday problem-solving inventories have been used in the group psychology literature. For example, group performance in problem-solving tasks was investigated in early studies by several researchers (e.g., Bales & Strodtbeck, 1951; Taylor, 1954; Thomas & Fink, 1961) and more recently by Williams and Sternberg (1988). Similarly, group performance in memory tasks has been investigated by many authors, some focusing on materials with little meaning (e.g., Hoppe, 1962; Perlmutter & de Montmollin, 1952; Ryack, 1965). More recently, collaborative memory performance has been investigated for meaningful, everyday materials such as prose, conversations, testimony, and films (e.g., Clark & Stephenson, 1989; Clark, Stephenson, & Kniveton, 1990; Edwards & Middleton, 1986b; Middleton & Edwards, 1990b). This latter trend is said to be related to the early work of

Bartlett (1932), an English psychologist often cited as a predecessor to contemporary contextual approaches to psychology (Edwards & Middleton, 1986a).

Four issues should be noted about the work on collaborative cognition. First, this work has shown that indeed in some (but not all) conditions, groups perform at a highly productive level (but not necessarily at a mathematically predicted optimal level). Second, this work has been largely independent of parallel work in child developmental psychology, especially that informed by the theories of Vygotsky (see Wertsch & Kanner, this volume). Third, this research has included tasks similar to those in a variety of intelligence and cognitive batteries, although not drawn directly from them. Fourth, although there is a very large literature of collaborative cognition studies, there is virtually no work focusing on research questions pertaining to intellectual aging and potential compensation. The reviews or studies just mentioned were almost uniformly conducted with young adults (usually college students), although some have a wider range of ages in their samples (e.g., Williams & Sternberg, 1988). With these issues in mind, it is apparent that contextual research on collaborative cognition and aging deserves further attention.

Collaborative cognition and aging: A research example

For this chapter, I have selected two illustrative tasks, chosen because of their similarity to tests associated with each of two dimensions of two prominent (and, in this regard, similar) theories of intellectual aging. The two theories are Horn's (1982) fluid and crystallized intelligence model, and the mechanics–pragmatics perspective of Baltes et al. (1984). The first task, digit recall, is similar to fluid and mechanics intelligence tasks. The second task, world fact memory, may arguably tap crystallized and pragmatics intelligence.

Notes on procedures. Details of the procedures and results for both illustrative tasks may be found in Dixon, Friesen, and Kurzman (1991). The digit recall task was adapted for group presentation. Four lists of 20 digits were randomly generated and presented to the participants via audiotape at regular intervals. Whereas for the first two lists participants were instructed to recall the digits in the order in which they heard them, for the last two lists the task was to recall the digits backward from the last digit they heard. In this chapter, I summarize only the results of the first two lists (i.e., remembering digits in their correct forward order). World knowledge or fact memory was measured via 40 trivia questions from the list of 300 compiled by Nelson and Narens (1980). As with the collaborative research already described, for both tasks we were interested in not only how many digits or facts they remembered but also the number of errors they made, the extent to which the groups performed better than individuals did, and how the individuals in groups worked together to remember the information. In addition, of fundamental interest were the patterns of performance for young and old adults.

Participants in the studies were 168 young ($n = 84$; M age = 24.3 years) and old ($n = 84$; M age = 67.9 years) adults who were randomly assigned to three group-size conditions: (1) individuals, (2) dyads (two participants), or (3) tetrads (four participants). Each same-age, same-sex group was tested separately, and, after first receiving practice in responding aloud, their responses were videotaped. Participants in the dyads and tetrads were unacquainted with one another. We chose to construct groups from unacquainted same-age and same-sex individuals so that we could minimize systematic effects of social power and persuasiveness. (In later studies, we examined collaborative cognition in dyads with substantial interactive experience.)

Remembering digits. Remembering digits in a particular order is not a task frequently practiced by adults in their daily lives. This lack of ecological relevance is an advantage, for we chose this task specifically to represent a dimension of intelligence that is characterized as being relatively content free. It should be emphasized that for the vast majority of young and old adults, this is a difficult task. Without special mnemonic training, few adults typically remember more than about 7 digits in the correct order. In remembering digits in the correct forward order, we expected and found that the individuals working alone recalled an average of about 6 digits in each of the two trials. The number of correctly recalled digits increased for both young and old adults with the addition of collaborators. Overall, dyads recalled about 10 digits, and tetrads recalled about 15 in each of the trials. Although beginning at somewhat different absolute levels as individuals, the zone in which collaborating young and old adults can improve in a fluid, intelligencelike task is relatively large. To illustrate, the top performances by the young dyads and tetrads was a perfect 20 out of 20 digits. The top performances by the old dyads and tetrads was 19 out of 20.

After finding that young and old adults accomplish substantial improvement in a social context, the next issue becomes the strategies of using social resources to accomplish such improvement. At a gross level, it is instructive to look first at how much time was spent on the task. Old adults did not spend more time than young adults on this task. All subjects spent more time on the first trial than on the second, without sacrificing recall performance, which suggests that they became more efficient with brief practice. In fact, the old adults decreased their time spent on the task more dramatically than the young adults. Hence, a key issue is that of how old adults could be more effective than young adults, not in terms of how much they remember per se but in terms of reducing the amount of time it takes to recall the same number of digits the second time around.

There are many possible measures of the qualitative characteristics of the actual interactions in the group contexts. In the dyads and tetrads, both the younger and older adults performed at a level of considerable expertise. They evidently use their collaborators as external memory aids, as had been predicted. One question to be addressed by a qualitative analysis concerns the process through which old (and young) adults collaborated on a difficult task so that they were able to attain a collective expert level. Among the major process variables are the following three: (1) strategies, that is, spontaneously produced strategies for maximizing recall performance; (2) negotiations, or discussions about how strategies could be implemented or which responses were correct; and (3) elaborations, or statements that are relevant to the task (or one's performance at the task) but are not recall, strategies, or negotiations. The results indicated that for each of these variables young and old adults performed differently across the dyadic and tetradic conditions.

Relatively few strategies were produced by the young and old dyads and tetrads. These strategies, however, were effective and made use of the human resources available. Their effectiveness, particularly for old adults, is indicated by a substantial correlation between number of strategies produced and number of digits recalled ($r = .3$ for young, $r = .5$ for old). A prominent strategy for both age groups was to divide up the 20 digits into manageable sets, with each individual in the group remembering one set. Some older dyads divided the digits in a given list into smaller sets, recognizing their individual limitations, whereas others tried to recall 10 (of the 20) each. In one older tetrad, one individual spoke of what really should be done to remember such information: "I write the numbers down to keep them in my mind." It is an oxymoron, but apt.

The dyads and tetrads negotiated primarily in the recall phases, and usually about the correct order of a set of digits. Whereas more such negotiations occurred for young dyads than for old dyads, the old tetrads negotiated their responses more than the young tetrads did. The number of negotiations produced was negatively correlated with recall for the young adults ($r = -.4$) but positively correlated for the old adults ($r = .5$). Representative comments include the following: "Was it 48 or 84?" At the conclusion of one older tetrad's testing, the following exchange was observed: "Have you guys learned something today?" "Yes, cooperation." "Yes, gang up." Unlike the elaborations observed in some other collaborative cognition studies (e.g., Gould et al., 1991), the elaborative comments in this study were just that – mostly commentary. Although young and old dyads, as well as older tetrads, produced an equivalent amount of elaborations, young tetrads generated relatively little commentary. In some previous narrative recall studies, elaborations have served as a functional retrieval structure (Adams, Labouvie-Vief, Hobart, & Dorosz, 1990; Gould et al., 1991). The comments observed with these materials were frequently about the difficulty of the task (e.g., "Five I can manage, but 20 . . ." and "I don't think Einstein could do that"). They included words of despair, joy at success, and congratulations for well-done jobs. One person offered the following concluding observation: "I'm a great believer in writing numbers down." (In examining the videotapes closely, we later discovered that he did occasionally seem to be making notes to himself.)

In sum, the young and the old adults accomplished their effective recall performance by using previously unknown collaborators in a strategic and cooperative manner. From dyads to tetrads, young adults decreased their use of elaborations and negotiations, whereas old adults increased their use of these two varieties of statements, as well as spontaneously produced strategies. Overall, the results indicate that adding even unknown collaborators results in improvement in performance for fluid intelligence tasks. In this way, it provides a parallel to the training studies on digit recall, which indicate that with training in the use of internal mnemonic devices younger and older adults can recall long strings of meaningfully encoded digits (Kliegl & Baltes, 1987). In the present case, of course, the level of analysis is shifted to the group context; thus, the interpretation is that old adults do, indeed, use each other as external memory aids and together – with no training and no prior introductions – produce impressive recall performances.

The results of the qualitative analyses indicate there may, in fact, be room for improvement. An interesting connection between the studies training old adults at this difficult fluidlike task (e.g., Kliegl & Baltes, 1987) and the present one might be suggested. What would the performances look like if one (1) gave old adults even the briefest training in how to use colleagues effectively or (2) selected naturally occurring groups (such as couples or bridge teams) who are experienced at collaborating on complex cognitive tasks? The terms *training* and *experience* should be reminiscent of at least two of the features of contextualism already mentioned. Indeed, the social context of performance and the use of naturally occurring memory aids are two contextual aspects of the present study, but future studies could consider even more. Next, we briefly summarize a study in which we used the same paradigm to investigate collaborative performance on a crystallized-like task, world fact memory.

Fact memory. The world fact memory task of Nelson and Narens (1980) presents questions that are like those one would find in games such as Trivial Pursuit. They range from difficult questions about obscure facts (of, e.g., geography and history) to quite well known facts that most North

Americans could immediately answer. We selected 40 of the questions and presented them to groups of same-age, same-sex individuals, dyads, and tetrads. Both correct and incorrect answers are of interest.

The results for the correct answers were just as expected. The young and old adults did not differ significantly, males ($M = 66.3\%$) answered more than females ($M = 50.5\%$), and tetrads ($M = 70.4\%$) answered more than dyads ($M = 58\%$), who answered more than individuals working alone ($M = 46.8\%$). We also examined the number of errors they made. Young adults ($M = 23.8\%$) actually committed more errors than old adults ($M = 15.3\%$). Overall, the presence of collaborators seemed to decrease the number of errors produced. Individuals and dyads gave more incorrect answers than did tetrads. Interestingly, older adults benefited more from collaboration than the younger adults, at least in terms of reducing the number of errors they made in answering these questions. Unlike the young adult dyads and tetrads, who failed to reduce the number of errors they made relative to young individuals, old adults reduced their error production with each increment in group size. The intriguing possibilities attendant on the observation of old adults answering world knowledge questions correctly at the same level as young adults, and then using one another to minimize their error production, deserve further qualitative analysis.

We considered four main strategy-related variables: (1) negotiations about how to answer a particular question, (2) requests for help or clarification from other group members or the interviewer, (3) elaborations or personal anecdotes that may lead toward or away from a correct answer, and (4) simultaneous speech, or the extent to which two or more group members contribute simultaneously to the conversations. Our analysis of negotiations and simultaneous speech indicated that these processes were not likely contributors to the explanation of the observed age differences. Instead, how old adults performed as well as they did in the group settings may be related to the dynamics indicated in the other two process variables. For example, in the request for help or clarification variable, younger adult dyads sought clarification, confirmation, or additional information more frequently than older adult dyads. Tetrads of younger and older adults, however, sought such information from each other at an equivalent rate. Unless it was a higher "quality" of information they sought – and we have no basis for judging that – this indicates only that older adults are using the same strategy in tetrads as the younger adults. In any case, number of requests for help was positively correlated with correct fact recall only for the old adults ($r = .5$).

We also noted that older adults produced more elaborations than younger adults, and this difference was most pronounced in tetrads. Again, number of elaborations was positively correlated with correct fact recall only for the old adults ($r = .5$). Elaborations may provide some insight into the successful performance of the participants in groups. Both young and old adults produced many elaborative comments of the following sort: "I have no idea," "I hate geography," or "Oh, they always ask that." Another category of elaborations – apparently more mnemonically useful – was also produced frequently. These elaborative comments were of the following sort: "Didn't he just have a birthday recently?" "It starts with an *O*," "Oh, he studied peas in the pod," or "He went through the Alps." In other words, through their production of elaborative statements, some individuals in groups were indeed using each other as external cognitive resources. Their statements were task-relevant and may have served as retrieval cues for other members of the group. We concluded elsewhere that elaborations play an important role in the effective use of collaborators by older adults in remembering personal narratives (see Gould et al., 1991, for similar conclusions regarding collaboration on a story-processing task).

Summary

Contextual approaches to intellectual development were described as emphasizing a flexible but coherent set of principles. Five of these principles are (1) multidimensionality of intelligence, (2) multidirectionality of intellectual change in adulthood, (3) the potential usefulness of investigating performance on ecologically relevant tasks, (4) the important role experience plays in intellectual aging, and (5) the theoretical and empirical significance of plasticity in adulthood. These five characteristics are not exclusively associated with contextual approaches. Indeed, researchers operating from several other approaches covered in this book share interest in one or more of these principles.

It is possible to consider a large proportion of the research results in intellectual aging in terms of these five principles. Such a consideration informs recent research on practical cognition and aging (e.g., Cornelius & Caspi, 1987), as well as the recent discussions of the relative gains and losses in cognitive skills with advancing age (e.g., Uttal & Perlmutter, 1989). Some researchers have argued that gains in some aspects of intelligence may "compensate" for age-related decrements in others. Because *compensation* is a term occurring with a growing frequency in the literature, there is a pressing need for theoretical analysis and empirical investigations. In this chapter, I have focused on this term, summarizing its definition and usage by several authors (e.g., Baltes, Charness, and Salthouse), as well as our own analysis (Bäckman & Dixon, 1991). When considered in terms of the dynamic relationship between the individual's changing cognitive skills and expectations of performance, on the one hand, and shifting contextual demands, on the other, compensation becomes a potentially central process in cognitive aging. In addition, when considered in these terms, its contextual characteristics are evident.

One example of compensation in everyday settings may be indicated by a set of findings suggesting that older adults use external aids to compensate for cognitive decline. They may, in fact, use memory aids in preference to the more cognitively complex (and perhaps less generalizable) internal mnemonics, although these can certainly be taught to normal old adults (Kliegl & Baltes, 1987; Kliegl et al., 1990) with impressive results. One common source of external cognitive aid – at least in everyday life – is other people. Much intellectual functioning occurs in the context of groups of various sizes and compositions.

In one set of studies we investigated the extent to which older and younger adults use (and use effectively) same-age collaborators in solving memory problems similar to those identified as fluid or crystallized intelligence tasks. This research was designed to blend aspects of research in cognitive, social, and developmental psychology. The results of two of these studies, summarized in the final section of this chapter, indicate the impressive extent to which older adults use previously unknown collaborators to boost their performance levels. Further research will indicate the extent and specific mechanisms of compensation of this sort. This paradigm is representative of a contextual approach to intellectual aging not because of the specific content of the tasks, but because it is consistent with the five features of contextual approaches. Not least important is the assertion that the context of performance – the collaborative groups – is ecologically representative.

These areas of contextual research on aging – practical cognition, collaborative cognition, and the expertise and compensation dynamic – will likely occupy many investigators in future years. The contextual approaches we have considered draw heavily on prominent theories of intelligence and cognitive aging, and use procedures honed in experimental cognitive laboratories. It would be inaccurate, however, to imply that these approaches are characterized exclusively by the application of extant cognitive theories to intellectual development in adulthood. As the discussion of compensation and collaboration indicates, these approaches may also be characterized by a tendency to explore the benefits of consulting a variety of neighboring disciplines. In so doing, unique research questions may be posed and new procedures to answer them may be implemented. It seems clear that these new questions and procedures are pushing the field in new and interesting directions. Still to be seen, of course, is the extent to which these approaches shed light on the problems and processes of intellectual aging.

References

Adams, C., Labouvie-Vief, G., Hobart, C. J., & Dorosz, M. (1990). Adult age group differences in story recall style. *Journal of Geronotology, 45*, 17–27.
Bäckman, L. (1989). Varieties of memory compensation by older adults in episodic

remembering. In L. W. Poon, D. C. Rubin, & B. A. Wilson (Eds.), *Everyday cognition in adulthood and late life* (pp. 509–544). Cambridge: Cambridge University Press.

Bäckman, L., & Dixon, R. A. (in press). Psychological compensation: A theoretical framework. *Psychological Bulletin.*

Bales, R. F., & Strodtbeck, F. L. (1951). Phases in group problem solving. *Journal of Abnormal and Social Psychology, 46,* 485–495.

Baltes, P. B. (1987). Theoretical propositions of life-span developmental psychology: On the dynamics between growth and decline. *Developmental Psychology, 23,* 611–626.

Baltes, P. B., & Baltes, M. M. (1990). Psychological perspectives on successful aging: A model of selective optimization with compensation. In P. B. Baltes & M. M. Baltes (Eds.), *Successful aging: Perspectives from the behavioral sciences.* Cambridge: Cambridge University Press.

Baltes, P. B., Dittmann-Kohli, F., & Dixon, R. A. (1984). New perspectives on the development of intelligence in adulthood: Toward a dual process conception and a model of selective optimization with compensation. In P. B. Baltes & O. G. Brim, Jr. (Eds.), *Life-span development and behavior* (Vol. 6, pp. 33–76). New York: Academic Press.

Baltes, P. B., Reese, H. W., & Lipsitt, L. P. (1980). Life-span developmental psychology. *Annual Review of Psychology, 31,* 65–110.

Baltes, P. B., & Smith, J. (1990). Toward a psychology of wisdom and its ontogenesis. In R. J. Sternberg (Ed.), *Wisdom: Its nature, origins, and development* (pp. 87–120). Cambridge: Cambridge University Press.

Baltes, P. B., & Willis, S. L. (1982). Plasticity and enhancement of intellectual functioning in old age. In F. I. M. Craik & S. E. Trehub (Eds.), *Aging and cognitive processes* (pp. 353–389). New York: Plenum.

Bartlett, F. C. (1932). *Remembering: A study in experimental and social psychology.* Cambridge: Cambridge University Press.

Berg, C. A., & Sternberg, R. J. (1985). A triarchic theory of intellectual development during adulthood. *Developmental Review, 5,* 334–370.

Botwinick, J. (1977). Intellectual abilities. In J. E. Birren & K. W. Schaie (Eds.), *Handbook of the psychology of aging* (pp. 580–605). New York: Van Nostrand Reinhold.

Bronfenbrenner, U. (1979). *The ecology of human development.* Cambridge, MA: Harvard University Press.

Camp, C. J. (1989). World-knowledge systems. In L. W. Poon, D. C. Rubin, & B. A. Wilson (Eds.), *Everyday cognition in adulthood and late life* (pp. 457–482). Cambridge: Cambridge University Press.

Cavanaugh, J. C. (1989). The importance of awareness in memory aging. In L. W. Poon, D. C. Rubin, & B. A. Wilson (Eds.), *Everyday cognition in adulthood and late life* (pp. 416–436). Cambridge: Cambridge University Press.

Cavanaugh, J. C., Grady, J. G., & Perlmutter, M. (1983). Forgetting and use of memory aids in 20 to 70 year olds' everyday life. *International Journal of Aging and Human Development, 17,* 113–122.

Cavanaugh, J. C., Kramer, D. A., Sinott, J. D., Camp, C. J., & Markley, R. P. (1985). On missing links and such: Interfaces between cognitive research and everyday problem solving. *Human Development, 28,* 146–168.

Ceci, S. J., & Liker, J. (1986). Academic and nonacademic intelligence. An experimental separation. In R. J. Sternberg & R. K. Wagner (Eds.), *Practical intelligence: Nature and origins of competence in the everyday world* (pp. 119–142). Cambridge: Cambridge University Press.

Chapman, M., & Dixon, R. A. (Eds.). (1987). *Meaning and the growth of understanding: Wittgenstein's significance for developmental psychology.* Berlin: Springer-Verlag.

Charness, N. (1979). Components of skill in bridge. *Canadian Journal of Psychology, 33,* 1–16.

Charness, N. (1981). Search in chess: Age and skill differences. *Journal of Experimental Psychology: Human Perception and Performance, 7,* 467–476.

Charness, N. (1989). Age and expertise: Responding to Talland's challenge. In L. W. Poon, D. C. Rubin, & B. A. Wilson (Eds.), *Everyday cognition in adulthood and late life* (pp. 437–456). Cambridge: Cambridge University Press.

Clark, N. K., & Stephenson, G. M. (1989). Group remembering. In P. B. Paulus (Ed.), *Psychology of group influence* (pp. 357–391). Hillsdale, NJ: Erlbaum.

Clark, N. K., Stephenson, G. M., & Kniveton, B. H. (1990). Social remembering: Quantitative aspects of individual and collaborative remembering by police officers and students. *British Journal of Psychology, 81*, 73–94.

Cornelius, S. W. (1984). Classic pattern of intellectual aging: Test familiarity, difficulty, and performance. *Journal of Gerontology, 39*, 201–206.

Cornelius, S. W., & Caspi, A. (1986). Self-perceptions of intellectual control and aging. *Educational Gerontology, 12*, 345–357.

Cornelius, S. W., & Caspi, A. (1987). Everyday problem solving in adulthood and old age. *Psychology and Aging, 2*, 144–153.

Craik, F. I. M. (1977). Age differences in human memory. In J. E. Birren & K. W. Schaie (Eds.), *Handbook of the psychology of aging* (pp. 384–420). New York: Van Nostrand Reinhold.

Demming, J. A., & Pressey, S. L. (1957). Tests indigenous to the adult and older years. *Journal of Counseling Psychology, 4*, 144–148.

Denney, N. W. (1982). Aging and cognitive changes. In B. B. Wolman (Ed.), *Handbook of developmental psychology* (pp. 807–827). Englewood Cliffs, NJ: Prentice-Hall.

Denney, N. W., & Pearce, K. A. (1989). A developmental study of practical problem solving in adults. *Psychology and Aging, 4*, 438–442.

Dixon, R. A. (1989). Questionnaire research on metamemory and aging: Issues of structure and function. In L. W. Poon, D. C. Rubin, & B. A. Wilson (Eds.), *Everyday cognition in adulthood and late life* (pp. 394–415). Cambridge: Cambridge University Press.

Dixon, R. A., & Bäckman, L. (in press). Reading and memory for prose in adulthood. In S. R. Yussen & M. C. Smith (Eds.), *Reading across the life span*. New York: Springer-Verlag.

Dixon, R. A., & Baltes, P. B. (1986). Toward life-span research on the functions and pragmatics of intelligence. In R. J. Sternberg & R. K. Wagner (Eds.), *Practical intelligence: Nature and origins of competence in the everyday world* (pp. 203–235). Cambridge: Cambridge University Press.

Dixon, R. A., Friesen, I. C., Kurzman, D. (1991). *Collaborative memory in young and old adults*. Unpublished manuscript.

Dixon, R. A., & Hultsch, D. F. (1983). Structure and development of metamemory in adulthood. *Journal of Gerontology, 38*, 682–688.

Dixon, R. A., & Lerner, R. M. (in press). A history of systems in developmental psychology. In M. H. Bornstein & M. E. Lamb (Eds.), *Developmental psychology: An advanced textbook* (3rd ed.). Hillsdale, NJ: Erlbaum.

Dobbs, A. R., & Rule, B. G. (1987). Prospective memory and self-report of memory abilities in older adults. *Canadian Journal of Psychology, 41*, 209–222.

Edwards, D., & Middleton, D. (1986a). Conversations with Bartlett. *The Quarterly Newsletter of the Laboratory of Comparative Human Cognition, 8*, 79–89.

Edwards, D., & Middleton, D. (1986b). Joint remembering: Constructing an account of shared experience through conversational discourse. *Discourse Processes, 9*, 423–459.

Gardner, H. (1983). *Frames of mind: The theory of multiple intelligences*. New York: Basic Books.

Gilewski, M. J., & Zelinski, E. M. (1986). Questionnaire assessment of memory complaints. In L. W. Poon (Ed.), *Handbook for clinical memory assessment of older adults* (pp. 93–107). Washington, DC: American Psychological Association.

Gillund, G., & Perlmutter, M. (1988). Episodic memory and knowledge interactions across adulthood. In L. L. Light & D. M. Burke (Eds.), *Language, memory, and aging* (pp. 191–208). Cambridge: Cambridge University Press.

Gould, O. N., Trevithick, L., & Dixon, R. A. (1991). Adult age differences in elaborations produced during prose recall. *Psychology and Aging*, *6*, 93–99.

Harris, J. E. (1980). Memory aids people use: Two interview studies. *Memory and Cognition*, *8*, 31–38.

Hill, G. W. (1982). Group versus individual performance: Are N + 1 heads better than one? *Psychological Bulletin*, *91*, 517–539.

Hoppe, R. A. (1962). Memorizing by individuals and groups: A test of the pooling-of-ability model. *Journal of Abnormal and Social Psychology*, *65*, 64–67.

Horn, J. L. (1982). The theory of fluid and crystallized intelligence in relation to concepts of cognitive psychology and aging in adulthood. In F. I. M. Craik & S. Trehub (Eds.), *Aging and cognitive processes* (pp. 237–278). New York: Plenum.

Hultsch, D. F., & Dixon, R. A. (1990). Learning and memory in aging. In J. E. Birren & K. W. Schaie (Eds.), *Handbook of the psychology of aging* (3rd ed., pp. 258–274). San Diego: Academic Press.

Hultsch, D. F., Hertzog, C., & Dixon, R. A. (1987). Age differences in metamemory: Resolving the inconsistencies. *Canadian Journal of Psychology 41*, 193–208.

Kliegl, R., & Baltes, P. B. (1987). Theory-guided analysis of mechanisms of development and aging through testing-the-limits and research on expertise. In C. Schooler & K. W. Schaie (Eds.), *Cognitive functioning and social structure over the life course* (pp. 95–119). Norwood, NJ: Ablex.

Kliegl, R., Smith, J., & Baltes, P. B. (1990). On the locus and process of magnification of age differences during mnemonic training. *Developmental Psychology*, *26*, 894–904.

Labouvie-Vief, G. (1985). Intelligence and cognition. In J. E. Birren & K. W. Schaie (Eds.), *Handbook of the psychology of aging* (2nd ed., pp. 500–530). New York: Van Nostrand Reinhold.

Lachman, M. E. (1983). Perceptions of intellectual aging: Antecedent or consequence of intellectual functioning. *Developmental Psychology*, *19*, 482–498.

Lachman, M. E., Steinberg, E. S., & Trotter, S. D. (1987). Effects of control beliefs and attributions for cognitive, physical, and social performance. *Psychology and Aging*, *2*, 266–271.

Lerner, R. M. (1984). *On the nature of human plasticity*. Cambridge: Cambridge University Press.

Lerner, R. M. (1986). *Concepts and theories of human development* (2nd ed.). New York: Random House.

Loewen, E. R., Shaw, R. J., & Craik, F. I. M. (1990). Age differences in components of metamemory. *Experimental Aging Research*, *16*, 43–48.

McCluskey, K. A., & Reese, H. W. (Eds.). (1984). *Life-span developmental psychology: Historical and generational effects*. Orlando, FL: Academic Press.

McGrath, J. E. (1984). *Groups: Interaction and performance*. Englewood Cliffs, NJ: Prentice-Hall.

Middleton, D., & Edwards, D. (Eds.). (1990a). *Collective remembering*. London: Sage.

Middleton, D., & Edwards, D. (1990b). Conversational remembering: A social psychological approach. In D. Middleton & D. Edwards (Eds.), *Collective remembering* (pp. 23–45). London: Sage.

Nelson, T. O., & Narens, L. (1980). Norms of 300 general-information questions: Accuracy of recall, latency of recall, and feeling-of-knowing ratings. *Journal of Verbal Learning and Verbal Behavior*, *19*, 338–368.

Paulus, P. B. (Ed.). (1989). *Psychology of group influence* (2nd ed.). Hillsdale, NJ: Erlbaum.

Pepper, S. C. (1970). *World hypotheses*. Berkeley: University of California Press. (Original work published in 1942.)

Perlmutter, H. V., & de Montmollin, G. (1952). Group learning of nonsense syllables. *Journal of Abnormal and Social Psychology*, *47*, 762–769.

Perlmutter, M. (1978). What is memory aging the aging of? *Developmental Psychology*, *14*, 330–345.

Perlmutter, M. (1988). Cognitive potential throughout life. In J. E. Birren & K. L. Bengtson (Eds.), *Emergent theories of aging*. New York: Springer.

Rabbitt, P. M. A. (1977). Changes in problem solving ability in old age. In J. E. Birren & K. W. Schaie (Eds.), *Handbook of the psychology of aging* (pp. 606–625). New York: Van Nostrand Reinhold.

Riegel, K. F. (1976). The dialectics of human development. *American Psychologist, 31,* 689–700.

Roodin, P., & Rybash, J. (1985). Social cognition: A life-span perspective. In T. M. Schlecter & M. P. Toglia (Eds.), *New directions in cognitive science*. Norwood, NJ: Ablex.

Rosnow, R. L., & Georgoudi, M. (Eds.). (1986). *Contextualism and understanding in behavioral science*. New York: Praeger.

Ryack, B. L. (1965). A comparison of individual and group learning of nonsense syllables. *Journal of Personality and Social Psychology, 2,* 296–299.

Salthouse, T. A. (1984). Effects of age and skill in typing. *Journal of Experimental Psychology: General, 113,* 345–371.

Salthouse, T. A. (1987). Age, experience, and compensation. In C. Schooler & K. W. Schaie (Eds.), *Cognitive functioning and social structure over the life course* (pp. 142–157). Norwood, NJ: Ablex.

Salthouse, T. A. (1988). Effects of aging on verbal abilities: Examination of the psychometric literature. In L. L. Light & D. M. Burke (Eds.), *Language, memory, and aging* (pp. 17–35). Cambridge: Cambridge University Press.

Salthouse, T. A., Legg, S., Palmon, R., & Mitchell, D. (1990). Memory factors in age-related differences in simple reasoning. *Psychology and Aging, 5,* 9–15.

Schaie, K. W. (1983). The Seattle Longitudinal Study: A twenty-one year exploration of psychometric intelligence in adulthood. In K. W. Schaie (Ed.), *Longitudinal studies of adult psychological development* (pp. 64–135). New York: Guilford.

Schaie, K. W. (1987). Applications of psychometric intelligence to the prediction of everyday competence in the elderly. In C. Schooler & K. W. Schaie (Eds.), *Cognitive functioning and social structure over the life course* (pp. 50–58). Norwood, NJ: Ablex.

Schaie, K. W. (1990). Intellectual development in adulthood. In J. E. Birren & K. W. Schaie (Eds.), *Handbook of the psychology of aging* (3rd ed., pp. 291–309). San Diego: Academic Press.

Scribner, S. (1984). Studying working intelligence. In B. Rogoff & J. Lave (Eds.), *Everyday cognition: Its development and social context* (pp. 166–189). Cambridge, MA: Harvard University Press.

Scribner, S. (1986). Thinking in action: Some characteristics of practical thought. In R. J. Sternberg & R. K. Wagner (Eds.), *Practical intelligence: Nature and origin of competence in the everyday world* (pp. 13–30). Cambridge: Cambridge University Press.

Shaw, M. E. (1976). *Group dynamics*. New York: McGraw-Hill.

Steiner, I. D. (1972). *Group processes and productivity*. New York: Academic Press.

Sternberg, R. J. (1984). Toward a triarchic theory of human intelligence. *Behavioral and Brain Sciences, 7,* 269–315.

Sternberg, R. J., & Berg, C. (1987). What are theories of adult intellectual development theories of? In C. Schooler & K. W. Schaie (Eds.), *Cognitive functioning and social structure over the life course* (pp. 3–23). Norwood, NJ: Ablex.

Taylor, D. W. (1954). Problem solving by groups. In *Proceedings of the 14th International Congress of Psychology*. Montreal: University of Montreal.

Thomas, E. J., & Fink, C. F. (1961). Models of group problem solving. *Journal of Abnormal and Social Psychology, 63,* 53–63.

Uttal, D., & Perlmutter, M. (1989). The dynamics of growth and decline across the life span. *Developmental Review, 9,* 101–132.

Wiener, P. P. (1949). *Evolution and the founders of pragmatism*. Cambridge, MA: Harvard University Press.

Williams, W. M., & Sternberg, R. J. (1988). Group intelligence: Why some groups are better than others. *Intelligence, 12,* 351–377.

Willis, S. L. (1985). Towards an educational psychology of the adult learner: Cognitive and intellectual bases. In J. E. Birren & K. W. Schaie (Eds.), *Handbook of the psychology of aging* (2nd ed., pp. 818–847). New York: Van Nostrand Reinhold.

Willis, S. L., & Schaie, K. W. (1986). Practical intelligence in later adulthood. In R. J. Sternberg & R. K. Wagner (Eds.), *Practical intelligence: Nature and origins of competence in the everyday world* (pp. 236–268). Cambridge: Cambridge University Press.

Yesavage, J. A., Lapp, D., & Sheikh, J. I. (1989). Mnemonics as modified for use by the elderly. In L. W. Poon, D. C. Rubin, & B. A. Wilson (Eds.), *Everyday cognition in adulthood and late life* (pp. 598–611). Cambridge: Cambridge University Press.

14   The princess grows up: A satiric fairy tale about intellectual development

Robert J. Sternberg

Once upon a time, in the thirty-first century, there lived a princess who wanted to grow up just as quickly as she could. She was tired of being a child and, at twelve years of age, wanted nothing more than to skip the teenage period so that she could get on with the real business of living. A determined young lady, she was ready to do whatever it took to grow up quickly. But she wasn't sure what it meant to "grow up." She did stretching exercises to make herself taller, but they didn't seem to work. Her elders laughed at her stretching exercises anyway, telling her that it took more than height to make a grown-up. She tried dressing in adult clothing, but again her elders laughed, reminding her that clothes don't make the person. She tried to act in adult ways, but adults treated her as a child nevertheless. When she stamped her foot in frustration, the adults glanced at her sympathetically and told her it was all just a stage. She had her whole adolescence to go through before she could really become a grown-up. But this was not a princess to be put off – one who would just wait because others told her to.

One day, she had what seemed to her a brilliant idea. She knew that people on other planets developed at different rates. Some grew up more slowly; others, more quickly. On some planets, people only twelve years of age were considered to be full-fledged adults. Perhaps some secret the people of these other planets knew about what it means to grow up enabled them to grow up sooner. If only she could discover the secret, she could grow up quickly too. So the princess surreptitiously chartered a rocket ship, a feat she was able to accomplish only because of her royal connections. She was determined to find out what it meant not just to grow up but to grow up *intellectually*.

Twelve-year-olds were not legally permitted to charter rocket ships. One day when no one was looking, she sneaked off to the rocket ship, started the engine, and flew away. She left her parents a note saying that she had gone to visit her auntie Graziella, and since everyone knew that Graziella was a recluse who avoided contact with the outside world as much as possible, the princess figured her note would give her time to discover the secret of growing up quickly. The princess started her voyage to the planets of her solar system on which she thought she might be able to unveil the secret of what it means to grow up intellectually.

Psychometrica

The first planet the princess visited was the planet of Psychometrica. She didn't know a great deal about it, but she did know that it was one of the oldest planets in outer space and that its civilization dated back to antiquity. The people she had known from Psychometrica were always precise: They seemed to assign a number to everything.

Upon landing, the princess used her royal status to arrange a visit to one of the wisest seers on the entire planet, Dr. I. Queue. Certainly he would know what it means to grow up intellectually, if anyone would. She was introduced to this seer, and his piercing eyes seemed to drill right through her. It was as though he was evaluating her on a number of dimensions, the nature of which she couldn't even begin to ascertain.

"So you want to grow up," chuckled the seer. "I'm afraid that there may not be very much I can do for you. But the first thing you must realize is that what matters is not how many years you have, or how tall you are, or how you dress. What makes a person grown up is how well the person thinks."

The princess wasn't sure what to make of the old seer. What he said made sense, but how could one change the way one thinks? Even if one did, how would that lead to one's being more grown up?

"Well first I'll have to see just how grown up you are," mumbled the seer. "Here, take this test, which will help me assess where you stand."

The princess looked at the items on the test. The seer had translated them from the language of Psychometrica to her own language. But in reading the test items, she wasn't sure the translation was good enough. Some of the items she did answer, but other items were strange indeed. Some of these items required her to know meanings of words, but the words were sometimes obscure, and the translations to her own language from Psychometrican of the multiple-choice answer options often didn't seem quite right: None quite described the word in bold print. Other items required her to know general information, but the information was about things and events that were part of the planet of Psychometrica, not of her planet. Still other items required her to indicate what response would be appropriate to an everyday social situation; but the princess knew that the customs of Psychometrica were different from those of her own planet, and wasn't sure whether to answer the questions in terms of the customs of her planet or the customs of Psychometrica, of which she was only vaguely aware. There were items that required her to remember things, but the things she was asked to remember were not things on her planet, so she found it much more difficult even to understand what she was supposed to remember than she would have if she had been asked to remember familiar things from her own environment. Then there were the items with strange geometric forms – points and lines and triangles and squares. But the objects of her own world were much more rounded, and she found it strange to think in terms of all these angular objects. Eventually, however, she finished the test and handed it to the seer. He scored it and frowned.

"I'm afraid, young lady, that your problem is not so much growing up beyond your years as it is reaching the point where you should be mentally for your own age of twelve. To be perfectly honest, and I will be honest because you have come a long way to see me, your performance is roughly equivalent to that of a ten-year-old on Psychometrica, giving you what we call an IQ of only about 83. The average on our planet is 100. But, then, we have repeatedly discovered that people from other planets don't do as well on our tests as people from our own planet. You should realize that you picked the most advanced civilization in which to start your quest, which may have been a mistake, because now I'm afraid you will start feeling bad about yourself."

The princess was taken aback. She felt unfairly judged because the test seemed to measure not the skills and abilities that were valued on her own planet but, rather, those that were valued on Psychometrica. Yet the old seer seemed so sure of himself, and in possession of so much knowledge, that it was hard to disagree with him. Maybe she just wasn't very bright after all. If that was so, what was the use of even trying to grow up? The princess then asked the seer, "But what does it mean to be intellectually more or less advanced? What is it that intellectually more advanced children have that children like me don't have? What is it that older, wiser people can do that even younger adults cannot do? What would I especially need to change?"

"Oh, there are many differences, my dear. We have found that intellectual abilities differentiate with age, so that children's abilities become more differentiated and also more diversified as they grow older. Eventually, it appears, abilities may de-differentiate in old age. We have found that the kinds of abilities that are important to measure are different at different ages. Higher-order mental abilities seem to become more important with age. We have even found that eventually, in later adulthood, some abilities seem to decline at the same time as others remain the same or even increase. For example, our ability to think quickly and flexibly often seems to decline in the later years, at the same time as our knowledge base keeps increasing. We develop compensatory strategies to maintain high levels of performance, using our greater knowledge of the world to offset declines in our flexible processing. Of course, none of this applies to me, because I am a seer. It only applies to other people. To be honest, I've heard other people say the same thing of themselves but, in my experience, without justification. You only have to hear them talk for a few minutes before you realize just how incompetent they have become!"

The princess kept thinking about her score of 83, and it depressed her. The more she thought about it, the more the ways in which she felt inadequate. Every inadequacy seemed to be summed up in that number. But then she had a thought, and she decided to confront the seer despite his obviously greater age and wisdom.

"Seer, I must ask you a question about these tests you use. How do you know that they measure all there is to intelligence? Are you saying that everything a person can do intellectually is wrapped up in that one number, what you called the IQ?"

"Child, of course it is not possible in any one test to sample every behavior in which a person might possibly engage. Nor do we try. Rather, what we do is sample a representative set of mental abilities and then derive a score from those. We have carefully researched our tests and have found that they are quite good at predicting almost everything a person does. Of course, they are not perfect, but we haven't found anything better. So we go with what we've got, which up to now has seemed to be about the best we can have. For you, dear, the prognosis is not that favorable. Perhaps there has been some inbreeding in the royal line of your planet, which has been shown to result in poorer mental performance."

This news depressed the princess even more. She thought of how the tests seem to predict so many things. Then she thought of all the things she didn't do as well as she wished. At the same time, it occurred to her that she had managed to outwit the people on her planet and to engage the rocket ship and actually fly it to another planet. But the test didn't measure that, so probably it wasn't very important.

"You mean that on the basis of this test, which took just about a half hour of my time, you can predict so many things about my life?"

"I'm afraid so," replied the seer. "In fact, we have found correlations with all kinds of life performances of about .2, meaning that we can predict four percent of the variation between individuals in their performance."

"Four percent! You call that prediction?"

"It may not sound like much, but it is a remarkably cost-effective procedure. When we predict the job performance of, say, thousands of people, that four percent edge can make us a whole lot of money, and save us and our potential job applicants a whole lot of heartburn."

The princess decided to leave Psychometrica. Her voyage to this planet had discouraged her enormously. She had gone with the hope of growing up, and now it was not even clear that she had grown up to the point she had thought she had. But she was a persistent young lady, and before giving up, she decided she should try other planets as well. So she launched her rocket ship and flew off to the next planet with which she was acquainted, Piagetica.

Piagetica

The landing of the princess on Piagetica was uneventful. She was welcomed and treated with the respect due royalty. Of course, the planet took some getting used to. Some features of it she could readily assimilate into her prior schemas. Other elements were less familiar to her, and she found she had to make some accommodations. But once she had adjusted to the change in gravity and the change in culture, she felt almost as though she were at home. She made inquiries as to whom she should see and was eventually brought to the house of a distinguished philosopher, Dr. Equil Bration, who specialized in something he called "epistemology," whatever that was – something about the study of knowledge, she was told.

The princess walked into a cramped study with books and papers strewn all over it, and a wizened old man sitting in a padded armchair that looked like a remnant of ancient times. It could have been from the twentieth century, for all she knew. She repeated her request to the philosopher: How could she grow up intellectually? She explained that she was in a hurry to get on with her life and had precious little time to waste.

The philosopher looked puzzled. "People from your planet are always in such a hurry. Hurry, hurry, hurry. Things never move fast enough for them. They always seem to want more of everything: more money, more power, more smarts. To be honest, it doesn't surprise me that a person from your planet would make what on this planet would seem such an unusual request. Here we are in no hurry, and let people develop at their normal rate. In fact, our experience is that it is very hard to change the rate at which children develop. Although there are some minor differences among children, we find that they all move through basically the same intellectual stages in the same order and at roughly the same rate. We are not so concerned here with the differences as they are, say, on Psychometrica, a planet for which we frankly have great distaste. We are much more interested in how people are similar than in how they are different. We are not so obsessed with trying to quantify everything under the sun. Leave people alone and let them grow. That's what we say."

The princess felt slightly embarrassed that her request seemed to displease the philosopher. But she had known when she had set out that on different planets there would be differences in people's perspectives.

"If people go through stages as you say, why can't I just accelerate my transition through the stages? That's all I'd have to do to grow up faster, and then I wouldn't have to waste my time being a maladjusted teenager."

"My dear, let me ask you a question," said the philosopher. "How many planets do you intend to visit?"

"Oh, not so many. Maybe four or five or six. It all depends on what I learn and when I figure out how to grow up faster."

"Well, suppose you decide to visit just four. Obviously, it is more convenient to visit them in some orders than in others. But suppose you were to consider all possible orders of four planets. What would all possible orders of the four planets be?"

The princess quite rapidly went through all twenty-four orders for her possible visits, making her task easier by systematically reviewing the possible permutations of the four planets. The philosopher was impressed.

"Princess, you are obviously a very bright child."

The princess was taken aback. She had just heard on Psychometrica that she was intellectually slow, and now she was being told she was bright. It didn't make any sense.

"You have just shown that you are what we call formal-operational. You reviewed the possible permutations in a systematic fashion, showing that you can think logically. Dear, you have reached the final stage of intellectual development. There really is nowhere for you to go. You are where you want to be."

The princess felt vaguely dissatisfied with this counsel. She didn't feel she had reached her intellectual peak. She knew many people on her own planet who seemed to be more complex thinkers than she was, and there were certainly others who knew a lot more.

"You see," the philosopher continued, "there are four basic stages of development, and you are in the last one. You don't need to grow up any more. Be happy with where you are."

"You talk about these stages, honored sir. But I am not sure exactly what you mean. To be honest, I haven't felt any major or sudden shifts in my ability to think about problems, and I know that my ability to solve problems in domains in which I'm knowledgeable seems to be a whole lot better than my ability to solve problems in domains I know nothing about. And then, sometimes I feel as if I go backward and have days on which I can hardly solve even the simplest problems."

"Yes, yes, my dear, all that may be true. But you are talking about truly not very important differences in your performance from one domain to another and from one day to another. What really matters is your competence to solve problems, and that, I can assure you, is not subject to these minor perturbations."

"But what difference does all this competence make if it is not reflected in performance? Besides, how can you really know a person's competence except through her performance?"

"You are a brilliant child indeed. Even many adults do not see these points. Yet, you miss the fundamental point, which is the importance of understanding the basic logical structures that underlie thought. Certainly people are not always perfect at executing these. But as they grow older they acquire more and more of these logical structures, and eventually they can think in the ways you show yourself so well able to do."

"Let me show you a little demonstration, Princess," said the philosopher. He clapped his hands, and in came a young child who could have been no more than four years old. The philosopher took a tray of marbles out of his desk drawer. Four of the marbles were green, and six of them were blue. The philosopher said to the child, "Look at my tray of marbles here and tell me something: Do I have more blue marbles or more marbles?"

The child looked perplexed. She didn't really understand the question. In fact, the question didn't make much sense to her. Then she smiled. Obviously the old geezer was losing his own marbles. What he really meant to ask, she thought, was whether he had more blue marbles or more green marbles. Now that was a sensible question. He had simply misspoken.

"You have more blue marbles, Great One," said the child.

"Thank you, my dear," said the philosopher, and he asked the child to leave.

"As you can see, Princess, this child is intellectually much less advanced than you are. She doesn't have what we call 'class inclusion.' As you know, you cannot have more in a part than in the whole."

"But mighty philosopher," said the princess, "I had the feeling that she didn't quite understand your question."

"But if she didn't understand the question," said the philosopher with a self-satisfied look, "all the more reason to conclude that she's got a long way to go."

"Well, I know you are busy, great philosopher, and I will not take up any more of your time. I understand that you are saying I shouldn't worry about growing up anymore, because I have already grown up, at least as far as my head is concerned. I appreciate your great wisdom."

So the princess went off, but satisfied she was not. She did not feel deep within herself that she was as grown up as the philosopher had thought, and moreover, she was perplexed by the difference between his evaluation of her and that of the seer on Psychometrica. She decided to move on to the third planet on her list, and so off she flew to Neo-Piagetica.

Neo-Piagetica

Neo-Piagetica was a very different planet indeed. What a change! This planet seemed much more modern, and from her interactions with them, its inhabitants seemed much more varied in their ways of thinking. They all called themselves "Neo-Piagetian," but whereas she had found a lack of diversity in the points of view on Piagetica, on this planet everyone claimed to have the same philosophy, but no one quite seemed to agree with anyone else as to what it was. The more she talked to the inhabitants, the more she became confused about just what their point of view was. They were obviously aware of the differences and that they applied the same label despite the differences. People seemed basically to accept the differences but at the same time made subtle digs at each other, suggesting that each believed he or she saw things the right way.

The planet was not all that different from Piagetica and obviously had drawn on the Piagetican civilization. It had started off as a colony of Piagetica, apparently, but the inhabitants had revolted and formed their own government. Perhaps it would be more accurate to say "governments," because they had apparently been experiencing disagreements among themselves and so had taken somewhat different paths on different parts of the planet. The princess was not sure to whom she should talk, because whenever she sought advice about finding an expert, she was pointed in the direction of a different supposedly knowledgeable person. Finally, she took one of the suggestions pretty much at random and found herself talking to what seemed to be a minor government functionary.

"Sir, I'm sorry to trouble you, as I can see you're very busy. But I'm seeking to grow up intellectually, and I'm trying to find someone on this planet who could help me. I was hoping you might be able to, or at least that you could tell me to whom I might turn. I've just come from Piagetica, and they told me that I was already quite grown up, but I'm afraid I'm not altogether convinced."

"Of course that's what they would tell you. They're so out-of-date, so fuddy-duddy. Yet, you know, our whole civilization is based on theirs, even though we don't always like to admit it. They were once a mighty civilization, but they couldn't change with the times, and so eventually we had to leave them behind, much as happened in the beginning of the twenty-first century on the planet Earth to a country called the United States."

"Sir, what do you think? Do you think I'm altogether grown up intellectually or that I've still got a way to go?"

"Oh, my dear, you still have quite a way to go. A mistake they have made on Piagetica is to believe that their so-called formal-operational stage is the end of intellectual development. But here on Neo-Piagetica we know better. For one thing, we know that not everyone even reaches their formal-operational stage. Besides, most people don't think all that logically anyway. Yes, we on this planet all would agree that you have a way to go. We might not agree totally on what way that is, or on how much farther you have to go. All of us believe that intellectual development continues beyond formal operations, but we can't quite reach a consensus as to how.

Clearly, people continue to develop intellectually in adulthood as well as in childhood."

"I suppose I'm a bit confused by all you are saying. Where could I go intellectually so as to grow up faster? What's left for me?"

"As I say, it depends on whom you ask, but in my own view, the really important thing is not how well you solve problems but what problems you choose to solve in the first place. Once you get a bit older, you'll learn that plenty of people spend lots of time solving the wrong problems, or at least problems that aren't very important. As a result, no matter what they do, it doesn't matter much, because they're on the wrong track. To be honest with you, I think you're on the wrong track yourself, but then, you're only twelve years old. Children develop in the ability to solve problems, but adults develop especially as they acquire a better sense of what problems to solve in the first place."

The princess had to admit that better advice would be hard to come by; yet she was not totally satisfied. She knew that what the man was saying was sound, but her desire to grow up intellectually did not leave her just because cognitively she knew she was getting good advice. This discordance between what she thought and what she felt and believed made her uncomfortable because it raised the question of just how rational intelligence was anyway. But that was scarcely a question for a twelve-year-old, and she put it out of her mind.

"Just out of curiosity," the princess said, "I understand that people from this planet have widely different views. Do you each think that you are right and the others are wrong?"

"Well, perhaps deep down we do, but we realize that there probably is no ultimate truth here, or at least that if there is one, we're a long way from reaching it. We see things in more dialectical terms. People propose one idea, then they decide the idea isn't so great, then they propose the opposite of the first idea, then they realize that that idea isn't so great either; finally they reach some kind of a balance. When we first rejected the rule of Piagetica, we had nothing good to say about our former masters. Everything they thought, we thought the opposite. Eventually we realized that they had some pretty good ideas, and that our goal ought not to be to reject everything we'd learned but, rather, to decide what we could use from it and what we wished to reject. So we have tried to achieve some kind of synthesis. Now, of course, the younger generation is rejecting much of what we say and coming up with their own ideas. And so it goes."

The princess had selected as her consultant only a minor government functionary, but she had the feeling that in some respects, there was a lot more wisdom here than in what she had heard from the seer and the philosopher on the other two planets. Maybe she should just turn around now. But her curiosity was not yet satisfied. She felt she was coming close to an answer to her question, and she couldn't stop when she was so close. So she decided to forge on and go to the next planet on her itinerary. So off she flew to Cognitiva.

Cognitiva

The trip to Cognitiva was uneventful, and when the princess landed she was hoping this world would prove even more instructive than the last. She looked around at the people of the planet and noticed they all looked very thoughtful. They seemed to be spending a lot of their time thinking, although not all of them seemed to be doing a whole lot. Apparently, on Cognitiva, the important thing was how you thought. She thought about it, and thought it made some sense, and the more she thought about it, the less she was sure of how she would act on it.

Eventually she was steered to Dr. Cerebro, a professor at the most prestigious university in the land. He had an unusually large head and not much hair. He wore thick glasses. They looked fake, almost as though they were there for the sake of appearance. He definitely had the "brainy" look. The princess explained to Dr. Cerebro her goal to grow up intellectually.

"Well that's one I'll have to think about," he chuckled. So he sat there thinking, and thinking, and thinking.

"I've thought this through, and there are lots of things we can do to help you grow up intellectually. For one thing, we can add to the number of mental processes you have available to you. For another, we can help you combine these processes into new strategies for solving problems. For another, we can help you better represent the information that you use in solving problems. For another, we can help you think faster. For another . . ."

The princess interrupted because she had the feeling that this list might go on forever. "But if you tell me how to do all these things, how is that going to make me any smarter? You will be telling me what to do; I won't be figuring it out for myself."

"Well, that's true but not so important. For example, on our planet we view computers as very intelligent, but basically we tell them what to do when we program them. The important thing is that they are able to do it, and often even do things beyond what we expect."

The princess thought about what she had heard. Then she tried to think a bit faster, hoping maybe she'd feel that much smarter. But she just became confused, and so she went back to her usual way of thinking.

"I certainly would be interested in learning some new ways of thinking, or how to think faster. Where would I start?"

"Well, we could have you do lots of different kinds of problems. We could teach you about comparing names of letters, or saying whether a digit we present to you is one you have heard before, or we could give you four-term analogies to solve, or three-term series problems like 'John is taller than Mary; Mary is taller than Susan; who is tallest?' or we could . . ."

"But what do all these problems have to do with anything I ever have to do in my life? I never do any of those things."

"Certainly you don't, but they are the kinds of tasks we study, and we think they are important because they contain the building blocks of thought."

"But are they the same building blocks of thought that we really use when we think about things in our everyday lives?"

"We think so. Even if they are not, they're what we can study with the methods we have."

There were other people whom the princess could talk to on the planet, but she was getting nervous. People on her own planet would begin to wonder where she was if she didn't get back soon. So she decided to move on to Learnia.

Learnia

The flight to Learnia was a long one. It was clear she was covering a lot of ground. But she was determined to hear what the denizens of this planet would have to say about her problem, because she was still determined to grow up faster. Eventually, the screen showed Learnia, and she set her ship down.

There was certainly a lot to learn on Learnia. The first thing the princess wanted to learn was to whom she should go for sage advice. Eventually she was steered to the home of Nol Edge, whom she was told was the most knowledgeable person on Learnia. Ms. Edge was perhaps seventy-five years of age. She was apparently considered the brightest person on Learnia because she had memorized both the encyclopedia and the dictionary. She not only had learned all of the facts in these volumes but could recite page numbers and even sometimes line numbers. The princess asked Ms. Edge what to do to grow up intellectually.

Ms. Edge replied, "It's really quite simple. All you need to do is what I have done – learn as much as you can, and the more you learn, the more grown up you'll be intellectually. I know almost everything there is to know on this planet, and that makes me the person to whom everyone turns.

"Now if you'll excuse me, I see that it is time for the news, and I must listen to the news so that I can keep on being the most knowledgeable person on the planet." Ms. Edge went to turn on the TV, but it didn't work. She exclaimed: "Oh dear, my TV doesn't work. What shall I do? There must be someone who can fix it."

The princess was taken aback. She remarked, "But I thought you knew all there is to know. You must know how a television works. Why don't you just fix it yourself?"

Ms. Edge looked puzzled. "Oh, you don't understand at all. Certainly I know everything there is to know about televisions, but it doesn't mean that I can use any of this knowledge. The important thing is what you know, not whether you can use it. I've never really been tested on what I can do, only on what I know. As you know," she said proudly, "I've memorized both the encyclopedia and the dictionary."

The princess was baffled. What kind of planet was this? To grow up mentally, she was being told, she should learn more, but the most respected person on the planet didn't seem even to know how to use what she had learned. What good is it to know things if you can't use them? Of course, other people on the planet might exploit their knowledge better. But the princess decided that this planet did not hold much for her.

"Well, I really appreciate your giving me your time. It certainly has been interesting talking to you."

"Oh, really, it was no trouble at all. Besides, I've learned yet more things talking to you, although I'm not quite sure what to do with them."

The princess hurried away to her rocket ship. As far as she was concerned, she couldn't leave this planet soon enough. Off she went to Contexta, the last stop on her trip.

Contexta

For the princess, Contexta was a new context indeed. It was a much more diverse planet than her own, with more different kinds of geographic habitats, more different kinds of people, more different kinds of everything. The princess had trouble figuring out whom to see. Whenever she asked for advice, she was told the right person to see would depend on just what she meant by "growing up," and just what it meant to be "smarter" on her planet. Even a person on the street was comfortable explaining to her that what they meant by "smart" on Contexta might be very different from what they meant on the princess's own planet, with the result that any information she gleaned on Contexta might be useless to her back home. She argued that there must be some things that are in common, but to no avail. The folk of Contexta assured her that whereas there might be some things in common, it was not at all clear in advance just what they would be. Moreover, how common they were depended on the context in which they were understood.

"But what does it mean to be smart on this planet?" she asked.

The reply she got was variable from one person to another. "It depends on whom you ask, and what they mean by 'smart.' After all," they would say, "what's smart in one place is stupid in another, and what might be smart for one person to do would not necessarily be smart for another."

The princess was relatively pleased by the appreciation on Contexta of relativity, but she was feeling relatively confused by all of the relativism. Eventually, she decided it was relatively close to the time to leave, and without ever finding her expert, she departed.

Back home

The princess came back home. People probably would have noticed her absence had it not been for the start of an interplanetary war with a notoriously aggressive planet, Earth. People were so busy fighting Earth that they had not had time to notice her absence. While others were busy fighting their war, the princess asked herself what she had learned. She came to an important realization: She was not going to obtain any one "right" answer by consulting experts about what she would need to do to grow up quickly. Every expert seemed to have a different opinion. She returned the rocket ship confident that journeys to other planets were not going to answer her question.

The princess had not been altogether happy with any of the responses she had received, but she realized each had its positive features. The approach of Psychometrica allowed wise men to construct a structural model of the mind, to measure the aspects of this structure, and to determine how each aspect changed with age. The approach of Piagetica allowed people to chart stages of intellectual development, especially regarding the more scientific aspects of thought. It also helped people understand the kinds of errors children and even adults make in their often less than successful efforts to think logically. The approach of Neo-Piagetica had more to say about adult development, especially about the progressive realizations during adulthood that solving a problem is less important than solving an important problem. The approach of Cognitiva was especially useful in detailing just how people think about problems at different stages of development, and what changes in their thinking. The approach of Learnia had more to say than the other approaches about the importance of both knowledge and its acquisition. It is important to understand not only the structures of development, but what content is acquired through these structures. And the approach of Contexta pointed out the key importance of understanding the role of the environmental context in intellectual development. What is considered intelligent and age-appropriate may vary from one place or time to another. The approaches, the princess realized, were largely compatible with one another.

She knew her trip had helped her grow up faster, because life is a process and not just a product. By exploring different solutions to her problem and even different formulations of the problem, she had not reached the final answer, but she had grown by the very process of exploration. It was in reflecting on, and mulling over, the problem, rather than in reaching any one solution, that she had helped herself grow up. The princess was happy, and of course she lived happily ever after.

Author index

Subject index

abilities: maintained, 59, 68–70, 90–1; organization of, 19, 49–58; practice and, 90; primary mental, 23, 52–65, *see also* structure of intellect model; structure of, 17, 51, 54, 92; verbal vs. nonverbal, 70–2; vulnerable, 59–67, 70, 87–90, 92

accommodation as transformation, 167

acculturation knowledge (G_c), 56, 68, 90–1; vs. G_f (fluid reasoning), 89; *see also* crystallized ability

action, internalized: regulation of, 106; in relation to thought, 101, 102, 113; reorganization of, 106, 108–10, 113–14

adaptability, 352–5

adult development, 188–9, 205–22; cognitive compensation and, 358–65; cognitive monitoring and, 211; creativity and, 204, 212; dialectical operations and, 205; interrelationships of, 219–21; judgment and, 209–10; knowing and, 208–11; organismic, 214–15; problem finding and, 212; relativism and, 205–6; and symbolic processing, 216; systematic thinking and, 206–8

affect: and cognitive development, 200–1, 250; and cognitive structures, 169; dimensions of, 217; experience of, 219; language of, 218–19; and motivation, 180, 250; regulation of, 217; and thought, 165

age cohort: differences of, 74, 154–5; education and, 83, 152–3, 156; effects of, 76, 77, 355–6

age differences, 76–87; in cognitive processing, 267–9; in executive processing, 269–71, 307; and experience, 355–6, 358, 360; and expertise, 286–7, 311; external vs. internal memory aids and, 364–5; in incidental learning, 308; in indirect tests of memory, 309; in intentional learning, 321; in knowledge representations, 266, 286–9; and knowledge retrieval, 311–15; in lab learning tasks, 310–11, 317–21; in learning, 303, 305–7; in processing resources, 271–4; and self-paced learning, 310; and speed, 311; and typing, 360

age of acquisition: conservation and, 117–18; practice, training, and, 118, 164–5, 185; task complexity and, 117–19; variation in, 116–19

aging: and attention, 85, 86, 313; and carefulness, 86; and cognitive compensation, 358–65; and

cognitive functioning, 264–74; and decline in G_f, 85–87, 93, 156; and depth of processing, 85, 304; and effectiveness or efficiency of processing, 266–9, 302–5; effects of, on G_c and G_f, 81, 313–15, 357; and environmental factors, 302, 361–2; forgetting and, 307; increase in score variance and, 81–2; and IQ, 83, 85; and learning, 301–5; and memory aids, 364–75; and memory loss, 85, 265–8; and mental rotation, 268–9; and plasticity, 356; and speed of processing, 240, 269, 271–4, 302, 311–15; and task complexity, 86–7; and use of strategies, 304; and verbal learning, 83, 304; and vocabulary, 313–15

analogy, 48; and education, 285; and induction, 284–5

appropriation, 335–6

arithmetic, mental: age differences in, 319–20; backup procedures in, 237, 238; computer simulation of, 237; development of, 234–40; and errors, 237, 319–20; model of, 235–7; and retrieval, 235; and working memory, 319–20; *see also* long division

assessment, *see* tests

association, 281, 284; strength of, and retrieval, 235, 238–40; word, 265–6

attachment, *see* social bonds

attention: and aging, 86, 92, 313; divided, 85

auditory processing (G_a), 67–8

autism (stage), 104, 202

automatization: of actions, 111–12; and G_f–G_c, 82; of processes, 247–8; in stage transition, 168; and task consistency, 82

autonomy vs. heteronomy, 200, 204

behaviorism, 280; critiques of, 281

bond theory, 23

canalization, 34

Cartesian model, 101, 102

change, levels and rates of, 352–4; *see also* cognitive development; cultural development; mechanisms of development; reading